THE
HISTORY OF ILLAWARRA

AND ITS PIONEERS

PORT KEMBLA, ILLAWARRA
Showing Red Point, where the first Convict Settlement was established

BY
FRANK McCAFFREY

THE HISTORY OF ILLAWARRA

CONTENTS.

	Page
Foreword	7
Early History of New South Wales	9
Our British Breeds of Cattle	62
Dairy Cattle Illustrations	76
Pioneers of Illawarra	126
Mendelism	205
Early Shows in Illawarra	213
Dairy Cattle Breeding	265
Cattle Sales	272
The Origin of the Bull "Major"	295
Licenses	297
Heredity	299
The Illawarra Dairy Cattle Association	304
Copy of Kiama Herd Book	309

CATTLE ILLUSTRATIONS.

	Page
Alexander Bros., Kiama	191
Alexander, George, Fairfield	107
Boxsell Bros., Myrtle Bank	203
Chittick, Henry & Sons, Alne Bank	259
Colley, Hugh, Greendale	61
Culburra	59
C. W. Craig's Test Cows	202
Daly, Hugh, Upton	199
Daly, Thomas, Woodbine	121
Dudgeon, H. & Son, Hillview	17, 23, 182, 183
Dudgeon, Wm. H., Glenthorne	51
Duncan, Alfred, Berkeley	239
Duncan, George, Brisbane Grove	203
Dunster Bros., Shellharbour	121
Eight Notable Red Bulls	146
Eight Notable Red Cows	147
Exrs. of late J. W. Cole, Coleville	164-165
Exrs. of late W. H. Cook, Glendalough	175
Gorrell, J. W., Unanderra	101
Gower, Mrs., Albion Park	229
Graham Bros., Mayfield	80-81
Grey, George, Greyleigh	23, 154, 155
Hardcastle, John, Jinbiggeree (Q.)	37
Irvine, Thomas, Minnamurra	23
James, John & Son, Kurrawong	65
James, Thos., Shellharbour	65
Johnston Bros., Marksville	249
Keys, Ernest E., Albion Park	23
Kiama A. & H. Society	45
Knapp, James R., Swanlea	209
Lamond, Alex. C., Numba	115
Lindsay, George & Son, Horsley	199
McGrath, Henry, Greenhills	275
Mears, R., Morden (Q.)	101
Musgrave, James W., Illawarra	101
Nestle's and Anglo-Swiss Co., Ltd.	31
N.S.W. Govt. Experiment Farm	93
O'Connor, B., Oakvale (Q.)	17
O'Donnell, Michael, Unanderra	87
O'Keefe, D., Kiltankin	139
O'Gorman, Roy, Albion Park	219
Payne, A. C., Springvale (Q.)	125
Pickles, Arthur, Blacklands (Q.)	131
Spinks, Henry, Culwalla	275
Spoors, D. & Sons, Mundubbera (Q.)	131
Scottish Australian Investment Co., Ltd.	72-73

A BRIEF WORD TO THE READER.

A direct and principal aim of the present volume has been to endeavour to make the history of Illawarra, its pioneers, and their dairy cattle a more interesting as well as a more useful study, by attempting to trace a well defined plan of events for the mind of youthful settlers on the broad acres of Australian soil, in place of presenting a mere mass of unconnected facts to the memory.

It would be a cause of joy, however, if as far as its scope may permit, this volume were able to lay claim to a second aim. The Abbot, Gregor Mendel has sounded a note which should vibrate through the minds of young stock breeders. He has discovered the secret of forming new breeds, and better types of animals and plants. It would then be good for the country if Mendelism was more closely studied with a view of still improving on the wonderful results achieved by the pioneer dairymen of Illawarra and their sons.

"Men," said Bacon, "have entered into a desire of learning and knowledge, sometimes upon a natural curiosity and inquisitive appetite; sometimes to entertain their minds with variety and delight; sometimes for ornament and reputation, and sometimes to enable them to obtain the victory of wit and contradiction, and sometimes for lucre and possession; but seldom sincerely to give a true account of their gift of reason for the benefit and use of man, as if there were sought in knowledge a couch whereupon to rest a searching and restless spirit, or a track for a wandering and variable mind, to walk up and down with a fair prospect, or a tower of state for a proud mind to raise itself upon, or a fort on commanding ground for strife or contention, or a shop for profit or sale, and not a rich storehouse for the glory of the Creator, and the relief of Man's estate." I hope then that my readers will benefit from my humble effort, as it is as the old aboriginal expressed it— "Coompartoo."

March, 1924.

EARLY HISTORY OF NEW SOUTH WALES.

WHEN the Vatican archives were thrown open by Leo XIII in 1881 to the peoples interested in historical studies that learned Pope wrote: "Let it be kept uppermost in mind that the first law of history is not to dare to say what is false, next not to fear to state what is true; nor to let arise any suspicion of partiality or animosity in writing." Now, by a vigorous application of these principles the writer is placing on record in readable form the transactions of the building of the Illawarra or Five Islands district of New South Wales.

To those who will be privileged to read this compilation I shall quote for them the great Napoleon's advice to his son: "Let my son often read and reflect on history; it is the only true philosophy." The reading and reflecting on history might have avoided some of the most calamitous mistakes in every age in every country. It would have helped us to solve many problems in stock breeding in Illawarra. Many at the present time are acting as if history had never been written for their guidance, for it must be borne in mind that every record that has ever been preserved, or that ought to have been preserved, represents, or did at one time represent, an important event—a link in the historical chain.

It is, then, plain that the agricultural and dairying industries, together with the mining industry at a later period, with their social influences, are all to be judged as being parts of the whole—each to be estimated according to its material worth to the State. It must, however, be kept in mind that our records have not been preserved as they should have been—men who were not by any means scrupulous in either their social or commercial dealings with the poor combined to influence the authorities to burn their most valuable portions: the records.

We have, however, left to us many traditions, which, the more thoroughly they are enquired into, and the more frankly they are brought under review, even though they display many flaws in the characters of those who amassed wealth regardless of whom they injured, the more unmistakably will be its benefit on future generations.

We need not dwell on the fact that Australian civilisation had for its origin "Transportation." The transportation of white slaves began in James II's reign—1633-1685—and was continued until it became a favorite pastime and a profitable industry, namely, to collect young white people and sell them when a favourable market was procured.

Before the commencement of the American War of Independence the introduction of the more docile and laborious negro had rendered the American planters hostile to the importation of white convicts. The war put a stop to the traffic in white flesh and crowded the English gaols.

There is nothing to be gained by going into the notorious Howard system. It failed, as all such schemes must fail. The annual accumulation of gaol birds had to be got rid of. How? That was the problem; and, so long as it was solved, few cared how. Hanging had been stretched to its utmost limit; transportation had been checked by the revolt of a country which had decided to employ no slaves who had not at least twenty-five per cent. of black blood in their veins, and to receive no rogues, except those who had escaped unconvicted.

Under these difficult circumstances a proposition for deporting English criminals on the shores of Australia, then but recently re-discovered by Captain Cook, was eagerly entertained. At that time it was presumed, on very insufficient grounds, a place of punishment could be rendered self-supporting; at any rate, the prisoners would cease to be a nuisance to life and property in England.

The value of Captain Cook's report on Botany Bay may be estimated when it is stated that he and his companions passed a few days on the intended site of the proposed penal colony, and had found a small river, a profusion of curious plants, and an indifferent harbour. They had not seen any plains or pastures fit to feed live stock. They had not found any large edible animals, such as deer, or buffaloes, or pigs. They had no means of testing the fertility of the soil. They could form no idea of its possibilities.

Be all this as it may, when the "first fleet" anchored in Botany Bay on 20th January, 1788, Captain Phillip did not take up much of his time enquiring about plant life or big game. He evidently got information about a better harbour, and quickly got into it.

Port Jackson, Sydney, N.S. Wales.

In the beginning the geographical features of the site of the port of Sydney and the adjoining country, on which now stands the city of Sydney, consisted of a picturesque panorama of water, with hills clothed with dense scrub, Sydney Cove the head of the harbour, into which flowed a pure stream of fresh water—the Tank stream. Eleven vessels, not more than 3800 tons aggregate, dropped anchor at this site in 1788.

Collins, one of the earliest writers, says:— "The confusion that ensued during the landing will not be wondered at, when it is considered that every man stepped from a boat literally into a wood. Parties of people were everywhere heard and seen variously employed, some in clearing the ground for different encampments, others pitching tents or bringing up some stores as were more immediately wanted; and the spot which had so recently been the abode of silence and tranquility was now changed to that of noise, clamour, and confusion." He also states: "On 1st May, 1788, the number of live stock in Australia was— 1 stallion, 3 mares, 3 colts, 2 bulls, 5 cows, 29 sheep, 19 goats, 49 hogs, 29 small pigs, 5 rabbits, 18 turkeys, 29 geese, 35 ducks, 142 fowls, 87 chickens." In the Illustrated London Library, an important publication in those days says: "In April, 1788, two bulls and four cows wandered away from the 'Pickpocket' herdsmen in the new settlement of N.S. Wales into the bush and were lost."

The progeny of those strays were never actually reclaimed by the several Governors that followed the regime of Phillip. They were the discoverers of many pathways into "fresh fields and pastures new." They proved the old adage—"Instinct oft prevails where science fails." Those dumb animals wandered apart as they increased in numbers, eventually getting into the ranges, and from there down into the gullies and gorges as far south as Jervis Bay. They were termed by the early settlers the Cape of Good Hope breed. They were of a variety of colours, many being creamy white. They were evidently of Indian zebu origin. They were undoubtedly the first discoverers of

the several gorges leading down from the coast ranges to the sea.

During April, 1791, Philip Schaffer, a German, arrived from England as a superintendent of convicts. He was, however, unable to speak a word of English, and, therefore, quite unsuited for the position. He retired, and accepted a grant of land—140 acres—at Rosehill. James Ruse, who was capable of supporting himself by means of crop-raising, got a similar grant of land. These two incidents, together with the arrival, in two detachments, of a regiment raised for the purpose of serving in the colony, under the title of the New South Wales Corps, were the most remarkable events during the latter years of the reign of Governor Phillip, who resigned his office to Lieutenant-Governor Grose, and returned to England.

The agriculturists prior to 1792 did not work so well for the joint-stock concern as those who got their liberty and were "working on their own." These were few in number, as nearly the whole population of the colony were being fed and clothed at the expense of the Government; all the bond and the majority of the few free were fed and clothed.

The following returns go to show the truth of the foregoing statement. At the close of 1792 the prices were:—Flour, 9d per lb.; potatoes, 3d per lb.; sheep (Cape breed), £10 10s each; milk goats, £8 8s each; breeding sows, £7 7s to £10 10s each; laying fowls, 10s each; tea, 8s to 16s per lb.; sugar, 1s 6d per lb.; spirits, 12s to 20s per gallon; porter, 1s per quart.

At those famine prices the mortality among the convict population was fearful. Between 1st January and 31st December, 1792, there died two persons of the civil department, six soldiers, four hundred and eighteen male convicts, eighteen female convicts, and seventy-nine children.

At this period and for more than twenty years afterwards spirits was the currency, and all extra labour was paid for in spirits. The tyranny of the convict overseers was terrible. Criminal assaults on women were common. Once assaulted a woman had no status in the colony. No wonder that even the best inclined were often goaded into rebellion.

"The Governor's Garden."

The garden which was established by Phillip in 1788, partly for his own use and partly for the use of the officials, until it was finally constituted the Botanic Gardens in 1816, has had for upwards of 130 years a peculiar interest to certain people, whose families settled in Illawarra upwards of 90 years ago. Without going into the fine details of this story, which has been a tradition among the families interested for all those years, the writer will be content with saying that on board the First Fleet there were people of mixed trades, professions and callings. Just to mention four names, viz.:— John Moss, Edward Pugh, John Nicholls, and Rebecca Poulton. These people settled in time in Windsor, Parramatta, and at the Cheshire Cheese Hotel. They married and intermarried, and drifted into life in different directions.

John Moss was a marine—a ship's carpenter. When Governor Phillip decided on the laying out of his garden a special day was appointed for the ceremony, and in due course a company was formed into square. There was a spade left ready for the turning of the first sod. When the Governor arrived at the scene Moss had given those present an exhibition of spade work. He was immediately put under arrest. He, however, had gained the honor of having turned the "first sod" of what in time became the oldest Botanical Garden in the world. Moss married, and his daughter Rebecca married John Pugh Nicholls. Prior to this latter marriage there were strained relations between Moss and surgeon De Arcy Wentworth, and Moss disappeared and never again returned to the bosom of his family in life. His spirit did so in death.

Governor Phillip embarked for England on December 11th, 1792, and settled at Bath on a pension of £500 per year, granted by British Government. He died in Bath in 1814. For nearly three years after Governor Phillip's departure the settlement was practically a military despotism. The government first devolved upon Major Francis Grose, and secondly on Captain Paterson, senior officer of the N.S.W. Corps, as Lieutenant-Governor. Incompetency and militarism were blazed on the face of their every act.

The official notification of the appointment of Captain John Hunter, R.N., being appointed Governor of N.S. Wales appeared in the "London Gazette" of 5th February, 1794, and the commission passed the Great Seal on the following day.

Governor Hunter's troubles began early; he complained that there was not a pound of salt provisions in the store, and that the colony was "destitute of every kind of tool used in agriculture." A few weeks later he complained that the military force was insufficient, and that there was no barn, granary, or store-house, and that he was so short of convict labour that he could not carry on necessary public works. Fully a thousand more male convicts were required. In fact he assured the Duke of Portland that he could scarcely call together twenty for any public service at Sydney, so entirely had they been absorbed by the military and civil officers and the principal citizens. Soon after those despatches followed other complaints of a reverse nature. He complained that in June, 1797, there were no less than 700 men, whose sentences had expired, who were a source of trouble; of these a number hung about the settlement procuring a more or less precarious living by casual labour for the officers or farmers; others betook themselves to the woods; others herding with the natives or living in bands.

Hunter's first conflict with the military was when members of the N.S.W. Corps off duty attacked the foreman carpenter, John Baugham, for causing one of their comrades to be arrested. After maltreating him, they broke up his furniture and razed his home to the ground. Hunter got no satisfaction from the Secretary of State. It is, therefore, plain that these two early Governors favoured those whom they considered useful settlers. Those who had influence employed men to obtain goods which they put to their own use. They were in a sense promoters of thefts or receivers of stolen property. When a case came before the Judge-Advocate Gore, as several did, and he committed the guilty ones to terms of punishment, the Governor over-ruled the Judge's decision. Hunter found soon after his arrival that 150 settlers were in possession of farms with no other title than a slip of paper on which the commanding officer had written: "A.B. has my permission to settle;" and numbers of these settlers were convicts whose sentences had not expired.

The summer of 1798-9 was remarkable for one of the first protracted droughts on record. For ten months scarcely a shower of rain fell. The drought was followed by a disastrous flood in the Hawkesbury River, of which local weather conditions gave no warning. The banks were "overflowing with vast rapidity." The Government store and all the provisions it contained were swept away. The river was more than fifty feet above its common level, and the torrent was so powerful that it carried all before it. Settlers' houses and furniture, live stock and provisions were alike swept away, and "the whole country looked like an immense ocean."

Governor Hunter was much concerned about reclaiming the progeny of the cattle that got away from the early settlement to the "Cow-pastures" and other localities. He had a survey made of the coast south of Botany Bay. The Shoalhaven River was explored and named. Hunter was also interested in the interior of the colony from information received from persons in contact with runaway convicts. Hunter had a desperate hatred against the Irish convicts who were sent out on the ship Marquis of Cornwallis. Then we learn that he applied for leave to appoint constables to act at Sydney, Parramatta, Toongabbie, and the Hawkesbury; each to have an additional suit of clothing annually in order to their having at all times a more respectable appearance; to have a pint of spirits served to each every Saturday; to have the same ration served to them which is issued to the military and free people.

Governor Hunter on March 2nd, 1798, wrote the Duke of Portland as follows:—"At this time, my Lord, we have many dealers; those, and such of the officers as are concerned in trade, pocket the whole products of the labouring part of the settlement by the extravagant prices charged for commodities—indeed, they are but too much engaged in this way—I wish it were otherwise; but whilst this destructive system prevails the unfortunate labouring man has no means of relief."

There was great mortality among the early convicts, especially so among those who came by the second fleet, which was formed of ten transports. On board those ten vessels embarked from England 1695 male and 68 female prisoners, of whom no fewer than 194 males and 4 females died on the passage out, and such was the state of debility in which the survivors landed that 114 males and 2 females died in the colonial hospital in six months. Of 122 male convicts who arrived by the Queen from Ireland in the year 1791, there were only 50 alive in 1793, and their death was looked upon as a perfect blessing to the colony. Colonel Collins said: "It was a blessing, as the stores were short." Captain Hunter, R.N.. ruled from August 7th, 1795, to September 27th, 1800.

The majority of the cases and abuses about which Governor Hunter was constantly complaining were assignable to a want of firmness on his own part. He was relieved by Captain Philip Gidley King in September, 1800.

Governor Hunter embarked for England at the close of 1800. The population of the settlement was then 5574 persons, including 776 children; in Norfolk Island there were 961 persons, making a total of 6535 souls. Of this population about one-third was located in Sydney, the rest at either Parramatta, Toongabbie, or Castle Hill, where land was being cultivated or being brought under cultivation.

The stock of the settlement in 1800 were:— Horses, 203; cattle, 1044; hogs, 4017; sheep, 6124; goats, 2182; 7677 acres of land was alienated or under lease to individuals.

The stories we listened to in our youth cling to our minds through life. We as boys enjoyed those old stories, hence the distance of memory alone cannot change the drops of time through which we used to swim into the rainbows of enjoyment. Two perspective painters have led us, poor mortals, through the whole theatre of colonial life—and those are memory and hope. Be great to despise the past, be greater to honour it. All the leaders of men in the past were better than their ebullitions of evil, but they were also worse than their outburst of noble enthusiasm. To make such men happy required not much less than everything; to make them miserable not much more than nothing sufficed. From the Governor down to the common flogger or hangman, the "system" was operating in various ways upon them like an opium—some it made mad, and they could eat their meals while watching their fellow-beings being flayed almost to death with the "cat-o'-nine tails" or hanged to the limb of a tree; some few became sleepy, weary, and disgusted. The most painful part of the whole of our early colonial history is that in no instance has it ever been exaggerated.

Governor King, 1800—1806.

Captain Philip Gidley King, R.N.. became associated with the civil and military powers in N.S.W. when he took up the duties of Governor on 28th September, 1800. He continued to hold office until August 12th, 1806. He began a weak man in many respects. His power over certain of the military authorities was such that they did much as they liked. He was nervous and frightened of troubles coming on him from within and from foreign parts.

In a letter to Lord Hobart, dated 1st March, 1804. Governor King states:—"I am sorry that during the last and present year we have experienced the greatest drought, with severe blight, which has much reduced our crops, although there is not the most distant appearance of any real want, except for our very increasing stock of swine, which will suffer for want of maize. The cattle have not escaped the inconvenience of this continued dry weather, which has not only dried up all the native grasses, but also most of the streams and ponds in the neighbourhood, insomuch that the Government herds are drawn off many miles to feed. They have also been afflicted much by a disease that has generally gone through all the cattle, viz., a spongy substance on the tongue, which, on being removed, occasions bad feet. From this disease the Government stock recovered, but, I am sorry to say, several belonging to individuals died."

This drought and cattle plague evidently caused Governor King much worry. The ship Lady Barlow, with 131 head of cattle and an Arab horse on board, and H.M. ship Buffalo, with 77 head of cattle and two Persian horses, had arrived in Port Jackson in the midst of all the trouble. King therefore at once despatched Captain William Kent, with a number of laborers and ample provisions, to explore the coast as far south as the Shoalhaven. We learn that "Captain Kent, of H.M. Buffalo, on Sunday, March 3rd, 1804, returned from a trip through the Shoalhaven district."

This bears out the often repeated statement that cedar getting and grazing were carried on by the favoured few in Illawarra in 1806. Cattle and horses were averaging big prices during the years 1804-6. Captain King, whose brand was K, possessed a large herd of cattle at Parramatta. Captain W. Kent had a large herd of cattle, Devon and Alderney crosses, and could lay claim to be the first to import pure merino sheep to N.S.W. Yet he suffered severely under the regime of Governor Bligh. Major George Johnston's cattle were sent to Illawarra during the drought of 1803-4, and were not interfered with by Bligh.

During the few years that Governor King held office he displayed an apparent tendency to favour certain of his friends—such, perhaps, is the weakness of the great. This weakness, however, brought troubles on his head in addition to the worries of droughts, cattle disease, and floods. It is recorded that in the month of March, 1806, one of the heaviest floods that up to that time had visited the Hawkesbury occurred. It rained every day for

a month, causing loss of life and property. The loss of property was estimated at £35,000. Several persons were drowned, and those who escaped with their lives had to face starvation.

"The Rum Rebellion" was brewing. King's real troubles were with the military authorities. These people went so far as to say: "The administration of Governor King was barren of good fruit." This was no doubt owing to his great antagonism to the military "ring," whose influence, owing to his previous concession, he found himself powerless to break. It was said that "the influence of the officers of the New South Wales Corps shortened King's period of service in the colony."

Bennett, however, says: "The six years of Governor King's rule, notwithstanding the serious civil disturbances and the prevalence of drinking habits to a degree never before witnessed in any community, were marked by a steady advancement in the development of the material resources of the colony. The sealing trade and whale fishery were carried on with energy and profit, the foundation of what proved a lucrative intercourse with New Zealand and the South Sea Islands." The whalers were evidently well acquainted with the seaboard of New South Wales during the years from 1800 to 1806 as we are to-day. It was also known that many hundreds of acres of land was good open forest country, and that much land along the seaboard was free from timber and covered with native grass that was only kept in check by hordes of marsupials.

The official returns for 1806 were given as follows:—Quantity of land occupied by Government or granted to private individuals, 125,476 acres; quantity of land cleared, 16,624 acres; land in wheat, 7118 acres; in barley, maize, etc., 5279 acres. Average production of wheat per acre, 18 bushels. Number of horned cattle, 3264; of sheep, 16,501; of pigs, 14,300; of horses, 458; of goats, 2900.

The population of the settlement was estimated at 9000, of which number 8472 were in N.S. Wales and 528 at Hobart Town.

Before his departure on 28th September, 1806, Governor King gave the incoming Governor, Captain William Bligh, R.N., a grant of 1000 acres of land. In return, on taking command Bligh gave Mrs. King 1000 acres, a grant as a token of mutual friendship.

The return of Government stock on 12th May, 1804, which included the returns from the five cattle stations, namely, Parramatta, Toongabbie, Castle Hill, Seven Hills, and Sydney, comprised 17 bulls, 678 cows, 735 male calves, 672 female calves, 129 bullocks.

The most vigorous, the clearest, and most fertile minds have been employed in search of facts. But one thing was ever present—the leading families had back histories—the histories of the accumulation of their wealth and subsequent importance. When one asked: "Why were certain records destroyed?" the usual reply came: "Our champions and teachers have lived in stormy times, social and commercial; even grave financial influences have acted upon those old settlers variously in their day, and have since obstructed a careful examination of their actions." In these histories lovers of history may be able to imagine our vast inheritance, without an inventory of its treasures. Nothing is given to us in profusion; there is little for us to catalogue, sort, select and complete.

We have more information in certain directions than we know how to use; stores of records, but little that is precise and serviceable about those brave pioneers of the bush or open forest country—the bushmen who penetrated the dense scrubs in search of cedar, and the cattlemen who took up the open country adjacent to those dense scrubs to raise bullocks to haul the timber to a market. From beginnings so small, from work so fortuitous, with prospects so unpromising, the early coastal settlers suddenly became important to the several merchants of Sydney and Parramatta. The originals would have found it difficult to say what they aimed at of a practical nature, if it were not to escape from the terrible conditions of town life, of which they had had a long experience before their arrival in Port Jackson. If they had stated the real facts they might be suddenly surprised any day by the earnestness of the authorities.

These hardy men penetrated the deepest gullies and ravines in search of cedar. The finest trees were at all times where vegetation was the most luxuriant, and where the scrubby undergrowths were always the thickest. Their position in such places was that of isolation—not at all times of a voluntary nature. These centres of population were not far apart, yet communication was not sought. The bullock-drivers, whose duty it was to haul the timber to the nearest port, were the carriers of the food supplies and the news. Many of these sawyers were half-fed, ill-clothed mortals, who had escaped from the "iron gangs," "stockades," or penal settlements, dreading capture.

Having experienced "torture," they were the prey of the more cunning members of the society, who used them for selfish ends. The heavy scrubs in many of the gullies and gorges were considered dank, damp, and unhealthy, consequently many of the early sawyers died off early owing to the want of sunlight. They left their records behind, and passed to the "Great Beyond."

Taking the old pioneer sawyers as a body of men, they were true and faithful to each other—no sacrifice was too great when duty called upon them to act.

> "From distant climes o'er wide spread seas we come,
> Though not with much eclat or beat of drum ;
> True patriots all, for, be it understood,
> We left our country for our country's good
> No private view disgraced our generous zeal,
> What urg'd our travels was our country's weal ;
> And, none will doubt but what our emigration
> Has proved most useful to the British Nation."

History goes to show that those lines gleaned from George Barrington's "The Convict's Ode," were in many instances prophetic. Take for example the assistance rendered to the dairying and pastoral industries of Australia by Joseph Holt—an ex-convict—to the Cox families—and Australia in general.

Captain William Cox was paymaster on the Transport "Minerva" which left "Cork harbour with prisoners on August 24th 1799. He had transferred from the 68th Regiment of Foot into the N.S. Wales Corps, and arrived in Sydney harbour on January 11th, 1800. On board the "Minerva" was Joseph Holt—known to fame as "General Holt." Holt was a farmer and stock-raiser in Ireland prior to the '98 rebellion—consequently, his services were of immense value to Captain Cox who placed him in charge of 100 acres at Brush Farm, Parramatta. The cattle raised subsequently by Captain William Cox were for years in demand by the old pioneer settlers in the County of Camden, of which Illawarra was a part; and, so far as cattle growing was concerned, an important part of that County.

Joseph Holt was transported to N.S. Wales as General Holt, a leader of the Irish Rebellion of 1798. "Who fears to speak of '98?" When he arrived in Sydney, he was not a criminal of the lower order, but a highly educated agriculturist in a general way. He was too valuable to the New Settlement to get his liberty as others of his class did almost immediately after landing. Others got government appointments and grants of land, while Holt had to serve his full time in order that he might educate those who were in good positions, how to farm and raise valuable horses, cattle and sheep.

The Wicklow Chieftain smarted under this unfair treatment with the result that as soon as he got his liberty he left on record a vivid sketch of his experiences in N.S. Wales, and the motley gang who called themselves officers of the N.S.W. Corps. Any one who could afford to buy a Lieutenancy, could buy one. The men of high military honour in England refused to serve as Convict Guards; therefore, a special Corps, with special officers, and special inducements, was called into existence. Drapers, clerks, low attorneys of the police courts of old Bailey, even light-fingered knights of industry secured positions, and commissions at Major Grose's price, and masqueraded as sworded paladins. They were, however, purely sordid tradesmen, and the special inducement held out to them was the monopoly in the spirit trade.''

The Rum hospital was built out of the proceeds of that monopoly; but they were three worthy gentlemen: De Arcy Wentworth, William Riley, Garnham Blaxcell who had the monopoly of the proceeds of the Rum hospital. John Macarthur came in for some satire. He was dubbed one of the Barrack Room Bullies, who had a Rum Keg on his shield, with the motto, ''With this we conquer'' painted in gold letters in the centre of a square.

For daring to defend their rights, thousands were slain, hundreds were starved to death, and hundreds that escaped those terrors were sent to Botany Bay.

''They rose in dark and evil days to right their country's wrongs.''

An eloquent speaker once said:—''Australians should give up much of their time to more general and better organised study of Australian history. The stereotyped methods which still dominate much of the historian's systems of conveying information of what took place in Britain and Ireland during the two centuries prior to the arrival of the First Fleet in Port Jackson, has to be written in plain English— as what has been passed down to us as history is too one-sided and unfair to be worthy of notice.''

The same charge may be laid against the writers of Australian history. The landlaws of Great Britain and Ireland were so unjust as to cause mankind, however honest minded the masses were, to rebel. Honest men and women were forced to rebel against the brutal land-stewards—men who desired their neighbour's holding, turned informers, and hundreds were sent to Botany Bay in felons' chains, to die at Pinchgut or fall into the trenches they were compelled to dig, weak and exhausted, never to walk on earth again beneath God's sun. Hundreds were destroyed in that way.

This state of things was patent in 1798, and continued up to the arrival of Sir Richard Bourke, and, after his arrival until the arrival of the State aid emigrants who poured into Australia in great numbers—poor, but brave and honest. When they learned of the treatment measured out to their countrymen, whose only crime was that of standing up bravely for their rights and liberties, they resolved to better things, and they did it. Many of those State aided emigrants were no better than they ought to be. Taking them, however, as a whole, they were proud of their political convict neighbours and worked with them in the bush and out in the open. Their children grew up to be men and women and intermarried, and in the course of years took possession of the lands of the convict masters, and then joined hands as one great people to make Australia what she is to-day—great, glorious, and free.

1806. In August 1806, Governor Bligh arrived in the Colony with his daughter and his son-in-law, Captain Putland, of the Royal Navy. Governor King therefore prepared to take his departure, his time having expired. Bligh had, it would appear, instructions from the Duke of York to the effect that all the officers and soldiers of the military detachment were to be paid in cash. This to a certain extent deprived the paymaster of the regiment and other officers of a lucrative living. In other words they were in future to live on their pay. The English Government had also sent out various articles of merchandise, which were placed in His Majesty's Stores, and the settlers were paid for their produce in goods which they needed, and for which they were charged very little more than the market price in England. It was subsequently stated that these reforms made the poor contented, as previous to this the poor had no redress. Many soldiers who objected to pay exorbitant prices for goods in the past had been sent to the guard-house, tried by court martial for mutiny and sentenced to terms of imprisonment. It was said that in Governor King's time there were two classes of people, those who sold rum, and those who drank it.

Captain John Macarthur did not like the new orders—his profits were reduced and he saw disaster staring him in the face and quickly convinced Major Johnston that Bligh's rule would soon ruin them all. The Governor saw through the plot that was being hatched by Macarthur, consequently he ordered Macarthur's arrest for disobedience to an order of the Judge Advocate, and committed him to prison. This brought Major Johnston to the rescue, Major Johnston rode into the Sydney Barracks from his private residence Annandale, called out his regiment, numbering about 300 men, and marched them in battle array to Government House. The Governor and party, which included the Rev. Mr. Fulton, were at dinner, and immediately placed Governor Bligh under arrest. The sequel of this story will no doubt form interesting reading to generations yet unborn.

When Admiral William Bligh took over the reins of Government in N.S. Wales in 1806, he did what most of our Governors did from the days of our first Governor, Captain Phillip, and since Bligh's time, right up to the forties of last century, he secured for himself a suitable piece of land and went in for dairying and dairy-cattle raising, with the assistance of a manager named Andrew Thompson. Thompson was born in Scotland in 1773, and arrived in Sydney in the ship Pitt. He worked at the stone quarry, Parramatta, and was in 1798 selected for the position of Constable at Green Hills, and was interested in shipping in 1805. Bligh made him his bailiff and overseer of his dairying operations on the Hawkesbury River. Andrew Thompson wormed himself into the good graces of Governors Hunter, King, Bligh and Macquarie. The latter made him a Justice of the Peace, and a guest at Government House. He died in 1810 at the early age of 37 years. He left his property—which was considerable in those days, to Governor Macquarie, and his associate in the days of his adversity, Mr. Simeon Lord.

It came out at the trial of Colonel Johnston, Captain Macarthur and others in England over the illegal disposal of Admiral Bligh as Governor of N.S. Wales, that when Bligh went in for stock-raising and dairying on the banks of the fertile Hawkesbury river, he used convict labour, which was free to all employers, so long as they could find plenty of employment for them. He, Bligh, was in consequence accused of having converted a considerable amount of Government property to his own use. In 1807, Governor Bligh's overseer Andrew Thompson estimated that the total profits during the ensuing year would be £1000. In ten weeks £60 was received for the sale of milk alone. Bligh was also accused of having cows, forward in calf, sent to his Hawkesbury farm from the Government herd, and after they had calved, these cows were returned to the government herd minus their calves.

At the historic trial, just mentioned, Colonel Johnston fared better than his friend and adviser Captain John Macarthur, as the Colonel returned almost immediately to N.S. Wales, whilst the Captain was forced to remain a few years in England. It is difficult however, judging by the sequel to those events which of the two fared best financially.

Admiral William Bligh.—In 1788 when on a visit to Tahiti in command of the ship Bounty, by order of the British Government to transport the bread-fruit tree of the South Sea Islands to the West Indies, the sailors were harassed to such an extent by Bligh, that they mutinied, seized the ship, and set Bligh and his officers adrift in a launch. This drastic action was the means of making Captain Bligh an Admiral and Governor of New South Wales a few years later. Bligh displayed such good seamanship that he covered 4,000 miles in the launch, and reached Timor safely. He was then considered a fit officer to rule the Convict Colony of N.S. Wales. He returned to England, and was dispatched again with two ships, the 'Providence' and the 'Assistant,' and in due course landed in Van Diemen's Land, and spent 12 days there planting fruit-trees, acorns, and vegetables. He was sometimes called "Bread Fruit Bligh." Bligh found trees did not flourish in Van Diemen's Land. His assistant botanist, Mr. Brown, however, landed at Adventure Bay, and after making himself safe with a black chief, planted the first apple tree on Tasmanian soil. Bligh's next visit to Tasmania was in 1808, immediately after the Rum Rebellion in Sydney. Between 1806 and 1808, Mr. Brown made botanizing visits to beautiful Illawarra, hence we have Mount Brown, and Brown's Mountain.

Andrew Thompson was not fated to benefit by his prosperity in the young Colony. Over zeal in his work caused a serious sickness, from which he eventually died. At the time of his death he must have had a very large herd of cattle that was in due course sold by public auction. Ex-Governor Bligh's herd must have remained in charge of his Colonial relations as, according to sundry traditions, his stud herd

B. O'CONNOR, Oakvale, Colinton, Queensland.

CHARM OF GLENTHORN (No. 213, I.D.C.H.B., Q'land).

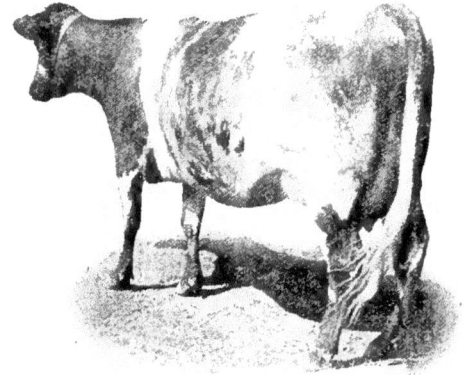

BLUEBELL OF OAKVALE (No. 202, I.D.C.H.B., Q'land).

WAKEFUL OF OAKVALE.

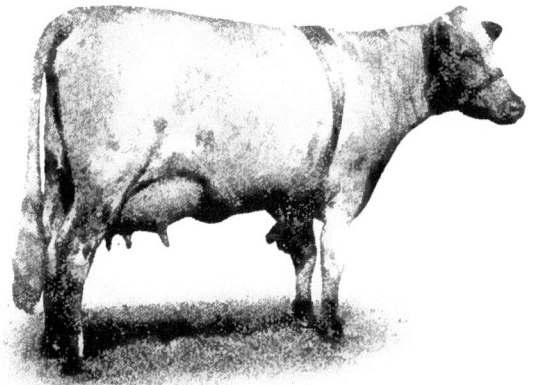

SHAMROCK OF HILLVIEW (No. 221, I.D.C.H.B.), Q'land.

HUGH DUDGEON & SONS, Hillview Stud, Jamberoo.

LOVELY II OF HILLVIEW (No. 68, I.D.C.H.B.).

GENTLE'S PRINCE OF HILLVIEW.

was one of the finest in the Colony. Be this as it may, in the Sydney Gazette for June, 1818, there appears the following notice:—"Strayed from Mr. Johnston's Black Cattle, near Liverpool, a red and white bull 14 months old, entirely bred from Admiral Bligh's herd." It will thus be seen that ten years had elapsed from the time of the Bligh rebellion to the date of the straying of this red and white bull. It is also of interest to note that in 1818 Colonel Johnston was in possession of the Macquarie Gift estate in Illawarra, where, from the earliest days of the settlement of Illawarra, valuable cattle were being constantly sent from his 'Georges Hall' estate, Liverpool, long before Bill West was overseer for the Johnstons. That the Red and White cattle were there when Joe Ross took charge; and that they were there in John Raftery's time and prior to the coming of the shorthorns that had been imported direct from England by Mr. David Johnston in the mid forties of last century is common history. In this draft of imported cattle came the Johnston show cattle. According to members of the Raftery family "these cattle were mostly roans, with good udders and teats. The best cows gave a good flow of milk after calving, much of which was froth and bubble."

Governor William Bligh R.N., 1806-1809. His task was a difficult one, almost the only unconvicted colonists at the time were the military and civil officers, and their relatives, who controlled the entire trading of the young colony; and, who had beside enjoyed the lion's share of grants of land and free use of labour. They had a monopoly of all tariff. Spirits formed the principal part of those cargoes which were registered as general merchandize. Bligh brought out instructions to put down this tariff. At an early period of the colony's history this would have been easily accomplished. Governor King had done things in such a careless manner that the settlement had got out of control of those who were paid to support the Governor, and uphold the law, and maintain order.

The Rum Rebellion did not prove that the Military and Civil authorities were imbued with the spirit of patriotism. The occasion of the conflict was that Governor Bligh showed a disposition, when carrying out his policy to side with the poorer classes against the rich. Nothing could be more offensive than conduct of this kind to the pride of men who had been accustomed to consider themselves the only rightful possessors of power and consideration in the colony, and when to the injuries he thus inflicted on the sensibilities of some, he added that of reducing the profits of others.

When Captain John Macarthur was arrested and charged with detaining two "still-boilers" against the expressed wish and instructions of the Governor; of promoting dissatisfaction; of using language calculated to bring the authority of the Judge Advocate into contempt; and allowing those who had formed the crew of one of his vessels to remain in Sydney contrary to the laws of the Colony, there was some hotstuff brewing for Bligh. The Rebellion.

"The Macarthur Memorial:—Sir, The present alarming state of the Colony, in which every man's property, liberty, and life is endangered, induces us most earnestly to implore you instantly to place Governor Bligh under arrest, and to assume the command of the Colony. We pledge ourselves at a moment of less agitation, to come forward to support the measure with our fortunes and our lives.

We are with great respect your most obedient servants.

To Major George Johnston, Lieutenant-Governor, and commanding New South Wales Corps."

This memorial was in the handwriting of John Macarthur, and signed by 83 persons. 24 of these were free on landing in N.S. Wales. There were 15 marksmen in the memorial, and 7 marksmen in the address of thanks. Major Johnston did not occupy Government House. He lived all the time in his own home at Annandale.

Among the old settlers—old hands, as they were generally termed—could be found many who possessed considerable literary ability—men of keen insight and knowledge of the races of mankind. To them, the children of Ham in Australia afforded food for reflection. One of these old hands often told the writer that the blacks made constant journeys to and from the Illawarra Lake from all parts of the coast and tableland. That they had certain secret missions to perform goes without saying, when we know from the lips of those who observed them on their march that these blacks never paused to speak to anyone during their journeying to and from the lake. They walked upright, and straight ahead they went until their mission was completed.

In the course of a few years the white settlers learned to follow the tracks of the blacks into the several valleys and gorges of Illawarra and the Shoalhaven River districts at a time when things were very unsettled under the regime of Governor Bligh. The story of Bligh and his times is of much interest to us Illawarra men, as our early pioneers would have been ruined if Illawarra had not afforded places of refuge for those alleged sinners whom Bligh was evidently prepared to crucify without waiting to study the great consequences that might and did follow. What was taking place in the settlement of N.S. Wales during Governor Bligh's regime may be easily gleaned from the Government orders that were issued and published by authority from his successor, Governor Macquarie:—"Applications to his Excellency the Governor—(a) By memorial, petition, or verbal will be received from individuals on first Monday in each month only. (b) Applications for land and cattle are to be made the first Monday in the month of June only; but if it be a holiday, then upon the second Monday in the month. (c) All petitions or memorials for the extension of the above indulgences are invariably to be countersigned by the principal magistrate and clergyman of the district the applicant resides in, certifying their opinion of their deserving the indulgence solicited; and the clergymen and magistrates are enjoined not to grant such certificates to persons with whose real character they are not acquainted, the certificate to express that they consider them sober, industrious and honest."

The granting of absolute pardons will be strictly confined to the industrious, sober, honest, and truly meritorious, and unquestionable proof of rectitude of conduct for a long series of years will in all cases be required. No person under sentence for transportation for life shall apply for an absolute pardon until they have resided fifteen years in the colony, nor for a conditional pardon until they have resided ten years in the colony; and those for limited periods are not to apply for an absolute pardon till they have resided three-fourths. nor for a conditional pardon until they have resided two-thirds of their original term of transportation in the colony.

Ticket of leave will not be granted to prisoners until they have been employed by Government or individuals they were assigned to for three years, and no application is to be made in future unless conformed to by the foregoing regulations; and the clergymen and magistrates granting certificates are to be well informed of the circumstances before they sign them. Applicants residing in Sydney to have their certificates signed by the resident chaplain and Superintendent of Police.

Cattle granted to individuals from the Government herds on condition of not being disposed of for three years. The sale, purchase, or disposal of such being prohibited on pain of prosecution, they being considered the real property of the Crown for the said term of three years.

Cattle to be marked and branded. All persons who have drawn or may hereafter receive cattle from the Government herds are to cause them to be immediately branded with their particular and distinctive mark, so that in case of their returning to the Government herds they may be distinguished from them and restored to their owners. And all cattle belonging to individuals, whether drawn from the Government herds or not, are in like manner to be branded in order to guard against mistakes in reclaiming them from the herds they may have joined. All cattle joining the Government herds in future will be deemed as forming part of those herds, unless distinctly marked or branded as private property. The Superintendent of the Government herds is enjoined to continue the practice of branding the young cattle with the broad arrow as soon as their strength will admit, and in no case to leave any unmarked beyond the age of six months; and also to renew the Government mark on all cattle if by time or accident obliterated.

The Government and private individuals offered bribes to those who would inform on all miscreants. The Government offered free pardons and grants of lands to those who laid information against their brother sufferers. In this manner many innocent men were led into traps and had charges laid against them of which they were in whole or part guiltless. Scores were hung, hundreds were flogged, receiving up to 1000 lashes. They became outcasts and died, and were buried in their chairs.

If such were the conditions of N.S. Wales under the rule of Major Lachlan Macquarie, what was the condition of things under the rule of Governor Bligh? If Captain John Macarthur succeeded in establishing a rebellion against the rule of Bligh, it was not because the Government and certain individuals were cruel to the convicts placed under them, nor was it on account of any sane reforms that were needed for developing the country. No! it was on account of Governor Bligh's orders prohibiting the military officers from trading with the convict population. and compelling them to pay 300 per cent. on the actual necessaries of life, and encouraging them to barter away their land grants and stock for rum. The military authorities and a few merchants had absolute charge of all stores. The military, under Captain Macarthur, rebelled when Bligh told them they must in future live on their incomes.

The First Stock Sent from Liverpool to Illawarra.

I remember being at the late E. H. Weston's home at Albion Park Illawarra in November 1878, when he showed me the oil painting of a roan Shorthorn bull, "Melmoth," that was imported to N.S. Wales by his uncle and father-in-law, David Johnston. I asked him if that was the first imported bull that reached Illawarra? His reply was, "No, not by a long way." He went on to say that "my grandfather, Major George Johnston, was one of the first to send cattle to Illawarra. During a drought all the country around Liverpool was burnt up, consequently, my grandfather and a few others who had good cattle asked Governor Kings' leave to send cattle to Illawarra. Captain Nicholls, a relation of the old Major. brought them down in a boat and put them ashore at Five Islands. Two ex-convicts were placed in charge. They were only yearlings at the time, and they remained in Illawarra long enough to survive the "Bligh Rebellion." From time to time, it is plain, that from land and sea Illawarra received draughts of valuable stock from Camden, Liverpool, and Parramatta for many years prior to the arrival of the Osbornes in Illawarra."

The foregoing remarks are quite in keeping with statements that have been made by the descendants of the old time sawyers, to wit. "that cedar was carried from the inner shores of Lake Illawarra, in small craft, during convenient periods to Sydney in 1810—and that the bullock teams used to haul cedar logs and planks to the edges of the Lake, at suitable centres for years before any real settlement took place.

The chief point is touched in the early history of Illawarra in the foregoing theme, as it goes to prove that our history is not a myth as it would appear to those who lived outside of the district. Most writers are compelled to study Illawarra from the outside, as the early Governors merely mentioned its existence, as viewed from the sea. It was not the case with the real settlers who took the risks and breathed the air of solitude. Such men saw instinctively what the authorities failed to understand.

The early pioneers of Illawarra did much to wear down the rage of Governors, and saved and preserved hundreds of valuable cattle from the ravages of disease, droughts, and floods. It was circumscribed by natural barriers, hence its difficulties of ingress caused it to be nature's granary and stockyard for a given number of cattle in all seasons.

Prior to Edward H. Weston settling in Illawarra, he was married to his cousin, Miss Johnston, a daughter of David Johnston. David was a son of Major George Johnston, and he had been Inspector of Stock in N.S. Wales since the death of his brother George, who died in 1820, owing to a fall from his horse on the Government Stock Station, at Brownlow Hill. Johnston's Meadows Estate had been in charge of the following pioneers:—George Simpson. William West, Joseph Ross, John Hockey, and John Raftery, before Weston took over the control. David Johnston naturally looked after his own interests in the property up to the time of his death, in 1866.

Edward Simpson had been in the employ of William Broughton at Appin. He and Billy Broughton (an aboriginal), acted as guides to those who desired to inspect the Illawarra or Five Islands district, while yet in its primitive state. Some years ago a square brass plate was found on the banks of the Shoalhaven river, bearing the following inscription, engraved in artistic style:—"Broughton, constable, 1822." He had evidently been employed by the military authorities as a tracker.

The Timberry family (aboriginal) were relatives of the Broughtons, according to the matrimonial rites of the old Illawarra tribe. Broughton Junr. and Timberry Junr. being cousins. In the early days of Illawarra they were expert horse and cattle men.

Those cattle men whom the early Governors permitted to depasture their young stock in the Illawarra or Five Islands district, did so undisturbed by their neighbours who had holdings in the drier parts of Cumberland. Selfishness, and the drought of the year 1813. which is reported to have been extremely dry in the County of Cumberland at any rate, caused attention to be directed towards Illawarra in real earnest, and we are informed that several applications for grants of land were received by the Governor of the Colony, Major-General Lachlan Macquarie, and favourably considered by His Excellency, who granted leases to those with starving stock.

On the 28th September, 1816, an inspired paragraph appeared in the New South Wales "Gazette" as follows:—"The natives of the new settlement at the Five Islands are described as being very amicably disposed to us, and the general mildness of their manners to differ considerably from the other tribes known to us. Several gentlemen have removed their cattle thither, as the neighbourhood affords good pasturing; and it is anxiously hoped that the stockmen in charge of their herds will be able to maintain the friendly footing that at present exists with them." Later on the following notification appeared in the "Sydney Gazette," under the heading Public Notices:—Government House, Sydney, 16th November, 1816. Those gentlemen and free settlers who have lately obtained His Excellency the Governor's promises of grants of land, in the new district of Illawarra, or Five Islands, are hereby informed that the Surveyor-General and his deputy have received His Excellency's the Governor's instructions to proceed thither in the course of the ensuing week to make a regular survey of the said district, and to locate the several promised grants. And in order that the locations may be made accordingly, those persons who have obtained promises of allotments are hereby requested to avail themselves of the approaching occasion of the Surveyors on duty in Illawarra, to get their locations marked out to them. And for this purpose they are required to meet the Surveyor-General at the hut of Mr. Throsby's stock-men, in Illawarra, or the Five Islands district, at the hour of twelve noon, on Monday, 2nd day of December next, at which time he is to commence on the locating the lands agreeable to the instructions which he will be officially furnished previous thereto."

By Command of His Excellency.
J. F. Campbell Secretary.

The settlement of those lands which to-day form the foreshores of Lake Illawarra has been the theme of discussion among the old hands in the past, and in reviewing the several arguments that were used it must be borne in mind that there were circumstances such as the limited scope for cattle-raising in and around the centre of population one hundred years ago which forced men of enterprise to adopt means of getting afield with their stock in times of drought at all hazards. Such circumstances are to be considered and carefully weighed in the balance of our judgment, with the object of diminishing difficulties. We are all aware that no human skill known to the old pioneer of Illawarra could turn the barren rocky passes over the Coast range into easy ways of ingress and egress for cattle—nor could they, with the material at their command, construct safe harbours. They had to take things as they found them; yet, it is evident by such skill and forethought as they possessed, they employed their limited resources to the best advantage, and thereby turned even the privations of their day into such blessings that in a short time they became a great power for good. It was by a simple means of organisation—a primitive form of co-operation—that a few settlers were enabled to endure and overcome difficulties, in a spirit, and with a success, which could not otherwise be attained. All the movements of these men, we may conclude, were neither hurriedly made nor done in a spirit of mere haphazard. Scouts—advance agents—such as the more daring convicts, assisted by aboriginals. were employed to report on the line of march. and the place to which it should lead. There were also labourers who did much of this pioneering work—who lie here and there to-day in unknown graves, whose duty it was to remove obstacles to allow the stock to pass along the narrow passes in dangerous places on the mountain range. The halts and advances were to a great extent regulated by these men according to the amount of labour required to remove Nature's obstructions. Let these considerations, therefore, be fairly weighed, and they will explain away much of the difficulties met with by the early pioneers and the perilous positions they were often in while engaged taking their stock to Illawarra by land. If, then, it should happen that there are persons in comparative ignorance of the geographical difficulties just let them stroll along the old tracks to-day which the old pioneers were forced to travel with stock and retravel. Take the early settlement of the Blackman's Paradise, the Kangaroo Ground, for example:—

It was with a view of preventing horse and cattle stealing that Captain Richard Brooks undertook the great task of stocking the Kangaroo Valley country in 1818. To do so he used the path which led from the Illawarra Lake, crossing the Macquarie Rivulet to the west of Johnston's Meadows, then up the range into the Pheasant Ground to a spot known to-day as

WHEN the Illawarra Dairy Cattle Association was being put into concrete form in 1910 those who were interested in their own private affairs did not care to give out to the dairy world the true origin of their herd. With them, and they were not a few, the word "Shorthorn" should cover up—yea, smother up—everything, regardless of truth. The illustration on this and other pages in this book will show what the admirers of the old breed are doing, not alone in Illawarra but throughout New South Wales and Queensland, since 1910.

GEORGE GREY, Kiama.

FOCH OF GREYLEIGH.

ERNEST E. KEYS, Albion Park.

TULIP'S HERO

HUGH DUDGEON & SONS, Jamberoo.

FUSSY'S JELLICOE OF HILLVIEW
(Grand Champion Dairy Bull, Adelaide Show, 1922.)

THOMAS IRVINE, Minnamurra, Jamberoo.

HONEYSUCKLE'S JELLICOE

Arguing from the basis of Bruce Lowe's figure system each of these four bulls carry large quantities of Hugh Dudgeon and Son's Hillview blood,—a blend of blood that has prevailed throughout Illawarra for sixty years. The old veteran breeder made no secret of his ideas. It is a pity that the words "pure Shorthorn" were ever added to the old Illawarra breed and type of dairy cattle, as it is farcical. What dairy cattle breeders admit in private conversation they should state publicly.

Hoddles' Track, and from thence along the range to the valley below. The Kangaroo Ground could also be reached from the County of Argyle, by path leading from Bong Bong, and by another path which led from Coura to Cambewarra. Jervis Bay and Coolangatta could also be reached by paths from the Kangaroo Ground; but it was the impression of old settlers that a convenient road could not be found to carry a wheel conveyance of any description in and out of the place. To-day, however, motor cars ply daily through there from Sydney to Nowra and Jervis Bay. In fact, fresh milk is now sent from there to Sydney twice daily.

Inducement is everything to an enterprising man with capital at his command. Governors Macquarie, Brisbane and Darling knew this when they offered the choice lands of New South Wales to bona fide settlers at a quit rent which was at the rate of 2/- per 100 acres per annum, to be paid to the officer in charge of the Internal Revenue. Men of means and energy got thereby every encouragement by way of large tracts of land and free labor to assist them in clearing and cultivating their holding, whether large or small. Free, wealthy emigrants, however, were not the only class of settler who obtained favours from those three Governors. Any man, whether he came bound or free, provided that he gave a pledge that his family would remain in the Colony, got a considerable concession for his wife and each of his children. Grants of from 50 to 100 acres were given to all children under a certain age coming into the Colony, as well as to those who were born within the Colony. Of course, the native born children obtained greater concessions, especially those who were reared in the Parramatta Orphan School. By this system it was easy for either father or mother, with a large family, to obtain a large holding, and by their united industry were enabled to build up a substantial home.

The earliest register for marriages dates from June 16th, 1820, a marriage having been performed on that date at Liverpool. The register is in excellent order, not in the handwriting of Fr. Therry, but in the handwriting of some individual who copied the records of all those early marriages, nearly all of which were celebrated by Fr. Therry.

The entries that interest us are the following:—

Date	Names.	Abode	Solemnised by	Witnesses
1829 Feb. 13	John Hart and Mary Broker	Five Islands	Fr. Therry	Henry Hart and Sarah Hart
1830 May 27	Garrett Donnelly and Mary Ann Cullen	Illawarra	Fr. Therry	Anne Shaughnessy Phillip Hughes

The land system from 1788—that is, from the foundation of the Colony to the arrival of Governor Bourke in 1831—is a matter of concern only to those who wish to study misfit administration. Up to the year 1824 the regulations for the disposal of land were left entirely in the hands of the Governor for the time being. Land was, in the early days of the Colony, bestowed on any man, bond or free, who could undertake to support himself. As the Colony progressed in wealth and population, certain situations became valuable, and were eagerly sought by parties of influence; but large portions were held, especially as pastures, under free licenses of occupation.

The Australian magnates emulated the white slave system by means of rum. Those who had grants of land bartered their holdings to the rum magnates. Hundreds of small land grants were allowed to pass unnoticed by the authorities into the possession of a few wealthy individuals. A keg or a bottle of rum purchased large and small holdings prior to 1831, not only in Sydney and its immediate surroundings, both north, south and west of the capital for at least a distance of one hundred miles. Our fair Illawarra did not escape the rum traffic, and many holdings could be pointed out as the result of purchase by a bottle or a keg of rum, sometimes a pig or a goat was substituted.

Grants of Land.—"Lands granted from the Crown prohibited to be sold, either directly or indirectly, for the term of five years, bearing date from June 8th, 1811."

In 1812 a committee of the House of Commons was appointed to examine the state of the Colony of New South Wales. After examining a number of witnesses, including ex-Governors King and Bligh, a report was printed, from which it appeared that the population amounted to 10,454, distributed in the following proportions:—The Sydney district, 6,158 Parramatta, 1,807; Hawkesbury, 2,389; Newcastle, 100 (of these, 5,513 were men and 2,200 women); military, 1,100; of the remainder, one-fourth to one-fifth were actually bond, the rest being free or freed from servitude by pardon. In addition, 1,321 were living in Van Diemen's Land, and 177 in Norfolk Island, but orders had been sent out to compel the voluntary settlers, who had adhered to that island after the Government establishment had been removed, to withdraw.

Shortly after the allocation of the first grants of land in Illawarra, in 1817, the Government formed a settlement at Red Point, Port Kembla. Dr. William Elyard, R.N., was the first Government visiting officer. The whole of the coast was policed by the military as far south as Jervis Bay. Hence we have Barrack Point at Shellharbour and Kinghorn Point near Jervis Bay. The powers invested in men like Elyard were most arbitrary. It was in their power to hang delinquents on the spot, and give others up to 500 lashes. They moved from centre to centre with a few of the military and a flogger in order to deal with each case that came before them. The stories of the old regime could not withstand the light of day, consequently they were collected and burned. After Alexander Berry got going at Coolangatta all the cases there were tried by visiting magistrates. On one occasion a flogger—a savage—was returning alone to Red Point; he was waylaid on Seven Mile Beach, murdered, and the body left for the dingoes to devour. What else could be expected from men who, after a severe flogging, had to sleep on their bellies for weeks? For a similar crime three men were hanged from the limb of a tree outside the old gaol in Wollongong. In October, 1817, David Allen, Richard Brooks, William Browne, Charles Throsby, Robert Jenkins, and Samuel Terry, who had obtained a footing in Illawarra by cattle raising, were much disturbed by gangs of cattle-stealers. They subscribed £5 each as a fund to secure the conviction of the evil-doers.

"In Illawarra in 1817," says a writer, "trees stood tangled and huge where life displays a vague and tenuous delight, separated, yet mingling in one great animal and vegetable kingdom. The mosses, under and attached to the giants of the forest, were thick and silent, which reminds one of that idolatrous prayer to the sun, 'From whom every good proceeds, of what we at least can discover, the most complete and glorious.'" Glades here and there, the trees no longer hiding them, these are the gates of Illawarra, and the valleys and glens through which the cattle pilgrims hobble along, unable to take advantage of any other means of transit.

C

In 1818 William Emmett was in charge of the Government station at Red Point. He was not a military man, but had the Government cattle under his charge. In 1818 a general order was issued, to begin on January 1st, 1819, calling upon all persons, bond and free, who were engaged cutting cedar in Illawarra, to get permits to do so. About this time we first learn of Charles Throsby, born in England in 1800. He was promised a grant of 1000 acres for finding a fresh track from the cow pastures to Bong Bong. His servants, Joe Wild and Jack Waite, got 100 acres each; another servant, Rowley, got 200 acres. Joe Wild and Jack Waite understood the bush tracks for years before 1819.

In 1819 all those who had merely the right to depasture their cattle and other stock in Illawarra got notice from the owners of the land to find fresh fields and pastures, and these owners settled overseers in charge in order to make their holdings good in the eyes of the Governor. The county of Camden was marked out in August, 1819. During same year Surgeon De Arcy Wentworth was shipping cattle to his Peterborough Estate, Illawarra.

In 1819 Charles O'Brien was appointed Government overseer of stock at Red Point, Illawarra, and Conor Wholohan was managing David Allen's farm at Five Islands. Among the places set apart for grants of land for small settlers was Coalcliff, Illawarra. Hamilton Hume took advantage of the neglect of those whose grants were there to take possession, and sent gangs of sawyers there from Appin to cut cedar thereon in 1823. Cedar getting was at that time an important industry in Illawarra. So extensive was this industry that the Government decided to cease controlling the affairs of the Illawarra or Five Islands district from Sydney, consequently arrangements were made to send a detachment of military to build barracks at Red Point. This took some time to complete in even a rough manner. However, in due time Captain Peter Bishop, of the 40th Regiment of Foot, one sergeant, one corporal, and 20 privates were duly quartered there. When the military got going in Illawarra they were victualled by the ship Schnapper for a short period. In 1820 Lieutenant Robert Johnston was in charge of the Schnapper. It was in the Schnapper that he carried Alexander Berry to the Shoalhaven River.

Up to 1820, the last year of Macquarie's Government, 400,000 acres passed into the hands of private individuals. Macquarie was generous to his friends; from him the settler frequently obtained with his grant the use of the Government gang, who not only cut down, but rolled the logs into piles, and burnt and cleared the timber off land that would not pay the settler to clear with hired labour.

Sir Thomas Brisbane granted 180,000 acres at a yearly quit rent of 2/- per 100 acres. He sold, between December, 1824, and 19th May, 1825, 369,050 acres at 5/- per acre, giving long credit, with, in addition, 2/- per 100 acres; and he also granted in two years between 1823 and 1825, 573,000 acres at 15/- annual quit rent per 100 acres. But it must be noted that all these grants and purchases were accompanied by an allowance of a certain number of convicts per 30 acres to clear and till them, and that these convicts, as well as the settler and his wife, were rationed for a limited period at the expense of the Government.

Sir Ralph Darling arrived in December, 1825. and continued to rule until the year 1831. Some authorities have stated that his six years' administration was singularly and deservedly unpopular. He was a man of forms and precedent of the true red-tape school. He obstinately evaded the control intended to be imposed on him by the secret official and nominee council, and perpetuated many acts of tyranny which had scarcely any parallel in English history. It was under his administration that the Australian Agricultural Company commenced operations. The story of Darling is not worth relating, and nothing that he did can be undone. He followed on the lines of Macquarie and Brisbane with regard to giving away land and supplying favoured settlers with cheap convict labour. 3,000,000 acres of land was disposed of in the manner mentioned by those Governors. In October. 1831, Darling resigned his Government, and Sir Richard Bourke took command. It was under the regime of Bourke that Sir Thomas Mitchell arrived in Illawarra in order to lay out a road through the centre of the district.

Governor Darling had ruled the convicts with a rod of iron. The times of the "first fleeters," the irresponsible floggers, and the short allowance of coarse food were revived, and carried out in Illawarra. The Legislative Council was supposed to be an advance from the Executive Council established by Charter in 1828, held its first meeting in 1829. yet its influence was of no value as regards the poor. Bourke tried to relieve the convicts under his care. All the same, there are long lists of floggings ordered by the several naval and military magistrates who visited, first at Red Point, Port Kembla, later at Wollongong, and from thence south to Kiama and Coolangatta. The first of these magistrates to visit at Red Point barracks was Dr. William Elyard, R.N., he being at the time superintendent of convicts, and stationed at Sydney. He came down in a gun-boat, the "Schnapper," and brought a sergeant, whose duty it was to count and record the strokes of the cat-o'-nine tails, and a flogger to administer the punishment.

The following land grants were issued by the several Governors under the following conditions:—Each person to whom a grant was given received a number of convicts in accordance with the area of land bestowed by the Governor. These convicts were clothed and fed by the Government. Thus the landowners had absolutely free labour provided for them. This state of things was not altered much until the mid-thirties.

Early Grants of Land in Illawarra. Vol. 2, Fol. 129.

52. Wollongong. — 1,000 acres granted to Robert Jenkins; date, 24th January, 1817; quit rent, £1. Commencing 24th January, 1822. Granted by Lachlan Macquarie. Condition: To cultivate 75 acres, and not to sell for five years.

53. Wollongong.—1,500 acres granted to David Allan; date, 24th January, 1817; quit rent, £2/4/-, from 24th January, 1822. Granted by Lachlan Macquarie. Conditions: To cultivate 75 acres, and not to sell for five years.

3. Jamberoo.—2,000 acres granted to Samuel Terry; date, 9th January, 1821; quit rent, £1, commencing from 9th January, 1826 (Mount Terry) Granted by Lachlan Macquarie. Conditions: To cultivate 100 acres, and not to sell for five years.

Kangaroo Ground.—800 acres granted to Richard Brooks on or before 21st February, 1821. Granted by Lachlan Macquarie; quit rent, £1. Not to sell for five years.

Coolangatta.—10,000 acres, granted to Berry and Wollstonecraft, county of Camden; date of grant, 30th June, 1825. Granted by Sir Thomas Brisbane.

Portions 4 and 8—Brundee and Numbaa.— Portion 4 granted to William Elyard, the younger, on 23rd April, 1841. being the land promised to William Elyard. the elder. on or before 23rd April, 1829. Portion 2,000 acres (Numbaa), granted to Alexander Berry on 30th

June, 1825. There was also a transfer of land at Greenwell Point from William Elyard to Alexander Berry, which was an exchange under Government supervision, Berry taking the Greenwell Point property in exchange for Bruudee. Anyone interested could possibly find the particulars in the Mitchell Library, where many of those peculiar transactions are stored. The Crow's Nest, North Sydney, transaction might be found there also.

The first grant of land on the south side of Lake Illawarra was given by Governor Macquarie to Lieut-Colonel Thomas Davey—generally known as "Mad Davey"—situated at Barrack Hill, Shellharbour, in the January of 1817.

Grantee—George Johnston, Esq., senr.; area, 1,500 acres; granted by L. Macquarie on 24th January, 1817; quit rent, £1 10s; quit rent commences 24th January, 1822; name of grant, "Macquarie's Gift."

The Dunlop Vale Estate, near Lake Illawarra, was a grant from the Crown to Mr. John Wyllie, bearing date 1822. It comprised 2000 acres. It was approved by Governor Darling on 13th October, 1829, about which date Mr. Wyllie had it somewhat improved and stocked with many valuable Ayrshire cattle. Mr. Wyllie then went into the employ of Mr. Alexander Berry at Coolangatta, Shoalhaven.

Mr. Bodenham, auctioneer, said Mr. John Wyllie's estate, situated at Five Islands, adjoining Lake Illawarra, was watered by Mullet Creek. This estate had been mortgaged to Mr. William Lang, and was being sold by the order of Dr. John Dunmore Lang, of Sydney. See "S.M. Herald" June 18th, 1832.

Carruth Bros. bought one half of Wyllie's grants.

Gerard Gerard purchased from Carruth Bros., then left Illawarra for New Zealand. Gerard Gerard became a prominent dairy cattle breeder. He sold to Robert Howarth, whose career in Illawarra was a most remarkable one.

Description.—At Illawarra, bounded on the north-east by a north-west line of 151 chains (commencing in a line with the point between Macquarie River and Johnstone's Creek), on the north-west by a south-west line of 80 chains; on the south-west side by a south-east line to the Macquarie River; and on the south-east by that river.

Conditions.—Not to sell or alienate the same for the space of five years from the date hereof, to cultivate 75 acres within the same period, and reserving to Government a right of making a public road through the same, and reserving for the use of the Crown such timber as may be deemed fit for naval purposes.

COLONIAL SECRETARY'S OFFICE, SYDNEY, 23rd OCTOBER, 1832.

Nos.	Persons to Whom Granted.	Grant of Lands. No. of Acres and District.			Governors Promised by, and Dates.
		Camden, as under.			
1	Cornelius O'Brien	300 acres, Illawarra			Governor Macquarie, 31st March, 1821. Quit rent, 6s., commencing 1st January, 1827.
2	Thos. William Warton	100 ,,	,,		Sir Thomas Brisbane, 14th January, 1825. Quit rent, 15s., commencing 1st January, 1831.
3	Michael Brennan	60 ,,	,,		Sir Thomas Brisbane, 14th January, 1825. Quit rent, 9s., commencing 1st January, 1831.
4	Patrick Callaghan	50 ,,	,,		Sir Thomas Brisbane, 29th August, 1824. Quit rent, 7s. 6d., commencing 1st January, 1831.
5	John Kelly	50 ,,			Sir Thomas Brisbane, 20th April, 1825. Quit rent, 7/6, commencing 1st January, 1831.
6	Robert Anderson	100 ,,	,,		Sir Thomas Brisbane, 28th October, 1823. Quit rent, 2/-, commencing 1st January, 1829.
7	John Cunningham	60 ,,	,,		Governor Macquarie, 10th September, 1818. Quit rent, 1/-, commencing 1st January, 1827.
8	Peter Mooney	50 ,,	,,		Sir Thomas Brisbane, 5th August, 1824. Quit rent, 7/6, commencing 1st January, 1831
9	William Underwood	70 ,,	,,		Sir Thomas Brisbane, 20th June, 1825. Quit rent, 11/6, commencing 1st January, 1833.
10	Joseph Underwood	70 ,,	,,		Sir Thomas Brisbane, 20th June, 1825. Quit rent, 11/6, commencing 1st January, 1833.
11	John Anderson	200 ,,	,,		Governor Macquarie, 1st January, 1827. Quit rent, 4/-.
12	Connor Bolan	200 ,,	,,		Sir Thomas Brisbane, 60 acres on June 30, 1824, and 140 acres, 7th April, 1825. Quit rent, £1 10s., commencing 1st January, 1831.
13	Denis Brien	60 ,,	,,		Sir Thomas Brisbane, 30th June, 1825. Quit rent, 10/-, commencing 1st January, 1833.

COLONIAL SECRETARY'S OFFICE, SYDNEY, 23rd OCTOBER, 1832—*Continued.*

Nos.	Persons to Whom Granted.	Grants of Land. No. of Acres and District.					Governors Promised by, and Dates.
14	Peter Lellis	40	,,	,,	..	..	Governor Macquarie, 31st March, 1821. Quit rent, 1/-, commencing 1st January, 1827
15	Richard Lellis	60	,,	,,	..	..	Governor Macquarie, 31st March, 1821. Quit rent, 1/-, commencing 1st January, 1827.
16	Timothy Fogarty	30	,,	,,	..	..	Governor Macquarie, 31st March, 1821. Quit rent, 1/-, commencing 1st January, 1827.
17	Thomas Martin	60	,,	,,	..	..	Governor Macquarie, 31st March, 1821. Quit rent, 1/-, commencing 1st January, 1827.
18	Thomas Trotter	80	,,	,,	..	..	Governor Macquarie, 31st March, 1821. Quit rent, 1/-, commencing 1st January, 1827.
19	John Drummond	280	,,	,,	..	..	Sir Thomas Brisbane, 15th July, 1824. Quit rent, 2/-, commencing 1st January, 1831.
20	George Tate	500	,,	,,	..	..	Sir Thomas Brisbane, 22nd June, 1824. Quit rent, £3 15/-, commencing 1st Jan., 1831.
21	Thomas Moran	40	,,	,,	..	..	Governor Macquarie, 31st March, 1821. Quit rent, 1/-, commencing, 1st January, 1827.
22	Malachy Ryan	30	,,	,,	..	..	Governor Macquarie, 31st March, 1821. Quit rent, 1/-, commencing 1st January, 1827.
23	Matthew Ryan	40	,,	,,	..	..	Sir Thomas Brisbane, 10th September, 1824. Quit rent, 6/-, commencing 1st January, 1831.
24	Isaac Cornwall	60	,,	,,	..	..	Governor Macquarie, 31st March, 1821. Quit rent, 1/-, commencing 1st January, 1827.
25	William Landran	60	,,	,,	..	..	Governor Macquarie, 31st March, 1821. Quit rent, 1/-, commencing 1st January, 1827.
26	John Harris	60	,,	,,	..	..	Governor Macquarie, 31st March, 1821. Quit rent, 1/-, commencing 1st January, 1827.
27	Thos. Simms	40	,,	,,	..	..	Governor Macquarie, 10th September, 1818. Quit rent, 1/-, commencing 1st January, 1827.
28	John Williams	50	,,	,,	..	..	Governor Macquarie, 31st March, 1827. Quit rent, 1/-, commencing 1st January, 1827.
29	Henry Brooks	600	,,	,,	..	..	Sir Thomas Brisbane, 6th July, 1824. Quit rent, £4/10/-, commencing 1st Jan., 1831.
30	Alexr. Monaghan	100	,,	,,	..	..	Sir Thomas Birsbane, 28th October, 1823. Quit rent, 2/-, commencing 1st January, 1829.
31	George Brown	300	,,	,,	..	..	Sir Thomas Brisbane, 26th June, 1824. Quit rent, £2/5/-, commencing 1st Jan., 1831.
32	George Brown	500	,,	,,	..	..	Sir Thomas Brisbane, 11th February, 1823. Quit rent, 10/-, commencing 1st January, 1829.
33	William Harper	50	,,	,,	..	..	Sir Thomas Brisbane, 21st April, 1825. Quit rent, 7/6, commencing 1st January, 1831.
34	James Neale	60	,,	,,	..	..	Governor Macquarie, 16th January, 1816. Quit rent, 1/-, commencing 1st January, 1827
35	W. F. Weston	500	,,	,,	..	..	Governor Macquarie, 30th March, 1818. Quitr ent, 10s, commencing 1st January, 1827.
36	Michael Stack	100	,,	,,	..	..	Governor Macquarie, 31st March, 1821. Quit rent, 2/-, commencing 1st January, 1827.
37	James Stack	100	,,	,,	..	..	Governor Macquarie, 31st March, 1821. Quit rent, 2/-, commencing 1st January, 1827.
38	Daniel Brady	145	,,	,,	..	..	Sir Thomas Brisbane, 12th May, 1825. Quit rent, 1/9, commencing 1st January, 1831
39	Michael Byrne	60	,,	,,	..	..	Governor Macquarie, 31st March, 1821. Quit rent, 1/-, commencing 1st January, 1827.
40	John Rudd	60	,,	,,	..	..	Governor Macquarie, 31st March, 1821. Quit rent, 1/-, commencing 1st January, 1827
41	Thomas Rudd	60	,,	,,	..	..	Governor Macquarie, 31st March, 1821. Quit rent, 1/-, commencing 1st January, 1827.
42	David Johnston	700	,,	,,	..	..	Governor Macquarie, 28th November, 1821. Quit rent, 14/-, commencing 1st January, 1827.
43	Isaac David Nichols	600	,,	,,	..	..	Sir Thomas Brisbane, 24th January, 1825. Quit rent, £4/10/-, commencing 1st Jan., 1831.
44	John Paul	1400	,,	,,	..	..	Sir Thomas Brisbane—600 acres, 16th May, 1823, and 800 acres, 4th June, 1824. Quit rent, £6/12/-
45	William Ralph	1000	,,	,,	..	..	Sir Thomas Brisbane, 14th March, 1822. Quit rent, 11/-, commencing 1st January, 1829.
46	William Bland	1000	,,	,,	..	..	Sir Thomas Brisbane, 14th November, 1825. Quit rent, £8/6/8, commencing 1st Jan., 1833.

COLONIAL SECRETARY'S OFFICE, SYDNEY, 23rd OCTOBER, 1832—*Continued.*

Nos.	Persons to Whom Granted.	Grants of Land. No. of Acres and District.	Governors Promised by, and Dates.
47	Richard Henry Browne	600 ,, ,, ...	Sir Thomas Brisbane, 5th June, 1824. Quit rent, £4/10/-, commencing 1st Jan., 1831.
48	John Cowell ..	800 ,, ,, ...	Sir Thomas Brisbane, 21st February, 1825. Quit rent, £6, commencing 1st January, 1831.
49	Denis Guiney	40 ,, ,, ...	Governor Macquarie, 31st March, 1821. Quit rent, 1/-, commencing 1st January 1827
50	William Elyard	1000 ,, ., ...	Sir Thomas Brisbane, 29th November, 1822. Quit rent, £1, commencing 1st January, 1829.
51	George W. Paul ..	600 ,, ,, ...	Sir Thomas Brisbane, 18th June, 1824. Quit rent, £4/10/-, commencing 1st Jan., 1831
52	William Smith	600 ,, ,, ...	Sir Thomas Brisbane, 19th April, 1825. Quit rent £4/10/-, commencing 1st Jan., 1831.
69	Mary Reiby	800 ,, Shoalhaven River ..	100 acres by Governor Macquarie, 15th March, 1815, and 700 acres by Sir Thomas Brisbane, 13th August, 1825. Quit rent, £5/18/6 stg. per ann.
73	John Cullen	300 acres, Illawarra	Sir Thomas Brisbane, 17th February, 1824. Quit rent, £2/5/-, commencing 1st Jan., 1831.
74	Michael Carroll	100 acres, Illawarra	Sir Thomas Brisbane, 28th October, 1823 Quit rent, 2/-, commencing 1st January, 1829.
75	Charles Macarthur ..	2800 acres ,, ...	Governor Macquarie, 800 acres, 31st March, 1821, and 2000 acres by Sir Thomas Brisbane, 1st Feb., 1825. Quit rent, £15/16/-, commencing 1st Jan., 1831.
76	Frederick Jones	100 acres, Illawarra	Sir Thomas Brisbane, 60 acres, 12th May, 1825, and Governor Darling, 40 acres, 6th October 1830. Quit rent, 15/8, commencing, 1st January, 1827.
78	David Bell	500 acres, Talawa	Sir Thomas Brisbane, 21st March, 1822. Quit rent, 10/-, commencing 1st January, 1829.

Following is a summary of the principal events in a matter which affected the Illawarra district during the years 1821 to 1826.

1821.—The boundaries of Argyle and Camden having been marked, received the Governor's assent. Mr. Charles Throsby is gazetted a Justice of the Peace for Argyle, 17th March, 1821. Charles Throsby had obtained broad acres in the vicinity of Bong Bong. Mr. Cornelius O'Brien notifies proprietors of land in Illawarra that he has discovered a shorter track with an easier grade from Illawarra to Appin Road, and suggests that £10 be subscribed by each settler to make this road available to cattle drovers. Mr. O'Brien thought that seven landowners giving £10 each would be sufficient for the purpose. Date of this suggestion, 29th May, 1821. Grants of land were promised to Alexander Berry, James Badgery, Thomas Campbell, James Donnelly, Thomas McCaffrey, Robert Marshall, Charles Throsby, jun., Edward Wollstonecraft and others, a list of whose names appear elsewhere.

1823.—In 15th February, 1823, "Gazette" there is an article deploring the drought which had visited the whole of the south coast of New South Wales. In 18th February "Gazette"

there appeared an article on the system adopted by the middlemen in the colony, in which those persons were termed "hungry shopkeepers and vulturine merchants." Another article in same paper had for its object the brutality of the officers over the various chained gangs throughout the colony. During this time a wordy war was raging between two press writers, "Old Emigrant" and "Colonist," relating to the middlemen and small settlers. It may be termed the dawn of freedom.

1823.—On 4th September Mr. Charles O'Brien is advertising for a practical man to take charge of the dairy herd at the Five Islands. Mr. Charles O'Brien had been placed in charge of the settlement after the departure of Mr. Dalrymple on August 20th, 1823, when there was a general muster of the cattle and stock belonging to the Government in Illawarra. C. O'Brien was dairying on the Government station at the Five Islands. Dr. Charles Throsby sent 10 fat bullocks to Cribb, a butcher in Sydney, from Bong Bong. Each produced 1000 lbs. of meat. Notice of cattle being stolen in

Illawarra was frequent, notwithstanding that Captain Bishop and a garrison had been entrenched for some time at Red Point, Port Kembla. A severe drought in Illawarra in 1827, and butter was 3/9 per lb. In 1829 there were 9000 head of horned cattle in Illawarra, and a total of 300,000 head in N.S. Wales. The drought continued from 1826 to 1829, caused great depression, and retarded enterprise. Little energy was displayed. Men were arriving in the colony with money and stock, and could find no openings. However, the salt beef and pork trade gave them the desired opening, and in a year or two the drought was forgotten. In 1829 James Pierce was appointed poundkeeper in Wollongong, which place has just been gazetted a postal centre. Prior to that date the buzz and hub of business was centred at Port Kembla. Grazing rights of 2/6 per 100 acres were obtainable from the Crown, such to be abandoned on a six months' notice. In 1825 Conor Wholohan was re-appointed overseer of the Five Islands Estate for David Allen. In same year Dr. Charles Throsby's herd, the progenitors of which were bred in Illawarra, was considered the best herd in N.S.W Wales, and equal to the best English herds. In 1825 the Jenkins Estate, Berkeley, was in charge of John Robinson, and Andrew Byrne owned the Ousdale Estate, where he had cattle grazing. John Wyllie was in possession of his Dunlop Vale Estate, where he had a magnificent herd of Ayrshire cattle. In June, 1829, a "Gazette" notice announced that the Five Islands, Kiama, Gerringong, Shoalhaven, Coolangatta, and Ulladulla were proclaimed post towns. Wollongong was prior to that date known as Bustle Hill, the whole of the land being owned by Charles Throsby Smith, who had a grant of 300 acres there. Among the list of places set apart for small settlers was Illawarra, between Bulli and Coalcliff, on the coast. This proclamation was issued in the year 1822. It must have been an inhospitable spot at that time. No wonder that poor men complained.

Wollongong. The barracks and gaol, which had been first erected at Red Point, Port Kembla, probably about the year 1825, were removed for the sake of convenience to Wollongong, from which Crown-street takes its name, in the year 1828. About this period of our history Mr. Thomas Macquoid was Chief Sheriff, Mr. Cornelius Prout was Under-Sheriff, Mr. Walter Rogers was Clerk. Mr. Alexander Murray was Governor of the Gaol, and Mr. Thomas Morton, Gaoler in Sydney,

where all important criminal matters relating to the Illawarra district had to be referred for final execution. In other respects the Gaol authorities in Wollongong had power to put into execution all the minor powers, such as starvation, the dark cells, and the lash. In the year 1830 Port Macquarie ceased to be a penal settlement; that is to say, no more prisoners were sent there after July 13th, 1830.

Prices in 1825.

Owing to the very extensive arrivals of wheat at our markets for some weeks past the trade has assumed an exceedingly dull aspect. However, the supplies this day were chiefly of a superior description, and sales were conducted at a trifling reduction from the terms of last week. There has also been a large supply of maize at market, but this article fully supports our last quotations. In barley and oats there is no variation.

Average price of wheat—6s 10½d.
Ditto of maize—6s 9d.
Ditto of barley—4s 9d.
Fine flour—22s 6d per cwt.
Seconds flour—20s 6d per cwt.
Potatoes—12s per cwt.
Ducks—7s 6d per couple.
Butter—2s 3d per lb.
Cheese—1s 3d per lb.
Fowls—4s per couple.
Geese—15s per couple.
Eggs—1s 9d per dozen.
Assize price of bread, sixpence per loaf. Selling price, fivepence halfpenny to sixpence halfpenny.

The cattle market has been very moderately supplied this week. A few fine milch cows were sold at extremely low prices, being from £5 to £7 each.

Beef, 2s 4d to 2s 8d per stone; mutton, 3s to 3s 6d per stone; pork, 2s 3d to 3s 3d per stone.

A Prophetic Poem.

"Yes, Master of the human heart, we own
Thy Sovereign sway and bow before Thy throne
In ages far remote, when Albion's state
Hath touched the mortal limit marked by Fate,
When Arts and Science fly her naked shore,
And the world empress shall be great no more,
Then Australasia shall thy sway prolong,
And her rich cities echo with thy song;
There myriads still shall laugh, or drop the tear,
At 'Flagstaff's' humour or the woes of 'Lear.'
Man, wave-like, following man, thy powers admire,
And thou, my Shakespeare, reign till Time expire."
　　　　　　　　—CHARLES SYMMONS, D.D.

Newstead Abbey, August 4th, 1825

NESTLE'S & ANGLO SWISS MILK CO., M.S. STUD, Toogoolowa.

GRACE OF NESTLES (No. 322).

NECKLACE (No. 171).

EMBLEM II OF NESTLES (No. 37).

DOT III OF NESTLES (No. 321).

"On 19th October, 1823," says Baron Field, "I rested on Mr. David Allan's farm—Mr. Allan being one of the officers of the Commissary General Department—and had the merit of settling the Five Islands district." Baron Field had arrived overland at the Five Islands from Sydney on 18th October, 1823, and on 21st October, 1823, was at Berry and Wollstonecraft's house, Coolangatta. A writer says: "Judge Baron Field in the journal of his excursions to the Five Islands and Shoalhaven in 1823 says: 'Illawarra is a fine district of good grazing and some excellent arable land close to the seashore; insomuch that, though distant and difficult from Sydney by land, it was settled in Governor Macquarie's time, when he refused to let anybody go on the other side of the Nepean.' The journal continues later: Walked over miles of the Illawarra farm, the property of David Allan, late Commissary-General of the Colony, who had the merit of setting the example of settling the Five Island district. Rode to Shoalhaven, 36 miles still further south, six or seven of which were through a mass of vegetation, requiring pioneers to penetrate it. Although we set out almost at sunrise, yet it was nearly sunset before we arrived at Shoalhaven, where Mr. Alexander Berry has taken his grant of land on either side of the Shoalhaven River Ascended with Mr. Berry the mountain called by the natives Coolangatta, under which he is building his house. One of the arms of the Shoalhaven is separated from Shoalhaven River by an isthmus not 150 yards broad, and across this Mr. Berry has cut a canal, being the first canal in Australia. Although I am afraid that these grants of land will hardly ever repay Messrs. Berry and Wollstonecraft for their outlay upon them, yet whoever extends the settling of New South Wales further than anybody has gone before him is a benefactor to the colony. I am afraid, in this case, the man has taken possession before nature has done her work. Immense swamps and lagoons have only just been left by the sea, and the forest land is yet indifferent for grazing, but, though the cedar grounds end before Shoalhaven, the sea is open for any exportable produce that can be raised on patches of alluvial soil on the alternate projecting points of the river; and Mr. Berry need not be alarmed lest any occupation of the immediate back country should shut in his cattle run."

Charles Throsby Smith arrived in Illawarra in 1825, having received a grant of 300 acres, comprising nearly half the present site of the town of Wollongong. He got the contract from the Government for victualling the garrison at Red Point in 1826. He used his influence with the authorities to get the military headquarters removed to land adjacent to his establishment, "Bustle Farm." He succeeded, and then tried to get the new settlement called Bustletown. The original name of the place was spelt Wullungah, Wollongong being the newer rendering. Lieutenant John Fitzgerald Butler, of the 39th Regiment. It was a Dorsetshire regiment, and had Captain Charles Stuart and members of the Innes family as officers of a higher rank. Charles Throsby Smith had influence and used it to advantage. In 1828 the garrison was taken from the Red Point establishment, and the settlement removed from there to the north side of the Tom Thumb Lagoon early in 1829. In 1829 there were 9000 head of horned cattle in Illawarra. Lieutenant Butler was appointed commandant and resident magistrate at Wollongong, Edward Corrigan was appointed chief constable, James and Patrick Garraty assistant constables. The penal settlement of Wollongong had full control over the convicts who were portioned out to settlers between Bulli and Jervis Bay. These convicts were not permitted to remain for long in any centre for fear lest they might form secret combines. All criminals were tried by military law. The floggers at Wollongong were Maddell, Roach, Francis (a black savage), and Davey Mott. They used the cat-o'-nine-tails, a military sergeant counted the strokes. The sergeants were usually very exacting. At Coolangatta, while the Government supported the several relays of convicts in the interests of Alexander Berry, a sergeant and five or six soldiers did duty there to uphold "law and order." The sergeant's duty, among other things, was to count the strokes ordered from time to time by the visiting magistrate. Henry Arthur Burton Bennett, clerk. James Pearce was appointed poundkeeper for Illawarra. Horned cattle were being sold at the pound to defray expenses at £2 per head. Gerringong was in 1829 owned by three persons, namely: Omega by Cornelius O'Brien (in trust for Thomas Campbell); William Smith, 640 acres, now known as Miller's Flats; Michael Hindmarsh's 640 acres.

1829.—On 1st June, 1829, among the list of towns published by proclamation were Five Islands, Kiama, Gerringong, Shoalhaven, Coolangatta, and Ulladulla.

1829.—On December 19th, 1829, arrived in Sydney the convict ship "Sarah," Captain Colombine in charge, with Alexander Osborne, Esq., R.N., as superintendent, there being in Sydney at that time also Messrs. John Osborne, R.N., and Henry Osborne. A lease was granted to Mr. John Wyllie of 2,000 acres in Illawarra in accordance with the proclamation issued 16th October, 1828. This land adjoined Mrs. Jenkins' property.

In 1830 the military forces were controlled by Major D. Macpherson, Lieutenants Butler and Sleeman, belonging to the 39th Regiment of Foot. Crown Street was being formed, and an hotel, "The Bull," was being erected for the convenience of the travelling public by Lawrence Timmins. Drs. R. M. Davis and William Elyard, Ms.D., were the visiting doctors.

From 1830 to 1840 many changes took place in connection with the district's rapid development. Roads had to be formed and such works as were considered necessary for the convenience of the settlers. These works were carried out by convict overseers with convict labour. Anyone who may be anxious to learn who they were who ruled over the destinies of the several batches of convicts (who were being constantly moved from centre to centre in the colony lest they might form close friendship) need but look up the names of the streets in each village and town between Bulli and Jervis Bay, and they will find the names of many of those convict overseers commemorated.

W. C. Wentworth, who had obtained the right from the Government to cut the timber off 5268 acres of land lying between the north bank of the Minnamurra River, near Jamberoo, and the top of Mount Terry, entrusted the duty of cutting the timber thereon and having it delivered at the little port at Shellharbour to his manager, John Pugh Nicholls. By this system the real settlers of Illawarra were robbed of their rightful inheritance, to wit, the finest timber in the world. If my readers will but examine into the real benefactors of the great Illawarra district, from Bulli to the boundaries of the original county of St. Vincent (which embraced but a margin of land adjacent to the foreshores of Jervis Bay), it will be found that the small landowners—those who got the crumbs from the tables of the several governors—were the real powers in the development of Illawarra. These men came on the scene after the large landowners had destroyed the wealth in timber that Nature had stored up for the use of future generations.

The following persons were registered in 1832 at the post office, Wollongong, as receiving letters:—Mr. James Allpin, Dapto, Wollongong; Mr. Gerald Anderson, St. Vincent, Wollongong; Mr. Henry Angel, Fairy Meadow, Wollongong; Mr. H. A. B. Bennett, Wollongong; Mr. Charles Bennett, Dapto, Illawarra; Mr. Edward Birmingham, Dapto, Wollongong; Mr. George Brown, Illawarra, Wollongong; Mr. Charles Campbell, Shoalhaven; Mr. Thomas Campbell, Kiama; Mr. William Clarkson, Dapto, Illawarra; Mr. Charles Clayton, Dapto Forest, Illawarra; Mr. Matthew Conroy, Kiama, Illawarra; Mrs. Hannah Cooke, Illawarra, Wollongong; Mr. Edward Corrigan, Wollongong; Mr. Thomas Cowper, Shoalhaven; Mr. James O'Brien Croker, Wollongong; Mr. Henry Davis, St. Vincent; Mr. Robert Dixon, Illawarra, Wollongong; Mr. Thomas Dundon, Illawarra, Wollongong; Mr. John Egan, Illawarra, Wollongong; Mr. Christopher Echlen, Dapto, Wollongong; Mr. Jonathan Eddis, Kiama, Wollongong; Mr. Alexander Elliott, Crown Inn, Wollongong; Mr. Phillip Elliott, J.P., Illawarra, Wollongong; Mr. William Elyard, sen., R.N., Brundee, Shoalhaven; Mrs. Bridget Farraher, Illawarra, Wollongong; Mr. Samuel Foley, Illawarra, Wollongong; Mr. William Garratt, Shoalhaven; Mr. William Gates, Illawarra, Wollongong; Mr. Humphrey George, Illawarra, Wollongong; Mr. Richard Glenvill, Shoalhaven; Mr. William Graham, Wollongong; Mrs. Sarah Greylish, Illawarra, Wollongong; Mr. Henry Harris, Fairy Meadow, Wollongong; Mr. Henry Harris, Illawarra, Wollongong; Mr. Michael Hindmarsh, Illawarra, Wollongong; Mr. John Hoare, Dapto, Illawarra, Wollongong; Mr. Peter Howell, Dapto, Illawarra, Wollongong; Mr. Michael Hyam, Sarah's Valley, Kiama, Wollongong; Mr. Thomas James, Illawarra, Wollongong; Mr. F. Jones, Illawarra, Wollongong; Mr. Thomas Kain, Illawarra, Wollongong; Mr. Michael Keefe, St. Vincent; Mr. Thomas Surflect Kendall, Illawarra, Wollongong; Mr. Joseph Kendall, Ulladulla; Mr. Hugh Kennedy, Illawarra, Wollongong; Mr. John Kennedy, Illawarra, Wollongong; Mr. John Layton. Wollongong; Mr. William Lloyd, Wollongong; Mr. Patrick Lysaght, Wollongong, Illawarra; Mr. James Martin, Illawarra, Wollongong; Mr. James Mitchell, Dapto, Wollongong; Mr. Robert Mitchell, Shoalhaven, Illawarra; Mr. Thomas Nash, Illawarra, Wollongong; Mr. John Nicholls, Shellharbour, Illawarra; Mr. Thomas O'Brien, Dapto, Wollongong; Mr. Cornelius O'Brien, J.P., Illawarra, Wollongong; Mr. Henry O'Neil, Appin, Wollongong; Mr. John Osborne, Garden Hill, Illawarra; Mr. Henry Osborne, J.P., Garden Hill, Illawarra; Mr. James Pierce, Wollongong; Mr. Charles Quinn, Dapto, Wollongong; Mr. Rae, St. Vincent; Mr. John Reddall, Wollongong; Mr. John Riddell, Peterborough, Wollongong; Mr. John Ritchie, Kiama, Wollongong; Mr. William Ritchie, Kiama, Wollongong; Mr. Benjamin Rixon, Charcoal Creek, Wollongong; Mr. William Roberts, St. Vincent; Mr. John Robins, Dapto, Wollongong; Mr. John Robinson, Mullet Creek, Illawarra; Mrs. Sophia Rogers, Kiama, Illawarra, Wollongong; Richard Rourke, Dapto, Illawarra; William Ryan, Charcoal Creek, Wollongong; James Shoobert, Illawarra, Wollongong; David Smith, Kiama, Wollongong; J. G. Spearing, Paul's Grove, Wollongong; Marcus Spearing, Belambie, Illawarra; John Spinks, Wollongong; Edward Swan, Mullet Creek, Illawarra, Wollongong; George Tate, Wollongong; Lawrence Timmins, Bull Hotel, Illawarra, Wollongong; Mr. C. Waldron, J.P., Spring Hill, Wollongong; William Wilson, Wollongong.

In 1833 there was a drought in Illawarra equal in severity to that of 1827-28-29. During these visitations many settlers left the district, and never looked back. In the early thirties great friction arose owing to the squatters memorialising Governor Bourke with a view of preventing ticket-of-leave men taking up large holdings or owning any description of stock. Counter-charges were sent along to the Governor, each charging the other with cattle-stealing and sly-grog selling, until there was little or nothing withheld, and the Governor was forced to believe that both cattle-stealing and sly-grog selling were common practices, and he was compelled to fall in with the views of the ancient, intrepid mariner, that it was the rule of the road. To show that Illawarra was by no means free of the contagion of cattle-duffing, in the year 1836 William Nairn Grey, Police Magistrate, Dr. John Osborne, R.N., Henry Osborne, Esq., J.P., and Colonel Leahy formed a branch of the New South Wales Cattle Association in Wollongong, and Messrs. John Lamb and David Berry formed a branch at Shoalhaven, with a view of preventing cattle stealing. Wollongong butter was selling in Sydney at 2/3 per lb.

The trustees in the estate of the late Captain Richard Brooks were offering Barrangery, 950 acres, at Kangaroo Valley, for sale on the ground at Brooks' stockyard, June, 1836. It was purchased by James Osborne, of Bong Bong, who in turn sold it to his uncle, Henry Osborne, of Marshall Mount, Illawarra. John Neale's farm at Dapto, Illawarra, 110 acres, with stockyard, cow-shed, piggeries, dairy and dwelling house erected thereon, was in the market for sale. The allotments of land in the newly-formed township of Wollongong were selling freely. Jas. Stewart bought 19 half acre lots and William Wilson 9 half acre lots on 8th October, 1836.

1833.—The Reverend Thomas Hassall performed Divine service in the Barrack Room, Wollongong. During the reverend gentleman's stay in Wollongong he expressed a hope that his people would soon hear the church bell ringing. The bench of magistrates received several complaints from other local magistrates and employers of labour in Illawarra to the effect that "Davy the Flogger" was not using the "cat and nine tails" with sufficient severity. Evil-doers, they contended, weren't frightened by his efforts at correcting their vices. Further, it was stated that some of the evil-doers would sooner have Davy at their backs all day than do the work they were put to.—Dated March, 1833.

1833.—In April, 1833, Reverend Father Therry celebrated Mass in the Barrack Room, Wollongong, christened a large number of children, and married two persons—in other words, joined in the bonds of holy matrimony the first pair in Wollongong! First school opened in Wollongong.

Through Father Therry's exertions the first building erected solely for the worship of God was erected by the Catholics and their friends in Wollongong. Rude in structure as it must have been in 1833, it displayed the depth of religious feeling that was present. It was the first place of worship on the south-eastern slopes.

1834.—In 1834 the list of magistrates in Illawarra comprised:—Phillip Elliott, Esq., William Nairn Gray, Esq. (Police Magistrate, Wollongong), Cornelius O'Brien, Esq., Henry Osborne, Esq., Captain Waldron, R.N. Postal arrangements had improved. The Campbelltown Royal mail left thrice weekly at 4 p.m. for Illawarra, leaving Wollongong for Sydney by return. Mr. Jas. O'Brien Croker was postmaster at Wollongong. Francis Allman, Esq., was

Commissioner for taking Affidavits in Illawarra. The Registrar stationed at Wollongong was Mr. James O'Brien Croker, and Mr. Edward Corrigan, Court Crier. The police establishment at Wollongong, Mr. William Nairn Gray was Police Magistrate, and Mr. Jas. O'Brien Croker was Clerk of the Bench. The Ecclesiastical Department in Illawarra was in charge of Rev. Frederick Wilkinson, A.M., and Mr. W. Davies was in charge of the primary school at Wollongong.

1836.—There were 6000 acres of land under cultivation in the Illawarra district, the labor of small settlers. The formation of the Australian Auction Company, 1836.

Extracts from "A Narrative of a Visit to the Australian Colonies," by James Backhouse, of the Society of Friends, consisting of a tour which lasted six years, commencing at Hobarttown, Tasmania, on 2nd March, 1832:—

Without attempting to follow the writer until the party began their journey to Illawarra, the narrative runs as follows:—"Stayed with a widow who had a large family at Appin. One of her sons guided James Backhouse to Illawarra (after describing the scenery, the flowering shrubs and timber, etc.) "A spot of cultivated land on the coast affords a treat to the eye, such as is seldom enjoyed among the vast forests of Australia. We descended by a rough track called the Bulli Road." (Then follows more description of the scenery.) "This road is difficult for horses, and impracticable for carts, except by the assistance of ropes passed round conveniently situated trees, by means of which in a few instances they have been brought down. After reaching the beach, our way for eight miles was along loose sand to Wollongong, near which our toils for the day found an end in the hospitable dwelling of Charles Throsby Smith, the chief proprietor of the place, which we reached when it was nearly dark, after a walk of 27 miles.

We went to Wollongong, which is on a small boat harbour. The buildings at present erected are a police office, two stores, two public houses, a Roman Catholic chapel, a few dwelling houses; a barn is also fitted up for an Episcopal place of worship. In the afternoon we met a large road party, in charge of a military officer, at a place a mile and a half from the town (date 21st September, 1836). They were assembled in a large open shed with a number of military, who were under arms, where they had their meals, the wives of the military being present. The prisoners were those sentenced

from Great Britain to work on the roads for certain periods before being assigned. They were at one time ordered to work in chains, and for periods as long as seven (7) years, but this excessive and injurious severity has been relaxed, and they are exempted from chains, unless as a punishment for improper conduct, and if they behave well they are assigned at the expiration of two years. Hope is thus kept alive, while strict discipline is likewise maintained, only three being flogged from 1st to 22nd September, 1836. The prisoners are lodged and guarded in the same manner as the ironed gangs. Though the station is called a stockade, there are no defences around it." (Then follows more descriptions of scenery, but more of a comparative nature than previously.) "Being furnished with horses by some of our friends, we accompanied a young physician a few miles off the coast, off which there are five islands that gave the district the name of The Five Islands, by which it is familiarly known by the lower class of the colony. On a little cleared spot of land near the margin of the Lake, is the habitation of a settler in humble life; it is a very rustic hut, covered with bark, and internally having much of the sombre hue. . . . . From this place we went to the hut of a friend to dine. It was of rough slabs, covered with bark, rustic, in the full sense of the word, and scarcely protecting his valuable library from the weather. Here he is superintending a flock of sheep, the joint property of himself and one of his friends, who is also temporarily dwelling in same habitation. But Illawarra not being favourable country for sheep, though a delightful climate, and fine soil, well adapted for agriculture, and which will no doubt become the Egypt of Australia, our friend is about to remove his flock, to one of the more elevated southern districts. The person referred to here was William Shelley, who had relatives at Parramatta. (Then follows more description of scenery, the word painting of which, like the narrative throughout is pleasant reading.) "Accompanied by two of my acquaintances, we proceeded to Dapto, a little settlement, on 25th September. 1836. on the following day we were detained at Marshall Mount. On that day we engaged a native black named Tommey, to be our guide to Bong Bong—a native of the Kangaroo Ground. He was of middle stature, rather broad shouldered, and had a depressed nose, through the cartilage of which he wore a bone." (More descriptions, and the mention is made of

JOHN HARDCASTLE, Jinbiggaree, Dugandan, Queensland.

CHAMPION RED BULL, JAMBEROO.

EARL OF DUNMORE.

WHITEFOOT 2nd OF JINBIGGAREE.

DARLING OF MAYFIELD.
(No. 684, Vol. II, I.H.B., Q'ld.)

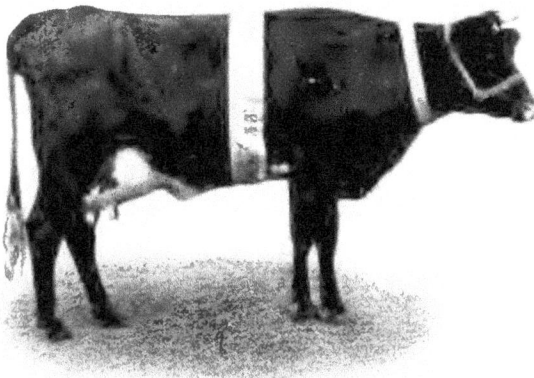

BUTTERCUP II OF JINBIGGAREE.

DIANA 7th OF JINBIGGAREE.

calling on a few settlers on the way to Kiama, which is described as follows):—"Kiama is situated on the Coast, at a little boat harbour; it consists of about a dozen cottages, built of wood, occupied by a blacksmith, a carpenter, a shoemaker, and a constable's house, where the police magistrate holds his court. We passed a mile beyond it to the house of a settler, where we were hospitably received," etc. (Then follows more descriptive reading matter.)"We left the rich district and emerged on the coast, about seven miles north of Shoalhaven, where we received much hospitality by Alexander Berry, the proprietor of extensive territory. When Coolangatta was approached religiously there was little response. Here black Tommey left without notice, and Lewis, an aboriginal from Tasmania, and Bani, a local black, became our guides. Broughton Creek station was under the charge of a respectable Scotch family. We reached the Kangaroo Ground, a stock station, before sunset. A man was in charge of a hut, who was a prisoner, in a bridge party, at Windsor, when we visited that place a year ago. Forty men of the Kangaroo Ground tribe were going to the cow pastures to learn a new song invented by the black people there. For this purpose they often travel great distances. All the men had gone through the ceremony of having a front tooth knocked out. There were 200 in the tribe. We reached Throsby Park, and were received with great hospitality by Mrs. Charles Throsby, of Bong Bong. An aged man named Joe Wild, who accompanied Robert Brown, in his botanical researches in N.S. Wales and Van Diemen's Land, and who discovered the district of Illawarra, was sent with us as a guide to Black Bob's Creek, and to bring back the horses on which we rode, as we wished to pursue our journey southward on foot, after visiting the bridge and road party. This part of the Colony is about 2000 feet above sea level. On 7th October, 1836, we visited the ironed gang at Marulan. The Marulan gang consists of such as have committed offences after assignment. Here the punishment, to which they are subjected, for misconduct in the gang is flagellation; and in some instances they have received 600 to 800 lashes within a space of eighteen months, at the rate of not more than 50 lashes for one offence." Reader, pause, and think of this punishment. The flogger was black Francis, a huge negro, who was employed by the authorities for that purpose. What must the state of things in Australia, prior to the arrival of that somewhat humane Governor, Sir Richard Bourke? Echo answers clink, clink! swish, swish!

The chains, the cat-o'-nine-tails, and the cuffs were much the same everywhere in N.S. Wales, wherever a gaol was erected. So was the system; 23 hours utter darkness in each day, one hour for daylight and exercise. This would continue every day for from nine months to three years, according to the sentence. In country gaols, a week or a month in the dark cells was the limit for magistrates. All those sentenced meant so many days on bread and water. Hence the vast numbers of what were termed run-aways, who faced death from starvation or life or death among the myall blacks. Run-aways and those who harboured them suffered severely when caught, yet, they demonstrated the possibility of a pure democracy. The only distinction to be won was that of being trustworthy to their benefactors. The good man was he who was kind and true; the bad man was he who was capable of betraying a confederate. In order to destroy brotherly love the system offered large bribes to the bad men.

The Illawarra, or Five Island District.

Mr. Surveyor Wells, in his Gazetteer of New South Wales, published in 1848, described Illawarra as follows:—

Illawarra as an Incorporated District.

Illawarra, an incorporated district of New South Wales containing 570,557 acres, of which 137,917 are alienated. It embraces the eastern portion of the County of Camden, and a small portion of the County of St. Vincent, bounded on the north, by a line west. to the head of the Cataract River, commencing on the shore near Bulli; on the west by the Illawarra Range, thence by a line to the middle sources of the Kangaroo River, thence by that river to its confluence with the Shoalhaven River, and by this river to its confluence with the Endrick River; on the south, from thence by a line bearing north-easterly to the source of the Yerrimong Creek, thence by Yerrimong Creek to a point from which a line due east would meet the north-west corner of Daniel Cooper's grant of 880 acres, thence by the south-eastern margin of Saltwater Lagoon to the northern point of Robert Lambert's grant on the sea shore, which forms the eastern boundary to near Bulli aforesaid. This council contains seven (7) members, including the warden.

Illawarra as a Police District.

2. Illawarra.—A police district of New South Wales, embracing the eastern portion of the County of Camden, and the northern portion of St. Vincent, bounded on the north by a line west to the head of the Cataract River, commencing on the sea shore near Bulli; on the west by the Illawarra Range, thence by a line to the middle source of the Kangaroo River, thence by that river to its confluence with the Shoalhaven River, and by this river to about two miles south of the Warreamungo, on the south by the range north of Endrick's River, to the source of Yalmal Creek; and again by a range to Lamb's grant, and by the eastern shore of St. George's Basin to Sussex Haven, and thence by the sea shore, which forms the eastern boundary to near Bulli. It contains 4210 inhabitants and 763 houses.

Note.—A few years after publishing the Gazetteer of N.S. Wales, Mr. W. H. Wells was drowned in Ritchie's Creek, Jamberoo, in a flood whilst endeavouring to reach his home—Kiama.

Illawarra, by David Christie Murray:—"A home of beauty which I visited was the Bulli Pass, and, if there is anything better worth seeing in Australia, I will go to see it, though it cost me a thousand miles of travel. Half way up the winding ascent we paused to look at a giant gum tree, which stands retired, as great beauties sometimes will, and hides its splendour in the lowly vale. We paid our homage to the giant—a living giant—and, making our way back to the road, resumed our ascent of the pass. The vegetation on either hand grew dense, and splendid cabbage palms, cactus, aloe, tree-fern, and scores of other families were there in glorious tangle. It was not until we reached the first outlook, that the rich beauty of the place we had come to visit declared itself, no word painter ever lived who could actually convey to the imagination of another the image of everything he had seen. But futile as the task must be, let me essay it. To begin with, picture to yourself a rough little paling at the precipitous edge of the road, lean over it if you have the nerve, and if you choose you may drop a pebble which will fall more than 200 feet without touching clay or foliage. Below to the front, the left and the right, lies the sea—a scene of most delicate azure fading on the horizon into palest torquoise. The sands are ever golden, and curved into innumerable bays. A line of white foam following the delicate outlines of the shore, breaks utterly unheard away and away; and away to the right waves this most undulating triple line of blue and white and gold until they are met together in the distance. The land sweeps boldly up in striking lines, and every hill side is a very riot of verdure, and every hill side is pleasing. The gum asserts itself here and there, but mixes its grim grey with many more cheerfully coloured growths, and in the mid-distance slender columns of blue smoke mark the whereabouts of some unseen manufactory or mine. On the extreme verge of the distance the white houses of the town of Shellharbour gleam softly with brightness chastened by the intervening air. An unbroken stillness broods over all, and though the atmosphere is as clear as crystal, as the vividness with which all objects at moderate distances are seen declares a tender blue gauze seems everywhere drawn across the distance. It seems half to shroud the brightness of the sunlit sky, and thickens softly towards the horizon, so that sea and sky melt one into the other."

According to the Picturesque N.S. Wales. published in 1901:—"In 1797 Surgeon George Bass saw the Blowhole (at Kiama) and was the first white man to give a description of it. He was obliged to stop during a coastal voyage, in a little bight just south of Illawarra, and found behind the shore, in a hollow circular space among the rocks, a hole 25 or 30 feet in diameter, into which the sea rushed by a subterranean passage."

This account was no doubt obtained from the log kept by Bass. But the old settlers used to tell us that the old black king—Captain Brooks—used to speak of having been present at the landing in Botany Bay of Captain Cook; and in Sydney when Captain Phillip landed; and also in Kiama when Bass landed under the old fig tree. It was a tradition among the old black-fellows—that in the long ago—a black-fellow was cast down the Blowhole for a crime, and a big wave cast him up again alive. The tribe never visited the place again.

Captain Brooks (an aboriginal king), native name unknown, claimed to have seen Captain Cook at Botany Bay, and to have been at the landing in Sydney of Captain Phillip; and in Kiama when Surgeon George Bass landed near the old fig tree in Kiama to explore the famous Blowhole. He got the name, Captain Brooks, from the sawyers who knew that he piloted John Cream and Captain Richard Brooks's cattle from Lake Illawarra to the Kangaroo Ground, in 1821. The old black king had, according to the old sawyers' views, tasted human flesh in various forms. He was a connoisseur and could describe roasting to a turn. He was in 1850 a very old man, totally blind, having to be led from place to place by the tribe. On July 4th, 1857, he was left alone in the camp near the lagoon, Kiama; a westerly wind blew the embers from the fire into where he was lying, and his charred remains were discovered there.

The Governor, Sir Richard Bourke, visits Illawarra, 1st May, 1834.

In 1834 an address was published from the residence of Illawarra to the Governor, Sir Richard Bourke, on his visit to Illawarra. In his reply, His Excellency said that his principal motive in visiting Illawarra then was to see how the beautiful fertile district could be opened up by road, and its communications with the Sydney market improved. Messrs. Cornelius O'Brien, George Brown, William Gart, Thomas Coaply, William Wood, Thomas Smith and others signed the address to the Governor.

When the land of New South Wales was thrown open for sale in unlimited quantities, at a minimum of 5/- per acre, all who had occupied superior land, with or without licence, sought to purchase their occupations; many rounded off their grants, and took in slices of barren land for uniformity, for pasture, or for water. Others who had neither influence, nor ability to wade through the dreary forms of the bureaucrats and martinets under Governor Darling indulged in freehold as soon as it became a matter of money, stimulated during the years from 1828 to 1836 by the offer of assigned servants, commissariat assurance, and a road-making Government, it paid the more wealthy settlers in Illawarra to improve their holdings and attempt better systems of cultivation and dairying. Thousands of acres were in a short space of time brought into an improved state. This system enabled the wealthy to overrun their poorer neighbours who could not find money to fence their grants of land. Hence the man who had money bought up for a few pounds sterling thousands of acres between those years that lay between 1830 and 1838. An alarming number of "land transfers" are to be found in our Lands Office, Sydney, dealing with lands lying between Bulli and Jervis Bay during those years.

The great ruin wrought through the financial failures of the late twenties compelled the authorities to issue practically a new map of New South Wales. It was commenced in 1831, and completed in 1835. Only a few men were strong enough financially to withstand that crash. Fat bullocks could be bought for £1 per head, and sheep were purchased in flocks at 1/- each. Henry O'Brien, who had removed from the Five Islands to Yass Plains found a way out by establishing the Boiling Down industry. Alexander Berry and others purchased scores of land grant orders and converted them to their own use at ridiculously low prices by means of barter. Influence was then brought to bear on the Government to issue deeds to the holders of these cheaply acquired lands. Applications for transfers of rights to such holdings followed, and a Court of Appeal appointed, consisting of Captain Peter Bishop (40th Regiment of Foot), Chairman; Captain John Moore Foley (3rd Regiment of Buffs); Lieutenant Henry Miller (40th Regiment of Foot); Lieutenant John George Richardson (40th Regiment of Foot); and Lieutenant William Wilson (48th Regiment of Foot).

Many applications were considered by this Court of Appeal. Scores of soldiers' grants in Illawarra passed into the possession of those who sold rum wholesale and retail. This caused another tribunal to be created in 1835, known as the commission for hearing and determining upon claims to grants of land within the Colony of New South Wales. President Sydney Stephen, Barrister-at-Law; Thomas Livingstone Mitchell, Surveyor-General; Roger Therry, Commissioner of Courts of Request, Secretary; John Dillon, Lower Elizabeth-st.; non-commissioned officers and privates who were discharged from the service for the purpose of settling in the Colony were allowed free grants to the following extent:—Sergeants, 200 acres; Corporals and private soldiers, 100 acres each. All officers desirous of becoming settlers after 1832 had to purchase it at public auction sales. They were, however, entitled to remission of the purchase money according to length of service— 20 years £300, 15 years £250; 10 years £200; 7 years £150. Crown lands, on the other hand, were leased to anyone from year to year.

Sufficient has been stated to show those who are in possession of the deeds of their farms how the said land came to pass through so many previous owners. In some instances land in Illawarra was in one way or other in the hands of six persons, not one of whom ever did a day's work on the land.

Illawarra.—What is the meaning of the name? In Governor Macquarie's first proclamation regarding the permanent settlement of the district he referred to it as "The Illawarra or Five Islands district." In the writer's school days the schoolmaster, a clever man, and a native of Sydney, used to say: "Illawarra is the black man's meaning for Five Islands." Later on Mr. Thomas Surfleet Kendall said: "Illawarra means happy place. I called my first home 'Happy Villa' on that account." Later still we are told that Illawarra means "Water far away." Methinks this same authority has given us other meanings for Illawarra.

With regard to the language of the pure-blooded blacks of Illawarra, all I have to say is this: In my schoolboy days when my hearing was as keen as any living white boy I could not catch the blacks' pronunciation of scores of places in Illawarra. I could not catch the words and passed on. I might as well add that at the old home on the banks of Jemara Creek, Kiama, we had black visitors back as long as my recollection can carry me.

To Begin My Story.—Between a dying system and one waiting to be born Major-General Lachlan Macquarie stood as Governor of New South Wales on December 31st, 1809. When he took over the rulership there were ahead of him difficulties that would have caused a weak man to falter.

Macquarie had this advantage—the naval rule in the young colony was doomed with the passing of Bligh, the old order had come to an end. Always advancing, the new ruler drove all before him over mountains and difficult river crossings. The pioneers under the favourable conditions offered them by Macquarie converted the Illawarra district into smiling homesteads in the course of a few short years. It was he who laid the foundation of Illawarra's first real settlement. He gave the land freely to those who desired to settle on it.

It has been repeatedly said "that the historical instinct among the English people has never been very keen. So that it is much more difficult to form an historical society among the purely English-speaking people than in any other country." It is, therefore, plain why so few of the objects of a truly interesting character have survived the life of one individual. Yet, there is a reason in nature as profound as the being of man why

we should always pride ourselves in our past, present, and future. It is simply this: No other creatures on this planet has ever been able to create a history of its kind. To man alone belongs the faculty of looking before and after, and considering the story of his race from the first human being that walked on the face of the earth. Our first forefather brought with him something new—the power to store up and celebrate memories of the great dead. His elemental pieties have become part of the whole tradition of our humanity; and that history which he began, and to which we add day by day, is our witness of the division of man from the other creatures of this world. When, then, we cherish this study we are proclaiming our pre-eminence among all living beings.

Illawarra has its own history, and it is with a view of putting that history on a sound basis that I have taken upon myself the task of recording solid facts. It goes without saying that at least two governors before the arrival of Macquarie shut their eyes and closed their ears to much of what their friends did. In this they were merely human. From 1813 to 1830 things were very different in Illawarra from Bulli to Jervis Bay, and as far south as Ulladulla was under civil and military rule. It is difficult to say how far south the district of Illawarra extended in those days. We have the assurance of Thomas Surfleet Kendall that Illawarra extended as far south as Ulladulla. He said: "The whole of the country between the mountain range and the sea was originally known as the 'Illawarra or Five Islands district.'" We can, therefore, as natives of the district, peacefully await the discovery of documents that may throw more light on the subject.

I am well aware that this book is open to a great multitude of criticism. It will be said for example, that it is unscholarly and unlearned, because to deal with a subject so sacred as the history of our first settlement demands a knowledge of partristic literature. It must not be forgotten, however, that this book is intended for the dairymen of Australia and their sons, who—after all has been said and done—can claim, and must claim Illawarra as the first great dairying centre in the Commonwealth. It is patent, or it should be, to all readers of this book that we are each and all unable to discourse on the primitive state of Illawarra prior to the arrival of, say, those who began to clear the land in real earnest. Its scenic beauty was prior to 1830, beyond the descriptive power of travellers who were evidently so overcome at the sights that met their view at every turn that they moved on and on—silently unable to comprehend the majesty of nature.

Who despoiled the beauty spots of Illawarra? At once let us say the most useful and progressive men that ever came to New South Wales, namely, the assisted emigrants who arrived in Illawarra between 1827 and 1857. Those who arrived between 1837 and 1847 faced the real solid bush, and cut it down, cleared the land and planted and reaped the crops. When they got going they helped those who came out year by year afterwards. These people and their families destroyed the scenery but they did for Illawarra what Illawarra required. They made grass grow where no grass ever grew before on many thousands of acres of scrub land.

It may be said, "Much of this history is rhetorical and inexact, emotional and uncharitable." Well, the book itself is its only defence. I stand behind the book, and if the biographies of our pioneers do not contain deep thoughts their histories are of a truly practical nature. These men, and women, too, had but one aim and one ambition. They wanted to get on the earth where they could make a living and build up honest homes. It is patent that the scrub lands with their scenic beauties was an obstacle in their progress. It was at once a cover for marsupials and wild cattle that raided their crops at night, so it was cut down and burnt regardless of its future value. After all scenery is merely for the idle rich to delight in. Fruit, maize, potatoes and wheat, a few dairy cows, pigs and poultry were the support of the early settlers in Illawarra. From twenty to thirty acres were found sufficient to keep a family of six or seven human beings in comfort. The soil was rich in humus and potash, so rich, indeed, that fruits and vegetables were full of merit. The plentiful supply of rich food produced great men and women. In the early days of Illawarra there were difficulties that had to be overcome with regard to getting produce to Sydney, and when it was delivered at a wharf there was no recognised system by which it could be disposed of. Consequently each of the farmers had to go with the boat on which his produce was carried to attend to its delivery and sale in Sydney.

Goods were bought with the proceeds of the sale and brought back to Illawarra. There were many small vessels trading in this way on the coast from the earliest times. Among those traders were Thomas Barrett and John Cullen, who in conjunction, owned the "Foxhound." Thomas Barrett owned by every right "Herne Farm," near the Figtree. His son, Thomas, was born there in 1824. In 1826 the "Foxhound" with a cargo of farm products left Illawarra for Sydney. She had on board Thomas Barrett, two soldiers, three convicts, several settlers, and the crew. She went down at sea with all hands (17 souls), and the Barrett family were later on cheated out of their property by a few cunning residents.

In 1836, ten years later, "The Black Swan," loaded up with farm products and cedar, left Illawarra for Sydney. She had—strange as it may seem—the same number of people on board as were on the "Foxhound," viz., 17, including Patrick Lysaght, of Fairy Meadow, two soldiers, and three or more convicts. She was never heard of again. She went to the bottom with all hands. The Lysaght family were fortunate to hold papers relating to their holding. It was a grant to Thomas Martin, who had sold it to Lysaght.

Many stories come down to us from the old families who had lost their rightful property owing to their forebears trading with very cunning settlers whose main object in life was to grab property.

The cunning people, whose names could be given, were always ready to bribe one set of convicts to lay false information against their fellow convicts. In this way useful men were compelled to serve an extra term of years. Certain convicts were bribed to steal produce. An unfortunate case of this kind happened near the "Figtree" where an ex-convict shot a fellow-convict. Another convict was duly hanged for being in the vicinity. Seldom did any of the ex-convict overseers remain long in Illawarra—a few certainly remained, but they were never respected. No one had a good word for them. The same may be said with much truth of the convict masters who had the reputation of sending their assigned servants to the triangles from Bulli to Jervis Bay.

"The Rust" in wheat gave the settlers in Illawarra their first set-back in 1860. This meant that more dairying had to be undertaken which at once demanded more scrub-clearing to get more grass for the cows. Apparently, there was no part of Australia on which nature's generous hand, benign and benedictory, seemed specially to have been laid in bountious blessing, than in Illawarra. As the train from Sydney to Nowra at the present time sweeps around Stanwell Park, what an unique enjoyment is at once obtained, as a western district man once stated the experience he had to the writer. "You come to a place where you can shoot wallabys from one side of the carriage, and catch schnapper from the other side."

Whilst enjoying, during that train route, the few rough patches of scenery that is left to us in Illawarra, how few there are who are capable of thinking of the labour and toil expended by men and women in making Illawarra what it is to-day from a commercial standpoint. Does anyone realise what it cost to clear these scrub lands. Methinks, very few could think it. Does anyone know what cheap convict labour did for the wealthy class in the Illawarra district? I doubt it. Do many know that convicts, working like bullocks in pairs, ploughed land in Illawarra? It is true that they did so.

One of the men responsible for these cruel acts caused one of his assigned servants, "a lifer," to be repeatedly flogged. On the last occasion the poor fellow was so severely punished that, when being marched back with others, he dropped dead on the road. A tyrant overseer, an ex-convict, used to cut the rations off those under him and sell them. He was found out, eventually, and sent for a term to Van Diemen's Land to serve another term. What of the over-lord? The convicts had to deal with him—in their spare time. They caught him one night, tried him by convict rules, found him guilty, and gave him an unmerciful flogging. He became more cruel, and he was followed towards the Monaro plains. He got another flogging which cut short his days in Illawarra. He must have been a vile tyrant as the old convicts forgave much in those days. Let us pause and rest while we note certain events. If the first church erected in Australia was largely the product of convict labour, and, if many of those convicts were afterwards flogged for failing to attend the worship that was conducted there, if those who were termed free mechanics were paid for their labour in rum and tobacco? What could be expected from those who had grants of land in Illawarra? Certainly

nothing more Christian could be looked for. As the tourist proceeds from Wollongong going south, he comes to Unanderra, the aboriginal name of this place was "Cullingung." In early times the Government erected a stockade at this spot. A man named Beaver built a house there in which he traded with the prisoners and settlers. George Brown was an interested party in another direction, so he gave Beaver much trouble. Among the charges laid against Beaver was that of sly-grog selling. This shop changed hands more than twice, and then George Lindsay, grandfather of the present family of Lindsays of Dapto and Unanderra, took it over and combined farming with store-keeping. Edward Hammond Hardgraves lived in the vicinity. His son William Henry was born there in 1839. Hardgraves went to Gosford in 1840, and then on to the Californian diggings in 1849. Richards, who established Richard's Tannery, was an old Sydney native, born before the year 1815. Woods opened a public house at Unanderra, and E. Way opened a public house on Barrett's Creek about 1853.

The Illawarra range when viewed from the sea is in great measure destitute of naturally systematic arrangement, consisting not so much of groupings as of utterly irregular amassments, and occasionally of isolated heights, such as Kiera, Kembla, Cooby, Koorinan, Nuninuna and Cambewarra.

The ravines and glens which fling the streams down to the sea, forming singular foils to the immense masses of rocks in fantastic or architectural forms. But the details of this magnificent series of slopes superbly adorned and opulently varied screens cannot be described by an historian beyond this. They must have been the scene of great events in former times.

To-day, a visitor is struck with the beauty of this mountain side country, subdivided and diversified with homesteads, grass paddocks, crops, and dairy cattle grazing right up under the most rugged peaks. Many forms and shapes, both natural and artificial, create a countless number of these landscapes, all agreeable, many pleasant, some highly picturesque.

The scenery of Illawarra viewed from Saddleback Mountain, is nought but intricacy, multiplicity, uniqueness, opulence, and has in consequence baffled every attempt at either verbal or pictorial description. The surface or ridge of this plateau may, in a general

KIAMA A. & H. SOCIETY, ILLAWARRA.

THE LANDSCAPE.

THE PAVILION.

The Kiama Showground—The most picturesque site in N.S.W.

FOUR PENS OF RED ILLAWARRA DAIRY CATTLE, EXHIBITED KIAMA SHOW, 1923. THE EQUAL OF THIS EXHIBIT HAS NOT YET BEEN SEEN ON ANY SHOWGROUND IN AUSTRALIA.

view, be characterised as being diversified with gravelly ridges sombrely patched, surrounded by a great variety of tiny, flowering shrubs. Some of these are beautifully gemmed. There are a variety of small bogs and swamps which in times of drought on the coast afforded a living for starving stock. The real view point of this range spur is that place where the grey-faced rocks stand overlooking, so to say, the Valley of Jamberoo. It commands, owing to its position and altitude, the one central position in the Illawarra range. A scenic power. If "Illa" means water, and "warra" far away in our native black language, one could easily imagine a young black accompanying his chief for the first time to the coast for a "fish feast," as was the old-time custom, exclaiming on reaching the summit of those grey, stately rocks, "Illa, Illa, Warra, Warra." The Pacific ocean in front, gorges and gullies, glens and ridges displaying escarpments, ravines, cliffs, pinnacles, with a general intricacy of outlines in sufficient amount to constitute both force and character in the higher orders of landscape, and around the whole is hung out one of the most magnificent natural panoramas in the Commonwealth. The land behind this elevation is not inviting. It is, however, a place unequalled as a prospective health resort in the future. It is right in the centre where nature blends mountain air with the sea air. All that is required to make it a tourist resort is good roads.

When Mr. Surveyor Hoddle was laying out the old tracks that led from Bong Bong Street, Kiama, to the chief town in the county of Camden, is it not a pity that he did not attempt a description of what he beheld from the summit of Saddleback, and from that great wall of white shaded rock that overlooked all the valleys and gorges below both north and south of the range.

One might easily imagine that the atmosphere, life and scenery of that ideal spot would adopt themselves to both the painter and the poet. A writer in his preface to Adam Lindsay R. Gordon's poems could have gained much had he visited that spot. However clever he may have been elevated to where sea and mountain air meet. As it was he wrote from an out-back position. "The dweller in the wilderness acknowledges the subtle charm of this fantastic land of monstrosities; he becomes familiar with the beauty of Loneliness. Whispered to by the myriad tongues of the wilderness, he learns the language of the barren and uncouth, and can read the hieroglyphics of gum trees, blown into odd shapes, distorted by fierce hot winds, or cramped with cold nights, where the Southern Cross freezes in a cloudless sky of icy blue. Thus the wild dreamland of the bush interpretes itself." Whereas on old Saddle-back there is an air of liberty, magnificence, and splendour that naturally inspires brilliant thoughts as she stands in her pristine beauty. Then there is the almost indescribable lyre-bird. The beauty in tints of other birds. The mountain wild flowers. It is truly from such places that poets should write. Where on a clear day one can see rivers and streams winding silvery to the sea. Just west from the summit of this range lie the Bishop's Lookout, and two very beautiful waterfalls—the Gerringong and Kangaroo falls. Some day there will be a famous health resort built up in the vicinity of these places.

The agricultural operations in Illawarra were for years carried out under great difficulties, and consequently in the roughest style with the crudest implements, and ploughing was done by single-furrow ploughs drawn by teams of bullocks. Reaping was done by hand with reaping hooks. Threshing was done by means of a flail until the Maguire-Comerford, Duncan Bros., Henry's, and Vidler's threshing machines came into use. Newer systems of agriculture followed until the soil was too much cultivated, especially on the hill sides. Neither the soil nor the climate were at fault originally in Illawarra. It was the system of farming and farm-leasing which combined to bring about degeneration. Crop after crop was being solicited year after year from the same enclosure without rest or manure of any kind to restore the elements of fertility in continual process of exhaustion. Rotation of crops, change of seed are good so far as they go, but they do not replace the soil that is washed off the hill sides. Heavy rains have washed off thousands of tons of rich soil into swamps and gullies. In the course of a few years the swamp lands became the richest possessions in Illawarra, while the uplands became useless.

Tobacco growing was tried in Illawarra. There were several plots on the banks of Mullet Creek, Dapto. The Messrs Black tried it at Jerrara, near Kiama, and Michael Hindmarsh tried it at Gerringong. So far as the writer knows it was not a commercial success.

Fruit and vegetable growing in early Illawarra was such a simple process that almost every home had an orchard and vegetable garden, and a page of names could be supplied of successful orchardists.

Flour Milling was carried out in many centres. Plants driven by wind power, water power, and later by steam power. Peck and Palmer, George Brown, Archie Graham, Henry Osborne, Captain Hart, I. Blay, John Sharpe. Berry, and Macpherson in far away Cambewarra.

Tanneries were plentiful. Nicholls had a tannery on the site of the present railway station, Wollongong. Allan followed, then Howarth, Richard Bros. at Charcoal Creek, Unanderra. Michael Hyam, Jamberoo, was followed by Harry Doddens, Greenwood at Kiama, where Blay's Creek was afterwards called Jack the Tanner's Creek.

Horse racing, the sport of kings, was indulged in by all classes.

Shortly after the arrival of Governor Sir Richard Bourke in the colony, a number of gentlemen held a meeting in Wollongong with a view of forming a race club. As the Governor was considered to be sympathetic George Brown applied to his Excellency for permission to hold a race meeting in Illawarra. The application was granted, and in due time a course was laid out on land originally granted to Edmond Burke on which George Brown had erected an hotel. The first race was won by George Brown's "Black Jack." "Black Jack" was the horse that Dan Sullivan, better known as Dan the Postman. was riding, carrying the mail between Campbelltown and Wollongong, when he was drowned trying to cross the Loddon river when flooded. George Brown's grey mare, "Fanny," won the third race. "Fanny" was the dam of George Brown's noted grey entire— a well-known sire—named Schnapper. George Brown used to ride Schnapper on his daily rounds watching his convicts at work on the banks of Mullet Creek. This first race meeting in Illawarra was on the flat due south of where the Commercial Hotel stands in Crown Street, Wollongong to-day, and was held on 17th March, 1832.

A series of pages could be written about race meetings held in Wollongong, Jamberoo, and Kiama during the early forties. The Church of England and the railway station are to-day on the old Kiama course. Shoalhaven had important meetings later on on the flat at Green Hills, and later at Numba, on the Shoalhaven River. Apart from those centres of sport and pastime there were a number of smaller meeting places where horses were tried on their merits.

The Timber Trade.—Possibly the first industry in Illawarra was the timber trade. Away back in Governor King's time cedargetters were working in the bush depending on floods to carry the planks out to sea to be picked up by boats trading along the sea coast. The trees nearest the banks of streams were the first disposed of. It was not for some years that bullocks were brought into requisition. Captain Hart's mill at Jamberoo, and Berry Bros.' mill at Broughton Creek (now Berry), were both driven by water power. Nothing remains to-day of those large concerns but two mill races which carried the water from the creeks to the water wheels. Saw pits were numerous. McIllraith Bros. opened a sawmill on Jerrara Creek, near Kiama.

Kiama.—The aboriginal names of this beauty spot is lost to us owing to its objectionable meaning. The first settler, David Smith— Davey the Lawyer—could not read nor write, and therefore, could keep no records. The military and then the postal authorities gave the place its present name, spelt Kiami and Kiama. The huge fig tree which stands to-day at the water edge has stood there for a long, long time. It was there that Surgeon George Bass landed when he discovered the "Blowhole." A beautiful sandy beach graced the foreshore then. The old town was as well known by the name "The Beach" as that of Kiama.

To "The Beach" the early settlers used to say they were going when they set out to meet the boats that called in, and lay off near the old fig tree. An old-time store stood on the shore adjacent to the fig tree, which was pulled down, re-erected and added to, decade after decade. It became a boat store, a Presbyterian Church, a commercial store, and a council chamber, and its timbers are now in a dwelling house overlooking the North Kiama railway siding.

The aboriginals had a story which they imparted to the first white settlers about one of their tribe, in the long ago, committing a great crime for which he was thrown alive down the "Blowhole," and that a big fellow gush of water threw him up again. The would-be executioners ran away in fright and never returned to the "Blowhole" again, which they associated with an evil spirit. Hence the origin of the word, "Kiama."

When shipping became more important a jetty was suggested. About 1844 the Colley Bros., James and John, got the job of erecting the jetty. After finishing this work an interesting case came before James Mackay Grey, J.P. Two men had been locked up in the old wooden lock-up by Constable Doyle. Next morning they were presented to the magistrate in a more drunken state than they were on the day before. This made the magistrate curious, so he investigated, and found that a friend of those in the lock-up, by means of two long straws, enabled the thirsty ones to get down a pint of rum each. As this was against the "Law of the Land" the Colley Bros. got the job of repairing the old lock-up. This was to the entire satisfaction of James Mackay Gray, J.P., and he then entered into an agreement with the Colley Bros. to build his home, "Omega House," on the Gerringong Road, which had a cellar on the lower side, and four secure cells, into which prisoners were placed when under arrest from Coolangatta and Numba, to be tried at Kiama, which was for years a police court centre.

Up to the mid-forties a military magistrate attended each month at Kiama. Then the lesser cases came before three local magistrates which included James Mackay Gray, Dr. Robert Menzies, and David Lindsay Waugh. Each of these local men were allowed a plain-clothed constable. Neither of these magistrates were permitted to order more than 25 lashes, and all three combined not more than 50 lashes. Quite a number of men were flogged in Kiama. Constable Doyle was for years chief constable. Eventually all four constables wore uniforms, which included jet black glazed helmets, short trousers, and white cotton sox.

Since 1860 dairying and pig farming became the chief industries in Illawarra. Very little change took place in the system in vogue from the thirties and forties. It was all the same, namely, setting the milk in pans, and skimming off the cream by means of a tin hand-skimmer. Churns changed from the stationary up-right to the revolving barrel churn worked by hand power. The factory system began with a cheese factory on Thomas McCaffrey's farm, near Jerrara Creek, Kiama. This was followed by a condensed milk factory at Omega, near Kiama. The pioneer butter factory followed near the old "Toll Bar," Kiama, in 1883. Albion Park opened in 1884. Two factories opened in 1887 in Jamberoo. From the Jamberoo centres the factory system spread over the dairy centres of New South Wales, Victoria, and Queensland.

The writer of these notes was the first manager of the Wanghope butter factory, Jamberoo. I have a diary of events going back to the beginning of the co-operative butter factory business since 1886. During the past 36 years there have been many changes. Fortunes have been made out of the sale of dairying and refrigerating machinery. What has the dairyman to show to-day for all the money expended on those things? I have piles of literature on the export of butter and the establishment of city milk supply companies extending over thirty years. Yet, finality has not been reached.

Kiama, situated midway between Wollongong and Nowra, and always in close touch with Gerringong, Jamberoo, and Albion Park, was throughout all those years of advanced thought the storm-centre. As it was the leading members of the Kiama A. & H. Society who were the chief movers in all matters connected with dairying and dairy cattle breeding. It was from Kiama and its immediate surroundings that the first real co-operative movement sprung. This goes to show that it was an intelligent place.

Kiama soon became an important centre, and then men and women, too, began to enquire about the meaning of the word Kiama. We have, however, conclusive proof that it is not the original name of the place from the diary of the Rev. Thomas Kendall as the following extract will show. "Illawarra, December, 25th, 1827, buried a Govern-man-servant of Mr. Ritchie, about 20 years old, on church reserve, named ————." The name was withheld by the Rev. Thomas Kendall and his son, Thomas Surfleet Kendall. The latter's explanation of the omission was that the original aboriginal name was a vulgar one, and that Kiama was substituted by somebody unknown to the Kendalls. That is what Robert Oscar Kendall told me when I returned the diary after carefully copying it. The spot where Ritchie's man was buried is the southeast corner of Bong Bong and Manning Streets. It is plain, then, that we would be to-day ignorant of this bit of his history were it not for an unfortunate man's death. As to when

John Ritchie settled in the neighbourhood of Jamberoo no one knows for certain. He was there in 1825, and at that period was well established. Near the Christmas of 1827 a boat arrived in Kiama with provisions and other wares, and was seeking consignments for Sydney. John Ritchie despatched his team in charge of a man known as "Big Will," and about the same time sent his stockman, "Red Jack," off with a mob of cattle that were to be delivered to Berry's stockman at the Crooked River, Gerringong. "Big Will" delivered his consignments in due course at the "Old Figtree," and re-loaded the goods for Ritchie. Afterwards he moved out to a spot a little to the west of the site of the Catholic Church to camp for the night. The bullocks were turned out on the adjacent point. He was joined later by Ritchie's stockman, who was hungry and thirsty. A jar of rum and a pint pot were convenient. Next morning when "Big Will" awoke he found his companion dead. He at once reported the matter at the barracks that stood due north from the present police quarters. An officer came from Red Point to hold an enquiry only to find that all the chief witnesses were drunk. so he locked them all up until they were sober enough to explain matters coherently. In the meantime Rev. Thomas Kendall had the unfortunate victim's last mortal remains buried as already stated.

Some people may be disposed to ask if there is really need for this sort of information. It would, however, be difficult, if not impossible, to find any given number of persons who are really agreed on anything important to mankind. Why! there are men who look upon records of many and repeated failures as being out of place in their advanced times. This latter class cannot see much that is attractive in any history book. Their experience to them is apparently everything. But experience is often a very narrow, dear school in which to learn. Wise men study the failures of others and thereby learn in time to avoid danger.

Unfortunately, too many writers and speakers who dwell upon by-gone days, and call back the heroes of the wild bush from the land of shadows, do not write or speak from out of the fulness of knowledge. On the contrary. their knowledge is often misty and dim, and they are ignorant of many things in the lives of those very men whose memories they invoke. With regard to the original or aboriginal names of places we are left to the mere imaginings of those who were not born when the aboriginal kings and queens ruled over their several tribes in peaceful Illawarra. What was old Illawarra when cruelty reigned supreme? Most of the inhabitants were at best mere slaves, and many were worse off than slaves. During the old slavery days the slaves were well fed; in old Illawarra the slaves were starved and then flogged for complaining. What of the newer Illawarra? Selfishness now takes command. The coal mines are owned by men who have no interests in the district outside the coal pits or coke stacks. The old type of dairyman is fast disappearing. Men who are on the best farms care but little for anything outside their own fences.

These men have no interest in settling people on the lands in other parts as they fear competition. True this is a characteristic of the men on the rich soil of Illawarra. The men struggling on the poorer lands are far more generous. Consequently a day will come when the people will demand equality. Then we will see justice meted out to the miners and small dairymen in Illawarra. Verily, the old pioneers were as a rule cruel, but those in their places are dreadfully selfish. They hate anything that tends to disturb their easy-going selfish habits. They have made the most beautiful spot in Australia a hum-drum place to live in.

Kiama Land Sales.—In 1835, fifty acres realised £50; in 1836, 558 acres realised £342 19s.; in 1837, 97 acres realised £331 8s.; in 1838, 252 acres realised £465 10s.; in 1839, 4675 acres realised £6,134 1s.; in 1840, 477 acres 3 r. 4 p. realised £14,943 12s.; in 1842, 100 acres £100; in 1843, 251 acres, £538 1s. 4d.; in 1844. 246 acres 3 r. 16 p. realised £389 11s.; in 1845. 118 acres 0 r. 24 p. realised £231 3s. 1d.; in 1847. 375 acres 2 r. 24 p. realised £578 10s.; in 1848. 212 acres 3 r. 12 p. realised £239 16s. 9d. The total land sold in Kiama from 1835 to 1859 was 25,792 acres 1 rood 37 perches which realised £81,535 18s. 1d. The total expenditure on public works from 1847 to 1859 was £1,323 6s. 9d. The remarkable high prices of land in Kiama in 1840 called for the attention of Governor Sir George Gipps who, in a report to the Home authorities, declared that a block of land comprising ½-acre had realised £400, and was the third highest price realised for land in New South Wales. The block in question is situate at the corner of Ferralong and Manning Streets, now in the possession of the Rural Bank.

WILLIAM H. DUDGEON'S STUD CATTLE, Glenthorne, Bangalow, N.C.

KITCHENER OF BURRADALE.
Sire, "Gus of Hill View"; Dam, "Fussy III of Hill View."

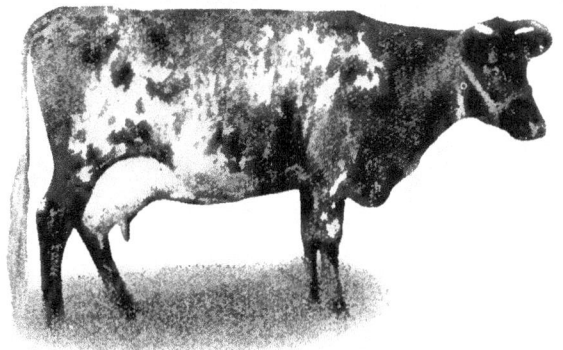

CARNATION OF GLENTHORNE.
Sire, "Kelso of Glenthorne"; Dam, "Posey of Hill View."

LADY KELSO OF GLENTHORNE.

MOLLY OF GLENTHORN.

MOLLY II OF GLENTHORNE.

BLUE BELL OF GLENTHORNE.
Test cow for full year:—17,809 lbs. of Milk; 3.9 per cent.

"**The Kangaroo Valley,**" originally known to the white population as the "Kangaroo Ground," is an extensive gorge in the South Coast Range drained by numerous streams that in turn drain several lesser gorges. Its history embraces the past and the present in its silent bosom. Under the green foliage of to-day, there lie, rotting slower or faster, the forests, and animals, yea, humans—black and white—of other years and days. Some have rotted fast, such as plants of annual growth, and are long since quite gone to inorganic mould, others like our gigantic cedars, growths that last a thousand years. You will find them in all stages of decay and preservation, down deep in the history of man. The "Kangaroo Ground" was, possibly, for centuries a black man's paradise. No one seems to be quite clear on the question, "When did the white man first invade this gorge?" It abounded in cedar. Who were, then, the first cedar-getters to enter upon the great task of getting it out? It was a secure place for cattle-stealers. To prevent cattle-stealing in Illawarra, Captain Richard Brooks got a grant of land, Barrengarry, which, by the way, is an Irish place name, and may have been associated with someone engaged in earlier times who raised bullocks for hauling cedar logs to the banks of streams to be convenient in flood-time to be floated down, down to the Shoalhaven River. Many may say: "The course of those streams were far too savage for cedar logs to survive the forces of Nature." Many now living can remember that a bullock was taken away by a big flood from Barrengarry, and landed safe and sound at Greenwell Point. Just one, out of a mob of twenty, owned by Daniel McIllraith. That being so, it is reasonable to suggest that cedar logs would be carried down safely.

Prior to the death of Captain Richard Brooks, the Rev. Parson Meares had a large gang of convicts engaged in "cedar-getting" in the Kangaroo Ground. To get at the situation of this important gorge we must take our survey from the range beyond Panton's Estate, Bombala, where the stations of Jenkins, Nicholson, Chisholm, Bell, and Dr. Hill adjoined. From these estates eastward the country broke into very deep ravines that feed the Shoalhaven River. They were, generally speaking, inaccessible in the early days. Into one of them, however, a path led down the Meryla Mountain into the valley of the Kangaroo Ground and the Bujjon River. Another path led from Bong Bong into the gorge, and then there was Jack Cream's track from the Illawarra side. In point of fact, the Yarringa Creek, Kangaroo River, and Bundanoon Creek joined the Shoalhaven River before it was joined by the Bungonia Creek. Near the head of Bungonia Creek there was a stockade. It was on Dr. David Reid's Estate, named "Inverary." It was from here that three soldiers and a flogger were sent into the Kangaroo Ground to carry out their duties in Parson Meares' time. A leaning tree took the place of the "triangles."

After the death of Captain Brooks, Barrengarry passed into the possession of James Osborne, a nephew of Henry Osborne of Illawarra, who placed an ex-convict named Ben O'Brien in charge. Later on Henry Osborne bought it. James Osborne then took up "Yacandandy" Station on the Murray River. About 1839 Henry Osborne sent James McGrath to take charge. He was the father of James McGrath of Cambewarra, and Henry McGrath, Green Hills, Shoalhaven. Horses and cattle were raised there in those days. About 1840 James McGrath went to Woolomi, on the shores of Jervis Bay. The country was wild in those days, with the exception of the meadow land where only a few scattered trees stood. English grasses soon displaced the natural grasses. All that was required then was to erect barns to hold the English grass hay. Each year the meadow was mowed and the hay cured and stored. No scarcity of any kind of food for man or beast. Wild bulls were man's worst enemy. A rifle soon drove them into the ranges. They were of the Cape of Good Hope breed, and they flourished in the ranges for many years.

Further down, the Shoalhaven River was joined by the Yarralla Creek, Werriamungo River, which is fed by Budgong Creek. (Grose had a station on Yarralla Creek). Curro Creek and Windella Creek (where Cartwright had a station).

Going back to Barrengarry. After James McGrath left, a man named Leech, took charge. He was a good judge of "beef Shorthorn," and bred for the station owners until 1840. In 1846 the writer's father took charge, commenced dairying on shares. He left in 1852. From 1852 until the death of Henry Osborne in 1858 the management was taken over in quick rotation by Johnston, Tritton, Wallace,

Brownlee and Swan. Then for a short terms the management was under the control of Henry Hill Osborne, the eldest son, who was living at Avondale, Dapto. Later on Alex and Ben Osborne took possession of Barrengarry and Glenmurray. "Murray" is an aboriginal name. The peace of the Osbornes was soon disturbed by a host of free selectors, who took up much land under Sir John Robertson's famous Land Act. Among these selectors came Daniel McIllraith from Sea View, Kiama. He succeeded in getting hold of a splendid block of meadow land on the Barrengarry holding. He surprised the Osbornes. Others got hold of good holdings in the Kangaroo Ground. The selectors had their difficulties—no roads, no bridges, dangerous crossings. The pack-horse was the chief means of getting produce in and out. The roads were mere tracks for years. When Mr. Alex Campbell was elected to Parliament in 1894, he proved himself to be a friend to the settlers. He worked hard to better their position. He obtained grants of money to form roads and build bridges. Shortly afterwards the town of Broughton Creek, Nowra, and Moss Vale could be reached by wheeled conveyances. A township sprung up, and the locality became known as the Kangaroo Valley.

Bendeela, an adjoining holding in the Kangaroo Ground to Barrengarry, was in charge of a man named "Conroy," in the interests of Alexander Brodie Spark, a Sydney merchant, in the late thirties. Conroy had previously been in charge of the stockade at Kiama. Samuel William Gray later on became the owner. Several people went to Bendeela from Coolangatta. Also a few newly-arrived emigrants from Great Britain. It was there where old Mrs. MacDonald was born in 1842. This good lady left her mark on lower Shoalhaven. She is now spending the evening of her days with her daughter, Mrs. James Watts, at Brundee. Many other children were born in that lonely gorge—the writer's two brothers, Charles in 1848, and John in 1850. Just how those children were taken over the ranges to be baptised in Wollongong is not easy of explanation. The strong faith of their parents faced the difficulties and accomplished much. We have heard of the pack-horses and pack-mules, and of coffins and butter being sent in and out empty and full astride a mule. We have heard of graves that the old pioneers fenced in, and of men who kept the fences in repair. Who could be found to point out

one of those old sacred spots to-day? In a lonely valley such may be expected. But if we go to Kiama there may be seen a plot of land where a cemetery was fenced in, tombstones erected over old pioneers. What has happened? The fence was taken away, the railing burned, the tomb-stones used for hearthstones in houses, and potatoes grown in what was once called "God's Acre." Full of grief for a time, then wanton destruction.

Jervis Bay is in the county of St. Vincent, and situated 80 miles south of Sydney. It forms a safe port for ships of all sizes, being large and commodious, easy of access, affording shelter from all winds, convenient to coal and fresh water. It extends about twelve miles inland. On one side there is a small inlet with a depth of five feet at low water, and in the past this was considered an excellent site for a dock—a natural dock, so to say. What is now called Bowen Island was named "Longnose Bay," by Captain Cook. Bowen Island, the most desirable spot in the bay, has a sea front formed of high vertical rock, in many places deeply rent, from which the land slopes gradually on the opposite side. In the early thirties it was moderately wooded or covered by long grass. Perpendicular Point marks the northern entrance of the bay, and rises from the sea in a perfectly vertical direction to the height of 600ft. It forms a conspicuous object on the coast showing neither tree nor shrub as viewed from the sea front.

We are told that Jervis Bay and the county of St. Vincent which was originally a small area of land around the foreshores of the bay were named after Sir John Jervis, who afterwards became Earl Vincent. Captain Arthur Phillip reported very favourably on Jervis Bay to Secretary Stephens, from information received from Captain Weatherhead, November 18th, 1791, who had called in there in the ship "Matilda," for repairs. Lieutenant Richard Bowen called in at Jervis Bay in the ship "Atlantic," November 8th, 1791.

In order to get at the origin of the old township, Huskisson, I wrote Mr. Hugh Wright, who is in charge of the Mitchell Library, Sydney. He suggests that the township of Huskisson "may have been named after the Right Hon. William Huskisson, who was Secretary of State for the Colonies when Darling was Governor of New South Wales." If that is the origin of the name it seems plain that Governor Sir Ralph Darling sent the soldiers, gangers, and convicts down to build wharves, erect houses, and cut the road, "The Gap," through the "Jerawangle" Mountain. The Right Hon. William Huskisson was killed by the first motive engine running between Liverpool and Manchester in 1830. The old jetty was built at the same time. Men of eighty years, who were born near Jervis Bay, speak of the old township as being of ancient origin. That the "Gap" was cut by convict labour in the long ago goes without saying. Upon the sandstone walls of the "Gap" were to be found many years ago the initials of human beings which were cut in the long ago. Fifty years ago no one could recognise the men whose initials were deeply cut in the face of the rock. These initials may not represent convicts' names, as the convicts. under a cruel taskmaster, were not permitted. nor allowed the time to indulge in such pastimes. We may, then, conclude that there is nothing left to us of the original of Huskisson beyond ruins that cannot be deciphered to-day. All we know about the old township is that it was at its zenith in 1829. with 1500 people formed into what was supposed to be a permanent settlement. About this time, or early in the thirties, a heavy easterly gale destroyed the jetty, carrying it away, together with much produce. The jetty was not rebuilt, and the old township was condemned. Edward Deas Thompson, who married a daughter of Sir Richard Bourke. owned the old township, or what was left of it, in 1841. He had a grant of 2560 acres on the foreshore. John Lamb had a grant of 2560 acres on "Wool Road," St. George's Basin, and on Cockrow Creek, Parish of Bhenwerre. Yet. nothing was done of note. The old inhabitants were hanging on waiting for future developments. In 1841, Edward Deas Thompson commenced to establish "South Huskisson." His land was in part sub-divided, and 100 lots sold by auction realising £3519, which would average £117 6s. per acre. Subscriptions totalling £800, came to hand to form a new road to the "Gap," and beyond it to Nerriga. Colonel Mackenzie was the first to send a load of wool from Nerriga. The steamer "Tamar" called for a series of cargoes. Later, the "Sophia Jane" took up the running between Sydney, Wollongong, and Jervis Bay. Yet this newer township did not progress. which makes the matter of getting at any definite history very confusing owing to those who did not see the old township, Huskisson, confusing it with the newer town, South Huskisson. The most reliable information comes from those who took notes on the spot and preserved them. No writer can expect to please everyone. There are always men who look at things from different angles.

A Valuable Diary.—A man named Bernard Brown, who entered the employ of David Berry in 1849 as overseer of the Jindyandy dairy, afterwards became a policeman, and finished up as an auctioneer, kept a diary up to the time of his death on January 1st, 1884, at the age of 72 years He never missed a day during all those years, and dated down everything that came under his notice. He placed on record many notes relating to Huskisson, and the several places around Jervis Bay. He has Edmonds. Joseph Ricketts, John Scott, William Lake. John Bascombe, John Payne, during 1837-8. which time he had entered into a private agreement with a Mr. Sly which was to last until 1839. In 1837 there is mention of an agreement between Mr. Wareham and Arnold Poole re an advance of £700 on a wool property.

There are names given as follows:—John Coffin. Robert Cox, Rev. Mr. Cooke, S. Saxby, James Gillingham, Richard Symonds, James Saunders and Mr. Head. Then we have Sly, Pitt, and J. W. Carter, Richard White, Robert Cox, and John Jarvis, Richard Hopkins and William Westbrook. These people had to do with Huskisson at Jervis Bay. He mentions in his diary horse racing, cricketing, law suits, accidents, a few deaths, and a case or two of murder. It's a valuable diary, and should be placed in safe keeping in the Mitchell Library.

Old men of to-day who saw the ruins of Huskisson in their youth are emphatic in their opinions that the old township was laid out with great care. and that some of the buildings were equal to those in Sydney at the time, which included numerous storied buildings, erected with bricks locally made. The locality abounded in excellent timber, so that sawn timber and shingles were easily obtained. At one time when Jervis Bay was an important place of call for masters of ships to replenish, there were several licensed hotels, and many persons were to be found who were prepared to risk the business without legal authority. Many people understood the "fine art" of making "poteen," (mountain dew). Illicit stills were numerous. A running stream, known as

Dawson's Creek, supplied the township with water, and higher up, supplied water for the "stills." These stills were kept going long after the township had disappeared in order to supply the ship masters.

The ruin of Jervis Bay may be put down solely to Sydney merchants. Ben Boyd applied for land on the foreshores of the bay. The combine blocked him. He was in consequence forced to go to Twofold Bay. Had he been given space there the Riverina trade would have been soon developed as he had the money at his command to build it up, whereas the Jervis Bay magnets had little or no capital at their command. Their stock-in-trade was selfishness.

The Berrys tried to make use of Jervis Bay. An old convict was supplied with the ways and means to cut a track through from Numba to Jervis Bay. His name was McNamara. He made his task light by composing doggerel about the people with whom he came in contact and on all passing events. The hides, salt beef and tallow from the Coolangatta boiling down works, and butter from Jindyandy dairy went to Jervis Bay. Bernard Brown was in charge at Jindyandy in 1849. William Robinson was in charge of the boiling down. Robinson married a girl named Drinkwater. Their son, Charles Drinkwater Robinson, was a storekeeper and butcher at Broughton Creek in after years. John Watts who had been a cooper at Jervis Bay, became the cooper at Coolangatta. Many names could be mentioned —men who settled here and there for short periods on the land: others who were usually in charge of small vessels on the river. Lieutenant-Colonel John Thomas Leahey, who was for some time a visiting magistrate, whose headquarters was at Wollongong, had a grant of 1000 acres within the Crookhaven and its branches up to the boundary of Monaghan's holding. "Red Jim" (?) was on part of it growing potatoes. Leahey was interested in land near the West Dapto centre of Illawarra. He passed out of memory long ago with the bursting up of the convict system in New South Wales.

Governor Macquarie was anxious to form a settlement at Jervis Bay, and on two occasions he made an attempt to do so; first in 1818 and again in 1820. His plans were not put into execution owing to the lack of military force. Colonel Erskine and Major Morrisch could not spare sufficient military men to take charge of both Jervis Bay and Port Macquarie.

CULBURRA.

The popular new Shoalhaven seaside township, near Crookhaven Heads, Jervis Bay, Lake Wollumboola and surfing beaches.

Most of the little bays upon the coast of Illawarra from Stanwell Park on the North to Jervis Bay on the south were originally as useless from a commercial point of view as they were beautiful. They are both healthful and delightfully picturesque. Select accommodation is now available for tourists, sightseers, nature lovers, and sportsmen.

If we consider that the shores lying between Greenwell Point and Kinghorn Point, or the Penguin's Head were practically unnoticed from 1822 to 1922, it will go to show that it was merely the lack of population and access that left these beauty spots so long isolated. Enterprising men have recently discovered their great worth. and are taking advantage of their opportunities and are opening up and developing this "Landscape" so that the people of the crowded cities can behold its great beauty which one might safely say is not excelled in any part of the world.

Famous as Illawarra is for its exquisite beauty and the ever, dazzling brilliance of its seaboard, one has to visit Culburra to get an insight into its real worth. Situated, as it is, at the estuary of the Crookhaven, there is great scope for fishing, with secure anchorage for small craft. The little bay with its islands, is surrounded by highly diversified and strangely picturesque shores varying almost from the sublime to the romantic. Yet it has been until quite recently frequented by comparatively very few tourists, and shamefully little known to men of refined tastes, owing, possibly, to the want of decently formed roads to and from it. If this was the chief obstacle in the way of sight and pleasure seekers it is being removed, and the fine broad new avenue with its sweeping curves, named by the Prince of Wales after himself as Prince Edward Avenue, is now available for all comers.

Nor is this all. Culburra's water attractions include both Culburra and Wairain beaches, with incomparable surfing, and Lake Wollumboola, a most beautiful inland sheet of water, teeming with fish and waterfowl.

Bay, ocean, and lake all within a mile of each other, and in between them all a skilfully planned area for man's occupation and pleasure. From obscurity it will become world famous.

The coast and for some few miles inland, with very few exceptions, is placed within a general view of the higher parts of the mainland where look-outs have been wisely reserved for the benefit of the public where a labyrinthine expanse of green and blooming herbage vie with each other in their beauty and variety.

The country around Jervis Bay is of an undulating character, well-drained and eminently suited for building purposes.

Much of the adjacent country near the Shoalhaven River having been successfully drained now forms the richest portions in Illawarra, which will grow in importance and value as towns arise to be served by its wonderful productiveness. Trees and scrubs— the most gorgeous features of our landscapes— and, which enter as much into the composition of picturesqueness as either hillside or dale as plumage does into the beauty of birds, is far from being meagre in these parts. We have then all that is capable of making a deep impression on the mind of a Britisher as we know the sea and the land differ as widely as light and darkness, yet in turn both have their exquisite charms.

The country around the present scene of operations in general conformation of surface possesses the singular character of a central plain surrounded by a seaboard and a mountain. If we take theoretic topography, or that which loves to fuse detached hills into ranges, and combine dispersed heights into systems, and to trace imaginary concatenations of mountain across valley and sea, we are confronted with this idea—a great upland falling on the Eastern side into valleys like ribs reaching into a basin, and fed by numerous creeks and streams, such is the Shoalhaven Valley. A systemising topographist is, therefore, required to do justice to my picture in order to describe the grandeur and loftiness of portions of the seaboard as compared to the undiversified lower declivities of the environing mountain ranges.

Historically, not much is left to us regarding the early settlement of the northern parts of Jervis Bay. It was used by settlers whose addresses were registered at the Sydney Post Office as St. Vincent. That much trading in cattle was carried on in that locality goes without saying. Gerald Anderson, an early settler, between Bulli and what is now Wollon-

D

gong, had two mustering yards south of what is now called Brundee. It was originally called Narellan. One of these mustering yards was at Falls Creek, and were both there in a neglected state sixty years ago; so neglected were those places of one time hustle and bustle that old residents only knew them as Gerald's yards. Adjacent to Falls Creek is the homestead, known as Cumberton Grange. It claims as owners in successive years, Captain Brooks, and a man named Blue, who owned a station property at the head waters of the Shoalhaven, where an early stockade was established to look after straying stock and wandering human beings. which goes to show that much traffic in stock was carried on between the Shoalhaven valley and the higher tablelands. It was the general opinion of the old settlers that many lives were lost in the wild mountain gorges that were and are to-day impenetrable. Among the lives said to have been lost there was that of a man named Huon of whom no trace has been found.

These mountains are rent and torn, gaps and gorges abound in them, thus forming great congeries that combine with a great aggregate of wild rugged broken hilly country. Much of the scenery might be technically termed as wild, savage, grand.

A writer recently described life in those wilds as follow: "Seek one of those ranges. There to be drugged into a luxurious scenic-coma by nature's anodyne by the fragrant perfumes of wild flowers—where contentment reigns amidst the unviolated realms of sweet scented musk—where creeks croon and bubble, and the permeating breath of golden wattle, outrival the scenes of the Orient." The variety of plants and shrubs in those ranges is very considerable indeed. Unfortunately, bush fires, the result of careless wanderers, have destroyed much of God's precious gifts to man.

The Shoalhaven River, whether tempest torn or placidly at rest, gilded by the rays of the sun, or silvered by the beams of the moon, foaming madly, or gently breaking over obstacles in its course to the sea, exerts a peculiar charm. Who has ever stood on the uplands and watched this river rushing on and on towards the great bridge opened for traffic in 1881, without feeling as the eye roams eastward to the great ocean, his soul expand and his mind inspired with a noble idea for

> " Oh wonderful thou art, great element
> And fearful in thy spleeny humours bent,
> And lovely in repose ; thy summer form
> So beautiful. And when thy silver sheen
> Laughs in its wildness, we think of the Unseen
> And harken to the thoughts Thy waters teach—
> Eternity! Eternity! and power."

The possibilities afforded by the waters of the Shoalhaven for important water supply and power schemes that will sooner or later be required on the eastern slopes are patent to those who have seen the great gorges that are to be found higher up the river. Deep valleys, mantled with velvety green, stupendous cliffs forming natural basins, that only require to be closed at the outlet to store up millions of gallons of the purest water, and pour out hundreds of thousands of horse power. No one should neglect an opportunity that would enable them to see what nature has done for man in this respect.

The Shoalhaven River, which is more than 250 miles long, takes its rise in a gully near Ballalaba at a height of 2800 feet above sea level. Its source is surrounded by lofty ranges including the Uranbeen Ranges. The Woulee Creek, between Jindulian and Uranbeen Mountains, is an important tributary. Hence the Shoalhaven is a phenomenon in the story of rivers, owing to its tortuous nature through an immense gorse or gap in the mountain where it takes the form of the letter "S."

The Macquarie Rivulet takes its rise in one of the morasses of the Wingecarribee, whence it flows through moors and bleak uplands, on through the mountain gorge, down through lowland farms to the south-western extremity of Lake Illawarra. It was crossed in the early times with much difficulty, especially so in wet seasons at Johnston's and Terry's Meadows. In more recent times these crossings have been bridged, and since then little or no inconvenience is experienced by the travelling public. The aboriginal name of "Terry's Meadows" was "Tupma." When John Terry Hughes came into possession of the estate he called the place "Albion Park," after his Albion Brewery, now Toohey's, in Elizabeth Street, Sydney. What is known as Johnston's Creek was the original "Yarra Yarra," so said old "Micky Nuninama," an ancient aboriginal, who ruled the destinies of his race in Illawarra. He was possibly the father of the old broom merchant of that name? On the John Terry Hughes'

Estate a dairy was established about the middle thirties. Mrs. O'Leary was in charge. She was an expert, and when several Scotch families, who were engaged in Scotland by an agent, arrived during the years 1839-41, Mrs. O'Leary was their guide, philosopher, friend. Included in these emigrants were the McGills, Russells, Frasers, Beatsons, etc. When they started dairying on their own accounts it was to Mrs. O'Leary they went to get the best cattle, and she did not deceive them. She afterwards married the manager, Jim Stroud, and tided him over his financial difficulties later on.

The first important sub-division sale at the Meadows was in 1860, when the executors of the John Terry Hughes Estate sold 3000 acres of land, watered by Cooback and Fraser's Creeks, in 48 lots. It would appear that the combined grants of Samuel Terry, Esther Marsh, John Terry Hughes and Andrew Allan extended from Harry Angel's grant on top of Mount Terry down either side of the main Jamberoo, Wollongong Road, right along to what is known to-day as Mathie's property.

It is easy enough to trace the relationship of all the parties, with the exception of Andrew Allan. He was a Sydney merchant, but whether he was a relation of David Allan who owned the Five Island Estate, or not, is not easily explained. Malcolm Mathie's property embraces about 51 acres, and 335 acres on Macquarie Rivulet, Albion Park (a) part 700 acres, portion 6, granted to Andrew Allan (b) part 2000 acres to Samuel Terry.

Among the first to buy land at the Terry Hughes Estate sale was Gabriel Timbs. His property was situated immediately under Mount Terry. He moved from Jerrara Creek (near Kiama) to his new holding in 1864, and brought with him a small herd of cows bred from the Osborne strains. He was a most successful dairyman as may be seen by the accounts given throughout this volume about the interest that was for many years taken by the dairymen in Illawarra in his strain of dairy cattle.

The auction sales of the Johnston's Meadows Estate took place at Kiama on January 20th, 1876. This would be about ten years after the death of David Johnston, second eldest son of Major George Johnston. D. L. Dymock was the auctioneer. He made a special day's gathering for Kiama: 1751 acres were disposed of in 12 lots. Lot 1, 100 acres, occupied by William

CULBURRA,

The new Shoalhaven Seaside Township, near Crookhaven Heads, Jervis Bay, Lake Wollumboola and surfing beaches.

THE MAIN ROAD TO THE NAVAL COLLEGE AT JERVIS BAY.

ACCOMMODATION HOUSE AT PACIFIC CITY, JERVIS BAY.

AN END OF THE OCEAN BEACH AT CULBURRA, NEAR JERVIS BAY AND CROOKHAVEN HEADS.

A PRETTY BEACH IN JERVIS BAY, RIGHT OPPOSITE THE HEADS, HALLORAN ESTATE.

BEAUTIFUL BEACH AT JERVIS BAY, SHELVING RAPIDLY TO DEEP WATER.

H.M.S. "RENOWN," AS SHE DROPPED ANCHOR IN JERVIS BAY WITH H.R.H. THE PRINCE OF WALES ON BOARD.

Swan; Lot 2, 140 acres, occupied by Herbert Bartlett; Lot 3, adjoining Lot 1, containing 120 acres, described as timbered country; Lot 4, 100 acres, occupied by Joseph Ross; Lot 5, 80 acres, described as Mrs. Howse's farm; Lot 6, containing 94 acres, occupied by James Reed; Lot 7, containing 126 acres, described as Rattery's farm and adjoined Lot 2; Lot 8, contained two 140 acre farms, described as Fraser's farm, adjoining Lot 7; Lot 9, 255 acres, described as Barker's farm, adjoining Lot 8; Lot 10, 70 acres, described as open forest country, adjoining Lot 2; Lot 11, 100 acres, adjoining Lot 4, and used as a run; Lot 12, 426 acres, known as the Middle Paddock, with a frontage to the Macquarie Rivulet. The vendors were Messrs. D. T., G. R., and A. A. Johnston, descendants of Major George Johnston, who put Governor Bligh under arrest. For this rash act he was tried by court-martial in England and deprived of all military honours. At the above sale John Russell of Croome, Illawarra, bought the homestead lot. Thomas Bateman bought it from Russell. In 1922, James O'Gorman of Albion Park, purchased it at Bateman's sale at £70 per acre, which is more than three times what John Russell gave for it in 1876. The O'Gorman farm, "The Gift," is the site on which Major George Johnston caused to be erected a house for his overseer and stockman to live in in Illawarra. The adjoining property has been purchased by John Dudgeon, late of Hillview, Jamberoo, at £75 per acre, which goes to show the value that practical dairymen place on the rich flats of Illawarra when it is a matter of feeding dairy cows to keep up the milk supply for the Sydney markets.

All the land round Albion Park is not rich, flat land; much of it is of very poor quality. This poor quality land is used for raising young stock which is a great mistake. The average quality of a dairy herd can never be kept up when young heifers are not properly nourished. To make this inferior land useful requires great intelligence, and a generous supply of lime to make the soil suitable for a still more generous supply of manure. Good soil means good grass, and good grass is necessary to raise young cattle. Adjacent to the township of Albion Park Johnston Bros. have a good dairy farm. Some of this land is equal to any land in Illawarra, being part of the John Terry Hughes' Estate.

When sold in 1861 the lot brought from £3 2s. 6d. to £43 per acre, averaging over £10 per acre, to wit, £30,519 4s. 6d. One of the most interesting peculiarities of good land is that its value is never stationary; it is constantly progressive and increasing in direct ratio to the growth of the population. The very cause that increase population multiply the demand on good land.

LOVELY OF GREENDALE (No. 38, I.D.C.H.B.).

MODEL OF GREENDALE (No. 186, I.D.C.H.B.).

OUR BRITISH BREEDS OF CATTLE.

A short, but faithful, account of the British breeds of cattle that formed the foundation of the original herds of dairy cattle in New South Wales. And from the blood of which, blended in various ways, our Illawarra dairy cattle have sprung. Men may write and talk as much as they may, but, facts are facts. If, after carefully reading these notes, the reader will turn to the notes on the origin of the Shorthorn taken from one of the best English writers, he will see that the Shorthorn did not drop down from heaven in her present form, nor did our Illawarra assume its present characteristics in one fell swoop.

The ancient writers were evidently trained upon the same model as the majority of our modern scribes, and found the occupation to be more genial to their tastes, and profitable to write about the affairs of those who moved on the higher paths of life, such as Senators and rulers. than the callings of pastoralists and farmers. Books on wars and invasions, courts and courtiers, are abundant. But when we turn up the English translations of the classic writers and strive to get a glimpse of the men on the land we find the springs of literature very, very dry. Prior to the dawn of the Christian era, say, 2000 years ago, when the Roman Empire was the world, internal troubles created strife, which produced frightful wars. The wars of Roman against Roman quite exhausted the Empire.

One wise statesman saw all the damage that had been wrought, and at once set to work to repair the damage. His name was Caius Cilnius Mæcenas, which name we are told is identical with that of patron of Letters and friend of Art. He saw that the sword would have to be beaten into a ploughshare if Italy was to be saved from the ruin. He resolved to ask the Virgil of the Ecloges to write a poem on Agriculture. The answer was given in a manner worthy of the subject, the patron and the poet. He gave us the "Georgies," which at once depicts the life of the Italian farmer, his daily and annual round of duties on his farm—among the animals of his farm. But what of the brindled cow? Here it is: Two rural singers, proud of their vocal prowess, challenge each other. See Virgil Pastoral iii.:—

"To bring to the trial will you dare,
Our pipes, our skill, our voices to compare ?
My brindled heifer to the stake I lay,
Two thriving calves she suckles twice a day,
And twice besides her milk never fail
To store the dairy with a brimming pail.
Now back your singing with an equal stake."

In Mr. G. K. Chesterton's "Short History of England," we learn that Feudalism was the main mark of the middle ages, and that the word "mediaeval" was used for almost anything from "Early English" to "Early Victorian." He also states: "Feudalism was not quite logical, and was never exact about who had the authority. Feudalism already flourished before the mediaeval renascence began. It was, if not the forest the mediaeval had to clear, at least the rude timber with which they had to build. Feudalism was a fighting growth of the dark ages before the middle ages—the age of barbarians resisting semi-barbarians. The feudal units grew through the lively localism of the dark ages, when hills without roads shut in a valley like a garrison. Patriotism had to be parochial: for men had no country, but only a countryside. In such cases the Lord grew larger than the King; but it bred not only a local Lordship, but a kind of local liberty, and it would be very inadvisable to ignore the freer element in Feudalism in English history. For it is the one kind of freedom that the English have had and held." We may thus take it as granted that "Feudalism" had much to do in forming England into counties and shires—and the general isolation of these counties and shires has give us the numerous breeds of British cattle.

It must have taken a long time to develop and perfect the several breeds of British cattle prior to the Peninsular wars. It has often been suggested that cattle are merely potters' clay, "ready to be moulded into any shape, form or colour at the whim of a skilled craftsman." Breeders, however, have not in the past, whatever they may do in the future, found it quite so simple as moulding bricks.

If we take a calm, unbiassed look at the varieties of colours that are presented before the cattle judges at any important show, we must at once admit that nature has an object in bringing about these varieties despite many efforts to obliterate certain objectionable show colours. The brindle streaks may have their virtues like the black hairs scattered through the white coat of the desert Arab, and through the cream coloured Russian horse so famous on the battlefields.

Anglesey Cattle.—Anglesey is the Mona of ancient times, the peculiar seat of Druidical superstitions, and long the rallying point of British independence, and is distinguished from other parts of North Wales by the absence of an irregular and mountainous surface. It is diversified only by numerous undulations, that scarcely deserve the name of hills—covered with grass—although not of a luxuriant nature, and on which a considerable number of fine cattle are raised.

Ayrshire (Scotland), 1790 to 1804; the old crumpled horn breed.—Ayrshire extends along the eastern coast of the Firth of Clyde, and the north channel from Renfrew to Wigtownshire, while it has Kircudbright, Dumfries, and Lanark on the south. Ayrshire was divided into three districts. But it is with but one of those three, viz., Cunningham, that we will treat on here, as it is the locality that claimed to have developed the Ayrshire breed of cattle. They were then called the Cunningham cattle, and were described as having a small head, rather long and narrow at the muzzle; the eye small, but smart and lively; the horns small, clear, and curved; neck, long and slender, tapering towards the head, with no loose skin below; shoulder thin; forequarter light; hindquarters large; back straight, broad behind, the joints rather loose and open; carcase deep, pelvis capacious, and wide over the hips; thighs thin, flat, and curved; tail long and small; legs small and short, with fine joints; udder capacious, broad, and square, stretching forward, and neither fleshy, long hung, nor loose; milk-veins large and prominent; teats short, all pointing outwards, and at considerable distance from each other; skin thin and loose; hair soft and woolly. The Ayrshire was then, as now, essentially a dairy cow—a few of them equal to four Scotch pints per day (a pint was 24 ounces).

In 1851 Sir John Sinclair, President of the Agricultural Society of England, said: "But one opinion prevails relative to the superiority of the Ayrshire cattle for the dairy, namely, they are the best."

The Bridgewater cattle.—These cattle are red, with white face, or spotted red and white. They are the produce of crossing Hereford cows with Devon bulls. In a herd of 40 cows the colours would be found to be 25 red ones, ten spotted ones, and five red with white face— and this was fairly constant throughout the locality—yet a Hereford bull was rarely seen, nor used in the herds.

A Mr. Wedge described the Cheshire breed of cattle in 1790 as follows: "A large thin-skinned udder, large milk-veins, shallow and light forequarter, wide loins, a thin thigh, a white horn, a long thin head, a brisk and lively eye, fine and clean about the chape and throat." Many such opinions could be quoted from those old-time writers on cattle which hold good at the present time. Let us take Aiton, in 1828, on the Ayrshire breed of cattle: "Head small, but rather long, and narrow at the muzzle; the eyes full, quick and lively; the horns small, clear, bended, and the roots as considerable distances apart; neck long and slender, tapering towards the head, with no loose skin below; shoulder thin; forequarters light and thin; hindquarters large and capacious; back straight, broad behind, and the joins of the chine rather loose and open; carcase deep, and pelvis capacious and wide over the hips; tail long and small; legs small and short, with firm joints; udder capacious, broad and square, stretching forward, and neither fleshy, long hung, nor loose; the milk-veins large and prominent; teats short and pointing outward, and at a considerable distance from each other; the skin soft and woolly; the head, horns, bones, and other parts of least value, small, and the general figure compact and well-proportioned. Dairy bulls to have a feminine aspect in their head, neck, and forequarter, not round behind. Broad huck bones and hips, with full flank."

The Celtic Shorthorn.—Professor Daw thus wrote on the Celtic Shorthorned breed of cattle of Great Britain and Ireland in 1898 as follows:—"This small short-horned breed was introduced by the Neolithic (Later Stone Age) herdsmen and farmers from the Continent as a domesticated animal. The place where it was originally domesticated is unknown for certain, but it may be inferred from the absence of any wild cattle of this species in Europe that it was introduced from the East, from some part of Middle Asia, into Europe. It was introduced into the British

Isles by the small, dark Iberic race, now mainly to be found in the western parts of our Isles, in Wales, Scotland, and Ireland, and still to be recognised elsewhere in our population by the small dark folk. These cattle were small and dark, with small horns, and were the only domestic breed in the country, so far as I know, throughout the whole of the Bronze and Iron ages, and during the time when Britain formed a part of the Roman Empire. There is no evidence of any large domestic cattle in Britain until the arrival of the English, who came over here with their families, their flocks and herds, and carved for themselves out of the province of Britain the land called after their own name." "The larger breed," according to Professor Rutimeger, "was domesticated on the Continent, in the Neolithic age, as proven by the discovery of their remains in Switzerland. This larger breed spread over the Continent of Europe through the prehistoric and early historic period, and became defined from all others by its white colour and red and black ears, not merely in the British Isles, but also in Spain. It cannot be traced further back in England than the coming of the Scandinavian Vikings. The Chartley Park white cattle and the Irish long-horned breed are considered by R. Hedger Wallace to be identical. The Chillingham Park white cattle are considered to be the forebears of the Ayrshire breed of cattle. Since the uninvited incoming of the peoples from the Baltic provinces into England the cattle have been contained within defined boundaries, and then each county formed its own breed. The colors varied from either black, black and white, white, red and white, and red, passing into reddish brown on one hand or dark on the other. Brindles were occasionally met with. Later on newer breeds were formed.

There is evidence to show that in Glamorganshire the Pembroke cattle are represented by an allied breed with red coats. The connection between the Pembroke and Glamorgan breeds is therefore of interest as showing how easily black passes into red among cattle. In Herefordshire, the home of one of the most unmistakable breeds of British cattle, we have a similar breed in point of colour of the skin and the medium length of horn, which gives them the appearance of being allied to the Pembroke, Devon, Sussex, and the older types of Yorkshire cattle, owing no doubt to the constant mingling of British cattle before they were arranged systematically into defined breeds. The old long-horns were originally a

western type, extending over nearly all the plains of Ireland, while in England their range reached from Lancashire northward to Cumberland and Westmoreland, and southward through Cheshire to the Severn district and parts of Somersetshire, whence it extended through the Midlands to Leicestershire and Derbyshire. The prevailing colour of the old breed was black and reddish brown, with more or less white on body, and invariably a white streak was seen along the middle of the back. Many theories have been suggested as to the origin of the long-horn Irish breed of cattle, but as the histories relating to Ireland and Egypt are silent regarding the cattle of those ancient countries, we may pass the query on to future historians. In those days, prior to the story of Jacob and his uncle Laban, cattle were evidently valued most that happened to be whole-coloured. We might, therefore, infer that four whole-coloured breeds were in existence, viz., black, white, red, and yellow. There is no mention of the colour of the bull which we can see in pictures standing with his horns touching the "Assyrian Symbolic Tree," otherwise we might claim him to be the forebear of one or other of our ancient breeds of British cattle. This may be considered too far-fetched. All the same, if anyone were to examine the illustrations of the several scores of breeds of cattle in Europe, it is certain that he would say, if born and reared on a dairy farm in Illawarra sixty or seventy years ago, "I saw all those types and colours of cattle during the early sixties." So mixed and diverse were the colours of the hair, shapes of horns, and types of cattle then.

The Chartley cattle show unmistakable signs of affinity with the long-horned breed on one hand, and the white Pembrokes on the other, the black Pembroke resembling the Hyland Kylocs. Yellow crossed with red gives light dun colour; dun comes crossing with black. The Norsemen introduced the polled, dun coloured Scandinavian cattle to the Orkney Islands. Hence we have Channel Islands, Orkney, Shetland, and Iceland. The Norman and Channel Island cattle are identical in shape, and present two colours—silver-grey and yellow.

The Derbyshire cattle.—This breed was originally a blend of the smaller size long-horned breed and the South Devonshire breed. They had wide outspreading horns of considerable length, red in colour, with traces of brindle in some of them. In 1830 they were essentially

JOHN JAMES & SON, "Kurrawong," Dunmore.

Champion group of M. S. Cattle at Nowra Show, 1922, and Grand Champion group open to all breeds

Reading trim left to right:—SNOWDROP VI OF KURRAWONG; SNOWDROP V OF KURRAWONG; SCARLET II OF KURRAWONG; SALLY IV OF KURRAWONG; CLARIE II OF KURRAWONG; PREMIER OF KURRAWONG.

BIRDIE V. OF COSEY CAMP, N.C.

MAY QUEEN OF COSEY CAMP, N.C.

THOMAS JAMES, of Rosemount, Shellharbour.

ZOIE OF ROSEMOUNT.

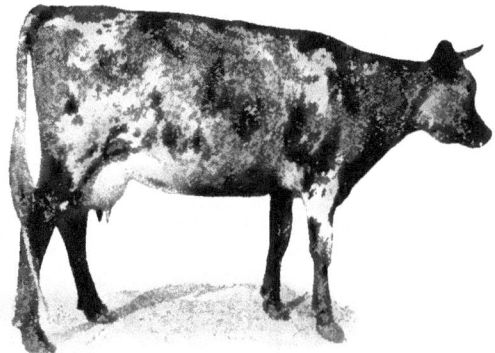

CASSIE OF ROSEMOUNT.
(No. 982, I.D.H.B., Vol. I.)

dairy cattle, equal to 17 lbs. of butter per week.

The Devon breed of cattle in England seems to be identical with the Salers breed of cattle in France. If so, it is not probable that the two breeds were separately evolved in different countries. History says: "Cattle from ancient Gaul of the Salers type were landed on the shores of England, and gave the colours and distinction of the Devon and Sussex breeds." There is at the same time a possibility that the origin of the Devon in England may be as remote as the landing of the Phoenicians in search of Cornish tin. If so, the breed would be Spanish, as the Phoenicians came to Britain from Spain, and their first settlement was in Cornwall, and, curiously coincident, the earliest notices of red cattle in the west of England places them in that country.

Sir Nicholas White, Master of the Rolls in Ireland, states, according to an ancient Irish manuscript of A.D. 1580, that Dingle Bay, in Kerry, was known as "Coon Edaf," which in Irish means "Red Ox Haven." The early peoples of Cornwall were a race of Gaels that first landed in Ireland.

In 1800 the Devon breed were distinguished by being of a high red colour, free from white spots, a light dun ring round the eyes, muzzle same colour. In 1808 Charles Vancouver stated: "The head of the Devon should be small, clean, and free from flesh about the jaws; deer-like, light and airy in its countenance; neck long and thin; throat free from dewlap; nose and round the eyes of a dark orange colour; horns thin and fine at the roots, of a cream colour." In 1830 a Devon bull was considered to be of good form when his horns were neither too high nor too low, tapering at the points, not too thick at the roots, and of a yellow waxy colour; the eye clear, bright, prominent, showing much of the white, encircled by an orange coloured fringe. Robert Bakewell, the celebrated improver of the Irish Longhorns, paid the Devons the highest compliment when he said: "The Devon cannot be improved by any alien race; yet they improve the other breeds." Devonshire being situated at nearly the western extreme of England, they flourished on the River Taw and towards the Bristol Channel, and more northwards, and prevailed in Somerset and Dorset, where a great supply of calves went to the Exeter market.

More southward there prevailed a larger variety—a cross between the North Devon and Somerset. In 1830 both Somerset and Dorset had a reputation for producing the larger-sized Devons. The pure Devon was then distinguished from other breeds by a full clear eye, surrounded by a gold coloured circle round the eye; yellow skin, muzzle yellow or orange colour, placid face. As late as 1835 or 1840 the Devons were whole-coloured, with the exception of a small star in forehead. The South Devons were plentiful in Tavistock and Newport, where the herds used to average 2lbs. of butter per cow per day.

The majority of the Shorthorn breeders of New South Wales kept a small herd of Devons. If these Devon cattle were not kept to give tone and colour to the stud Shorthorn, it is difficult to assign any reason for their presence. Without pressing the case to any logical conclusion, we will await a tangible theory from Shorthorn breeders.

Glamorganshire.—This was the favourite breed of cattle of His Majesty George III., who was considered in his time one of the few best judges of cattle in England. He kept and bred a herd of Glamorgans at Windsor Castle. Old chroniclers agree that they were produced by crossing Norman bulls with Devon cows, and that the progeny were generally of a reddish colour, large framed, excellent milkers. A few were pied, and some were brown, with a dorsel streak; clean heads and tapering necks; silky hair.

The Hereford breed, from 1750 to 1800, were described as being light red in colour, white face, dorsel streak, middle horned, wide on hips, rump and sirloin, tolerably straight back, flat on ribs and sides, thin thighs, middle line, forequarters heaviest.

The Holderness cattle were plentiful on the banks of the River Tees in 1750. An old oil-painting of a cow on the tower walls of Durham Cathedral may have been very old, but judging by an illustration of that painting, if it is a true representation of the orignal Durham cattle, there has been remarkable changes in the breed as we knew them, say, fifty years ago in Illawarra.

The Holderness breed were thin quartered, too light behind, and too coarse before; large shoulders, coarse necks, and deep dewlaps. In 1810 they were described as being thick, large-boned, clumsy animals, large behind; thick, gummy thighs; always fleshy, but never fat. In 1835, on the banks of the Tees, in Yorkshire, they were much improved, and developed into good milkers by judicious crossing with the Ayrshire breed. They then became the Yorkshire cattle of a variety of colours.

The Kyloe.—The origin of the term Kyloe is obscure. Sir John Sinclair traced it to the word Kyloc, which meant a ferry, which abounded among the west islands of Scotland, and used for taking cattle across from island to island. Others say that it is a corruption of the Gaelic word spelt Kael, signifying highland. Be that as it may, Malcolm McNeil, of the Isle of Islay, says: "The Highland bull should be black, the head not large, the ears thin, the muzzle fine and rather turned up, broad in the face, the horns tapering to fine points, but not rising too high, neck fine." They were introduced into England by a Mr. Moorhouse, of Craven, Yorkshire, in 1763. He came to the Hebrides, and was entertained by Miss Flora McDonald, in the absence of the Lord of the Clan, and slept in the same room that 17 years before was occupied by Prince Charley. Moorhouse purchased 1600 head of Kyloes at £2/5/6 per head.

Kyloe cattle were, according to the traditions of the **West Highland and Hebrides** farmers, originally of two colours—white and dun—and as such were prized. The white Kyloes were called the "Fairy cattle" of the Fairy folk. These were the "Firbolgs" of Ireland—the early inhabitants of Scotland—known as Turanians, Aryans, and Picts, or mixtures of all three men. The owners or raisers of the original West Highland cattle were evidently a very stern race of people, as Sir Walter Scott tells us that in the reign of Malcolm IV., A.D. 1153, the Lord of the Hebridian Islands scarcely acknowledged even the nominal allegiance either of the Crown of Scotland or that of Norway, though claimed by both countries. Alexander II. died in the remote island of Kerrera, when trying to force his authority. Alexander III., in A.D. 1263, succeeded in inducing the the Lords of the Isles to submit to the rule of the Kings of Scotland. The cattle were then throughout the islands of the West Highland breed. Later on, by crossing upper Fifeshire cows with **West Highland** bulls, they were improved for dairy purposes, and in 1830 four gallons of milk per day per cow was the recognised production.

The Lincoln Reds.—"Modern breeders," says Primrose McConnell, "claim that the breed is a Shorthorn—not merely an off-shoot of the breed, but a breed with a history of its own, developed alongside the others, introduced

from Jutland, Holstein, and Friesland; the same breed, with a distinction in colour.

The Lincolnshire cattle, in 1835, were regarded as fair specimens of the best of the Dutch cattle. So prevalent was the opinion that that was the origin of the breed that metropolitan butchers dominated the Dutch cattle. There was a coarseness about the head and horn that was not observable in the common Holderness or in the improved Durham. The bones were comparatively larger, the legs higher, and the hips and loins wider—approaching ruggedness. Captain Thurnill improved them, and they were afterwards called the Thurnill breed. Their colour was red, and red and white spotted.

The Longhorns were first produced into Craven (Eng.) from Ireland, and gradually spread along the western coast of England. They were to be seen in Craven, as in Ireland, in two sizes, and were considered, in 1750, as being two distinct breeds. But the difference in size was the result of the pasture lands on which they were raised being different, such as highlands and lowlands provide.

A man named Webster, of Canley, near Coventry, purchased bulls from Lancashire, and in time established the Canley breed of Longhorns. It was he who bred the bull Bloxedge out of a three-year-old heifer. When one-year-old this bull was discarded and sold to a man named Bloxedge, hence the bull's name. His dam was by a Lancashire bull. Bloxedge became a noted stock-getter. Robert Bakewell, of Dishley, in Leicestershire, born in 1725, became a noted breeder of Longhorns in 1750 by purchasing two Longhorned heifers from Webster and a Longhorned bull in Westmoreland. One of the heifers was known in after years as Old Comely, and was the dam of the noted bull "Twopenny." Readers of cattle history are familiar with the histories of the bull D (dee) and Fowler's bull "Shakespere." The latter was said to be "a striking specimen of what naturalists used to term accidental variation." To look for the origin of these animals in Ireland is useless, because when the English merchants took possession of the graziers in England they were compelled to fall into line with the English graziers, and all records were lost.

The Norfolks were the native breed of Norfolk, and they belonged to the middle-horn cattle. Their colour was usually red, and they possessed many of the characteristics of the Devons on a smaller scale, with pointed turned-up horns.

The prices of British cattle when New South Wales was being peopled may be of interest here. At a sale of Mr. Fowler's herd at Little Rollright, in Oxfordshire, on 27th March, 1791, six bulls and two cows were sold as follows: Garric, a five-year-old bull, sold at 205 guineas; Sultana, a two-year-old bull, sold at 201 guineas; Washington, a two-year-old bull, sold at 205 guineas; Young Sultan, a one-year-old bull, sold at 200 guineas; a one-year-old bull sold at 145 guineas; a one-year-old bull sold at 100 guineas; Brindled Beauty, a cow, sold for 260 guineas, and Washington's mother sold at 185 guineas. At a subsequent sale of Mr. Paget's stock in 1793, Shakespere, a bull bred by Mr. Fowler sold for £420. In 1792 Mr. Bakewell leased his bull for the sum of 152 guineas, to be used from May to September.

The Pembroke cattle.—These cattle were considered the most useful cattle in Great Britain. They were black, and the great majority of them were entirely so; a few had a white face, or a little white on the belly and tail brush. The horns were white, and turned upwards. They were shorter on the leg and deeper bodied than the Montgomeries; a keen look and a beautiful eye; small horns, and were good milkers when cared for.

The Shorthorns.—Taking Coates' herd book as our guide with regard to the origin of our Shorthorns, we find that there are 710 bulls mentioned in Volume I. of Coates' English Shorthorn Herd Book. No mention is made regarding the cows, which were bought on general appearance, at Fairs, and scarcely one of them had a pedigree.

James Brown's red bull, No. 79 C.H.B.; the date of his birth is not recorded, nor is his dam mentioned, or any mention of her breeding. Going back to Hubback, the Abraham of the Shorthorns, calved in 1777, colour yellow and white, No. 319 C.H.B.; his sire was Snowdon's bull, No. 612 C.H.B.; his dam's breeding was not given, nor was his pedigree enquired into until the year 1822. Then we have Lady Maynard, dam of Young Strawberry; she was first registered as Favourite; no pedigree given of either her dam, g. dam, or g.g. dam; yet she did more to found the Shorthorns than any other female. Lady Maynard was the dam of Phoenix and Favourite bull No. 252 C.H.B. Phoenix was the g. dam of the bull Favourite. Foljambe had a dark face, yet Colling Bros. thought more of him than any bull of his time. Charles Collings purchased several of his best cows, sired by Fawcett's bull, and also a Stan-wick cow—regardless of pedigree, so far as we know. The Stanwick cow was described as a yellowish red and flecked; she was the forebear of the Duchess tribe.

The American cow, Red Rose, and Red Rose I., established another family of Shorthorns. Why Rose was termed the American cow is this. She was sold to order and shipped by her owner in England to an American buyer, who rejected her on account of her colour. Deep red was not a recognised colour according to the American view at that period, and in consequence she was returned to England, and became the foundress of the Red Rose tribe of Shorthorns that afterwards became famous.

Assertion is one thing, proof is another. We have to depend for our information from those authors of books who were on the spot and wrote first-hand information. If Foljambe was white, with a few red spots, and had a dark face and nose, we have often seen similar cattle, and no one questioned their pedigrees. We can, therefore, conclude that our informant may have stated what was true.

Cherry, a fine cow, bought at Yarm Fair, no pedigree, was foundress of the Cherry tribe. A yellow cow, by Punch, produced a white heifer that was exhibited over England; no record was given of her birth; no pedigree on dam's side. Same yellow cow put to Favourite, 252 C.H.B., produced North Star, 459 C.H.B. Beauty, dam of Punch, 53 C.H.B., was a yellow red. Punch was the sire of the dam of Charles Collings' celebrated cow, Old Daisy. What was the cause of all these varieties? It amounts to this. The original Shorthorns were a very mixed lot, of which history is silent. If the Wildair or Hubback tribe could be traced to the stock of Sir William St. Quintin they would then be mixed and of no defined colour or breed.

The truth is, Culley, Bakewell, and the Collings Bros. all believed in in-and-in breeding sire to daughter, and son to mother. They selected the best animals within their reach, and bred from them in this manner. Albion, for example, was both a son and a grandson of Favourite, No. 252 C.H.B. At the Ketton sale in 1810 16 head of the Phoenix tribe averaged £221/3/-. Comet brought 1000 guineas at Bramton sale, 1818; the Red Rose tribe averaged £269/3/6; Lancaster, 621 guineas; and 13 head of the Favourite-Wildairs averaged £142/17/6. This average included the bulls mentioned.

The Durham ox that was exhibited weighed 3024 lbs. at five years old. His sire was Favourite, No. 252 C.H.B.; dam, a black and white cow, no pedigree. This points to Sir William St. Quintin's Dutch cattle being used in the breeding of the ox.

When the first Shorthorns were being raised the calves got new milk till they were three months old; then they got whole and half-skim milk and linseed or other meal and porridge. Nurse cows were kept for the choice bull calves.

Dairy Shorthorn's Record Yield. For the first time in the history of the breed, a Dairy Shorthorn cow has produced 2000 gallons of milk in a lactation. The animal is "Lady," belonging to Mr. William Ewing, of Gate Street, Bramley, Surrey, a well-known member of the Dairy Shorthorn Association and of the Surrey Milk Recording Society. "Lady" calved on 9th May, 1920, and her lactation period ended on 15th April last, having lasted forty-eight weeks and three days. During that time her yield of milk was 20,163¼ lbs., and on the last day of the period she gave 44 lbs. She is 7½ years old, and this was her fourth lactation.. She was bred by Mr. Ewing, and her ancestry is strong in milking capacity. Her sire is a Bates bred bull, "Claremont Red Waterloo," 114,714, Vol. 59, p. 100, whose sire, "Waterloo King," 97,628, and dam, "Red Rose 19th" (of T. Bates' noted old Rose family) by "Cardinal," were both bred by the late George Taylor. "Waterloo King" and the dam's sire were both successful in breeding heavy milkers in the Cranford herd. The dam of "Claremont Red Waterloo" was "Waterloo Rose 2nd," who gave 1184 gallons of milk in 1905. and won second prize at the Tring Show in 1906. "Red Rose 19th," the dam of "Lady," gave 9677 lbs. of milk for the year ending 30th September, 1911. In the production of her 2000 gallons "Lady" has received no extra ration.

Milking Shorthorns.—The English Dairy Shorthorn Association was established in London possibly in or about 1905, as the members held their tenth annual meeting on 30th October, 1915. Sir Gilbert Grenall, Bart., was elected President for 1915-16.

Much notice was taken of the cow Liberty, the winner of the Spencer Challenge Cup for the best dairy cow giving the greatest number of points by inspection, milking trials and butter test. She won the Durham Challenge Cup and Lord O'Hagan's champion cup. She is described as a "non-pedigreed Shorthorn. the

property of Mr. S. S. Raingill, The Grange, Cheshire." Another non-pedigreed Shorthorn, Silverton Verona, at the same show, won first prize for inspection, reserve for the Spencer Cup, and reserve in both milk trials and butter test. She is owned by Mr. J. L. Shirley, Silverton, Blatchley (Eng.).

The theory about the breeding of these animals is not definitely defined; neither is their milk or butter tests available at the present moment.

It will be seen that the first volume of the English Shorthorn Herd Book gives us but little history anterior to the year 1780. Twenty years later New South Wales was making cattle history with the best material at the command of its pioneer settlers. Even at that time nothing much was known about the pedigree of the best English Shorthorn bulls beyond the name of the sire and grandsire. For example, we can read of Ralph Alcock's bull No. 19. Allison's grey bull No. 26, Bartle No. 63. J. Brown's white bull No. 98, Dalton Duke No. 188, Danby III. 190, Davison's bull 192, Dobson's bull 218, Harrison's bull No. 292 (his record only says bred by Waistell), Hill's red bull No. 310, Hollon's bull No. 313, Hubback No. 319, Jolly's bull No. 337 (nothing but the name is recorded), Kitt No. 357 (nothing but the name recorded). Then we have Lady Kirk No. 355, Mansfield No. 404, Masterman's bull No. 422 (got by Studley bull No. 626), Paddock's bull No. 477, William Robson's bull No. 538, Signor No. 588, Sir James Pennyman's bull No. 601, Jacob Smith's bull No. 603, T. Smith's bull No. 609, Snowdon's bull No. 612 (sire of the bull Hubback No. 319), Studley-White bull No. 627 (got by Studley bull No. 626), Waistell's bull No. 669. The same as Robson's bull No. 558, Walker's bull No. 670. The same as Masterman's bull No. 432.

Of the 710 bulls recorded in Vol. I. of the English Herd Book lived prior to 1780, and belonged perhaps to the blood of the breeders mentioned. But it would be wild conjecture to attempt to define the blends of blood in the "Foundation Shorthorn."

What is known as Coates' English Shorthorn Herd Book was being talked of in 1818, but it was kept back through want of funds until 1822. When the first volume appeared the number of bulls recorded was 710, with an equal number of cows, a few of which had gone to America. The second volume appeared in 1829, with 891 additional bulls, and a proportionate number of cows. The third volume ap-

Scottish Australian Investment Co.

THE DARBALARA STUD HERD had its origin at Bolaro, on the uplands of West Monaro, in the year 1899. At that time, dairying on the share system had been carried on by the Scottish Australian Investment Co., Ltd., at Bolaro, for some years, and also at Talgai West, on the Darling Downs, Queensland. The chief object in starting a stud was to breed bulls of good quality and constitution to improve the producing standard of the dairy herds then in use on the Company's properties.

On the Coast the proposal to breed high-class stud cattle on the bleak, icy plains of the Monaro was considered to be a hopeless project that could only end in failure ; but the Shorthorns found something in the climate that agreed with them, and the young stock bred there developed a robustness of constitution combined with a capacity for high productivity that has never left them, and may have much to do with their present day success.

For profitable dairying the growing season on the Monaro was altogether too short and the winters too severe, and, for that reason, the change to Darbalara was a welcome one. At the same time, this writer will always maintain that as a nursery for young dairy cattle the volcanic tablelands of Monaro have no rival in the sunny land of Australia, and it would pay coastal farmers well to make more use of this country for that purpose.

However, this is by the way—to get back to my subject. Thirty years of experience with Milking Shorthorn cattle had taught me that, for dairying purposes, the old dual purpose type has no superior, and I pinned my faith on that type, and carefully avoided the modern "beef" type as far as possible, and any admixture of other blood.

The chief foundation cows of the old Bolaro Stud were selected by me in 1899 on the South Coast. Four of these were special heifers purchased from Mr. George Tate, of Kangaroo Valley, four from Mr. C. Lamond, who at that time had a high producing Shorthorn herd, and ten were purchased from Mr. Harry McGrath, of Terrara, Shoalhaven, who had previously bought them from Mr. E. McClelland, of Kiama.

The four Tate cows are entered in Vol. I. of the Milking Shorthorn Herd Book, as follows :—

Madame of Bolaro (406)	Heatherbelle of Bolaro (291)
Champion of Bolaro (90)	Myrtle of Bolaro (502)

The Lamond cows were :—

Daisy of Bolaro (136)	Primrose of Bolaro (568)
Rose of Bolaroo (630)	Shamrock of Bolaro (672)

The heifers bred by Mr. E. McClelland were :—

Dolly of Bolaro (159)	Priscilla of Bolaro (586)
Marie of Bolaro (421)	Florrie of Bolaro (249)
Emma of Bolaro (195)	Camellia of Bolaro (83)
Matilda of Bolaro (433)	Daphne of Bolaro (147)
Sophie of Bolaro (690)	Eva of Bolaro (205)

These heifers were specially selected to mate with " Banker of Bolaro:" (5), a bull of my own breeding, by " Victor " ex " Violet." Their progeny were mated with " Heather of Bolaro " (27). This bull was bred by R. W. Moses, of Myra Vale, and his sire was of the Tate strain of " Major." The best producing blood on Darbalara at the present time is that which has the strongest infusion of the blood of these two bulls.

Other good bulls used in the Stud were :—" Combat of Coleville " (163), " Musket II. of Bolaro " (43), " Abram of Bolaro " (1), " Shoalhaven of Bolaro " (63), " Theodore of Bolaro " (72), " Chancellor of Bolaro " (12), and others.

A close system of " line " breeding has been followed out since the foundation of the Stud, and all bulls used since were bred in the stud.

In Official Testing the strongest family is the " Melba," the foundation cow of which was by " Banker of Bolaro " (5) ex " Madame of Bolaro " (406). " Madame " is also the dam of " Emblem of Darbalara " (100)— one of the chief sires. She is also the dam of " Madame II.", " Madame VI.", and " Madame X.", and others all good breeders, and she bred till she was 22 years old.

Next to "Madame," comes "Champion of Bolaro " (90), by the same sire, " Heather of Bolari " (27). This cow's females were all good under test, and her son, " Sunrise of Darbalara " (228), has proved himself outstanding as a sire of heavy producers.

" Daisy of Bolaro " (136) comes next to " Champion:" as a producer and breeder. Mated with "Banker" (5), she bred " Surplus "—a bull that did good work in the Talgai West Stud, and " Silver King of Darbalara " (130), that did equally good work at Darbalara. She was also the dam of " Lily of Bolaro " (366), " Daisy II. of Bolaro " (141), " Daisy III. of Darbalara " (1354), " Daisy VI. of Darbalara " (1355). " Lily of Bolaro " (366) produced " Lily II. of Darbalara " (1019) from a union with " Heather of Bolaro " (27) and mated with " Carbine " produced " Lily III. of Darbalara " (1020), both great producers and breeders. Mated with " Emblem of Darbalara " (100) " Lily II." bred " Kitchener of Darbalara " (419), and " Lily III." produced " Lily's Cupid of Darbalara " (431), two bulls that have done good work in the Stud and were hard to beat in the Show ring.

" Rose of Bolaro " (630) mated with "Banker of Bolaro " (5) bred " Banker II. of Bolaro " (6), " Prince of Raleigh " (52), " David Harum of the Hill " (93), and " Souvenir," all outstanding sires, and mated with " Emblem of Darbalara " (100) she bred " Rose III." (1703), " Rose IV." (5253) and " Rose V." (5254).

SCOTTISH AUSTRALIAN

DARBALARA STUD OF MILKING SHORTHORN CATTLE,
GUNDAGAI, NEW SOUTH WALES.

EMBLEM OF DARBALARA (No. 100, M.S.H.B.).
Banker (5) ex Madame (406).
Sydney R.A.S. Records:—1st and Champion, 1910, 1911, 1912, 1913, 1914, 1915 and 1916. First in Bull and Progeny, 1913, 1915 and 1916. Unbeaten for 7 successive years.

KITCHENER OF DARBALARA (No. 419, M.S.H.B.).
Emblem of Darbalara (100) ex Lily II of Darbalara (1,019).
Sydney R.A.S. Records:—1st, as yearling, 1914; 1st, 2 years old, 1915; 1st, 3 years old, 1916; 1st and Champion, 4 years old, 1917; 2nd and Reserve Champion, 1918; and 1st in Bull and Progeny. Unbeaten for 5 years, except once by Elected of Darbalara, bred by the same stud.

MELBA III OF DARBALARA (1058 M.S.H.B.).
1st and Champion Cow in milk, 4 years and over,
R.A. Show, 1914 and 1916.
Govt. Official Test—9 months, 13,818lb. Milk; 585lb. Butter.
„   „   12 „   15,223 „   653 „

LILY III OF DARBALARA (1020 M.S.H.B.).
1st Prize Dry Cow, 4 years and over, R.A. Show,
1914 and 1915.
Govt. Official Test—9 months, 14,742lb. Milk; 580lb. Butter.
„   „   12 „   17,576 „   689 „

CAMELLIA II OF BOLARO (85 M.S.H.B.).
2nd to Melba III and Reserve Champion Cow in Milk, 4 years and over, 1914.
1st and Champion Cow, 1915 and 1917.
Govt. Official Test—9 months, 10,896lb. Milk; 463lb. Butter.

CHAMPION III OF DARBALARA (839 M.S.H.B.).
Winner of the "Sydney Morning Herald" and "Sydney Mail" Test Prize, R.A. Show, Sydney, 1914.
Yield, 10,299 lb. Milk; 563 lb. Butter.
Period of lactation, 9 months.

Bred by and the Property of the Scottish Australian Investment Co., Ltd., Darbalara Estate, Gundagai, N.S.W.
PURE BRED YOUNG BULLS FOR SALE.
For full particulars, apply The Manager at Darbalara.

INVESTMENT CO., LTD.

LIMELIGHT OF DARBALARA (1105).
Sire—Lily's Cupid of Darbalara (431).
Dam—Melba VII of Darbalara (4181).

EXPERT OF DARBALARA (Vol. VI).
Sire—Lily's Cupid of Darbalara (431).
Dam—Melba XVI of Darbalara (10059).

MELBA VII OF DARBALARA (4181).
Sire—Emblem of Darbalara (100).
Dam—Melba IV of Darbalara (1576).
Official Test—
  6 years, 14,371 lb. Milk; 836 lb. Butter; 273 days'
  6 years, 17,364 lb. Milk; 1,021½ lb. Butter; 365 days

MELBA XV OF DARBALARA (4188).
Sire—Kitchener of Darbalara (419).
Dam—Melba VII of Darbalara (4181).
Official Test—
  4 years, 18,131 lb. Milk; 931 lb. Butter; 273 days.
  4 years, 21,635½ lb. Milk; 1,150 lb. Butter; 365 days.

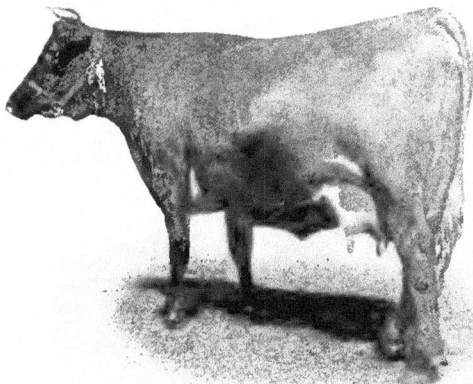

MELBA XI OF DARBALARA (4185).
Sire—Union Jack of Darbalara (634).
Dam—Melba VII of Darbalara (4181).
Champion Cow of R.A.S., Sydney, 4 years in succession.

MELBA XXI OF DARBALARA (10064).
Sire—Silvermine of Darbalara (592).
Dam—Melba XI of Darbalara (4185).
First 2-year-old M.S. Cow Dry, Sydney Royal, 1920.

Scottish Australian Investment Co.—*Continued.*

Of the McClelland heifers the most outstanding were:—" Camellia " (83), " Dolly " (159), " Daphne " (147), " Priscilla " (586), and " Eva" (205). " Eva," mated with " Banker " (5), produced the famous Champion bull " Kingston of Sea View " (187).

" Priscilla of Bolaro " (586) bred " Victor II.", a Champion in the Show ring, and the best sire used in the Talgai West Stud, also " Dividend,"another good Show bull and sire.

" Dolly of Bolaro " (159) bred " Tarquin of Bolaro " (70) and " Redwood of Bolaro " (57) to " Banker " (5) and to " Emblem of Darbalara " (100) produced " Wellington of Darbalara " (1438), one of the best dual purpose bulls in the Commonwealth.

" Daphne of Bolaro " (147) bred high testing stock, one of which has done pretty well in New Zealand.

" Camellia of Bolaro " (83) to " Banker " (5) bred " Camellia of Bolaro " (85), and " Camellia IV. of Darbalara (837), two great producers, and, as Show cows, were hard to beat. Both these cows are breeding regularly now at 19 and 17 years old respectively. " Camellia II." was eleven years old when she was first exhibited in Sydney at the Royal Show of 1914. and when she was second and Reserve Champion to her herd mate " Melba III. of Darbalara " (1058). The following year " Camellia II " was First and " Melba III." Second. In 1916 " Melba III." again took preference, and in 1917, when 15 years old, " Camellia II." once more came to the front.

For 12 years in succession the Darbalara bred bulls, " Emblem " (100), " Kitchener " (419), " Elected " (358), and " Melba's Emblem of Darbalara " (461) have held the Championship of Sydney Royal Show. For 8 years " Melba III." (1058), " Camellia II." (85), and " Melba XI." (4185) have held in continuously.

The following are some records of Darbalara cows under Official Test by the Department of Agriculture of New South Wales :—

NAME	AGE	LACTATION	MILK	BUTTER
MELBA XV.	4 years	273 days	18,131 lbs.	931 lbs.
"	4 years	365 days	21,635½ lbs.	1150 lbs.
MELBA VII.	6 years	273 days	14,371 lbs.	836 lbs.
"	6 years	365 days	17,364 lbs.	1021½lbs.
SHAMROCK XIV.	7 years	273 days	13,263 lbs.	689 lbs.
MELBA X.	4 years	273 days	11,773 lbs.	591 lbs.
MELBA III.	8 years	273 days	13,818 lbs.	585 lbs.
MELBA IV.	11 years	273 days	11,763 lbs.	582 lbs.
MELBA XVI.	4 years	273 days	10,996 lbs.	575 lbs.
LILY III.	7 years	273 days	14,742 lbs.	580 lbs.
CHAMPION III.	8 years	273 days	10,299 lbs.	563 lbs.
MELBA XVII.	3 years	273 days	11,747 lbs.	551 lbs.
MINNIE VIII.	8 years	273 days	10,775 lbs.	489 lbs.
MELBA IX.	2 years	273 days	9,361 lbs.	471 lbs.
CAMELLIA II.	11 years	273 days	10,896 lbs.	463 lbs.

The above cows were fed on bran, chaff, and boiled maize in addition to pasture.

NAME	AGE	LACTATION	MILK	BUTTER
RAPTURE II.	6 years	273 days	11,062 lbs.	564 lbs.
BLOOMER	8 years	273 days	10,827 lbs.	556 lbs.
BESSIE II.	10 years	273 days	10,455 lbs.	548 lbs.
CHAMPION VIII.	6 years	273 days	10,626 lbs.	541 lbs.
MELBA VIII.	3 years	273 days	11,295 lbs.	516 lbs.
VIRGINIA IV.	4 years	273 days	10,221 lbs.	485 lbs.
BUTTERFLY II.	10 years	273 days	10,378 lbs.	472 lbs.
SLIPPER II.	8 years	273 days	9,732 lbs.	452 lbs.
SYBIL	10 years	273 days	9,639 lbs.	452 lbs.
VIRGINIA II.	7 years	273 days	8,896 lbs.	449 lbs.
POSEY	12 years	273 days	8,570 lbs.	447 lbs.
CAMELLIA VIII.	9 years	273 days	11,396 lbs.	504 lbs.

These cows were fed on pasture only, no hand feed of any kind, and they formed part of a herd milked by a share farmer in the ordinary way.

peared in 1836, with the American breeders included, which contained 2897 bulls and an average number of cows. The fourth volume appeared in 1843; and even at this date the colours of the English Shorthorns were of many shades, and the black-nosed ones were the best milkers everywhere they tested. Our fathers who understood the Shorthorns of the forties and fifties always maintained that they were larger-framed, coarser-boned, more mixed in colour than the modern type, and that the drab-coloured nose was a sign of constitutional vigor and dairy quality.

Whatever difference of opinion may prevail respecting the comparative merits of the several breeds of cattle in England during the year 1750 to 1800, it must be admitted that the Shorthorns presented themselves to notice in 1810 under circumstances of peculiar interest, possessing in an eminent degree a combination of qualities which have generally been considered irresistibly attractive to the eye, owing to their beautiful frame and varied colours. The only way to get an idea of the great improvements in this breed is to compare the old type animals with the newer type.

The Somerset cattle betrayed their Devonshire origin. They were, however, remarkable animals, and may be accounted for in this way. The Somerset farmers were said to be the best cattle judges in England from 1770 to 1830, as they were in close touch with the breeders on one side and the graziers on the other. The farmers' cattle were sheeted—the head, the neck, and hindquarters were red, while the body was white, as if a sheet was passed around their body. In 1835 the old Somerset cows were sold to make nurses for the improved Shorthorns.

The Sussex cattle were in 1750 to 1800 of a red colour, but middle-horned, and similar to the Hereford. While the horns of the Hereford were turned downwards, those of the Sussex were turned upwards. They were said to be of west country extraction.

Westmoreland cattle.—In that part of England bordering on Lancashire and Yorkshire and in the neighbourhood of Kirby Lonsdale, the breeds of cattle most favoured were, in 1800, Longhorns, Teeswaters, and Shorthorns, and were being slowly introduced by fanciers. The smaller Craven also had admirers. It was

a sort of battling ground for the breeds and the blends of breeds which in time, say, 1835, gave the world the Longhorned Durham, the Teeswaters, the Yorkshire Shorthorn. About Manchester the Holderness cows gave nine quarts of milk per day, and the Longhorns seven quarts per day. The old Longhorn breed of cows gave the most butter, and in 1835 the Earl of Derby gave it as his opinion "that the Lancashire dairy cattle deteriorated with the loss of the Longhorned breed in that country." Note.—It will be remembered that both the late Mr. James McGill and the late Mr. John Russell gave it as their opinion that we never had cattle in Illawarra to equal D'Arcy Wentworth's Longhorns.

A writer who has given us his opinions recently on Cumberland cattle says: "In the English counties of Cumberland, Westmoreland and Yorkshire there is a race of cattle distinguished for special dairying qualities. They are described as being uniformly of Bates' Shorthorn character, with a definite reminiscence of affinity with the heavier and stronger Ayrshire types. This resemblance is not to be attributed to any established relationship between Ayrshires and these cattle. It is rather that in both breeds or varieties there has been a constant striving after dairying merit, and consequently there is a certain measure of common resemblance in type. These north of England cattle, for the lack of a better designation, are usually spoken of as non-pedigreed Shorthorns." This is exactly in accordance with Professor Robert Wallace's views. As Professor of the Edinburgh University in 1914 he wrote to say that the milking Shorthorns of England were non-pedigreed animals, similar in type to what he had seen in Illawarra in 1888-1889.

If, after carefully reading these notes, the reader will turn to the notes on the origin of the Shorthorn, taken from one of the best English writers, he will see that the Shorthorn did not drop down from heaven in her present form; nor did our Illawarra assume its present characteristics in one full swoop. Mr. John Larkin, of Galway Farm, West Dapto, Illawarra—a native of the district, born in 1835—told the writer that "the original dairy cattle in Illawarra were coarse, large-boned, large-framed animals, with long horns, and variegated in colour."

DAIRY CATTLE ILLUSTRATIONS.

Our Dairy Cattle Illustrations.—Histories make men wise, and in proportion, as their minds are influenced by a natural love of the districts in which they have been raised, so they will always feel a desire to become more and more familiar with the most authentic accounts of the origin of their birth place, and the development and progress of that particular centre. With Illawarra men, who have any ambition to know anything outside their home—there are few things more fascinating than to study the improvements from decade to decade of the animals and plants of the district generally.

The most careful investigations are diverging roads; the further men travel upon them, the greater the distance by which they are divided. In matters of dairy cattle development, the mind as well as the eye adds something of its own before an image of the clearest type can be painted upon it. In this we have many opinions as to which is really the better of two or more types, and in historical enquiries, the most instructed thinkers have but a limited advantage over the most illiterate. Those who know the most approach least to agreement. This is patient enough when we study the "Battles of the Breeders."

It is thirty years since the writer of these lines went forth to preach to the settlers of the North and South Coasts and tableland districts of New South Wales and Queensland the advantages of dairying and the improvements of the herds and methods of dairying. Bitter opposition, north, south, and west, was my experience. I took my experience with me everywhere, and at all times advocated the importance of Illawarra dairy cattle to dairymen.

I am proud of the stand I took during the past thirty years, and am proud to say that the breeders of those old type cattle thirty years ago, are still to the fore, as the grand illustrations herein go to prove. Thirty years ago, one class of dairymen were constantly finding fault with their old neighbour's cattle. Unfortunately that state of things still exists. No one knows it better than the writer. Where are those fault-finders' cattle to-day, as in the past? You, dear reader, would search the pages of any illustrated journal in vain to find one animal worthy of a place, owned by such men. Envy is an ill-natured vice, and is made up of meanness and malice. It wishes the force of goodness to be strained and the measure of success abated. It laments over the prosperity of better things and sickens at the sight of progress. When the illustrations in this volume are seen by the envious dairyman he will go forth and say "If I only had my cattle ready in time to be photographed they would out-do the best in that book." All one can say in reply is that no man is expected to send along that which he hasn't got.

The author can, with confidence, recommend those in search of stud animals, be they M.S., I.D.C. or Ayrshire breeders, to those whose cattle are illustrated herein, as they are each breeds of real worth. The breeders of high-class dairy cattle are few, while the peddlers of dairy cattle are many.

The Founding of Poplar Grove Stud Herd, Jamberoo, Illawarra.

The Cole Family.—About the year 1847, William Cole purchased Poplar Grove, Jamberoo, from John Ritchie. It is situated at the junction of Drawalla Creek, and Minnamurra Rivulet, where he carried on farming and dairying until 1867, when he passed away, leaving a widow, five daughters, and three sons. James W. Cole, the eldest of the boys, was then 14 years old, J. T. Cole was 12 years old, and Ebenezer 7 years.

At the time of William Cole's death the dairy herd consisted of long-horned and other breeds chiefly purchased from John Ritchie with the farm. Among these animals were a line of Durham heifers, purchased in the early fifties—quiet docile cows, easy to milk and appreciated by the boys. On that account, which doubtless created a liking for Shorthorns, the Cole boys took an interest in cattle, displaying the Shorthorn type.

Thomas McKenzie had been farming and dairying on the Terrara Estate, Shoalhaven, prior to 1860. The flood of 1860 sent him up the river in search of drier country. McKenzie sold his daughter, Mrs. William Cole—

a few Durham type heifers. Among these were two very superior animals, "Roany" and "Mushroom." The whole line were more or less inbred, and therefore displayed the roan colour and Shorthorn character. From Thomas McKenzie, junr., came a very fine dairy bull called "Whisker," a bull of uncommon length and size—a strawberry roan in colour. He was the sire of the cow "Roany" already mentioned.

In 1874 a roan bull was purchased from Edward Smith who was dairying on Druwalla Creek. This bull was bred by George Tate. His sire was said to be by a bull owned by John Boxell, who had purchased him from Lowe, of Mudgee, and Tate called him "Boxer." This Edward Smith bull was the sire of "Slasher," whose record for one week, tested under the supervision of the Kiama A. & H. Society, produced 420lbs of milk, yielding 18¼ lbs. of butter. The Smith bull's progeny were healthy, good feeders, and all true to colour and quality. He, however, became a rambler which soon ended his career.

The next bull was a strawberry roan of good size, purchased from John Tate, of Broughton Village, of George Tate's Boxer strain. He was a good bull, but not equal to the Smith bull. Then came the purchase of Henry Frederick Lame's bull, by Major. This bull was bred by Evan R. Evans, junr., from a Cox-bred cow. He was a soft roan, with a rich soft skin, and was of outstanding Durham type. His head was of perfect shape, and he looked all over a dairy bull. He did service in the Cole herd for six years. This bull left his stamp on the quality of the Cole Bros.' herd.

Stud breeding was, after the Major period, taken up seriously, good cows were secured, gave the improved Shorthorn cattle a trial, and although good dairy cows were purchased of the old Osborne and McGill strains of blood, the produce from the improved Shorthorn bulls were not up to standard for dairying purposes, and were soon discarded.

In dairy bulls the Cole Bros. kept solidly to the Major strain until the brothers separated. Three other bulls were purchased from Evan R. Evans, one which was closely inbred, and was much like the original bull.

Then came a bull called "Creamy Jim," owing to his rich yellow skin. He was purchased from James Mann, of "Carraghmore," Jamberoo, purchased by D. L. Dymock, and had come along from Evan R. Evans' stock. Following this bull came "Commodore," from

a McGill bred cow. He was a typical Durham, of splendid size and frame. Rich roan in colour. His daughters, "Queen," "Violet," "Snowdrop," and "Nonsuch" are recorded in the A. & H. Society Show records, together with his bull produce, "King Slasher," Slashem," "Sir Robert," and "King Cole." All these animals caught the judge's eye, and won at the several Illawarra shows.

A cow that made fame for the brothers Cole was "Butterfly." She was purchased by D. L. Dymock from Patrick Tierney, who got her, a young heifer, from Osborne's Barrengarry Estate, Kangaroo Valley. She had lost one quarter of her udder, and advanced in years. She produced 15lbs of butter per week under the old pan-setting system. The loss of her young bull, and that of the test cow, "Slasher," was considered by the Cole Bros. their greatest misfortune in dairy cattle raising. Another noted cow purchased by D. L. Dymock was "Lady-bird." She was the grand dam of William Graham's "Sir Robert." Other foundation cows came from the herd of Thomas Armstrong, of Oak Farm, Albion Park, of the Osborne-McGill strain.

The parting of the ways. J. W. Cole got married, and took a share of the cattle, and settled at "Coleville." In 1887, Ebenezer Cole married and took a share of the herd to "Colewood." A few years later J. T. Cole sold out his interests to his brother James, and so the brothers drifted apart, after using consecutively seven roan bulls in the Poplar Grove herd. The last being "King Slasher."

The Founding of the Coleville Stud Herd.
Jamberoo, Illawarra.

The Coleville Herd.—James W. Cole began operations at Coleville by purchasing a stud sire. A red bull, bred by the Messrs. Black, of Genera Vale, Kiama, sold by them to Jules Schreiber. This bull was used until he secured the bull "Slashem," sold as a calf by Cole Bros. to Kenneth McKenzie, of Cambewarra. "Slashem" was by "Commodore," from a daughter of "Slasher," by a youthful son of the cow "Butterfly." "Slashem" was a show bull as well as being a good stock getter.

Following "Slashem" came "Major V." bred by Henry Nixon, of Kangaroo Valley. Sire "Major IV." bred by George Tate, of Oakdale, Kangaroo Valley, and purchased by Edward Moses, of Barrawang, near Moss Vale. "Major V." won show ring prizes until he was thirteen years old. Then followed "Major VI,," also a show bull, and a winner of many prizes.

Contemporary with "Major VI." was the bull "Comet of Coleville," No. 15, M.S.H.B. He was bred by Thomas McCarthy, from Michael O'Gorman's bull, "Volunteer," from a cow purchased at Samuel Huxley's sale, Kangaroo Valley. (See particulars elsewhere in this volume).

"Comet" was the sire of "Gold of Coleville," No. 215, M.S.H.B., a continuous champion prize winner for nine years in succession at the Illawarra shows, and winner of several prizes at R.A.S., Sydney.

"Comet" was followed by "Signal of Coleville," No. 65, M.S.H.B., bred by S.A.I. Co. Sire "Musket II.," No. 43, M.S.H.B.; dam "Scarlet," bred by John Otton of Bega. This bull suited the Coleville cows, and was in use in the herd for a number of years. Contemporary with him was the bull "Jeweller of Coleville," No. 184, M.S.H.B., bred by owner. "Sir Admiral of Coleville," dam, "Jewel of Coleville," No. 991, M.S.H.B. "Jeweller of Coleville" was hurt at R.A.S., Sydney, and never quite recovered

Then we have "Goldleaf of Coleville," No. 389, M.S.H.B., sire, "Signal of Coleville," No. 65, M.S.H.B., dam "Gold of Coleville," No. 275, M.S.H.B. This bull's heifers are reported to be very promising. They should be good on account of their breeding, coming from a long line of show animals as our records go to prove.

Many of the late J. W. Cole's old neighbours did not see eye to eye with him in his methods of dairy cattle breeding. He, however, bred cattle and carried on dairying according to his own ideas, and in this he was successful as he won many valuable prizes at the best shows, and sold large numbers of young bulls each year. By this means he purchased and paid for much land around his original holding, which shows that he made his system pay.

The Dudgeon Hillview Stud, Jamberoo, Illawarra.

Hugh Dudgeon, senr., and Hugh Dudgeon, junr., and now Hugh Dudgeon and Son, have been carrying on dairying and dairy cattle breeding in continuation since 1857. In 1857 the father of the Dudgeon family began dairying in a small way at the source of Jerrara Creek, Kiama, with cattle purchased from the Messrs. Black. The first start was with seven cows, 1 roan, 2 red and white, spotted, and 4 reds. The roan cow was a failure. Those six cows made a keg of butter per week, and helped to pay for more cows. After a time a move was made to a farm at "Hell Hole," so named by the early sawyers. It is now known as "Fountaindale." From "Hell Hole" a move was made to Dr. Menzie's farm, Hill View. Before going up to the top of the hill, Hugh Dudgeon, junr., settled on Johnny Bradney's farm, "Plough Weary," on the roadside leading from Jamberoo to Mount Terry. Here the subject of this sketch began on his own account with a few cows, the progeny of the original purchase, and a roan bull called "Bob," which he purchased from Robert Graham, of Jerrara. Graham's herd was a good one, composed largely of the Osborne strain. All the members of Hugh Dudgeon's family were born at "Plough Weary" before he moved up to his present home, "Hill View." Some people have twitted Hugh Dudgon with "not being capable of seeing good cattle in his neighbours' herds." Such is not true, for, during his long career as a breeder and exhibitor, he has gone outside his own strain of cattle to select both bulls and cows. Take the Calvert bull, the Coughrane bull, the Reid bull, the McGuhen bull, the Antill bull, and the bull Noble, all these animals were from outside breeders. True, he never fancied the beefy Shorthorns. His bulls that were descended from the Gordonbrook Station stock were all crossed from Illawarra cows. The Gordonbrook cattle in 1892 were of a blend of Shorthorn and Devon. Of this the writer is speaking from personal observation.

Hugh Dudgeon always believed in large-sized roomy cows, and medium-sized bulls with well-sprung ribs. He never once disputed the fact that from a good type of Ayrshire bull large bodied cows could be produced. The men who found fault with Hugh Dudgeon and his opinions on dairy cattle breeding had, generally speaking, no opinion of their own. We will take for example three bulls, "Noble," "Red Prince," and "Gus." Each of these animals were placed in the Hill View herd for a wise purpose, and each in turn was a big success owing to the stern fact that the cows were there that suited them. It is possible that any one of those bulls in other herds would have been a failure. It goes to show that inbreeding, out-breeding, and cross-breeding, and line breeding are all useful in the hands of a man who understands his herd of cows, and who desires to see them carrying good udders.

GRAHAM BROTHERS, Mayfield, Dunmore, Illawarra.

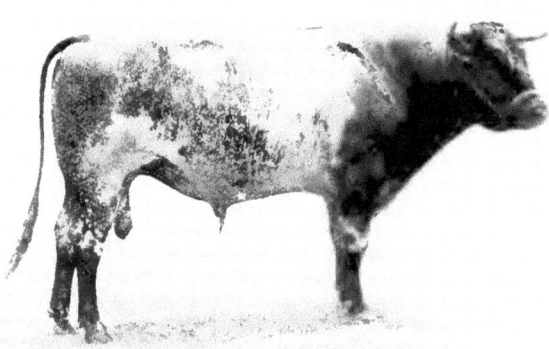

WARRIOR.

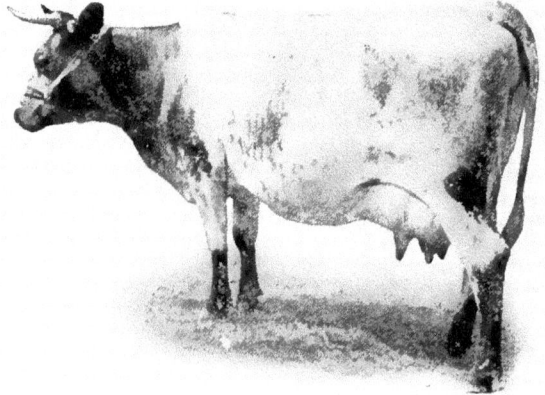

MODEL OF MAYFIELD.

ROOSEVELDT OF MAYFIELD
(No. 552, Vol. 4, M.S.H.B. of N.S.W.).

HANDSOME OF MAYFIELD
(No. 3446, Vol. 4, M.S.H.B. of N.S.W.).

DEFIANCE OF OAKDALE
(No. 340, Vol. 4, M.S.H.B., N.S.W.).

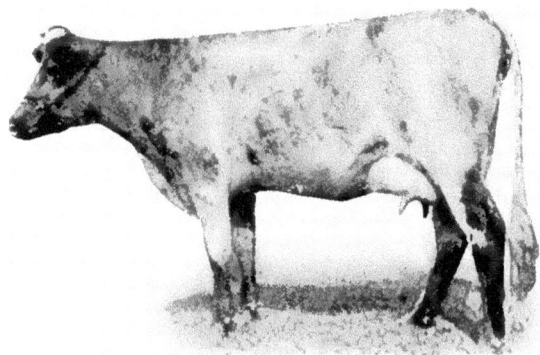

FAIRY OF MAYFIELD
(No. 340, Vol. 4, M.S.H.B. of N.S.W.).

GRAHAM BROTHERS, Mayfield, Dunmore, Illawarra.

FLOWER OF MAYFIELD.

FLOWER II OF MAYFIELD
(3249, Vol. 4, M.S.H.B. of N.S.W.).

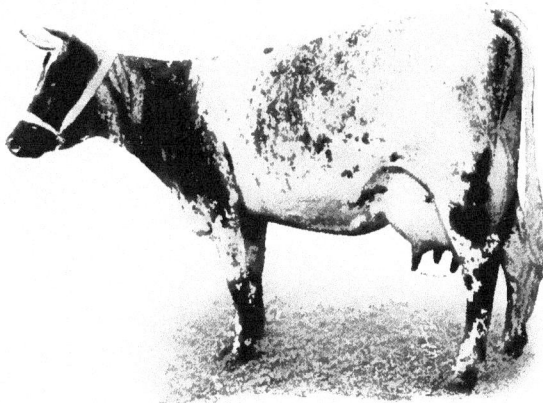

PINK PEARL OF MAYFIELD.

MODEL III OF MAYFIELD
(No. 4354, Vol. 4, M.S.H.B. of N.S.W.).

MILK MAID'S LAD OF MAYFIELD
(No. 1152, Vol. 5, M.S.H.B. of Australia).

MILK MAID OF MAYFIELD (No. 4225, M.S.H.B of N.S.W.).

John Dudgeon is at the present time entirely in charge of the Hill View herd, and, need we say, few there are in the dairy cattle line with a keener insight into the science of mating dairy animals than he. No other member of the Dudgeon family has grasped the ideas of the head of the family as John has, owing, no doubt, to his continued association with his father.

Hugh Dudgeon and Son have raised by careful attention to details many valuable test cows. Among the list we find Fussy III., No. 139, I.D.C.H.B. As a two-tooth cow she gave 48 lbs. of milk in 24 hours, equal to 17 lbs. of butter per week At 6 years old for lactation test she gave 80 lbs. of milk in 24 hours, equal to 25 lbs. of butter per week; three months later she gave 62 lbs. of milk in 24 hours, equal to 19 lbs. of butter per week; six months after calving 44 lbs. of milk in 24 hours, equal to 17 lbs. of butter per week. Same year she was placed first for cow in milk at Kiama Show. She is also the dam of several valuable cows and bulls.

The cattle illustrations, in this volume, from the Hill View Stud prove beyond doubt that advancement on a large scale is going on and on in dairy cattle breeding despite the fact that the soil on which these animals are raised is of an ungenerous nature, which goes to show that a keen knowledge of the soil on which dairy cattle are bred is as essential to the system of mating of the animals as any other factor.

John Hardcastle's "Jinbiggaree Stud," Dugandan, Queensland.

In the year 1898 Messrs. Lewis Thomas and Samuel Grimes, members for Bundamba and Oxley, in the Queensland Legislative Assembly, accompanied by Professor Shelton, of Gatton Agricultural College, visited Illawarra, and purchased a number of the famous Illawarra dairy cattle. After their return Mr. Grimes gave a lecture in the Corinda School of Arts, at which the subject of this sketch was an interested listener. The following year, being on a visit to Sydney in connection with the Rifle Association fixture, he made a flying visit to Kiama and was quite convinced the cattle there were far superior to the dairy cattle of Queensland. The bull, "Jamberoo," and 16 heifers were purchased, and laid the foundation of the herd which in later years was instrumental in giving many a young dairyman a start in the right direction. Messrs Waters, Pickels, and Dunn all obtained their foundation stock from this stud. In 1908 the bull "British Admiral" and 16 heifers by the famous sire, "Admiral," were purchased from Graham Bros. The "Jamberoo" and "Admiral" strains of blood appear to blend to perfection, and some of the progeny are giving very satisfactory results. For several years Mr. Hardcastle had an uphill fight to get the breed recognised by the National Agricultural Association of Queensland; he held the office of first President of the Illawarra Dairy Cattle Association, and fought strenuously against amalgamation. Ill health, however, caused him to retire from the post about four years ago.

We find that some of Mr. Hardcastle's stock have proved themselves in the show-ring after passing into the possession of other dairymen. For instance, "Blossom III." was bred by John Hardcastle, and sold to David Dunn, Beaudesert. She had an extraordinary record in the show ring, and won the championship four times at the National Show, Brisbane, 1912, 1914, 1915, and 1916, and also won the milking competition at the same show in 1912 and 1916, a record no other cow has yet beaten. At the age of 15 years she gave 15 lbs. of butter per week. "Buttercup II." was champion at Brisbane, 1911, and was the first Queensland-bred cow to win that honour. "Earl of Dunmore" and three of his progeny won the bull and progeny class in 1913, being the first Queensland bred group to win that prize. They were all bred and owned by the exhibitor, who considers this his most brilliant win in the show ring, having beaten the champion bull and progeny out of sight.

"Darling II.," one of the group from "Darling," an "Admiral" cow, bred by Graham Bros., holds the 2-tooth record of Queensland—86½ lbs. milk in 48 hours, Vol. I, I.D.C.H.B., Q. "Diana VII.," from another "Admiral" cow, has just been tested, and gave 57½ lbs. milk on second calf, which will go very close to a record for 6-tooth cows. "Damsel II.," another "Admiral" cow, bred by Graham Bros., has just been tested for the herd book at the age of 14 years. She gave 54½ lbs. milk and 2.25 lbs. butter, equal to 15¾ lbs. per week. She has now been milking 70 days and has given 3223 lbs. milk, a convincing proof of the great milking qualities of the Jamberoo and "Admiral" strain.

T. S. Mort's Great Enterprises.

Bodalla.—About twenty miles south of Moruya a traveller in search of the beauty spots of New South Wales will find himself in the heart of the great dairy estate known as Bodalla throughout the dairy world. Prior to 1858 it was one of that sturdy, old-time pioneers—John Hawdon's cattle stations. It was in charge of a stockman, and in a state of neglect, practically speaking, unimproved.

In 1858 it was taken in hand by that enterprising and liberal colonist, Thomas Sutcliffe Mort, and persevered with until Bodalla became the model dairy establishment of Australasia. All that active intelligence, supported liberally by capital, could do for Bodalla, was done by its new and spirited owner. True, the land, the climate, together with its magnificent water supply, was all that men with capital and intelligence could desire. Much ridgy open forest and valuable timber belts surround the rich well-watered flats on which grow a variety of the best English grasses. Bodalla was then, by nature and care, capable of generous response.

The Bodalla Estate comprising an area of 22,000 acres, 5000 acres of which, by well-directed labour, were converted into the richest dairying and agricultural land in New South Wales. When the great farm was in working order, one of the first batch of cheese was brought to Mr. Mort's table, at which quite a number of guests were seated. "Do you like this cheese?" he asked. "Yes, it is excellent." "It ought to be so," remarked the host, "for it has cost me £40,000."

In 1891, when Bodalla took the National for farms on the South Coast, it was pasturing 3000 head of cattle, of which 2000 were cows (1020 of which were being milked), 134 horses, 414 sheep, and 2348 pigs. The general returns were about £20,000 per year, principally from cheese and bacon; 1000 acres of land were under cultivation.

The milking was done at eight stations, five of which were furnished with cheese-making plants. The bacon factory was supplied with the most modern refrigerating appliances, so that the curing could proceed all through the year. Silage pits held immense stores of fodder, and all which could be done to make the settlement profitable to its owner and the workers was effected under skilled management. Since 1891 no silage has been made on the estate—grass, good, fresh healthy grass with the addition of fodder crops has sufficed ever since.

The writer visited Bodalla several times since 1891, twice while it was under the management of Mr. Grierson, and at least five times since it has been under the able management of Mr. Douglas Hutchison, and can safely say that Bodalla has not only held its own, but in many instances, like its good cheese, improved with age. The grasses and fodder crops are growing luxuriantly, and the dairy cattle reflect the value of the soil in their contour.

If at any time a subdivision of the Bodalla Estate takes place it should be borne in mind that there is only one Bodalla in New South Wales: furthermore, there is no estate superior to it in Australia. He who purchases a farm on that great estate, should an opportunity of doing so offer itself, he would succeed straight away, with the necessary energy and intelligence at his command, as the soil will respond quickly to generous treatment. The climate is genial, the rainfall abundant, and the water supply plentiful and good.

Annual returns from ten out of fourteen dairy farms comprising the Bodalla Estate, New South Wales, for year ended March 31st, 1921. It is difficult to draw a correct comparison between the different breeds and grades as the farms are not of equal value. The Friesians occupy the best farm, yet the Red Shorthorns are on a farm of lesser value.

Name of Farm.	Breed of Cows.	Average Cows Milking.	Average Cows Dry.	Total Cows	Total Milk.	Average Galls. per Cow.	Test.	Butter Fat.	Average duration of Lactation.
Home Farm	Friesian	71	20	91	63,710	700	3.54	247	285
Comerang ..	Friesian grade (yellow and white)	76	13	89	61,891	695	3.65	253	311
Widgett	Shorthorn (red) ..	48	14	62	37,132	598	3.52	210	282
Long Point	Guernsey grade ..	49	15	64	37,053	578	3.95	227	277
Greenway	Friesian grade (black and white)	57	19	76	43,389	570	3.81	217	273
Central Bails ..	Shorthorn grade ..	63	16	79	44,521	564	3.83	216	291
Trunketabella ..	Ayrshire	59	23	82	46,164	563	3.77	212	262
Greenwood Park ..	Shorthorn (roan) ..	61	18	79	40,692	515	3.71	191	281
Long Flat ..	Ayrshire grade ..	65	19	84	42,520	506	3.89	196	282
Gannon's Point ..	Ayrshire (red) ..	32	10	42	19,655	468	3.95	184	277

George Lindsay's Ayrshire Herd, Horsley, Illawarra.

The Lindsay Family.—John Lindsay, the founder of a very excellent family of dairymen, settled down to dairy cattle breeding in 1851. This herd comprised the cattle that were bred in Illawarra for dairy purposes. They were very good milkers, while the ground was new and clover and rye grass plentiful. He, in a few years' time, raised a large herd and acquired more land. The pure sire craze came his way, and he purchased Shorthorns from Jenkins and others, but soon found that their milking qualities were not satisfactory. He got a "Major" bull from Evan R. Evans, whose dairy quality was good, and he bred bulls for his own use from this bull until the progeny became delicate. He then introduced a Devon bull which proved to be unsuitable although his progeny had good constitutions and gave rich milk. He then went to Victoria and purchased the "Earl of Beaconsfield," a pure Ayrshire bull from James Buchanan, of Berwick. This was early in 1878. This bull, mated as he was on cows of mixed breeding, soon proved himself a wonderful sire. Later he returned to Victoria and purchased three bulls and five cows, and the result was so satisfactory that John Lindsay became a prominent exhibitor at Illawarra Shows. His three prize cows, "Honeycomb," "Whiteback," and "Buttercup" won many show-ring and milk and butter test prizes on the Coast, and in Sydney prior to 1891.

Since the death of John Lindsay, of Kembla Park. Unanderra, the Lindsay Bros. have followed the breeding and exhibiting of pure-bred Ayrshire cattle. George Lindsay, of Horsley, Dapto, has been a successful Ayrshire breeder. Now the breeding and exhibiting is carried on under names of George Lindsay and Son. If the reader will turn to page 199 he will see the present types of Horsley. Ayrshire (No. 1), "Pansey II., of Horsley," sire "Glen Elgin's Royal Scot," No. 587, dam, "Pansey." She is a very consistent milker; (No. 2) "Duchess II of Horsley," sire, "Glen Elgin's Royal Scot," No. 587, dam "Duchess," descended from "Earl of Beaconsfield," a very heavy milker (No. 3). "Polly of Horsley," No. 5341, sire, "Glen Elgin's Royal Scot," No. 587, dam, "Mary of Horsley." She was champion cow, competing against all breeds, Dapto Show, 1921, and has a record of 9543 lbs. of milk. (No. 4) "Mary Scot of Horsley," No. 5339, sire "Glen Elgin's

Royal Scot," No. 587, dam "Mary of Horsley," champion Ayrshire cow, Dapto Show, 1920, "Mary Scot" gave 7850 lbs. of milk in eight months.

It will be seen from the foregoing records that the business of breeding and exhibiting Ayrshire cattle at Kembla Park has been continued in ever since the death of the good old pioneer, by his son and grandson at Horsley, Dapto.

"Horsley," Dapto, Illawarra, is an old-time place. It was a grant to Lieutenant William Frederick Weston, who was born at West Horsley, Surrey, England, and who died at Dapto on April 26th, 1826, aged 33 years. Many old-time memories cluster around those ancient homes in Illawarra.

All those early grants of land were cleared and worked by convict labour. When the lord and master appeared on the scene it was hats off every time. The tenant farmers, however, came on these lands with their dairy cattle, and, in a few years, most of the original owners became but a memory throughout Illawarra. The late John Lindsay and his family with their Ayrshire cattle have secured many of those early holdings.

Michael O'Donnell's Ayrshire Herd, Allendale, Illawarra.

The O'Donnell family have been for many years large and important dairymen on the Five Islands Estate prior to any developments in and around Port Kembla. The old home of the family has been pointed out to the writer fifty years ago as being the site of the "Hut of Dr. Throsby Stockman," where the first meeting of bona-fide settlers took place in 1816, and where the first division of the lands in Illawarra was decided by Surveyor John Oxley, by order of the Governor, Sir Lachlan Macquarie.

When those old sites are not marked out at the proper time, there is always a difference of opinion as to the exact spot. As the Five Islands Estate was given on that occasion to David Allen who was anxious to secure for his own use that which Dr. Charles Throsby was merely using on sufferance, people may or may not be able to read between the lines. David Allen was, however, a resourceful man.

Their early cattle were of the general run of Illawarra dairy cattle until the beef boom set in, when they secured stud bulls from

William Warren Jenkins and Henry Hill Osborne. The usual result followed in their case—increases in the carcase, and decreases in the milk bucket. The Ayrshire became the ideal dairy animal. The mere carcase of an animal at so much per lb., as against the yearly return in butter at, say, 1/- per lb., the cost of raising each animal being about equal, has caused many graziers to think since those beefy days down about the region of their pockets.

The late Frank O'Donnell evidently followed up success after success with his Ayrshires. The Illawarra "Mercury" of May 27th, 1897, states: "Mr. Frank O'Donnell, of Five Islands, has sold two bulls by champion Ayrshire bull, 'Sir James,' and two Ayrshire heifers by the Ayrshire bull, 'Noble,' to a northern district buyer. Three years previous to this the same buyer took away a few head of 'Noble's' heifers, and pooled the shows in his district. 'Sir James,' after five years' service at Five Islands, went to McKenzie's herd at Moss Vale. At Moss Vale Show he lowered the colours of the South Coast champion. Hugh Dudgeon, of Hill View, Jamberoo, having purchased heifers by 'Noble,' and found them so good that he came back for more, and secured 'Noble' for his Hill View stud. About the breeding of 'Noble' there hangs a doubt. At the time 'Noble' was sired, the Woodhouse's of Mount Gilead, Campbelltown, had a noted Devon bull of superior dairy quality named 'Nobleman,' and a herd of Ayrshire cows that were kept to provide milk to feed stud Shorthorn calves for show purposes. There may be nothing in the name, but the colour of 'Noble' and the colour of his progeny, especially the reds, accounted for much suspicion."

Going back to "Berkeley House" things were carried on there in fine style. The best of everything. On race days and show days a drag, four well-groomed horses, coachman and footman, left for the scene of pleasure. Picnic parties were formed under the ti-trees and honeysuckle tree clumps. Yes, everything was carried out in a big way by the Jenkins'. It has been said that much of this pomp was kept up by means of free convict labour in the earlier times. In those bad old days, good, brave men were compelled by the military authorities to take off their hats to these lordlings and their families. Eventually the dairyman with his cattle pushed the original owners over the edge.

With regard to Michael O'Donnell's experiences of Ayrshire cattle, he frankly states: "I have been breeding and using Ayrshire cattle for forty years, and have not any desire to change for other breeds. I claim no records over other breeds, nor do I aim at world's records. I just demonstrate year in and year out their ability, as a uniform, persistent producer, and their ability to produce for a longer period of years than any other breeds of dairy cattle. I am at the present time keeping 40 Ayrshires on a back run where 20 Shorthorns failed to get a living. In proof that Ayrshires remain productive over a long period of years (the cow 'Jaunty,' whose photograph I enclose with others for illustration), was photographed at the age of 21 years. She is still hail and hearty, and looks as if she will be useful for some years to come. She is one of a number I have in use who have reached this age."

The foregoing statement is made by a gentleman whose veracity no Illawarranian would for a moment doubt. An honourable exhibitor and a modest winner.

The founder of the family, Michael O'Donnell, was born, reared, and educated for commercial pursuits in the County Tipperary. Ireland. His wife, whom he married in 1840, was a native of County Cork. In January. 1841, the young couple decided to try their luck in Australia, sailing from Queenstown for Botany Bay. They arrived in Sydney in the following May. Business not being too bright in Sydney Mr. O'Donnell got a position in the Education Department at Wollongong. This country was in a most disturbed state owing to the large number of convicts and ticket-of-leave men who were becoming masters of the situation. Mr. O'Donnell's Wollongong experience caused him to relinquish teaching. He formed the acquaintance of W. C. Wentworth, the owner of the Five Islands Estate; was joined by another school teacher from Jamberoo named James Rigney, and the firm of O'Donnell and Rigney took over the management of the estate comprising 2,200 acres as a farming and grazing proposition. After a short period Rigney withdrew and went into business in Sydney. Michael O'Donnell took over the whole concern and ran it successfully until the time of his death, 1861. His widow and her fine family took charge. She was a very superior woman, and carried on successfully until her death in 1887. Prior to

MICHAEL O'DONNELL'S AYRSHIRE STUD CATTLE, Allandale, Unanderra.

SIR JAMES II OF FIVE ISLANDS.

JAUNTY OF ALLANDALE (aged 22 years)

NOBLE OF FIVE ISLANDS

SIR DOUGLAS OF PORIRUA, (435, A.H.B. N.Z.)

FAWN 4th OF ALLANDALE.

JAUNTY II OF ALLANDALE.

MYRA OF EUMARALLA.

CHOICEST OF LYNBARN.

the death of Michael O'Donnell much land was sub-let as clearing leases. In consequence many families were raised on the Five Islands Estate. Since Mrs. O'Donnell's death large areas of the estate has been resumed for harbour accommodation.

The Mayfield Milking Shorthorn Herd, Dunmore, Illawarra.

Graham Bros.—This stud of milking Shorthorns was started over half a century ago by William Graham (who was born near Jamberoo, Illawarra, 78 years ago), at "Waterside," a snug little farm adjacent to the picturesque Minnamurra Falls, about three miles from Jamberoo.

During his years as a dairyman and a dairy cattle breeder he always stood for Shorthorn dairy-type bulls. He purchased no other type of bull, and strictly avoided the beef-type animals. After a few years at "Waterside" he removed down to one of the Menzie farms adjoining Dr. Robert Menzie's old homestead, Jamberoo. It was on this farm that he used "Sir Robert," bred by J. W. Cole, and "Comet," bred by Mat. Reen. Both of these were Shorthorn type animals.

Then came the founding of the "Warrior" family by the purchasing of "Robin Hood" from Thomas Fredericks. Going back to Faulks Bros.' stockyard mountain and their bull, "Sojer Boy." The Faulks Bros. purchased a very fine roan cow from William Williams, of Foxground, and mated her with "Sojer Boy," and her calf, a bull, was purchased by Thomas Fredericks, and he grew up to be a very excellent animal indeed. Thomas Fredericks purchased a heifer from Patrick Creagan, of Shellharbour, of William James' "Robin Hood" strain. She was mated with the Faulks' bred bull, and produced a red roan bull which William Graham fancied, and eventually purchased. He called this bull "Robin Hood." "Robin Hood" was mated with "Old Flower" (sold later to the New South Wales Government). The produce of this mating was the celebrated bull, "Warrior." "Warrior" grew up to be an ideal type of milking Shorthorn bull as his photograph pictures him. "Warrior, mated with a cow named "Rat," alias "Robina," produced another cow named "Flower." "Flower" mated with "Admiral" produced George Grey's "Togo."

Now we come to some show-ring experiences. William Graham sent "Warrior" to a Berry show. Two expert dairy cattle judges turned him down as not being of the true dairy type according to their ideals. Graham said but little, simply waited until the "Warrior" heifers showed up. He then confronted these two experts with a few heifers. Their opinion was: "It would be difficult to find better dairy animals." "Well," said Graham, "they are by the bull you gentlemen rejected at Berry."

In 1905 the Graham Bros. took over the Minnamurra herd from their father, and removed to their present home, Mayfield, Dunmore, where they continued the breeding of high standard cattle. Their first sire was "Young Warrior," bred by their father. They then decided to purchase the noted bull, "Admiral," who blended in an unique manner with the "Warrior" and "Young Warrior" cows. He was a wonderfully successful sire, bred as he was on true dairy lines by Denis Kelleher, sire "Sir Henry," dam "Dairymaid." The next sire was "Rooseveldt," bred by C. J. Cullen, of Rose Valley, Gerringong. He was champion Shorthorn bull four years in succession at Illawarra shows. Mated with the "Admiral" cows, "Rooseveldt" sired excellent cows, many of whom were prize winners. "Champion of Mayfield" was champion Shorthorn cow at Kiama Show, 1921; also at Albion Park Show same year, "Model V.," another great cow, and a heavy producer. Both these cows display the old Illawarra Shorthorn type. It is plain that in this type of cow Graham Bros. have aimed at Shorthorn type and character. Next bull placed in the Mayfield herd is "Defiance of Oakdale," purchased at the R.A.S. Show, Sydney, for 200 guineas, and was bred by George Tate, of Oakdale, Kangaroo Valley, and is descended from that noted cow, "Tot of Oakdale," and, therefore, a half-brother of "Tot VIII. of Oakdale," purchased at the late sale by auction for 246 guineas.

"Defiance of Oakdale," has won many prizes, including first and champion at Albion Park, and Kiama in 1920 and 1921, and 3rd prize at R.A.S. Show, Sydney, in milking Shorthorn classes. Contemporary with "Defiance of Oakdale" in the Mayfield stud, is "Milkmaid's Lad of Mayfield." He is being mated with the "Defiance" cows, a beautiful red, sire, "Kitchner of Mayfield," dam "Myrtle of Mayfield," going back to "Warrior" and "Milkmaid." No one possessed of a milking Shorthorn type eye could fail to grasp the outstanding type and character of the Mayfield M.S. cattle illustrated in this volume.

E

Ben O'Connor's Oakvale Stud, Colinton, Queensland.

Ben O'Connor has not been before the public of Queensland as a breeder and exhibitor of dairy cattle for many years; he has nevertheless made rapid progress, and has gained a good reputation for his Oakdale stud. Perhaps, he was fortunate in getting hold of the progeny of the blend of two noted bulls, "Gentle's Prince of Hill View," and "Gus of Hill View." A glance at the illustration in this volume of "Gentle's Prince" and "Lovely II" will, no doubt, suffice to show the quality and type of the blood "Gus" was mated with at Hill View. This blend of blood has been successful in the prize ring of Queensland, New Zealand, South Australia, and throughout the North Coast of New South Wales.

No. 1. "Charm of Glenthorn."—No. 213, I.D.C.H.B., Queensland, is the winner of 24 milk and butter competitions; also the winner of 20 champion prizes. She has a 48-hour record on the Brisbane Show Ground for 1918, producing 139.60 lbs. of milk. On the same ground in 1920, she produced 6.76 lbs. of butter in 48 hours. In a six months' test she produced 12,394 lbs. of milk, equal on test to 650 lbs. of butter, producing a calf each year.

No. 2. Bluebell of Oakdale—No. 202, I.D.C.H.B., Queensland, is the winner of several prizes in the show ring, and a few milk and butter tests. She defeated her stall companion, "Charm of Glenthorn," at the Ipswich Show. She has a test record of 19.81 lbs. of butter per week; and in a nine months' test, produced 11,607 lbs. of milk, equal to 649 lbs. of butter.

No. 3. Wakeful of Oakvale.—She is by "Gundagai," by "Abram," ex "Heatherbell," by "Victor II." Her test is 19.59 lbs. of butter per week.

No. 4. Shamrock of Hill View.—No. 221, I.D.C.H.B., Queensland, sire "Gus of Hill View," ex "Biddy," dam "Silky," by "Prince Larry," by "Gentle's Prince." At three years of age she produced 20.40 lbs. of butter per week, and gave up to 74 lbs. of milk in 24 hours; she has also won several show ring prizes.

George Grey's Greyleigh Stud, Kiama, Illawarra.

George Grey, of Greyleigh, Kiama.—His grandfather, as may be seen elsewhere, settled on the Robb Estate, Kiama, 1843, and later on settled at Omega Retreat, and eventually purchased "Mount Salem," adjacent to the town of Kiama. His son, William, in due course settled on an adjoining farm. Both father and son carried on dairying, and were closely associated with the original A. & H. Societies, and helped to push on the best interests of the district. They bred good dairy cattle. William went in for the Jenkins' Shorthorns when the beef cattle boom was on in Illawarra, and soon regretted having done so.

At an early age, William Grey's son, George, of Greyleigh, learned to discriminate between beef and dairy types of cattle. At the age of, say, 10 or 11 years, George Grey's ideal cattle were six cows his father purchased at Boyd Bros.' sale at Broughton Creek, and two cows purchased at Booth's sale, near Kiama, in the year 1876. The descendants of those eight "clinking cows" in after years formed the foundation stock of the Greyleigh stud. Another choice cow was purchased from W. H. Grey, of Saddleback. She was of the "Boxer" strain from Mrs. Lee's herd, Gerringong, a roan cow of good dairy type, but her progeny were more productive at the pail than she was. "Florrie II" is descended from that "Boxer" cow. The first bull of note was M. N. Hindmarsh's show bull, bred by Evan R. Evans, a roan Shorthorn. His progeny were passed out. Then came an "Earl of Beaconsfield" bull, colour red, bred by John Grey, of Berry, out of a red cow bred by William James. This was the first stud bull at Greyleigh in 1891. The next bull to move the herd forward was "Rupert," bred by Hugh Dudgeon. He was a red bull of great merit. A blood-red cow called "Redman" and "Rupert" produced "Princess." "Princess" was mated with "Ranji" and produced "Red Prince." Either before or after those two bulls, there was in the Greyleigh herd a red bull bred by William Graham called "Rupert II." This bull was by "Robin Hood," alias "Fredericks." He left some full red animals behind him which goes to show that there was plenty of red blood in the veins of his sire and dam which can be very easily accounted for owing to William Graham having purchased a line of heifers from William Musgrave that had the blood of P. H. Osborne's Devon bull in their veins. George Grey, however, had much red blood in his herd from sources which would develop under varied conditions.

Going back to the nucleus of the Boyd cattle, they had, at the beginning of their cattle breeding, purchased ten prime red heifers from Dr. Kenneth McKenzie, of Bundonau, and a red bull from Thomas Black. In a conversation with the late Hugh McKenzie about his father's red cattle, he said: "My late father purchased a mob of dairy cattle with calves at foot, of the Rev. Samuel Marsden breed. The majority of those cattle were blood-red, and were of the red Sussex breed, with horns of various shapes."

With the best cattle at his command George Grey began with energy to build up a dairy herd. The females from the "Red Prince" and "Rangi" matings proved to be full of vitality and dairy quality. He was then most fortunate in his choice when he secured "Togo," whose sire was "Admiral," and his dam "Flower," from Graham Bros. "Togo" put the real dairy type and quality into the Greyleigh herd. Then came "Rufus" with much of the Hugh Dudgeon strain of blood in his make up; sire, "Dudley," dam "Empress." "Dudley" was by "Gentle's Prince," ex "Ruby."

The "Rufus" blood, like good wine, "requires no bush." The "Rufus" cows, illustrated on pages 78-79, will be a sufficient explanation. "Foch" is at the head of the Greyleigh herd to-day. His sire is "Fussy's Pride," and his dam is "Gentle," and as "Gentle" was by "Togo," it is plain that George Grey is not going too far away from the foundation blood of the herd.

Much is expected from "Foch" as a sire, and those interested in dairy cattle breeding will watch with interest the result of the mating of this bull with the "Rufus" cows.

David Dunn's Valley View Stud, Beaudesert, Queensland.

David Dunn, Valley View, Beaudesert, Queensland, has had a life-long experience among the best Shorthorn breeders of Southern Queensland. When his mind was centred on dairying and dairy cattle breeding he visited Illawarra and made several purchases. His greatest success was with "Blossom III," No. 57, I.D.C.H.B., Queensland. "Blossom III" was bred by John Hardcastle, Jinbiggaree, Dugandan.

First Prize, National Show, Brisbane, 1906, for Illawarra Heifer under 15 months (15 entries). First Prize, Boonah and Beaudesert. Third Prize, Milking Competition, National Show, Brisbane, 1909 (16 entries). Reserve Champion, Beaudesert, 1912, Dry, and beaten by her stable mate, Ruby. First Prize, National Show, Brisbane, 1912;

Illawarra Cow, over 4 years in milk. First Prize, 1912, Home Milking Competition, 48 hours; best on farm; 4lbs. butter. Champion Illawarra Cow of Queensland, 1912, and winner of Trophy value 10 guineas. Champion Butter Cow of all breeds, Brisbane, 1912. First Prize, National, Brisbane, 1912; Class 263; First Special. XVI, First Special; XVII, First Special; XVIII, First Class. 164 First Special XIX; First Special XIXa; also Certificate of Queensland Chamber of Agricultural Societies. First Special Prize, National, 1912; B.N. Cash Prize, £2/2/-, National Butter Fat Best. First Prize, Beenleigh Show, 1912; Illawarra Cow. Champion Illawarra Cow, Beenleigh Show, 1912. Not shown in 1913. First Prize, National Show, Brisbane, 1914; Illawarra Cow. Third Prize, National Show, Brisbane, 1914, House Milking Competition, being badly scalded from dipping while competing. First Prize, Pair of Illawarra Cows—"Blossom" and "Jemima"—Brisbane National Show, 1914. Champion Illawarra Cow of Queensland, Brisbane, 1914-15. First Prize, Brisbane National; Illawarra Cow in Milk. First Prize, Brisbane National; Home Milking Competition; 48 hours on farm; 5,092 lbs. of butter; having been down with milk fever three weeks before competing in this competition. Second Prize, Brisbane National Show, 1915, for cow yielding largest supply of milk in 48 hours. Champion Illawarra Cow of Queensland, Brisbane National Show, 1915. Second Prize, Brisbane National Show, 1915, for Butter Fat Test. 1916, First Prize Brisbane National Show, Illawarra Cow, 4 years old and over in milk. First Prize, Brisbane National Show, Home Milking Competition, Test on Farm, 48 hours, 16 ozs. Butter. 2 First Prizes, Class 1331-134, Brisbane National Show, Butter Fat Tests, all breeds, 26 entries. Second Prize, Brisbane Show, Largest Supply of Milk in 48 hours, 100 lb. 12 ozs. Champion Illawarra Cow of Queensland, Brisbane National Show. 1916, Champion Butter Fat Test Cow, all breeds competing. 1912, Winner of Two Trophies (Cups). 1914, Winner of One Trophy (Cup). 1915, Winner of One Trophy (Governor's Cup). 1916, Winner of Two Trophies (Cup and Case of Cutlery). 1916, Brisbane National Show (Cash Prize, £2/2/-. Also First and Champion Illawarra Cow, Beaudesert, 1919.

Hugh Colley's Greendale Stud, Jamberoo, Illawarra.

The Colley Family.—Four brothers, John, James, William and Hugh settled on dairy farms near Kiama in the early fifties. They took up separate holdings, and being of a practical turn of mind they soon became possessed of good dairy cattle. They took a very prominent part in the founding of public institutions, and a very keen interest in the Kiama A. & H. Society. Their names are written on the many pages devoted to agricultural and dairying progress. For years John William and Hugh Colley had herds of cattle second to none in New South Wales. They made money out of their cattle.

At Jamberoo, after Michael Hyam left "Sarah's Valley," property became the possession of the Howard family, and what is now Greendale, was known as Howard's Flats. In 1865 John Colley purchased Howard's Flats, and for years it was known as Colley's Flats. It was considered a spirited purchase in those days. At present the property is owned by John Colley's son, Hugh, who, like his father and uncles, has taken a keen interest in public matters. He has been for years an important member of several of our best institutions. He helped in no small way to carry out the milk and butter tests for the Kiama A. & H. Society's herd book. In this he neglected his own interests to serve his neighbours.

Hugh Colley took a leading part at the founding of the Illawarra Dairy Cattle Association in 1910, and had a number of very excellent types of dairy cows tested for the I.D.C. Herd Book. Two of those cows, "Lovely" and "Model," whose illustrations may be seen on page 61 of this volume, suffice to prove their value. And one would be safe in stating to-day that no better types of Illawarra dairy cows could be found within the Commonwealth. The trouble, however, lies in the difficulty of getting men who are appointed to act as judges of dairy cattle at agricultural shows being able to pick out the salient points of a dairy animal when low in condition. Such persons are not judges of dairy cattle who go into a show ring looking for what has gone down the throats of each animal. The method adopted by the majority of our A. & H. Society committees when judges are being appointed has not by a long way advanced the best interests of these institutions. A judge of stock should be capable of educating the visitors, not a mere automaton, to serve his friends.

The following records have been put up by cows bred at Greendale by Hugh Colley. Their breeding goes back to cows tested for the Kiama A. & H. Society's Herd Book, founded in 1879. See page 309.

LOVELY.—Tested for I.D.C.H.B. in 1910; produced 59 lbs. of milk per day, equal to 16.93 lbs. of butter per week

MELBA.—Tested for I.D.C.H.B. in 1911; produced 41¼lbs. of milk per day, equal to 18.65 lbs. of butter per week.

GAZELLE.—Tested for I.D.C.H.B. in 1911; produced 50½lbs. of milk per day, equal to 15.39 lbs. of butter per week.

VENUS.—Tested for I.D.C.H.B. in 1911; produced 54½ lbs. of milk per day, equal to 16.43 lbs. of butter per week.

FORTUNE II.—Tested for I.D.C.H.B. in 1912; produced 19 lbs. of butter per week.

MODEL.—In six months' test for Kiama A. & H. Society's Show in 1913; produced the grand average result of 20.82 lbs. of commercial butter per week. She was the winner of butter test for Royal Show, 1914, with 156 lbs. of milk—average test of which was 6.2912 lbs. of butter fat. For entry in I.D.C.H.B. she produced 23.62 lbs. per week.

James W. Musgrave, Illawarra.—The Musgrave family have been dairying and farming in Illawarra for upwards of sixty years. William L. Musgrave, the founder of the family, came from the County Tyrone, Ireland, in the fifties, and commenced farming at Dapto when wheat growing was a profitable industry, and continued to do so up to about 1860, when he turned his attention entirely to dairying.

He was successful because he was always on the look-out for any improvements that suggested to his mind the uplifting of his herd, and his herds of dairy cattle were always good. He fancied the old Shorthorn type. At the same time he had no objection to the dairy types of Devon and Ayrshire, and used animals of those breeds in his herd profitably. In this way it was always noticeable that the Musgrave herds had many notable deep red cows, and a bull of same colour, grazing in paddocks adjacent to the milking bails. He admired the red and roan dairy cattle.

The subject of this sketch, James W. Musgrave, as a boy took a keen interest in what his father had to say about the old types of dairy cattle owned prior to 1860 by Messrs. Johnston, J. Terry Hughes, and Henry Osborne, and when he started to found, on his own account, the "Riverside" herd, he followed, as far as possible, on the late father's ideas. The cow, "Lily II.", illustrated in this volume, could be traced by him generation after generation to a cow purchased by his late father at a sale, mentioned in this volume, of John Beatson's herd on the north bank of the Macquarie Rivulet, Albion Park. She may, therefore, be considered a true type of the old Illawarra breed of dairy cattle.

The bull, "Belmont," was by James W. Musgrave's champion bull, "Belmore," bred by by William Moles, Tongarra, Albion Park, whose sire, "Orion," was bred by Hugh Dudgeon, Hillview, Jamberoo. "Belmont" had been successful in the show ring and won championship prizes before being sold to Patrick Walker, of Mullimbimby, North Coast. Needless to say "Lily II." won several prizes. James W. Musgrave was a member of the Albion Park Show Committee from its first year up to 1923, a period of 35 years. He sold his farm, "Riverside," during April, together with his dairy herd. The young stock, by a Dudgeon and Son bull, sold remarkably well. He now retires out of the business for an honourably earned rest.

The "Riverside" farm was part of a grant to William Browne who was known in the early days of Illawarra as "Yallah Browne," and as Merchant Browne. Henry Osborne bought the estate in the thirties, and at his death in 1858 bequeathed a large area of it to his son, George, from whom the Musgrave family leased it. George Osborne died in

MILKING SHORTHORN STUD

AT

BERRY EXPERIMENT FARM

OWNED BY

N.S.W. DEPARTMENT OF AGRICULTURE

Irish Milking Shorthorn Cow, "GIBSON GIRL" (imp.) (1465 M.S.H.B.).

Milk yield when 15 years old, 10,702 lb. milk and 494.79 lb. butter in 365 days.

Won 3rd Prize, Dry Cow, R.A.S. Show, 1918.

Milking Shorthorn Bull, "MELBA'S EMBLEM OF DARBALARA (461); sire, Emblem of Darbalara (100); dam, Melba 3rd of Darbalara (1058) by Musket 2nd (43); g. dam, Melba of Darbalara, by Banker (5); g.g. dam, Madame of Bolaro (406).

Melba 3rd of Darbalara yielded 15,239 lb. milk and 653 lb. butter in 365 days.

Melba's Emblem of Darbalara won 1st Prize and Champion Milking Shorthorn Bull, R.A.S., Sydney, 1921.

Young Bulls from tested stock always on hand—apply Under Secretary and Director, Department of Agriculture, Bridge Street, Sydney.

March, 1920, and the property was sold in farm lots. James W. Musgrave purchased his holding, and in less than two years sold out, as already stated, at nearly double the price, he paid for it, which goes to show the unstable nature of land values even in such an old settled district. When Patrick Larkin settled on that farm, away back in 1834, its value was estimated at £3 per acre. J. W. Musgrave purchased it at, say, £23, and sold at £40 per acre. A man named Blackman was an early settler on the north bank of the Macquarie Rivulet. He occupied a portion of the Musgrave holding. Farms were small in the early times in Illawarra. Few, indeed, were rich in those days. Want, however, was nowhere to be found. The old families have passed out and newer men are in their places. To-day 'Riverside'' is the property of Ernest Keys, and he is worthy of it owing to his industrious habits.

Henry Spinks, Culwalla, Jamberoo, Illawarra.—The founder of the Spinks family, James Spinks, takes us back a long way in the history of Illawarra. Although born at Campbelltown. N.S.W.. in 1816, his people had been residents of Illawarra a few years prior to that date. He was a tall, straight, powerful man, a thorough bushman in every sense of that term. In the course of years he married a daughter of Peter Joseph Fredericks of Jamberoo (who had had the unique experience of having fought in turn under two of the greatest generals in Europe, namely, Wellington and Napoleon) by whom he raised a large and highly respectable family.

James Spinks commenced dairying on the Wauchope property, Jamberoo, made money, and purchased a holding of his own on the northern slope of Saddleback, which he named ''Woodgrove,'' where he established the afterwards noted J.S.P. brand of cattle. He early in the fifties joined his brother-in-law, Henry Fredericks, and their neighbour, John Colley, in the purchase of thirty dairy heifers from Henry Osborne of Marshall Mount, at £10 per head. They drove them to Colley's Flat Rock farm, Jerrara, tossed for pick and picked turn about. Not one bad animal in the mob All three were satisfied, and all three became good dairymen and cattle breeders. James Spinks took a great delight in his home, and saw to it that all work done on the farm was done

well. If he bought cattle at a sale he bought the best. In this way he purchased some excellent cows. He was an early member of the Kiama A. and H. Society, as was his father, of the old Illawarra A. and H. Society, and always exhibited high quality horses, dairy cattle, farm and dairy produce.

The subject of this sketch, Henry, was his fourth son. He married a superior girl, a Miss Mitchell of Kiama, and commenced dairying at Kiama. A good judge of dairy cattle, in truth, all the Spinks family were good judges of cattle. The brothers got hold of a bull called ''Boxer,'' bred by Peter Quinn of Gerringong.'' He was by an Evans bred bull out of a Robb bred cow. In colour he was a sooty red, with a white flank, and of the lean kind. He was the sire of a noted roan bull called ''Musket.'' ''Musket'' was the sire of ''Musket II.'', a bull that figures frequently in the pedigrees of the Darbalara stud cattle, and. no doubt, the blue streaks are noticeable in the fleshy part of the nose of ''Musket II's'' descendents as recent as the Royal Show of 1923.

Henry Spinks has made money on the land by means of honest dairying, and has purchased and paid for the Culwalla property, comprising 250 acres. where. with his wife, son and daughter he enjoys much human comfort. Henry was one of those who helped to found the Illawarra Dairy Cattle Association, and for a number of years since then has been the inspector, whose duty it is to see that all animals entered in the herd book are true to colour, type, pedigree and dairy quality. In this he has been one of the most careful of those who have undertaken such duties. He has been a successful dairyman, which at once goes to show that he has, throughout his dairying operations, kept good, profitable dairy cattle.

The two cows. ''Daphne'' and ''Mabel,'' illustrated on page 275 were bred and owned by Henry Spinks, and their type and quality has been influenced by the upland nature of the soil on which they were bred and raised. Had those animals been bred and raised on rich, low-lying land they would have been different. The soil has more to do with the distinction between the milking Shorthorn and the Illawarra than persons unacquainted with cattle raising under varied conditions can imagine.

"Sam," the sire of Henry Spinks' cows, "Mabel" and "Daphne," was exhibited by the Spinks family, and won several prizes. He was bred at the old home, "Woodgrove," and was considered by good judges to be a true type of the old Illawarra breed.

The James Family of Shellharbour, Illawarra.

—The founder of this family, William James, was born in St. Ives, Cornwall, England, and migrated with a trade at his command in the early fifties, and came direct to Illawarra where he erected several important buildings, including a "flour mill" for William Wilson at Shellharbour. He became interested in farming and dairying and decided to settle on a portion of the Bassett Darley Estate, Darley having married one of the daughters of Surgeon D'Arcy Wentworth he got some broad acres with his, on which were settled several tenant farmers. George Osborne, who died recently at Holly Lodge, Burwood, was the agent for the property for years.

William James was a good settler, and made good quickly, and purchased his land at the first opportunity and called his home, "Bravella," after his native home in England. He became a prominent dairyman and cattle breeder. He was a consistent member of the re-constructed Kiama A. and H. Society in 1867. The writer's brother, Thomas McCaffrey, was a fellow committeeman for several years, and always spoke in the highest terms of William James' uprightness and unselfish motives throughout the seventies. He was one of those who spent time and money trying to place Illawarra butter on the London market, and helped to establish the Shellharbour S. N. Coy. to carry produce direct to Sydney. As an exhibitor of dairy cattle he was always consistent. In the mid-eighties he took a trip to England to buy two or more dairy bulls. He failed to see anything so good as was then to be found in Illawarra, so he did not buy any stock. He died in 1888, leaving his family well on the way to success.

John James and James James went to Alne Bank, Gerringong, and carried on dairying on a large scale before their father passed away. Thomas James and other members of the family remained at "Bravella." The firm of James Bros. sold out their herd at Alne Bank at the expiration of their lease, and had, at the time, the best sale of cattle (up to that time) in the old district. Cows carrying bull calves were sold at that sale whose progeny have commanded attention to the present day, including some of the best types of the Darbalara stud animals.

The James Bros. then went to Rose Valley, Gerringong, and later on to Cosey Camp, Richmond. From Cosey Camp John James returned to Illawarra, and settled in the old home in a new and up-to-date house. The firm is now John James and Son, Kurrawong, Dunmore. Throughout all those years John James, as head of the firm of James Bros., was a constant exhibitor of dairy cattle. The two cows, "May Queen of Cosey Camp" and "Birdie V. of Cosey Camp," have won honours at the best shows on the North Coast. They are illustrated in this volume. The bull, "Premier of Kurrawong," is now at the head of the stud at the old home with his prize-winning progeny at Nowra Show, in 1922, competing against all breeds. "Premier of Kurrawong" was also placed at the Royal Show, Sydney, in aged M.S. bull class. This bull has many fanciers, while others equally versed in M.S. bull type do not admire him as a dairy bull.

John James and Son's M.S. cow, "Maggie of Kurrawong", has just completed her 273 days' test, producing 8379 lbs. of milk, testing 4 p.c.: equal to 334½ lbs. of butter-fat.

Thomas James of Rosemount, Shellharbour, was born at "Bravella," and grew up with his father on the old farm, an education which carries its own worth through life. When the father of this family went to England, he was capable of taking his father's place on the farm as chief director. He had been associated with his elder brothers at Gerringong and at Bundanoon, until he was 18 years. Having left school when 14 years old this would give him four years of extra experience. After his father's death he had complete control of "Bravella." It is only fair to say that Thomas James is of a modest and retiring disposition, yet, withal he possesses much sound sense in his dealing with show animals. He rarely misses an opportunity, when offered, to exhibit, and he invariably, through a long series of years, got his dairy cattle exhibits placed. He has often won coveted prizes, twice winning championships for dairy cow at Albion Park and Kiama, and twice carried off the prize for six dairy cows at Kiama.

For seventeen years Thomas James lived at "Bravella," now Kurrawong, and for seventeen years he has been at Rosemount. Since 1893 he has been a most consistent member of the Kiama A. and H. Society, and was its president in 1911. The James family, it will be seen have been not only consistent supporters of Illawarra A. and H. Society shows, but also important exhibitors. Thomas James' two certified test cows are illustrated in this volume. They are "Zoie of Rosemount," tested from April to December, 1919, at the age of two years yielded for 273 days, 238.975 lbs. of commercial butter. "Cassie of Rosemount," No. 982, I.D.C.H.B., yielded 400.489 lbs. of commercial butter, in 273 days, tested from July, 1921, to April, 1922. His other two cows, "Daisy of Rosemount," winner of first and champion prizes at Albion Park and Kiama Shows in 1902, and "Easy of Rosemount," that won first and champion prizes back in 1896 at Kiama were illustrated in the first volume of the I.D.C.H.B. Both animals as illustrated are typical of the Illawarra breed and type. Thomas James is spreading out, and has recently purchased the old home of the late William Moles at Tongarra, where members of his family has gone to reside. It i. a neglected farm, but can be much improved by intelligent energy.

It will doubtless seem strange to many of my readers how it has come to pass that two brothers reared on the same farm, and using the same cattle jointly and separately for years, should find themselves in rival breeding camps, John being a leading light in the M.S. Association, while Thomas has all through stood for the Illawarras. On this subject nothing more need be said at present.

William H. Dudgeon's stud herds of milking Shorthorns are the result of careful mating of the best sires procurable with the best types of dairy cows. There is much to be learned from a careless breeder of dairy cattle because the law that governs that subtle science, "The study of heredity," is apt to manifest itself in a neglected state. Who has not observed from time to time in our show rings a classic looking cow that upon investigation had no written pedigree. She came by chance, and these "come by chance animals" give an investigator much food for thought. In the building up of the Glenthorne and Burradale stud herds W. H. Dudgeon did not risk the chance system of herd building. He looked for the best and

tried to improve on certain well-defined lines from his first start.

William H. Dudgeon was born on his father's (Hugh Dudgeon) farm, "Ploughweary," Jamberoo, Illawarra. He from early boyhood had the opportunity of becoming an expert dairy cattle breeder because his father always owned good cattle, as the show records in this volume go to show, especially so after his removal up the hill to Hillview.

Miss Dudgeon married John T. Young of Jamberoo, who had leased J. T. Coles' Poplar Grove farm, where he carried on dairying until about 1898 when he sold out his herd and joined his brother-in-law, W. H. Dudgeon, as partner in a dairy farm at "Newrybar" in the "Big Scrub," North Coast. They took with them from Jamberoo 43 heifers and four bulls, one half bred by J. T. Young, the other half bred by Hugh Dudgeon of Hillview. In September, 1901, they dissolved partnership. J. T. Young remaining at Newrybar, and W. H. Dudgeon taking over Glenthorne, near Bangalow, and placed "Dairyman," a bull bred by H. Dudgeon at the head of the stud. Since then the Glenthorne stud has commanded notice. This bull's stock were mated with a noted prize winner, "Kelso." The writer of these notes gave "Kelso" his first champion prize against much opposition. Since then he won both medals and cups. He was not an easy bull to mate. W. H. Dudgeon states, "My best successes with "Kelso" were all inbred to him. They were excellent testers." He was followed by "Red Prince," bred by H. Dudgeon, and "Young Kelso," bred at "Glenthorne." The latter bull is the sire of "Bluebell II. of Glenthorne." Then came "Captain" by "Vain Captain" (imp.). This bull has left some very good stock after him. Then followed "Westbridge," whose sire was "Gentle's Prince of Hillview." A bull called "Noble," bred by J. E. Noble, Jamberoo, was also used.

The bull at present in W. H. Dudgeon's herd is "Kitchener," bred at the present home. Burradale, sire, "Gus of Hillview," dam, "Fussy III." g sire "Togo," and g sire "Gentle's Prince," a noted combination for milk quality.

In March, 1920, W. H. Dudgeon bought J. T. Young's farm, known as Burradale, together with the stud herd thereon, about 50 head, including the bull "Kitchener." W. H. Dudgeon now owns three herds, one at Burradale, and two on Glenthorne. His No. 2 herd is fully registered and tested by the Government officers. Part only of No. 1 herd is registered. The Burradale herd is registered and tested according to the rules of the United Breeders' Union. His cow "Molly II." recently put up a splendid 273 days' test under droughty conditions—13,788 lbs. of milk, average test, 4.1, equal to 560.68 lbs. of butter. "Bluebell II." is, under similar weather conditions, going strong in the 273 days' test, which is at once worthy of interest to those who are bent on improving their dairy herds, and thereby setting a noble example for the younger dairymen to follow; and, if possible, surpass.

Dairy cattle breeding under the closer settlement conditions of the past in Illawarra brought out all that was best in the old pioneers. The energy that the more successful ones put into the business has been reflected in their families on the North Coast. Hence we are not surprised at the progress in breeding high-class dairy cattle by W. H. Dudgeon.

Thomas Daly, Woodbine Stud Farm, Bolong, Shoalhaven.—The father of the above-mentioned dairy cattle breeder was Michael Daly, who arrived in Jamberoo, Illawarra, from the County Cork, Ireland, in the early forties. He was a clever man among horses and cattle, and soon found an opening for his energy in those lines at Cambewarra where David Berry had a cattle run during the year 1857. He then got into a larger job at Meroo where he had many cattle and horses to look after for David Berry. It was at Meroo that his son Thomas was born in 1862. Twenty-six years later we find him on Burraga, pig island, a married man, farming and dairying on his own account. His first dairy cows came from Alex. Emery, of Glen Murray, Kangaroo Valley, early in 1889. A bull was obtained from James Willey, of Meroo, who was then a prosperous dairyman. Thomas Daly carried on very successfully on Pig Island where he worked hard, long hours, day by day. He was fortunate in not being washed out by a big flood as was Dr. George Underwood Alley in 1860, who lost everything, including a valuable library and all his cherished papers and documents that would be valuable to-day.

Thomas Daly lost nothing on Pig Island; on the other hand he made money, and at the Berry Estate sales he purchased Dr. Grant's farm. Dr. Grant was a Presbyterian minister who supported himself and his family by farming. He preached alternated Sundays in Gaelic and in the English languages. His rent was fixed at one shilling per acre during the life of David Berry. Thomas Daly called his newly-acquired home "Woodbine." It was an uphill undertaking, but he and his good wife faced it and made money and to spare. They are living retired at their cottage home, "Glenore," Bomaderry, while their sons are carrying on at "Woodbine" the good work so well worked up by their parents.

The present stud at Woodbine, Bolong, contains many M.S. registered animals, descended from a bull called "Donald," bred by Henry McGrath from his Knightly III. by Knightly II. After the third cross with the old Illawarra dairy cattle the Knightly blood gave good results. He used a bull called "Hector," by "Sunnyvale of Bloomfield," bred by James W. Gorrell, who left a few good cows after him. On these cows he used a bull called "Ikey," bred by Harry King of Tabbegong, Kiama. This bull was full of Earl Beaconsfield blood. Good results always came from the descendants of the Earl of Beaconsfield no matter how they were mated. "Ikey's" dam, "Princess," was a remarkably fine cow, bred by R. V. Boyd. Her sire was a Beaconsfield bull, and her dam was of the Boyd strain.

Michael O'Gorman was born in "Ennis," County Clare, Ireland, in 1844, and arrived in Illawarra at the age of 16 years. Six years later he was farming and dairying on his own account. He gained his experience from Gabriel Timbs, who had married his sister (second wife). He obtained his cattle locally, and when he bought cattle they were invariably of good quality. His first noted bull came from Gabriel Timbs' herd, and was by the bull mentioned freely elsewhere. That went into George Tate's herd at Broughton Village. O'Gorman called his bull "Volunteer," owing to his peculiar markings. From "Volunteer" he bred an excellent dairy herd. They were greatly admired by Thomas Fredericks, senr., who had carried out testing for the several A. and H. Societies. That is to say, he was interested to see that everything was done properly and free from suspicion which is, after all has been said, the better plan.

Going back to history, the Anderson Bros. owned Bannockburn Station, Inverell, in 1870.

They bred high-class Shorthorn cattle, and bought good Shorthorns. They had learned of the high prices of pedigreed Shorthorns in Illawarra, so they sent a young man, Jonathan Lambert, to a farm on Mullet Creek with sixteen head of stud Shorthorns. Six more animals came through from Victoria with a consignment for W. W. Ewen of Ulladulla. The stud bull in Lambert's charge at Dapto was called "Viceroy," a beautiful roan, an attractive-looking animal. Lambert was milking a few locally bred dairy cows of good quality. From one of these coms Michael O'Gorman selected a bull in 1878, under two years old, which he called "Clare Boy." "Clare Boy" gave colour and type to his progeny, and he bred a bull from him out of a "Volunteer" cow that sired very fine dairy stock. From this latter bull he bred a pen of six heifers that won first prize at Wollongong Show in 1885, in class, one year and under two years, beating that noted Illawarra breeder, Simon Dudgeon, who had to be contented with second prize. These and other young heifers bred by Michael O'Gorman grew into excellent types of dairy animals, and when the first show was held in Albion Park, Michael O'Gorman entered two pens of three cows each. William Sharpe, who lived adjacent to the show ground, admired these animals, and twitted O'Gorman with having made a great search among the neighbours to get the collection together. O'Gorman resented the remark, though it was made jokingly, and offered to lay a wager that he left three better cows in the paddock at his home. The wager was taken, and away O'Gorman went, returning with three extra cows. The result created no little stir among the cattlemen when it was found that O'Gorman won the wager and first prize with the pen he had left behind on the farm. John Lindsay got second place with a pen which included the celebrated cow, "Honeycomb." Apart from the prize money, O'Gorman won three trophies as special prizes, which included a silver cup, which is in the possession of his widow. Michael O'Gorman did not trouble about pedigree. He simply followed up what, in his opinion, produced the best results. In this he succeeded. His sons were much of the same opinion as that of their father, and bought largely from their neighbours. They have also been successful as business men and cattle dealers.

Following one's judgments instead of studying out pedigrees is, we know, often criticised without much reason. On this question the writer of these lines had much to say during the eighties and nineties of last century. At the beginning of these disputes there were six bulls to which cattlemen strove to base the success of their test and show cattle, to wit— Three Illawarra Shorthorns, and three Ayrshires. These arguments were rife during the early stages of cheese and butter factory developments between Unanderra and Gerringong. After being away for some years from Illawarra on the North Coast of New South Wales and Queensland, I started on a task in 1905 to collect as far as possible first hand the pedigrees of the prize animals at our several shows, and got hold of a large collection of written and verbal statements from "all and sundry." What are my conclusions? They are as follows: The three Shorthorn type bulls gave the general outlines; the three Ayrshire type bulls gave the vitality and dairy quality. The rich, red colours, yellow circles around the eyes, and on the fleshy part of the nose came from a mingling of Devon blood if not by direct mating by that blood being in those Shorthorn and Ayrshire bulls as shown in the long list of cattle sales in this volume.

As will be seen in the article on the "Macquarie Rivulet" James O'Gorman is now the owner of Major George Johnston's old homestead farm, which is a portion of the historic 1500 acres, known as the "Macquarie Gift." Mrs. C. Gower has leased portion of it. Master Roy O'Gorman, an enterprising youth of 18 years, is conducting successfully a dairy farm on the other portion, and will doubtless be the owner of the whole block, 150 acres, of rich meadow land in the course of a few years.

At present Master Roy O'Gorman's prospects are bright. What he may develop into as a dairy cattle breeder has yet to be seen. If, however, we are to judge by the page of dairy cattle illustrations in this volume which cover the last few years of the O'Gorman Bros.' cattle breeding efforts as well as animals at present in Roy's possession, it should not require a great stretch of one's imagination to predict a bright future for him, especially as he has an astute father to guide these early stages of his dairy education.

Robert Mears, Morden Farm, Toogoolawah, Queensland.—Robert Mears landed in Queensland from England in April, 1910, with his wife, three sons and one daughter. He was a brickmaker by trade, but his ambition was to get on the land. He bought a farm in the following September from J. H. McConnel, on the Cressbrook Estate, about 4½ miles from Toogoolawah. and set about getting a dairy herd. He picked up a few fairly good cows and a Shorthorn bull. There were many disappointments which was but natural as he was learning.

In January. 1917, he purchased "Belmont of Nestles" (No. 125, M.S.H.B.). He had previously used two unregistered bulls bred by Nestle's Coy. "Belmont" was by "Belmore II." ex "Sweetheart II.", by "Royal Standard" (22). On February, 1918, he purchased "George of Nestles," No. 126, M.S.H.B. He then, during the following year, purchased three good heifers from Nestles Coy., and three more at the disposal sale of the Cressbrook herd. In 1922, Robert Mears journeyed to New South Wales, and bought three heifers from Walter James, Cosey Camp, and two from W. H. Dudgeon at Burradale—both recognised breeders on the North Coast. His more recent purchase is from Nestles Coy., viz., "Lady Rose," a grand-daughter of "Rose" (140); and "Pansy VIII.", related to "George of Nestles." She goes back in line to a Sydney Royal Show champion bull, "Melba's Emblem," illustrated in this volume, owned by the New South Wales Department of Agriculture. "Tulip of Morden" seems to be one of the most successful cows in the Morden stud. She is a half-sister to "George of Nestles," sired by "Royal George" (50), dam, "Minnie II. of Grasstree" (263). She won two firsts and reserve champion at Toogoolawah, 1921; first at Ipswich, 1921; first and

special in all breeds in Brisbane in 1921; first in home milking competition with 63½ lbs. of milk, 3.53 lbs. of commercial butter in 24 hours, Brisbane Show, 1922. In class, 3 years and under 4 years, 273 days test, all breeds, she was head of the list with 12,187¼ lbs. of milk, 609.72 lbs. of butter. Her first calf was "Rufus of Morden," sire "George of Nestles." Sold at Brisbane Show, 1922, for 98 guineas.

"Hazel of Morden," purchased from Nestles Coy., sire "Royal Standard," dam of "Hazel II." illustrated in this volume, in 273 days, beginning at 4½ years, produced 13.516 lbs. of milk, equal to 657 lbs. of butter. "Buttercup of Morden," bred by owner, has in 273 days, produced 12,144 lbs. of milk, equal to 631,93 lbs. of butter. "Bonnie II. of Morden" a grand-daughter of "Buttercup" (1083), by "Belmont" (125), ex "Bonnie of Morden" (977), has commenced a 9 months' test at 2 years, and has every appearance of carrying the test through for 273 days successfully. "Hazel II. of Morden" was the first "George of Nestles" heifer to calve. The second heifer to freshen was "Norah III." ex "Norah" (771), at the age of one year 10 months. She has yielded 5.453¾ lbs. milk, 263.38 lbs. com. butter in 166 days, and is still under test. This heifer was second at the last Brisbane National Show. "Nina III." ex "Nina" (1082), is the only other "George" heifer in milk. She was just two years old when she calved, and gave 34½ lbs. milk, 1.565 lbs. com. butter in 24 hours. This will be the first test for 273 days' record. The following cows have been officially tested for 24 hours with results as shown:—

Name of Cow.	Sire.	Dam.	Age.	Lbs. Milk.	Lbs. Com. Butter.
Norah of Morden (771) ..	Mayflower's Prince ..	Fiery	5 yrs. 2 mths.	44	2.07
Silver of Mordon (1008) ..	Royal Standard (22) ..	Silver of Gunyah Farm	3 yrs. 5 mths.	35½	1.74
Cressbrook Bridget II. (1096) ..	Discount (67)	Bridget of Cressbrook ..	3 yrs. 8 mths.	52	2.44
Cressbrook Myrtle II. (1097) ..	Redgum (68)	Myrtle of Cressbrook ..	3 yrs. 6 mths.	47½	2.00
Bonnie of Morden (977) ..	Mayflower's Prince	Buttercup of Morden ..	5 yrs. 2 mths.	43	1·955

HEIFER'S HIGH RECORD. ("Sydney Morning Herald," 19/10/'22.)

The secretary of the Illawarra Milking Shorthorn Herd Book advises that "Hazel II. of Morden," an Illawarra Milking Shorthorn heifer, bred and owned by Mr. R. Mears, Morden Farm, Toogoolawah, Q., has completed her 273 days' test with a yield of 8,794 lbs. milk, and 460.41 lbs. commercial butter. She was one year 250 days old when she started her test, and as far as the secretary is aware this is the best Australian performance to date for an

animal of any breed of her age. "Hazel II. of Morden" is by "George of Nestles" (126), from "Hazel of Morden" (1009).

When the average Australian dairy farmer has studied the foregoing results he ought to blush to think that a man trained to make bricks in England, came to Australia in 1910, and in the very short period of twelve years has set them a task they are, apparently, unable to follow.

JAMES W. MUSGRAVE, Illawarra.

BELMONT OF WATERVIEW.

LILY II OF WATERVIEW.

J. W. GORRELL, Unanderra.

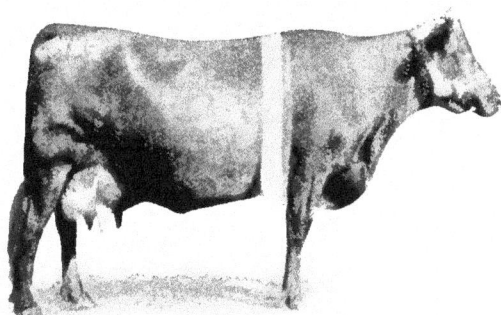

TULIP II OF SUNNYVALE.

TULIP III OF SUNNYVALE.

R. MEARS, Morden, Toogoolawah, Queensland.

HAZEL II OF MORDEN.
(No. 154, I.M.S.H.B., Qld.)

GEORGE OF NESTLES.
(No. 126, I.M.S.H.B., Qld.)

Mrs. Charles Gower, "The Meadows," Albion Park.—It is but seldom that one gets the opportunity of writing an appreciation on the merits of a lady in connection with dairy farming and the dairy cattle raising industry. Such an opportunity has, however, come to the writer. It is an easy task as the lady in question belongs by birth and marriage to two very old Illawarra dairying families. Mrs. Gower is a daughter of Levi Raison, who was born in Somerset, England in 1828. He arrived in Illawarra in 1852, and finally settled in Albion Park in 1867 where he died after a useful and honest career in October, 1904. The Gowers were an old family as regards their association with Illawarra and its dairy cattle. Charles Gower was a member of that family, and was born at Tongarra," Albion Park, in 1874. Tongarra was originally part of the dominion of a celebrated aboriginal king named "Tullumbah." That was when Major George Johnston sent his cattle down the range out of the reach of Governor Bligh. It was on portion of the Johnston "gift" holding that Charles Gower, after his marriage with Miss Raison, commenced dairying on his own account. The young couple moved along in keeping with the times. Young Gower was a cattle fancier, and always bought the best available animals. He was a hard working man who spent much energy in forcing his way to the front. The pace began to tell on his spent energies. Yet, he continued to force things until it was too late, and passed out on 26th June, 1921. Right here the great work of a woman with a small family begins. She carried on in the face of difficulties. She had a large herd of dairy cattle left on her hands and a high rent to meet every quarter. She had to pay labour at current rates. Yet she never faltered. She took the helm in her own hands and steered on and on through every trouble. What is the result? She is comfortably and free from all worries. The farm on which she and her husband had lived being sold (John Dudgeon being the purchaser) she moved into the adjoining farm owned by Mr. James O'Gorman of Albion Park, where it may be said with all truth she is prospering, has one of the best dairy herds in New South Wales; can meet her liabilities with a smile. The bull at the meadow farm is "Triumph," bred by Hugh Dudgeon and Son (late of Hillview, Jamberoo. Sire, "Fussy's Lad," dam, "Miss Jean," "Fussy's Lad," by "Gentle's Prince," dam "Fussy II."

In Mrs. Gower's page of illustrations in this volume may be seen the following animals, and there are many more equally good ones in the herd:—"Myrtle of the Meadows," sire, "Charmer," bred by W. H. Cook, Unanderra. Dam, "Daisy," bred by Charles Gower. "Silky of the Meadows," sire, "Prince," bred by Hugh Dudgeon and Son. Dam. "Ruby," bred by Charles Gower. "Amy of the Meadows," sire, "Prince," bred by Hugh Dugeon and Son. Dam. "Muriel," bred by Charles Gower. "Gwen of the Meadows," sire, "Prince," bred by Hugh Dudgeon and Son. Dam "Silky," bred by Charles Gower. "Dolly of the Meadows," sire, "Prince," bred by Hugh Dudgeon and Son. Dam. "Princess," bred by Charles Gower.

The bull, "Prince," the sire of these cows, was by "Fussy's Lad," dam "Emma II," which goes to show that he is closely bred to the present bull, "Triumph," illustrated in this page of Mrs. Gower's. The constitution of these animals being all that could be desired, a little in-breeding is sure to prove good.

In the effort put forth to carry on the work her husband left in an unfinished stage, Mrs. Gower gave the Illawarra dairymen an example of a woman's pluck. Her success in finishing the work and carrying it on to a profitable state has set an example that but few men have been capable of performing, and in doing so she has also gained much in the way of womanly dignity.

The writer visited Mrs. Gower's home in November, 1922. She was then sending seventeen ten-gallon cans of milk daily to Sydney off a farm containing 140 acres of land. Those figures speak louder than fancy returns from a few highly fed cows here and there throughout Australia. It is easy to pick, say, five or six cows out of a herd of 100, and force them up at the cost of the keep of a dozen animals. It is not so easy to get big returns for a herd of cows in a profitable manner.

James Robert Knapp, Swanlea, Bolong, Shoalhaven was born on the south side of the Shoalhaven River at Berallen, 1859. Since then the name has been changed to Brundee owing to confusion in the postal department. His father was a well-known agriculturalist and a prize ploughman. Stephen Knapp's ploughing successes are mentioned in this volume, not only on the banks of the Shoalhaven River, but in the Ulladulla district, where he settled with his family in later years and carried on both farming and dairying there with success

The subject of this sketch commenced dairying at Moruya in 1881, and obtained his first dairy cattle in that district, and bred from a bull bred by Cole Bros., Jamberoo. He obtained a red bull of the "Mariner" strain bred from Francis McMahon's dairy herd when that noted Shorthorn breeder owned a valuable herd of dairy cattle. He then got a Wilford bred bull. The late William Wilford often explained to the writer of these lines his theory of breeding dairy cattle, which, briefly, meant his ideas of blending the Shorthorn with the Aryshire. He used Shorthorn and Ayrshire bulls in his herd alternately every three years, and was always careful to select a Shorthorn bull with a prominent backbone, a type of animal that has not been plentiful since the introduction of the beef breed in the South Coast districts.

As soon as James R. Knapp got an opportunity of buying a farm in the Shoalhaven district he did so. His home, Swanlea, is situated at the junction of Broughton's Creek with the Shoalhaven River, almost under the morning shadow of Coolangatta hill. Here he carried on dairying and farming combined. He had learned cheese-making, and made money out of his cheese, rearing calves on the whey, which has been found to suit the purpose very well when other ingredients are used with it.

At Swanlea James R. Knapp soon moved forward, and has 230 acres of very choice land. The floods annoy him occasionally, especially so when they get out of control. Floods are, however, not without blessings, as at Swanlea where large deposits of rich silt is spread over the flats. In this way, if a crop is swept away, the next year's crops pay for it.

The Swanlea stud of dairy cattle have been improved very much by the introduction of Illawarra bred bulls and heifers. Those who meet the Swanlea animals in competition at our leading shows find that it is not an easy matter to get the judge's eyes away from them. A few of them may be viewed in this volume where they are illustrated. No. 1, "Jock of Swanlea," colour, red, brand K.J., sire "Joffre of Greyleigh," g sire, "Daisy's Heir of Hillview," from "Tulip of Hillview," dam, "Cinderella II. of Greyleigh," g sire, "Rufus of Greyleigh," g dam, "Cinderella of Greyleigh."

"Gwen of Swanlea," colour, red, with little white, No. 1146, I.D.C.H.B.; sire, "Fairy Boy of Fairfield," g sire, "Fairfield," gg sire, "Togo," dam, "Empress." "Jessie IV. of "Swanlea," colour, roan, No. 1148, I.D.C.H.B., sire, "Togo of Greyleigh," dam, "Jessie III. of Greyleigh." "Blossom II. of Swanlea," colour, red, No. 1139, I.D.C.H.B., sire "Fairy Boy of Fairfield," dam, "Blossom of Swanlea," g dam, "Spot." "Flossie of Swanlea," colour, red, sire "Patey of Swanlea," g sire, "Togo of Greyleigh," dam, "Blossom II.", g dam "Blossom," gg dam, "Spot." "Velvet IV. of Swanlea,," colour, red, No. 1148, I.D.C.H.B., sire "Patey of Swanlea," etc., dam, "Velvet III. of Swanlea," g dam, "Velvet II.", gg dam, "Velvet." It will thus be seen that the Swanlea stud is an Illawarra breed which has flourished in every new dairying centre in Australia. To-day animals from the Swanlea stud may be seen doing well for their owners as far north as the Atherton Tableland in Queensland. Call them whatever name you may they are still Illawarra. They are like a square block of wood, roll it as you may it will turn up square. Turn over the pages of this volume and study the types of dairy cattle in it, and you cannot fail, dear reader, to pick out an Illawarra. Yes, and as soon as James R. Knapp got his eye set on the Illawarras he determined to make them his ideal cattle, and he is doing so.

James R. Knapp's I.M.S. cow, "Flossie of Swanlea", has just completed her 273 days' test. Result: 8,982 lbs. of milk, testing 4.6, equal to 410.31 lbs. of butterfat. This cow was only two years and nine months old when she began this meritorious test.

Henry McGrath, The Green Hills, Shoalhaven, was born on a farm adjacent to his present home in 1850. His father, James McGrath, was born in Co. Tyrone, Ireland, and came to New South Wales in the early thirties, and went into the employ of Lieutenant Lawson of Veteran Hall, Prospect. In his youth he was a schoolmate of Mrs. Henry Osborne of Marshall Mount, Illawarra. In or about the year 1838, Henry Osborne sent him to Barrengarry, Kangaroo Ground, then a cattle run. About 1842 he went to Woolomia, on the shores of Jervis Bay, where his son, James McGrath of Cambewarra, was born in 1846. He then took a farm at Green Hills where the subject of this sketch, Henry, was born. He died, the result of an accident in 1879, aged 81 years.

Henry McGrath grew up on the land, always among horses and cattle. He never had any particular fancy in dairy cattle, nor had he much respect for pedigreed animals. His theory of breeding can be explained away in a simple manner. He, working on the experience of many old-time dairy cattle breeders, to wit—That the bull gave the progeny their outward appearance, colour, etc., while the cow conveyed to them their nervous, milk-producing qualities. A case in point, when Dr. Hay imported his Shorthorn bull, ''Knightly,'' he was mated with quite a number of high-quality cows bred in Illawarra. Their male progeny showed the Shorthorn type, and roan colour. These young bull in turn were mated with other Illawarra cows of superior dairy quality. Henry McGrath got a beautiful roan bull calf called ''Knightly III.'' who was about the third remove from ''Knightly'' (imp.). This bull mated with heifers purchased from C. W. Craig, and other Illawarra dairy cattle breeders gave him his first great lift upward in dairy cattle breeding at ''The Green Hills.'' Of course he had been cattle breeding and dealing in cattle for years before that in Cambewarra.

To get at the Green Hills property we must go back a long way in the history of old Illawarra, when William Graham was managing things for those cruel taskmasters, Major Druitt, Captain Rossi and Lieutenant William Sheaffe in turn. Just how William Graham came to be called by some of the old settlers ''Terrible Billy'' need not be mentioned here. In the course of time he got to Shoalhaven where his two eldest sons, James and William, obtained a grant each of 60 acres, owing to having been born in New South Wales prior to a certain date. They settled at Mayfield. James' grant was dated July 6th, 1841, quit rent £5 6s. 8d.; William's grant was dated December 12th, 1841, quit rent, 9s. per annum.

So far as can be ascertained William Graham, senr., did not receive a grant of land in Illawarra, although he was early on the scene. So far as the old maps guide us there is no such place as ''Green Hills,'' so it must have been so named by local residents. This particular property comprised a grant of 640 acres to J. Layton, generally known as Parson Layton. Portion 5 on the southern bank of the Shoalhaven River, opposite Pig Island. Native name, Burraga. Layton did not fulfil the

necessary conditions, and William and James Graham occupied it as tenants in common. It was then granted to them on January 30th, 1843. As time moved on the Grahams increased in numbers until at one time the clan was represented by about six generations. William Graham, junr., died in 1849, and trouble arose among the several families. The law courts were leased for a term to settle these disputes. The majority soon felt that law at best was a losing game. Then a sub-division of the 640 acres was agreed upon. In this sub-division appears the names of James Graham, John Graham, James Monaghan, David Hyam, Maria Hyam, Christina Williams, and others. Then James Monaghan found himself in possession of one of the finest dairying properties in New South Wales containing 183 acres 1 rood and 28 perches, on which he erected a fine house, and things went on swimmingly with him. He bought out the interests of others who were interested in the Green Hills property, and thereby increased his holding to 359 acres. He then either rode or walked over a dairyman's gold mine for a number of years. But the ''Green Hills'' was his ruin. He made money on this farm and craved for more; went into a gold mining spec at Yalwal, and became involved and lost the best gold mine on the Shoalhaven River.

All who knew James Monaghan were sorry for his ill luck. He was a useful, honourable public man. At the same time no one begrudged Henry McGrath his slice of good luck because he made his money by close attention to the business he understood. Henry McGrath kept on the old beaten track. He understood the land, horses, and cattle. He made much money on horseback as a dealer in stock. On page 275 we have him at the age of 72 years seated on his favourite horse, ''The Cob,'' just starting off to inspect a line of dairy heifers. And again we have him holding a mare whose pedigree goes back to a black mare owned by his father, sired by a blood horse imported by Henry Osborne of Marshall Mount, Illawarra. There were such sires as ''Merry Pebbles,'' ''Deerfoot,'' and ''Grandmaster'' in her back breeding. She is a chestnut and her sire is ''Game Boy.''

Henry McGrath has a family of three sons and seven daughters, and carries on in a large way both agricultural and dairying pursuits. His hobby is, however, to get out in the open among the stock. A keen judge of cattle values. Small profits and quick returns on large mobs bring him in substantial returns.

Denis O'Keefe, Kiltankin, Jasper's Brush, South Coast.—Many will be anxious to learn the origin of the name to be seen on the Illawarra railway line, "Jasper's Brush." In the early days of the Berry regime men were stationed at several centres to watch the movements of men and things. They received rations and rode about the open country in order to see that no cattle nor timber were removed without the overseer's orders. One of these men whose name was "Jasper Brush," was located at this part of the Berry Estate. Hence the name, as he was only known as "Jasper."

Denis O'Keefe was fortunate in getting hold of some good land in the vicinity which he named "Kiltankin," after his native place in the Co. Tipperary, Ireland, where he was born on July 22nd, 1868. It will be seen, then, that Denis is not a pioneer, nor the son of a pioneer of Illawarra, but he did what a wise man would do if he got the chance, viz., he married the daughter of one of Illawarra's pioneer dairymen, namely, Miss Timbs, whose father was Samuel W. Timbs. The Timbs family are mentioned elsewhere in this volume. Samuel was a brother of Gabriel Timbs.

On July 12th, 1884, Denis O'Keefe landed in Sydney and came down to Illawarra determined on making a home. He started dairying at Kangaroo Valley on November 1st, 1892, by purchasing a few cows and a red and white bull called "Hero," bred by E. J. Condon of Kangaroo Valley. He won several prizes with this bull which gave him a taste for show ring fame. He then decided on following up the Shorthorn type of dairy cattle, and purchased from his father-in-law "Monarch," a bull of much merit. The progeny of this bull had made a name for their sire in Johnston Bros.' herd on the Richmond River, North Coast. "Monarch" did much good for the Kiltankin herd after Denis O'Keefe purchased at Jasper's Brush from the Berry Estate people. "Monarch" was also a successful bull for his owner at South Coast shows, including the champion prize at the National Show, Berry, in 1914.

The next sire put into the Kiltankin stud was "Denial," registered in the IV. volume of the M.S. herd book of Australia. This bull was bred by James Gilroy. He was evidently inferior in regard to dairy quality to "Monarch," under more favourable circumstances, and "Gayfield," bred by James W. Musgrave, of "Riverside," Yallah, was placed at the head of the stud. This bull is also registered in Vol. IV. of the M.S.H.B., No. 878. This bull has been exhibited for a number of years with varied success and failure according to the opinion of one man (the judge for the time being). He was placed second, and got reserve champion award at Nowra and Berry in 1921 and 1922. Won first for bull and progeny at Nowra in 1922; second in same class at Berry in 1923. On his sire's side he goes back to Spinks Bros.' Musket strain. He has, however, much of the Knightly blood in his mixture in "Daphne" (2721, H.B.).

The present stud bull at Kiltankin is "Renown," whose sire is "Standard of Oakdale," his dam being "Rachael of Oakdale," as registered in Vol. VI. M.S.H.B. Both "Gayfield" and "Renown" are illustrated in this volume. Critics may, therefore, form their separate opinions of their respective merits for dairy purposes.

Denis O'Keefe has been breeding and exhibiting dairy cattle at South Coast shows for 27 years, and for several years past at the Royal Show, Sydney. His success as a dairy cattle exhibitor is by no means so important as his advancement in the ownership of good dairying and agricultural land in Illawarra. His Kiltankin property at Jasper's Brush contains within its boundaries soil that will produce, with a small amount of labour in comparison to other farms, an abundance of food for man and beast, and is the result of the combined energies of himself and his good wife during a short time.

George Alexander, The Fairfield Stud Farm, Kiama, Illawarra.—George J. Alexander may be at once described as a progressive man of the younger school of Illawarra dairymen. He began operations in 1910 as head of the firm of Alexander Bros. at Fairfield, Kiama, and has since taken charge of the whole of the Kiama interests as well as being a shareholder in Alexander Bros.' holding at Numba, Shoalhaven. At the Fairfield home he has bred

GEORGE ALEXANDER,
The Fairfield Stud Farm, Kiama, Illawarra.

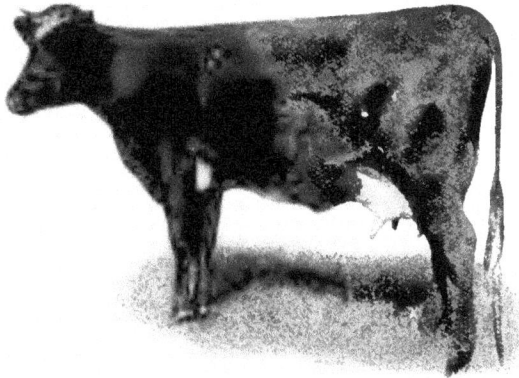

BUTTERFLY II OF FAIRFIELD.

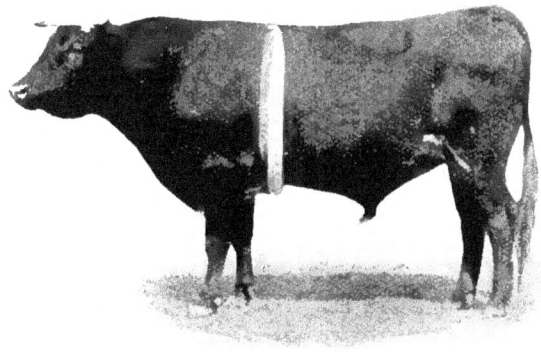

CHARMER OF FAIRFIELD.

FLORRIE OF FAIRFIELD.

BEAUTY II OF FAIRFIELD.
(No. 115, I.D.C.H.B.)

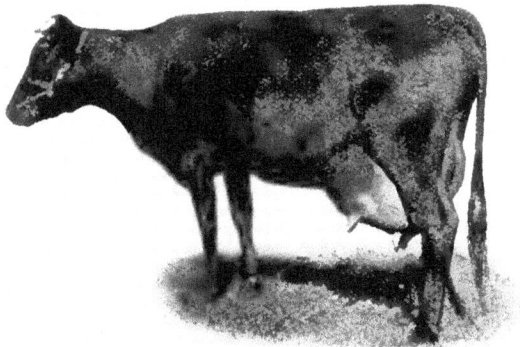

MAYFLOWER OF FAIRFIELD.
(No. 23, I.D.C.H.B.)

DUCHESS OF FAIRFIELD.
(No. 10, I.D.C.H.B.)

several very fine animals, including "Fairy of Fairfield," a record breaker in her day. She was disqualified by what may be termed a committee of opposition breeders because milk was part of her daily ration. This may have been right. At the same time it is generally believed that chemical compounds can be used to take the place of milk—the compound having this advantage; it can be used secretly. It has been stated in the past that it is not practical to materially change the per cent. of butterfat in milk by feeding, but the milk flow can be increased to an enormous degree by giving cows the right amount and kind of food. Breeding experiments have, however, shown that butterfat production can be bred into a cow. Thus it may be seen by those who desire to see that "Fairy" should not have been disqualified.

To possess an ambition to breed high-class dairy cattle and at the same time to attain a marked degree commercially requires a great amount of physical and mental energy, as they often run on what may be termed devergent lines. In perfecting the plan of a herd requires constant attention at home, while commercial enterprises take men away from home. George Alexander has entered upon this dual career, and has so far been successful in both undertakings.

Every man may have at times the ideal, in his mind, what he should be. This ideal may be high and complete, or it may be moderate and unsatisfactory. Perhaps no one is so satisfied with himself that he never wishes to be wiser or better. Such men are not likely to benefit their neighbours.

To understand dairy farming in its many ramifications a man must be observant and quick to size up and sum up the commercial side of every branch of the industry. That is George Alexander's aim in life.

It is a sterling character that makes a man architect of his own circumstances. Men of this stamp succeed by keeping abreast of the times. The subject of these remarks kept to the fore by securing good bulls and selecting good cows to mate with them. Fairfield, No. 2, A.R. I.D.C.H.B., laid the foundation desired. Fairfield whose sire was Togo, thus giving at once a blend of "Admiral" and "Warrior" blood. Then there was "Illawarra Prince," a massive red bull that combined the "Gordonbrook," N.C., and the "Hillview" blood, together with "Red Prince" with "Beaconsfield"

blood in every vein. The next bull at "Fairfield" was "Fussy III's Pride," the sire of George Gray's stud bull "Foch."

Passing on to the present sire in the Fairfield Stud "Charmer of Fairfield," bred by owner, it may be noticed that his position is in common with all stud animals, that is, certain strains of blood come to the fore. "Charmer's" official pedigree is given as follows. Sire, Fairfield, No. 2, I.D.C.H.B., and his dam, Phyllis, goes direct back to "Marquis II." No. 6, I.D.C.H.B. This bull holds an unbeaten show record for 1922 and 1923 at leading coast shows as well as at the R.A.S., Sydney.

Fairfield of Fairfield, sire of Charmer, is also sire of Fairy of Fairfield, who gained the following prizes, viz.:—Second and reserve champion, R.A.S., Sydney, 1917; first, dry cow, and reserve champion at Kiama, 1919; first in pen of dry cows at Kiama, 1919; second, Nowra 1919; first and champion at Berry, 1919; first and champion at Nowra, 1919; second and reserve champion at Kiama, 1920; and first and champion at Nowra, 1920. Tested for the Kiama Show, 1920, she produced the following, viz.:—April 24th, 1919, 80.5lbs. milk, equal to 4.143 lbs. butter, averaging 29.001 lbs. per week; June 21, 1919, 72 lbs. milk, equal to 3.608 lbs. butter, averaging 22.341 lbs. per week; September 1st, 1919, 54.2 lbs. milk, equal to 2.364 lbs. butter, averaging 21,476 lbs. per week; in addition she was first in six months' test, three stops as per figures given; first in milk test with 80.5 lbs. in 24 hours, and second in butter test with 29.001 lbs. in seven days; for best dairy cow in the show, 1920, she gained second on points for utility and production, with 96 points.

Under the United Pure Bred Dairy Cattle Association Herd Test she produced 17,130 lbs. milk for eight months, equal to 70.4 lbs. per day, daily average test, 3.4, equal to 712 lbs. butter. She also produced in 365 days 21.972 lbs. milk, equal to 947.201 lbs. butter, and she is half sister to Duchess of Fairfield, who produced 18,277 lbs. milk, equal to 793.121 lbs. butter.

Fairfield of Fairfield is also sire of Fairfield IV., who has an unbeaten record, and gained first prize at Berry, 1921; Commissioner of Fairfield, who has an unbeaten record and was purchased at Kiama Show sales for 151 guineas; Duchess of Fairfield, a successful show cow, and who produced 68 lbs. milk daily for six months; and Princess of Fairfield, who was sold for 80 guineas.

The cow illustrations in this volume from the Fairfield Stud and their performances are of the highest merit. The herd comprises 170 head of dairy cows, and 70 head of young cattle; 130 cows being milked on the average daily. The Fairfield farm contains 340 acres.

At the late Royal Show, Sydney, Fairfield had 21 cattle exhibits for which 19 ribbons were secured worth £81 3s, which, after all, did not pay much over expenses. There is evidently too much show about the R.A.S.

Arthur Pickles' Stud of I.M.S. Cattle, Blacklands, Wondai, Queensland.—To get an idea of the far-reaching influence of the old pioneers of Illawarra one must wander far away from the grave plots that hold the ashes of those sturdy men, heroes in the true sense of the term, for they risked life and limb to build homes in the bush—a bit of thick bush land—then a few cows and a horse gave them their first homes.

How many are there to be found to-day who do really respect those old heroes? Methinks they are few in number. Now the subject of this sketch was reared in Queensland on a dairy farm, and can bring to mind the cattle used by his father. As he says, "They were called dairy cattle." That was thirty years ago. The writer can remember that between thirty and forty years ago dealers were engaged in the business of taking cattle from the dairying centres of Illawarra to Queensland. Cattle in those days could be purchased for small sums. They were often brought back over the border to the Richmond and Tweed Rivers by other dealers.

Mr. Pickles informs me that it was a common practice on stations to cut off two teats from a cow's udder in order to relieve the strain, and still allow the udder to contain enough milk for the calf. That never happened in Illawarra, as milking twice, and in some instances thrice a day, was generally adopted in Illawarra in the very early thirties, and the calves "poddied" and sent out to the stations at from 9 to 12 months old. Butter was everything to the early dairyman; and it was a common thing for a dairyman to ride ten or twenty miles to get a bull calf of a well-known strain, and those who had no horse carried the calf in a bag on his back. Yes, they were everlastingly after butter. Hence the beef, Shorthorns, introduced in 1870, and

the following ten years upset many good men.

It was the first Illawarra cattle brought into Queensland over thirty years ago that took the eye of the subject of this sketch. He loved them in his early youth, and when he grew up he decided to own some of them. In 1902 the Blacklands Stud was started by means of a bull and heifer, from John Hardcastle's Jimbiggaree Herd—"Jamberoo II." and "Diamond II." He secured a blue-ribbon with each animal at the Rosewood Show which made him a very proud man indeed. "Jamberoo II." was by the noted bull, "Jamberoo," No. 1, I.D.C.H.B. His dam was "Whitelegs," a very fine cow. "Jamberoo II." is No. 22 in the same herd book. His next purchase was a bull bred by Graham Bros. of Illawarra. Sire, "Admiral," dam, "May." "May" was sold to Tyson Donnelly of Darling Downs, Queensland, for 80 guineas. She was a spotted cow of great merit, and a prize winner in New South Wales and Queensland. The next bull was by "Federal of Mayfield," dam, "Milkmaid," bred by Graham Bros. One could not speak too highly of "Milkmaid of Mayfield." She was by "Admiral." Her record was 71½ lbs. of milk in 24 hours, equal to 25¾ lbs. of butter. She is the dam of the Reserve Champion I.M.S. bull at the Royal Show, Sydney, 1923. On the progeny of those bulls a great bull was placed, "Sir Hugh," No. 26, bred by Hugh Dudgeon and Son of Hillview, Jamberoo. "Admiral" was sold foolishly, and the sire of "Sir Hugh." "Guss of Hillview" was also sold far too soon. How many great bulls have been cast out foolishly in Illawarra? Scores of them. "Sir Hugh" is recognised to-day as the leading bull for production and show purposes in Queensland, over fifty of his daughters having qualified for the herd book test. His place is being filled gradually by "Florrie's Victory," out of the noted cow, "Florrie"; and "Fussy's Monarch," bred by H. Dudgeon and Son, out of "Fussy III.", a very superior cow indeed. A youngster from the Hillview stud, by "Hero," ex "Princess," is coming on later. "Florrie's of Blacklands" record is 74 lbs. of milk per day, equal to 24 lbs. of butter per week, 19.374 lbs. of milk, equal to 900 lbs. of butter in 365 days. (Official). A glance elsewhere at Graham Bros. and Dudgeon and Son's dairy cattle illustration is sufficient to show the quality of the Blacklands stud, of which there are 26 cows averaging 51 lbs. of milk daily, and an average of 16.83 lbs. of butter per week. "Royal IV." is the winner of the butter test at the Brisbane National Show. Just turned four years, making 5.96 lbs. butter in 48 hours, which is an excellent performance.

The lesson to be learned by breeders throughout New South Wales and Queensland from the success of the Blacklands' system of dairy cattle breeding is plain. Arthur Pickles had been taught early in life the differences between common station-bred cattle and the Illawarras for dairying purposes; when, therefore, he began to exercise his own judgment, he looked for the Illawarra type of dairy animal, and afterwards bred that type. He did not cast about looking for what did not exist, to wit, a dual purpose animal. In his effort to get hold of the best strains of dairy cattle in Illawarra the builder of the Blacklands herd, Arthur Pickles, made several visits to the old dairying centre, and has secured the "Gentle Prince," "Guss of Hillview," the "Fussy," and the "Royal Prince of Hillview" blood. "Hero of Blacklands," No. 52, H.B., is out of "Buttercup II. of Alne Bank," and was bred by Henry Chittick and Sons whose cattle are duly recognised in this volume.

Alexander Campbell Lamond was born at Oakbank, Shoalhaven, in 1865, on a farm belonging to his father. He has, therefore, been associated with farming and dairying all his life. In the year 1890 he commenced farming and dairying on his own account. He turned his attention to cheese making, and was successful owing to close and careful attention to the business. He did not for some few years devote his attention to cattle breeding; used all sorts of breeds and their crosses until 1903, in which year he speculated in a few grade Friesians. He was so impressed with their dairy qualities that he at once decided to adopt the Friesian breed, and has worked on those lines ever since. He purchased the best available animals from Bodalla, Coolangatta and Numba to which places Friesians had been imported direct from Holland. Mr. A. C. Lamond surprised his friends by purchasing high-priced land on the Shoalhaven River. He evidently had confidence in his dairy cattle as he continued buying high-priced land until to-day he owns 1150 acres of the rich Numba flats and two other holdings between Numba and Jervis Bay containing 900 acres and 700 acres respectively of grazing land. The Friesians are his sole study, and a glance at the illustrations on page 115 in this volume will at once convince breeders that there are quite a large amount of dairy quality in the animals that have been and are now used by Mr. Lamond in building up his herd.

From whence came these animals which are admired by so many dairymen in New South Wales.

Silesia.—This fertile country prior to the late war belonged in part to Prussia, Austria, and Poland. Since the late war Poland has claimed the better part of it. It has been for centuries rich in dairy cattle, apart from its great coal measures. From an historical point of view we need only state that it would be to the ancient annals of Silesia we should turn if we wished to get at the Friesian breed of cattle. It may be questioned as to whether we should give to one variety of cattle the name of the whole group, comprising as it does, Dutch, Friesian, Oldenburg, and Holstein. The trouble, however, lies with the constant feuds between these neighbouring peoples. The winning side always carrying away the stock of those who were forced to submit to the yoke of the strongest power. If history is correct, the Silesian cattle were a few hundred years ago yellow and white spotted. The mixture with other races gave this superb breed of cattle a variety of colours without taking from them their size or dairy quality. Hence we find black and white, and red and white spotted, many blue roans, and sooty-grey animals. In order to overcome difficulties of the nature just described about 1875, two cattle associations were established in the fertile lands of Holland. In the beginning no distinction was made in colours, all were regarded as pure. Later on the Friesian Association advanced the classification of colour, and adopted the black and white as the distinct colour. Professor Isaachsen, a noted Norwegian authority, says: "Passing from Scandinavia to the lower countries, a well-known and characteristic breed is the one commonly bearing the name of Dutch cattle, although termed in America Holsteins-Friesians, the latter title referring to the Dutch province of Friesland. It is represented in the German province of Holstein. In general appearance and colouring these cattle seem to present a considerable resemblance to the old black and white Ayrshire breed, with which they also agree in being mainly reared for dairy purposes." Following Professor Isaachsen one might easily conclude that these cattle prevailed throughout Denmark and Jutland. "Where," he states, "Black and white cattle owing to their albinistic nature are found with the white markings arranging themselves along the lines of the limbs, extending to the front pair as high up as the shoulder blades, and in the hind-quarters to the pelvis, and in many instances the red colour displaces the black. These animals are termed the red and white Baltic cattle. In size all these cattle run very large, and scientists point out that the change in colour from black to red is a kind of retrograde evolution as demonstrated in the "Malay bantin," in which the cows and calves are red, while the old bulls are black, which goes to show that black is a specialised type of colouring in cattle, whereas red is the primitive or original colour. The jumping from black to white is albinism.

Be all this as it may be. A. C. Lamond has made a success of dairying and Friesian cattle breeding. On his home farm, Numba, he has a number of remarkable fine animals and several high testers which include:—"Woodcrest Johanna Tepee" (imp.), No. 451, born, 14/1/'12.—Milk 256.285, butter 104.5 in 365 days; and "Johanna Mercedes of Lyndholme," No. 453, tested at 3 years old:—Milk 18909.75 lbs., butter 751.934 in 273 days.

The Berkeley Estate.—The Berkeley Estate, as may be seen elsewhere in this book, was originally a grant to Robert Jenkins. After his death his widow, Mrs. Jeminia Jenkins, added to it by purchasing other smaller grants from soldiers and their sons. In this way the estate spread westward and grew in size until it contained about 5000 acres. It lay just west of the Five Islands Estate, and was bounded on the north by Allan's Creek, and on the south by Lake Illawarra. The old South Coast road passed through it at Unanderra, the western portion becoming what might be termed North Dapto. A small township sprang up at "Charcoal," now Unanderra, watered by a stream of fresh water. Dapto proper lay about three miles further south. With regard to the meaning of the word Dapto, one might search in vain to solve the problem. An aboriginal king, "Old Bundle," gave it as his opinion that it wasn't derived from the aboriginal language, possibly then from Di Pieto or D'Petro, a foreigner, who settled there in very early times and carried on shoe-

making and tanning, and dealt largely in fur skins with the blacks.

Immediately around this enlarged Berkeley Estate, moving round from Allan's Creek towards the range west, and then south, lay the properties in early times of several military men including Captain Waldron, Colonel Molle, Lieutenant Sheaffe, Captain Plunkett, Colonel Britten, Captain Hopkins, Colonel Leahy, Major Druitt, Lieutenant Weston, Captain Cole, R.N. We have it on the best of authority that these men considered themselves a superior class, and carried on farming and dairying operations by means of cheap convict labour, and, employed as a rule, an ex-convict as an overseer, who did not practice those fellow feelings that go to make man wondrous kind. If, then, tradition reminds us that convicts were shot in those localities when suspected of stealing food it only recalls to mind a lecture delivered in Sydney during December, 1864, on the history of New South Wales by the late Sir Henry Parkes, then Mr. Henry Parkes, M.L.A., when he stated, "Thomas Barrett, Henry Lovell and Thomas Hall were hanged in Sydney for stealing beef, and John Freeman was hanged for stealing flour. These unfortunate men," said Mr. Parkes, "were starving when they stole the food and should not have been hanged." Who knew more than Sir Henry Parkes the state of things in England when his countrymen were being transported in chains to Botany Bay? Who knew more than he about the state of things that existed in New South Wales in the early days? He, himself, had to toil alongside of men who had served under cruel overseers, and Sir Henry came to Australia a free man. What Sir Henry Parkes saw and heard in Sydney on his arrival could be seen and heard in Illawarra. No wonder then that every effort was put forth to destroy our records. But somehow tradition keeps alive dreaded memories. Whereby the sins of fathers are recorded against their children. There is but little left to us of ancient Illawarra in the form of buildings. In the forties of last century quite a number of new homes were erected. The old homes erected by means of convict labour have either disappeared or were remodelled in such a manner as to appear quite different to the original design. This it at once patent to those acquainted with the increase of families. A modern investigator moving through Illawarra with his camera would certainly be able to snap many old buildings, but would find it most difficult to locate the site on which the original buildings stood. Some few who lived a solitary life did not attempt to alter things. That was not, however, the spirit of the age. Scores of old homes were swept by fire, and a few by floods. Change. There is nothing more certain than change.

Of the old military caste which once ruled in Illawarra very little remains. It was peculiar to the Hindoos, hence military officers who had served in India did not look upon the officers of the old New South Wales Corps with much respect. Illawarra was not the place for such distinctions. Consequently, the pride of man was short-lived. The next blow that felled the pride of these haughty ones was the granting of land to "ticket-of-leave men." They left one by one, leaving nought behind but a fig or a pine tree to mark the spot from whence their convict slaves went forth to toil in sunshine and in rain.

Among those old-time military men Captain Hopkins appears to have settled down to farming and dairying on fairly solid lines. His home, "Benares," was of an up-to-date character.

"Benares" did not escape its share in the form of tragedies. A fine young girl was murdered there by a man named Pritchard in a fit of dire revenge. Another sad happening was the death from thirst of a father and son, relations of the Hopkins' family, who had developed a craze for cattle-droving in the interior of New South Wales—

Far, far beyond, prolific region spread,
Where whispering winds have made their balmy bed,
Disturb'd but by a Leichhardt's daring thread!
   *   *   *   *
"O'er his dominion the emu wanders wild,
And deems himself fond Nature' fav'rite child;
Bears his high head and o'er each wavy chain,
Shoots his bright gaze, the monarch of the plain.
  Yon barren desert's broad and drear expanse,
Checked the bold Sturt and dar'd him to advance
Awed with its sterile majesty of space,
And warn'd him backward from the fatal place"
  *   *   *   *   *

In 1867 Captain Hopkins sold out his dairy herd at "Benares" and leased his farm. It was at this sale that the Bartletts bought Captain Hopkins' imported Durham bull which they put among the cows purchased from Andrew McGill, with a view of improving the herd and bringing it up to a higher standard of purity. They improved the colour but not the dairy quality.

The Cook Family.--The founder of this family, William Manning Cook, was born in Cambridgeshire, England, in 1834, and arrived with his parents in Illawarra at an early age. He, therefore, saw much of the early life of Wollongong, and was present when the first load of coal was delivered from the Mount Kiera mines. A procession was formed at 10 a.m., Monday, August 27th, 1849. (A copy of the invitations sent out to the principal residents of Wollongong to attend the celebration of that important event is in the possession of the writer.) There has been many developments in coal mining since then.

William Manning Cook married early in life and settled for a time near Mount Kiera. Then he removed to Avondale where he carried on dairying until Edward Gibson gave up the lease of Benares. He secured the lease from Captain Hopkins, and then commenced dairying and farming on a large scale as his family had increased considerably in numbers. Benares contained 470 acres, was well watered by two running creeks, with a splendid house erected thereon. He was a hard-working, progressive man, and milked as many as 140 cows, which goes to show he was a good manager. He introduced, fifty years ago, horse works for churning butter which relieved his family of much labour.

It was at Benares that the first butter was made which was sent to Sydney to compete in the open market in the new colony. It was made by John Kennedy, packed in the butt end of bangalow leaves which had been specially treated for the purpose. The old black inhabitants taught the whites how to make this material just as pliable as leather. It was by this means that water was carried, and the butter reached Sydney in perfect condition.

William Manning Cook soon made sufficient money to buy Benares, which estate is in possession of his family to-day. He died February 6th, 1921, aged 87 years.

William Henry Cook was born in Illawarra in 1857, and worked on his father's farm where he had many opportunities of studying farming and dairy cattle raising, which, judging by the use he made of his opportunities, was taken advantage of. He, like his father, married early in life, and at once went to live at "Glendalough," where he and his good wife raised a very fine family. He went into dairying with a gay, full heart, bred and purchased the best types of dairy cattle, made money, purchased, when an opportunity offered, adjoining farms until he increased his holding stage by stage into many broad acres.

He was as well as being a good father, a good dairyman, and a good dairy cattle breeder, an upright public man. He went full hearted into co-operative dairying, and was one of the first to move in the matter of establishing the Co-operative Butter Factory at Unanderra in 1887. A director of the Farmers' and Dairymens' Milk Coy., Sydney, and a consistent member of the Dapto A. and H. Society. He died, the result of an accident, March 30th, 1922.

The estate of the late W. H. Cook, which is in four farms, is practically under the control of Albert, Stanis and Harry Cook, who like their father, were brought up to the business of farming, dairy, and cattle raising, which, is at all times, a great advantage to the man on the land. It is impossible to calculate the amount of knowledge a boy gains on his father's farm year in and year out.

If a young man, like Albert Cook, had to learn at a college what he has already learned, he would find it very difficult, whereas, all he has to do on his farm is to study books on Mendelism, heredity, and those diseases that are peculiar to the cow under domestication to enable him to overcome any difficulties that call forth his attention. A good father on a good farm is a wonderful guide.

At "Glendalough" there are 100 cows milked daily. All these cows are of choice colours, being either red or roan, and registered in the M.S. or the I.M.S. herd books. On the estate there are 300 head of dairy cattle. The two sires in use are "Rufus of Glendalough" and "Admiral of Glendalough." For bull and progeny prizes at local shows these two animals were awarded several prizes. The Rufus group won eight times; the Admiral group six times. The bulls that sired most of the aged cows were "Bloomfield of Glendalough" and "Advance of Greyleigh." The cows from these two bulls are of good quality. Several of them have show tests to their credit as well as show ring prizes.

During the present year, 1923, "Rufus of Glendalough" was awarded first and champion prizes at Albion Park; was first at Wollongong, and grand champion of all breeds at Dapto against 13 competitors. The Cook Bros.' stud of dairy cattle is worthy of the men who spent so many years in bringing it up to its present stage of perfection.

The Duncan Family of Unanderra and West Dapto.—The originals of this family were very old colonists. John, the founder of the Illawarra family, was one of six brothers and one sister, and was born outside of Sydney harbor in 1837, and was, therefore, an old Australian native. He was brought into Illawarra by his parents in 1841, who had taken up a clearing lease from William Warren Jenkins on his Berkeley Estate. In the course of time they began to grow wheat and other farm products. The original home is now the property of George Lindsay, of Horsley, Dapto. John Duncan, together with two other brothers, Alexander and Thomas, purchased a bullock power threshing plant from an old Illawarra identity named Darough, and threshed wheat and other cereal crops for the farmers as far south as Jamberoo during the years that wheat flourished in Illawarra, free from rust. After the rust trouble had made wheat growing impossible the Duncan brothers separated, and John Duncan and his family settled down in common with his neighbours as a dairy farmer which he continued in up to a period when old age called a stop. He died at an advanced age after having spent 66 honourable years in Illawarra.

Alfred W. Duncan, of Berkeley, Unanderra, was born on the Berkeley Estate in 1860, and has been dairying on his own account for some considerable time, and has always taken a keen interest in dairy cattle raising. He always looked out to use none but dairy quality bulls. The bull illustrated in this volume is "Play Boy of Berkeley," and was bred by Hugh Dudgeon and Son, of Hillview, Jamberoo. The champion test cow, "Prize of Berkeley," was bred by Alfred Duncan. She is an excellent type of dairy cow from a practical dairy farmer's point of view, inasmuch, as she requires no pampering to force up her dairy yields of milk and butter. She is in this respect the poor man's cow.

Alfred Duncan is in a large way as regards dairy farming as he runs two dairy farms, one on the old Berkeley Estate, and the other on the old Five Islands Estate. In this way he milks on the average 90 cows.

A glance at the cattle illustrations in this volume will suffice to prove two things:—First, that Alfred Duncan has well-bred dairy cattle, and, second, that his cattle were photographed under very trying conditions that prevailed in Illawarra during the latter part of 1922 and the early part of 1923, when the camera man

ALEXANDER CAMPBELL LAMOND'S FRIESIAN STUD.
Numba, Shoalhaven.

OLDA XII OF COOLANGATTA.

WOODCREST JOHANNA TEPEE (Imp.) (No. 450).

LUNTA I OF BRUNDEE.

OLDA XIV OF COOLANGATTA.

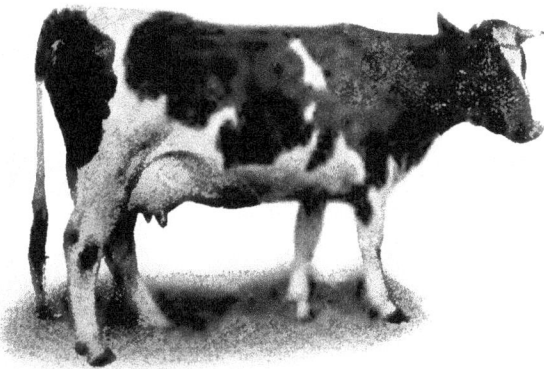

JOHANNA MERCEDES OF LYNDHOLM (No. 453).

FANNY KING OF ROCK.

The animals illustrated on this page are the foundation stock of the now
celebrated Friesian Stud at Numba.

came on the scene. To a judge, the quality is plainly visible. It is then merely a matter of feeding to bring them up to a higher standard of production. It has been shown by repeated cow tests in America that scores of cows that were producing from 500 to 600 gallons of milk per year, viz., Each milking period were by judicious feeding made to produce from 1000 to 1200 gallons of milk during each milking period, which is generally recognised as 9 months.

In reviewing Alfred Duncan's cattle illustrations, then it must be borne in mind that the photographs were taken when some of the animals were well run in milk. All the Unanderra cattle were photographed under similar difficulties. That, however, does not influence the mind of a man acquainted with dairying under all sorts of conditions.

George Duncan of Brisbane Grove, West Dapto, was born on the Berkeley Estate, and has been associated with dairy farming all his life, and for several years has been dairying on his own account. The animals exhibited in this volume were all bred by him, and they are a credit to him as they show excellent dairy quality. No. 1, The roan Shorthorn bull, "Noble Lad of Brisbane Grove," calved December 25th, 1914, at Brisbane Grove, sire, "Young Bloomfield of Sunnyvale," dam, "Beauty II." "Young Bloomfield" was by "Bloomfield of Sunnyvale, dam, "Lovely of Sunnyvale." "Beauty II." was by "Noble," dam, "Beauty of Mount Nebo." No. 2, "Becky of Brisbane Grove," calved March 2nd. 1914, a roan Shorthorn cow, sire, "Young Bloomfield of Sunnyvale," dam, "Cherry of Brisbane Grove," whose sire was "Tim" and her dam was "Gertie." "Becky" was shown at Dapto A. and H. Society Show five times, winning four first prizes and one second prize; and four champion prizes in Shorthorn dairy cow class. No. 3, Red and white Illawarra cow, "Blossom of Brisbane Grove," calved April 12th, 1914. Sire, "Young Bloomfield of Brisbane Grove," dam, "Trixie of Brisbane Grove," sire, "Tim," dam, "Beauty II." "Blossom" was placed first as heifer two years and under three years; twice first as cow in milk, and twice champion, and was twice successful in pen of three cows in milk. No. 4, "Star of Brisbane Grove." An Illawarra dairy cow, colour red, calved July 29th, 1914. Sire, "Young Bloomfield of Sunnyvale," dam, "Brownie II. of Brisbane Grove," whose sire

was "Prince Ivanhoe," dam "Brownie I." It will be seen that George Duncan is the breeder of all four animals in the Brisbane Grove page of cattle illustrations, and by reviewing the career of the Duncan family since the head of the family settled in Illawarra, it will be patent to my readers that as a family they have each and all been good citizens who have by their honest industry made Illawarra richer by their presence at a time when labour was required to make ends meet.

Henry Chitticks and Sons.—Henry Chitticks arrived in Illawarra in 1880 at the age of 18 years. He spent a few years among the dairymen seeking experience and earning a little money with a view of starting on his own account. In 1886, Henry made his first start at "Woodbrook," Jamberoo. "Woodbrook" belonged to an old Conservative pioneer named James Wallace. After the death of James Wallace his daughters remained in the old home and leased the farm to whomsoever they considered likely to pay them the highest rental on the day the rent was due, if not quarterly in advance. In this way the subject of this sketch found favour in their eyes.

A wise man hath said: "Perseverance, dear my lord, keeps honour bright. To have none is to hang quite out of fashion, like a rusty nail in monumental rockery." By perseverance Henry plodded on and on until he found himself on a better farm on "Flat Rock Creek" (Clinton's old farm), near Kiama, in 1892. He remained there until 1898 and then moved down to John Colley's farm and leased the adjoining farm owned by Moses King.

Henry Chitticks moved into a position that enabled him to purchase in 1904 Moses King's 55 acres, John Colley's farm, the Glenburn farm, 145 acres, situated on north bank of Minnamurra River, Jamberoo; McIntyre's farm at the Foxground, 151 acres, and, then in 1905, Alne Bank, Gerringong. Alne Bank was the old home of the Hindmarsh family. Anyone interested can see in this volume under "cattle sales" that several large heads of cattle were disposed of by the tenants who had occupied "Alne Bank." Henry Chitticks' latest purchase was a farm on the late James Robb's Riversdale property. On this farm a man named Scott experimented with sugar cane in the early sixties. The cane when cut was taken to Riversdale and put through a primitive crusher which only crushed one stalk at a time. When improvements were being executed the sugar crop failed and Scott moved northwards.

Henry Chitticks married in 1885 and had three sons and two daughters for whom he has worked ever since. His wife died in 1905. The Chitticks' herds were practically founded by purchased cows and heifers. He purchased a cow called "Lovely," in calf to an Antill bull, "Dunlop." That "Lovely" bull was the best bull he ever owned. He then purchased a bull from Hugh Dudgeon of Hillview, Jamberoo, by Red Prince; he then fancied a calf called "Royal Prince" whose dam was a plum one of Dudgeon's choicest cows by "Gentle Prince." He then turned his attention to George Grey's bull, "Togo," and secured a bull by that great sire out of "Primrose," a very superior cow. Henry Chitticks and Sons have been exhibiting dairy cattle at local shows, and at the Royal Show in Sydney since 1910 with satisfactory results. The number of first and champion prizes won by the firm ran into huge figures. Of course they followed up the shows year by year from Wollongong to Nowra. One cow, "Buttercup II." produced in 1914, in class, cow giving greatest quantity of commercial butter per week: 17.514 lbs.; in 1915, 17.480 lbs.; in 1916, 18.418 lbs.; in 1917, 17.480 lbs.; in 1918, 18.404 lbs.; in 1919, 14.175 lbs. She was tested under careful supervision. Had this cow's dam been raised on rich flats instead of on poor hilly country, and had she in turn been raised on country rich in bone forming constituents, she would have been a large-framed animal; instead of that, was delicate looking in 1914, and she continued on the medium size right up to the year 1919. All things being equal, size and constitutional vigour is everything in cow-testing as such animals can consume large quantities of rich foods. "Buttercup II." is illustrated on page 259 in this volume, together with other types of Chitticks and Sons' stud dairy cattle. Their appearance go to show that a dairyman can breed handsome, profitable cattle. Others of their neighbours who were on the land in Illawarra away back in the seventies have neither farms or presentable cattle to show to a visitor.

James W. Gorrell, Sunnyvale, Unanderra.— James Gorrell, senr., was born in Armagh, Co. Tyrone, Ireland, and migrated in common with hundreds of his countrymen to New South Wales in the early fifties. He was not long in getting on the land, and settled on the Avondale Estate, West Dapto. Avondale was a grant to Alfred Elyard, of whom we know but little beyond the fact that all the Elyards of that period were associated either with the convict barracks, or the law courts in Sydney, where they occupied good, easy jobs. None of the Elyards were agriculturalists or commercial men. They sat tight like barnacles and leased their grants to military gentlemen who worked them by means of convict labour.

In the mid-thirties Henry Osborne of Marshall Mount, purchased Avondale from Elyard and leased it out to the small settlers. After his death it went to his eldest son, Henry Hill Osborne, who carried on farming and dairying for a few years.

It was on his father's farm at Avondale that James W. Gorrell was born in the year 1862. His father, being both an agriculturalist and a dairyman, the subject of this sketch, had the opportunity of getting closely into touch with those industries. He evidently took advantage of his opportunities as we find him in 1883 striking out on his own account. He was an energetic man who took to work as being part of his nature, and about the year 1890, he was settled on his own farm, part of the Berkeley Estate. Unanderra, containing 84 acres, with a very excellent wife.

To show what the small settlers have done for Illawarra as compared with the large landowners, let my readers think this over. The Jenkins family, prior to this sub-division, owned 3500 acres, some of it the finest land in Illawarra, yet they failed to make ends meet. It was cut up into about 20 farms, and all those who settled on it became independent of financial worries.

It is safe to say that few men have been more successful at dairy farming than James W. Gorrell. To his 84 acres he added 121 acres, and since then purchased 84 acres on the Canterbury Estate. Part of John Wyllie's Dunlopvale grant which fell into the possession of Dr. J. D. Lang, D.D., here we have the name, Canterbury.

James W. Gorrell is not a man to cultivate fancies in dairy cattle breeding. He always believed in practical results, and the Illawarra breed suited his purpose. Consequently we find him with a herd of good, working cattle. He cultivates 30 acres of land, feeds his soil, and fills two large silos every year for winter supply besides growing green fodder for direct feeding. Each silo contains 110 tons of silage.

He milks from 50 to 80 cows throughout the year. The results from his stock are a sufficient guarantee that dairying is a paying concern on Sunnyvale. From 20 to 30 heifers are reared on the farm each year to replace the old cows as they pass out to be fattened off for the butcher. He may rear a bull for his own use, but as a rule he buys from his neighbours. The bull at present on the farm is "Douglas," bred by Hugh Dudgeon and Son.

Mr. and Mrs. Gorrell have a very excellent home wherein they have raised a family of seven sons and three daughters. The sons have relieved their father of much of the farm work. He has, in consequence, been able to devote much of his time to the public. He has been for years an active public man, and Mayor of Central Illawarra Council for a number of years.

The Johnston Bros. of Albion Park.—The builder of this Illawarra home was born in the County Fermanagh, Ireland, in 1838. His name being John Johnston, and the last of his brothers to seek a fortune in New South Wales. Consequently he did not arrive in Illawarra until 1865. He, however, like many of his countrymen, was prepared to face difficulties, and got on the land first at "Crawley Forest," Kiama; then removed to Jamberoo; from Jamberoo he removed to Omega Retreat, where he found himself solidly on his feet.

It has been said with a considerable amount of truth, "They who acquire a position with much difficulty, retain it the longest; as those who have earned property or money are usually more careful of it than those who have inherited those luxuries." It was certainly the case with John Johnston who worked very hard, made money, and took care of it while he lived.

A great number of the North of Ireland men who came to found homes in Illawarra were well acquainted with buying and selling cattle for years in connection with the "monthly fairs" that were held throughout their respective counties. When, then, they arrived in Illawarra, they hadn't much to learn in that direction. John Johnston was one of those shrewd men who noticed where the best sires were to be found. He attended auction sales and always bought his fancy in dairy cows which gave him the best material to work on. He made a great forward move in dairy cattle breeding when he secured an excellent bull by "Earl of Beaconsfield." From this bull and the best of his cows he bred

money-making stock. It was from this bull and a cow named "Florrie of Coral Cottage" that he raised a bull named "Florrie's Pride," an excellent type of Illawarra, and was a prize-winner at local shows. From "Florrie's Pride" and a large-bodied roan cow named "Lovely," he bred "Lovely's Prince," a roan of much quality. From "Lovely's Prince" and a very handsome roan cow which he purchased at Messrs. James Bros.' sale, Gerringong, he bred another roan bull named "Omega." From this bull and a cow of his own breeding he bred "Omega II.". He had, by this time, brought around him a family that were ready to take on a farm and a dairy herd on a larger scale.

The next move was his last. He leased and afterwards bought a large holding at Albion Park known as Marksville, a part of the noted John Terry Hughes' estate. It contains about 300 acres. Some of this land is of a very rich nature; the other portion is dry forest land. Taking its convenience to a market and its proximity to the village of Albion Park, it may be termed a very excellent holding constantly increasing in value.

The Johnston Bros. have taken advantage of their opportunities, and are interesting themselves in the breeding of good dairy cattle. They have an intelligent grip of the value of good cattle, and are not likely to be led off the lines laid down by their late father, namely, always seek out the best dairy strain and hold on to it until some better strain can be secured. This is patent in their conversation, as they still look back with pride to the great worth of the "Earl of Beaconsfield" blood.

To the man who can think for himself the example of a man like John Johnston is worthy of attention. He placed more value on quality than on pedigree, and following on those lines made money without much capital to start on. Such efforts are the true object lessons.

Messrs. Johnston Bros. purchased a bull named "Richmond of Kalube" from M. E. Hindmarsh of Robertson. It is from this bull's strain that they are now breeding. A photo of the bull bred by Johnston Bros. is illustrated on page 249, named "Dairymaid's Prince." His dam, "Dairymaid," is illustrated on the same page. By a survey of the outlines of "Dairymaid's Prince" it would appear plain that his line breeding going back to "Florrie's Pride" with occasional out crosses has not impaired his constitution, altered his back sires' type.

nor impaired his dairy quality. He is, therefore, an object lesson for young breeders to study.

D. Spoor and Sons, Illawarra M.S. Stud, Mundubbera, Queensland.—The writer is forced to clip from the "Gayndah Gazette" the following account of the rapid advance in dairy cattle breeding of the above-named dairymen:—"Situated within a short distance of Mundubbera is the 'Aurora' dairy farm, owned by D. Spoor and Sons, the home of some of the highest class Illawarra M.S. cattle to be found in the State. In 1918 Spoor and Sons set out to establish a dairy herd on high-class lines. The herd was gradually founded with the best females obtainable from the herds of such noted breeders as A. Pickles, P. Biddles, E. Moses, and a bull thrice champion of Queensland named 'Young Richmond' was purchased from W. G. Curran; two cows from D. Doran by auction. A heifer in calf was also obtained at Doran's sale by 'King's Counseller.'" The writer says: "Although this heifer looked very promising, it was little thought she would develop into such a great producer. She is now known as 'Handsome of Hillcrest.' Her completed nine months' test has stamped her one of the best, and has a weekly record for the Gayandah Show of 17¾ lbs. of butter. Spoor and Sons' cattle have been successful at several shows, carrying off seven championships, fifty firsts and fourteen second prizes; also a silver cup at Biggenden Show. The bulls used in the 'Aurora' stud are 'Hugh's Prince' and 'Florrie's Boy II.' They are line bred to each other, both having for g sire 'Federal of Mayfield,' out of 'Milkmaid of Mayfield.' bred by Graham Bros., Dunmore, Illawarra, who are well known as dairy cattle breeders.

"The following is a list of some records put up by Spoor and Sons:—'Gold of Blacklands,' A.R., 333 lbs. of butter in 9 months as a two-year-old; 101½ lbs. of butter in seven days at 28 months. 'My Love of Home Park,' A.R., 396 lbs. of butter in 9 months as a four-year-old: 14 lbs of butter in seven days. 'Handsome of Hillcrest,' A.R., 506 lbs. of butter in 9 months as a four-year-old; 17¾ lbs. of butter in seven days. 'Handsome II. of Hillcrest,' A.R., 389 lbs. of butter in 9 months as a two-year-old. 'Joyce of Blacklands' produced 121 lbs. of milk equal to 5.96 lbs. butter in 48 hours on Brisbane Show ground. 'Dora of Blacklands,' 'Kiama of Blacklands,' and

several other cows have passed into the I.M.S.H.B. of Queensland.

It is to be hoped for that Messrs. Spoor and Sons will continue to move on swimmingly when they decide to frame their own ideals by breeding their own fancy in cattle independent of outside influences. Men with large areas of land, a variety of soil, many cattle, and money at their command, can do much. Small landholders must walk circumspectly.

Dunster Bros.' M.S. Dairy Herd, "The Hill," Shellharbour, Illawarra. The Dunster family came from Kent, England, and settled at Dapto, Illawarra. The late Humphrey Dunster was then two years old. The family removed to Shellharbour in 1856, and settled on the top of Stoney Range where they carried on farming and dairying for a number of years.

Joseph Dunster, junr., was born in Kent in 1826, and as a young man went into the storekeeping business at Tullimbar, near the head of the Macquarie Rivulet, where he married Miss Jane Elizabeth Stratford. They had for neighbours the Wilsons, Crawfords, Kirtons, Colemans, McGills, and John Beatson. The old butter track from the Kangaroo Ground (now Kangaroo Valley) passed through there to Wollongong, near Tongarra.

The Tongarra climate did not suit Joseph Dunster, junr., so he determined to seek out higher land. Enoch Fowler at that time lived on "The Hill" farm, and Dunster waited until Fowler was ready to remove to Sydney, and in the meantime carried on a butchering business.

Joseph Dunster, junr., carried on butchering for a time at the junction of the Albion Park and Kiama roads, near Shellharbour. Dairy farming, however, claimed his attention, and he moved up to "The Hill" farm in 1860.

When the Joseph Dunster family settled on "The Hill" property they had for neighbours the Allan and James families, who, in time, became connected by marriage.

Joseph Dunster remained on "The Hill" farm until the time of his death in 1877.

Right here we may pause and refer to the origin of the Scotch Jock cattle of Illawarra. The disputes about the original Scotch Jock bull have been numerous. Alex Fraser, now well up in the years beyond the three score and ten, states that as a boy he took cows to the McGill bull, and that he was

"THE HILL," Shellharbour, Illawarra.

The home of Messrs. Dunster Bros., where a high-class herd of
M.S. Cattle is being established.

MILKING SHORTHORN HERD, ESTABLISHED IN 1860, BY JOSEPH DUNSTER,
and successfully carried on by his son, W. C. Dunster, and now the property of C. R. and K. R. Dunster.

THOMAS DALY, Woodbine Stud Farm, Bolong, Shoalhaven.

F

a big, massive, red and white spotted bull, with large upturned horns.

These large framed spotted, red and white Ayrshire-like cattle were owned and bred on three Illawarra estates — Johnston's, Terry Hughes' and Osbornes. Consequently, the McGills, Colemans, Kirtons, Trittons, Dunsters, and James' families had them.

At Joseph Dunster's death in 1877 the widow and family carried on the farming and dairying operation on "The Hill" for a period of seven years, when Mrs. Dunster died. At the winding up of the estate the brothers, W. C. and R. Dunster, took over the farm (a leasehold) and the stock. Later on they divided the stock between them, taking pick about. They divided the farm and carried on separately. When the Bassett Darley Estate was sold, W. C. Dunster purchased "The Hill," together with his brother Robert's holding. That was in 1899.

William C. Dunster died in 1919, and his widow died in the following year. The estate had then to be wound up in March, 1921. The farm, together with 40 head of the stud herd, were purchased by C. R. and K. R. Dunster in the name of Dunster Bros.

The Shorthorn type of Illawarra always took the fancy of the Dunster family. This type of animal is now and has been for the past twenty years been termed milking Shorthorns. In a conversation with the late W. C. Dunster a few years before his death, he stated that the best bull the family ever owned was purchased by his father early in 1872 from Evan R. Evans. This was a roan bull of great length, full of dairy quality; then he (W. C. Dunster) got another good bull from Williams of Robertson. This Williams' bull sired his fine cow "Ada." "Josephine," a noted prize winner and the dam of several fine animals was purchased at James Bros.' sale, Alne Bank, Gerringong. There is a fancy descendant of "Josephine" in Dunster Bros.' herd at the present time which much is expected from.

Among the bulls owned by W. C. Dunster was "L'Aglon; he was fancied by show judges, and his progeny turned out well. The writer has a photograph of this bull which, apart from his red colour, displays many of the outstanding characteristics of the Devon breed. After this bull came a Coolangatta Estate-bred bull called "Alex Knightly." How his progeny turned out cannot be ascertained. Of course, on "The Hill" farm, there were several bulls, including one of the "Musket's" named by one

who knew no better. "Mikado," when he was put into "The Hill" herd he must have been very old as he had been previously in at least three herds. All the same he was a half-brother of "Musket II." of Darbalara fame.

The illustration of "The Hill" farm in this volume does not do justice to its worth as a dairying proposition. It is an excellent holding for the purpose for which it is used, namely, dairying and dairy cattle raising. The soil is of a very rich volcanic nature. Young cattle grow into good form on it.

Messrs. Dunster Bros. have, therefore, plenty of opportunities of showing to the New South Wales dairymen what they are capable of during the next few years.

Messrs Boxsell Bros., Myrtle Bank, Meroo Meadow.—The Boxsell family have been long and favourably known as dairy farmers and dairy cattle breeders—first at Omega, Kiama, and afterwards at Berry in the Illawarra district, covering easily a period of seventy years. Over forty years ago the writer of these notes saw John Boxsell's herd of dairy cows in the Berry district. They were of the Longhorned Durham type. A number of them showed their old Longhorn origin, having fairly long hooped horns and a dorsal streak on the back. They were certainly dairy cows of great merit. Anyone passing down Harris street, Ultimo, Sydney, might notice the model of the Golden Cow over the Farmers and Dairymen's milk depot. That model was taken from the photo of the late John Colley's great cow "Easy of Jamberoo." She gave over 18lbs. of butter per week, grass-fed, under the old pan-sitting system. No one need doubt this as the writer supplied the photo of "Easy" to the model maker. Now it is also true that all, or nearly all, John Boxsell's cows were of that type. Once the Lowe-bred bull—a Mudgee-bred Shorthorn—went into the Boxsell herd, that old Longhorned-Durham type gradually disappeared.

Boxsell Bros.' Myrtle Bank Stud of dairy cattle at Meroo Meadow was established in 1893. The foundation bull was bred by Hugh Dudgeon, of Hillview, Jamberoo, and was by his noted bull "Charmer", illustrated in this volume.

"Charmer" was out of the test cow "Charmer," and by the Faulk's bred bull, "Sojer Boy II." The influences of the Charmer blood is patent in the I.M.S. cattle to be seen at Myrtle Bank to-day.

Following on the Charmer bull was a bull bred by Jennings, of Cumberton Grange, near Jervis Bay. This bull was soon displaced by a bull called "Nelson", bred by James Sharpe, of Gerringong, of the "Barney" strain, named after the breeder, Barney McGucken, of Kiama. Few better bulls than the old Barney bull was ever raised in Illawarra. His dam was a beautiful blood-red cow, breeding unknown. She was all the same, a good cow, and produced a good son, and Boxsell Bros. benefited much by using that blood on the Charmer strain.

Then came "Red Prince II.", bred by A. Binks, of Berry; a large, red, loose sire. The progeny of this bull won many prizes at local shows, against much competition, besides giving many sires to other dairymen. The majority of the cows now in the herd are by "Red Prince II".; the young stock are by "Earl II. of Sedgeford," a bull of nearly the same blood.

The bull at the head of the Myrtle Bank stud to-day is "Charmer's Warbond of Myrtle Bank", whose sire is George Alexander's bull, "Charmer of Fairfield". Few bulls have taken the dairymen's eyes so keenly as this bull, and show-ring critics dub him, "The coming bull". He is illustrated in this volume; he is only three years old, and is growing into form rapidly since this photo was taken. He has not been beaten in the show-ring—only by his sire in the aged classes—while in his own classes he has won twenty-three first and champion prizes. Better still, his calves are giving great promise. Of course he is well bred, as he goes back to "Togo", and through "Marquis II." to old "Charmer".

The cow illustrated in this volume, "Pigeon of Myrtle Bank," bred by the owners; sire, "Nelson"; dam, "Beauty", is a dairy cow of merit, with a record of 70lbs. of milk in 24 hours. She was neither pampered nor forced, like those world wonder cows. Just a good profitable dairy record animal. Three of her sons, by "Red Prince II.", are at the head of profitable herds at the present time.

Boxwell Bros., all through, have looked ahead and used their eyes before buying a sire. They have just purchased a bull calf from George Grey, of Greyleigh; sire, "Foch"; dam, "Coronation". They are moving onward.

A. C. Payne, of Spring Vale, Chatsworth, Gympie, Queensland, was born at Gerringong, Illawarra, and spent most of his early life in the coast districts. In 1905 he commenced dairy-farming on his own account. He had some good cattle of the Hindmarsh strain, and purchased a bull from Thomas Nelson, of Kangaroo Valley, his first start being on the North Coast of New South Wales. In 1915 he took up land on the Mary River, near Gympie, Queensland, to which place he removed his young cattle. He then got bulls from W. H. Dudgeon, of Glenthorne, of the Hugh Dudgeon strain, and a few heifers bred by Joseph E. Noble, Jamberoo. At the present time (1923) his herd consists of 100 head of dairy cattle, with a bull, "Raleigh's Reflection of Glenthorne", as the chief stud animal. His farm, Spring Vale, contains 200 acres of rich scrub land, well grassed, with abundance of water, and is situated within six miles of the township of Gympie, on which there is erected every dairying convenience on the best scale. The cattle are doing remarkably well, and are all registered in the Queensland I.M.S. Herd Book.

The test cows illustrated in this volume are as follow:—

Heather II. of Hillcrest.—This heifer at 2 years 8 months produced under Official Test 54 lbs. milk, yielding 2.145 lbs. c b f, or 15.015 lbs. in 7 days, and has been successful at all leading Shows, including National. An official 273 day test gave a yield of 12,903¼ lbs. of milk, and 469.31 butter fat; equal to 552.13 commercial butter in the period. She was 2 years and 9 months old at the beginning of her test, and now holds the Queensland record for I.M.S. cow under 3 years of age. Heather II. of Hillcrest was bred by Jos. E. Noble, of Jamberoo, Illawarra, and is by "Jellicoe," ex "Kate of Hillcrest." "Jellicoe" is by Fussy's Lad of Hillview," ex "Mermaid of Glenthorne."

Darling III. of Springvale—Official test at 2 years and 6 months, 37¾ lbs milk, yielding 1.5 lbs C.B. fat. Bred at Springvale Stud by A. C. Payne. Sire, Cherry Boy II. Dam, Darling II.

It is plain from the foregoing facts that A. C. Payne is a man who is aiming at high averages, not only in milk and butter records, but in the quality of his young cattle. If a dairyman succeeds in putting together a herd of cows that give good average returns according to the monthly cheques from the factory, he is at once considered a successful dairyman. More, however, is required of him if he is going to be a recognised breeder. He must look to it that he is not raising too many culls. A good cattle breeder has but few culls each year. Buyers may then feel secure when they visit a farm of this nature that the stock are the goods. This is doubtless A. C. Payne's object, as his advertisement states that inspection is courted. The value of inspection to a keen judge of dairy-cattle lies in the ultimate understanding between buyer and seller, for with young dairy cattle no one can be positive of results. The buyer, then, pays the price, and takes his pick, with all the risks. All the same, no ambitious breeder likes to hear of failures. He is invariably anxious to learn that his stock has turned out well.

TWO OF THE HERD OF A. C. PAYNE,
Springvale, Chatsworth, via Gympie, Queensland.

DARLING III. OF SPRINGVALE.

HEATHER II OF HILLCREST.
(Registered I.M.S.H.B., Q'ld.)

PIONEERS.

The Original Johnstons.—George Johnston at the age of 17 years was gazetted to the 24th Regiment of Foot, and saw a lot of fighting. In 1763 he was elected member for Westminster and in 1764 he was appointed a colonel in the army, and A.D.C. to King George III. During the American war the duke commanded the camp at Boston under Sir John Gage. It was while serving in America that his Grace the Earl Percy, was brought into contact with Captain George Johnston of the 4th King's Own Regiment of Foot, who was appointed his A.D.C. Captain Johnston was mortally wounded at the battle of Bunker's Hill where his son, Ensign George Johnston greatly distinguished himself by recovering the colours of his regiment and carrying them away from the enemy into action again. On the advice of his Grace Earl Percy Ensign Johnston was at once appointed lieutenant, and afterwards volunteered for service under Captain Phillip. He was appointed by Phillip A.D.C. in 1788. His Grace Earl Percy never forgot Captain Johnston, and sent him in 1801 a pure-bred Merino ram and a thoroughbred stallion named Northumberland. In 1803 he sent him in the ship Calcutta a ram and four ewes of the finest Teeswater breed.

We are told that early in the eighteenth century the title of Earl of Northumberland became extinct by the death of the last male heir of the Percy family. The proud Duke of Somerset, as he is recorded in history, married the daughter, then representing the Northumberland title and estates. The Duke of Somerset's Percy wife died early, and he again married a lady of lesser rank in the peerage. The duke being one day closely engaged in his room looking over some papers, his wife quietly stepped in and put her hand on his shoulder. He turned round and said: "Madam. your familiarity is altogether inopportune. Recollect my first was a Percy." This woman was a daughter of Sir Hugh Smithson, and, having children, Sir Hugh was raised to the peerage in 1766 with the title of Duke of Northumberland. He was the great Shorthorn cattle breeder, and the peers dubbed him the Yorkshire grazier. Hugh, 2nd Duke of Northumberland, was born in 1742.

It has been said that the Earls and Dukes of Northumberland came from an ancient family. Their family name was Percy, and the Barony of Percy was founded in the year 1299. The family, through its successive barons, earls, and dukes were rich, powerful and influential. Located near the Scottish border, and subjected to wild raids of the northern clansmen, they were brave by instinct, warlike by necessity, enterprising by education, and rich by inheritance. Their estates were vast, and to their earlier grants from the Crown, they added largely both by purchase and marriage. They had the means to apply the agricultural improvements through the generations of which they had passed, and it would appear that the heads of the family were most sagacious in worldly affairs. Among those improvements none was more apparent than the excellence of their grazing lands, the quality of their horses, cattle and sheep.

As lieutenant Johnston sailed from England for Australia with Captain Phillip in 1787. On the death of Captain Shea. of the New South Wales corps he was promoted to the captaincy. He fought at Castle Hill, New South Wales, in 1804, and as a mark of bravery Governor King gave him a present of 2000 acres of land near Parramatta, known as the King's Grant.

Captain George Johnston rose in rank to that of lieutenant-colonel of the 102nd, or the old N.S.Wales Corps as it is generally termed. The arrival of Governor Bligh caused the military authorities of New South Wales considerable anxiety, and eventually Captain John MacArthur of the old New South Wales' Corps rose the rebellion of which mention is made elsewhere. Lieutenant-Colonel George Johnston's friend Earl Percy exercised great influence in his behalf, and although he returned to New South Wales robbed of his rank in the army, he was allowed to return immediately, and found on his arrival all his property and stock in his possession, whereas Captain John MacArthur was detained in England for eight years. After his return to New South Wales he lived in retirement at his home, Annandale, near Sydney, where he died 5th January, 1823. His son, Mr. George Johnston, junr., held the position of chief inspector of the Government herds in New South Wales from the year 1815. In this capacity he had visited the Illawarra or Five Islands district. He was inspecting the Government herd at Brownlow Hill, and was thrown from his horse against a tree and died at Annandale a few days later, February 28th, 1820, aged 32 years. His brother, Mr. David Johnston, was immediately appointed as chief inspector of the Government herds of New South Wales, and held the position for many years, keeping in touch during the whole of the time with Johnston's Meadow Estate, Illawarra. Lieutenant Robert Johnston, R.N., was born in the old George Street Barracks, Sydney, in 1790. In the year 1797 he was sent by his father to a strict naval school in England and returned to New South Wales in 1816, and placed in charge of the "Schnapper," a Government boat which was placed at the disposal of the military authorities for conveying soldiers, convicts, provisions, and material to and from the gaols to the several penal settlements. In this capacity Lieutenant Robert Johnston, R.N., often visited Red Point, now Port Kembla. In 1819 he took Messrs. Alexander Berry, Hamilton Hume, and James Meehan in the cutter Schnapper from the Five Islands on a tour of inspection as far as Mount Dromederry. In 1822 Lieutenant Robert Johnston, R.N., in the cutter Schnapper, took Messrs. Alexander Berry, Hamilton Hume, and John Oxley from the Five Islands to the Shoalhaven. On this occasion Messrs. Berry and Oxley returned to Sydney in the Schnapper, but Mr. Hume went through the Shoalhaven Valley to Braidwood. In 1823 Lieutenant Robert Johnston, R.N., after the death of his father, entered into possession of the home at Annandale, near Sydney, where he lived almost a retired life. He died there full of years in September, 1882, aged 92. Isaac Nicholls, who arrived in Sydney in the ship Admiral Barrington in October, 1791, was a brother-in-law of Major Johnston, of the old New South Wales Corps. Nicholls worked his way out of servile toil and became superintendent of convicts. Then he was brought more prominently under official notice. He became the first postmaster, married Miss Rosetta Julien in February, 1805, received a grant of land at Calderwood, Illawarra, and died November, 1819, aged 49 years. An old tradition held good in the early days that a Captain Nicholls piloted a schooner in and out of the Illawarra Lake for cedar cut on Major Johnston's estate in 1810. If such be true, it

would be simple to explain how the early settlement of Illawarra was accomplished. New South Wales was terribly policed during the early part of Governor Macquarie's reign. He and Johnston, however, were friends, and cedar was new in those days and a valuable asset.

Mr. David Johnston lived at George's Hall, near Liverpool, New South Wales. He had in addition to the imported creamy stallion, "Northumberland," which Mr. E. H. Weston said was the progenitor of the celebrated hurdle horse, "Creamy Jack" and other valuable stallions. Re "Creamy Jack" was bred by Mr. John Johnston on the banks of Jerrara Creek, and was certainly of mysterious origin. Johnston was my neighbour and an honest man, but who owned the sire of "Creamy Jack" it was difficult to say. Mr. David Johnston owned a horse named "Providence," a bay stallion standing over 16 hands, imported by a Mr. Wilson, by the white sire "Alma," dam "Pauliness." Alma's sire was "Old Grog," and "Pauliness'" sire was Mr. D. Halady's "Venture." He also owned "Protector," an imported stallion, and won 1st prize at the agricultural shows at Parramatta in 1861 and 1865. He was also owned by Tom Ivory and George Tindel. Mr. Johnston also imported the celebrated blood horse "Æther," sire of Mr. James McGill's "Hopping Joe." The imported Shorthorn bull "Melmoth" came to Johnston's Meadows, Illawarra, where valuable cattle were bred and sold by auction at saleyards by local auctioneers. In 26th January, 1876, ten years after the death of Mr. David Johnston, Johnston's Meadows Estate was sold. The break came in 1866, and the Johnston's Meadows property was ready for division. Mr. George K. Waldron, auctioneer, sold at his yards, Kiama, 50 head of pure-bred cattle, brood mares, colts and fillies. Later still we have a record dated 20th January, 1876, when D. L. Dymock, auctioneer, sold from the verandah of George Adams, Steampacket Hotel, Kiama, on behalf of D. T. G. R. and A. A. Johnston a number of lots of land, part of Johnston's Meadows Estate, Albion Park. Note—Frederick R. Cole was a son of Captain Cole, an old Wollongong identity, who had a farm on Bundarra Creek.

Samuel Terry came out to New South Wales in common with many of our early pioneers as the guest of the Imperial Government about the year 1795. After a term he went into business, and although he could neither read nor write he succeeded exceedingly, and evidently managed to keep his best side turned towards every Government official. He was wealthy on the arrival of Governor Bligh, yet he dodged every enquiry and defeated silently the designs of all who attempted to get the better of him. He kept in close touch with Major Johnston. He became the owner of an extensive property on the banks of the Nepean River, and had a secure place for a few of his choicest cattle in Illawarra when the Bligh regime was put into force. Mount Terry, in Illawarra stands to-day, as it may do for all time stand, as a monument to his memory. He died in 1838 worth £500,000, equal then, to probably four times that amount to-day. He made small use of his Illawarra Estate beyond running stock on it in charge of a stock-keeper.

It would be an impossible task to describe the system followed by Mr. Samuel Terry on Terry's Meadows since the days from the arrival of Admiral William Bligh as Governor of New South Wales. Many old records have been lost, and the stories of the old settlers were usually conflicting; they praised and condemned for mere trifles. He had originally been a dealer and storekeeper in a small way at Parramatta, when he married Mrs. Marsh, a widow. He developed into a brewer and wholesale wine and spirit merchant. Cattle were in those days, next to rum, used as as means of bartering for other goods, and no doubt in this way Mr. Terry found himself in possession of many cattle. After Governor Lachlan Macquarie had settled down calmly in the Sydney corner of this territory he permitted certain of the better conducted, according to his idea of conduct, to move outside the county of Cumberland and settle in various centres of the county of Camden, mostly on sufferance. Colonel George Johnston was the only one who got a free grant in Illawarra. That is, if we can call his grant free when all the timber thereon was reserved for naval purposes.

Samuel Terry carried on his Illawarra Estate in accordance with the customs and usages of the men of his time, by means of a manager and an overseer. The manager lived in Sydney, and an overseer, a stockman, and a few blackfellows looked after the stock which consisted of a few horses and many cattle in Illawarra. The overseer's duty was to keep an account of the increase and decrease of the stock, send the fats to market, and brand all the "clean skins" he could muster. As the estate was kept to a great extent for breeding

purposes, the young males would be dressed and sent to stations on the southern tableland.

On September 19th, 1825, Samuel Terry's nephew, John Terry Hughes, married Samuel Terry's step-daughter, Miss Esther Marsh, and the pair took the world easy and lived in fine style until the year 1838, when Samuel Terry died aged 62 years After 1838 the Illawarra Estate was called Albion Park, and instead of Terry's Meadows, the name Terry Hughes' Estate was substituted by the new arrivals who by this time became numerous in Illawarra. His brand was ITH, and he had about a score of cattle stations in New South Wales.

After John Terry Hughes entered into possession of the estate there were many overseers and stockmen employed. We have learned of the deeds of daring of the brothers Stevenson, Billy Hipkins, Johnny Ritchie, Billy Broughton, Ned Swan, and we have read of Haslem, Stroud and Duncan Beatson, as being experts in their respective lines among stock.

He had a property at Bringelly (Camden) called Shancamore, where he kept both stud horses and cattle. The management of the Terry Hughes' Estate became supporters of the early Illawarra shows, principally in agricultural produce. It was principally from the management of the Terry Hughes Estate that Messrs Duncan Beatson and Andrew McGill obtained the foundation of their dairy herds.

John Terry Hughes died October, 1851, aged 49 years. At the time of John Terry Hughes' death there were several Scotch families settled on the Albion Park Estate, including Messrs. Andrew McGill, Alexander Fraser, Ebenezer Russell, and Mrs. Archie Beatson. After the death of John Terry Hughes' son, Samuel Terry Hughes, who died in 1865 at the age of 36 years, other portions of the estate were cut up and sold, when the families just named were the purchasers of much of the estate. The first sub-division:—The following paragraph appeared in the "Herald" of June 21st, 1860: "Great Land Sale. The whole of the celebrated Terry's Meadows Estate comprising about 3000 acres, in the famed Illawarra district, subdivided into 48 farms from 20 to 150 acres each on the Dapto and Shellharbour roads, 15 miles from Wollongong, and 12 miles from Kiama, was disposed of on Monday, the 18th inst., by Messrs. Richardson and Wrench, of Sydney, at the Queen's Hotel, Wollongong, at prices ranging from £3/2/6 to £43 per acre. The total sale realised £30,519/4/6, averaging a little over £10 per acre.

The first sub-division of the Albion Park Estate was entrusted to a clever surveyor named Wilton Henry Wells, who was drowned in a flood in Ritchie's Creek, Jamberoo, June 1861, aged 43 years. He was the author of "The New South Wales Gazetteer."

John Terry Hughes' only son (Samuel Terry Hughes, born 1829), died in 1865, and one of his daughters who married Captain Malcolm Melville MacDonald retained interests in portions of the Albion Park Estate which were not disposed of at the above mentioned sale. The lands thus resumed were sold in lots at different auction sales and privately until recent times, and have been purchased by local residents at satisfactory prices.

John Terry Hughes had a partner in the person of John Hoskings, a relation by marriage. The business offices were in Sydney, and it was known as Hughes and Hoskings, merchants, Sydney. This firm had large estates and town and city allotments in New South Wales, and carried on an extensive trade. They held a grant of land containing 850 acres which abutted on to the town of Kiama. After cutting out the cedar and much of the choicest hardwoods, they sold out to Henry Osborne.

From 1831 to 1840 Mr. John Terry Hughes made purchases of cattle anywhere a bargain was to be seen, and he also sold large mobs of cattle. Consequently on his Albion Park Estate in 1840 he had numbers of Messrs. Wentworth and MacArthur's Long-horned cattle. Mr. Richard Jones' cattle from Fleurs, South Creek. He found employment for many settlers in Illawarra who afterwards owned portions of his Albion Park Estate. In 1838 he purchased a pure Durham bull at the Segenhoe Estate sale in Sydney; and in 1840 he purchased two red and white Yorkshire Shorthorns in Sydney at £420. One was 17 and the other 18 months old. But whether any of those three bulls came to Illawarra no one seemed to know.

Mr. Henry Osborne had for years set longing eyes over the Albion Park Estate, and once offered £10,000 for the homestead and 1500 acres attached thereto—a big price in those days. There had, however, been a considerable amount of ill-feeling existing at that time between them over the mysterious disappearance of a celebrated white bull bred by Mr. Osborne. Old Billy Wright used to say: "I know what became of Osborne's white bull!" Perhaps he did; if so, old Billy knew how to keep the secret.

In 1860 the wheat growing industry which had been of great importance to the small settlers in Illawarra began to show signs of failure. Rust had begun to destroy the crop— and wheat-growing had to be abandoned. Dairying was not a paying concern, prices had been dropping year by year owing to an irregular market. Although the Illawarra A. & H. Societies had been doing good work to improve the method of cultivation, and had endeavoured to improve our breeds of horses, cattle, pigs, etc., no effort was put forward to find oversea markets for the farmers' produce.

Dr. James Mileham came out to New South Wales in the ship "Ganges" on June 2nd, 1797, and was appointed assistant colonial surgeon. Ruled over the convicts at Parramatta, Newcastle, and Sydney until 1808. Went as a presiding magistrate to Pitt Town, June 8th, 1811, and went to Wilberforce from 1815 to 1820, and then became police magistrate at Windsor. He received a grant of 700 acres at Shellharbour on south side of Lake Illawarra, where a stockade was erected, and soldiers sent down from Sydney to protect the interests of the cattlemen and cedar getters. Barrack Swamp is near the site of the old stockade. Dr. Mileham's grant is dated 24th July, 1817. He sold out to Surgeon De Arcy Wentworth, and died September 28th, 1824, aged 60 years.

Mr. Moses Brennan, of Vinegar Hill, 1798 veteran, who owned a grant of land in Jamberoo, was, prior to 1821, farming on his own farm about two miles beyond Appin. In 1821 he was appointed a constable for that district and pound-keeper. He is buried at Campbelltown.

Mr. John Cullen was a friend and associate of Moses Brennan. He owned a grant of land adjoining that of Moses Brennan in Jamberoo, on which the old Woodstock mills and brewery were erected on behalf of Captain Hart by Captain John G. Collins of the 13th Dragoon Guards in 1835. John Cullen was a cattle breeder at Appin, and the JC brand was well known to the early settlers. He became one of Sydney's publicans, and was a racing man. His horse "Favourite" was matched against Thomas Hammond's 3-year-old colt. Cullen won the wager, £50 aside.

Dr. John Dunmore Lang writing in 1856, says: "My late father had a grant of land from the Crown, 2000 acres at Bong Bong and Sutton Forest, for which I received £1500. I am not aware of the value of such land at the present time. At all events it would be four times that amount at least. I possessed 1200 acres on the Illawarra Lake. It was a splendid property, and is now worth from £20 to £30 per acre. It brought me only £2 per acre." What of poor John Wyllie who was forced to take £1 per acre for it?

The Wentworths.—According to reliable authorities the name was of Saxon origin, and was known as Winteworde in York, England. The list of twists is a long one, until the family name of De Arcy Wentworth emerged from Athlone, County Roscommon, Ireland, and passed from there to Ardreagh and Truin, County Meath, as steward to the 4th Earl of Roscommon, and captain of the Meath Militia, a commission dated 1st October, 1690. This De Arcy Wentworth died in 1710, leaving a son George, who married into the family of Longfields, of Meath. His son Robert married a Miss Walsh, and they had a son named De Arcy, who also married in Ireland, and had a son named William.

De Arcy Wentworth was, according to our records, in the years 1765, an ensign in an Irish Yeomanry Regiment, the 1st Ulster Provincials, a regiment founded to defend the unjust claims of those who had usurped the lands of the old Irish families. Wentworth was the son of De Arcy Wentworth, of Portadown, and was married, and the father of one child, a son. Finding that his regiment was about to be reduced he decided to forego the army and study medicine, and with that intention he left his wife and son in Ireland and enrolled himself at the institution since known as the Royal College of Surgeons. Being successful in his studies he was promised a vacancy in the East India Company's service. His young spirit could not wait, and as he was short of funds he decided to force the pace which led to a conflict with the laws of England. Lord Fitzwilliam came to his assistance, and at once became his patron. Application was made for leave for the young surgeon to go to Botany Bay. The Secretary of State then charged with the care of the colony, furnished the necessary permit, and added a letter of introduction to Governor Phillip. Accordingly Surgeon De Arcy Wentworth sailed for Port Jackson in the "Neptune," one of the transports in the second fleet in January, 1790. After a short stay with his associates in New South Wales,

he was sent as assistant medical officer to Norfolk Island. Surgeon De Arcy Wentworth was the fourth and youngest son of De Arcy Wentworth, of Portadown, County Armagh, Ireland. In 1791 he became superintendent of convicts at Norfolk Island. Appointed assistant surgeon in New South Wales on December 1st, 1796, a justice of peace for New South Wales on May 15th, 1810. Surgeon to the settlement by Royal Warrant, May 31st, 1811; superintendent of police at Sydney, May 8th, 1815; resigned March 31st, 1820; treasurer to the police fund, June 3rd, 1820, superintendent of police and treasurer of Colonial Revenue in 1821, and retired from public in 1825.

We are not concerned with Surgeon De Arcy Wentworth's transactions while at Norfolk Is. He returned to Sydney, and worked himself into several good jobs, anyone of which would have satisfied a less ambitious man. He, Surgeon De Arcy Wentworth, evidently ingratiated himself into the good graces of the Governors and acting governors of his period. Tenders were called in May, 1811, for the building of a public hospital, which for certain reasons has since been termed the "Rum Hospital." He was chief surgeon and police magistrate. He obtained many grants of land. On a 140 acre grant at Homebush he erected his private residence. He became wealthy, and retired into private life in 1825. By Catherine Parry who died at Parramatta in 1810, and had three sons and one daughter, of whom William Charles was the eldest. De Arcy joined the army and went to Tasmania, where he rose in rank; John entered the navy and was drowned at sea in 1820; the girl, Martha, died young.

With regard to his dealing in Illawarra very little is of much local interest as he was merely represented by an overseer and a stockman. He had cattle and horses depastured on his holdings, much of which was open forest country. On May 21st, 1819, he had a notice in the Sydney "Gazette" calling on "all owners of cattle or stock that were depasturing on his Five Islands Estate, Illawarra, to remove them at once as he was preparing to send his own stock there." On July 19th, 1819, a general order was issued relating to "persons, bond and free, cutting cedar in Illawarra." De Arcy Wentworth did not enter into the cedar trade. The cattle or stock referred to would most likely be James Badgery's cattle.

By a will made 5th July, 1827, we find that De Arcy Wentworth's Illawarra Estate contained 13,060 acres which works out in accor-

ARTHUR PICKLES' STUD OF I.M.S. CATTLE,
Blacklands, Wondai, Queensland.

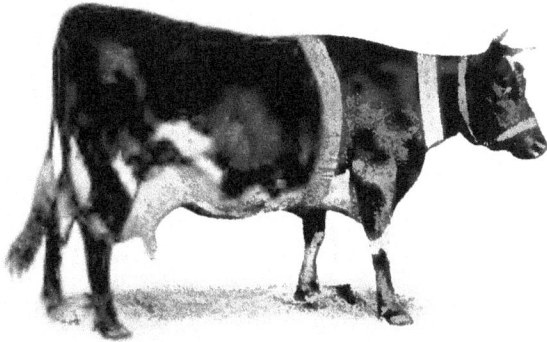

FLORRIE OF BLACKLANDS.
(No. 16, I.M.S.H.B., Q'ld.)

JEAN 5th OF BLACKLANDS.

PRINCESS III OF BLACKLANDS (Adv. Reg. I.H.B.).

ROYAL 4th OF BLACKLANDS.

D. SPOORS & SONS, Illawarra M.S. Stud, Mundubbera Queensland.

FLORRIE 2nd's BOY OF BLACKLANDS.

GOLD OF BLACKLANDS.

dance with the plan of the estate as follows:—His daughters, Martha, Sophia, Catherine, and his son Robert were to enjoy the whole of the Illawarra Estate, 13,060 acres altogether. R. C. Wentworth, called Robert; Martha Reddall, who died in 1847; Sophia Wentworth who married Robert Towns in 1833; Mary Ann Wentworth who married Stephen Addison in 1840, and remarried Charles Hollings 10th June, 1854. Edward Druitt and James Hart had each £4000. As a result of this will Hugh De Arcy Addison, son of Stephen Addison, received lots 6, 7, and 8 in village of Shellharbour, and 12 acres, 12 perches adjoining Barrack Swamp. Thomas Alexander Reddall's interests came in in 1851, together with Robert Towns and Sophia Towns, his wife, and Robert De Arcy Wentworth Towns, their eldest son as beneficaries in the will of De Arcy Wentworth; as also Robert Towns and Stephen Addison and Mary Ann Addison (formerly Mary Ann Wentworth); also Benjamin Darley and Catherine Darley (formerly Catherine Wentworth), and Catherine Darley, their eldest daughter; also Robert Towns and Alexander Donaldson Kellie, and Randolph John Want, a ninth and tenth part each. There were interests elsewhere to William Charles Wentworth and De Arcy Wentworth, his whole brother, William Charles, George, Martha, Sophia, Robert John, Mary Ann, and Catherine Wentworth.

He owned at the time of his death the following properties in Illawarra:—1650 acres, Peterborough, granted by Governor Macquarie, 9th January, 1821. The Governor's signature was witnessed by H. C. Antil, of Picton. 2000 acres, a grant from the Government of New South Wales to De Arcy Wentworth on or before the year 1825; 1500 acres, a grant from the Government of New South Wales to De Arcy Wentworth, on or before the year 1825; 2000 acres, Barrack Point, transferred from Lieutenant-Colonel Thomas Davey to De Arcy Wentworth; 1000 acres, a grant from the Government of New South Wales to De Arcy Wentworth; 1200 acres of land, transferred from John Horsley to De Arcy Wentworth on or before 1825; 700 acres land, transferred from Dr. James Mileham to De Arcy Wentworth, on or before 1825; 1000 acres land, transferred from Surveyor Ralph to De Arcy Wentworth on or before 1825; 2000 acres land, transferred from De Arcy Wentworth to De Arcy Wentworth, Oak Flats property.

Further explanation might be out of place here. We shall give a little attention to William Charles Wentworth. When he arrived back from England; New South Wales was confined to a small area not more than forty miles wide along the coast from Port Hacking to Port Stevens. During the drought of 1813 William Charles Wentworth, then only 20 years of age, in company with Blaxland and Lawson organised a party to find a track over the Blue Mountains. They were also accompanied by John Tye, Thomas Gorman, William Dye, Samuel Freeman, Samuel Eyres, Thomas Hobby, Richard Lewis, James Kelly, William Mucklow and Thomas Green. William Charles Wentworth was called to the bar in 1822. When Sir Ralph Darling took over the affairs of the colony in 1825, considerable friction had been worked up by the free settlers against the emancipists. Wentworth championed the cause of the emancipists with such force of character that the Governor was forced to yield. Yet, Governor Darling had friends. Perhaps it was because he (Darling) ruled the convicts with a rod of steel?

Surgeon De Arcy Wentworth did not at any time own the Five Islands Estate, Illawarra. It was a grant dated 24th January, 1817, under the hand of Lachlan Macquarie, Governor, for 2200 acres of land originally granted to David Allan; 1827, November 1st, David Allan sold to Richard Jones; 1828, Jones sold to William Charles Wentworth.

There was a reservation in the grant of 200 acres with the right to erect fortifications at any time by the Crown.

Andrew Byrne was born in the County Wicklow, Ireland, in 1774. He was one of the patriots of '98 which caused his removal to Botany Bay. He arrived in the "Minerva" on January 11th, 1800, at the age of 26 years. He was evidently an intelligent man, of good behaviour as he soon became a trusted colonist. He received a grant of land, 100 acres, at Appin, and established a half-way house there with secure paddocks attached thereto. It was patronised by travellers and drovers passing to and from Sydney, Bong Bong, and Illawarra. He also had grants of land at Port Hacking, and 500 acres at Kiama. He established a dairy in Sydney, and had his milking yard on the spot where David Jones and Coy's warehouse stands in George Street. His office was at 82 Pitt Street. Prior to 1825 he sold his half-way house property, 100 acres, at Appin, to D'arcy Wentworth. And prior to 1828 he sold his Kiama Estate, Barroul, consisting of 500 acres to Rev. Thomas Kendall. He went into the hotel trade at the Haymarket, Sydney, and had interests in stock depastured on the Dapto side of Lake Illawarra in 1835. Those who knew him well said that he could tell many startling stories of the old regime and racy tales of those days when bullock teams were provided with board and lodgings at Haymarket, George Street, Sydney, whilst their conductors were unloading and loading goods. These teams came from Bong Bong and Goulburn through that terrible turnpike of the early teamsters—the Bargo Brush. Of Andrew Byrne's transactions in Illawarra very little is known. He, nevertheless, must have had considerable business transactions with the early Illawarra settlers as he owned land and stock apart from his Barroul property which he sold to Rev. Thomas Kendall in 1827. In 1825 Byrne was interested in Ousdale, Illawarra, and in 700 acres in Ulladulla, and had cattle grazing at Minnamurra. He was evidently expert in cattle raising as it was from Andrew Byrne that Edmond Woodhouse obtained the foundation stock of the celebrated Shorthorn and other studs of Mount Gilead, Campbelltown. He knew much of the history of New South Wales by personal experience and died at Haymarket, George Street, Sydney, on April 22nd, 1863, aged 89 years.

Mr. James Badgery was born in the County Devon, England, in 1764, and arrived in New South Wales in or about 1800. He settled on a farm at South Creek, where he died on December 1st, 1827. He had three sons—Henry, born at South Creek, William, born at South Creek, died August 1st, 1841, and James, born at South Creek, died 1844. He was a cattle breeder, and had some valuable dairy cattle that were bought after by the early pioneers. He never, so far as we know, visited Illawarra. He had the use of all the clear land from the southern shores of Lake Illawarra to the Minnamurra Rivulet, now known as Shellharbour. He sent his cattle down to Illawarra in charge of a trusted stockman, named Bob Higgins, and he remained in possession until 1819, when Higgins had the cattle and horses removed to Bong Bong. From Bong Bong James Badgery's stock moved southward. Mr. James Badgery and one of his sons, Andrew Badgery, were racing men when races were held on what was known as Grose's Farm, south of the present University Grounds, Sydney. He owned Molly Morgan and Molly Maguire. When he was having his stock removed from Illawarra to Bong Bong, they were taken up via Dapto through Jack Waite's or White's Gap. In a swamp between the "Gap" and Bong Bong, the race mare, Molly Morgan, was bogged and had to be shot. Hence the place has been called Molly Morgan's swamp to this day.

"The late Henry Badgery, when about 21 years of age, and in the year 1825, was advised to apply to the Governor for a special grant of land as his father had a very good breed of horses and cattle, and he, being born here, would improve his property, and not sell it and return to England as some other grantees had done. The governor quite agreed, and told him he could go anywhere into the interior and take 1920 acres (3 square miles). He had some knowledge of the South Coast, as his father in 1817 used to send their spare stock to near Shellharbour, on the south side of the entrance to Lake Illawarra, and upon what is now called Weston's or Terry's Meadows. They used to pass to Wollongong and swim the cattle across the neck of the lake, because if they took them round by Dapto they would make back on the same track. Upon one occasion as this was being done a calf got carried out to sea by the current, so far that it was sometimes hidden by the waves, and was considered to be certainly lost, but much to the surprise of all on the following day the calf was with the cattle by its mother's side."

The Kendall Family.—The coming of the Rev. Thomas Kendall to Illawarra takes us back to convict days. His father was said to be interested in the American slave trade prior to the war of independence. Be that as it may, the late Robert Oscar Kendall of Barroul, Kiama, Illawarra, wrote on 23rd October, 1914, to say: "My grandfather, the Rev. Thomas Kendall, was born in England, but I can't find out what part of England; none of us seem to know. Father was born in the same place June 14th, 1806, and died on the 2nd November, 1883, aged 77 years. This is all I can ascertain about him. My father was with grandfather at New Zealand for a while before he married mother."

Mr. H. T. Purchas, M.A., has written a book dealing with the Rev. Thomas Kendall's missionary efforts among the Maoris in New Zealand, and states therein much that is not, let us hope, peculiar to men of the missionary turn of mind.

The whole story of the early attempt of civilising the Maoris by those missionaries is, indeed, a sad one. Then, there were the captains of ships trading between New Zealand and Sydney, who were deceitful, and often trustworthy honourable chiefs were betrayed. This takes us back to the days of Governors King and Bligh when there was much disorder, and disastrous licence was being taken by masters of ships trading between Port Jackson, England and New Zealand, where seal skins were to be obtained in large quantities. Trade was brisk. The Rev Parson Marsden purchased 200 acres of land from the Maoris for twelve axes, and set about Christianising the Maori chiefs and their people.

Captain Dalrymple was a well-known trader between Sydney, New Zealand, Illawarra, and Van Diemen's Land. Hence we have Port Dalrymple, now Launceston, Tasmania. He had a grant of land there, "Mount Leslie."

By referring to Rev. Thomas Kendall's diary we find that he traded largely, and visited many settlements. He eventually settled at 68 Pitt-street, Sydney, in 1825. His family consisted of six sons, Thomas Surflect, Laurence, John, Joseph, Basil and Edward! his daughters were Mrs. Florence and Mrs. Bowden.

In Rev. Thomas Kendall's diary we read that on 25th December, 1827, he buried a servant of Mr. Ritchie's at a place—. Right there he stopped short, without mentioning the name of the place. On enquiring from members of the Kendall family why the name was omitted, I was informed that Thomas Surflect Kendall said: "The original name of Kiama was a most objectionable one, hence the real name was omitted."

The story of this burial comes down to us from the old hands, as follows:—John Ritchie was located at Jamberoo prior to 1825. On this occasion he had sent his man, "Big Will", in to meet the boat with a team of bullocks and dray, with a load for Sydney, and to bring a load back to the homestead. About the same time he sent another servant, "Red Jack", on to Gerringong with a mob of cattle to be delivered to Berry and Wollstonecraft's man at the Crooked River. Big Will got rid of his load, and then loaded up for the return journey. He moved out to a spot west of where the Catholic Church stands, turned the bullocks out on the point, and prepared to camp for the night. He was joined later on by Red Jack. There was rum on the dray, and a pannikin was handed to Red Jack to

help himself. He did so freely. Next morning, when Big Bill woke up, he found his companion dead. He gave information to the Stockade, which was in turn sent on to Red Point, Port Kembla, from which place a military officer came to hold an enquiry. On this officer's arrival, he found all hands drunk, so he locked them up until they became sober enough to give evidence.

The Rev. Thomas Kendall in the meantime, had the last mortal remains of Red Jack buried, together with the original name of Kiama, on the south side of Bong Bong street and the east side of Manning street. On the site of that grave was erected the first Church of England, which was afterwards used as a school-house by an old-time teacher named Willy.

Extracts from Rev. Thomas Kendall's diary:

ILLAWARRA.—February 3rd, 1827, baptized at the house of John Fitzgerald Butler, Esq., Commandant—James, the son of Herbert and Atty Green, born 27th December, 1826.

ILLAWARRA.—February 24th, baptized at the house of Messrs. Berry & Wollstonecraft, Margaret, the daughter of Thomas and Jane May.

ILLAWARRA.—March 2nd, 1828, baptized Maria, the daughter of Charles Throsby and Sarah Smith, born 11th January, 1828. Baptized at their house, Wollongong.

SAINT VINCENT.—May 2nd, 1830, baptized at Narra Walla, Mary Jane, the daughter of Thomas and Elizabeth Florence, born 7th April, 1830.

CAMDEN.—May 30th, 1831, baptized Jane Caroline, the daughter of Thomas Surflect Kendall and Caroline Blake Kendall, born April, 11th 1831.

BURIALS.

ILLAWARRA.—December 25th, 1827, buried a Government servant of Mr. Ritchie, about 20 years old, on Church reserve, named—(see page 49).

ILLAWARRA.—February 5th, 1831, buried George Bates of Illawarra, aged 55 years.

MARRIAGES SOLEMNIZED.

October 31st, 1825, John Martin married to Sarah Amy Jarrett.

June 5th, 1826, Charles William Wooster, married to Mary Ann Wilkinson.

September 2nd, 1826, Moses Glover, married to Emma Hills.

January 29th, 1827, Thomas Leighton, surgeon, married to Angola Martha Fredericks.

REV. THOMAS KENDALL'S COMMERCIAL TRANSACTIONS AS PER DIARY.

No. 29/220.—Colonial Secretary's Office, Sydney, February 18th, 1829.

Re Application for permission to rent land dated, 21st August, 1828

Signed ALEX. McLEAY.

Rev, Thomas Kendall,
　c/o Mr Barker, Sydney.
No. 1002.—Co'lonial Secretary's Office, Sydney, 6th November, 1827.

An order to select 1,280 acres according to regulation of 5th September, 1826.

　　　　　　　　　　　　Signed ALEX. McLEAY

Rev. Thomas Kendall,
　68 Pitt Street, Sydney.
Surveyor-General's Office, Sydney, 11th February, 1831.
　Grant of Land to Mr. Thomas Kendall of 320 acres.
　　　　　　　　　　　Signed R. MITCHELL.

No. 30/607.—Colonial Secretary's Office, Sydney, 17th April, 1830.
　Re Grant of 100 acres as a marriage portion from the Crown to Miss Caroline B. Rutter, now Mrs. Kendall, c/o Thomas Kendall, Sydney.
　According to Government Order, Sydney, 19th August 1829.　　　　　Signed J. C. HARRINGTON.

Certificate of Sale of Cattle, 8th March, 1826, at Stonequarry.
　　　　　　　　　　Signed W. C. ANTILL, J.P.

No. 930.—Colonial Secretary's Office, 18th October, 1827.
　Re Application dated 5th October, 1827, calling on the Rev. Thomas Kendall to be in readiness with the necessary proofs of the actual capital available in his possession, and informing him that the Authorities would not allow his sons to select land.
　　　　　　　　　　　Signed ALEX. McLEAY.
Mr. Thomas Kendall, 68 Pitt St., Sydney.

COMMERCIAL MATTER IN WHICH THOMAS SURFLECT KENDALL WAS INTERESTED.

Grant of land to Thomas Surflect Kendall at Darling Forest, situated north bank of Narra Walla Creek. Date, 24th October, 1840.　　Signed HENRY HALLERAN.

County of St. Vincent, 320 acres, promised by His Excellency Sir Ralph Darling, in 1831.
　Date, 1840.　　　　　Signed GEO. GIPPS.

Internal Revenue Office, Sydney, 8th April, 1833.—No. A 33/414.
　In reference to A No. 31/622, 29th May, 1831, requesting him to take up 500 acres of land, situated in County of Camden, purchased by Rev. Thomas Kendall from Andrew Byrne of Sydney. Pay fees and quit rent and take out deeds.
　Re the above.—Fees due at Surveyor-General's Office from 20th May, 1828 to 31st December, 1832—£3 16s.
　　　　　　　　Signed WM. MACPHERSON,
　　　　　　　　　Collector of Internal Revenue.

A. No. 32/891.—Internal Revenue Office, Sydney, 28th June, 1832.
　To Rev. Thomas Kendall—Deed of Grant promised by Major-General Lachlan Macquarie, 31st March, 1821, situated in County of Cumberland, in compliance with Government notice, 14th September, No. 13, in Londonderry. Fees due, 15/- and 5/- quit rent from January, 1827, to 31st December, 1831.　　　　　Signed WM. MACPHERSON,
　　　　　　　　　Collector of Internal Revenue.
Rev. Thomas Kendall,
　Narra Walla, Illawarra.
Sydney.—The Estate of the late Rev. Thomas Kendall.
　　　　　　　　　Signed C. & F. WILSON.

NOTE.—Rev. Thomas Kendall always considered the Ulladulla district part of Illawarra.

Prior to 1833 Rev. Thomas Kendall was engaged in cedar getting at Ulladulla, whilst his son-in-law, Mr. Florence, a surveyor, and a party were busy allocating grants of land there.

The whole of the survey party with Mr. Kendall left Ulladulla, Five Islands, in a cutter named "Brisbane" during the year 1833 for Sydney. The cutter foundered off Jervis Bay, and all hands were lost. Nothing belonging to the party came ashore with the exception of Mr. Kendall's trunk and shoes. Not one of the party came ashore to tell the tale.

Of the sons of Rev. Thomas Kendall we know little beyond Thomas Surflect who settled on the Barroul Estate, Kiama, and Basil Kendall who settled in Ulladulla. Thomas Surflect Kendall remained on the Barroul Estate until his death when his sons and daughters married and went out from the old home, he divided the land among them, leaving Robert Oscar Kendall in possession of the homestead. Barroul is now the property of Mr. Kieran Ryan, solicitor, Kiama, who bought it from R. O. Kendall.

Referring to the great disaster that caused the loss of the cutter "Brisbane" with all hands on board, we are reminded that no mention is made of the master who was in charge of her at the time. In 1832, Basil Kendall was registered as being the master and owner of the "Brisbane." He was not in command during that fateful trip. He lived, and in consequence he gave to Illawarra in due time Henry Clarence Kendall, Australia's sweetest singer, who clothed the simple elements of his life in a dress full of great and fundamental characteristics. His nature was so refined that he mastered intricate tasks—and crystallised his ideas into forms and into such sweet tones that possess a charm and grace which are to be found in no other Australian poet. Basil Kendall married the daughter of an Irish policeman named McAnnally, and went to reside at Ulladulla where Henry was born. The Kendall family did not appreciate the poet's mother, yet, methinks, that if ever a scientist is found who will apply the science of genetics to trace the origin of Henry Clarence Kendall's poetic genius, he will quickly centre his mind on the the origin of that sweet force in Kendall's mother. Alas, poor Kendall, with all his faults we, as Illawarrites, love him still. Ulladulla, where the poet was born was considered a part of the Five Islands or Illawarra district by the Rev. Thomas Kendall and his eldest son, Thomas Surflect Kendall, of Kiama.

Henry Clarence Kendall wrote his sweetest verse while he was assisting William Allen in John Allen's store in Jamberoo, about the year 1860. In those early poems he has woven the memories of his young manhood, like rays of light, into the tenderest and sweetest verses.

A writer with claims to a literary training, says:—"Henry Kendall is a poet who owes everything, except his poetry, to Australia." Poor Kendall, in later years, made mistakes. "To err is human, to forgive divine." He confessed his faults with a candour all his own in the following lines:—

> "So take these kindly, even though there be
> Some notes that unto other lyres belong,
> Stray echoes from the elder sons of song,
> And think how, from its neighbouring native sea,
> The pensive shell doth borrow melody."

Henry Clarence Kendall lived in Illawarra at a time when the old aboriginals were numerous enough to enable him to gather from them material for an epic that would have traced for other generations that vein of purest gold that we are told runs through our Indo-Malayan mythology. His training ought to have given him that insight which was necessary to free it from its gross materialism and repulsive fanaticism and clothe it in language that would live as long as the English race will remain on earth.

No one can claim to be a true interpreter of Kendall's early poems who did not see the natural features of Illawarra as Kendall saw them prior to 1860. Those who saw the primeval bush could alone succeed in transfusing the oppressive stillness and brooding melancholy of the few bush scenes that were being preserved here and there in the vicinity of Kiama. He saw the night fires of the old clearing lease days, and set himself expressly to shadow it forth into song.

The Throsby Family.—They were a Leicester family of considerable standing in England. The first member of the family to arrive in New South Wales was Dr. Charles Throsby who was appointed superintendent of convicts at Newcastle. In 1807 he had two dairy cows shipped from Sydney to Newcastle for his private use at the settlement. This Charles Throsby died suddenly in 1809. Then we learn that the executors in the estate of the late Charles Throsby had advertised on October 15th, 1809, to obtain a suitable person to take charge of the late Charles Throsby's dairy farm at Parramatta.

Another Dr. Charles Throsby arrived in New South Wales, said to have been barrister at law who never practised in New South Wales. He was born in Leicester, England, in 1774.

He is the man who made history. He took charge of the Throsby Estate in New South Wales, and settled at Glenfield, near Liverpool. He acted as agent for settlers who had to return to England, including Sir John Jamison, who, before he went to England to receive a knighthood, was the Squire of Regent Ville on the Nepean River. After the return of Sir John Jamison to New South Wales, October 1st, 1814, Dr. Charles Throsby was declared a "Free Settler" from 3rd February, 1816. It meant that he could go inland at any time in search of fresh fields and pastures new. It must be borne in mind that the settlement was then, in every sense of the term a gaol from which no one bond or free dare move without a pass. He is said to have been the first to bring cattle down the range into Illawarra. He was possibly the first to bring cattle down openly, that is, with the authority of the Government. He had three trustworthy servants named respectively, Joseph Wild, John Waite, and George Rowley who were acquainted with the blackfellows' tracks from Sydney to the tableland and the surrounding country. It was these men who brought the Throsby cattle from Glenfield to Illawarra in about 1813.

On October, 1819, Dr. Charles Throsby was granted 1000 acres of land for finding a fresh track across the cow pastures to the Bong Bong. His servants, Wild and Waite, got 100 acres each, whilst the other servant Rowley, got 200 acres. Mr. Charles Throsby, after doing much for the commercial life of this country, died in 1828, the result of a fall from his horse. He was a man of many parts: established the Throsby Park Estate at Bong Bong, and bred the finest beef cattle in the colony.

General Orders, 31st May, 1819.

"His Excellency the Governor, having received and perused the journal of a tour lately made by Charles Throsby, Esq., by way of the cow pastures to Bathurst, in the new discovered country, west of the Blue Mountains, takes this early opportunity publicly to announce the happy result of an enterprise which promises to conduce in a very eminent degree to the future interests and prosperity of the colony.

The necessity which Mr. Throsby appears to have been under of accelerating his progress through the country he was exploring, did not allow him to dwell minutely in his journal on the various productions and properties of the soil he traversed. His Excellency, therefore, adverts with pleasure to his general report of the capabilities, qualities and features of the country intervening between the cow pastures and Bong Bong; which he represents to be, with a few exceptions, rich, fertile and luxuriant, abounding with fine runs of water, and all the happy variety of soil, hill and valley, to render it not only delightful to the view, but highly suitable to all the purposes of pasture and agriculture.

"The importance of these discoveries is enhanced by the consideration that a continuous range of valuable country, extending from the cow pastures to the remote plains of Bathurst, is now fully ascertained, connecting those countries with the present settlements on this side the Nepean.

"His Excellency the Governor, highly appreciating Mr. Throsby's services on this occasion, offers him this public tribute of acknowledgment for the zeal and perseverance by which he was actuated throughout this arduous undertaking, and desires his acceptance of one thousand acres of land in any part of the country discovered by himself, that he may choose to select.

"The Governor also in acknowledgment of Mr. G. Rowley's services on this occasion, will assign him two hundred acres of land in the same country; and to Joseph Wild and John Waite, servants to Mr. Throsby, who accompanied him on the expedition, and whose fidelity and exertions are particularly noticed and commended by Mr. Throsby, His Excellency will assign one hundred acres of land each.

"The services rendered by the two native guides, Cookoogong and Daal, and to whom much of the success of the undertaking may be ascribed, being very meritorious, His Excellency will order a remuneration to be made to them in clothes and bedding; and will further appoint Cookoogong chief of the Burra Burra tribe, to which he belongs, and over which he appears to have very considerable influence, together with the usual badge of distinction. And on Daal, His Excellency will confer the badge of merit as a reward due to these natives, for their respective exertions and services. By His Excellency's command, J. T. Campbell, Secretary."

Mr. Robert Jenkins was born in the County Gloucestershire, England, in 1777, where he received a very liberal commercial education. He arrived in New South Wales in 1808, and re-

visited England twice before finally settling in Australia. He entered upon the business of an auctioneer in Sydney and at Parramatta, and was one of the first to join in the the sending of cattle to the Illawarra district in 1813, where he later on obtained a grant of land in conjunction with Mr. David Allan, of the Commissary Department of Sydney. Mr. Jenkins' grant was 1000 acres. and Mr. Allan's grant was 2200 acres, gazetted in January, 1817. A gang of cedar getters was sent down from Sydney. In 1821, Mrs. Robert Jenkins had a dairy farm at Berkeley; an enterprising man of business.

Robert Jenkins was married on 22nd March, 1813, to Mrs. Jemima Forest, relict of the late Captain Forest, R.N., of Richmond Hill, N.S.W. Captain Forest had been an officer of distinction in the naval service of the East India Company, and acquired much wealth. It was he who purchased the estates of Captain John Hunter, ex-Governor of New South Wales, on April 5th, 1805. These properties had been held in the Governor's nephew's name, to wit: Captain William Kent, who transferred them to Captain Forest on date named. Captain Austin Forest arrived in Sydney in charge of Mr. Robert Campbell's ship, Sydney, 900 tons, from Calcutta, and shortly afterwards married Miss Jemima Matchem Pitt. Captain Forest was killed by a fall from his horse on December 12th, 1811. The widow afterwards married Robert Jenkins, who became the owner of Eagle Farm, Campbelltown, and the Berkeley Estate, Illawarra, and several station properties inland. As will be seen Robert Jenkins lost his life by a fall from his horse whilst riding in to his place of business in Sydney. His horse shied at a mob of blacks at Surry Hills and threw him. Then we had his son, Mr. Robert Pitt Jenkins, who married Captain Patrick Plunkett's daughter (Miss Alice Frances Plunkett). They were lost in the ship "Royal Charter" on the Irish coast. Captain Plunkett belonged to the 80th Regiment, and was for a term in charge of the stockade in Wollongong, and was the visiting magistrate of Kiama and Coolangatta. He owned the "Keelogues" Estate, near Wollongong. Keelogues is the Irish name for a narrow stripe of land. Captain Patrick Plunkett arrived in the ship Lloyds, in 1837, and was a cousin of Hon. John Hubert Plunkett, of Sydney.

After the death of Mr. Robert Jenkins, his widow, Mrs. Jemima Jenkins, carried on the

D. O'KEEFE'S REGISTERED M.S. CATTLE,
Kiltankin, Jasper's Brush.

GAYFIELD OF KILTANKIN.
(No. 378, Vol. IV, M.S.H.B.)

DULCIE OF KILTANKIN.
(Vol. VII, M.S.H.B.)

RENOWN OF KILTANKIN.
(Vol. VI, M.S.H.B.)

RACHAEL OF KILTANKIN.
(No. 10456, Vol. V.)

DINAH OF KILTANKIN.
(No. 2795, Vol. IV, M.S.H.B.)

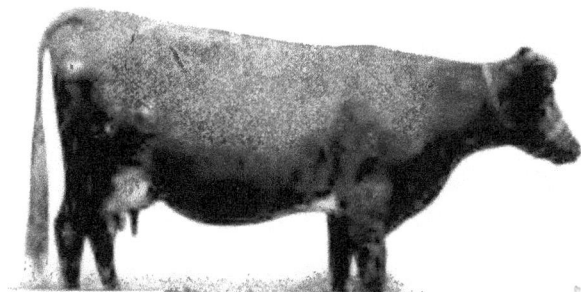

BETTY OF KILTANKIN.
(No. 2084, Vol. IV, M.S.H.B.)

Illawarra Estate which she had increased considerably in area, and we learn of William Shelley and John Robinson being in charge, until the marriage of Mr. William Warren Jenkins to his cousin, Miss Matilda Pitt Wilshire, July, 1838. She was the fourth daughter of Commissariat Officer Wilshire of the First Fleet. It was Mr. James Wilshire who purchased the first stud cattle for Mr. W. W. Jenkins, Illawarra Estate, just prior to his death in 1840.

Mr. William Warren Jenkins lived in fine style in Illawarra. He was an Australian, having been born in O'Connell Street, Sydney, on 11th July, 1816. He died in 1884, aged 69 years. Mr. William Warren Jenkins was a member of the 1st Illawarra District Council, September 3rd, 1843. It being as follows:— Warden, Dr. John Osborne, and Messrs. Gerard, Dapto, John Berry, Shoalhaven, Henry Osborne, Marshall Mount, Chas. Throsby Smith, Wollongong, and James Mackay Gray, Gerringong. In 1854 Mr. Jenkins became warden. Robert Thomas Jenkins became heir to the Berkeley Estate. Like his father he supported racing, and bred cattle, principally beef Shorthorns. During a drought he lost thousands of pounds worth of Shorthorn cattle. He kept racehorses, owned Skylark, Irene, Minx, Fernando, Churn, and Unanderra. He also owned the stud horse "Velentia." He died in 1913, aged 73 years.

Robert Thomas Jenkins lived to see the Berkeley Estate grow and prosper, and finally decay until the name of Jenkins ceased to represent an acre of land in Illawarra.

The Westons.—Captain Edward Nicholas Weston, of His Majesty's East India Company, and who afterwards became a Judge in India, came to Sydney on furlough, and before his return to India, married Miss Blanche Johnston, youngest daughter of Colonel George Johnston, of Annandale, New South Wales. Miss Blanche Johnston was two years old at the time of the Bligh Rebellion in 1808. Captain Weston, together with his wife and family, returned to India in 1832, merely to return and settle on 2,000 acres known as the King's Grant, near Parramatta. He renamed the place "Horsley," and at once set the pace as a country gentleman. He kept a pack of hounds, and hunted in good English style No wonder that our old Illawarra friend, Mr. Edward H. Weston, got the gift of horsemanship, which he sustained through life.

Captain Edward Weston died many years age, but his widow lived to a ripe old age. She died in 1914, aged 98 years, leaving to her descendants her father's estates. Her sons, Major Edward H. Weston, supervised Johnston's Illawarra Estate for many years, and died at Military Road, Mosman, in 1913, aged 81 years. The following letters were received by me from the Major of my old Cavalry corps, which he established at Albion Park, Illawarra, in the eighties of last century, under the direction of Major Malcolm Melville MacDonald. Such things merely return to memory to pass again like shadows.

As a breeder of dairy cattle in Illawarra, he was a failure. Had a fine property, but let things drift. Always a horseman, he died one, as his communications will show. A man of the world, but his world was his own. A good neighbour and a true friend, as these letters go to show:—

Copy. "Dear Sir,—I must apologise for not replying to your letter sooner, but the only person who knew anything about the importation of pedigreed cattle is Mr. Percy Johnston, and he has been laid up, and not able to attend to anything. However, I received a reply to my letter to him, in which he tells me Major Johnston never imported any pedigreed cattle at all. The Duke of Northumberland sent him out a few Leicester sheep and a stallion (a creamy), hence the creamies in Illawarra district in after years. Mr. David Johnston, youngest son of Major Johnston, imported a very fine Shorthorn bull, who was the progenitor of the magnificent cows bred by Messrs. Johnston Bros. This was many years after the arrival of the sheep and the creamy stallion. I shall be glad to give you any information I can. I remain, yours faithfully, E. H. Weston, 14th Oct., 1912."

Mr. E. H. Weston, of "The Meadows," Albion Park, stated in 1896: "Having paid a good deal of attention to cattle breeding during the last thirty years, and brought into the district during that time several high class bulls, viz., the Devon bull 'Victor,' the Durham bull 'Nonsuch,' bred by George Lee, and the pure Shorthorn bull by 'Imperial Purple,' I have noticed within the last few years that the breed of cattle in Illawarra is deteriorating in constitution. All writers on cattle-breeding concur that there is nothing like a cross of the Devon blood to remedy this defect. I have therefore purchased one of the best Devon bulls in the

Colony, viz., 'Prince William,' from Mr. Frank Reynolds, of Tocal, Paterson River, N.S. Wales, etc.''

Lieutenant William Fredrick Weston was born at West Horsley, County Surrey, England, and was a brother of Captain Edward Weston of Parramatta. He had a grant of land, West Horsley, Dapto, Illawarra, where he died on 25th April, 1826, aged 33 years. His widow married a man named Williamson. Richard Brooks, son of Captain Richard Brooks, and who owned an estate on Maneroo Plains, was connected by marriage with the Westons. He died at West Horsley, Dapto, on 10th July, 1855, aged 43 years. The West Horsley property passed into the hands of Mr. Andrew Thompson, who proved himself an up-to-date settler in every respect. It is now owned by Mr. George Lindsay. The Westons were all military men. One was Chief Gaoler at Lower George Street, Sydney, and at Parramatta.

Mr. Alexander Berry was born in Fifeshire, Scotland, 3rd November, 1781, and was educated at Cupar School, St. Andrews, and Edinburgh Universities where he studied for the medical profession. He went to India in the service of the East India Coy. After some few years in the East India Service he entered upon mercantile pursuits. He chartered a ship and visited places where he could obtain suitable merchandise for New South Wales. Eventually he called at False Bay, Cape of Good Hope, and took on board a small shipment of wine and sundries.

Alexander Berry left False Bay, Cape. of Good Hope, 4th September, 1807, for Port Dalrymple, now Launceston. Van Diemen's Land, now Tasmania, was then in charge of William Paterson of the New South Wales Corps. Captain Hunter having lost the ship Sirius at Norfolk Island, was afterwards discovered by Captain Dillon who had also discovered the wreck of the ship La Perouse at Samoa lost no time in causing the penal settlement at Norfolk Island to be transferred to the River Derwent. All this was learned by Berry on his arrival at Port Dalrymple, and as his cargo was more valuable in Sydney he steered for Port Jackson. He soon found himself in a family circle. Robert Campbell, of the wharf, was the harbour master. Mr. Commissioner Palmer was looking after the stores. Captain John MacArthur, Captain Kemp and Mr. Simeon Lord were business men as was also Captain Piper. Governor Bligh

understood the rules of the road followed by all those gentlemen of rank, and immediately sent for Alexander Berry. He was not pleased with Berry's line of conduct, or the lines he had for sale. Major Johnston wished to buy a cask of wine from Berry. It was not sold, but Major Johnston received a cask of wine as a present from Alexander Berry. All this took place in Sydney in 1808.

Alexander Berry and Governor Bligh.

Governor Bligh wrote in a despatch to Viscount Castlereagh, dated April 30th, 1808: ''On the 12th a ship called 'The City of Edinburgh' arrived from Cape of Good Hope laden with about 22,000 gallons of spirits. A leaky ship, which rendered it necessary for her to discharge her cargo immediately; but as the quantity of wines and spirits seemed enormous I ordered it into the store until I could consider what quantity ought to be distributed; and this precaution was the more necessary as two American ships — the Jenny (Captain Dorr), and the Eliza (Captain Corry) were in the harbour—whom I had been under the necessity of restricting from issuing their spirits, but had permitted them to dispose of their wine and merchandise before the City of Edinburgh arrived.'' Spirits were selling in Sydney at 50 shillings per gallon in 1808. Consequently Alexander Berry had large capital when he arrived in New South Wales, and although he was a great advocate of the temperance cause he had an eye to business, and sent a cask of wine ashore to Mayor Johnston's mess-room. Governor Bligh heard of this, and, had not Major Johnston declared solemnly that the wine was a present, it is certain that Alexander Berry would have been put under arrest.

The sequel to Berry's present to the military authorities can be understood by the following statement:—''After the deposition of Governor Bligh, Major Johnston, acting-Governor of New South Wales, with Captain John MacArthur Colonial Secretary, entered into a contract with Alexander Berry to convey all the settlers from Norfolk Island to the Derwent, Hobart Town, Van Diemen's Land. The vessel was hired at 23 shillings per ton per month to be paid for in timber. It was verbally agreed or understood by the contracting parties that the time should not exceed ten weeks. Berry, however, took twenty-seven weeks to perform the service. He presented Lieutenant - Governor Foveaux, who as senior officer superseded Major

Johnston, with a bill of freight of £3,600, offering to take the timber already prepared, estimated value £2,830, with cash or goods out of the King's store for the balance. Foveaux offered Berry £2000 which offer Berry refused.

In 1819 Berry and Wollstonecraft determined to settle in Australia, and for that purpose chartered a vessel and took her out to Australia. The venture proved successful, and Mr. Berry returned to London to enlarge the firm's connection, and was informed at the Colonial Office that Sir Thomas Brisbane had been appointed Governor of New South Wales. Berry chartered the ship, "The Royal George," 500 tons burden, and the Governor and staff came out to New South Wales with him. On arrival Berry, without locating the grants, made an offer to Sir Thomas Brisbane to keep 100 convicts free of expense provided he gave 10,000 acres on the banks of the Shoalhaven River. This tender was promptly accepted as it was costing the Government £16 per annum for the upkeep of each convict at that time. In May, 1822, a suitable vessel was secured and Berry and Wollstonecraft commenced operations at Shoalhaven. Young Davidson, whose life he had saved in New Zealand, was one of the ship's crew. He, his mate and two sailors were drowned in the breakers in endeavouring to inspect the channel that led into the river. A native black gin swam ashore. There were three native blacks on board. Two were chiefs of Jervis Bay and Numbaa, named respectively Lager and Wagin; 200 convicts dug the canal in six weeks, and created an island where none existed before.

Alexander Berry made his first rise in Australia owing to the wreck of H.M. ship "Sirius" at Norfolk Island. Lord Wyndham decided on a report from ex-Governor Hunter to remove the penal settlement from that island hell to a place to be called New Norfolk on the Derwent River, Van Diemen's Land. Alexander Berry refitted his ship, the City of Edinburgh, and took a hand in that costly work. No one knows for certain what he actually made out of that contract.

Alexander Berry in explanation of the canal being cut near the entrance of the Shoalhaven River in 1822 said: "At the upper part of the Crookhaven River there was an arm which approached within one-eighth of a mile of the Shoalhaven. I therefore immediately determined to make a new entrance to the river from Crookhaven, and next day I put spades and axes and pickaxes into the hands of all the men, and showed them where to dig. When I did so I hardly expected that I should be able to accomplish my object; but as idleness is the parent of mischief it was necessary to keep my people employed, especially as they were nearly all convicts. The only free persons there with me were a young man, Charles Campbell, a convict superintendent, and Hamilton Hume. After the canal was cut Mr. John Wyllie took Mr. Charles Campbell's place as superintendent of convicts, Mr. Hall, manager, 1836. In 1822 Alexander Berry read a paper before the Philosophical Society of Australia, which contained the results of his own explorations of the coast line from Port Stephens to Jervis Bay. Of Jervis Bay he said: I have found good land both forest and alluvial. The access to the bay is safe and easy; and although it is not such a magnificent harbour as Port Jackson, still it affords good shelter and safe anchorage, and is superior to many of the best-frequented ports in the world.

Although Alexander Berry had been granted during 1821 the regulation limit of convicts for his Shoalhaven venture, probably not more than twenty or thirty. He desired many more to carry out his plans in the valley of the Shoalhaven. Brisbane sent them also a few soldiers, together with overseers to control them.

Joseph Townsend, writing of his visit to the Coolangatta Estate in 1842, says: "Great pains have been taken to improve the breed of cattle on this estate, and bulls have been imported from England at great expense. 'Ella,' a Durham, is a splendid creature, and cost £500; and there are also some beautiful Ayrshire bulls: choice animals of this description are kept for sale in an extensive clover paddock devoted to them alone. And to the place they become so much attached that there is a great difficulty in removing them even in the company of cows. Some of the bullocks reared and fed on this country attain a great size, some as much as 15cwt., and the rolls of fat on their backs forms hollows something like a saucer. One beast yielded 250lbs. of caul and kidney fat, and 5cwt. of tallow was obtained by boiling down two of them. Drafts of cattle are being constantly sent from this estate to Sydney, and many dairy cows are sold to other settlers. A large dairy is kept on foot where often 200 cows are milked, but only once a day.

After the morning's milk is taken from them, the calves are allowed with them until night, and the cows yield about two gallons of milk per day, which, under another system would be doubtless more. The skim milk feeds a little army of pigs. Many beautiful mares are to be found among the herds of horses, and a stallion from the English turf was in the stalls. The horses bred on this property attain a great size; their points are well developed, and many have been sent to India.''

Lieutenant Henderson, in describing the process of boiling down at Coolangatta during the "panic" when stock were at zero, considered the system "a very happy idea" as it not only at once made sheep and cattle worth the price of their "hides and tallow," but acted beneficially by thinning out the stock. He further states the owners of this estate reside in an excellent brick house which crowns a rising ground, and well built cottages have been erected in convenient situations for the accommodation of the several superintendents. The produce of the estate is sent to Sydney in vessels built on the river; 2000 bushels of barley were harvested on the estate, but no sale for that quantity could be found in Sydney. The dairy was returning at the rate of £70 per week for butter alone.

Hon. Alexander Berry, M.L.C., died at North Sydney on 16th June, 1873, aged 93 years. His greatest opponent during 1857 and 1860 was the Rev. Dr. Lang, M.D.

According to a reliable authority Charles Throsby Smith, of Wollongong, acting as agent for Berry and Wollstonecraft, secured 25,000 acres of land for the firm in Illawarra. Hence the origin of Broughton Head Farm.

"Mr. David Berry died in 1889, and the trustees, Mr. John Hay and the Hon. Dr. Norton, M.L.C., have, among numerous legacies, to provide for two sums of £100,000 each for the erection of a hospital for the district of Shoalhaven, and for the University of St. Andrews; and it is to make payment of the bequests that the trustees are selling portions of these large and hitherto intact properties.''

The Shoalhaven Estate.

For the purpose of selling the Berry Estate sub-division, the following paragraphs were used: "The Shoalhaven and Illawarra districts of New South Wales are famed throughout Australia for their rich and fertile lands, for their special breed of dairy cattle, and for their general scenery. Occupying the com-

paratively narrow strip of coast line between the mountain range and the Pacific Ocean. These lands receive the moisture wrung out of the sea breeze by the hills and thus are ever fertile and prolific.''

"The Illawarra country commences near Wollongong, 48 miles south of Sydney Heads, but it is not until the districts round Kiama, Jamberoo, Gerringong, Nowra, and especially Shoalhaven, are reached that the unbounded fertility of the soil, and its adaptability to dairy and cereal farming can be fully realised. Shoalhaven, without dispute, is the Queen of Illawarra, and it is from here that so much of the dairy and farm produce is supplied to Sydney and other parts of the colony.''

"The Shoalhaven Estates comprise some 60,000 acres of rich agricultural and grazing land on both sides of the Shoalhaven and Crooked Rivers, and are intersected by Broughton Creek which is navigable for small steamers to near the village of Berry, formerly named Broughton Creek.''

First sale, 4 Gerringong farms, comprising 21 acres 2 roods; 27 acres; 28 acres 3 roods; 97 acres, 3 roods. To be sold at D. L. Dymock's sale rooms, Kiama, Tuesday, 29th March, 1892. Terms 25 per cent. cash, 15 per cent. in two years, the balance in five years from day of sale, bearing interest at 5 per cent. per annum. Second sale, the township of Bomaderry, consisting of 300 acres. Laid by Messrs. McCabe and Ewing, surveyors, situated on the banks of the Shoalhaven River, at the entrance of Bomaderry Creek, opposite the town of Nowra. Sale Wednesday, March 30th, 1892, on the ground. Same terms as No. 1. No. three sale. The Numbaa farm lands which are bounded on the east and north by the Shoalhaven River, and on the south by the Crookhaven, comprising from 5000 to 6000 acres, and close to the townships of Terrara and Nowra. In farms from 20 to 200 acres each, laid out by Messrs. Atchison and Schleicher, surveyors. The whole of this property was under municipal government having been incorporated in 1868. The Shoalhaven River forms the boundary of the property on the north, and runs from west to east into the South Pacific Ocean. It rises in the coastal range, flowing northerly through deep gullies, and turning sharply to the east it enters the alluvial plains which are counted amongst the richest and most productive in the country. This river is 260 miles in length, but is naviga-

Notable Red Bulls in whose Veins Circulated good Devon Blood in more or less Quantities.

ADMIRAL (at the age of 12 years).

ROBIN HOOD.

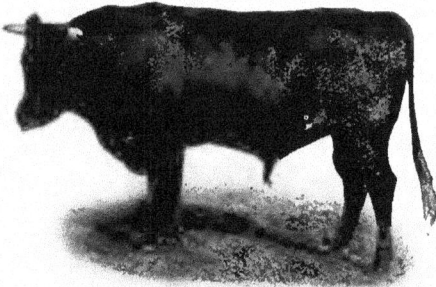

RED PRINCE OF HILL VIEW.

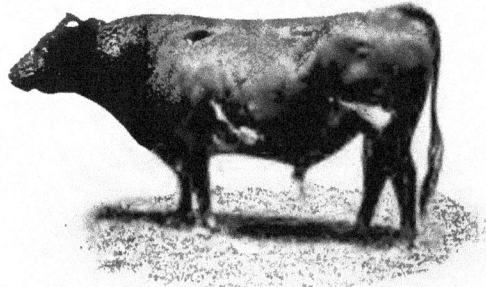

RED PRINCE OF GREYLEIGH.

NOBLE OF GILEAD.

GUS OF HILL VIEW.

J. HARDCASTLE'S CHAMPION BULL JAMBEROO.

DAIRYMAN OF GLENTHORNE.

Eight Red Illawarra Type Dairy Cows of Merit.

GEM OF GREENVALE.

VISION III OF BLACKHEATH (No. 1257, Vol. 2).

DAISY OF HILLVIEW.

TOT 11 OF OAKDALE.

MARCHIONESS OF COOBY.

EMPRESS OF HILLVIEW.

FLORRIE II (No. 368, I.D.C.H.B.).

PLUM OF MAYFIELD

ble only for a few miles, draining a distret of 3,300 square miles in area. The Numbaa farms were sold in the long room, Numbaa, Tuesday, March 31st, 1892. Same terms as No. 1 and 2. H. G. Morton was land steward.

The Nowra bridge cost £42,000, and is 411 yards long.

Auctioneers, Hardie and Gorman, Sydney, D. L. Dymock, Kiama, and Stewart and Morton, Berry.''

Dr. Kenneth Mackenzie was born in Scotland on 29th August 1806. He was a medical doctor and came out to Sydney in the early thirties. In 1837 he purchased Bundonan, on the upper Shoalhaven, from R. H. Brown containing 600 acres, and commencing farming operations which he later on combined with cattle raising. In the early fifties it was a common thing for Illawarra men to visit Dr. Mckenzie's farm with a view of purchasing dairy heifers. A reference to the records of the old Illawarra A. & H. Society will show that Dr. Mackenzie was one of its founders. In 1838 he married a Mrs. Cliffe by whom he had five children, namely, Helen, Mary, Murdock, Hugh, and Julia. Mrs. Mckenzie died in 1858. In 1870 Dr. Mackenzie and his eldest son, Murdock, sailed for Scotland in the ship Ann Duthie, and the father settled and died at Dundonald, Scotland, in the year 1878. Murdock Mackenzie did not live long after his father's death. He passed out in London in 1881. His remains were taken for burial to Dundonald. A relation of the Mackenzie family, Murdock Ross, was manager for the Berry family at Meroo, and also for the Osborne family at the Kangaroo Ground.

Miss Mary Mackenzie married James Thompson, a grandson of Mrs. Mary Reibey, so that much of the upper Shoalhaven properties became a joint family concern. Dr. Kenneth Mackenzie and Mr. James Thompson were for years the local magistrates for the Shoalhaven district, acting in conjunction with Mr. James Mackay Grey, of Kiama, or Captain Plunket, of Wollongong, according to the gravity of the cases to be tried by them.

Of the great men of modern times Mr. Hugh Mackenzie stood high and strong in stature and moral force among the native born of old Illawarra. He was born in Bundonan in 1845, and was educated in Sydney. He like his father took a keen interest in all matters that had for their best object the well-being of his district. After the death of his brother in London, he took a trip to Dundonald, Rosshire, Scotland, to settle up his brother's affairs. A few years later he took his wife and children to see the Scottish home. He did not like the climate. About 1887 he purchased the Terrara Estate from the Executors of the De Mestre family for £40,000. Although his father was fond of a race horse he did not inherit a love for the sport of kings. He did more good by helping in a big way the betterment of the man on the land as president of the Shoalhaven A. & H. Society. He died in November, 1917, aged 72 years.

In October, 1879, Hugh Mackenzie purchased 100 acres at Terrara from W. H. Lovegrove at £40 per acre, and Lovegrove removed to Sydney.

Mr. Charles Throsby Smith came out a mere youth to New South Wales from England to his uncle Dr. Charles Throsby, of Glenfield, Liverpool. He claimed to have done much pioneering for his uncle. No doubt he assisted in many ways but Dr. Throsby's chief guides were three experienced servants, John Waite, Joseph Wild, and Rowley. It was those three men who brought the first cattle into Illawarra overland from Liverpool for Dr. Throsby. It was John Waite, or as he was sometimes called, Jack White, who had entire charge of Dr. Throsby's cattle in 1813.

The first notice we have of Mr. Charles Throsby Smith's entry in the lands in Illawarra is in 1825 when he is advertising in the ''Gazette'' for a cow lost from his farm, ''Bustle Farm.'' There was evidently Wollongong at that time. The settlement being at ''Red Point.''

Mr. Charles Throsby Smith, however, did this, he married a Miss Broughton at Parramatta as first wife, and obtained a grant of 300 acres in what is now the town of Wollongong. He called his farm ''Bustle Farm,'' and took the contract from the Government to provision the garrison at Red Point, Port Kembla. Floods occasionally interfered with his operations, and he had often to pass round by Spring Hill to avoid the Lagoon. He, after a little time, got influence enough at his command to have the stockade and garrison removed from Port Kembla to Wollongong. And hence we have Crown Street, Wollongong. The gaol and soldiers' quarters were situated at Lower Crown Street.

Speaking of Early Illawarra—

Mr. Charles Throsby Smith says:—Dr. Charles Throsby, of Glenfield, near Liverpool, was my uncle, and when I first started for Illawarra with a mob of cattle, two white men and two black men were in charge of the cattle. We reached Appin on the first day. Next day we took an easterly direction for four days, when we reached the top of the Bulli Mountain. We rested there overnight. Next day we came down the range to where the township of Bulli is to-day." Speaking of Wollongong after he had commenced farming at Bustle Hill, Mr. Smith said: "All the land between what is now Crown Street and the Lagoon was thickly covered with a honeysuckle and ti-tree scrub."

By his Broughton wife Mr. Smith was connected by marriage with Lieutenant Carne, Dr. Charles Throsby, and Dr. Clayton. The latter gentleman resided for some years in Dapto. In the diary of Rev. Thomas Kendall, we find that he visited Illawarra and baptised a child born 27th December, 1827, belonging to Herbert and Atty Green, at the house of the Commandant, John Fitzgerald Butler, on 3rd February, 1829. Nearly twelve months before he had baptised Maria, daughter of Charles Throsby Smith and Sarah Smith, at their house; date of birth, 11th January, 1828; date of baptism, 2nd March, 1828. This goes to show that the date of the arrival of Mr. Smith in what is now Wollongong, would be about 1825. He evidently knew much more about early Illawarra than he ever told to even his immediate friends. He was married four times, and once visited England. He was appointed Government Lands Commissioner. He had an up-to-date farming plant in what is now the town of Wollongong. It was in his barn that the Church of England service was held prior to 1837. He died 25th September, 1876, aged 78 years.

Petersham,
February 28th, 1914.

I regret to state that my health has been so bad during the past twelve months that I am unable to comply with your request as to the early history of Wollongong. The records of which are among the Smith family and out of my reach at present. I am in my eightieth year. In answer to your query re the name of Broughton, it was named after my late uncle who took down a draft of cattle for Berry Bros., to Broughton Creek about the year 1824, and is reputed to have taken up for Berry 25,000 acres at Broughton Creek.

Unfortunately there are none of my relations, Throsbys, living who could give much information re the taking up of the town of Wollongong, then portion of the County of Camden. My elder sisters, the late Mrs. F. R. Cole, who died at eighty-four years, Mrs. A. A. Turner, now resident of Leichhardt, 86 years. I fear her memory has become faulty or information could be obtained through her, Mrs. Turner was born in 1828. Mrs. Cole previously. Our mother was born at Parramatta in 1799. Our father came to Wollongong in 1824 or 5. Pray excuse my scribbling. After I write for ten minutes my hand gives way. Hope you will make out what I have written. Wishing you success in your undertaking.

I remain, Yours faithfully,
Chas. F. Smith.

Dr. Thomas Montgomery Perrott, a retired staff surgeon, of first class, who served during the Peninsula Campaign, at Walchren, and first Burmese War, in H.M. First 41st Regiment of Foot. He received a grant of land, 500 acres, on Druwalla Creek, and purchased a farm on the Jamberoo road, bordering the Terragong or Mango Swamp, where he built a house and had a fine orchard. He practised his profession and carried on dairying. His brand was a globe surmounted by a cross. His servant was John G——y, who did not admire the cows. "They were too tough to milk." One day John was doing some tree felling, and a large tree smashed up several cows. John immediately gave himself up. When asked by Dr. Robert Menzies, J.P., what he had done, he said: I have broken up the "Globe and Crosses." Dr. Perrott was killed by a fall from his horse—whilst hurrying to save a man who had cut his throat—on 12th June, 1853, aged 62 years.

A writer possessed of much knowledge regarding the history of England, and the people thereof, once wrote: "I speak of the name Perrott, not a very common one, and which, it occurs to me, is historical also in another sense as it was borne by an officer very distinguished in the conquest of Ireland under Queen Elizabeth, viz., Sir Thomas Perrott, who was said to have been a natural son of 'bluff King Hal.' I don't know whether there is any other connection than the identity of name; but when I first came to Jamberoo there used to be a good deal heard about a certain Dr. Perrott, then recently dead, and formerly an army surgeon, a gentleman whose professional skill and peculiar manners furnished the subject of a good many anecdotes. He left some two or three hundred acres which were cleared by tenant farmers."

None of the old Jamberoo identities accused the old doctor of being so ambitious as to consider himself a more important man during the Peninsular war than the Duke of Wellington. They, however, considered that no man hated the "Iron Duke" more in every respect than did Dr. Thomas Montgomery Perrott. The doctor also hated the French, and possessed a large flake of a Frenchman's skin as a species of trophy from the war.

Mrs. Mary Reibey was a very old colonist and a friend of Governor Macquarie who assisted her to prosper in the new colony. He (Macquarie) promised her a grant of land in 1813; she did not, however, take possession of her grant at that period. Evidently she followed the custom of the time, viz., she took up the best available cedar country when it was opportune to do so. We learn that Mrs. Mary Reibey travelled on horseback from Sydney to Burrier in order to take possession of her Shoalhaven River grant in 1828. She must have travelled via Bong Bong, and then down a spur of the Meryla Mountain to Burrier. It would appear to have been the only trip she made south as she constantly kept that journey on her mind, and repeatedly mentioned it to her children and grandchildren. To her it was a great feat. But many Australian mothers performed remarkable feats in those days—often on foot—no horses to be had. No grass in the early bush to feed a horse; cows and bullocks were more useful to the struggling settlers who had to make grass grow where no grass grew before.

Mr. James Thompson was born on August 26th, 1824 in Launceston, Tasmania, and was the eldest son of Lieutenant Thomas Thompson of the Royal Marine Light Infantry. He was educated in Sydney and became clerk to his uncle, Captain Innes, then police magistrate at the Hyde Park Barracks, Sydney. He then entered the service of the Bank of Australasia in Launceston, Tasmania, and in 1847 returned to New South Wales and settled at Burrier, which was a grant to Mary Reibey in 1824. The Burrier grant had been settled in 1833 with Mr. Alexander MacKay as manager. Mrs. Mary Reibey was Mr. James Thompson's grandmother, and she gave Burrier and her other grant Illaroo, to her two grandsons—Messrs. James Thompson and John Atkinson. Mr. James Thompson bought out his cousin's interests and took possession of the whole of the upper Shoalhaven properties. Mr. James Thompson was a horse fancier, and owned

Euclid as a stud sire. His cattle were of the James Atkinson Oldburg breed, and were always in demand.

He was elected to the first Parliament under responsible government in New South Wales, and only sat during the first session of that Parliament which cost him £800. He suffered serious loss owing to the Shoalhaven flood of 1860. He had Andre de Mestre, of Terrara, and Charles Moore (of the Botanic Gardens, Sydney) under his hospitable roof, together with other friends, and although no rain had fallen on February 9th up to 9 o'clock p.m. on the 10th at daylight the river was a banker and they all had to rush for their lives and camped that night in a fowl house owned by a neighbour. The river rose 15ft in 15 minutes at one period of time. In 1870 the flood washed the old house away. He married Miss Mackenzie, daughter of Dr. Kenneth Mackenzie, of Bundonan, Shoalhaven, who owned an estate in Scotland, named Dundonald, in Rosshire, about which hangs a tale of ye olden days. However, Dr. Mackenzie and James Thompson were resident magistrates for Shoalhaven and endeavoured to act justly.

William Browne, of Athanlin, Yallah, Illawarra, belonged to an old Irish family whose estates were in Sligo. Most readers of Irish history would know of the Marquis of Sligo and his associations with law and order in Ireland. William Browne of Yallah, or Merchant Browne, of Sydney, as he was usually termed, was born in Galway, Ireland, in 1762, and became an officer in the Hon. East India Company. He resigned his position and came to New South Wales from Calcutta with possibly £20,000. With such a sum at his command Governor Macquarie made him welcome, and gave him advice. He had only to ask for Government aid to find it showered on him, according, of course, to regulations. It is just possible that Mr. John Thomas Campbell, the Governor's secretary, went on board the ship "Mary" on her arrival from Calcutta, in the harbour of Sydney in 1816 to point out a few of its beauty spots.

Soon after arriving in Sydney Mr. Browne received a grant of 2800 acres of land for the erection of a wholesale wine and spirit store. A little later he obtained a grant of land on the shore of Lake Illawarra, between Dapto and the Macquarie Rivulet, of 1000 acres. He was married in Calcutta to a daughter of Lieutenant Colonel Forbes, and so far as can be ascertained neither he nor any of his own family ever settled in Illawarra. He sent an overseer down from Sydney who carried on dairying and farming in a small way. Horse-breeding may have interested him to a certain extent, as he was a racehorse owner. So, far, however, as Illawarra was concerned, he did little towards developing its resources, and eventually it fell into the hands of Mr. Henry Osborne, whose son, Mr. George Osborne, of Holly Lodge, Burwood, owned the southern portion of the Browne Estate.

According to Mr. John Brown, of Dapto Dr. Alexander Imlay, of Bega, and a nephew of Mr. William Browne, used to pay Yallah a visit occasionally, and that the first pole-dray ever seen in Illawarra was built to the order of Dr. Imlay. Prior to that a single bullock worked between two shafts like a horse, with a horse collar turned upside down causing an odd number of bullocks in a team.

It is a wonder that Dr. Alexander Imlay was not knighted for this innovation as it is on record that one wealthy Australian gentleman received a knighthood for introducing a new method of burning out stumps.

Mr. John Brown has informed us that the high range situated north of the Yallah Estate is called "Mount Browne" after the original owner. But as our old Illawarra resident had no knowledge of the celebrated botanist, Mr. Robert Brown who accompanied Governor Collins to Tasmania in 1803, and who was in Admiral William Bligh's expedition to that country, being in Illawarra on a botanising expedition in 1806, he was evidently confused in the name.

Be that as it may the dwelling house and outbuildings that were erected by Mr. William Browne for his overseer have long since disappeared. The manager of the Yallah Estate, Mr. Cornelius O'Brien, had frequently to ride over the mountain to Appin. He set about to discover a new route which has since been known as "O'Brien's Pass." This route turned off what is now the main South Coast road at the Figtree Bridge, and passed then over the mountain to Appin; and, it like the Bulli Pass, was used as a bridle track only, and these were the only pathways in and out of Illawarra for years. In the course of time the Mount Kiera Pass was discovered and opened up for traffic by bullock drays; and many of the early settlers of Illawarra came with their families by this route. Among them were Mr. William Spearing who received a grant of land known

as the Mount Kiera Estate. He founded a homestead at the foot of the mountain. Mount Kiera house and orchard were old land-marks. It was down the Mount Kiera Pass that Mr. George Brown, of Dapto, came from Liverpool to settle in the Illawarra district in 1829. Mr. Cornelius O'Brien was a qualified surveyor.

Mr. Cornelius O'Brien was a brother-in-law of Mr. William Browne, and Messrs. Charles and Ben O'Brien were relations. Their names appear in the management of many of our Illawarra Estates as far south as Terrara, Shoalhaven. They were associated with the first race club in Illawarra in 1834, when we learn of George Brown's "Blackjack" and William Browne's "Kauri Gum."

The Imlay Bros., of Tarraganda, Bega, were closely associated with William Browne, of Yallah, Illawarra. They were largely interested in blood horse breeding under the patronage of Sir Richard Bourke.

We then hear of Dr. Imlay, he is entertaining Major-General Sir Richard Bourke at Tarraganda in the Twofold Bay district. His Excellency after visiting Wollongong, and giving instructions to have the roads and bridges made, and the placing of a police magistrate permanently in Illawarra, boarded his frigate and went south to Twofold Bay. Before returning to Sydney his Excellency spent a good time in the extreme south of coastal development. After settling for a time in the Goulburn district Dr. Alexander Imlay returned to Tarraganda where he was joined by his brothers Dr. George and Mr. Peter Imlay. They quickly launched out in a large way and imported some of the finest horses and cattle England could produce. The following thoroughbred horses were imported by the Messrs. Imlay Bros., of Tarraganda, Bega, then known as the Twofold Bay district. For the pedigrees of whom we must refer the reader to the English Stud Book:—

No. 1, "Young Camel," bay, bred in 1838, sire, "Camel," dam, "Miss Kate"; No. II. "The Prince of Wales," bay, bred in 1838, sire, "Newtown," dam, "Holbrook"; No. III, "Merry Pebbles," chestnut, bred in 1837, sire, "Saracen," dam, "Lady Cauford"; No. IV, "Cerberus," black, bred in 1836, sire, "Defence," dam, "Charlotte"; No. V, "Hambledon," brown, bred in 1838, sire, "Ishmael," dam, "Babel"; No. VI, "Almanack," bay, bred in 1836, sire, "Camel," dam, "Miss Skin."

This was possibly the most important importation of blood horses that was ever recorded

GEORGE GREY, The Greyleigh Stud, Kiama.

TOGO.

CINDERELLA OF GREYLEIGH (No. 333, I.D.C.H.B.).

PLUM OF GREYLEIGH (No. 61, I.D.C.A.H.B.).

CARNATION (No. 178, I.D.C.H.B.).

MODEL II OF GREYLEIGH (No. 29).

EMPRESS OF GREYLEIGH
(No. 77, I.D.C.H.B.).

GEORGE GREY, The Greyleigh Stud, Kiama.

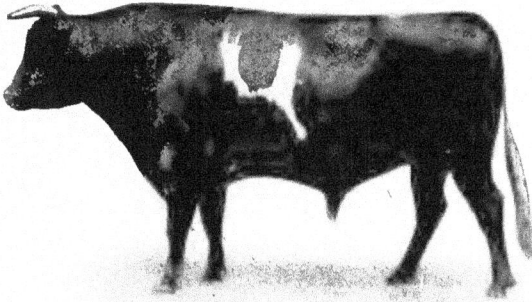

RUFUS OF GREYLEIGH (No. 7 I.D.C.H.B.).

DANDY IV (No. 746, I.D.C.H.B.).

JUDY III.

GEM II (No. 443, I.D.C.H.B.).

DUCHESS IV OF GREYLEIGH.

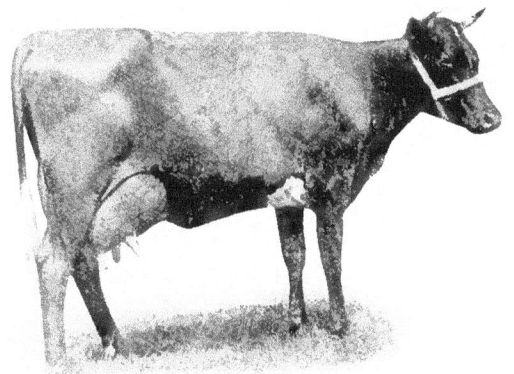

MODEL IV OF GREYLEIGH.

to Australia prior to 1840. The result of this importation was soon felt, and Mr. David Johnston took a leaf out of the Messrs. Imlay's book and imported £1600 of stock to New South Wales including the finest types of horses and cattle procurable in England. The result of these importations enabled the small settlers to get into their possession good stock which they preserved. Young foals and calves were easily transferred from one dam to another mother, and from one owner to another man. Flogging and starving a few unfortunate men for small crimes never had the slightest influence on those who were transferring stock from one part of the Illawarra district to another. It was to prevent free trade in horses, cattle and sheep the city merchants and large landed proprietors formed associations.

Dr. Thomas Foster.—Leaving John Terry Hughes' station, Albion Park, and travelling south, the spur of a mountain range is crossed which runs towards the sea. The northern side of this spur is called Mount Terry, and the southern side Mount Foster. At any part of this mountain spur splendid views of the several localities may be obtained.

Going south to the Minnamurra Rivulet, W. C. Wentworth's timber leases lay on the eastern side. To the right lay Dr. Thomas Foster's grant of 2560 acres, call Curragh-more. Dr. Foster belonged to the Marquis of Waterford's regiment in Ireland, and he called the property after the Marquis' private residence. In New South Wales the doctor was attached to the 46th Regiment of Foot, and married the eldest daughter of Gregory Blaxland in 1817. He never had much interest in Illawarra beyond selling the timber on his grant to the Woodstock mills. He was the father of William Foster a leading politician. The doctor died at Brush Farm, Parramatta, in 1882.

Mr. James Atkinson obtained the appointment of Chief Clerk in the Colonial Secretary's office in Sydney in 1818. He also received a grant of land in the County of Argyle, not far from Sutton Forest, which he called "Oldbury" after his native village in England. In 1824 he resigned his office and returned to England. While there he purchased a number of pure-bred horses, cattle, and sheep. He chartered the ship Cumberland (Captain Caruri), loaded her with agricultural stores and live stock, and arrived in Port Jackson, Sydney. 24th January, 1827. Among the several passengers who came with him to settle in N.S. Wales, was Miss Throsby, who afterwards married Dr. Patrick Hill.

James Atkinson on Cattle Breeding.

Mr. James Atkinson had no direct interests in Illawarra, but his descendents had later on. and the settlers in Illawarra took a keen interest in him and his imported stock. The cattle which he imported comprised the best dairy strain of the Sussex, Devon, Ayrshire, and Shorthorn breeds; and furthermore, as his writings show, he had his own opinion about dairy cattle breeding. Unfortunately he passed away too soon to be able to put his ideas into practical effect. His death is recorded in 1834. We find in the Records of 1828 that according to Mr. James Atkinson, "The horned cattle of the Colony were derived from various countries— England, Cape of Good Hope, India, and other places—and have been bred with little discrimination and were a mixed lot. Some few breeders, however, paid more attention, and soon possessed very good herds, though possibly not the best adapted to the country. Mr. John Macarthur's are of the Lancashire, and the Rev. Mr. Marsden's of the Suffolk or polled breed. These two, perhaps, are the finest and least unmixed in the Colony. Mr. Throsby possessed a strong and large variety, and the heaviest oxen yet produced have been from his herd."

"A very large proportion of the horned cattle of the Colony are derived from the Bengal breed, which are easily recognised by their Buffalo appearance. They are remarkable for their large hump on the shoulders, thick skin, and smooth shining hair. They are small and of little or no use for the dairy; fatten readily upon inferior keep; strong and hardy working stock; the quality of the beef is very fine."

"It is hardly possible to trace the other varieties introduced at different times; the pure English breeds of the large kind are not suitable in the early stages of the Colony's history, whilst depending upon the natural grass, unless when they have a large tract of country to range over. The smaller breeds, such as the Devons, South Wales, and Galloway Scots are more suitable, and would produce big beef, more milk than the Herefords, Sussex, or large Yorkshire breeds."

"The Yorkshire breed is the best for crossing with the Colonial cattle, the majority of which may be described as large-boned, thick-skinned, coarse-necked, heavy fore-quartered, deficient hind-quartered, and badly milking stock. The short-horned Yorkshires are the reverse to all this. The prices of horned cattle are extremely various. and have been declining for years; notwithstanding, good dairy cows are still in great demand, I have known lately £100 offered for five cows, a choice of forty in a herd, and refused, in Sydney." See "British Farmers' Magazine," 1826.

According to James Atkinson, of Oldbury, Sutton Forest, N.S.W., he was the first of his time, to wit, 1828, to advocate the Red Sussex breed of cattle as a means of crossing with other dairy breeds to bring about the ideal dairy animal. At that time it was considered that "the bull ought to be the most handsome of his kind; his eyes sprightly and prominent; his ears long and thin, hairy within and without, his horns long, clean, and bright, and standing low at the crown, his mouth small, and muzzle fine; nostrils wide and open; the head not looking coarse or large, as all fineness about the head denotes a great inclination to fatten; his neck near to the head fine, both above and below, but gradually thickening until it joins the breast and shoulders, and not encumbered with a coarse, wreathy skin. What is termed the neck vein should be very full; the upper parts, called the withers, broad and strong, and well fleshed where it joins the chine, which is a certain criterion of any animal being fat in its upper parts. The neck, in length, should bear a proper proportion to every other part of him, be grown well out of his shoulders, rising with a gentle curve, giving a lofty appearance; his forehead broad, and set with close, short, curled hair, standing up, with very little dewlap or loose skin in any part. Further, his shoulders should be deep, high, and moderately broad on top, the forelegs open; the breast large and projecting well before the legs. From the top of the head to the tail should be nearly straight, the little rise on the upper part of the chine excepted; the back of hoof broad, so as to carry the greater weight on all his fine parts; the ribs standing out round from the chine. but not in the extreme, nor should they be broader below than on top, but forming a proper depth on the sides, and the rib should be near the huck, so as not to show a hollow, even with an empty belly. The huck-bone should be globular at the end, standing a little higher than the ribs or the rump, which latter should be long and level, with the back and ribs, carrying width near the tail; the two

bones on each side of his tail, by some called the 'tut-bones,' should be about two inches lower than the tail, and not far asunder. The highest part of the tail should be about one inch higher than the chine at the rump, and the upper end of the tail, giving the rump a considerable thickness, but tapering downwards to become very small at the bottom, with much lank hair on the under part of it; the forethighs strong and muscular, tapering gradually to the knees; the legs straight, short-jointed, full of sinews, clean, fine-boned. The hind-thighs should be well-covered with flesh, so as to form a good round or buttock of beef, but not so fleshy on the outside as to be what is termed 'Dutch-thighed'; the hair not hard or stubborn to the touch, but elastic to the feel like buck-leather; the hair uniformly thick, short, curled, and of a soft texture. His walk should be light and nimble, moving with his hind feet wider from each other than his fore-feet, showing much light between the legs. The carcase, taking a side view, should appear long, with small shoulders, to be of great length from the back of the shoulders to the tail; the body deep and round, filling well up to the shoulder, so as not to show hollow or weak places in any part—great shape being required in the ribs of all animals, which ought from the first to the last, to show a little farther out than another, so as to form, which is not improperly termed, a barrel-like carcase."

"The marks of the cow, proper to fatten. so far as they relate to the head, hide and general figure, are much the same as those already stated. In the cow, the flank is a part of much consideration, and the more it is thrown out in width, the better, being in some measure round, but deep, as there is a material difference between a deep-ribbed beast and a gutty one. Those termed gutty are wider below than above, whilst the proper shape in the body of a beast is to be wider above than below. so as to carry the greater weight upwards in its fine parts; consequently the shoulder of a fattening beast cannot be too small, nor is the animal ever too long, if one part bears proportion to another. The neck, although it should be fine and thin at the back of the horns, ought soon to become thicker in every part, joining the shoulder. There is nothing in which the cow for milk and the cow for fattening vary more than in this, as the cow for milk cannot have too thin a neck. It is presumed that whatever be the breed intended to fatten, the above applies to all."

Captain William Howe was a very old and valuable colonist. He got a large grant of land from the Crown in the Campbelltown district and called his home there Glenlee. He, by means of cheap labour, converted his holding in a few years into a large dairy farm, and the "Glenlee" butter and cheese were always in demand at advanced prices He seems to have had the idea from the commencement of his operations in New South Wales that it was the correct thing to breed crosses of at least four distinct breeds of dairy cattle for dairy purposes. He either imported or purchased pure bred Shorthorns, Devons, Sussexs, Ayrshires and Alderneys. It would be almost impossible now to come to any other conclusion. Nearly all the early settlers went to "Glenlee" for the nucleus of their dairy herds. This will be patent to readers of this book as they follow its pages. The Red Sussex cattle in the early days of the colony are described as being "harder-haired than the Devon, and of a deeper red than even the North Devon, cherry red, larger-framed and tip-top milkers." The first acquaintance we get with Captain Howe and his cattle is a "Gazette" notice as follows: "Mr. Bavin, auctioneer, sold at his paddock, known as Haymarket, Brickfield Hill, on 28th June, 1818, Captain Richard Brook's cattle, William Howe, Glenlee, being the chief purchaser." These cattle were described as being Durham, Ayrshire, and Devon crosses.

Captain William Howe carried on his operations with his wife as chief overseer. Very little, therefore, of the ways and means of those operations got outside the Glenlee homestead. We learn, however, that at the great cattle sale held at Segenhoe, near Singleton, on January 20th, 1838, Mr. William Howe, of Glenlee, purchased the chief Shorthorn stud bull, Jupiter, for £85, the highest priced bull at the sale, Segenhoe being the estate of the Hon. Potter MacQueen. In 1841 (April) Mr. Samuel Lyons had for sale at his bazaar, Sydney, the celebrated pure Durham bull, Jupiter, bred by Mr. Potter MacQueen, of Segenhoe, Singleton. His sire was Comet, and his dam Durham Nancy. His age was stated to be 7 years, and if fat would weigh 2000lbs. Also four bulls by Jupiter, out of Glenlee cows that have been judiciously crossed by imported bulls for the last twenty years. This gives us a fair idea of the class of cattle that many of our Illawarra dairymen began dairying with in 1840.

The Tate Family.

George Tate and Elizabeth Kell were married on the 1st June, 1815, and recorded in the parish book of Bowden, by the Revd. Belfour, Roxburghshire, Scotland. Their eldest child, Elizabeth Tate, was born at Shawburne, Roxburghshire, on 3rd day of March, 1816. John Kell Tate, the second child, was born at Eastfield, Roxburghshire, on 13th January, 1818. Both Elizabeth Tate and John Kell Tate were baptized by the Revd. W. Belfour, Minister of the Gospel, at Bowden.

George Tate, the third child, was born at sea on the way out to Sydney, on September 12th, 1819. Edward Kell Tate, the fourth child, was born at Kirkham, Camden, N.S. Wales, on December 5th, 1821. Mary Kell Tate was born at Campbelltown, N.S. Wales on 26th July, 1825. George, Edward Kell, and Mary Kell Tate were baptized by Revd. Dr. Lang at the Scots' Church, Sydney.

Mrs. Elizabeth Tate died at "Springhill," Illawarra, next to Berkeley estate, near Wollongong, N.S. Wales, on the 1st June, 1827, aged 36 years. George Tate, her husband, was gored by a bull and killed at Haymarket, Sydney, 27th December, 1835, aged 41 years. Mrs. James Donnelly (nee Elizabeth Tate), died at Cowell's Farm, Kiama, N.S. Wales, on December 30th 1854, aged 38 years.

George Tate, on arriving in Sydney, became manager for Surveyor John Oxley, at Kirkham, in the Camden district, where the fourth member of his family was born. He took an hotel at Campbelltown where his fifth child was born. On 22nd June, 1824, he received a grant of 500 acres at Springhill, Wollongong, on which he built an hotel. He was, therefore, the first recognised publican in Illawarra. He carried on cedar getting and cattle breeding, principally raising bullocks for hauling timber. After the death of his wife, in 1827, he remarried a Mrs. McDermott, mother of MacDermott, who opened the first hotel in Jamberoo, "The Man o' Kent," Woodstock. In 1832 he sold the Springhill property to Captain Charles Waldron of the 39th Regiment of Foot, and took over the Wheatsheaf Hotel, opposite the old Toll-bar in George-street, Sydney. From the Wheatsheaf Hotel he went to the "Forbes" Hotel, near the salevards, Haymarket, where he was gored by a bull as stated, and died 27th December, 1835. Two of his sons, George and Edward, learned trades, blacksmithing and wheelwrighting respectively, with Fowler Bros., Campbelltown. John was a storekeeper. All three came to Jamberoo in 1841. George and Edward at the side of an old track that led past where the Catholic Church now stands, John opened a store on the hill adjacent thereto. Mrs. James Donnelly who died on Cowell's Farm, near Kiama, was the mother of that celebrated jockey and racehorse trainer at Randwick, George Donnelly. James Donnelly intended buying Cowell's farm. It so happened that the property was in the hands of Daniel Cooper for disposal. Cooper living in London in 1853 gave Samuel Charles the chance of his lifetime, and he took advantage of it, purchased the property and called it "Eureka." Samuel Charles had been sent to England at that time to bring out the steamship Kiama. He put Captain Grainger in charge, he himself not being a deep sea captain.

In the year 1848 there came to Jamberoo an up-to-date Yorkshire farmer named George Wood. About ten years later another English farmer named George Wood settled on a farm on the Robb estate, near Kiama. So they were styled as George Wood, Jamberoo, and George Wood, Springhill. The elder Wood settled on Moses Brennan's holding, near John Ritchie's farm, where he farmed successfully for a few years, and then combined dairying with agriculture. John Tate and Edward Tate married daughters of George Wood, of Jamberoo, and George Wood, jun., of Jamberoo, married a daughter of James Donnelly. John Tate, Edward, and George Wood, junr., settled down to their respective callings and carried on dairying in Jamberoo. It is with George Tate, however, that the Illawarra district had the greater concern, as he launched out in several ways. He became a cattle breeder and a cattle dealer on a larger scale than the majority of his neighbours, and passed the dealing instinct on to his sons. Hence we have records of four George Tates in Illawarra. We will then confine our remarks to the careers of the Georges as being prominent cattle breeders and cattle dealers, as well as being successful exhibitors at the Illawarra A. and H. Society shows; not always in the Shorthorn type classes. In 1856 George Tate was carrying on dairying in conjunction with his trade (in fact all three brothers combined dairying and farming with business), his farm was leased from Dr. Robert Menzies. The site is that now known as Hugh Dudgeon's Hillview Farm. George Tate was in every sense of the term a busy man. His first stud bull was purchased from John Marks at Terragong, on the Kiama-Jamberoo road. He got to work at Broughton Village, buying all the village lots there, and set then to work to fell the timber

and clear the land, as did all the original settlers in Illawarra. As soon as the land was ready and a house erected he left Jamberoo and took up residence at Broughton Village. A few years later he made a plunge. Ben and Alex Osborne had Glenmurray-Kangaroo Valley on the halves. Their respective brands were B.H.O. and A.H.O. George Tate bought all Ben Osborne's cattle. He engaged Harry Thomas and two blacks, including the clever bushman, Owney, to collect the cattle. These experts collected upwards of 500 head by scouring the ranges, most of them unbranded, which he sold in lots wherever he found a market. The choicest he reserved for his own farm at Broughton Village. In 1869 he bought a bull from Evan R. Evans, afterwards known as the old E.E. bull. He later went in for pedigreed Shorthorns, "Prodigal" from Lee, of Bathurst; "Napoleon" from Barnes and Smith of Richmond River; "Boxer" from John Boxell, of Berry, who had bought his sire from Lowe, of Mudgee. None of these Shorthorns pleased him. In 1875 he purchased Gabriel Timbs' bull. In 1876 he had an auction sale, reserved some yearling heifers, and the calves by E. R. Evans' bred bull, which he sold at the sale, and also reserved from sale the Timbs' bull. He leased the farm for a year to George Thompson, and put him right into possession at the end of that term. At the end of twelve months he sent the Timbs bull and the young heifers over the range to his son George, at Oakvale. George, junior, commenced dairying there, and purchased an Ayrshire bull by a very superior Ayrshire bull purchased by Henry Hill Osborne, of Avondale, New Zealand. George in a few years put together a fine herd of cows. His health failed, and in 1882 he leased the farm to William Kelleher, and sold his cattle at great prices for those times, and went dealing for five years in conjunction with Jerry and Paddy Sullivan. In 1887 he sent the Messrs. Sullivan out to buy up cattle to commence dairying again. They moved towards Jamberoo and Shellharbour, and on the tableland around Moss Vale. The majority of the cattle were purchased by Jerry Sullivan around Shellharbour at £4 and £5 per head. These animals were actually the foundation cattle of the Oakdale herd that was dispersed by public auction in 1919 at enormous prices.

John Wyllie, of Dunlop Vale, Illawarra, little is known beyond his early association with Governor Sir Thomas Brisbane, Mr. James Dunlop (an astronomer), Mr. Alexander Berry,

M.C., and the Rev. John Dunmore Lang, D.D. These associations, it is very evident, did not pan out at all satisfactory as far as Mr. John Wyllie was concerned. He did not survive the ordeal, and left no relations here to fight his cause or to preserve his memory. He (Wyllie) received a grant of 2000 acres of land on the shores and in the vicinity of Lake Illawarra, and carried on farming and dairying in the usual way; that is, in plain English, by means of convict labour, the Government supplying the men and assisting to feed and clothe them. As the intrepid mariner said, "It was the rule of the road."

The late Alexander Berry claimed the honour of bringing to Australia Sir Thomas Brisbane and his train of attendants. He also had on board his ship Mr. James Dunlop, the astronomer, and Mr. John Wyllie. What was the relationship between the two latter gentlemen is not easily defined. Suffice to say here, Mr. Wyllie called his place Dunlop Vale, and imported what the old hands used to term "the choicest types of Ayrshire cattle that graced Illawarra before or since."

The sequel to this history is a very sad one, so we will let it rest for the present. Mr. Wyllie became acting manager at Coolangatta for Mr. Alexander Berry, where he got involved in a law suit with a neighbour, with the result that he (Wyllie) was cast into, for that period, heavy expenses. Alexander Berry took over Wyllie's choice Ayrshire cattle, and Messrs. Carruth Bros. and Rev. John Dunmore Lang divided Dunlop Vale between them, giving the name Canterbury to the lake side, and Kembla Grange to the western portion of the estate.

Mr. William Thompson, of Belseyvale, Dapto, born County Fermanagh, Ireland, same age within a few weeks of the late John Russell, of Croome, says: "My uncle, Andrew Thompson, worked for a time with the Messrs. Carruth Bros. on a portion (1000 acres) of Wyllie's 2000 acres on Mullet Creek. He was a shipmate of Robert Harworth, and worked on the farm with him. When Wyllie sold his cattle to Alexander Berry and went to the Coolangatta Estate as overseer (when Wyllie was in charge there) James Graham took a vessel up the Canal, contrary to Berry's wishes. Wyllie reported this to Alexander Berry, who wrote Wyllie instructing him to bore a hole in the bottom of the boat. Wyllie did as instructed. Then Graham entered an action against Wyllie. Alexander Berry came on the scene, went to Wyllie's drawer, took away the

letter he wrote him, and left Wyllie to fight out the case on his own. Wyllie was cast in £200 expenses. He hadn't the cash, so he went to Dr. Lang's father (Andrew Lang), and mortgaged his property. Wyllie sold to Carruth Bros. They sold 1000 acres to Gerard Gerard, and Dr. Lang, on behalf of his father or brother, took the other 1000 acres. Carruth Bros. went away to New Zealand, as they thought they had bought the whole lot, 2000 acres, for £1000.

Wyllie died of a broken heart in Sydney, through worry contracted at Coolangatta.

Prosper de Mestre was of French extraction, and claimed to belong to folk at one time associated with a British man-o'war under the command of the Duke of Cambridge. He was one of Sydney's early merchants, and married a widow in Sydney with at least three children by previous marriages. Prosper John de Mestre, his eldest son, was born in Sydney in 1821. There were two other boys of the union, namely, Andre Cotterell de Mestre, and Etienne Livingstone de Mestre, and several daughters, all of whom were entitled to grants of land varying from 60 to 100 acres, as was the rule in those days, having been native born.

Mr. Cornelius O'Brien, J.P., of Bulli, was the Government land agent for Illawarra. With his assistance all these grants were centred into one block of land at Worrigee, Shoalhaven, which was named "Terrara." Prosper de Mestre, senr., was much worried about financial matters in 1845, in which year he died suddenly, and certain members of the family came to reside on the Terrara Estate in 1846. Farming and dairying was carried out as at other centres in Illawarra. It was at Terrara that reaping machinery was first used on the coast.

The following copy of an agreement entered into between Mrs. de Mestre, widow, of Terrara, and others concerned as trustees or guardians of the Terrara Estate, and of the late Prosper de Mestre family on the other part, and the trustees of the two acres of land at Worrigee belonging to the Wesleyan Church, on the other part, will go to show that there were at least four marriage interests in the said Terrara Estate.

That Mrs. de Mestre, which evidently refers to the widow of Prosper John de Mestre, and the said trustees of Terrara, agree to make an exchange of 100 feet frontage by 242 feet more or less in depth, bounded on the north by Wheatley's allotment at Terrara, as shown to Mr. Holme (surveyor), and absolutely to convey same to trustees for the benefit and full possession of the Wesleyan Methodist Church on the condition that the said trustees or any other authorised persons shall convert to her or her heirs or assignees the two acres of land situate at Worrigee as aforesaid.

Further a conveyance of the said Worrigee land may require some time to complete, Mrs. de Mestre and the trustees of Terrara will give a lease of 21 years which shall be made null and void, as if not made, when the conveyance of the said land is completed. The lease to take effect fourteen days after this date, March 9th, 1857. Witness, Samuel Wilkinson, Thomas Holme, M. A. de Mestre.

Abstract of title of Edward and Francis Lord, Esqs., trustees of the lot within mentioned, 25th February, 1836, grant from the Crown to Prosper de Mestre Esq., of thirteen hundred acres at Terrara, Shoalhaven, 13th January, 1844, indenture of release of 1300 acres. George Edmond Griffiths, Clarke Irving, James Holt, of the first part, Prosper de Mestre, of the second part, Francis Lord and John Henry Black of the third part, and Mary Ann de Mestre of the fourth part;. 30th September, 1859, indenture of release of the said 1300 acres from Francis Lord and John Henry Black to the said Mary Ann de Mestre.

Will, bearing date the 3rd day of July, 1861, whereby the said 1300 acres were conveyed to the said Francis Lord and Edward Lord upon certain trusts therein mentioned.''

In this de Mestre Estate old Simeon Lord, of Sydney, took a hand. Andy Collone was interested in Terrara, when Simeon Lord joined in as part owner. Lord's vineyard was south of Terrara, and was called "Warra Warra." To this place he consigned Andy Collone. In the late Mr. Bernard Brown's dairy there are several references to Collone's bush. Further we need not go into the matter.

The Terrara Estate, as the training ground of many noted race horses, is only too well known. Terara was a township for years. Scores of people employed in caring for and training horse stock. Perhaps the de Mestre's were never really their own masters. After the death of Prosper John de Mestre, his widow married Thomas Richards, a well-known solicitor. Andre Cottrell de Mestre died at Greenwell Point, Shoalhaven, 15th December, 1917, aged 95 years; Etienne de Mestre died at Moss Vale 22nd October, 1916, aged 84 years.

The loss to racing men and to sections of the Shoalhaven district must have been considerable when Mr. Etie de Mestre's operations ceased. But generally speaking, the influence of Mr. Hugh Mackenzie, who was also a broadminded sportsman, operated more widely locally for the good of the district. He was as president of the Shoalhaven A. & H. Society a princely man, and did good everywhere silently.

Dr. William Elyard, R.N. came to New South Wales early in our history, and became a superintendent of convicts in various centres. We learn of him at the Carter's Barracks, at Brickfield Hill, Sydney, and at Red Point, and Coolangatta, Illawarra. He, in due time, received a grant of land at what is to-day Greenwell Point, Shoalhaven, and 37 acres 28 perches, portion 7, parish of Bhererre, St. Vincent. No one but trusted Government officers got these stray positions on the sea border as land grants.

Dr. William Elyard, R.N., was the first superintendent of convicts at Five Islands, Illawarra, now Port Kembla. He visited there from Sydney with a flogger, a large framed man, whose name was Waddell. Dr. Elyard resided there afterwards from 1822 to 1823. He received a grant of 500 acres of land at West Dapto, which he called Avondale. His two sons, William and Alfred Elyard resided on the farm, which was managed by John Derrett. Elyard, some years later sold the farm to Henry Osborne, of Marshall Mount. Dr. William Elyard, R.N., had another grant of land at Crookhaven Heads, which Alexander Berry fancied would become important so he brought about an exchange with Elyard for his (Berry's) Worrigee grant. Berry shortly afterwards found that he had made a gigantic mistake. Then followed a series of costly law court cases which almost ruined Elyard. He, however, held on to Worrigee, and his sons, Alfred and William finally settled there. Part of the estate was called Narellan, and remained under that name for years until the postal authorities became confused owing to an older settlement claiming priority. Then the Shoalhaven district Narellan was changed to that of Brundee.

After Mr. Alexander Berry had cut the canal at Crookhaven, he evidently intended to form a township at the entrance to the Shoalhaven River, and induced Dr. Elyard to exchange his grant for his (Berry's) grant at what is now Brundee. The exchange had to go through the Government offices in those days of officialism. Evidently, also, the boundaries of Brundee were not well defined, and as the days passed into

Types of the Coleville Stud Milking
The Property of Executors of the Late

VIOLET OF COLEVILLE.

QUEEN OF COLEVILLE.

SLASHEM OF COLEVILLE.

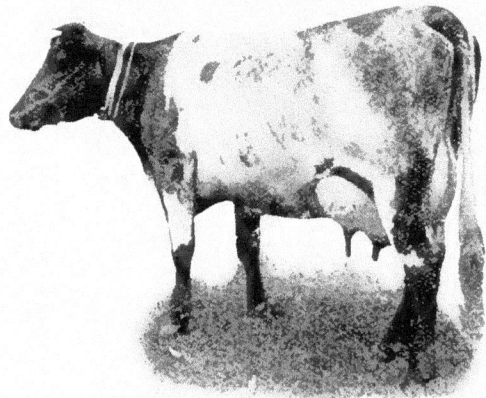

DIADEM OF COLEVILLE.

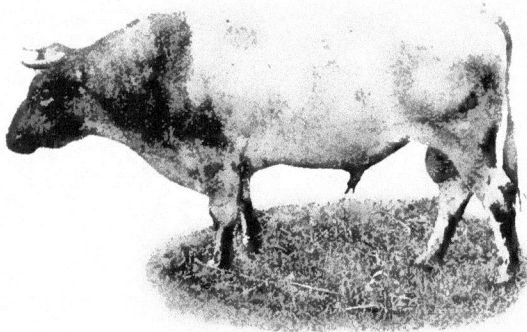

MAJOR V OF COLEVILLE.

PRINCESS OF COLEVILLE.

Shorthorn Cattle of Australia.

J. W. Cole, Coleville, Jamberoo, N.S.W.

MAJOR VI OF COLEVILLE.

JEWELL OF COLEVILLE.

GOLD OF COLEVILLE.

ELSIE II OF COLEVILLE (No. 189, Vol. I).

GOLD II OF COLEVILLE.
(No. 1472, Vol. III, M.S.H.B. of N.S.W.).

POSEY III OF COLEVILLE.

years, Mr. Berry saw that he had made a huge mistake. A house in which a constable lived formed an excuse, if such were necessary, for a quarrel between two men capable of ruling with an iron hand. Berry claimed the house and land occupied by the constable. Elyard resented his claim. The case was engineered by lawyers into the Privy Council in London. It matters little who became the constable's landlord. Dr. William Elyard, R.N., suffered financially. He, however, held on to his Brundee property.

In 1834 there were three members of the Elyard family in New South Wales. Dr. William Elyard, R.N., whose address was Brundee, Shoalhaven, Alfred Elyard, and William Elyard, junr., Surry Hills, Sydney. Alfred Elyard was possibly a brother of William Elyard, of Brundee. Alfred had a grant of 600 acres at Dapto, Illawarra, which he called Avondale, after his native heath in Scotland. He sold it to Henry Osborne, and went to reside at Berrallan, Shoalhaven, where he died 23rd December, 1879, aged 80 years. We also have Arthur Elyard, of Brundee, Shoalhaven, Samuel Elyard, died at Nowra in 1910, aged 94 years. William Elyard, junr., died in 1865. He joined the Government Service in Sydney, in 1822. William Arthur Gilbert Elyard died at Bomaderry, 7th July, 1914, aged 73 years.

John Thomas Lardner was overseer for Dr. Elyard at Brundee, and Thomas Chester was his coachman.

David Smith (Davey, the Lawyer), arrived in Kiama in 1822, and went in for cedar getting and cedar buying. He was piloted into Kiama by Captain Stewart, who was for years trading on the coast. He could neither read nor write, yet he understood much law, and was a capable calculator regarding the value of a cedar log. He opened a public house in Kiama — "The Traveller's Rest," and owned many bullocks which he used to depasture on Cowell's grant. His brand was JS, and his shipping agents' brand was also JS. The Railway Commissioners took away the old Smith Estate. It was opposite what was for many years called Smith's Bay. He erected a storied house on the stream opposite the bay which he leased to those who required a private home. He died in what was the old public house on 13th December, 1883, aged 84 years. Many considered he was older.

Michael Fitzgerald was born in Ireland in 1812. Died at Stockwood, Dapto, April 13th, 1908, aged 86 years, which property he had pur-chased from Robert Edward Stack on 5th February, 1838. He figured in the Agricultural Show rings of Wollongong and Kiama during the early forties and fifties. He owned two noted blood mares, Cantata and Beeswing, and bred good cattle, as will be seen by looking over the Illawarra A. & H. Society's prize lists.

William Davis, senr., had an order from the Governor to take up two 50 acre blocks of land, one each for his sons William and Joseph. He selected at Jamberoo, the aboriginal meaning of which is said to be a "cluster of stars." After William Davis, senr., died, his son Joseph, whose block is now part of the village of Jamberoo, got mixed up with the "rum merchants." His brother came to his assistance. In this matter William made a great self-sacrificing effort. We need not dwell further upon this subject.

William Davis, Junr., was born in George Street, Brickfield Hill, Sydney, in the year 1815. He arrived at Port Kembla, Illawarra, with his brother Joseph and parents in 1822. Mrs. Jenkins had a family dairying at the time on the Berkley Estate. William Davis, senr., took a job of sawing cedar there. Twelve months later he moved on to Jamberoo. The halts were many as he had to earn money as he moved on and on. The old road or track after crossing Mount Terry inclined to the west through Curraghmore, and went to John Ritchie's station, Poplar Grove, near the range. It then twisted round to the east keeping to the south of the present Jamberoo-Kiama road until it became known as the Longbrush road. It crossed or joined the Bong Bong road about a mile south of the boat harbour, Kiama, and then turned north near Andrew Byrnes' 500 acre grant, Barroul.

Dec. 1st., 1821.—On or before 1st December, 1821, a promise of 100 acres grant at Jamberoo was made by Crown to William Davis, who on 1st January, 1833, by deed of gift, made over and transferred it to his sons, William and Joseph Davis, and their heirs and assigns for ever. (Description of said 100 acres is attached hereto.)

April 26th, 1839.—Joseph Davis then sold 50 acres of said land (being his half share in said 100 acres) to Michael Hyam (the part under lease to James Donnelly, Patrick Garretty and Harry Williams).

Nov. 9th and 10th, 1840.—Michael Hyam, dealer, of Sarah Valley, Illawarra, sold to John Wright and Alexander King, of Campbell Street, Sydney.

July 27th, 1842.—It now appears that in order to promote the due settlement of the territory of N.S. Wales (colony), and in fulfilment of a promise made on or before 1st day of December, 1821, by his Excellency Major-General Lachlan Macquarie, and in consideration of the quit rent thereafter reserved, her Majesty Queen Victoria did, on 27th July, 1842, by deed, poll, or grant from the Crown, under the hand of his Excellency Sir George Gipps, Captain-General and Governor for the time being of the colony of N.S. Wales, and under seal of the said colony, grant to James Mackay Gray 100 acres (hereinbefore mentioned) **upon trust** for William Davis, of Jamberoo, and John Wright and Alexander King, of Campbell Street, Sydney, and to their heirs according to their respective rights, etc.

You will note that a report on this case (that is, the title to the 100 acres) was numbered 1017, 15th December, 1841, and the report of the Commissioner was acted upon in the manner before been described, William Davis, the original grantee, being deceased before 1842. It is surmised that his family or next-of-kin wished to prove William Davis' claim, or those interested therein. This should enlighten one as to how this land was obtained and divided by John Wright an Alexander King.

Names of some of the tenants of an area, 100 acres of land (part of which also appears to join Thomas Barker's selection, which was in occupation of J. Cromer, tenant), adjoining land then owned by Thomas Wood on the north, on west by Mr. Hyam's land, south and east by other land owned by Mr. Hyam, and also on the west by Earra Creek. and now occupied by John Dully and Denis McCarthy as tenants thereof.

Wright and King owned 100 acres originally as tenants in common, and divided as above as far as we know no one is quite clear on this point as other Sydney land is mentioned in the deal.

Description of Davis Bros.' Land When Under Trust to James M. Grey.

All that piece or parcel of land in our said Territory containing 100 acres more or less, situated in the County of Camden and parish unnamed, at Minnamurra, Illawarra, bounded towards the North by John Cullen's 300 acres, being a line extending best 40 chains on the South side from the South-East corner thereof to the North-East corner of John Wheeler's 50 acres towards the East by a line extending South 8

chains from the South-East corner of John Cullen's 300 acres to the South-West corner of William Ritchie's, and from that corner by a line extending best 24 chains, the said lines being the boundary of Michael Hyam's 1280 acres on the South-East and on the West by a line extending Northward 40 chains on the East side by of land adjoining John Wheeler's 50 acres to the North-East corner thereof, against John Cullen's 300 acres, being the land provided to William Davis, deceased, on or before the date above mentioned, but now granted in accordance with the report on Case No. 1017, on the 15th December, 1841, by the Commissioner appointed under the Act of the Colonial Legislature 5, William 4th, No. 28, unto the said James Mackay Grey upon trust for William Davis, of Jamberoo, in district of Illawarra, Settler, I John Wright and Alexander King, both of Campbell-street, Sydney, and to their heirs, according to their respective rights of interest with all rights, etc. In trust as hereinbefore recited and to his heirs and assignees for ever at yearly quit rent at 2/- per annum from 1st January, 1827, unless the same should be rendered by the grantee his heirs or assignees within 20 years from that date.

Hamilton Hume was born at Toongabbie on 15th June, 1797. His father was Andrew Hume who was a commissariat's offier in that terrible convict centre. His mother was Elizabeth Kennedy. It was Sir Francis Rawdon, the Marquis of Hastings, who got Andrew Hume his job at Parramatta. Mrs. Andrew Hume, about 1802, became associated with the Parramatta Orphan School, and later became matron.

Hamilton Hume's association with Illawarra is not easily explained. He was by no means the first to discover the district lying to the east of the Five Islands, viz., "Red Point." Illawarra was a place of call for whale boats. and it was under the protection of the Governors long before he (Hume) accompanied Alexander Berry to the Shoalhaven River. In fact we do not hear much about his visits to Illawarra until 1823 when he was in charge of a number of sawyers who were engaged cutting cedar on the slopes north of Bulli. Many might be inclined to say that he was the first to enter upon the cedar industry in Illawarra were it not that the records show that licenses were issued to the bond and free to cut cedar in Illawarra on 1st July, 1819. Timber getting was carried on for at least ten years before that date according to the old sawyers.

For all we know to the contrary Hume may have been like many others, a dummy for Alexander Berry, as he never fulfilled the necessary conditions of occupation. Beyond the name "Hume Island" nothing is recorded of Hume.

In 1824 Hamilton Hume joined W. H. Hovel in an expedition of exploration. On October 3rd of that year Hovel met Hume at the latter's college in Appin. Hovel had three men, Thomas Boyd, William Bollard, and Thomas Smith. Hume had Claude Bossawa, Henry Angel, and James Fitgerald. Of those men the only one to settle in Illawarra was Henry Angel. He got two grants of land, and we have to the present day Angel's Creek, near Wollongong, and Angel Home, joining Sam Terry's grant, Mount Terry.

Many of our writers claim for Hamilton Hume wonderful powers, almost equal power with the native bee that is capable of winging home from any direction. He was different to the "bee" in this—he invariably had a guide—an aboriginal—when travelling.

Captain Richard Brooks took charge of the ship "Atlas" and quarrelled with Surgeon Jamieson. She was a convict ship, and 70 convicts died; it was said for want of proper accommodation caused by too much space being taken up by the Captain's merchandise. On August 21st, 1806, Captain Brooks was in charge of the ship "Alexander," 278 tons, and a crew of 24 men and 12 guns. In 1808 we note he was in charge of the ship Rose, Robert Campbell and Company part-owners. He had on board a cargo of fermented and spirituous liquors without having a port clearance from H.M. Customs, London. He had to return and face this charge before the Right Honourable Robert Stewart, Viscount Castlereagh, for the common crime of smuggling. The charge was laid by John Blaxland, a native of Kent, England, then a wealthy farmer and grazier in New South Wales. D'Arcy Wentworth was his friend, and taking advantage of Captain Richard Brooks' return to England was entrusted with the care of his son, Willliam Charles, who was then 17 years of age, to be educated in England. Captain Brooks continued in the trade, and was in Sydney in March, 1810, in command of the "Simon Cock," 184 tons; and again in September, 1811, in charge of the "Argo," 200 tons. Later on he purchased the brig "Spring," and made much money trading in cattle and merchandise, finally settling in Sydney in 1814.

Captain Richard Brooks.—"The Illawarra Lake," Woonawarry, is said to be the Aboriginals'—of Illawarra—name for the black swan. Hence we have Woonawarry Bay on the western shores of the said lake. It was here that Captain Brooks founded his homestead. It was a weatherboard house. The timber for it was sawn by Thomas Williamson on the land once owned by John Robins in the year 1816, adjacent to Abbott's old home. There was the homestead and a large number of out-buildings. Near where a native fig-tree was planted some years later, in about 1853, by Benjamin Marshall, Captain Brooks had two grants of land near the lake; his own grant of 600 acres and one of 1500 acres, which he obtained in the name of his son Richard Henry Brooks. Captain Brooks and William Browne had grants adjoining, and a stone wall was run out into the lake waters to mark the boundary there between the two estates. Captain Brooks' 600 acre grant was on what was called Brooks' Creek. In 1823 young Richard Henry Brooks, then a youth of about 11 or 12 years old, who was in delicate health, was sent down to Koonawarra to live under the care of a private tutor named Lloyd. The Captain sent a small boat down for the use of his son, described as a natty craft, with the name "Fewsuch" painted on her in bright letters.

A man named William Neal was the manager of Captain Brooks' Goonawarry estate, whilst his brother, John Neal, was general manager at Denham Court, near Campbelltown. James Neal, their father, obtained a grant of land on the north side of Brooks' Creek, and is said to have purchased other land from a man named Harper. In 1822 Edward J. Swan came to Illawarra and leased James Neal's farm, and his two sons, Edward and Henry, helped him to clear it, and thereon grew crops of wheat and maize. Their residence was a little further down the creek than the present dam. Therefore, the young Swans and young Brooks were next-door neighbours at Koonawarry; and, being about the same age, went out often on the lake boating together. About the year 1824 a man named Tom Barron, a sailor, arrived at the lake, and commenced fishing at the mouth of a small stream, afterwards called Barron's Creek. He was a net fisherman, caught and salted mullet, dried them in the sun, and sent them to Sydney via Red Point and Shellharbour, as opportunity offered. Barron sailed his own fishing craft to and from Sydney and the lake with fish in 1825, and on one occasion took a quantity of wheat grown by E. J. Swan on Neal's land, Barron and Swan being the only two occupants of the boat. They sailed through the entrance on the north side of Windarry Island. Barron carried on fishing till about the year 1828. Then the Swan family removed to a farm of 500 acres, which was a grant to George Brown, a cousin of George Brown, of Dapto. This property afterwards was sold by Brown (who was connected with the Commissiary Department in Sydney), to Dr. Alexander Osborne, R.N., who called it Daisy Bank.

From the western shores of the lake is to be seen the Bong Bong mountains, over which the old road passed to the then chief town in the County of Camden, the township of Bong Bong. This mountain is about 1700 feet high, and is formed of three bluffs on the main range, which with their rocky cliffs give the whole a very prominent appearance when viewed from the main South Coast road when passing through Dapto. The road to Bong Bong passes between the first and second of these cliffs, and the bluff as shown to the right, by one acquainted with the locality, is one of the best look-out points on the Coast range, taking in as it does a very extensive view of the north and south with a full view of Lake Illawarra and the ocean in front. The aboriginal name of this mountain is Wangarill (where the Swifts build.)

Captain Richard Brooks had a servant in his employ named John Cream. It was he, and an aboriginal, afterwards known as "Captain Brooks," who had discovered the track for cattle and other stock from Lake Illawarra to the Kangaroo Ground. It was known for years as "Jack Cream's" track. About September, 1846, the writer's father packed the first butter from the Kangaroo Ground, via Marshall Mount to Wollongong. Since then the old track was known as the "Butter Track." The old "Butter Track" was not an easy task to take on in 1846, yet men and women who never saw a bush like Illawarra was in those days, faced it with stout hearts. Children were brought on horseback over the old Butter Track to be christened in Wollongong. What of the times, and what of the men and women who lived the life the wild bush afforded? They are, generally speaking, forgotten!.

Mr. William Keevers was one of the famous Inniskillian Dragoons, and was present at the battle of Waterloo. He came to New South Wales and was appointed drill instructor to the first troop of mounted police which were placed in charge of Captain Francois Nicholas De Rossi, from 1824 to 1834. Captain Rossi was connected with the trial of Queen Caroline, wife of George IV., and his appointment carried with it that of superintendent of police, and comptroller of customs. William Keevers had a grant of 100 acres of land at West Dapto, Illawarra, which he eventually sold and came to reside with a numerous family in the vicinity of the Woodstock mills and brewery, Jamberoo. He died on 11th November, 1871, aged 84 years. Two days before his death he was presented before Earl Belmore, Governor of New South Wales.

The Mounted Police.—A Government order was issued from the Colonial's Secretary's Office on March 21st, 1826, as follows: "The Governor has been pleased to direct, re the mounted police. This force is specially charged with the suppression of convict outrages, and has been drawn from the infantry regiments serving in Sydney." It was first established in 1825 by Governor Brisbane, and began with two officers and thirteen troopers. In 1839 it had increased to 9 officers, 1 sergeant-major, 156 non-commissioned officers, with 136 horsemen and 20 foot-men. The officers were magistrates. All the others were subject to military law and discipline although appointed to serve as police. They were armed with sabre, carbine and horse pistols, and wore the dress of Inniskillian Dragoons, light horse uniform. The head-quarters division consisted of Commandant, the adjutant, and 25 men remained in Sydney. The others went to important centres and the road gangs.

The Coopers.—Mr. Robert Cooper, junr., of Juniper Hall, Sydney, died suddenly, leaving a widow, two sons, and three daughters. The sons were Robert and William Cooper: of the daughters, one married William Kendall, one married John Jewel Rutter, and the third went to England. Mr. Thomas Chapman married Mrs. Cooper, and lived in a storied house built by Carnell, for the term in which he was building Hartwell House, Kiama. Mr. Thomas Chapman had a brother, Mr. William Chapman, who had two sons, William and George Chapman. Mr. William Chapman, junr., went to Ulladulla and went in for breeding Shorthorn cattle. Mrs. Caird is a daughter of William Chapman, senr., and has the old home Hartwell, at Kiama. Mr. Thomas Chapman was married three times. No family. Died at Hartwell, Kiama, on 7th November, 1874, aged 78 years.

The Coopers, Robert, senr., and Robert, junr., were distillers in Sydney, and the Chapmans, Thomas and William, were largely interested in the sugar business. Both families were connected by marriage with the Hindmarsh, Kendall, Evans and Rutter families.

John Ritchie was an early settler in Jamberoo. He was born in Edinburgh, Scotland, in 1775. What he was before coming to N.S. Wales no one seemed to know, nor did any one find out from him the date of his arrival in Sydney. He must have been an early colonist, and was favourably known to the early Governors as he claimed the right to three blocks of land in Sydney, one in King-street, one in Druitt-street, and one in Kent-street. He married several times. His first wife died, leaving him with two children. His grant of land comprising 300 acres bears date 30th June, 1825. On 13th April, 1827, his brother, William Ritchie, obtained a grant of 60 acres near the same locality, called "Figtree Flat." Moses Brennan had 300 acres adjoining dated 29th August, 1834; and John Cullen got 300 acres 1st January, 1831.

John Ritchie occupied all that area under lease for years, on which he grazed cattle. His son, Johnny Ritchie, became an expert stockman and bushman. He used to deal in horses and cattle, using the Yalwal gully, south of the Shoalhaven river as a place for grazing his stock. John Ritchie lost his first wife by death prior to 1830. Then he remarried Mrs. Wright, who had three sons. The elder one, Thomas, married his stepfather's daughter, Martha Ritchie. Mrs. Wright had money when she married John Ritchie. Later on William Ritchie died or was killed, leaving by will his farm, Figtree Flat, to William Wright. A few years later the second wife of John Ritchie died, and he married another widow with two children. Their names were Fred and Nellie B. Morgan. Fred Morgan kept the Wheatsheaf Hotel opposite the old Toll-bar in George-street, Sydney. After the death of the third Mrs. Ritchie, John Ritchie remarried a young woman, who was the mother of George Ritchie and two girls, one of whom became Mrs. Jabez Smith. Johnny Ritchie eventually took a job of stockman for Henry Osborne at Point Station on the Murrumbidgee river, and never looked back at Illawarra. His half-brother Georgie Ritchie, went to Midkin Station, Morce. Then, we find that John Ritchie after having lived to see his station property grow out of the wild bush into a prosperous settlement and pass out of not only his possession, but of his descendants; and, many of those who knew him well said: "He lost his property through no fault of his own making." He died in 1860, aged 85 years.

From information received from the old Jamberoo settlers one might venture the opinion that John Ritchie and John G. Collins both belonged to the same regiment, the 13th Dragoon Guards. Captain J. G. Collins belonged to that regiment and, we learn that in 1832 he was at Ritchie's Station, Jamberoo, buying horses for India. Captain Collins in the following year was commissioned by Captain Thomas Frederick Hart, of the Light Dragoon 2nd Life Guards and 94th Regiment, to come to Ritchie's Station, Jamberoo, and establish there, on a gigantic scale, a village on a 99 years' lease. This Collins did, and called the place Woodstock, after a village in England.

This was one of the most ambitious undertakings entered upon up to that date in N.S. Wales, as it was backed up with capital to the amount of £82,000. Money was spent freely, and soon absorbed men of all classes and callings. A saw-mill, a flour-mill, and a brewery, the Kent brewery. Much of the power came from a water-wheel. A water-course was cut into the works from the Minnamurra river. Large boilers and engines came from sea and land from Sydney. Brick-making, and charcoal-burning were carried on in the vicinity. Horse-teams and bullock-teams did the hauling between the primitive ports of Wollongong, Shellharbour, and Kiama, along roads of the most difficult nature. The early roads went up and down the hills, no money available for side-cuttings or zig-zagging to save bullock or horse-power. True co-operation in those days, when they came to hills, one teamster unhooked his bullocks and helped to haul the load to the top. Timber was hauled out of gullies and deep ravines in the same way.

The flour mill at Woodstock, Jamberoo, was on a large scale for the period. It was presided over by a good miller named Henry Hughes, and wheat was brought from as far south as Gerringong in the forties, and from Shellharbour to be ground into flour. No roads in those days, only cedar tracks. Bullocks, with a set of harness on the one chap who worked in shafts, collar and hames, the collar turned upside down. Seven and nine bullocks in each team. The dray was like an ordinary horse dray—only on a much larger scale. It took three days to travel from Gerringong to Woodstock mill and back. As the land was cleared more wheat was grown—60 bushels per acre. Three other small flour mills were erected. One on Griffiths' Hill (now Pike's Hill, Kiama), and one at Blay's Creek towards Gerringong. A few years later, one was erected by John Sharpe at Bush Bank, Kiama. John Sharpe afterwards erected a large mill in the town of Kiama, and William Wilson erected a flour mill at the water's edge, Shellharbour. Of all those flour mills nothing remains but two stone buildings, one at Bush Bank, Kiama, and one at Shellharbour. Of the Woodstock mills and brewery nothing remains but the mill races which supplied the water power for the water-wheel. The water-wheel and machinery were built up under the supervision of George Atkinson. He was brought from Tasmania for this purpose where he had some experience in the convict settlement of Van Diemen's Land. He settled in Kiama after a time, and established an orchard, in which he was buried.

The first church erected south of Wollongong, the old R.C. Church at Jamberoo, by voluntary labour from the Woodstock mills. Small settlers were pouring in then, and in a few years' time a village was formed and named Jamberoo, on a portion of a grant of 50 acres to William Davis.

Mr. Alexander Macleay was born June 24th, 1767, and was the eldest son of Mr. William Macleay, of Caithness, Scotland. At the age of 58 he was selected by Earl Bathurst for the position of Colonial Secretary for New South Wales. He resigned in 1837, when in his 70th year. Mr. William Sharp Macleay was a son of Mr. Alexander Macleay, and was born in London, July 21st, 1792. Mr. George Macleay was probably a nephew of Mr. Alexander Macleay. He (Alexander Macleay) died, the result of a carriage accident 19th July, 1848, in his 31st year. He established the Croobar Estate, Ulladulla, in the year 1828. His A.M.L. cattle were good, resembling the Ayrshire, yet they were larger, and more pronounced in type than the Ayrshire. In the early fifties of last century Messrs John Marks, of Terragong, Jamberoo, and Henry Grey, of Gerringong, purchased exceptionally fine dairy cows from Macleay's Ulladulla Estate.

We learn from the Sydney "Gazette" of 12th February, 1824, that Captain Watson, of the ship Aquilar, imported a fine bull and cow of the Norman breed. These animals have been over and over again stated to have been the foundation animals of the Macleay breed. Be it as it may the Macleay cattle were in the mid-sixties quite distinct in type and character from either the McKay or Robb Ayrshire.

At the Kiama Show of 1857 the late Mr. Henry Grey won 1st prize with a Macleay-bred cow. From that cow the Love and Moses families got foundation stock. To name but two bulls will suffice here — "Curly" and "Cardigan," as both figure in the catalogue of Messrs. Fraser's and Morton's Greystaine, pure milking Short-horn cattle sale, April 21st, 1906, lot 102.

The Hindmarsh Family consisted of Messrs. Michael, George, and Miss Hindmarsh. They were old colonists, and were born at Anakie, Northumberland, England, and on arriving in New South Wales, about 1825, settled in Sydney. Mr. Geo. and Miss Hindmarsh remained in Sydney several years. Mr. Michael Hindmarsh, who was born on 1st of January, 1800, went out Campbelltown way before he came to Illawarra. When he came to Illawarra he stayed with Mr. George Tate at Spring Hill, near Wollongong, where he gained much knowledge of the district from the old sawyers. He then purchased 640 acres at Gerringong at 5/- per acre, and his request was granted by Governor Darling, which was the rule then.

He married in Parramatta a Miss Rutter, and settled at "Alne Bank," Gerringong, and commenced clearing his land by means of free convict labour, the custom at that time. And we soon learn of him as a grower of maize and potatoes, and a raiser of pigs, which, in due time, were converted into salted pork packed in casks and sold to shipping men. Cedar and other timbers were plentiful, and much trade was carried on in this way. Mr. Hindmarsh's first born son, Mr. George Hindmarsh, junr. (born in 1828), was born in Campbelltown, and was brought back by his mother overland to Gerringong on horseback. The shipping trade and the general development of Kiama induced Mr. George and Miss Hindmarsh to come and settle in the town. Mr. George Hindmarsh owned a fast sailing ship called "The Vision," William Geoghegan, skipper. During one of her many trips to Sydney Mr. Hindmarsh was on board. A storm arose. Mr. Hindmarsh got very sick, and insisted on going in to Kiama, against the protests of the old skipper. Result: "The Vision" was wrecked, and all hands got safely ashore. Mr. Hindmarsh then purchased the "Charles Webb." He continued in the trade and in other forms of business until his death in 29th February, 1871, aged 75 years. Miss Hindmarsh took up school teaching; had a ladies' school in Kiama, where many of the early settlers' daughters received their scholastic training.

Returning to Mr. Michael Hindmarsh. He left Gerringong in 1832 and took a milk run in Campbelltown. He used "Glenlee" cattle, and in time had a herd at Gerringong, where he commenced dairying. He and his wife were fortunate, had 14 children of the marriage, 2 died young, 12 have lived to be men and women. He died suddenly 25th January, 1867.

Mr. Murtock Farraher came from the County Mayo, Ireland. Early in the history of Illawarra. He settled in Bulli where Mr. John Farraher was born in 1826. In the course of a little while the home was established at Bellambi, a picturesque spot, and may be easily located by persons travelling by either road or train through Illawarra. The old couple acquired much land in the Illawarra district which passed into the hands of their sons. Mr. Thomas Farraher settled at Stoney Creek, Jamberoo, James and Patrick settled at Bulli, Denis settled on the north side of Terragong Swamp, Shellharbour, and John settled at Holly Mount, Kiama, and eventually went to Candelo, Bega.

Mr. John Farraher was possibly better known than any member of the family owing to the fact that he was fond of honest horse racing, and owned and bred several good horses including the celebrated race horse and sire, "Trump Card." He became a breeder of Jersey cattle, and made more out of them than the majority of men have done. His judgment in getting possession of "Lucius," imported by the Messrs. Tooth, added to his fame as a breeder.

Michael Hyam.—Michael Hyam was born in London in 1799, and arrived in Sydney in 1827 with a capital of £2000, and received a grant of 640 acres at Lochinvar, Hunter River. He then heard of the cedar lands of Illawarra and obtained a grant of 1280 acres at Jamberoo and called it Sarah's Valley, after his people in the Land of Goshen. He got married in Sydney in 1833, and arrived in Jamberoo a few months later with about 30 convicts and commenced clearing his land, cutting whatever cedar was on it and sending it to Sydney via Kiama. He built a store and public house, established a tannery, and in a sense, went to work on a large scale. The road to Kiama was then a cedar track. Hyam's establishment was adjacent to where Hugh Colley's house stood, a little more to the east. The road from Ritchie's Station passed round the south side of William Wright's 60 acres grant, and passed through Hyam's Estate, keeping the same route as the present road through a portion of Malcolm Campbell's 500 acres until it reached the eastern bank of Fountaindale Creek, where it turned south and east, passing up the hill to the site of Henry Spinks' house. A large figtree stood there in those days and formed a camping ground for the teamsters. Called by the blacks Culwulla, whisky, fresh as mountain dew, was to be had there at all times. From Culwulla the track passed down into Hughes and Hosking's grant past the site of the Jerrara School, and up an easy incline till it reached Wright's Creek, called after John Wright, a publican in Campbell Street, Sydney, near the present homestead of Mr. George Grey, called "Greyleigh." This road was called the old Longbrush road, and followed the ridge down to the boat harbour at Kiama, where the old fig tree stands. That road was used until about 1839, when Mr. Gerard Irving, who was placed over a gang of convicts, had formed a road from Hyam's Station direct to Kiama. Two houses on wheels used by the chained gangs on the road from Wollongong to Hyam's were taken over by Gerard Irvine, and one of them was left on the eastern bank of Fountaindale Creek, and occupied by old Poll Rogers for years. The other was sold to a settler. The road formed by Irvine and his gang of convicts passed through the properties of Malcolm Campbell, James Marks, Dr. Thomas Perrott, and James Robb's Riversdale Estate. It passed over Spring Hill, and into the Kiama township reserve over Griffith's Hill, and about five chains to the left of Terralong Street to the site of the public school to the north west of the figtree. A gaol and the harbour store stood on the bank above high-water mark. The old gaol, with a gumtree for a triangle, was ordered to be taken away by Captain Perry, after some score or more convicts had been flogged, tied to the gumtree, and a slab lockup erected near the site of the present courthouse. The old gaol was built of red stone, quarried on the spot. A man named Conroy was in charge of the station. A warder named Gates and a matron named Rogers attended to the wants of the prisoners who were sent there in 1835 and 1837. The only lawyer in those days in Kiama was David Smith, who kept the "Traveller's Rest" Hotel at a spot now occupied by the yards adjoining the railway sheds.

Michael Hyam prospered in Jamberoo, and cut cedar away to the range and had it hauled by teams to Kiama. He also employed shoemakers and cobblers. His tannery was in what is known to-day as Minnamurra Lane, where Martin Piermont, known in literary circles as Martin the Tanner, presided over other workmen. In 1844 Hyam had formed a racecourse which Martin the Tanner immortalised in verse.

Michael Hyam sold out his Sarah's Valley property to Captain William Wilson for £7000, and took his passage for England expecting to have all the purchase money paid over before leaving Sydney. Heavy storms set in and Wilson lost several boats, and had to forfeit the deposit to Hyam, and Hyam forfeited his passage money, and the ship he was going home in was lost at sea with all hands, and Hyam then considered he was a lucky man. He then got into business transactions with Parson Meares, and it is evident these transactions were not to his liking, as he immediately sold out to Robert Owen, and came in to Kiama and lived in a storied house opposite the storm-bay beach in Manning Street. He was then negotiating with a storekeeper in Gundagai for the purchase of a store, and would have purchased it but for the advice he received from Dr. Menzies, of Jamberoo. Hyam was once more lucky as the store with its contents, inmates and goods were lost forever in the great Gundagai flood. In 1847 Michael Hyam and his family left for the Shoalhaven district. Prior to leaving for the Shoalhaven district, during the years that Martin the Tanner was poet laureate of Jamberoo, Michael Hyam had a score of sawyers and teamsters working in the vicinity of Flash Bob's Flat collecting cedar. He followed up racing, and occasionally made matches. Raced on the flat £50 aside, Hyam's Jerry and Wright's Pedro, Hyam won, with young Burke in the saddle. When he left Jamberoo and went to live in Kiama, he had another match £50 aside—Hyam's Corinthian Kate and Dr. Kenneth Mackenzie's Duke, on the Kiama course. Hyam lost. Burke again in the saddle. This Burke family lived in Jamberoo for many years, drifted away to Sydney, then went up to Murrurundi to take charge of a station, at which place the whole family, with one exception, was murdered by the blacks. In 1846, Michael Hyam went to Dapto to race. The chief event was contested between three noted horses—Brown's "Grey," Kennedy's "Grey," and Hyam's "Jerry." Result—Hyam 1st, Kennedy 2nd, and Brown 3rd. The result was not considered final, and there was much talk of another match. No money, however, changed hands. In 1846 the Hyam Estate, "Sarah's Valley," was purchased by Mr. Robert Owen, who cut it up into farms, and

formed the village of Jamberoo. The chief part of the estate was purchased by the Howard family. Hence we had the Howard's Flats. These flats were later on sold to the Messrs. Colley, and the property has remained in possession of that family since that date.

Needless to say, Michael Hyam experienced much of what may be termed the early, rough bush life in Jamberoo, and his dealings with the convicts brought him into contact with men whose past life had been more or less shady, and it might become a habit with him to suspect all men. His name, however, does not often appear in the records. Yet, when it did, he seems to have finished the career of those he sent back to the authorities. For instance, a convict named Growner stole his grey stallion out of the stable at Jamberoo, and was arrested in Wollongong. Growner was sent to Norfolk Island, which really meant death in those days. Yet another example. When James Modie Marks kept the Steampacket Hotel, Market Wharf, Sydney, in 1834, he (Marks) got hold of 50 acres of land adjacent to Terragong Swamp, and purchased the adjoining 50 acres from an old hand named Walker at 5/- per acre. He (Marks) sent down two ex-convicts to look after his interests. At that time an old soldier named Duke who had got into trouble for brewing whisky near the Argyle Cut, Sydney, had an orchard on the south-east corner of Marks' 50 acres, and was living in this garden. Things moved on slowly until early in the year 1836. James Marks' two ex-convicts, Patrick Fox and John McNamee, were living together in a hut in the north-west corner of the 50-acre grant, right at the edge of the swamp, when one morning Patrick Fox was found murdered in the hut. McNamee was at once placed under arrest. He, however, was able to show that on that identical night he was at a friend's place at James Mackay Grey's homestead, four miles away in a straight line. McNamee was discharged, and, on 5th April, 1836, the Government offered "£200 reward for the conviction of some person or persons unknown who murdered Patrick Fox, in the house of Mr. James Marks, near Kiama, where he had been employed as overseer." It so happened that another ex-convict named John Tobin called at Hyam's Hotel, Sarah's Valley, and told Michael Hyam of the murder. Hyam at once suspected him, and laid information against Tobin, who was arrested and hanged. He, Tobin, was attended by Rev. Father Therry, and he stood calmly on the scaffold and protested before God his innocence of the crime.

Exors. of late WM. H. COOK'S REGISTERED DAIRY CATTLE.
Glendalough, Illawarra.

ADMIRAL BLOOMFIELD OF GLENDALOUGH.

BELLS OF GLENDALOUGH.

PEARL OF GLENDALOUGH.

CHERRY II OF GLENDALOUGH.

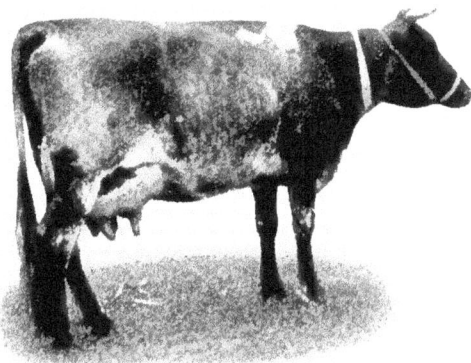

GEM OF GLENDALOUGH.

FUCHSIA OF GLENDALOUGH.

This event created a terrible sensation at the time, and the hanging of John Tobin was resented on all sides. The population of Jamberoo continued to increase. A considerable number of settlers who had taken advantage of grants of from 50 to 100 acres given by the early Governors to boys and girls born in New South Wales, took up land in the vicinity of Hyam and Ritchie's grants, and commenced growing wheat. Houses were few, huts were plentiful. Dr. Robert Menzies purchased a grant, built a good house on it, and combined farming with his medical practice.

Alexander Stewart was 85 years old at the time of his death, having arrived in Wollongong in 1828. Being a resident of 67 years, his experience of old times was often sought by those in search of information about old Illawarra. He said on one occasion: "There were only 10 women and 16 children between Bulli and Jamberoo at the time of my arrival. The land between Crown-street and Tom Thumb Lagoon was densely covered with swamp oaks, and was all Government land. In 1828, going south from Crown-street, Wollongong, was a hut upon Edmond Burke's land, in which Burke himself lived. Sterling Jones' land came next. Next place was George Tate's Spring Hill. Heron farm was a Crown grant, and was the property of Thomas Barrett, sen." Beyond this we need not follow Alexander Stewart.

Gerringong.—The early pioneers of this locality form an interesting chapter in our history of its own in Illawarra. A Sydney merchant named Thomas Hyndes, was a friend of Alexander Berry and John Wright, the brewer of Sydney. Hyndes was, among other things, a timber merchant. He had the right with Aspinall and Brown to cut timber. Their holdings were originally leaseholds, which they converted into real property prior to selling to Berry and Wollstonecroft about the year 1836. A soldier named Antony Finn was placed in charge of the sawyers to keep order. He had a grant of land at Broughton Vale known as the little meadow. Finn got the credit of having captured Broger, the outlaw, after which Broger's Creek (now Harper's Creek) in the Kangaroo Valley is named.

Thomas Hyndes owned "Cockmaleg" Forest, and it was his intention to form a village there and name the site "Hyndeston." Geering, who was John Wright's brewer, used to trade with Hyndes, hence we have Geering Bay, from which Gerringong has been evoluted. The original name of the locality was Jaron Gong. The first settlers were William Smith and a man named Googley, who held a lease of what is now Miller's Flats, at about two shillings and sixpence per 100 acres. Smith was at one time overseer of convicts at Wollongong. He afterwards converted the property into a freehold about 1829 at 5/- per acre. Lieutenant Thomas Campbell had 1280 acres as a grant from the Crown on the northern boundary of Smith's land, Michael Hindmarsh taking up the Alne Bank Estate in 1828, 640 acres at 5/- per acre, lying on the western boundary of Smith's grant. These properties were termed grants, although purchased at the upset price from the Crown, for the reason that the Governor had to give his sanction just the same as if they were granted by him. On Smith's land there was much swamp. Hindmarsh's land was well timbered. A large figtree on the hill was the guide for skippers to steer into Geering Bay. Between the years 1828 and 1832 Michael Hindmarsh devoted his attention to the timber trade. He employed a number of convicts and cut the timber, mostly cedar, in saw-pits. About 1832 he decided to take up dairying, purchased a number of cows from the Glenlee herd, but found the business was not profitable, so he decided to go to Campbelltown (where he spent some time before returning to Illawarra) and started a milk run. In 1835 James Mackay Grey purchased the interests of his brother-in-law, Lieutenant Campbell, and named the estate "Omega." He considered it the last settlement south of Sydney. Michael Hindmarsh then returned to Alne Bank and went in for maize growing and pig raising, maize always commanding a good price. The pigs were not killed until they would reach 300 or 400lb. in weight, then the pork, when salted and placed in casks, found a ready market among the shipping agents. Potato and tobacco growing was also followed with success. The brothers Rainey went in for potato growing on portion of Smith's land.

A cobbler named Staypleton occupied a hut on the south-east corner of Smith's land, and the settlement was completed by the arrival of Robert Miller and his family. Robert Miller sold his farm at Terragong to Dr. Thomas Montgomery Perrott, and purchased William Smith's interests. Then for many years Michael Hindmarsh, James Mackay Grey, and Robert Miller, together with their respective families, carried on successfully farming and dairying pursuits. The Hindmarsh families became horse and cattle breeders, introducing draught and coaching stallions into the district, and Durham bulls and heifers at very high prices, not that the farming population benefited thereby, but lack of judgment was not lack of enterprise in those families. From the year 1845 until 1855 the clearing lease system brought into the Gerringong portion of Illawarra many valuable families who left their footprints on the soil.

The Hindmarsh and Miller families helped to develop that part of Illawarra by the manner in which they helped to develop their own personal interests. Maize, potatoes, tobacco, wheat and barley were largely grown and hauled by their teams to the sea port at Kiama, and the Woodstock mills and brewery. The cedar and pork trade was carried on also; many hundreds of barrels of salt pork were sent out to the trading ships along the coast.

The old Illawarra A. & H. Society, and later on the Kiama A. & H. Society, had for founders Messrs. James Mackay Grey, Michael Hindmarsh, and Robert Miller, whose estates joined at a point a short distance from the present site of the present railway siding, Omega.

James Robb, Riversdale, Kiama, was born in Perthshire, Scotland, in 1805 and came to Sydney, New South Wales, about the year 1828, and established himself as a builder and contractor in Bathurst Street. In 1830 he was the architect for a number of buildings in Sydney. The Sydney "Gazette" of 21st September, 1830, has the following notice:—"Court of Claims—Case No. 371, James Robb, of Bathurst Street, builder, by his attorney, John Smith, 1280 acres, County of Camden, at Kiama, Illawarra. commencing at the north-west corner of Cowell's farm, on the west by the swamp called Terragong, on the north by part swamp and Minnamurra River, to the north-west corner of Cowell's farm. This land was located by an order of Governor Darling, dated 26th October, 1829, in favour of William John Collis, who, it is alleged, sold to William MacDonald, who sold to Peter Haydon, who sold to Charles Coates Fenton, who died intestate, and whose eldest brother and heir at law, Michael Fenton, sold to claimant."

James Robb did not come to live on this property for several years after he became possessed of it. He built a storied brick house to the east of the Kiama public school which was occupied by an officer who was in charge of the barracks in Kiama; one of the very early constables named Sutherland also lived in

it. The Riversdale Estate was, in the meantime, denuded of its cedar which, cut on sawpits, and hauled by bullocks to the boat harbour in Kiama and despatched on by boat to James Robb in Sydney. About 1840 James Robb decided to build at Riversdale and to establish an orchard and vineyard. He appointed Nicholas Craig, an expert gardener who had come to New South Wales with a letter of introduction from Sir William Molesworth to James Macarthur, of Camden, in 1839.

In 1843 George Grey, then living in Wollongong, leased 1000 acres of the Riversdale Estate from James Robb with the view of settling a number of emigrants, relations and acquaintances of his own from the County Fermanagh, Ireland. In this respect George Grey was very successful. After the discovery of gold in New South Wales labour became very scarce, and in order to meet the difficulties that arose, about a dozen German emigrants were introduced and carried out their engagement satisfactorily At one period of the development of dairying on the portion leased by George Grey there were 22 families resided on that area now occupied by six. In March, 1861, Mr. James Robb landed in Kiama from Scotland a noted Ayrshire bull and two fine Ayrshire cows. The name of the bull was "The Duke of Argyll," and was highly prized by dairy farmers. All the papers connected with this importation were burned in the Riversdale house fire.

When Mr. Robb landed his cattle in Illawarra, March, 1861, consisting of one bull and two cows, one cow was just at calving point. When she calved her calf was stolen and another substituted. Although one bull calf was taken and another bull calf put with its dam, it was not by any means a fair exchange. The calf taken away was a superior animal, the one left an inferior one. In the course of a few years much comment was made regarding this inferior bull's progeny which in some quarters gave Robb's Ayrshires a bad reputation. Even the columns of the Press became in time filled with long letters condemning the Ayrshires. Those, however, who got the "Duke of Argyll" blood always swore by them. Since then the secret was given up, and the man who stole the calf admitted having done so to a member of the Robb family. "Let the dead past bury the past."

The leaseholders on Riversdale were 24— George Grey, Henry Grey, William Grey, William Vance, Joseph Vance, James Hetherington, John Hetherington, Christy Hetherington, Thomas Wilson, James Irvine, Gerard Irvine, James Irving, D. Lindsay, Donald Robinson, Alexander Robinson, Edward Bryant, John Francis, John McClelland, Robert McClelland, William Burless, Lanty Nethery, John Noble, Thomas Kent, Mrs Martin.

Henry Osborne was born in County Tyrone, Ireland, on 8th February, 1803—a son of Archie Osborne, of Dairaseer, Tyrone, and was the youngest of ten children, three of whom emigrated to New South Wales. Henry Osborne arrived 9th May, 1829, and gained a little colonial experience and advice from Captain Thompson, of Liverpool, New South Wales, prior to settling on a grant of land which he obtained from the Crown in Illawarra, containing 2560 acres, which entitled him to receive from the Government from twenty to thirty free labourers. He called his estate Marshall Mount (after his wife's maiden name, who was a Miss Marshall), and set to work, as all pioneers had to do in those days who wished to succeed. He went in for dairying, and obtained his first cattle from William Howe, of Glenlee, Campbelltown, and branded their produce HO. There was much of the land open forest, and good for grazing, where young cattle could be raised. The same condition prevailed in other centres, and cattle became plentiful in the course of a few years. The spirit of speculation quickly asserted itself in his nature. He saw broad acres, and delighted in open space cattle dealing. On 2nd December, 1839, he started from Dapto, Illawarra, with a few stockmen, comprising one free settler, three convicts, and three aboriginals, with a mob of cattle for South Australia. He was four months on the journey, and was very fortunate in striking a good market. Sir George Grey, writing of these overlanders, said: "The overlanders are, nearly all of them, in the prime of life, and their occupation is to carry out large herds of stock from one market to another. They have overcome difficulties of no ordinary kind, which have made the more timid-hearted quail and relinquish these enterprises, in which many were engaged, whilst the resolute and undaunted have persevered, and the reward they have obtained in wealth, self-confidence in difficulties and danger, together with a fund of accurate information in many interesting points, is considerable. Hence almost every overlander you meet is a remarkable man." He continued his cattle-dealing enterprises. No mob of cattle was either too big nor too small for his own

personal inspection. About 1840 he began to acquire large holdings inland, so as to move his stock into convenient centres, and set about improving the quality of his herds. He gave a free exhibition of his imported cattle in the Market Square, Wollongong, in October, 1843, which laid the foundation of our present-time A. & H. Societies in Australia.

A volume could be devoted to the life and times of Henry Osborne. The writer, from information received first hand from my father during his ten years' close association with Henry Osborne, to wit, from 1841 to 1852, could supply a few score of pages. To sum the man up: Had he lived the allotted span of life, namely, "three score years and ten," he would have been by far the richest man that ever settled in Australia, as he was naturally very clever, keen, and immensely energetic, and, above all, he was successful. Every act of his life, all his dealings and transactions, were for himself. He died at Marshall Mount, Illawarra, during the year 1859, aged 56 years. He passed out at a time when his energy would have been worth much to his family. The Osborne Memorial Church at Dapto stands as a monument to his memory. His possessions in Illawarra were considerable at the time of his death. He had secured both Captain Brooks' and Mr. William Browne's grants at Lake Illawarra and The Elyard grant (Avondale) at West Dapto. He was largely interested in coal lands in Illawarra and elsewhere. May one add: It took an act of Parliament to deprive him of much of the land on which the township of West Maitland stands. He had secured several large cattle stations inland, and was in a large way at the time of his death, caused by an internal growth.

In 1841 Mr. Henry Osborne imported a cow called "Brutus." She was a large-framed roan Durham, produced twins twice (once a pair of white bulls). He refused £700 for her in 1843 when on exhibition in Wollongong. In 1843 he imported two bulls, "Duke" and "Marquis." "Duke" was a roan Durham of great quality, and "Marquis" was a blood-red—Sussex—an animal of striking appearance with hooped horns.

In 1844 he (Mr. Osborne) imported two cows, "Blossom" and "Daisy." "Blossom" was a red and white spotted cow; "Daisy" was a light roan cow.

The ship "La Hogue" arrived in Sydney with a consignment of cattle for, possibly, various owners, which included Durham bulls and cows and a two-years-old draught Entire horse. As Mr. Osborne did import a horse of that description from England, we may reasonably infer that it was the ship "La Hogue" that brought the cow "Charlotte" and her daughter to New South Wales. After the arrival of the ship "La Hogue" there were for sale at the wharf, Sydney, one bull 2 years and 3 months old, one bull 2 years old, and one bull 4 years old.

To attempt to describe the transactions in cattle as carried out year in and year out by Messrs. Johnston, Hughes and Osborne in Illawarra, without touching upon their outside station business, would be as futile as it was gigantic. They each and all purchased and sold cattle in hundreds. Mr. Henry Osborne, with whose cattle transactions I am familiar, owing to my father being in his confidence for many years, bought cattle as far north as New England and as far south as the border of the Murray. In this way he had to import for stud purposes but few cattle. He could at any time take advantage of the times and buy either imported cattle or the progeny of imported cattle at a quarter the price it cost to import or even breed them. In this way he obtained several very valuable imported bulls and cows, whose names and pedigrees are lost to us owing to his papers being mislaid prior to his death.

For some years there was a little rivalry between Mr. Henry Osborne and his neighbour, Mr. David Johnston, as the old Illawarra A. & H. Society shows, as will be seen by the old records—not that they were directly interested in these competitions on all occasion. The stock they bred drifted among the settlers, and they as breeders were anxious to see the animals they bred coming to the fore. In these contests the descendants of cattle bred in Campbelltown by Mr. William Howe, and at Bringelly by the J. Terry Hughes Estate, came in for the show honors, which gave a healthy stimulant to the breeding of high-class cattle.

The Somerville family settled at Dapto in 1840-41, and commenced dairying on the west bank of Mullet Creek, and while being engaged in this business the founder of the family (Mr. George Somerville) secured the lease of a run near Lake Illawarra. During the drought of 1849 Mr. Henry Osborne arranged to send his stud cows to the Lake farm, and when the drought broke he went in person to take the cattle away. He insisted on old Mr. Somerville accepting the present of a white bull calf in return for the obligement. This white bull calf was called "Major." The Somervilles continued dairying on the bank of Mullet Creek until the year 1856, when the father and eldest son, Robert, sold out and removed to Bulli, where they became interested in coal-mining industry.

It will be seen that prior to his death Mr. H. Osborne had quite a number of pure-bred cattle on hand at Marshall Mount, Illawarra. These animals had been bred for station supply. He was constantly sending drafts of young stud bulls inland. He, therefore, seldom sold any bulls locally. When he desired he could command big prices. He did not believe in using pure-bred cattle for dairying purposes. His dairy herds were at all times a mixed quantity, some very fine animals of choice colours, but, generally speaking, they were of every variety of colour. Dairy quality is what he aimed at, and he certainly got it.

His first purchases were from Mr. William Howe's famous Glenlee herd. He secured early in the forties three imported bulls, one a strawberry-Durham; another was a blood-red bull with hooped horns. The late Mr. Gabriel Timbs described this bull as being "very like a Devon, yet he was much bigger than a Devon." This bull may have been a red-hooped horned Sussex. The third bull was a large red and white spotted bull, with high commanding horns, an old type Ayrshire bull. The progeny of this spotted bull were highly prized in Illawarra and in the Kangaroo Ground. His favourite cow was the celebrated roan cow "Brutus." She was said to be the best cow ever seen in Illawarra.

He made, as just stated, other important purchases, and when he joined the Australian Importation Company he had at his command the best cattle available in Great Britain and Ireland. After the sale of the Osborne stud herd in 1860, Mr. Alex. Osborne took charge at Marshall Mount, Illawarra for a few years. He, however, did not trouble about the business very much—he merely used the H.O. brand, and used the name, and lived on his father's reputation.

Late in the sixties we find that Messrs Ben and Alex. Osborne were carrying on dairy-cattle breeding in the Kangaroo Ground. They divided the lots equally, Ben's brand was B.H.O., and Alex.'s brand A.H.O. Henry Osborne, a brother, settled at Avondale, Illawarra; his brand was H.H.O. There were several brothers who settled elsewhere in New South Wales. Marshall Mount was subdivided and sold in 1872, and so passed out one of the finest dairying centres in Australia.

HUGH DUDGEON & SON, Hill View Stud, Jamberoo.

CHARMER.

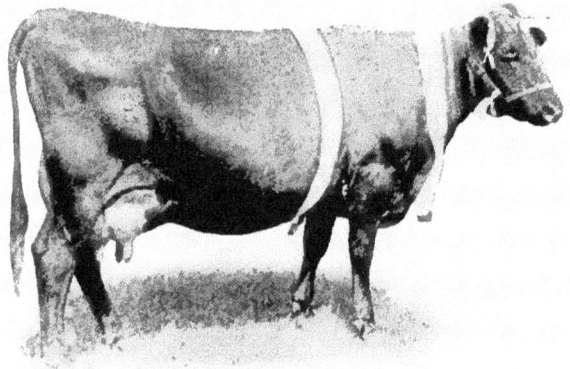

FUSSY II OF HILLVIEW (2).

FUSSY III OF HILLVIEW (No. 542, I.D.C.H.B.).

FUSSY IV OF HILLVIEW (No. 541, I.D.C.H.B.).

FUSSY VI OF HILLVIEW (No. 543, I.D.C.H.B.) (4).

LADY JEAN OF HILLVIEW (No. 99, I.D.C.H.B.).

HUGH DUDGEON & SON, Hill View Stud, Jamberoo.

LOVELY OF HILLVIEW (No. 68, I.D.C.H.B.).

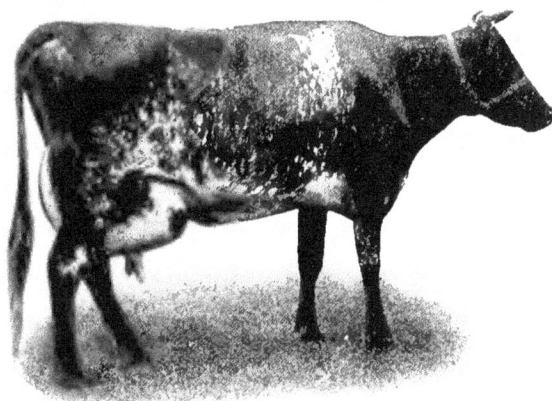

LADY MAY OF HILLVIEW (No. 289, I.D.C.H.B.).

MAYFLOWER OF HILLVIEW (No. 554, I.D.C.H.B.).

PRINCESS OF HILLVIEW (5) (No. 564, I.D.C.H.B.).

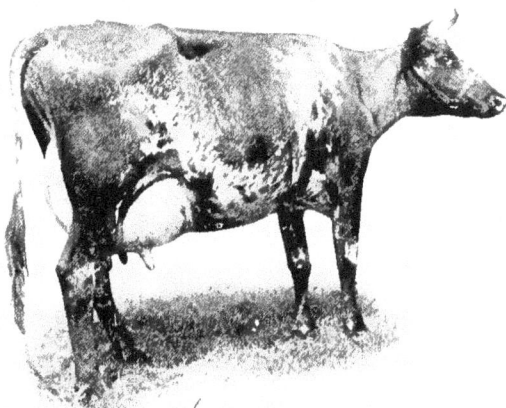

EMMA II OF HILLVIEW (No. 341, I.D.C.H.B.).

VIOLET OF HILLVIEW (No. 73, I.D.C.H.B.).

Dr. John Osborne made three trips to New South Wales as Superintendent of Convicts on board transports. In 1836 he purchased 300 acres, through Charles Throsby Smith, and called it "Garden Hill." He let it on clearing lease terms. Like Smith's grant, it became part of the township of Wollongong.

Dr. Alexander Osborne was also a Superintendent of Convicts. Both belonged previously to the Royal Navy. Alexander Osborne purchased 300 acres from William Brown, a cousin of George Brown, of Dapto. He became a very useful citizen, and resided on his farm, Daisy Bank. He was a prominent public man for some years. Daisy Bank has been in the possession of the Marshall family for a long period of years.

Captain Robert Marsh Westmacott was A.D.C. to Governor Sir Richard Bourke, who arrived in New South Wales in 1831. In 1834 Governor Bourke visited Illawarra and shortly afterwards Captain Westmacott settled on a small farm in the vicinity of Bulli. He went in for fruit growing and kept a few racehorses. He discovered a path up the range which became known as "Westmacott's Pass." He was the first secretary, of, perhaps, the first Agricultural and Horticultural Society as we understand such institutions in New South Wales. He only remained a few years in Illawarra, and passed on to Sydney.

Mr. George Brown, of Dapto, was born in Fifeshire, Scotland, on 21st November, 1794, and arrived when a young man in New South Wales, and after a time got married and opened a hotel at Liverpool. He succeeded in getting a grant of 300 acres of land at Dapto, Illawarra, where he settled in 1829. About 1832 he placed a man in charge of his farm at Dapto, and he opened a public house, "The Ship Inn," on a fifty acre grant of land to Edmond Bourke. His hotel stood on the flat, due south of the sites of the Commercial and Royal Alfred Hotels in Wollongong. While he was there Governor Bourke visited Wollongong, and sent Sir Thomas Mitchell down to survey a road from about the foot of Mount Kurd to James Mackay Grey's Estate, Omega, Gerringong. Between Mr. George Brown and Mr. M. Grey the money granted for this road was largely absorbed. They had the use of convict labour. Mr. Grey worked his contract from Dr. Thomas Foster's Curraghmore Estate to a gully on the northern side of Mount Pleasant. This road was only proclaimed to where the road formed by similar labour branched off at

H

Hyam's public house for Kiama. Going back to Mr. Brown, he had a cousin named William Brown, who was in the commissariat department, Sydney, who also got a grant of 300 acres at Dapto, Illawarra, which he sold to Dr. Alexander Osborne. Dr. Osborne called it Daisy Bank, and carried on farming there for years. George Brown in the meantime grew tired of hotelkeeping in Wollongong. He found his place of business was getting out of line. He tried a get a block of land near the proposed harbour but failed, and then decided to erect a fine hotel on the hill overlooking the valley below the Illawarra Hotel. When this hotel was completed in 1837, it was far in advance of country hotels. It was, however, mysteriously burned in 1838, and Mr. Brown took the cottage on the present site of Brownville, and opened up what was known as the Illawarra Hotel. He had a wind-power flour mill working on the hill for a little time, so he decided to erect a steampower mill near the Illawarra Hotel. This flourmill was a landmark, as was also the old hotel for years.

Returning again to Mr. George Brown. If Brownsville never advanced it may be attributed to his over-zeal on its behalf. He died on 26th November, 1853, aged 53 years, and his sons and daughter took over the management of the business.

Road Tenders in 1834.—No. 1 tender dated 22nd November, 1834, James Mackay Grey, from Minnamurra Rivulet to Bonna Hill, £3/10/- per acre; No. 2 tender dated 24th November, 1834, J. S. Spearing, from the fence separating John Osborne's and Spearing's farms to the foot of the mountains, £2/15/- per acre, and from the foot to the top of the mountain £4/15 per acre; and from the commencement of the road northwards to the corner of Gillies' (now Spearing's) land, £2/17/6 per acre. From that point to the extent of Spearing's land £2/10/- per acre. From that point to the old Bulli Road £3/10/- per acre. From a marked stump southwards to Figtree Rivulet, a little beyond Spearing's fence, £2/15/- per acre. No. 3 tender, dated 24th November, 1834, John Osborne. From Wollongong to Osborne's and Spearing's boundary, £2/15/- per acre. From Mullet Creek to the marked stump about two miles from Wollongong, £3/5/- per acre. No. 4 tender, William Osborne, from Mullet Creek to Macquarie Rivulet, £2/16/- per acre. From the Macquarie Rivulet to the Minnamurra, £3 per acre. No. 5 tender, 21st November, 1834, George Brown. The line near Wollongong extending northwards to Bulli, £1/12/6 per acre. No. 6 tender, 21st November, 1834, George Brown. From the Macquarie Rivulet to the Minnamurra, £1/15/- per acre. No. 7 tender, George Brown, from the marked stump about two miles from Wollongong to Mullet Creek, £1/15/- per acre. No. 8, 21st November, 1834, George Brown, from Mullet Creek to the Macquarie Rivulet, £1/12/6 per acre. These tenders were opened on 25th November, 1834, in the presence of and considered by Alexander McLean, Colonial Secretary Williams, Lithgow, Auditor-General, and J. A. Cary, Deputy Surveyor-General, who recommended the tender of James Mackay Grey No. 1 and the tenders of George Brown, Nos. 5, 6, 7, 8, the same being considered by the Surveyor-General to be reasonable in references to the respective lines of road. The document was then sent to the Governor for approval, and returned on the 2nd December, 1834, with the following memo written on it:—''Approved of with respect to Nos. 1, 5, 6, 7, 8. The other numbers to stand over until I have some further information on the subject.—Signed Richd. Bourke, December 2nd, 1834.'' The following memo is also written on the document—''The tenders for the lines not included in the recommendation having been considered by the Surveyor-General to be too high, it was recommended that fresh tenders be advertised for.''

A good number of men were set to work at once by Mr. Brown to clear the roads, and about a year or so afterwards, 1835, or early in 1836, a gang of prisoners were sent down from Sydney to form the streets in Wollongong, and also to form and make roads and erect bridges and culverts thereon. Stockades for the prisoners and soldiers who were in charge of them were built at the cross roads on the north side or corner where Robson's house now stands, and afterwards at the Figtree on the south side of the creek where the cottage now stands, on the eastern side of the main road, at Charcoal Creek, at the rear of where George Lindsay now resides; and later on again at Mullet Creek on the western side of the main road at the northern end of the north bridge. The first stockade and headquarters were at the cross-roads, and Lieutenant Otway was the first officer in charge. The other stockades were built further on as the work of making the road progressed southwards. Wollongong was standing bush at the time, and the first work commenced by the prisoners was to clear Crown Street from the green to the junction of the Bulli Road, where the Royal Alfred Hotel

now stands, which was the western end of termination of Crown Street.

Captain Robert Towns was born in Northumberland (England) in 1794, and went to sea at the age of 16 years. Was with a trader for some years, and got the command of a brig in the Mediterranean. He saved money and then started to make money, and after building a boat for himself named ''The Brothers,'' he took up the business of trading between England and New South Wales. In 1833 he married a daughter of Surgeon De Arcy Wentworth, and settled in business in Sydney as Towns and Co. He went into the cotton growing business in Queensland, and worked his plantation with black island labour, and collected beche-de-mer, cocoanut oil, sandalwood, and other products from the natives. He was joined by his brother-in-law, Captain Samuel Addison, and the firm in Illawarra was known as Towns and Addison, and their stock brand was TXA. Captain Samuel Addison settled on the shores of Lake Illawarra, near Shellharbour. (Land sale at Sydney, May 29th, 1865, by Richardson and Wrench, by orders (?) from Hugh de Arcy Wentworth Addison. 2560 acres at Minnamurra and 2000 acres at Oakflats, Illawarra; no title. G. L. Fuller chanced it, got it cheap, and won). Nor is it at all necessary to follow out to the end the career of Captain Samuel Addison, suffice to say that the late Mr. George Laurence Fuller, of Kiama, became the owner of nearly all the Illawarra estates of the late Surgeon De Arcy Wentworth, which at one time amounted to 10,050 acres The prices paid by Mr. Fuller were extremely low. He, however, got the chances and took advantage of them. Hence the Dunmore Estate.

Captain Towns never lived in Illawarra, but his partner, who was also his brother-in-law, Mr. Samuel Addison did. Mr. Addison was a useful pioneer, and his name is recorded in the proceedings of the old A & H. Society of Illawarra. He had two sons, Hugh and John Addison. After Mr. Addison's death the family went to England Mrs. Addison re-married and became Mrs. Hollings. A grandson of Captain Samuel Addison is secretary to the Tasmanian Government

John Hawdon was born in County Durham (England) in 1801, landed in N.S.W. in 1823 with a wife and two sons. In 1833 he went to Kiora. Later he took up Howlong Station on the River Murray. He also took up Kulwyne, near Mildura, Victoria, where his son John

Hawdon died, aged 20 years. His grave, as well as Armour Forster's (a brother-in-law of Hawdon's overseer), are within three-quarters of a mile of old Mildura Station. The Hawdons were among the first to overland cattle to Adelaide. He received as a grant from the Crown 1,280 acres, called Kiora, on the Moruya River, and eventually took up Bodalla and Bergalia. He owned some of the finest Shorthorn cattle in Australia, and stocked Bergalia with sheep under the care of a Mr. Campbell. Captain McKay took up Eurabodalla, and a Mr. Carr took up an adjoining station. A younger brother of Mr. John Hawdon, Mr. Joseph Hawdon, arrived in New South Wales in 1834. He became famous as a pioneer and overlander with cattle to Victoria. A copy of his diary was kindly placed at my disposal by the late Mr. William Hawdon, of Kiora, Moruya, with whom I corresponded for years. It will be seen elsewhere that many cattle found a ready sale in Illawarra, bred by the men just mentioned.

When the Sir John Robertson Land Act came into existence the Hawdons were deprived of their cattle runs. They had often been deprived of valuable cattle by a gang of cattle duffers. The bull 15th Duke of Cambridge, made famous by "Robbery Under Arms," was once owned by the Hawdons. The shanty on the creek, immortalised by Henry Clarence Kendall, was on one of the Hawdon runs. Passing on a Mr. William Wilson, whose sale is mentioned elsewhere as being held on the Macquarie Rivulet, Illawarra, was a son-in-law of Mr. John Hawdon. He however, purchased most of his cattle from the late Mr. Henry Osborne under whose guidance he worked. At Mr. Wilson's sale my late father and the father of the Armstrong family purchased largely. I quite remember my father bringing from that sale a white bull with a few small blue spots on his neck. He had a golden skin, and was said to have been descended from the imported cow "Brutus" that was on exhibition in Market Square, Wollongong, suckling four calves, two of which she had just previously given birth to. Brutus was a large framed roan Durham. She had twins three times, on one occasion two white bulls, one of which was stolen. The late Mr. William Wright, of Jamberoo (old Billy), used to wax eloquent on the dispersal of Harry Osborne's and Mr. Jack Terry Hughes' choice cattle, including the white bull. He always drew a long breath when emphasising the feats of horsmanship on

stockyard and mountain. Messrs. Cole Bros. and William James got possession of the descendants of William Wilson by purchases from Armstrong family and my late father respectively. The late Mr. Thomas Alexander Browne (Rolf Boldrewood) was a personal friend of the Hawdons, and collected much colonial experiences under the roof of the Kiora homestead. The late Mr. William Hawdon possessed a fine store of reminiscence and had a clear lucid style of impression.

Mr. James Mackay Grey was born in Eneagh, County Armagh, Ireland, October 3rd. 1800, and was in his youth educated for the Church at Edinburgh University. He drifted into a brewery, and marred a widow, a sister of Lieutenant Thomas Campbell's wife. Campbell had, for certain reasons, been deprived of his commission in the Navy, and came to New South Wales, where he obtained a grant of 1280 acres, immediately to the south of Captain Farmer's grant, south from Kiama. Something went wrong at the Armagh brewery, and James Mackay Grey decided quickly to leave for New South Wales, and landed first at Tasmania in 1833. He remained there but a very short time, as he was in Kiama in 1834. In 1834 he purchased his brother-in-law's grant for £400. and called it Omega Retreat, as he thought no one would ever pass over the swampy land that lay between his purchase and the lands of Messrs. Berry and Wollstonecraft. The then swampy land was in a few years' time the richest possession in Gerringong, and is generally known as Millers' Flats. Thomas Campbell purchased Grange Farm, Druwalla Creek, Jamberoo, and there made more mistakes. In the meantime James Mackay Grey worked into the good graces of the New South Wales authorities, obtained about a dozen convicts, and set about putting his house in order, with a view of bringing out his wife and family. They arrived in 1835. His son, Samuel Wiliam Grey, then 12 years of age, a schoolboy. Captain Hart's mill and brewery were in course of erection, and James Mackay Grey at once saw where he could make money, which was very scarce at that time in his immediate neighbourhood. He wrote the Authorities in Sydney, stating that his neighbours desired a road to the new settlement at Jamberoo. The Sydney Authorities granted his request, and gave him the contract. Being wise in his day and generation, he began operations on the Jamberoo side, and cleared a track two chains wide from Hyam's Hotel, passing along towards the site of the road marked out by Sir Thomas Mitchell. Mr. Robert Young's house and Wauchope House were afterwards erected on the old track. He then took up the old Cedar track, on which Culwalla's house is built. He went down the gully by an easy grade, turning to the right, he worked up the Jerrara Valley to where Mr. John Colley's house was erected, which was known to the sawyers as the "Flat Rock." Much "poteen" was brewed there in the early days. He then followed the banks of Jerrara Creek until he reached Genera Vale. Here James Mackay Grey halted and reported that he had discovered an unpassable barrier —between his last camp and his own land. This road was never either gazetted nor used as a road, but portions of it had been used by settlers who came to reside in the locality some years later. This led many to believe that a gazetted road was there, and, owing to this notion, some few lost considerable sums at money trying to prove their notions in the law courts.

James Mackay Grey went in for farming by means of convict labour, and quite a long list of men worked out their ticket-of-leave terms on the Omega Retreat Estate. He went in for wheat, maize, potatoes, kept pigs, and manufactured salt pork. In 1844 Messrs. John and James Colley built a fine house for that time for James Mackay Grey. He became a Magistrate, and Land Commissioner for the Kiama district. He leased his land on the Clearing Lease system, and had in 1856 no less than twenty tenants. "We," said one of the old identities, "all knew when rent day came round for the Omega Retreat tenants, James Mackay Grey could be seen standing at the corner of Manning and Terralong Streets, Kiama, saluting each tenant as he passed to the I.S.N. Coy's. wharf with his produce. What a change has taken place there during the last 50 years, in common with a majority of similar settlements in Illawarra, that were built up, so to speak, with the sweat and blood of convicts. Mr. James Mackay Grey's family consisted of Mr. S. W. Grey, Mrs. Samuel Charles, Mrs. William Marks, and Mrs. William Osborne. Two girls died when young, one in Ireland, and the other shortly after landing in New South Wales. James Mackay Grey died at Omega House, Gerringong, on July, 1877, aged 77 years, leaving much wealth and property to his son, Mr. Samuel William Grey, who became a member of Parliament, and spent it freely.

Lieutenant Thomas Campbell, R. N., was born in Belfast, County Antrim, Ireland, in 1778, and fought under the British Flag, married Miss Burton in 1816. One child was born, who came to join her father with her aunt, Mrs. James Mackay Grey, in 1835. She married a Mr. Yarnold, who lived on Druwallah Creek, Jamberoo.

We need not follow the career of Lieutenant Thomas Campbell further as he did very little to forward the interests of his adopted country. His son-in-law James Yarnold, on the other hand, gave much promise of usefulness. His efforts were, however, cut off owing to an unfortunate tragedy over which he had no control driving him into oblivion. In this we will let the dead past bury the past.

AN HISTORIC LETTER.

Wollongong Hotel,
27th October, 1840.

My Dear Sir,—

You will, perhaps, be surprised when you see where I have dated this letter from, but I daresay you will be more surprised when you know the occasion. My last letter contained nothing but bad news. I now mean to make this contain only good news. When we came in to the Sacrament to Goulburn last month my father found a letter laying for him from **William Hart** (brother of Miss Hart) stating that he had a principal share in a saw mill concern with Captain Collins down at Illawarra wherein he had advanced about £8000 and never got any return, but on the contrary always getting new bills drawn upon him. The gentleman he sent out to represent his interest in the concern is very anxious to give it up and requested to have some one put in his place. **Walter Jollie** had met Mr. Hart at Brighton and told him of my father and my having gone out to this country, the object of his letter was to give my father a power of attorney to examine into the books of the establishment and requesting me to take the place of Mr. Otley, the gentleman he sent out before; indeed so anxious was he that he sent out duplicates of his letters, the last more pressing than the first. We accordingly corresponded with Mr. Otley, and the result was our coming down to inspect the mills personally before finally accepting the situation. The result was such as to make me accept the situation at once, as I think it may be an opening perhaps for something else afterwards. We breakfasted with Captain Collins this morning here, and he promises me £150 per annum, board and lodging. How long it would have been ere I could have got **such** at **home**. My

father will be paid by Mr. Hart, I, by the Concern. There is a good cottage attached to the place where if Captain C. goes to Sydney, as he intends to do, my mother and Eliza will reside, but we are also in terms for a small farm two miles from the mill where they will reside, my father farming and looking after the mill at the same time. We are on our way back to Goulburn to report, and are wearying to get home. The situation is six miles from the coast where they have coasters for transporting the timber to Sydney, distant about 70 miles, so that if we take a farm we could send in our produce to the Sydney market. David is still at Port Phillip and knows nothing of all this. He has had sad work, he says, in keeping the rest of his men from running away. We are wearying much to see him. We have had plenty of rain this season, and the country is most beautiful. There is so much wheat in the ground, and it is so cheap just now that it will never pay the cutting down. Men's wages are most extravagant; getting 30/- per week just now for common labourers, and at the mill a man gets 42/- per week for doing nothing but sharpen saws! I think, but am not quite sure, that your brother will have to pass our way every time he goes to Sydney, but he is more at the Shoalhaven. My next letter will be a dissertation upon **Timber**. I don't know what I will take up next. Do you remember when I came away you gave me a present of a measuring line? You had surely been gifted with a sense of seeing into futurity. We received Dr. Muir's pamphlet with your pencil remarks. Did you read the other side of the question?
Your Affectionate Brother,
JAMES W. WAUGH.

Mr. D. L. Waugh.—David Lindsay Waugh was born in Edinburgh, Scotland, in 1810, and came to Sydney, New South Wales, in the ship Isabella, in 1834, and settled for a time in Victoria, and then came to Jamberoo, Illawarra, in 1840; purchased the Waughope property in 1845. Other members of the Waugh family came out in 1838 and 1840, and the Dymock family in 1845. Mr. D. L. Waugh married a Miss Hope, of Camden, hence the name "Waughope" in 1851. Mr. Waugh became a magistrate in 1849, and was appointed chairman of directors of the Illawarra Steam Navigation Coy. in 1853. His correspondence with friends in Scotland will give readers an idea of how things were moving in the Illawarra district at the time the Waugh and Dymock families settled here. Mr. D. L. Dymock was

a nephew of Mr. D. L. Waugh, and having married a daughter of Dr. Robert Menzies, of Jamberoo, became at once a public man of note. As an auctioneer he stood high for many years. As a public man he did much for his adopted district. He did more in a short space of time for the Kiama A. & H. Society than a number of men could have done in a life-time. Mr. David Lindsay Waugh was a good man in his way, but Mr. David Lindsay Dymock was a great man. Copies of Mr. D. L. Waugh's letters:—

Waughope, Jamberoo, N.S.W.,
14th March, 1857.
To R. Scott Moncrieff, Esq., Edinburgh.
My Dear Sir,—Your letter of 11th December last reached us here on the 6th February, the new line of mail steamers doing their work well. The one that brought your letter reached Sydney exactly two months from the date of its departure from England, after having called at Melbourne, Port Phillip, and left their mails which occasioned a delay of nearly a day. This is doing the work well and the Glasgow Company that have got the contract are deserving of great praise, as it is a gigantic undertaking. Their vessels are all above or about 3000 tons. yet the people here are not content, and are anxious to have the news faster expecting by ———— to shorten the term to 45 days. We are by the Electric Telegraph Union, in course of erection, connecting the capitals of four Australian colonies, and expect by way of Singapore to be joined to London before any very long course of time.

I am glad that you like any scraps of news or information that I can give you from this land, for to tell the truth, I am sometimes puzzled to know what I can say sufficiently interesting to you in the Old Country, etc.

We have had most extraordinary wet weather for more than the last 12 months, and great abundance of everything, not much to the benefit of farmers as prices go. From the great influx of population into the colonies during the last three years, and the fact that it always takes time, generally at least one season before a new arrival can become a producer to any extent, the consequence was high prices and large imports. But now wheat is only about 48/- a quarter instead of from £5 to £6, butter 9d. to 1/-, instead of 1/8 to 2/6 per lb.. and other things in proportion. Potatoes that 18 months ago were £12 to £20 per ton were sold at £2. In many places hundreds of tons were never dug at all. It was found that after paying for taking them up and sending them to market the owner had to pay expenses over their receipts. For, strange as it may appear, wages have not fallen. Men cannot be had under £35 to £50 a year, lodgings and rations found them. The high price of wool and the continuance of gold digging I suppose is the cause. But if we have a large influx for the next year wages must fall, but I don't think that they will ever fall very much.

Meanwhile increased population increases our improvements rapidly in our district. Our Steam Navigation Coy. of which I have been chairman ever since its commencement has had difficulties which crippled us very much. We have absorbed another company and extended our capital to £22,000. I have been re-elected chairman, and am glad now I did not get into our colonial Parliament.

(Signed.)   D. L. Waugh.

The district has long felt the want of steam communication with Sydney, and nine months ago we started a company to raise £7000, in shares at £5 each. I took 40 shares and each of the family have a share or two between them. Upwards of £6000 were taken by the inhabitants of the district. We had a charter of incorporation from the Legislative Council, and among the directors I was elected chairman which has given me a great deal to do. We sent an agent home to bring a steamer out in June last, to be called the "Kiama." We expect it to return at present rates from 25 to 50 per cent. when fairly started. Property has increased enormously in value. I could get £6000 for this farm at present. We are brought within six hours of Sydney. Two boys. the youngest 7 months old. Robert and Goulburn have a daughter. James is single in Sydney, in a good business.

David L. Waugh, July, 1853,
State Account, £475 borrowed.

Waughope, Jamberoo,
12th November, 1853.
To R. Scott Moncreff, Esq., Daltreith,
Edinburgh.

My Dear Sir.—I received your letter of the 28th July, /'53, on the 9th inst., and letter to acknowledge the receipt of it and its enclosure of £130. I need not again express our united thanks for the continued kindness you show in taking not only so much trouble but taking into consideration what you think would be best suited for us.

There has been a great change in this colony since the effect of the gold has become more generally felt. In regard to the value of money it still leaves a higher rate of interest than in Britain. But even here it is found that it is getting superabundant. I believe that there is at present about three millions of deposits in the Sydney banks, and mortgages of the first character have gradually fallen from 10 to 8, 7 and 6 per cent. There are few ways of investing money to live on the interest, but for one who wishes to employ it himself there are still ample ways of investing it most profitably. As the money borrowed on the credit of insurance forms partly the old funds. Both Elia and Ann possess allotments in the rising town of Kiama, four miles from here, on which they wish to erect some suitable buildings, which are very much wanted. But to get anything done at present is exceedingly difficult; wages are very high; carpenters get 12/- and 15/- a day; plasterers and bricklayers can easily earn £1 a day. Two sawyers, father and son (Irish) earn between them £6 per week.

Provisions have risen in the colony. At Jamberoo beef 3d. per lb; flour 25/- to 30/- per 100 lbs.; tea 1/6 per lb., sugar 4d. per lb. Potatoes at present not to be had. They were 12/- per cwt. Butter was 2/6, now 1/6 per lb. The chief manufacture in the district is butter. I am milking between 30 to 40 cows and making about £400 a year which will increase every year.

Melbourne, 16th November, 1859.
To David Waugh, Esq.,
Waughope, Jamberoo, Sydney.

My Dear Sir.—I had a letter by this post from our mutual friend, Mr. Alex. Bremner, in which he says: When in New South Wales I was asked by Mr. David Waugh to give plans for a harbour at Kiama, the port of the district. He of course was led to believe from his worthless neighbours that they were to pay the expenses along with him. I, at a great deal of trouble and expense, made the survey and plans for which I ought to have got £280 at the very least. When, however, they got the plans they would not come forward to pay. Mr. Waugh asked me to take his acceptance for £120, which I did without any understanding of any sort to refund any part of it in instalment. Learning from the Rev. Dr. McKay when here that the main burden was left on Mr. Waugh's shoulders I wrote to him asking a statement and find that he is minus £54 by the transaction.

ALEXANDER BROS., Kiama.

FAIRFIELD OF FAIRFIELD (No. 2, I.D.C.H.B.).

FAIRY OF FAIRFIELD (No. 345 I.D.C.H.B.).

HUGH DALY, Upton, Alstonville.

PIGEON OF UPTON (Vol. 1, I.D.C.H.B., No. 423).

He then says: Taking into account Mr. Waugh's very excellent character of a most consistent Christian, one who serves our Lord in the church, etc., and the worthless of the others, will you send him £54., etc.

Very Truly Yours,
David Ogilvy.

Reply by the Governor to an address from Kiama residents re breakwater. Date 1855-61.

Gentlemen— I feel deeply grateful to you for your kind expressions of sympathy for me under my late bereavement.

I should, had circumstances permitted, been glad to make a longer stay in a part of the colony which has been so singularly favoured by nature, and I trust upon some future occasion to be able to devote more time to the examination of the many remarkable features which characterise the Illawarra district.

The delay which has taken place in considering the plans for the improvement of your harbour has not been owing to any want of appreciation by the Government of the claims of the inhabitants of Kiama to such assistance as the Government can afford, but to the difficulty of determining on the best plan to be adopted.

I trust that in a short time the Government will be able to submit to the Legislature an estimate for the funds required to complete a work which will give full security to the vessels employed in a trade which will yearly increase, and that the result will be increased prosperity to Kiama.

W. Denison.

Ballater,
Aberdeenshire, August, 10th, 1859.

My Dear Sir.—I have just returned from a ramble to Balmoral and had a peep at the interior of the Highland seat of royalty. It is very beautiful and grand, but I do not envy them for they are on a slippery place. I beg to acknowledge yours of 12th May, Old friend, you have omitted to mention Mr. and Mrs. James, of Sydney. To David Waugh, Esq., Waughope. The appointment of Sir W. Denison to the governship of these colonies is a great calamity as could well befall a country, in an engineering point of view. I would wish you if you will preserve my plans from the hands of the spoilers. It may be that some day hence they will tell their own tale.—I am, etc.,

Alex. Bremner.

Mention is again made of Sir W. Denison and his "Star of Bidablea." You will observe that the bay is so circumverted that a few blunders arriving out of the first grand one will fill it up so as to render it useless. I am in the ship St. George, and from the Clyde, 1838.

Aberdeen, February 16th, 1859.

Mr. Dear Sir.—I was sorry to hear that your old minister, Rev. George McKie, had left Kiama. He had many good parts about him, some difficulty in getting his equal. I saw Rev. Dr. McKay very shortly when in Great Britain. I heard there is nothing doing towards Kiama harbour. Your kind neighbours do not show themselves able for such improvements otherwise they would move better in the right direction. Did you succeed in recovering from them the £120? My address is c/o Archd. Ritchie, agent of the Scottish Equitable Life Insurance, 26 Poultry Street, London.—From Alex. Bremner.

The Evans Family. — Evan Robert Evans, senr., arrived in Illawarra in the mid thirties of last century, and shortly afterwards commenced store keeping. Later he purchased a farm which he called Penrosevilla, and began horse breeding. He purchased in 1841 the foundation of his dairy herd from Mr. William Howe, of Glenlee, Campbelltown, and later still joined in with Mr. Henry Osborne, of Marshall Mount, in the business of trading in cattle. Mr. Evans bought the young cattle from the settlers, and these would be sent in drafts as far as the borders of the Murray River. As times moved he moved with them. Carried on dairying on a large scale at Penrosevilla, Dapto, leased Murramarang, a fine cattle run near Ulladulla, to which he sent his own bred heifers. He was in touch with a Mr. Carr, of Moruya, and they did a lot of cattle dealing in combination. He was a modest, upright man, and a consistent supporter of the old Illawarra A. & H. Society. After the death of Mr. Henry Osborne, he was interested with Mr. Alex. Osborne in Murramarang, on the South Coast.

He had two sons, Mr. John Evans, of Shellharbour, and later of Ulladulla, and Mr. Evan Robert Evans who became heir to the Penrosevilla property, and five daughters, Mrs. William R. Hindmarsh, Mrs. Nesbet, M. Hindmarsh, Mrs. Robert Ritchie, Mrs. Joseph Ritchie, and Mrs. Frank Badgery. So it will be seen that the Evans family formed a wide connection. He owned several bulls and tried many different blends and crosses. He purchased many young bulls including the bull, Billy, which was several years after Mr. Evans' death named

"Major" (imp.).   Mr. Evans died at Penrose-villa in 1863, aged 58 years. His son, Mr. Evan R. Evans, took charge of the estate and tried as best was in his power to follow in his father's footsteps, an honest, honourable man, a lump too soft-hearted for the crowd that were ever ready to make use of him.

A considerable amount of thoughtless history has been centred on the Evans' family over the alleged purchase of an imported bull calf at Martyn's bazaar, Sydney. The writer heard the Hindmarsh Bros. and others talking freely at the sale yards in Kiama and other public places about the cause of Evan R. Evans' death being grief and worry owing to his son-in-law, Robert Ritchie, getting the better of him over the possession of the first batch of the Major bull's heifers that were sent away from Dapto as poddies to his Murramarang holding, and then taken on to Robert Ritchie's property, Jellet Jellet, Bega. They were of the primest quality.

As Evan R. Evans, junr. had stated over and over again: "It was my late father, not I, who bought the bull Major as a calf in Martyn's bazaar, Sydney." No one questioned the Hindmarsh Bros.' story. It is, however, a good plan to keep on and on investigating dates. Strolling through the old burying ground at Dapto, the writer noticed a head-stone erected to the memory of Evan Robert Evans, senr. There in plain letters is to be seen: "Died June, 1863, aged 58 years." This at once gave the impression that if Robert Ritchie became possessed of heifers of great dairy quality they were by a bull in the Penrose herd prior to 1863. The Martyn bazaar purchase was even then a mere calf scarcely 12 months according to Evan R. Evans' junr., statement.

There are other statements that have been taken for granted for years, and then passed into the newspapers and books as truths, which cannot be accepted as been free from grave doubts. Take J. W. Cole's stud bull "Commodore" as an example.

John James, of Rose Valley, Gerringong, under date 17th July, 1907, as follows: "Re the bull Major. At or after a Kiama show about 1873, Mr. W. E. Williams bought him for his father the late Thomas Williams. My father had a notion to buy but Bill Williams put him off as his father wanted a bull and father had Robin Hood in his prime, about 2 or 3 years old at the time. Cole's Commodore was sired after this. Evans said the Major came home

and served the McGill cow, while Joe Williams says he was milking for Evans where this cow was, and that one of the A. A. Co.'s bulls, 'Solon,' gave service."

Mr. Evan E. Evans bought in 1872, 2030 acres of land at Sutton Forest at fifteen shillings per acre, and commenced cattle dealing in combination with dairying. No pedigrees of cattle bred or purchased were kept. Nor were there any account of sales, so that it is bare justice to say that prior to this date the only pedigree any man got with any of Mr. Evans' bulls was, "He is by the old bull and out of one of my best cows." Since that date Mr. Evans, up to the time of his death, could not be certain of the breeding of any animal as there were always three or more bulls running with the cows. If then the dairymen of Illawarra who have been at all times considered keen critics of dairy cattle characters were often dissatisfied with the results obtained from certain bulls, no one is to blame but those who sold and bought bulls and cows without written statements regarding their breeding. Bull breeding for show purposes, and, ultimately for the sale of their progeny, has in the past and at the present time, given rise to much ill-feeling among dairymen. J. W. Cole's "Commodore" was not, generally speaking, admired, yet he sired good animals when suitably mated, including William Graham's "Sir Robert."

It is plain that the Mendelian law has come to stay in stock raising. Going back to Evan R. Evans' Devon bull, "Red Rover," bred by Reynolds of Tocal, full of red colour and dairy quality. There were dominant characters in that bull, and were passed on to William James' bull, "Robin Hood," a very superior bull indeed, a far better bull than his photograph pictures him. Say what people may, most of the red dairy cattle of Illawarra described by their owners as being of the "Scotch Jock" strain were of the Robin Hood strain. Take another example. A Devon bull, "Nobleman," owned by Woodhouse, of Mount Gilead, Campbelltown. That bull was noted for his red colour and dairy quality, which gave such good results in the herds of Yeo, Lackey and Morrice in the Moss Vale district. The Woodhouse "Nobleman" blood was in Hugh Dudgeon's noted bull Noble, although it is not mentioned in the pedigree given by the original owner.

Ayrshire Cattle for Illawarra.—According to the Illawarra "Mercury" of 1st June, 1883, Mr. Evan R. Evans, of Penrosevilla, Dapto, had purchased an Ayrshire bull and cow from Mr. John Wood, of Sydney, a red and white heifer from Victoria; also a red and white bull and a cow with female calf at foot. Mr. John Lindsay, of Kembla Park, Unanderra, had on 11th May, 1883, stated that he then owned 100 head of Ayrshire cattle, and had just sold his Ayrshire bull, Earl of Beaconsfield, at Kiama Show, to Mr. John Grey, of Broughton Creek, and intended purchasing another Ayrshire bull. The Earl Beaconsfield blood had evidently greatly improved Mr. Lindsay's herd.

The Illawarra "Mercury" of July 8th, 1884, states: "Excelsior appears to be the motto of Messrs. John Lindsay and Evan R. Evans, in regard to the transformation of their dairy herd into the Ayrshire breed. The former gentleman introduced the Ayrshire blood into his stock a few years ago, and being satisfied in his own mind after a trial that that breed was the best adapted for the district under present circumstances, he has kept on obtaining and producing more and more of that kind of cattle ever since. Mr. Evans being determined that his herd should not lose its prestige as the premier one of Illawarra, also decided upon giving the pure Ayrshires a trial, and the result, so far, is that he, too, is launching out still further in the same direction. Others of our dairy farmers in this end of the district are also experimenting with Ayrshires, principally among such being Messrs. W. M. Cook and Edward Gibson, of Dapto. Both of whom maintain that they have Ayrshire animals equal if not superior, to the best of either of Mr. Lindsay or Mr. Evans. On Tuesday last, however, the last two mentioned gentlemen took another step forward in the Ayrshire line by making important purchases at an auction sale of pure stock of that kind of cattle, held at Kiss's yards, Sydney. These cattle came from New Zealand. Mr. Lindsay secured a bull "Teviot," at 113 guineas. Mr. Evans purchasing three heifers at 39 guineas, 29 guineas and 23 guineas. Note, some of the New Zealand Ayrshires of that period were ill-bred, and notoriously pedigreed.

Malcolm Campbell arrived in New South Wales early and was connected with the settlement at Coolangatta as an overseer over convicts. For services rendered he received a grant of 500 acres along the eastern boundary of Michael Hyam's grant, and bounded on the north by the southern boundary of the Terragong Swamp. He built a brick cottage on the northern end and about five chains from the swamp boundary, and placed a man named Black in charge of it. Malcolm Campbell then went to reside in Sydney, and was found dead, sitting in a chair of the parlour of James Modie Marks' hotel adjoining the Rocks area in 1837. Two claims were put in in connection with his estate, one by James Modie Marks for board and lodging, etc., and the other by Ewen Campbell as next of kin. The transaction works out as follows according to the deeds: 250 acres granted to James Marks on 28th March, 1843, annual quit rent £2/1/8, commencing 1st January, 1838; 250 acres granted to Ewen Campbell on 16th December, 1844, annual quit rent £2/1/8, commencing 1st January, 1838. Malcolm Campbell had obtained possession of the above-mentioned 500 acres on 24th April, 1830. Ewen Campbell, as heir at law of Malcolm Campbell, sold the 250 acres to David Lindsay Waugh who lived for a time on James Modie Marks' property. Captain John G. Collins, of the 13th Dragoon Guards, while managing the Woodstock mills, lived in a house to the south and east of Black's residence and not more than 50 yards' distance therefrom. The main road in 1838 separated these two houses, leaving Black's house on the swamp side. As the years passed on John Marks married Mrs. Arthur Little, a very rich widow who was a daughter of William Moffitt, a bookseller and stationer, who made lots of money in various ways according to the customs of the times. His shop stood in Pitt Street, near King Street. James Marks also married a daughter of William Moffitt. John Marks built Terragong House, and James Marks built Culwalla House. David Lindsay Waugh built Waughope House (a mud wall storied house with shingle roof) erected by a man named Carnell. Carnell built a lockup in Kiama, and a storied house for a superintendent of convicts in Kiama, Captain Perry's home overlooking Smith's Bay.

The clan Campbell were also represented in Illawarra. Charles was at Coolangatta, and Ewen was at Numbaa in the early days as overseer of convicts.

After James Modie Marks sold out the Steampacket Hotel, Kiama, to William Gard, he resided for a time on side of Jamberoo road in the house previously occupied by Captain John G. Collins. D. L. Waugh, after coming from Victoria where he had an overseeing job, at what was at that time termed Port Phillip, lived near Terragong.

Many changes since those days. Few indeed

are left of the old school boys who can remember those old roadside homes; how many
are there on earth to-day who can remember
"old Duke's garden" that flourished in the
early forties on the west bank of Jerrara
Creek, immediately to the south of Terragong
house? Few still could recall the old military
man whose once straight frame had become
stooped.

**Lieutenant William Lampriere Frederick
Sheaffe,** of the 39th Regiment H.M. Foot, arrived in Wollongong to relieve Lieutenant Ottway, who was in charge of the Government
chain gang, who were making a road from
Wollongong towards Mount Kiera. Ottway
resented it, and shot himself next day, April,
1836. Lieutenant Sheaffe was accompanied
from Norfolk Island by Sergeant Harris and
Corporal Smith. Harris received a grant of
200 acres at West Dapto, and sold 100 acres
of his grant to Sheaffe. They went in for
farming and dairying. Sheaffe's portion was
in charge of a settler, whom the blacks troubled
by stealing his maize. He set himself the task
of dealing with them. He, therefore, secreted
himself in the maize one night, and cut the
hand off a blackfellow. The blacks never had
much love for Scotchmen in Illawarra after
that "terrible" deed. Lieutenant Sheaffe died
in 1860, aged 59 years.

Mr. Robert Haworth spent seven years feeding pigs and calves for Robert and William
Carruth, on one-half of John Wyllie's Dunlop
Vale Estate, Dapto, Illawarra. He was a shoemaker by trade, and made boots for the settlers
in his own hours. By the time the Carruth
Bros. had sold out the property to Mr. Gerard
Gerard, Robert Haworth was preparing to own a
tannery in Wollongong. He prospered, and when
Mr. Gerard Gerard was prepared to sell out
Mr. Haworth was prepared to buy. He bought
and called the farm "Kembla Grange." He
built a fine house and lodge on it which remain
to his memory. He entered Parliament. He
was ruined, however, by foolishly going security for the completion of the Wollongong Harbour Works.

Mr. Abraham Lincoln was an important per-
sonage at the old Woodstock brewery at Jamberoo, in the early forties. He was a native of
Suffolk, England, and was a very excellent
authority on farming. He was practically the
founder of the Illawarra Agricultural Societies.
He left Illawarra about 1850, married a widow
in Melbourne. Had an office in Kirk's bazaar.

Melbourne. He was found dead seated in his
office chair; heart failure. He had been on
the agricultural staff of a London journal.

Mr. William Timbs and his family arrived in
Illawarra from England in 1838, and entered
into the employ of Mr. Henry Osborne, of
Marshall Mount. They were placed in charge
of some stud dairy cattle purchased from Mr.
William Howe, of Glenlee, Campbelltown. They
remained there for several years. Father and
son (Gabriel) had sole charge of the imported
cattle that were on exhibition in the Market
Square, Wollongong, in 1843, when the first
attempt was made to found the Illawarra A.
& H. Society. At that time an A. & H. Society
had been established at Parramatta. But as
the Illawarra, as part of the district included
in the original scheme, could not compete owing
to its isolation, several progressive settlers decided to establish an A. & H. Society in
Wollongong.

In connection with these references to the
cattle of Messrs. Henry Osborne, William
Timbs and his son, Gabriel Timbs. The Timbs
family were the neighbours and friends of the
writer throughout a long period of years.
Hence this information came direct from the
men who played the chief part in these dairy
cattle transactions.

William Timbs was born in England and
arrived in 1838, died at Jamberoo, Illawarra, 1882, aged 91 years. His son Gabriel
Timbs arrived with his parents in Illawarra
1838, and father and son found employment
with the late Henry Osborne, of Marshall
Mount, and were at once placed in charge of
the H. O. stud dairy cattle. The greater portion of the Marshall Mount H. O. cattle were
bred at Glenlee, Campbelltown, by William
Howe, a noted breeder during the late twenties,
thirties, and early forties of last century. The
Timbs family were with the late Henry Osborne
when that noted pioneer made an overland
journey from Dapto, Illawarra. (See notes elsewhere).

William Timbs and family settled on land
on the banks of Jerrara Creek, near Kiama, in
1849, and commenced clearing the dense bush in
that locality; 40 acres was sufficient to provide
all necessary comforts for large families then.
Gabriel Timbs took up an adjoining block, and
commenced dairying in a small way. He prospered, and when the John Terry Hughes Estate
was subdivided and sold in 1860, he purchased
a large holding at the foot of Mount Terry,
Albion Park. He was a sound judge of dairy

cattle, and purchased good bulls at all times. (See account of his sale.) He died at Albion Park in 1912, aged 79 years.

Andrew McGill was born in Kintyre, Argylshire (Scotland). He farmed at Musedale for a time. His intention was to migrate to Canada, but got involved in a lawsuit—McGill v. Ferier —which altered his design, but not his resolve to leave Scotland. He engaged with an agent who represented the estate of John Terry Hughes, and came to Sydney with his family in the ship St. George.

In conversation with Mr. Duncan McGill, of Kangaroo Creek, North Coast, during 17th and 18th June 1892, he said: "The foundation bull of my father's (Andrew McGill) herd was called the "Bally Bull"—A bald-faced, white-backed bull bred on the Terry Hughes Estate, hence the majority of the McGill herd were of that description for some years. The "Gardiner bull" was bought from William Curtin, an orchardist who lived at the head of the Macquarie Rivulet. The Blucher bull was a red bull with brindle stripes, and was bred and used on the Terry Hughes' Estate. The roan McGill cattle were the Davey Johnston strain." He added that in his opinion the Davey Coleman cattle were at all times of a very superior type and of good quality. With regard to cattle sales Mr. McGill said: "My father never called a clearing out sale. Sometimes he sent stores and culls to Duncan Beatson's yards. The prize cow 'Queen' was sold as a store. She was not supposed to be in calf when she was in calf."

Going back to the year 1839, Mr. McGill said: "The cows on the John Terry Hughes' Estate when we arrived there were a mixed lot. The dairy cows had been purchased in Sydney from the executors in the estate of George Howes, who was a relative of Edward Lee. They carried the GH and EL brands. Our family arrived at the Albion Park Station in 1839. My father did not commence dairying on his own account until 1846. At the homestead at the time we went to live on Hopping Joe's Meadow there were three bulls. A long-horned bull of the Craven breed, with hooped horns, white face, a dorsel streak, and reddish brindle sides. He was known as the "Bally bull." A red bull with brindle streaks, named "Blucher," and a large strawberry Durham had just been leased for a season from Henry Osborne. To the best of my belief those three bulls laid the foundation of my father's herd. My father's first great cow was called "Betsy"; she was out of

the same cow and by the same bull as the ITH Bally bull, and her calf, a white-faced white-backed, long-horned bull, with reddish brindle sides, was my father's foundation bull. After we left, the Terry Hughes Estate leased a white bull from Mr. Ben Marshall, of Dapto. My father was accompanied from Scotland by a very clever cattleman named John McQuilter, who was known on Terry's Meadows, Illawarra, as 'Scotch Jock.' It was 'Scotch Jock' who supervised the upbringing of the young cattle and who had much to do with the matings of the sires and dams of my father's cattle."

Mr. Duncan Beatson commenced dairying on portion of Terry's Meadows about the year 1846 where he established the celebrated DB brand. Mr. Duncan Beatson was a bosom friend of John McQuilter. Which of the two was the more capable man it is difficult to say, but this I believe. Duncan Beatson was the best judge of dairy cattle in Illawarra in his time. His purchased cattle were at all times tip top. At Duncan Beatson's sale my father purchased the cow "Lofty," carrying the DB brand for £21; an enormous price in those days. He also bought a cow called "Reddie" at £15. These cows, in addition to the cow just mentioned (Betsy), founded the AMC brand. The cow Lofty calved a red bull calf which was called "Lofty's Boy." The red and white spotted bull was McGill's show bull of 1860. He was purchased from Mr. William Kirton, a gardener, who lived up "Calderwood" side. This bull was called "The Gardiner's bull." There was another bull purchased shortly afterwards from Peter Coleman, a neighbour and an exhibitor at the Illawarra shows. After my father's second marriage we separated, and then lost interest in the old herd. With regard to the disease termed Pleura, I cannot say from memory what animals were taken off at the time of the outbreak; but always thought that some of the choicest animals kept in a reserved paddock died off with it."

In May, 1916, I journeyed in company with Mr. Thomas Armstrong, of Oak Farm, Albion Park, to interview Mr. Andrew McGill, of Tullumbah, and whilst chatting over the McGill cattle, the question of the bull "Scotch Jock" cropped up. Mr. Andrew McGill gave it as his opinion that "Scotch Jock" died of pleura in 1862. There may, however, have been more than one bull called after old John McQuilter as he was the guide, philosopher and friend of many of those in search of young bulls from the McGill herd. This must be so as I hold in possession no less than four different descriptions of the bull "Scotch Jock" all claiming to have obtained such first hand.

Mr. Alex. Fraser who was a neighbour of the McGills states: "The bull Mr. Andrew McGill was using in his herd in 1852 was a red bull with a bald face, iron rings on horn tips. I think the next bull was purchased from Peter Coleman. In 1860 he had a big spotted red and white bull with a yellowish tinge in the hair, very large spots. He took some prizes with this bull. When Mr. Duncan Beatson sold out McGill bought several of the best cows." Mr. D. L. Dymock states: "My recollections of the McGill cattle take me back to a big white faced bull. They had many ballies in my time, not red colour of the present Hereford, more yellow with beautiful spotted faces, good milkers. I was several times in the McGill herd when they went to the Green Mountain to live after their father's second marriage. I think the McGill ballies had a lot of Ayrshire blood in them from the beautiful fine heads they had and fine horns."

Evidently a big change took place in Mr. Andrew McGill's herd between the year 1862 and 1867, at which date he sold out to the Messrs. Bartlett and came to live in Kiama. Mr. John Bartlett writes: "I do not recollect Mr. Andrew McGill having a sale at any time; my father bought him out, prize cattle included. The cows were reds and roans. The bulls were roans, said to be of the David Johnston breed. My father then bought Captain Hopkins' imported bull, and later a Shorthorn bull from Mr. Henry H. Osborne, sire Alexander (imp.).

The best dairy cattle my father ever owned he purchased from Mr. Duncan Beatson. My brother, Mr. Wyndham Bartlett, came to Illawarra and spent five years gaining colonial experience with Mr. Duncan Beatson on the Meadows. At Beatson's sale my brother purchased 20 head of cows and heifers at an average of £17 per head, an enormous price at that time, but he knew the animals and they were the best dairy cattle we ever owned."

With reference to the outbreak of pleura among the McGill and Johnston cattle, George Reed, who knew those herds, having been in the locality from childhood, and had milked cows for Andrew McGill for years, states: "There cannot be any doubt about the seriousness of the disease on those farms. Both McGill and Johnston lost many cattle. Johnston could withstand the loss, McGill could not. Consequently McGill never seemed to settle down again to cattle breeding." It would appear that McGill lost several of his prize animals including a valuable two-year-old bull. Johnston was burning and burying carcases of cattle for weeks.

Dr. Robert Menzies was born in Edinburgh, Scotland, in 1812, and came to reside in Jamberoo, in 1838, on 300 acres of land purchased from John Lewis Spencer in 1835, at 5/- per acre, where he practised his profession and carried on dairy farming, until his death in 1860, aged 48 years. Dr. Menzies was a useful colonist, and helped to found the Kiama branch of the Agricultural and Horticultural Society, and became its first president in 1848.

Mr. J. S. Lomax came to Illawarra from Lancashire, England, about 1839. His son, J. R. Lomax, was born at St. Aubin's, London. The Lomax family settled on Colonel Britain's farm, near the Keelogues. Mr. Lomax, senr., brought with him a valuable Shorthorn, a rich roan, named "Mars." His foundation stock he purchased from the estate of Mr. George Rouse, of Parramatta. He also obtained a red bull from the herd of Governor Gipps that were being depastured on the estate of Messrs. Towns and Addison, of Shellharbour. He did not remain more than six years in Illawarra as his son, J. R. Lomax, was only 9 years old when the family removed to Victoria.

Colonel Britain's farm was situated between Unanderra railway station and the hillside on the west. At the time Mr. Lomax lived there it was rich and fertile. He lost a lot of valuable cattle during a severe drought, and then decided to try his luck in Victoria, where he procured an estate and carried on beef cattle raising—the Lomax Shorthorns, and his noted red cattle regarding which we have no reliable facts. They were deep red, medium-sized animals displaying good dairy quality. Mr. John Brown said they were Devons of a larger size than usually seen in Illawarra at that time, which gives one the impression that they were of the Sussex breed. Unfortunately we have no records to show to what breed they really belonged. Mr. J. R. Lomax, a son of the above-mentioned gentleman settled at Yandilla, Darling Downs, some few years ago, and with his family carried on beef Shorthorn breeding.

Charley Ransome, better known as "Charley the Cobbler," described as a short, stout, red-faced man, who settled in the long ago in Illawarra. He for a time carried on farming near Wollongong, then took on dairying at Stoney Creek, near Jamberoo. Mr. G. K.

GEORGE LINDSAY & SONS, Horsley, Dapto.

DUCHESS II OF HORSLEY.

PANSEY II OF HORSLEY.

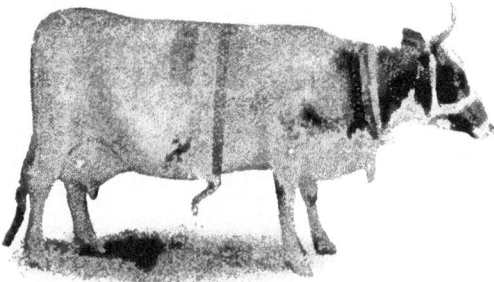

POLLY OF HORSLEY (5341).

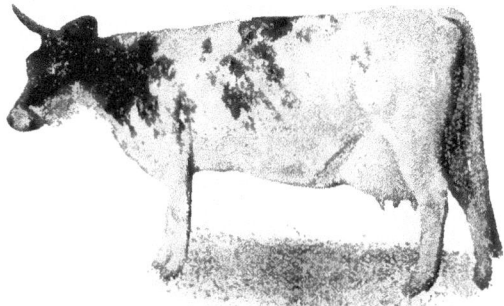

MARY SCOT OF HORSLEY (5339.)

Waldron sold out his herd in 1857, and Charley came to live in Shoalhaven Street, Kiama. He, however, continued to own cattle of various breeds, generally very good of their kind. He owned one noted bull that was known as "Charley the Cobbler's" bull. This bull was a black and red brindle throughout with the exception of the brush of the tail which was white. How Charley got possession of him no one seems to have bothered. But some say he was the descendant of a Polish breed of cattle imported by Mr. Richard Jones of "Fleurs," near Penrith. He was possessed of great quality, and laid the foundation of Mr. Thomas Black's herd, Omega, Gerringong. When his progeny were mated with a blood-red bull purchased by Mr. Black in Sydney, the brindle disappeared but the dairy quality was sustained. The Cobbler's bull was, according to those who saw him in the fifties, a model of beauty as regards form. Charley Ransome died suddenly in Kiama in 1859, leaving no issue. A man with a history before coming to Illawarra, and who made history while he lived there. Just where or how he got that noted bull is not known. Mr. Richard Jones, of Fleurs, imported a bull and three cows in the ship "Hope," 8th July, 1824. It was the same ship that Mr. John Terry Hughes came out to Australia in. Mr. Jones we know once owned the Five Islands Estate, Port Kembla.

David Williamson Irving was born in Edinburgh (Scotland) on January 5th, 1819, and was the fifth son of John Irving, W.S. (writer to the signet), who was an early personal friend of Sir Walter Scott. He was, therefore, a nephew of Alexander Irving, one of the Supreme Court Judges in Edinburgh, and known by the title of Lord Newtown. He had an elder brother named John, who set sail in the "Terror" in 1845 with the ill-fated Franklin expedition, and whose body was found and identified after being in the snow for 30 years by means of a silver medal which was in his possession. David Williamson Irving studied at St. Andrew's University for the medical profession, but came to New South Wales at the age of 20 years. He shortly afterwards married a daughter of that celebrated dairy cattle breeder of Glenlee, Campbelltown, and later on purchased a part of John Wyllie's Dunlop Vale Estate in Illawarra, and named it "Newton," where he resided and carried on dairying and bred cattle on the lines of his father-in-law, Mr. William Howe, who was

a visiting magistrate in the Camden district under the old regime for many years. David Williamson Irving was associated with the old Illawarra A. & H. Society, and was appointed the first president of the Dapto A. & H. Society. He was a consistent and honourable exhibitor for years in both those society show rings. The following note is of interest. "His bull 'Sportsman,' was a bull of the pure Durham and Devon extraction, was the winner of the 1st prize, and was bred by Mr. Evan Evans, of Penrose, Dapto. His other bull 'Glenlee,' was bred by Mr. William Howe, of Glenlee, Campbelltown, from a pure Alderney cow." See sale report 22nd February, 1859, in Illawarra "Mercury."

Mr. D. W. Irving was appointed police magistrate at Tamworth, where he died May, 1892, aged 73 years. Mr. Irving's brother-in-law, Mr. Ephrium Howe, also settled in Dapto, Illawarra, where he carried on dairying pursuits, but did not enter into the public life of the district. It is plain that for many years Messrs. Irving, Evan R. Evans, senr., and other dairymen in Illawarra followed closely the lines of breeding and systems of dairying as that followed at Glenlee.

Dr. Richard Lewis Jenkins was born in Monmouthshire (England), and came to Sydney in 1841 as medical officer on board the ship "James Moran." He practised his profession for a time in the Hunter River district, and soon became a station owner on the Peel and Namoi Rivers. In 1857 he removed to Sydney, and then purchased Nepean Towers Estate, near Penrith, and went in for breeding pure pedigreed Shorthorn cattle. He had married on 1st January, 1852, Miss Mary Rae Johnston, eldest daughter of Major Edward Johnston, of H.M. 50th Regiment. His career as a cattle breeder in New South Wales is well and favourably known to fat cattle breeders. But not so favourably known to the Illawarra dairymen. He died in Brisbane, Queensland, on 13th August, 1883. He may have been a relation by marriage of Mr. Edward H. Weston, of Albion Park. They were, however, close friends, and Mr. Weston purchased bulls from him. That great prize winner at nearly all the Illawarra A. & H. Society Shows, John Dudgeon's bull "Reddie," had on his dam's side the Nepean Towers' blood in his pedigree which easily accounts for his lack of power to put udders of average quality on his female progeny.

Captain Charles Waldron, of H.M. 39th Regiment of Foot, arrived with his wife and family in 1828, and settled in the city for a time. In 1832 he purchased Spring Hill, Illawarra, consisting of 500 acres, with an "all cedar" house erected thereon, for £500, which is an indication of the depressed conditions then prevailing. He did not, however, live long in his new home to enjoy and admire the beauty of its surroundings. Towards the close of the following year, 1833, he found much trouble with his assigned servants. The result is quickly told. Two of his female convicts attacked and mutilated him in such a manner that he died on 28th January, 1834.

1834.—On January 28th, 1834, Captain Waldron, of Spring Hill, near Wollongong, was murdered by two female convicts. They were tried before Judge Burton and reprieved. Judge Burton after this trial proceeded to Norfolk Island, which he described as a hell.

His widow, Mrs. Jemima Waldron, carried on the farm with the assistance of her family. Several of her descendants are interested in portions of Spring Hill at the present time. Of Captain Waldron's family, the only one who took a lead in public affairs in Illawarra was George King Waldron, who was born in the Isle of Jersey in 1827. He joined his brother-in-law, Thomas J. Fuller, and they bought out John Graham, who had a store on the site of the Kiama Public School. Fuller and Waldron afterwards moved into premises where the E.S. & A. Bank stands. George L. Fuller, who had kept a post office in Gerringong and a commission agency business in Sydney, came on the scene and bought out his brother and

brother-in-law, and began by combining a wine and spirit business with general storekeeping. He succeeded, owing to the influence of his brother and brother-in-law. Information came easy, as T. J. Fuller became the first manager of the City Bank, at the corner of Terralong and Manning streets, and G. K. Waldron became a prominent auctioneer in the Kiama district.

George King Waldron as an auctioneer was a man of many parts. He was a sportsman, and owned and raced good horses, including "The Maid of Erin" and "Lady Benson." He was for years in close business friendship with Andrew McGill, James Robb, Duncan Beatron, and J. M. Antill, whose strains of dairy cattle he admired. His presence as a salesman was of the finest style. He was outspoken, and at all times advocated the introduction of the Devon and Ayrshire blood with the Shorthorns. He sold many young Ayrshire bulls at his Kiama yards. It was he who induced James McIntyre, of Gerringong, to give £50 for J. M. Antill's champion Ayrshire bull, "Dunlop." At James McIntyre's sale Henry Frederick purchased a blood red cow in calf to "Dunlop." That calf became the property of Simon Dudgeon. From that bull came "Sir Henry," the sire of "Admiral." "Admiral" in Graham Bros.' herd produced dairy cattle.

Waldron helped many struggling farmers in Illawarra and on the Richmond River. He died in the midst of work, suddenly, in 1888, at the age of 61 years. His bad debts at the time of his death were upwards of £3000.

C. W. CRAIG'S TEST COWS.
Winners of National Test Prize, £20, in 1896.
Reading from left to right—PRINCESS, EMPRESS, VIOLET, REDDIE, DANDY. 120¼lb. milk in 12 hours—. 4.51 per cent. average butter fat per cow. *See page 254*

GEO. DUNCAN, Brisbane Grove, Dapto, Illawarra.

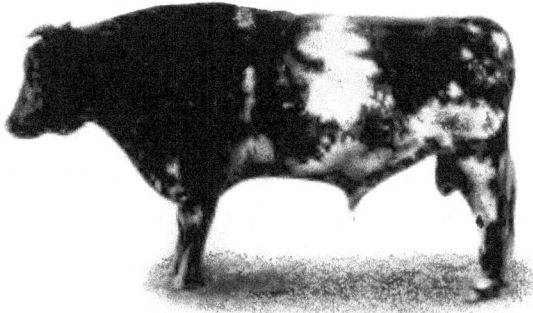

NOBLE LAD OF BRISBANE GROVE.

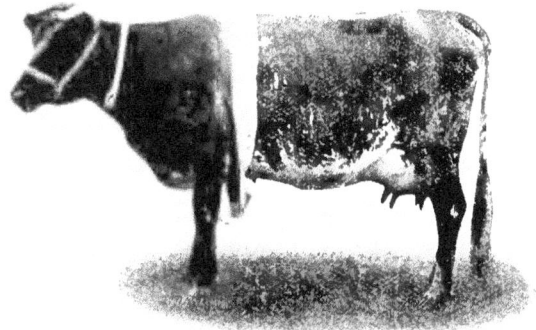

BECKY OF BRISBANE GROVE.

BLOSSOM OF BRISBANE GROVE.

STAR OF BRISBANE GROVE.

BOXSELL BROS., Myrtle Bank, Berry.

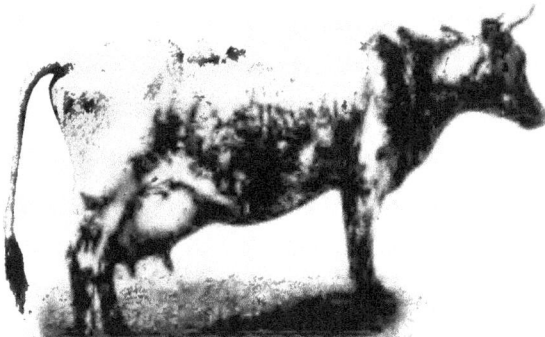

PIGEON OF MYRTLE BANK.

CHARMER'S WARBOND OF MYRTLE BANK.

MENDELISM.

Mendelism has no doubt given the key to open the door to a certain extent, and has therefore enabled several of our noted scientists to explain away many difficulties in cattle breeding. Until Mendel's discovery, which might be summed up in one word "segregation." In the segregation of factors Mendel saw that in order to obtain clear results it was absolutely necessary to start with pure breeding homogeneous material, and consider each character separately, and on no account to confuse the different generations. Then he realised that the progeny of distinct individuals must be separately recorded. All these ideas were entirely new in his day. The fact of segregation was the essential discovery which Mendel made, such segregation is normal phenomena of nature, according to the erudite Professor Bateson, and the Professor then came to the plain conclusions, "purity of type has thus acquired a precise meaning," inasmuch as it is dependent on genetic segregation, and has nothing to do with a prolonged course of selection, natural or artificial. He furthermore states:—"The red roan in shorthorn cattle is what is called heterogene in character caused by the meeting of the factors of red and white. The blue roan is often met with in the cross of the black Aberdeen Angus and the white shorthorn cattle. Many examples could be enumerated. Nothing of a definite nature was suggested to breeders by the scientific world that would enable them to solve the breeding problems, until Mendel's theory was properly explained. Every breeder was on the lookout for a wonder bull that would be capable of mating successfully with every cow in the herd. Such wonder animals do come occasionally. Nothing of a very definite nature was suggested to breeders that would enable them to work out.

How could any man then settle down to the idea that such continuous red colouring matter as found in Boyd's herd could be conveyed from sire to son for forty years, unless the foundation bulls were full of good red blood? We have ample proof of the importance of whole colours in blood horse breeding, where we find that the chestnut colour will always breed true to chestnut. Moreover, the fact is,

I think becoming every year more widely recognised that to breed full red cattle great care must be exercised in selecting sires true to pedigree. The uniformity of the laws of Nature is of such a character as under few circumstances to cause breeders to marvel over the simplicity of breeding stock true to colour. To argue then that Boyd's blood red cattle were the product of spotted red and white, or roan bulls is to set up a fetish, and, then call upon one's neighbours to worship a fantasy, or a tiresome idol, or one who may happen to be a romancer.

By the laws of uniformity of Nature we understand that the phenomena of Nature follow a regular sequence, and is therefore commonly defined as a uniform mode of acting which a natural agent observes when under the same circumstances. The Universe, as daily experience bears witness, is not a chaos of objects unrelated one to another, but is organised in a series of types. Each individual belonging to any one of these possessive properties similar to those of all other examples of that type. In the same circumstances they all act in the same way. So too, in regard to objects imbued with life, whether vegetable or animal. Trees of the same species will always produce fruit of the same sort, and wood of similar texture. So will red cattle produce red cattle. These uniformities are called 'Laws of Nature.' The Law of Continuity is also a valuable truth. But both must be argued with caution, as the only qualities which we can prove to be uniform to all matter are the Laws of Motion and Gravity.

Every theory of cattle breeding is based upon, and must take into account, two prime factors: Heredity and Variation. To put the thing into simple language, it must be obvious, even to the most unobservant, that the offspring of any couple, whilst more or less resembling that couple, also more or less depart from their standard. In other words, they inherit a general resemblance, but they have varied slightly, so that they do not present absolute facsimilies of their parents; but this is taking a very narrow view of the matter. The real wonder of heredity, which has ceased to be a wonder because it is universal, is the fact that species breed true. That there are small differences, which may be either absolutely or relatively small, is the result of the second factor, that of variation.

There are only two ways in which a biologist can deal with these problems, he can try to explain them, or he can assume them, and pass to the laws of both or either of them, so far as such can be observed. Let us consider, Heredity, of which it may at once be said that whilst we know a good deal about its operations, we know little or nothing about its mechanism. We may turn to the other question, that of Variation, and we are confronted with a similar difficulty. No one doubts that the thing is there; but can we in any way account for it? Another tangled tale.

When we mention such names as Darwin, Galton, Mendel, and Bateson, in connection with the science of breeding domestic animals it must be kept in mind that the views of those great investigators are by no means universally accepted, and that in the course of time further facts may come into notice which may utterly upset their varied hypotheses. Sir Bertram C. A. Windle has stated:—"Scientific opinion on any particular point is apt to waver from view to view, as new acts swim into one's ken; it swings from one side to another like a pendulum, and is sometimes found, after a long interval of time, to have returned to a position which it might have been supposed had been abandoned for ever." That such must necessarily be the case will not require much demonstration to an astute cattle-breeder who has experienced similar difficulties to that experienced by Mr. Boyd—conscious of the fact that a change of type was absolutely necessary, yet unable to decide as to which would be the better of several suggested ways of bringing it about.

That segregation is an important factor in cattle may, or may not be successfully demonstrated as our knowledge of heredity is defective. The term segregation is commonly used to denote the splitting out of the parental characters amongst the offspring of hybrids, but in dairy cattle it means bringing in an outcross, and then getting back on to the original strain with a view of increasing the size and vigor of the herd without sacrificing the colour to any serious extent.

The methods of a breeder are two. They are, as a matter of fact, nearly always used in conjunction, and not separately; but they are nevertheless essentially distinct. They are

selections and crossing. Pure selection, operating on material which is not the immediate result of a cross, modifies the form of an animal, and leaves it different from what it was when the selection began; something has to be added or taken away; something created or destroyed. The primary object of crossing is to combine within one strain two desirable qualities existing in distinct strains. Selection, however, may create something new, or bring forth character which had long been hidden and long separated.

The breeder who gets rid of his first crosses because they did not display the character he was working for would be acting foolishly. First crosses are, however, not always bred, because they may possess new characteristics, yet, they often possess greater vigour when the parents crossed. If say, a red bull is mated with white cows, the progeny will be termed hybrids if they display red and white, and roan colours. It is then a point with the breeder as to whether it would be better to continue using a red bull on white cows, or a white bull on red cows, in preference to mated, the red and white animals or the roan animals separately, with a view of raising a spotted red and white herd, or a roan herd, according to his fancy. In theory, if a breeder were to purchase a pure bred red Sussex or a Norfolk bull and a dozen white shorthorn heifers, some of the progeny, in the course of a few years, would be red, others white, others roan, and others of the cross would be red and white spotted. Then, in the selection of the future stud sires and dams it might be wise to use the full coloured animals.

As Derbyshire states:—"The student of heredity aims at finding out how the characters of animals are handed on from generation to generation. The breeder is not concerned with the interpretation of what he achieves; he does not care how the character of his stock is handed on from generation to generation, so long as the change which he effects tends in the direction of an improvement." The student of heredity, thus, is seldom interested in immediate profits. But there cannot be any doubt that both the practical breeder and the student of heredity would profit much by exchanging ideas constantly. There is a wide field for investigation. Hybrids are as sterile as they ever were. New specimens have failed to materialise. Artificial variations are still puzzling breeders who have not yet grasped the idea of Mendelism—dairy cattle as we understand them, unless fixed by the crossing of Mendel's dominants with dominants or regressives with regressives, (of which Darwin knew nothing) still tend to revert to original conditions.

That many of these newer ideas have had their origin in older ones, is shown by Dr. Thomas Dwight, where he states:—"Trustworthy of serious consideration is the theory of changes, by sudden leaps, advocated by Mivart and the Duke of Argyll, and in old times by St. Hilairs. It has since become known as the mutation theory of De Vries. According to Osborne, a very competent critic, De Vries has demonstrated the law of saltation, and, that saltation is a constant phenomenon in Nature, a vera causa of evolution. Professor Bateson shows that it harmonizes with Mendel's conception of heredity, and it may be regarded as par excellence the contribution of the experimental method." "It is to this theory," says Dr. Dwight, "that I myself incline very strongly, always with certain reservations and limitations." Further, he implies, "That the saltation theory implies vitalism, or the existence of something in the organiser which directs its growth under normal and unusual circumstances, allowing it to adapt itself to changed conditions."

Be all this as it may, head and shoulders above most workers in the science of evolution stood "Abbot Mendel," who, trusting not to theory, but to experiment, discovered a law, which has stood the test, concerning the working of variation through inheritance.

The one great, outstanding difficulty confronting all experimenters who may attempt to Mendelise our domestic animals is the lack of a sufficiency of really pure bred animals. All, or nearly all our domesticated animals are the blends of several breeds or sub-varieties, which give no end of trouble, under the most favourable circumstances to their masters to get them to breed true to type. The conditions become more and more complicated when an array of fancy points have to be worked into any given breed, namely:—type, size, colour, constitutional vigor, and quality.

The trouble with the majority of our stock breeders is, they are a little of almost everything, and not much of anything for very long. Certainly not long enough to prove any of the many rules demanded in stock raising.

Mendelism.—The question, What is Mendelism? has been asked through the press of the world during the last twenty years, and although the answers come with equal promptitude, but few seem to be able to grasp its great importance to breeders. All we can do is to give the old stereotyped answer, namely, "Mendelism is the name of the discovery of Abbot Mendel, a peasant boy who turned monk, and died in Brunn in 1882. This priest-scientist carried out a series of experiments with the common pea, crossing varieties, with astonishing results." Mendel's work has been taken up by several enthusiasts during the last twenty years. Professor Biffen began experimenting with wheat to find a variety of wheat which would be rust-resisting. Then the whole wheat question in its relation to milling and yielding properties came into the limelight, and experiments on a large scale have been conducted everywhere.

As soon as a wheat which produced a fine, stiff, upstanding straw and a high quality of yield of grain was established, experiments were tried on the animals of the farm. When the writer read of these results, it flashed with irresistible force on his mind that it was possible to produce better types of cattle than hitherto in Illawarra. Professor Biffen had to cross good wheat liable to rust with poor wheat not liable. He succeeded in his wheat breeding experiments. Why, then, if all flesh is grass, could not the Illawarra dairymen produce good results by judiciously crossing breeds of cattle? The practice of crossing was not new in Illawarra, but it was always carried out by blind chance, and was in consequence constantly falling into disrepute. It had, however, been continued in long enough in so many quarters that the theory of long-dated pedigrees had been shaken to its foundations, and the continual clamouring of some dairymen for the introduction of new blood did not improve matters. Nature and nurture work hand in hand when understood and practised. As with wheat so with cattle. It is a matter of a much longer time with cattle owing to the slowness of the maturing of cattle. Time is money, and money is everything with the great majority of our dairymen. Hence the difficulty of keeping a sufficient number of them together to form a strong one-idea cattle association. If the theory is not first sensitised on the brain, it is too much to expect much earnestness in the pursuit of the objective.

Types of dairy cattle vary, and no doubt this variation has been noticed by dairy cattle fanciers who have followed up the A. and H. Society shows held in the different dairying centres of N.S.W. and Queensland during the last thirty or forty years. It may have occurred to many how different in certain characteristics certain of these types are.

Needless to say all have been moulded by Nature for a purpose. Hence it is that good cattle judges in one locality fail to satisfy the views of judges a few hundred, or even fifty, miles away. "Use is second nature," and, therefore, when a dairyman gets a type fixed on his mind's eye he is constantly looking for that type. This is a mistake when the judge follows it up in another locality where the true dairy type is different, however small or great that difference may be. There is a very old saying, "Handsome is as handsome does," and it applies with considerable force in dairy cattle breeding; unfortunately too often!

This brings us face to face with each other in regard to defining a general type for all dairymen to follow. At once I should say such a thing is impossible. What, then, is the way out? It is this—each district should decide for itself, and then each breeder should try and prove or disprove the correctness of that type to his own entire satisfaction.

The difficulty in arriving at conclusions is begotten of lack of concentrating one's brain power sufficiently long on any given type to be able to draw a clear, honest opinion therefrom. With some breeders it is impossible to reason, as whatever type they may have in stock for the time being is the best. Such men have really no fixed ideas. They can tell you the cows that are giving them the most milk, but that is about all they can tell you. When it comes to a matter of breeding good cows true to a given type or colour they fail.

If our dairy cattle breeders were more sincere, and less inclined to find fault with their neighbours' cattle, we would get nearer a correct solution of the best types to follow in our several localities than we are doing in a much quicker time. It is now forty years since the first conference was held in Kiama, embracing as it did delegates from Bega to Bulli on the coast, and was extended to the tableland. Its deliberations were good apparently, but evidently lacked sincerity.

Size, it has been said, though we might suspect such remark may have emanated from those who owned large cattle, is everything in a dairy cow. It is difficult to arrive at a definite settlement of this question, as many medium-sized cows have been long and consistent producers of rich milk. Many experiments have been entered upon to prove which is the more profitable cow, the large, or the medium, or the small sized, without definite results.

It is generally recognised that the soil on which dairy cattle are raised has all to do with the size of a breed, as where the bone-making constituents are present in large quantities in a soil the animals raised there are sure to be larger, and that the progeny of these large animals will deteriorate in size when removed to a less congenial soil as regards bone-making proclivities.

Without stopping to gainsay an opinion so manifestly apocryphal, I will content myself with the observation that to my certain knowledge all big cows are not good dairy cows, nor are all medium or small sized cows bad dairy cows. Trees and plants are supposed to stretch themselves upwards in quest of air and light, but the upward growths of cows and bulls cannot be said to be free from objections, and spring from a different origin.

We have ample proof that deficiency in appearance is by no means a proper object of reproach in either bulls or cows, for a plain frame may contain remarkable vitality, and angular bodies often contain great producing powers. The unfortunate thing about this is that when a breeder brings one of these typed bulls into a show ring, its mean appearance is at once the object of scorn and derision, and becomes the target for the shafts of ridicule.

It has been over and over again wished that a scale of excellence could be made to accompany degrees of quality, and that the higher the quality rose the higher should be the scale of excellence. Experience has, however, taught us many lessons in this respect, one of which is very patent, namely, we can adjust points to suit for general appearance, but when show excellence is placed in a dairy quality balance the appearance theory is found wanting in a large majority of cases. It was these thoughts now expressed that caused the writer to found the I.D.C. Association in 1910.

There are many cases that could be recorded where bulls on which no value was placed while they were in the Illawarra district as bulls, yet their progeny in every respect far excelled the prized ones, but space does not permit to record them here. There are also many cases that could be mentioned of bulls whose pedigrees have never been satisfactorily explained, owing to the fact that a host of breeders either claimed to have bred one or more such animals, but who had notwithstanding never produced anything so good themselves.

JAMES R. KNAPP, Swanlea, Bolong, Shoalhaven.

JOCK OF SWANLEA.

GWEN OF SWANLEA.
(No. 1146, I.D.C.H.B.)

VELVET 4th OF SWANLEA.

BLOSSOM 2nd OF SWANLEA.
(No. 1139, I.D.C.H.B.)

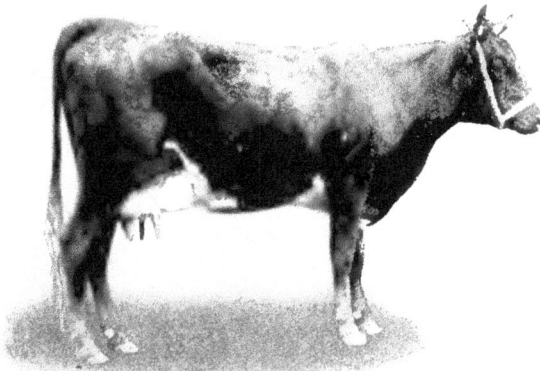

FLOSSIE OF SWANLEA.
Test for full year:—10,650 lbs. Milk; 4.8 per cent. Butter
Fat; 508.68 lbs. Butter Fat.

JESSIE 4th OF SWANLEA (No. 1148, I.D.C.H.B.).

The stories of dairy cattle breeding are only interesting when they are true. There are also many vexed questions that should always demand truth, such as Reversion or Atavism, which is the reappearance of ancestral traits which have been absent or latent in the race for one or more generations. Next in order we have telegony, or the influence of the first sire with a female, or the sire of another breed, maternal impressions. Before one is carried away with these theories, it would be wise before giving way to such arguments to carefully study the natural photograph to see what influence the sun or moon's rays have regarding the color of animals, as nearly all the evidence brought forward as proofs of acquired characters is capable of being interpreted in another way. Many characters in plant and animal life depend on the presence of determining factors behaving as units.

Now, supposing that these determining factors have been persevered in for years—generations, in fact—by the art of breeding, what would happen if that art was relaxed? We will submit a case in point: On a stretch of tableland in Queensland, situated between the Bulloo Downs station, on the Bulloo River, and the Nocatunga station, on the Wilson River, which may be termed at the time no-man's land, as it was considered to be useless country for grazing purposes. Both the stations were shorthorn cattle stations. No other breeds were ever introduced, and pure sires were being constantly supplied. It is said that "instinct prevails where science fails." Be that as it may, a number of cows in charge of a bull or two found their way to the tableland from Bulloo Downs station, and established themselves there. They bred freely, evidently on the lines of consanguinity, regardless, perhaps, of consequences; certain they were free from the law of the patriarchal devices of father Abraham. This society of friends occupied the tableland for about twenty years. When discovered there was approximately an equal number of males and females of variegated colors. The earlier generations had died off, and the remaining family were of brown, brindle, and yellowish-red colors, with long, coarse horns. Now, if you were asked what breed did they belong to, all that could be said is that they were of no particular breed, but representatives of the several units from which the shorthorn breed had been made up! When, however, we come to the question, supposing all the males were taken away and pure shorthorn bulls used, how long would it take to bring the progeny back to their sires' status? This is a question scarcely worth arguing, as it would be better to kill off the whole lot, and start with fewer and purer stock. Mention has been made of "Charley the Cobbler's" red and black brindle bull, and "Andrew McGill's" red bull with the brindle stripes. In the case of the complete brindle that colour disappeared and never reappeared in his descendants. On the other hand Blucher's descendants according as they were mated displayed the brindle stripes. Yet, in both instances the dairy qualities, and general appearances have been sustained.

It will be seen from the foregoing facts that if the atoms that go to build up an animal had the power of choice it would be impossible to be certain of one's breeding experiments, and breeding could not be successfully carried on, as it is a game, not of chance, but one of playing with stacked cards. He is a smart man who can predict the future of his herd 20 years hence. For be it known, "heredity is a vexed problem." No animal can inherit the whole of its ancestors, nor, need it be wholly dominated by traits descending to it from any one of them. It will have its own individual attributes to nullify these, and its own environment to influence what shall not be. Calculate the fragments scattered here and there through the pedigree of Mr. George Grey's bull Togo. These fragments would remind one of a house built of various kinds of bricks—a mosaic, so to speak. Perhaps, purity of types as regards Togo acquired a precise meaning, and had nothing to do with a long prolonged course of selection, natural or artificial. His great characteristic depended on the result of the meeting of two gametes bearing similar factors. When they met, the product, Togo, was a distinct animal, with its own characteristics.

It would therefore seem that every egg is a law unto itself, and has the power of reaching an individual end according to its environment. Few have not formed an opinion as to whether or not new features do appear—as they certainly, to our untrained minds, do seem to appear. But according to the authorities who have studied Mendelism, they are not really new qualities in any proper sense of the word. They are qualities which have all the time been there, but have been prevented from coming to the front. Yet, if these theories are pushed too far it will be found that what appears to be a gain was really a loss, for until the retaining qualities have been removed the hidden qualities could not appear. Added characters are never permanent, on the other hand mutations are lost characters, and can be comprehended. Example, polled cattle.

Facts and theories require proofs. and at times proofs are elusive things. It has ever been the tendency of man to measure himself by the expanse of the universe, yet the cell from which he sprung may be defined as the smallest particle of organic matter capable of life.

Perhaps, when the Mendel law, as it is now termed, comes to be better understood by practical breeders, it will be found applicable to all kinds of animal characters. Nature and nurture working from within and without.

Hence it is that all cattle breeders, in truth all animal breeders, have to exercise care when selecting a sire, and equally as much care with regard to their systems of feeding. In 1913 Sir Oliver Lodge spoke strongly of "a critical examination of scientific foundation, and of a growing mistrust in purely intellectual processes." Professor Bateson, in 1914, speaking from the stand-point of a biologist, said:—"The age is one of rapid progress and profound scepticism in scientific thought," and added, "we must confess also to a deep, but irksome humility in the presence of great vital problems." Alexander Pope hath said: "The bliss of man could pride that blessing find, Is not to act or think beyond mankind; no power of body or of soul to share, But what his nature and his state can bear."

EARLY SHOWS IN ILLAWARRA.

THE FIRST AGRICULTURAL SOCIETY OF NEW SOUTH WALES.

The first Agricultural Society of New South Wales was established in 1821. The following gentlemen were the first duly appointed office-bearers:—President, Sir John Jamieson; Vice-Presidents, Rev. Samuel Marsden, Dr. Townson. LL.D., and William Cox, Esq.; Secretaries, Messrs. E. T. Palmer and Alexander Berry; Treasurers, Messrs. Alexander Riley and William Walker.

The prospectus of the Agricultural Society of New South Wales for 1821-2, set out to give the merino fleece to 300,000 sheep; to improve 400 horses, and breed them for exportation; and to give the Hereford and Devon carcase or the Suffolk udder to 100,000 head of cattle. This was considered no mean undertaking, for the Colony then had only been 35 years under British rule. The original Society became defunct in 1833. The old committee had 118 subscribers; 31 of those came from Newcastle. A stock fund was formed, of which £1000 was sent to England, and absorbed in the purchase of merino ewes £500, £200 on horned cattle, and £300 in horses from the general fund. Captain King, R.N., expended a sum of money in the purchase of grass and corn seeds, together with a collection of agricultural literary works. The first show was held at Parramatta on the first Thursday in October, 1822, when £100 was distributed—prizes for the best sheep, lambs, horned cattle, and stallions. Prizes were also given for the best shepherds and farm servants. Jonas Bradley won a silver tankard for exhibiting 1 cwt. of negro-head tobacco, grown by himself at Windsor. Premiums were offered by the Society of Arts, manufactures, and export, to persons who could manufacture and export no less than 10 gallons of oil during the years 1824-5-6, and to persons who during the years 1824-5 should export the best wine, not less than 20 gallons, the produce of their land. In 1821 726 bales, or 181,500 lbs., of wool was exported, also a small quantity of lambs' wool, from New South Wales.

The annual subscription was five guineas each member, and a subscription fund of £25 each was started, with a view of introducing from the mother country more important breeds of horses, cattle and sheep. This was owing to the better types of stock in the Colony not being considered equal to the demand. The number of breeders were few, and most of those who bred the better class of stock bred for their own use. The following is a list of the subscribers in 1823 to the Stock Importation Fund:—Major Goulburn and Sir John Jamieson, £100 each; Messrs. Alexander Berry, Edward Wollstonecraft, and William Walker, £50 each; Messrs. James Atkinson, John Blaxland, Richard Brooks, John T. Campbell, James Chandler, William Cox, sen., William Cox, jun., Robert Crawford, Prosper de Mestre, John Dixon, William Howe, Captain King, R.N.. William Lawson, Robert Lowe, Hannibal Hawkins Macarthur, Thomas McVitie, Rev. Samuel Marsden, William H. Moore, James Norton, John Oxley, John Palmer, John Piper, Edward Riley, Charles Throsby, Robert Townson, Thomas Walker, De Arcy Wentworth, and Major West, £25 each. Allan Cunningham was corresponding secretary.

The Agricultural Society of New South Wales.—The premiums awarded were presented at Walker's Inn, Parramatta, on 17th October, 1824, consisting of plate value equal to 40 Spanish dollars each to Edward Riley and William Howe for five best 2-toothed Australian merino ewes; to Rev. Samuel Marsden for best colonial bred bull; to George Cox for best colonial bred heifer; a piece of plate valued at 30 Spanish dollars to John Buckland for best team of bullocks; to William Howe for best colonial made cheese; a piece of plate valued at 10 Spanish dollars to John Thomas Campbell for best colonial bred stallion; a piece of plate valued at 40 Spanish dollars to John Pye for best colonial bred boar; a piece of plate valued at 10 dollars to John Pye for best colonial bred sow.

Taking advantage of this show of stock, Mr. Robert Cooper, the distiller, offered for sale eight capital English-bred cows (milkers) off the first dairy farm in the Colony, and one thoroughbred English bull. Note.—Had the name of the farm been mentioned in the above advertisement it would have been possible for us to describe the breeding to which the above animals belonged. The sale took place at Parramatta on 28th October, 1824.

Early Show in Parramatta, 13th October, 1825.—Neither cattle, sheep, nor horses were present as exhibits. A few horses were brought there for sale. Mr. John Macarthur sold two at 50 guineas, the other at 40 guineas. We read of medals being awarded to Messrs. John T. Campbell, H. H. Macarthur, and John Peisley, and of Mr. Lethbridge having a fine ram on exhibition on one occasion, but no prize was awarded, as it was the only exhibit in its class. Mr. Bayly had a bull on exhibition the same day. It was the only exhibit in its class, but as the judges declared it to be "much above mediocrity" the owner pressed his claims and a prize was awarded.

Very little has come down to us from the ruins of the first agricultural shows that were held in Australia—mere items. For example: "In October, 1833, after the exhibition at Parramatta, for sale, two pure-bred Durham bulls."

THE HISTORY OF AGRICULTURAL SOCIETIES IN ILLAWARRA, N.S.W.

When a writer takes upon himself a duty such as this—to wit, the publication of a book of historical importance—it may be inferred that he is going to give the world, in readable form, his own personal experiences. Few writers, however, confine themselves to their own personal experiences; as a rule they are men possessed of a keen perception, always observant, good conversationalists, and deep readers. Where many writers err is when they listen to clap-trap on subjects about which they have had no personal experience, and thereby taking for granted stories that have little or no historical foundation. Such is the free and easy way of writing. But what is its real value? Just what it pans out in the washing, namely, a few grains of gold, out of tons of waste material, or non-facts.

Too much ink has been wasted by writers on matters relating to soil, climate and environment, and their influence on animal life, without a thought as to whether the owners of the animals ever used, or knew how to use, those natural advantages for the purposes of demonstration. What is here being alluded to is the often foolish way in which incapable press representatives—self-chosen of course—make fatal havoc with these subjects through not being able to study the true history of animal life on the farms. Too much theory has been set down in cold type about the origin of our

cattle, and far too much has been taken for granted. No one in the past set himself the task of collecting facts.

Fortunately the writer went through the old records, and is now in a position to give them to the public for the benefit of the present and future generations of Illawarraians. There is nothing to be gained by referring to Homer nor to Virgil to learn that the animals of the farm were domesticated and raised to a high standard of excellence not only at the dawn of the Christian era, but for centuries before the dawn of our era. It suffices for the present purpose to go back about a century and a half ago, when the only inhabitants of Australia belonged to the stone-hatchet age, and to the landing of "The First Fleet." No horses, no cattle, no sheep, no goats nor pigs were then on Australian soil.

What do our Australian histories tell us about that period? See early chapter of this volume.

THE ILLAWARRA A. & H. SOCIETY.

As will be seen elsewhere, the beginnings of this Society are traditional, owing to the absence of a local newspaper or a recognised press correspondent. The story of its founding is none the less true, as the writer's father, who landed in Wollongong on the 17th of March, 1841 (in company with quite a number of other immigrants from the North of Ireland), and went direct into the employ of the late Mr. Henry Osborne at Marshall Mount, Illawarra, was at that first exhibition in the Market Square, Wollongong, in 1843. It was purely an exhibition of the cattle imported into Illawarra by the Osborne family, which comprised three brothers—Dr. John Osborne, R.N., Dr. Alexander Osborne, R.N., and Mr. Henry Osborne, of Marshall Mount.

The object of this Osborne exhibition was what should be the prevailing principle of all our A. & H. Societies, namely, an honorary display, with a view of bettering the district, the reward, if any, to come from the sale of the animals, plants, fruits, and vegetables thus exhibited.

There were at least two such exhibitions of stock in the Market Square, Wollongong, before the Agricultural and Horticultural Society of Illawarra was founded, which can honestly be placed on record as being the first and oldest of its kind in Australia. This statement is borne out by the minute books of the Illawarra Agricultural and Horticultural Society, and run as follows: "On the 15th April, 1844, a meeting of the landed proprietors and others took place in the new school house, Wollongong, to take into consideration whether it would not be advisable and advantageous for the general interests of the district to establish an Agricultural and Horticultural Society. The proposition was favourably received, and it was unanimously agreed that such a Society should be forthwith formed, the subscription being limited to one shilling per month, in order that all classes might be enabled to subscribe.''

In June, 1843, the Cumberland, Cook, and Camden counties combined to form a Society on the lines of the English county shows, and began its operations by holding a ploughing match at Parramatta on 6th June, 1843. This was the beginning of Agricultural Societies as we understand them to-day. Prior to this date shows were practically wealthy pastoralists concerns, in which the small landowners and settlers generally had no interests—in truth, they were not considered, as small settlers had little or no standing then in New South Wales.

Owing to its isolation, Illawarra was out of the running in this Society. There were no macadamised roads to any given centre. Bong Bong was then the chief town in the County of Camden, and Hoddles' track along the crest of Saddleback the only way to it in a direct line. The Dapto people did not feel disposed to come so far south, and set to work to reach Bong Bong in their own way, with a view of course, of forwarding their own personal interests. Nature was, however, against the advocates of either track, and as the years rolled by the old cattle tracks used in the early days by Colonel George Johnston and John Ritchie's stockmen became the recognised roads.

The Wollongong-Dapto-Berrima road was for some years known as Jack Waite's track; then the Bong Bong road up to 1843. In 1842 Dr. George Underwood Alley, a clever man, with a taste for writing combined with progressive ideas, conceived the idea of forming a road capable of bringing trade to the seaboard at Wollongong. He was joined in his efforts by Mr. George Brown, of Dapto. Dr. Alley's letter to the ''S.M. Herald'' of 27th January, 1843, stands as a memorial to his effort. He and Mr. Brown could not see eye to eye, so Dr. Alley removed to Hyam's Flats, Jamberoo, and then Mr. George Brown induced the Government to send a batch of convicts from Sydney, 30 in number, to form a dray track from Dapto across Molly Morgan's Swamp to Berrima.

When the late Mr. Henry Osborne and others caught the idea of shows for the benefit of themselves and the small settlers they set to work in a practical way to benefit their own district, and allowed the people in all the other localities to look after their own affairs in like fashion.

On 15th April, 1844, in a public school building, at that time unoccupied, in Crown Street, Wollongong, and, after discussion, was adjourned to the 21st April, 1844, on which date a Society was formed, to be called the Illawarra Agricultural Society. E. F. Wood was elected first President, and R. M. Westmacott was the first hon. secretary. The following gentlemen were members of the first committee: Gerard Gerard, J.P., Charles Throsby Smith, Captain William Lampriere, Frederick Sheaffe, Michael Hindmarsh, Edward Palmer, James Mackay Grey, J.P., James Shoobert, J. R. Comins, Dr. Robert Menzies, J.P., Robert Miller, Thomas Way, Dr. Alexander Osborne, J.P., Henry Osborne, J.P., George Brown, James Robb, Captain Samuel Addison, William Warren Jenkins, Captain Plunkett, and Dr. Charles O'Brien. The first show was held in the verandah and house next to the present Telegraph Office on Thursday, 27th January, 1845. The exhibits were good, but the room spaces being too small much inconvenience was felt. The first ploughing match was held at Dapto in Mr. George Brown's paddock, on the bank of Mullet Creek.

There was a time, not many years ago, when the residents of the Shoalhaven Valley considered that they at no time formed part of the great Illawarra district. The Shoalhaven Valley having had its beginnings at Coolangatta very likely led many to form that conclusion. However, there is now sufficient evidence to show that it then, and is now, a part of one great centre of production.

The part played by those who were associated with Captain Hart's great enterprise at Woodstock, Jamberoo, is not generally known. It was this:—

Abraham Lincoln came to the Woodstock Mills, Jamberoo, in about 1840, from Suffolk, England, where he had been trained in agricultural pursuits in his youth. He was a writer and contributor on agricultural subjects before coming to Australia. Contemporary with Lincoln at the Woodstock Mills was James W. Waugh, who had been prior to coming to Australia a publisher in Edinburgh, Scotland. He afterwards founded and published Waugh's Almanac in New South Wales. Those two men were the real founders of the old Illawarra A. & H. Society. They understood the business, and furnished for the guidance of those who followed them the propaganda on which every society of the kind has been worked out. The staff of Captain Hart's Woodstock Mills and brewery were men of great worth to Australia. They were in the forefront of matters relating to agricultural progress. Hop-growing, fruit-growing, as well as root crops and cereals of every kind, were carefully experimented with at the old Woodstock-Jamberoo establishment. One might with every confidence say that the Kent Brewery, established there in 1835 with the capital supplied by Captain Thomas Frederick Hart, was the forerunner of Tooth's Kent Brewery in Sydney, as John Tooth was associated with Hart's Brewery in its later stages.

As mentioned elsewhere, the last mortal remains of Captain Hart are lying in a neglected grave at Unanderra, Illawarra. Yet few, if any, of our old Australian pioneers were more worthy of a public monument.

The people who nestled around Captain Hart's great enterprise came from the chief centres of Great Britain and Ireland, bringing with them the newest ideas of the old lands. True, an Agricultural Society had been formed in New South Wales as early as 1822, but it had not the same ideals as the Illawarra Society had. This is plain when we know that the former was under the domination of the city merchants and large landed proprietors, whilst the latter has been controlled and supported through all the years of its existence by the dairy farmers and small agriculturists.

The following gentlemen were proposed to conduct the general arrangements of the Society, viz.: Chairman, Henry Osborne, Esq., J.P.; Committee, Gerard Gerard, Esq., J.P., Messrs. Edward F. Wood, Michael Hindmarsh, Thomas Way, Edward Palmer, Charles Throsby Smith, James Shoobert, James Mackay Grey. Dr. Robert Menzies, Captain R. M. Westmacott, Robert Miller, Dr. Alexander Osborne, George Wood, George Brown, Thomas Atchison, James Robb, Captain Samuel Addison, and William Warren Jenkins; Secretary and Treasurer, Mr. William Taylor, C.P.S.

At the next meeting of the Committee Mr. Henry Osborne resigned his position as Chairman of the Society, and Edward F. Wood, Esq., was appointed Chairman; and Mr. William Taylor resigned the position of Secretary and

Treasurer, and Captain R. M. Westmacott (who had been A.D.C. to Governor Sir Richard Bourke) was appointed, and the names of Captain Francis Plunkett and Charles James Tindall were added to the Committee.

At meeting held on May 7th, 1844, the following gentlemen were appointed to arrange a list of prizes:—Edward F. Wood, Esq., chairman, Dr. Alexander Osborne, William Warren Jenkins, Captain R. M. Westmacott, Henry Osborne, Captain Samuel Addison, W. Crawford, and Edward Palmer. Another meeting was subsequently held at the Wollongong Hotel, and rules were drawn up and adopted for the first ploughing match, and the following was the list of prizes for live stock:— Horse section: Best two-year-old colt £2/10/-, best two-year-old filly £1/10/-, best entire horse in exhibition (naming the purpose for which bred) £2/10/-. Cattle section: Best two-year-old bull £2/10/-, best two-year-old heifer £2/10/-, best calf (two months old) £1/10/-. Swine: Best boar under 12 months old £1, best sow under 12 months old £1, best fat pig 10/-, best sow and litter 10/-. Then followed a list of prizes for grain and dairy products, fruits, vegetables and flowers, for which liberal prizes were offered.

At meeting held July 7th, 1844, the date of the show was fixed for the third Thursday in January, 1845. The system of voting adopted was suitable to capitalists. In the voting Clearing Lease exhibitors and such as occupied small farms of not more than 20 acres were allowed but one vote.

The prizes for ploughmen and drivers:— Bullock teams, six bullocks, 1st prize £1/10/-, 2nd prize 10/-; fat bullock team with four bullocks, 10/-; driver of six bullocks, 1st prize 7/6, 2nd prize 2/6; driver of four bullocks, 4/-. The judges were Messrs. Henry Osborne, W. W. Jenkins, and Jas. M. Grey in all the agricultural classes; Mr. H. Heathorne, Dr. Alexander Osborne, and Captain William L. F. Seaffe were in charge of the awards in the horticultural classes. Judges for the ploughing matches were Dr. Alex. Osborne and Messrs. Way and Hindmarsh, who also acted as judges of stock.

At a meeting of the Society held on 10th December, 1844, Dr. Robert Menzies spoke on behalf of the subscribers from Captain's Hart's mills and brewery, Woodstock, to the effect that Mr. Heathorne requested that £3 out of the £25 collected there be devoted to a first prize for barley, and that Mr. Lincoln requested that his donation of £2 should be added to the prizes for ploughing. A sub-committee, consisting of Gerard Gerard, Edward Palmer, Captain R. M. Westmacott, and James Shoobert, were appointed to make all arrangements about the show and ploughing matches. Messrs. Black and McKay were appointed judges in place of Dr. Alex. Osborne, W. W. Jenkins, and James M. Grey in the ploughing matches. The report of show dated February 10th, 1845, missing.

A general meeting was held in Wollongong on March 11th, 1845, when the accounts for 1844 were laid before the committee. The meeting then proceeded to elect a chairman, secretary and treasurer for the year 1845. E. F. Wood, Esq., was again elected Chairman, and Captain Robert March Westmacott was elected Secretary and Treasurer; Committee, E. F. Wood, Henry Osborne, Michael Hindmarsh, William W. Jenkins, Gerard Gerard, Edward Palmer, Dr. Jerrett, Dr. Alex. Osborne, James Shoobert, Edwin Gerard, Thomas Black, Captain R. M. Westmacott (five to form a quorum). The annual meetings were fixed for the 11th March in each year. The following notices were dealt with, viz.: (1) To make the floral show at such season as flowers can be obtained; (2) to allow small farmers whose lands do not exceed 20 acres to pay sixpence per month; (3) no person be allowed to exhibit unless a subscriber; (4) entrance money to be one shilling for first and second horses; (5) no person to touch any article exhibited; (6) day and place to be both mentioned for both the show and ploughing matches; (7) to consider prizes for 1845. These propositions had been duly submitted, and, 14 rules in all, had been adopted on that date, which were the foundation rules of every A. & H. Society and Ploughing Match Committee since established in Australia.

During April, 1845, Mr. E. F. Wood resigned from the Society owing to his departure for England. It was then suggested to appoint Captain Westmacott, but on a motion by Dr. O'Brien and Captain Sheaffe, Mr. Gerard Gerard was appointed Chairman. The appointment of Mr. Gerard Gerard was warmly supported by Captain Samuel Addison, who had become a strong supporter of the Society.

The following members were appointed at a meeting held January 6th, 1846, to arrange matters in connection with the show to be held on 28th January, 1846, also for ploughing matches on 27th January, 1846:—Dr. Alex. Osborne, C. T. Smith, James Shoobert, Edward Palmer, J. T. Lomax, Gerard Gerard, and Captain Westmacott. It was also agreed that a dinner should take place on the 28th January, 1846, and that the tickets were not to exceed 5/- each, to which the judges should be invited.

A sub-committee, consisting of Messrs. W. A. Crawford, J. T. Lomax, Thomas Palmer, J. McDonald, and Captain Westmacott, were appointed to arrange the dinner; prizes to be awarded after dinner.

A general meeting was held on February 15th, 1846, and accounts were submitted. Mr. Gerard Gerard was elected Chairman, and Captain Westmacott Secretary and Treasurer. A committee was appointed, consisting of Gerard Gerard, Dr. Alex. Osborne, Edward Palmer, Captain W. Sheaffe, James Shoobert, Dr. Robert Menzies, W. A. Crawford, Captain Addison, W. W. Jenkins, Captain Westmacott, Dr. J. Jerrett, H. Heathorne, C. T. Smith. Next meeting was held in Wollongong on 26th March, 1846, when the Chairman, Mr. Gerard Gerard, and the Secretary, Captain Westmacott, resigned their respective offices, thus leaving the Society without officers. Then we find the following notice in the "Sydney Morning Herald" of that date: "To Edward Palmer, Esq. We the undersigned members of the Agricultural Societies of Illawarra request that you will act as Secretary for the time being to the Society, also that you will communicate with Captain Westmacott, the late Secretary, and obtain from him such documents, or books, as belong to the Society, and that you will report upon them at your earliest convenience. (Signed) Alex. Osborne, C. T. Smith, Henry Heathorne, George Brown, Andrew Thompson, Edward Elliott, John Osborne, Robert Haworth, Bernard McCauley, Edmond Bourke, Edward Corrigan, John Gilligan, Thomas W. Palmer, Gerard Gerard, Thomas Jessett, and James Commins. Dated Wollongong, 9th April, 1846." A meeting was called for 19th May, but it was postponed until the 21st of same month, when Mr. Charles Throsby Smith was voted to the chair. After the books had been duly examined, Mr. C. T. Smith was appointed Chairman of the Society, and Edward Palmer Secretary for the remainder of the year 1846; Committee, Messrs. Guion, John Osborne, William Ahearn. It was then decided to erect a shed in the Market Square, Wollongong, in which to house the exhibits. Drs. O'Brien and John Osborne carried a motion of thanks to Captain Robert March Westmacott. The following memorial was also drawn up for presentation to the Governor for leave to erect a shed in Market Square:—"To the Governor,—I beg leave to inform you that the members of the Agricultural Society of Illawarra propose to erect a shed in the Market Square of Wollongong for general purposes, but particularly for the use of the Society, to enable them to hold their half-yearly meetings, and to have their annual show there. (Signed) Edward Palmer, Secretary. 4th June, 1846." "Sir,—In reply, I am directed to state that His Excellency regrets that he has no authority to grant the required permission, as to do so would be virtually to give the ground on which the shed is to be erected. (Signed) E. Deas Thompson." On July 1st, 1846, at a meeting held in the store of the I.S.N. Company at the wharf, Wollongong, it was decided to postpone the idea of building in the Market Square, Wollongong. Then followed the revision of the prize list, as between fifty and sixty pounds sterling were forthcoming for prizes. On motion by Captain Addison and Captain William Sheaffe it was decided to allot prize-money as follows: Horse stock £7, horned cattle £8/10/-, grain £12, swine £4/15/-, poultry £2, butter £2/10/-, cheese £1/15/-, honey 10/-, wax 10/-, wine £1, mead 10/-; horticulture, fruit £5, vegetables £2, flowers £1; ploughing matches, £8; total, £57.

At a meeting held on 29th September, 1846, it was decided to hold a meeting 14 days before the show; the ploughing match to come off in Mr. George Brown's paddock at Dapto. Mr. Gerard handed in a memo. to the Secretary to the effect that he wished his donation of two pounds to be given as prizes to farm servants who have been taught in the services of their masters, and known to be of sober and industrious habits (£1), and to best cheese (£1). Mr. George Brown stated that he would give £1 as a donation, to be divided among the plough drivers. On motion by Dr. Alex. Osborne and Captain W. Sheaffe a dinner was to be arranged for at the Marine Hotel, tickets not to exceed 10/-; the dinner to comprise such gentlemen as are willing to express their appreciation of the comfort and advantages of the establishment of a good hotel in Wollongong, and the advantage to the community at large from the increased inducement for strangers visiting the district. The following committee was appointed to receive names for the dinner:—Dr. Alex. Osborne, Captain Addison, C. T. Smith, Edward Palmer, Dr. John Osborne, Captain Richard Hopkins, Henry Heathorne, and Captain Westmacott, when all the members, numbering 21,

gave in their names. Captain Westmacott proposed to present the Society with two paintings, to be hung up in the room of the Society. It was considered a very handsome gift, and would be cherished as a memento of the first Secretary of the Society. The stewards for show dinner were Dr. O'Brien, Captain Addison, Captain Westmacott, Dr. Jessett, Edward Palmer, C. T. Smith, and William Taylor. Dinner to take place at 3 o'clock. Cattle judges and horse judges were to be selected from Messrs. Eaken, Creagh, Gerard, Guion, Field, Westmacott, M. Hindmarsh, Curry, Beatson. Judges for ploughing matches, Messrs. Turkington, Dr. Jessett, and Andrew Thompson. Re medal for first prize cow, it was agreed that the owner of the first prize cow should be at liberty to take either the medal or £1/10/- (the prize-money), and that the same should apply to the winner of the second cow prize. The show was held on 28th January, 1847, and, according to report, was marred by rain—it was very wet—and in many classes, namely, wheat, barley, tobacco, hops, poultry, wine, and mead, were poorly represented; many of the fruits were not ripe. Prizes, however, were awarded for articles that were decidedly good, or where the competition was considered worthy of the name. The prize-list was read out as follows:—Best carting stallion (£1/10/-), George Brown; best thoroughbred stallion (£1/10/-), Captain Westmacott; best carting mare (£1/10/-), George Brown; best thoroughbred mare (£1/10/-), Henry Osborne; best bull, any age (£1/10/), Henry Osborne; best two-year-old bull (£1/10/-), Evan Evans; best cow (medal), Henry Osborne; second best (£1/10/-), Henry Osborne; best heifer (£1/10/-), Evan Evans; best bullock (£1/10/-), George Brown; best mangel wurzel Dr. Jessett; best potatoes, Alex. Mackenzie; best hops, Dr. Jessett; best boar, Dr. Alex. Osborne; best sow, Dr. Alex. Osborne; best fat pig, Thomas Black; best sow and pigs, Gerard Gerard; best fowls, Dr. Jessett; best butter, Thomas Black; second best, J. R. Lomax.

Ploughing matches: 1st prize, Stephen Lynch (bullocks); 2nd prize, Hudson; 3rd prize, Jacob Bucket; 4th prize, Mossop. The judge considered that the second prize for horse team should be awarded to the four-bullock team owned by Dr. R. Menzies. There was also a long list of awards in horticultural and floral exhibits. The show dinner was held in Russell's Marine Hotel; owing to the rain only 40 persons sat down for dinner.

ROY O'GORMAN, "The Gift," Albion Park, Illawarra.

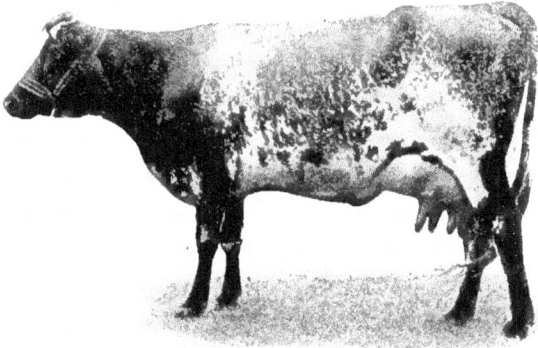

FAVOURITE OF THE GIFT.

BLOSSOM OF THE GIFT.

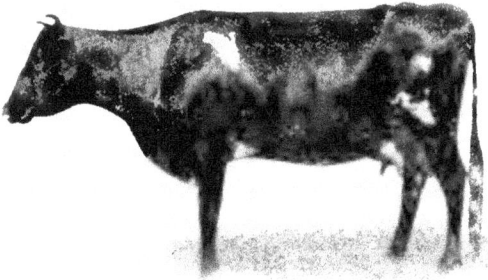

MODEL OF THE GIFT.

BEAUTY OF THE GIFT.

SHAMROCK II OF THE GIFT.

DAIRYMAID OF THE GIFT.

A meeting of the Society was held on 1st March, 1847, at the Marine Hotel, at which Mr. Charles Throsby Smith was elected Chairman, and Edward Palmer Secretary, on motion by Captain Sheaffe and Dr. Alex. Osborne. It was decided, on motion of Dr. Alex. Osborne and Henry Heathorne, that the next ploughing matches would be held near the Woodstock Mills, Jamberoo, in season 1847-48. This evidently disturbed Mr. George Brown, of Dapto. who moved at next meeting that the ploughing match shall take place on 2nd January, and another show on the 21st of January, 1845, and that in case the show shall take place at my inn I will offer every facility in the shape of show-room and stalls, without cost to the Society. This motion was also seconded by Mr. Henry Heathorne and carried. It was moved by Captain W. Sheaffe and seconded by Edward Palmer, that Mr. Henry Osborne be requested to act on the Committee. The Committee consisted of Messrs. Gerard Gerard, Dr. Alex. Osborne, Captain Sheaffe, Dr. Robert Menzies, Dr. Thomas Jessett, Henry Osborne, and George Brown. All members who paid one pound were then entitled to sit on the Committee of the Illawarra A. & H. Society. Note.—At this period of the old Society the people of the Kiama district put in their claim for a show, as it was understood that the shows were for Illawarra, and Illawarra extended to the shores of Jervis Bay. The members of the Society were gathered in from almost every part of Illawarra; hence each centre had its claims on the Society. Wollongong had had the shows; Dapto the ploughing matches.

At a meeting held at George Brown's Illawarra Hotel, Dapto, on 2nd August, 1847—Mr. C. T. Smith in the chair—it was decided to approach Mr. Owen with reference to selection of a suitable paddock at Jamberoo in which to hold a ploughing match. At this meeting it was moved by Mr. Henry Osborne, seconded by Dr. Thomas Jessett, that medals instead of prizes be awarded by the Society in the following sections:—Best stallion, best mare, best bull, best cow, best butter, and the design of medals be obtained. Prize-list: Horse stock £3, cattle £7/15/-, grain £7/15/-, swine £3, fowls £2, butter £4/10/-, honey £2/10/-. Judges in horticultural section, Messrs Brewer, Goodall, Creagh; in butter, Mr. Micklejohn; in horses, Messrs. Jones and Stewart (they were also to act as cattle judges). In the ploughing matches the judges were Mr. John Berry and Mr. Thomas Hall, of Shoalhaven. Mr. Micklejohn sent a donation of £2, to be awarded for butter, as a special prize. Messrs. J. R. Lomax, Thomas Hall, and Williams were regulated extra judging duties.

Meeting held 18th January, 1848, to receive report on ploughing matches that took place in John Ritchie's paddock, adjacent to the Woodstock Mills, Jamberoo, when James Hukins, sen., George Woods, sen., and William Wright were appointed judges. The following teams were on the ground:—William Keevers, Edwin Vidler, John Bradney, Captain Addison's man, Dr. Robert Menzies' man, and James Swan. The judges awarded the prizes as follows:— 1st prize (£2/10/-), won by Dr. Menzies' man; 2nd prize (£1/10/-), Captain Addison's man; 3rd prize (£1), won by Edwin Vidler; 4th prize (10/-), won by William Keevers; 5th prize, (5/-), won by John Bradney; 6th prize (5/-), won by James Swan.

Show held on 21st January, 1848, at Dapto. This was the fourth show of the Society, Mr. George Brown having made preparations in his mill for the agricultural and horticultural products, and the mill ground was set apart for horses and cattle. Four judges were appointed for inside exhibits and four judges for outside exhibits. Best stallion (silver medal), awarded to Michael Fitzgerald; best bull, any age (silver medal), Gerard Gerard; best two-year-old bull (£1), Henry Osborne; best cow (silver medal), Henry Osborne; second best cow (£1), Evan Evans; third best cow (15/-), Dr. Thos. Jessett; best heifer (£1), David Johnston; best fat beast (£1), David Johnstone; best boar (silver medal), Captain Hopkins; best sow (silver medal), Dr. Jessett; sow and pigs, Black; best fowls, Dr. Jessett; best ducks, George Brown; best butter (£2/10/- and silver medal), Mr. J. R. Lomax; second prize, James Shoobert; best cheese, Gerard Gerard; best wine, Guion. Cost of medals, £10; prizes for ploughing, £6.

At next Committee meeting Mr. Charles Throsby Smith was re-elected Chairman, and Mr. Edward Palmer was re-elected Secretary. On motion by Mr. Gerard Gerard and Dr. Menzies, it was decided to hold the fifth show in Wollongong. Mr. C. T. Smith offered 20 acres of land for show purposes on the banks of the Macquarie rivulet. It was then moved by Captain Sheaffe and Dr. O'Brien that a sub-committee, consisting of the Chairman and Secretary, Messrs. F. R. Cole, James Shoobert, Creagh and Gerard, to report at next meeting.

The foregoing offer of land was made on behalf of Captain Samuel Addison.

The question of altering and amending the rules of the Society was being considered, and a suggestion to offer cups instead of medals was being considered. The prize-list for the fifth show was as follows:—Horses £5, cattle £10, grain £10, swine £4, poultry £2, butter £4, honey £5, fruit £5, vegetables £3, flowers £2, ploughing £7, bacon £1, leather £1/10/-; total, £57/10/-.

The sub-committee appointed to alter and amend the rules of the Society brought forth 18 alterations and amendments on December 28th, 1848, and the next show meeting was fixed for 22nd January, 1849. It was also decided that the next ploughing match should take place on Mr. James Shoobert's land at the Cross Roads, near Wollongong.

The Show Committee met on 22nd January, 1849, to appoint judges and stewards, and it was decided to hold the show in the Market Square, Wollongong, and to use Mr. Palmer's store for inside exhibits. The stewards appointed were Dr. Alex. Osborne, Henry Osborne, Dr. Thomas Jessett, C. T. Smith, and T. S. Palmer; the dinner to consist of cold meats, hot vegetables, plum pudding, ale in abundance, two bottles of wine between two persons; price 7/-. Mr. Andrew Elliott, an opposition hotelkeeper, offered to do it for 5/ and got the job. It was decided to appoint Messrs. John Marks and David Johnston : judges.

Meeting held 2nd July, 1849. Mr. C. T. Smith and Mr. Edward Palmer were again re-elected Chairman and Secretary, when it was decided to hold the next show at Dapto, and that the ploughing match should be held on the 12th and the show on the 14th February, 1850, and Dr. Jessett, Messrs. Newnham, Fred R. Cole, and George Brown were appointed a sub-committee of management. Subscriptions to be paid before 1st January, 1850.

Meeting held at Brown's Illawarra Hotel on 6th February, 1850. Mr. Henry Osborne in the chair. A serious drought prevailed, and it was decided to postpone the ploughing match. The show dinner was to be at Brown's hotel at 4 o'clock p.m. Stewards, Dr. Alex. Osborne, Captain Sheaffe, Dr. Jessett ,and Mr. Gerard Gerard. Judges to be invited to dine, and advertisements to be sent to the ''S.M. Herald'' and ''The People's Advocate.''

It was plain that the Dapto influence had created trouble in the Committee of the Illawarra A. & H. Society. It was evidently resented by the officers of the Society, as no report of this show is to be found in the books of the Society. These feuds—or storms in teacups—must have been very bitter, as leaves have been torn out, so to say, from the pages of our history. If there was anything wrong it is just as well they are missing; on the other hand, if it was merely spite, it is regrettable.

Meetings were resumed on 28th October, 1850, at Wollongong. The first was called by the Warden to ascertain whether it was desirable that the Society should be continued. It was held at Mr. Tom Evans' Inn, when Dr. Alex. Osborne, the Warden, was called to the chair. It was at that meeting decided to carry on the Society, on motion by Dr. George Underwood Alley and Mr. Gordon. Mr. C. T. Smith was elected President, and, on motion by Messrs. Gerard Gerard and Thomas Atcheson, Mr. Edward Palmer was re-appointed Secretary, with the following gentlemen as Committee: Messrs. Charles Fairs, George W. Brown, James Wilshire, Thomas Atcheson, Evan Evans, Gordon, Robert Haworth, Bernard McCauley, and Dr. G. U. Alley. Mr. Henry Osborne proposed to call tenders from publicans who were members of the Society for the show dinner, and that the best offer be accepted. Messrs. William Taylor, James Shoobert, Guion, Lea, Meares, Evan Evans, and Dr. Alex. Osborne to act as stewards.

Messrs. C. T. Smith and Edward Palmer were once more Chairman and Secretary of the Society. Mr. Andrew Elliott carried a motion to have cattle show and ploughing match held on same day. At a meeting held at the Farmers' Inn, Wollongong, on 1st September, 1851, it was decided to hold a show on the 4th February, 1851, in Wollongong, and a ploughing match at Dapto on the Friday before the show.

Meeting held at Mr. Tom Evans' Farmers' Inn, Wollongong. Mr. C. T. Smith was appointed President. As Mr. Palmer had resigned the secretaryship of the Society, Mr. George William Brown was appointed Secretary. It was decided, on motion by Messrs. Charles Newnham and Thomas Atcheson, that the Secretary write Henry Osborne, Esq., M.C., and all the magistrates of the district soliciting funds for the Society, and that the next meeting would be held at Barney McCauley's Inn, Wollongong. Appointment of collectors: Messrs. Edward Palmer and Thomas Atcheson for Fairy Meadow; Messrs. C. T. Smith, Barney

McCauley, and Sam Russell for Wollongong; Captain Sheaffe and Mr. Yates for West Dapto; Messrs. Evan Evans and Andrew McGill for Dapto. A vote of thanks was carried to Mr. C. T. Smith, who had acted as Chairman for the Society for a period of six years.

Meeting held at Barney McCauley's hotel, Wollongong, on 6th September, 1852. It was decided, on motion by Dr. Alex. Osborne and Mr. McKenzie, that the next show be held on 3rd February, 1853, in Wollongong, and the ploughing match at Dapto on Tuesday before the show. Prize-list: Horse stock £9, cattle £10, swine £4, grain £9/5/-, poultry £5/12/6, flowers £2/5/-, ploughing £5/5/-; conditions of ploughing, furrow 5in. x 9in. Tent or booth, 10/-. Fifteen amended rules and regulations were considered by the Society. Mr. George W. Brown offered the ground for the ploughing match, provided no other publican's booth but his was allowed on the ground.

Kiama Show, held 5th December, 1848.—The inside exhibits were housed in a building owned by William Gard, who had first erected it for flour milling purposes, and changed his mind and converted it into a brewery. It stood on the flat a little to the east of the present Masonic Hall. The cattle were enclosed where Tory's hotel stands. James Barton had bought and cleared the block, and was about to erect the Fermanagh Hotel thereon. The horses were shown where Terralong Street and the Presbyterian Church grounds join. What is somewhat out of order in prize descriptions could be seen in that old prize-list. The sum of 10/- was awarded for the "best sucking bull." It was practically for a male calf that was at the time sucking its mother. Cows with calves at foot were often exhibited. The prize was won by Mr. Michael Fitzgerald, of Stackwood, Dapto. Mr. D. L. Dymock, then a mere youth, held a rope to which a similar calf was attached, owned by his uncle, Mr. D. L. Waugh, of Jamberoo.

List of stock exhibited at the Kiama A. & H. Society's Show. 1851:—Mr. Nicholas Craig, Orange Grove, Kiama, 1 draught mare; Messrs. Charles and William Newnham, Woodstock Mills, 1 heifer, 1 boar, 2 sows; Mr. George Hindmarsh, jun., Gerringong, 1 cow, 1 fat beast, 1 draught mare; Mr. Henry Osborne, Marshall Mount, 1 bull, 1 cow, 1 blood colt (2 years), 1 blood mare, 1 draught mare, 1 boar, 1 sow; Mr. Charles Beck, Kiama, 1 blood mare; Mr. Thomas S. Kendall, Barroul, Kiama, 1 fat calf; Mr. Michael Hindmarsh, Alne Bank, Gerringong, 1 bull, 1 cow;

Mr. Henry Grey, Omega, Gerringong, 1 bull, 2 cows, 1 fat cow, 1 draught mare, 1 heifer, 1 boar, 1 fat pig.

Much maize, potatoes, fruits, flowers, butter, cheese, and bacon was exhibited. The stock at this show were exhibited where the Public School stands to-day.

BY-LAWS OF KIAMA AGRICULTURAL SOCIETY, 1848.

Agreed upon at a general meeting of subscribers, December 6th, 1848.

I. All subscribers to pay 10/6 per annum, but any person subscribing one guinea to be qualified to act on the Committee and have a voice in the general management of the Society, taking date from 1st October in each year.

II. Donations will be received of any amount, and the same may be awarded in any way the donor may think proper.

III. Any person not having paid up his subscription on or before the 1st of February will not be entitled to compete for any of the prizes.

IV. All articles for exhibition to be delivered over to the care of the officers of the Society, or other responsible persons appointed for that purpose at the place of show, previous to the hour of 10 o'clock a.m. on that day. And each exhibitor to give in writing list at the same time to the Secretary of the various articles he has brought for competition.

V. All persons intending to exhibit stock to give notice to the Secretary at least a week previous to day of show, and also to state how many and what animals they intend to exhibit.

VI. Any non-subscriber may exhibit by nomination of a subscriber, but he will not be entitled to a prize.

VII. All agricultural, horticultural and floricultural produce, and all manufactures, must be grown or made by the party so exhibiting them; and all stock must have been the property of the exhibitor at least six months previous to the day of show.

VIII. That no prize shall be awarded without competition, unless the article exhibited be such as in the opinion of the judges shall be considered possessed of merit and good of their kind; and it will not follow that prizes shall be awarded unless the judges approve of the article so exhibited.

IX. No person shall be admitted during the time the judges are awarding the prizes.

X. On the day of the show all subscribers

and their families will be admitted free; adult non-subscribers will be charged 1/- per head; children 6d.

XI. In case of dispute, the decision of the judges to be final.

XII. To prevent confusion, the prizes will be paid the day after the show.

The Illawarra A. & H. Society held a show in Kiama during February, 1848. The inside exhibits were stored in William Gard's new brewery building, situated near where the present Masonic Hall stands, near Collins Street. The cattle were penned in yards erected upon the site of the present Public School. The horses were shown where the Presbyterian Church stands. The best stock exhibitors at the time exhibited animals to give a stimulus to the objective of that old society, which was to encourage the breeding of horses, cattle and pigs, and the production of all classes of grain, vegetables, and other farm products.

The amount of prize-money distributed was £31/4/6, but there is no record of the individual amounts won. The following list is all that is available, so it looks as if a debt was incurred. In that case, such an encumberance would be paid off quickly by private subscription, as names appear here and there which indicate that they came on the scene to help the old Society along after the event. Horses: Best blood horse, David Johnston, 1st prize; best blood horse, Henry Osborne, 2nd prize; best blood mare, Michael Fitzgerald, 1st prize; best blood mare, Henry Osborne, 2nd prize; best blood two-years-old colt, Henry Osborne, 1st prize; best draught mare, Dr. Thos. Jessett, 1st prize; best draught filly, George Hindmarsh, 1st prize. Cattle: Best bull, Henry Osborne, 1st prize; best bull, William Haslem, 2nd prize; best cow, David Johnston, 1st prize; best cow, Evan Evans, 2nd prize; best heifer, Henry Grey, 1st prize; best fat calf, Michael Fitzgerald, 1st prize. Pigs: Best boar, Henry Osborne, 1st prize; best sow, Henry Osborne, 1st prize; best fat pig, Henry Grey, 1st prize. Frederick R. Cole, bull, cow, heifer, 2 mares; David Johnston, fat bullock, 2 cows, 1 heifer, 1 fat calf, 1 blood horse; William Haslem, 2 cows, 2 bulls, 2 heifers; Evan Evans, 2 cows, 1 bull, 1 two-year-old entire colt; Dr. Thomas Jessett, 1 draught mare; Hugh Colley, 2 cows; James Colley, 1 fat calf; Dr. Menzies, 1 fat cow; Samuel Forward, 1 two-years-old filly; Nicholas Craig, 1 draught mare; C. and W. Newnham, 1 heifer, 1 boar, 2 sows; Haslem, maize (2 bushels); Charles Beck, 1 blood mare;

Thomas Kendall, 1 fat calf; Michael Hindmarsh, 1 cow, 1 bull; George Hindmarsh, jun., 1 cow, 1 fat beast, 1 draught mare; Henry Grey, 1 fat cow, 1 bull, 2 cows, 1 draught mare, 1 heifer, 1 boar, 1 fat pig; Henry Osborne, 1 bull, 1 cow, 1 entire blood colt (two years), 1 blood mare, 1 draught mare, 1 boar, 1 sow.

Ploughing match held in Jamberoo in 1850 (February 19th).—Hugh Boyle, 1st prize, valued £3; Edward Spinks, 2nd prize, valued £2/10/-; John Keevers, 3rd prize, valued £2; John Bradney, 4th prize, valued £1/10/-; James Keevers, 5th prize, valued £1.

List of stock exhibited Illawarra A. & H. Society Show, 1850, held in Kiama:—Mr. Frederick R. Cole, Herne Farm, Figtree, 1 bull, 1 cow, 1 heifer, 2 mares; Mr. David Johnston, The Meadows, 2 fat bullocks, 1 heifer, 1 fat calf, 1 blood horse; Mr. William Haslem, Terry's Meadows, 2 bulls, 2 cows, 2 heifers; Mr. Evan R. Evans, Penrose Villa, Dapto, 1 bull, 2 cows, 1 2-years-old entire colt; Dr. Jessett, West Dapto, 1 draught mare; Mr. Hugh Colley, Muskfield, Kiama, 2 cows; Mr. James Colley, Antrim Hill, Kiama, 1 fat calf; Dr. Robert Menzies, Minnamurra, Jamberoo, 1 fat cow; Mr. Samuel Forward, Spring Hill. Kiama, 1 2-years-old filly.

KIAMA AGRICULTURAL SOCIETY, 1851.

President, James Macarthur. M.C.; Robert Menzies, Vice-President; D. L. Waugh, Secretary.

List of prizes to be competed for at the Kiama Agricultural Society's ploughing match and show meeting on Tuesday and Thursday, 18th and 20th February, 1851.

Ploughing match: Without regard to the number of oxen employed in the team; best executed work £3, second best £2/10/-, third best £2, fourth best £1/10/-, fifth best £1. For two horses with reins, best executed work £2, second best £1/10/-. Any party having carried off a first prize at a previous show not being allowed to compete. Tent booth on ground, £1/1-. The match will take place on Tuesday, 18th February, in a paddock belonging to Mr. Miller, Gerringong, and the competitors will be required to cut out and back up one whole land and two halves, but the ground marked out will not exceed ½ acre; the work to be done with a furrow of 4in. deep by 7in., and properly finished off. All teams to be on the ground by half-past 9 a.m.; start at 10, and finish not later than 4 o'clock. The farmer who has his land ploughed shall pay to the treasurer at the rate of 10/- per acre for the quantity of land ploughed, out of which he shall pay to the competitors who gain no prize the price of ploughing half-an-acre. The ploughmen shall be provided with refreshments in the middle of the day by the Society. The prizes will be awarded as soon as the judges give their decision. No one will be allowed to compete who is not a subscriber.

Prize-list for Kiama A. & H. Society's show, held on 20th February, 1851:—Horses: Best blood horse £1/10/-, best draught horse £1/10/-, best blood mare £1, best draught mare £1, best 2-year-old colt 15/-, best 2-year-old filly 15/-. Cattle: Best bull (any age) £1/10/-, best cow £1/10/-, best cow £1, best heifer under 3 years old £1, best fat calf under 6 months 10/-, best beast (grass-fed) £1. Pigs: Best boar £1, best sow £1, best porker under 6 months 10/-. Grain: Best collection of cereals, £1. Wine: Best two bottles of wine £1/10/-, best two bottles of wine £1, best two bottles of wine made from other fruit 15/-. Mead: Best mead 10/-. Vinegar: Best vinegar 5/. Miscellaneous: Best side of bacon £1, best ham 10/-, best five gallons of ale (made of malt and hops only) £1, best cured pork (in cask, not less than 2 cwt.) £1; samples of silk, cabbage-tree hats, plaits of straw, and cabbage-tree plant; agricultural implements in variety.

Ploughing match in connection with the Kiama A. & H. Society was held in Mr. Robert Miller's paddock, Renfrew Park, Gerringong, on 18th February, 1851. The following was the prize-list:—First match, two horses with reins, best executed work, £2 first prize (if bullocks are used, driver allowed no limit as to number used); £1/10/- second prize. Note.—Any person having carried off a prize at a previous match not to compete. The competitors will be required to cut out and back up one whole land and two halves, and the ground marked out not to exceed ½ acre; the work to be done with a furrow 4in. x 7in., and properly finished off. All teams to be on the ground at 9 o'clock a.m.; to start at 10 o'clock a.m., and to finish not later than 4 o'clock p.m. The farmer who has his land ploughed shall pay the teamster at the rate of 10/- per acre for the quantity of land ploughed; those who gain prizes to be paid extra. The ploughmen shall be provided with refreshments in the middle of the day by the Society. Bullock teams were also allowed in this match. All competitors must be subscribers.

The only record obtainable regarding this match is to the effect that Mr. James Mac-

arthur, President of the Society at the time, was present with the secretary, Mr. D. L. Waugh, and that Abraham Kent won first prize, and William Burless won second prize. Mr. Miller paid £2 for land ploughed, so there must have been several entries, especially in the Clearing Lease settlers class, of which there is no record beyond James Lees, first prize.

Tuesday, 1st February, 1853. A ploughing match in Mrs. Brown's paddock, Dapto. The following entrances were received by the secretary:—No. 1, ploughman, William Evans, driver, Thomas Edwards; No. 2, ploughman, Patrick Gorman, driver, John Gorman; No. 3, ploughman, Thomas Barrett, driver, Thomas Carwood; No. 4, ploughman, Robert Hutson, driver, Phillip Town; No. 5, ploughman, Archie Colville, driver, Neil McGill; No. 6, James Rixon, driver, John Rixon; No. 7, ploughman, Adam Dennis, driver, Reuben Dennis. Judges: Andrew Thompson, John Nunan, and Joseph Ritchie. Winners—1st prize, £2, Adam Dennis; 2nd prize, £1/10/-, James Rixon; 3rd prize, £1, Robert Hutson; 4th prize, 10/-, Thomas Barritt; 5th prize, Archie Colville.

Entries for show, February, 1853, were as follows:—Messrs. George Somerville, 1 two-year-old bull, 2 cows, 1 two-year-old heifer; George Buchanan, 1 fat beast; James Armstrong, 1 draught stallion; Andrew McGill, 1 blood stallion, 1 draught stallion, 1 two-year-old heifer; Evan R. Evans, 3 cows, 2 bulls; James R. Cummins, 1 two-years-old draught colt; Joseph Derrett, 1 draught mare, 1 two-year-old draught colt, 1 blood mare; Henry Harris, 1 blood mare; Captain Hopkins, 2 two-year-old heifers (branded RH), 1 draught mare (branded WL); Henry Osborne, 2 aged bulls, 1 two-year-old bull, 1 cow, 1 fat beast, 1 blood mare. This show was held in the Market Square, Wollongong.

List of prize-winners at show held February 3rd, 1853. (This was the ninth annual show of the Illawarra A. & H. Society, and was held in Wollongong. Other shows of the Society were held in Kiama. (See other pages). The judges were Messrs. Michael Hindmarsh, Robert J. Marshall, and Joseph Moon for agriculture; Messrs. Robert Rutter, Thomas Black, and Andrew Thompson were the judges of all stock.

Protests.—Best draught filly (£1/10/-), awarded Joseph Dunster; protest lodged. Vegetables and cereals, award Richard Dennis (£3/5/-) at stake; protest lodged. Blood filly (£1), awarded Mrs. E. Williamson; protest entered.

EXHIBIT	PRIZE	OWNER	PRIZE
Best Draught Stallion ..	£1/10	Michael Hindmarsh	1st
Best Blood Stallion ..	£1/10	Andrew McGill ..	1st
Best Draught Mare	£1	Evan R. Evans, sen.	1st
Best Blood 2 yr. old Colt	£1	Evan R. Evans, sen.	1st
Best Draught Colt ..	£1	Henry Grey ..	1st
Best Bull, any age ..	£2	William Yates ..	1st
Best Cow ..	£2	Evan R. Evans, sen.	1st
2nd Best Cow	£1/10	David Johnston	2nd
Best Bull, 2 years old ..	£1/10	David Johnston ..	1st
Best Heifer ..	£1	Joseph Derrett ..	1st
2nd Best Heifer ..	10/-	David Johnston	2nd
Best Fat Beast ..	£1/10	David Johnston ..	1st
Best Calf ..	10/-	Willaim Yates ..	1st
Best Boar ..	£1	Archie Graham ..	1st
2nd Best Boar	12/6	Dr. Alex. Osborne ..	2nd
Best Sow ..	£1	Archie Graham ..	1st
2nd Best Sow	12/6	Archie Graham	2nd
Best Young Boar ..	7/6	Captain Hopkins ..	1st
Best Young Sow ..	7/6	Captain Hopkins ..	1st
Best Cheese ..	£1	Joseph Derrett ..	1st
Best Butter (in cask) ..	£1	C. T. Smith ..	1st
Best Salt Butter (in cask)	£1	C. T. Smith ..	1st

After the show a meeting was held in the show-room, Market Square, Wollongong, date 14th March, 1853, at which meeting the secretary showed a credit balance of £7/13/4. Mr. C. T. Smith was appointed President, and Mr. George William Brown Secretary, for the current year. At meeting held at Tom Evans' Farmers' Hotel, Wollongong, it was decided, on motion by Dr. Alex. Osborne and Mr. Evan Evans, sen., to increase the prize for best two-year-old bull by an additional £1. The next show to be held on 8th February, 1854. The prize-list was reviewed and slightly altered. The ploughing match to take place at Dapto. The report of the ploughing match held at Dapto during 1853 was read out before the Committee, and the following is the statement: Tuesday, 1st February, 1853.

THE ILLAWARRA AGRICULTURAL SOCIETY OF 1854.

Chairman, Charles Throsby Smith, Esq.; Hon. Secretary, George William Brown, Esq.; Committee, Thomas Hales, John Musgrave, Fred. R. Cole, William Kirton, Robert Haworth, Robert Osborne, Alexander McKenzie, Even Evans, Thomas Hobbs, Henry H. Osborne, James Achison, Andrew McGill, Dr. J. D. Kinear, Alexander Elliott (subscribers of one guinea and upwards). Other subscribers: Barker and Wyatt, Stephen Lynch, Duncan Beatson, Phillip Town, John Manning, Matthew Ryan, Thomas Wholohan, Thomas A. Reddall, John Hetherington, Patrick Larkins, George Buchanan, John Tighe, James Hetherington, James Kidd, James Scott, Benjamin Marshall, William Yates, Joseph Staff (sub-

scribers of £2/2/- and down to 10/6). The design of the institution was to give encouragement to husbandry, servants, and others in the district of Illawarra by granting rewards and prizes annually for skill in ploughing, and to improve the produce of the district generally.

List of prizewinners at the Illawarra A. & H. Society's show, 8th February, 1854. Horses: best draught stallion, £1/10/-, D. McKinney 1st prize; best blood stallion, £1/10/-, Henry Osborne 1st prize; best draught mare, £1, Evan R. Evans 1st prize; best blood filly, £1, Henry Harris 1st prize. Note.—The other horse exhibits were considered by the Judges unworthy of a prize. Cattle: best bull (any age), £2, David Johnston 1st prize; best bull (any age), £1/10/-, Evan R. Evans, 2nd prize; best bull (2 years old), £1, Evan R. Evans 1st prize; best cow, £2, David Johnston 1st prize; best cow, £1/10/-, Henry Osborne 2nd prize; best heifer (2 years old), £1, Evan R. Evans 1st prize; best heifer (2 years old), 10/-, Evan R. Evans 2nd prize; best fat beast, £1, David Johnston 1st prize; best fat calf, 10/-, Henry Osborne 1st prize.

Note.—In butter honours were divided between Messrs Evan R. Evans, Andrew McGill, Jas. R. Cummins and Henry Gordon. Bacon, Flitch, Evan R. Evans—only one prize. There was also a fine display of cereals, vegetables, fruits and flowers.

Entries for show of 8th February, 1854 were as follows: Henry Osborne, 4 cows, 2 calves, 1 horse, 2 pigs; David Johnston, 1 cow, 2 fat beasts, 1 bull, 1 heifer; Evan R. Evans, 1 two-year-old bull, 3 cows, 2 two-year-old heifers, 1 mare; D. McKinney, 1 blood stallion; D. Guion (an orchardist), fruits, etc.

Kiama Show Committee for show, February, 1854. The Kiama A. & H. Society held a meeting at the Kiama hotel, January, 1854—Mr. Joseph Pike in the chair—when the following office-bearers were appointed for the year 1854: President, Mr. Robert I. Perrott; Vice-President, Mr. Nicholas Craig; Treasurer, Mr. James Colley; Committee, Messrs. John McMahon, George Turner, Joseph King, Robert Morris, John Black, Alexander Gordon, Thomas Tempest, George Wood, jun., James Harrison, John Sharpe, William Rutter Hindmarsh, John Miller, James McGill, William Moles; Mr. William Irvine, Secretary. It was the custom in those early days to appoint all committees of management on motion at first meeting each year, and, as the mover always concluded with these words, "With power to add to the number," it is impossible to get hold of many of the best workers for the Society in each year. The formation of the Kiama Society was much criticised by the northern section of the Illawarra Society.

Kiama Show held February, 1854, was considered to be a success as the quality of the exhibits, although not numerous, was of good merit. The cattle were exhibited in the sale yards on west side of Shoalhaven Street, and the grain, produce, fruits, flowers, etc., in a shed on the east side of the same street. The awards. Horses — Best draught stallion, £1/10/-, Michael Hindmarsh, 1st prize; best draught 2-year old colt, £1/10/-, James McGill, 1st prize; best draught mare, £1, Patrick Daly, 1st prize; best blood stallion, £1/10/-, Henry Osborne, 1st prize; best blood mare, £1, Michael Fitzgerald, 1st prize; best blood filly, 10/-, Robert Miller, 1st prize. Cattle—Best bull, any age, £2, Henry Osborne, 1st prize; best bull, any age, £1/10/-, Andrew McGill, 2nd prize; best cow, £2, Henry Osborne, 1st prize; best cow, £1/10/-, Henry Grey, 2nd prize; best heifer, 10/-, Thomas Black, 1st prize; best fat beast, £1, Robert Miller, 1st prize; best fat calf, 10/-, Michael Fitzgerald, 1st prize. Pigs— Best boar, £1, Thomas Black, 1st prize; best sow, 10/-, James Harvison, 1st prize; best fat pig, 10/-, Michael Hindmarsh, 1st prize.

The ploughing match for 1854 came off in the same paddock as previous years. It was of a boggy nature, and suitable for certain types of ploughs and ploughmen. No, 1, ploughman, James Swan, driver, Charles Gower, 3rd prize, £1; No. 2, ploughman, Adam Dennis, driver, William Thomas, 1st prize, £2; No. 3, ploughman, James Rixon, driver, John Rixon, 2nd prize £1/10/-. The judges were James Hukins, senr., Michael Hindmarsh, and Samuel Rowley.

The 10th Annual Show of the Illawarra A. & H. Society took place in the Market Square, Wollongong. The Judges for inside exhibits were E. Gerard, W. Hindmarsh and W. Yates. No report available of this show (1854), nor the following year, 1855.

It would appear that there were more disputes, and the disappearance of records.

In 1855 a meeting of the Illawarra A. and H. Society was held in Mr. George Hall's Commercial Hotel, Wollongong, 15th October, 1855, Mr. G. W. Brown, Secretary. No report at this 12th annual meeting of the Illawarra A. & H. Society. The President, Mr. Charles Throsby Smith, delivered an address on the benefits of agriculture, which he considered was "a social agent, which would be found to have more humanising influences over the mind than any other occupation. The practice of agriculture had softened the forces of nature among our ancestors, and prepared them to rule over a large proportion of the inhabited world." The Secretary, Mr. George William Brown, however was not convinced that "Agriculture, as a social agent, had by any means worked out to the satisfaction of the Illawarra A. & H. Society, the financial side of which had always been a serious difficulty.

The Illawarra A. & H. Society's ploughing match took place in Mr. Wiliam Ryan's paddock, opposite the old Dapto R.C. Church on Thursday, November 8th, 1855—¼ acre of land to be ploughed in equal furrows 5in. x 8in. wide, land when finished to be in two equal halves. First match, horse teams, no competition. Second match, bullocks teams, result: No. 1, ploughman James Swan, driver James Swan Jnr; No. 2, ploughman, James Rixon, driver, Ben Rixon Jnr., 2nd prize; No. 3, ploughman, Adam Dennis, driver, Reuben Dennis, 1st prize. Third match, with oxen, for ploughmen who never won a prize: No. 1, ploughman, Charles Gower, driver Isaac Edwards, 2nd prize; No. 2, ploughman, John Rixon, driver Archie Gillespie, 1st prize; No. 3, ploughman, John Gorman, driver John Town; No. 4, ploughman John Russell, driver, John Preyhoe, 3rd prize. Note.— The John Russell mentioned here eventually became the Squire of Croome, Shellharbour. The Judges were Messrs. John Baker, John Nunan and Robert Hutson.

The formation of a separate A. & H. Society in Kiama, which practically meant the breaking away from the old Illawarra A. & H. Society, of which Kiama had been from its foundation a part, caused the "Illawarra Mercury," of November 19th, 1855 to wince, and say: "Individual exertion will never accomplish much, and our agricultural friends in Kiama may be assured of failure.'' The Kiama Society held a meeting on November 22nd, 1855, in Mr. James Barton's Fermanagh Hotel

1855.—The funds were supported by donations, and monthly subscriptions of members to the amount of one shilling. E. H. Wood was chairman, and Robert Marsh Westmacott, Hon. Sec. The following gentlemen were members: Roger Therry, Esq., M.C., William Foster, Esq., M.C., George W. Allen, Esq., Dr. John Osborne, R.N., J.P., John Hubert Plunkett, Esq., M.C., W. H. Kerr, Esq., William Manning, Esq., J.P., Dr. Alexander Osborne, R.N., J.P., Captain William Frederick Lampriere Sheaffe, Ed. Way, Esq., William Warren Jenkins, Esq., Ed. Rowe, Esq., Capt. Plunkett, J.P., Henry Osborne, Esq.. J.P., Revd. W. B. Mears, William Cummings. Esq., George Brown Esq., Abraham Lincoln, Esq., Edward Palmer, Esq., Dr. Cox, Joseph Ross, Esq., William Taylor, Esq., D. L. Waugh. Esq., J.P., Captain Cole, R.N., J.P., Gerard Gerard, Esq., J.P., Michael Hindmarsh, Esq., George Hindmarsh, Esq., Captain R. M. Westmacott, Dr. Gerard, Thomas Black, Esq., J. Jeffries, Esq., Dr. O'Brien, E. Widgett, Esq., James Mackay Grey, Esq., J.P., Benjamin Marshall, Esq., Captain Aitken, William Herne, Esq., David Johnston, Esq., J.P., Frederick Elliott, Esq., Samuel Clarke, Esq., Captain William Weston, Matthew Ryan, Esq., Edmond Gerard, Esq., Fincham, Esq., S. A. Bryant, Esq., Dr. Robert Menzies, J.P., Captain Innes, J.P., Robert Hancock, Esq., Charles I. Smith, Esq., J.P., A. Crawford Esq., Captain Robert Towns, Hugh Coulston, Esq., John Collary, Esq., Bernard McCauley, Esq., Hugh Kennedy, Esq., R. H. Tweedie, Esq., D. Aitken, Esq., John Terry Hughes, Esq., J. H. Hebden, Esq., Thomas Holt, Esq., James Shoobert, Esq., Michael Keele, Esq., H. Calvert, Esq., Alexander Elliott, Esq., Thomas Smith, Esq., Captain Stephen Addison, Dr. Kenneth Mackzie, J.P., Henry Heathorne, Esq., Rev. Mr. Atchison.

A meeting of the Kiama A. & H. Association was held in James Barton's Fermanagh Hotel, Kiama, on 22nd November, 1855, which was fairly well attended. It was decided to form an independent Society, to be called the Kiama Agricultural and Horticultural Society, and that the first exhibition was to take place on the first Wednesday in March, 1856. Owing to the loss of the Society's books and the opposition towards the movement by the Illawarra press, no report of the show was published in the press.

A Society, to be named the Kiama Horticultural Society, was duly established in Kiama on December 20th, 1855. Kiama had then practically two societies. The Horticultural Society decided to hold a flower show on the first Wednesday in March, 1856.

The Illawarra A. & H. Society's show was held in Market Square, Wollongong, 7th February, 1856, when the awards were made: Horses: best draught stallion, £2/10/-, Evan R. Evans 1st prize; best draught mare, £1/10/-, George Somerville, 1st prize; best blood mare, £1/10/-, Edward Graham 1st prize; best draught two-year-old colt, £1, William Lindsay 1st prize; best draught two-year-old filly, £1, Andrew McGill 1st prize; best blood two-year-old filly, £1, John Beatson 1st prize. Cattle: best bull (any age) £2/10/-, Edward Graham 1st prize; best bull (any age) £1, Andrew McGill, 2nd prize; best two-year-old bull, £1/10 McGill 2nd prize; best bull (2 years old) £1/10/, Andrew McGill 1st prize; best cow, £2/10/-, David W. Irving 1st prize; best cow, £1/10/-; Thomas Barrett 2nd prize; best heifer, (2 years old), £1/10/-, David Johnston 1st prize; best heifer (2 years old), £1, David Johnston 2nd prize. For pigs honours were divided between Messrs. D. W. Irving and Evan R. Evans. Mr. John Nunan was awarded a special prize for a plough of his own make.

James R. Cummins was living at Hopefield, Illawarra.

A meeting was held on 23rd September, 1856, at Brown's Illawarra Hotel, Dapto, Mr. C. T. Smith in the chair. Mr. Smith was elected President, and Mr. George William Brown, Secretary for the ensuing year. The accounts—receipts, £89/13/2; expenditure, including prizes, £83/9/11; balance in hand, £6/3/3. It would seem that £26/15/- of prize money had not been paid, thus showing a debt of £20/11/9. Committee appointed for ensuing year: Messrs. J. R. Cummins, John Davis, Evan Evans, Senr., Andrew Thompson, James Wright, S. S. Roggers, Robert Osborne, R. T. Hales, Andrew McGill, Frederick R. Cole, William Kirton, J. B. Clyne, Patrick Gorman, Joseph Ritchie, James McGill and George Buchanan. Next meeting to be held at R. T. Hayles' Sportsman's Arms Hotel. Wollongong, on Monday, 6th October, 1856.

But without going further into details than was necessary it is plain that they were affected by certain troubles such as lack of duties, negligence, and petty jealousy.

The Kiama Show Committee decided to hold its show of inside exhibits in Mr. John Car-

MRS. GOWER, "The Meadows," Albion Park, Illawarra.

SILKY OF THE MEADOWS.

TRIUMPH OF THE MEADOWS.

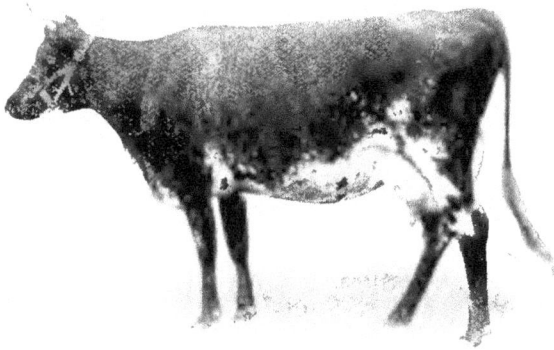

GWEN OF THE MEADOWS.

MYRTLE OF THE MEADOWS.

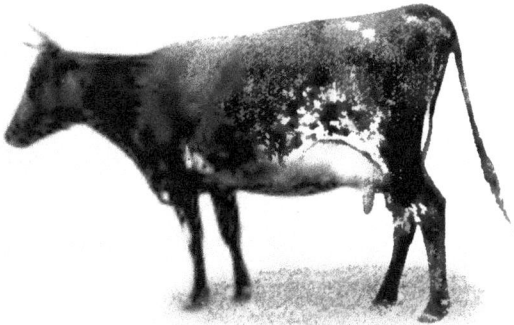

AMY OF THE MEADOWS.

DOLLY OF THE MEADOWS.

ruthers' Kiama Hotel, just erected in Shoalhaven Street. The cattle were shown at the rear of the hotel, the horse stock near where the Presbyterian Church stands. At this show which was not held until 1st Wednesday in March, 1856, Messrs. Atkinson, Craig, Kendall, King, Bullen, Turner and Hindmarsh showed to advantage in the inside exhibits. The cattle were shown at a great disadvantage.

A ploughing match in connection with the Kiama A. & H. Society took place in Mr. George Wood's paddock, Jamberoo, on 4th March, 1856. The hours allowed for performing the work were from 10 a.m. to 2 p.m., ¼ acre to be ploughed in two equal parts in even furrow, 5in. x 8in. The following was the result: No. 1, Henry Fredericks, first prize, £5; No. 2, George Yates, 2nd prize, £3; No. 3, George Wood, 3rd prize, £2; No. 4, Robert Young, 4th prize, £1. Note.—The work was carried out excellently.

The 13th annual ploughing match, under the auspices of the Illawarra A. & H. Society to take place at Dapto. A meeting was held at Brown's Illawarra Hotel, Dapto, at which the following gentlemen were present: Messrs. S. S. Rogers, Jas. R. Cummins, J. Davis. Andrew Thompson, Evan Evans, J. Wright, Robert Osborne, R. T. Hales, W. Kirton, Joseph Ritchie, J. Buchanan, P. Gorman and Captain Clymo, date of meeting, 21st September 1856. A report of the last show was read, which showed that a balance had been carried forward, and from the previous show of £17/12/8. From subscriptions, and money taken at the door, £72/0/6, total, £89/13/2, and of this, £83/9/11 had been paid out in prizes, leaving a balance of £6/3/3. There were, however, unpaid accounts amounting to £26/15/-, leaving a debit balance of £20/11/9. There was £30 of unpaid subscriptions.

The Kiama A. & H. Society was founded as an independent Society on 17th December, 1856. It had for President Dr. Robert Menzies, J.P.; Mr. Joseph Pike was Treasurer, and Mr. William Irvine was Secretary. Committee, Messrs. Robert Miller, John Black, James Marks, sen., George Tate, James Spinks, George Wood, sen., Nicholas Craig, William Colley, John Colley, James Colley, Neil Sharpe, George Turner, George Grey, Henry Lee, James Robinson, Joseph Blow, John Carruthers, Joseph King. Edward Moses, and James Harvison.

The Dapto A. & H. Society held its first show near the present site of Brownsville. The inside exhibits were housed on the second floor of the Steam Flour Mill, and the Illawarra

Hotel saleyards were used for the cattle. The horses were exhibited in a paddock at the rear of the hotel. £140 had been subscribed for the show.

New subscribers to the Illawarra Show held in Wollongong on 12th February, 1857, were: Messrs. Gerald Anderson, Duncan Beatson, John Beatson, and Captain Benjamin Darley, Dr. Robert Davison, and Mrs. Geraghty. The new subscribers to the Dapto A. & H. Society were: Hon. Daniel Cooper, M.L.C., John Marks, Esq., M.P., James Thompson, Esq., M.P., and Dr. John Gerard, the amount of their subscriptions being one guinea each.

Robert Campbell, Esq. (per Captain Daniel Leahy), W. Carr, Esq., Ellis, Esq., James Robb, Rev. Father Rigney, Joseph Barrett, Esq., Captain Hopkins, B. Marshall, Esq., Lyons, Esq., Guion, Esq., Thomas Palmer, Esq., Robert Jenkins, Esq.

Prizes: Best 2-year-old colt, £1/10/-; best 2-year-old filly, £1/10/-; best entire horse (the exhibitor naming the purpose for which it was bred), £2/10/-; best two-year-old bull, £2; best two-year-old heifer, £2; veal calf (two months old), £1/10/-; prizes for 2-horse teams, £1/10/-; prizes for 6-bullock teams, £1/10/-; prizes for 4-bullock teams, 15/-; prizes for bullock drivers of 6 and 4 bullock teams.

It was arranged that the next annual show should take place in Wollongong on Thursday, 12th of February, 1857, and that the ploughing match should be held at Dapto about the 10th of February, 1857. There was some influence used to have this ploughing match held on the farm of Mr. Patrick Larkin, known as Galway Farm, West Dapto. Mr. Brown reported against it, and again recommended his brother's Swamp paddock, leased to Mr. Buchanan, who was favourable to it being used for the purpose. Eventually Dapto formed an A. & H. Society, as the following letter shows (Mr. Francis Peter McCabe had been appointed President of the Illawarra A. & H Society for 1857; Dr. Robert Menzies had been previously appointed President of the Kiama A. & H. Society):—"Dapto Steam Mills, 6th August, 1857. Sir,—I have the honor to inform you that at a meeting of the Dapto A. & H. Society, held at the Illawarra hotel on the 5th instant, your communication of the 3rd ultimo, respecting the amalgamation of the Illawarra and Dapto A. & H. Societies, was duly laid before the members of the Society, when the following resolution was unanimously agreed to, viz.: 'That the Dapto A. & H Society be continued in its integrity.' (Signed) John Brown, Hon. Secretary Dapto A. & H. Society," and addressed to Francis Peter McCabe, Esq., President of the Illawarra A. & H. Society. Mr. David Williamson Irving was then appointed President of the Dapto A. & H. Society.

The Illawarra A. & H. Society held a ploughing match at Kembla Grange, the property of Mr. Robert Haworth. The spot on which the match took place was held by lease by Mr. John Armstrong. The following is the result:— No. I., ploughman John Dixon, driver Archie Gillespie; No. II., ploughman Stephen Lynch, driver Phillip Town, 2nd prize £2; No. III., ploughman James Rixon, driver Ben. Rixon, jun., 1st prize £4; No. IV., ploughman Adam Dennis, driven Reuben Dennis, 3rd prize £1/5/-; No. V., ploughman Robert Hutson, driver John Town, 4th prize £1; No. VI., ploughman Thomas Berrett, driver John Kelly.

The following were members of the Committee of the Illawarra A. & H. Society for the term 1857-8:—Messrs. J. R. Cummins, Evan Evans, sen., Andrew Thompson, James Wright, S. S. Rogers, Robert Osborne, R. T. Hales, George Hewlett, Andrew McGill, William Kirton, James McGill, William Hales, Charles Fairs, sen., C. T. Smith, Dr. Lambert, A. McKenzie (Ellengowan), A. McKenzie (Bulli), James Hetherington, Thomas Garrett, and Edward Johnston. It was decided that Messrs. G. W. Brown and James R. Cummins be joint secretaries for the ensuing year. It was decided that the 14th annual show should take place in Wollongong, 19th January, 1858, and that the ploughing match should take place at Fairy Meadow on the Thursday before the show. This show was very successful. The exhibits of horned cattle were not numerous, but of good quality. Mr. David Johnston, of The Meadows, Albion Park, and his neighbour, Mr. Henry Osborne, of Marshall Mount, won all the leading prizes. Patrick Larkin, of Galway Farm, West Dapto, exhibited a beautiful grey draught horse, and Mr. James Hetherington exhibited the blood stallion "Sir Charles." Mr. Alexander Elliott won for blood mare, Mr. Andrew McGill won for best draught mare, Mr. John Graham won for best blood filly one-year-old, Mr. John Musgrave won for blood filly two-years-old.

Cattle—Best bull, any age (£3), Mr. Henry Osborne, 1st prize; second best (£1), Mr. David Johnston; best bull, two-years-old (£1/10/-), Mr D. W. Irving, 1st prize; best cow (£3),

Mr. David Johnston, 1st prize; second best cow (£1/10/-), Mr. D. W. Irving; best heifer, two-years-old (£1/10/-), Mr. Evan Evans, sen., 1st prize; best fat beast (£1), Mr. David Johnston; best boar, Mr. Edward Graham; second best, Mr. Thomas Armstrong; best sow, Mr. Edward Graham. The stock exhibitors were:—Mr. Evan Evans, 1 bull, 2 cows, 1 two-year-old heifer, 1 fat cow; Mr. Patrick Larkin, 1 draught stallion; Mr. George Buchanan, 1 draught mare; Mr. F. Darragh, 1 two-year-old filly, 1 draught mare; Mr. D. W. Irving, 1 two-year-old bull, 2 cows, 2 two-year-old heifers; Mr. Alexander Elliott, 1 blood mare; Mr. James Hetherington, 1 blood stallion, 1 blood mare; Mr. David Johnston, 1 bull, 1 cow, 1 two-year-old heifer, 2 fat bullocks; Mr. Andrew McGill, 1 draught stallion, 1 two-year-old bull, 1 fat bullock, 1 draught mare; Mr. Edward Graham, 1 two-year-old colt; Mr. William Coughrane, 4 two-year-old heifers; Mr. John Maxwell, 1 draught mare; Mr. P. McHugh, 1 two-year-old colt, 1 two-year-old filly; Mr. James McGill, 1 blood mare; Mr. Henry Gordon, 1 two-year-old draught colt; Mr. Henry Osborne, 1 draught stallion, 2 bulls, 1 imported cow, 1 cow, and 2 fat heifers; Mr. John Graham, 1 two-year-old draught filly; Mr. John Keys, 1 two-year-old draught filly; Mr. David Payne, 1 draught mare; Mr. Andrew Lysaght, 1 blood mare, 1 two-year-old blood filly. The judges of stock were Messrs. Joseph Sullivan Smith, Archibald Beatson, and William Keele. In farm produce the judges were Messrs. D. Aitkin, William Wilson, and William Ritchie. The dinner was held at Mr. Johnstone's hotel, Wollongong, and passed off quietly. The ploughing match at Fairy Meadow was a failure, owing, no doubt, to the nature of the soil. The ploughmen who had been trained on the Swamp paddock had no show in the stiffer clay soils where formation was difficult to attain.

Kiama A. & H. Society's show, held February 28th, 1857, in the Market Square, Kiama. Heavy rain almost prevented the show being held. There were no less than 67 exhibitors, a building 100 feet long being well filled with exhibits. The building was owned by George Bullen, and Bullen and Turner's displays of flowers were very superior. The stock were located behind John Carruthers' hotel, occupied by host John Reed. The prizes were awarded as follows:—Horses: Best draught stallion, £5, Michael Hindmarsh; best draught mare, £3, Alexander King; best blood mare, £2, Larry O'Toole; best draught two-year-old colt, £2, Patrick Daly; best draught two-year-old filly, Patrick Daly. Cattle: Best bull. two-years-old, £2, Francis Grey; best dairy cow, £3, Henry Grey; second best dairy cow, £2, William Vance; best heifer, £2, Thomas S. Kendall; best fat beast, William White; second best, Thomas Black. Swine: Thomas Black, James Harrison, and R. Busknell won the prizes.

FOUNDING OF THE DAPTO A. & H. SOCIETY.

The first exhibition held under the auspices of the Committee of the Dapto A. & H. Society at Shorn's Point on January 28th, 1857. Reported in "Illawarra Mercury" of 2nd February, 1857. The President of the Illawarra A. & H. Society, Mr. Charles Throsby Smith, and Dr. Robert Menzies, President of the Kiama A. & H. Society, were present by invitation. The report states: "The examination of stock and agricultural and horticultural produce occupied a considerable time, and it was about 4 o'clock when the names of the successful competitors were read out by the Secretary, John Brown. Previous to this the President of the Dapto Society, David Williamson Irving, addressed those present, thanking them for their attendance, taking it as an evidence of their approval, not only of the committee, but in showing that Dapto was the best place for holding a meeting of the kind in the district."

The show of horned cattle was said to have been the most numerous ever shown in the district. From the quantity enumerated our readers may judge for themselves, but they certainly exceed in number any show it has been our privilege to attend, and we will venture another opinion—that in their quality they have been unequalled, of all ages. They were composed of draught horse stock, 4 horses, 4 colts, 7 mares, 3 fillies; total 18. Blood horses 1, colts 3, mares 9, fillies 2; total 15. Horned cattle, aged bulls 8, two-year-old bulls 5, cows 54, heifers 22, fat bullocks 9, calves 4; total 102. Swine, boars 4, sows 6; total 10. The total number of articles entered for exhibition were 355, entered by 65 competitors.

Awards.—Horse stock: Best draught horse, Evan R. Evans, sen.; best blood horse, James McGill; best draught mare, Joseph Dunster; best blood mare, Thomas Wholohan; best draught two-year-old colt, George Tate; best draught two-year-old filly, James McGill. Cattle: Best bull, any age, Edward Graham; second best, Robert Ritchie; third best, Andrew McGill; best bull, two years, David Johnston; best cow, David Johnston; second best, Ed-

ward Graham; third best, David Johnston; best heifer, two-years-old, William Wilson; second best two-year-old heifer, David Johnston; best fat beast, David Johnston; second best, Joseph Ritchie; best fat calf, Mrs. Fitzgerald.

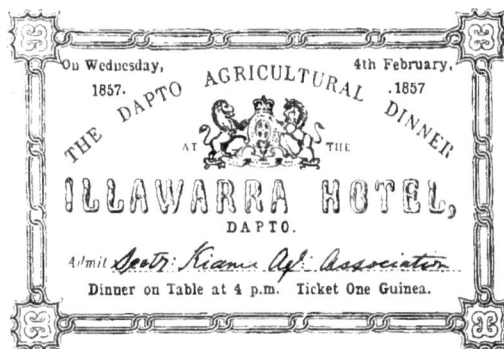

On Wednesday, 4th February, 1857. 1857. THE DAPTO AGRICULTURAL DINNER AT THE ILLAWARRA HOTEL, DAPTO. Admit *Sec'ty Kiama Agl. Association* Dinner on Table at 4 p.m. Ticket One Guinea.

The Dapto A. & H. Society held a ploughing match on 10th February, 1857; oxen only to be used. The result was as follows:—Entries: No. 1, ploughman Adam Dennis, driver Raebur Dennis, 2nd prize £3; No. II., ploughman Robert Hutson, driver Edward Dawe, jun., 3rd prize £1; No. III., ploughman James Rixon, driver Ben Rixon, jun.; No. IV., ploughman Stephen Lynch, driver Phillip Town, 1st prize £5; No. V., ploughman John Rixon, driver Archie Gillespie.

Ploughing match in connection with he Kiama A. & H. Society was held on 20th February, 1857, in Mr. Thomas Tempest's paddock (near the Jamberoo Recreation Ground), Jamberoo. This match was conducted under difficulties owing to the uneven nature of the ground at the time. The drawing for places decided against four of the competitors, who retired. Rain also operated against the men. The boys were, on the other hand, quite happy, and put in good work. The following is the results:—Thomas Campbell won 1st prize, valued at £7/10/-; George Wood, jun., won 2nd prize, valued at £4; Thomas Gould won 3rd prize, valued at £3. These ploughmen were at the time of the match under 20 years of age, hence the term boys.

During the time the match was in progress it was witnessed by a large and orderly crowd of interested farmers. A shooting match had been arranged with Colt's revolvers; distance 84 yards. Eighteen shots were fired, and Mr. William Black was declared the winner. At the conclusion of this match a meeting was held, at which it was decided to meet later at Mr. John Reed's hotel. Kiama. This meeting took place, as arranged, on 10th March, 1857, when a Gun and Revolver Club was formed.

At the Dapto Show held on 28th February, 1857, there was a fine display of horned cattle, and the most numerous ever seen in the district. The stock display was good and was composed of: Horse stock: horses, 4; colts, 4; mares, 7; fillies, 2; total 18. Blood Stock: horses, 1; colts, 3; mares, 9; fillies, 2; total, 15. Horned Cattle: aged bulls 8; two-year-old bulls, 5; cows, 54; heifers, 22; fat bullocks, 9; calves, 4; total, 102. Swine: boars, 4; sows, 6; total, 10. The gross number of entries 355; 65 competitors. Prizes—Horses: best draught horse, Evan R. Evans 1st prize; best blood horse, James McGill 1st prize; best draught mare, Joseph Dunster 1st prize; best blood mare, Thomas Wholohan 1st prize; best draught two-year-old colt, George Tate, protest entered; best draught two-year old filly, Henry Lee, protest entered; best blood two-year-old colt, George Buchanan, 1st prize; best blood two-year-old filly, James McGill 1st prize. Cattle: best bull (any age), Edward Graham 1st prize; best bull (any age), Joseph Ritchie 2nd prize; best bull (any age), Andrew McGill 3rd prize; best bull (2 years old), David Johnston 1st prize; best cow, David Johnston 1st prize; best cow, Edward Graham 2nd prize; best cow, David Johnston 3rd prize; best heifer (2 years old), William Wilson 1st prize; best heifer (2 years old) David Johnston 2nd prize; best fat beast, David Johnston 1st prize; best fat beast, Joseph Ritchie 2nd prize; best fat calf, Mrs. Fitzgerald 1st prize. Swine: John Armstrong, D. W. Irving, John Graham, Stephen Lynch and G. W. Brown divided honours.

A meeting of the Society was held at Mr. Jim Heatherington's Hotel, Wollongong, on March 18th, 1858. It would appear that the dignified, courteous, and kindly disposed President, Mr. Francis Peter McCabe, had accidentally trod on someone's pet corn—there was a considerable amount of fuss. Then Mr. George William Brown resigned, and Mr. James R. Cummins took over the entire control of the books of the Society, and lasting peace was restored.

The Illawarra A. & H. Association held meeting at Commercial Hotel, Wollongong, on October 4th, 1858, Robert Haworth in the chair. A report was laid before the meeting. £50 was collected, of which £20 was collected at Terry's Meadows by James McGill and Evan Evans. Next meeting was held at Davis' Harp Inn, on 31st January, 1859, when arrangements were made to hold the show in Market Square, Wol-

longong on 9th February, 1859, ploughing matches to be held on 7th February, 1859. Messrs. McCabe, Hales, Stemmel, Evans and Elliott were appointed a sub-committee to appoint Judges.

The faith of the farmers in the possibility of holding the Illawarra district shows under one central committee. The year 1856 was fruitful of discontent.

The Committee for 1859-60 comprised: Mr. F. P. McCabe (President), Mr. James R. Cummins (Secretary), and Mr. George Hewlett (Treasurer); Mr. Thomas Hale was elected Vice-President; Messrs. C. T. Smith, Evan Evans, Dr. Alex. Osborne, Thomas Garrett, F. Stenell, S. D. Lott, John Somerville, William Kirton, Dr. G. P. Lambert, Andrew McGill, William Spence, A. McKenzie (Ellengowan), A. McKenzie (Bulli), Andrew Elliott, Robert Osborne, G. G. Rogers, and Andrew Thompson. It was decided to hold the show in Wollongong on 12th February, 1859. Ploughing match to take place at Mr. Andy Lysaught's Hotel, Fairy Meadow, on 5th January, 1859. Messrs. R. Haworth, Robert Longmore, Patrick Higgins, Percy Owen, and Evan R. Evans, jun., were added to the Committee. For the ploughing match only two teams started. James Rixon ploughman, John Rixon driver, 1st prize (£3), won by Rixon; Ben Rixon, jun., ploughman, A. Robertson driver, 2nd prize (£2), won by Ben Rixon, jun.

The 15th annual show took place in the Market Square, Wollongong, on February 12th, 1859. Horse stock: Judges, Messrs. Burke, Gallaway, and Kerr. Best draught stallion, no prize awarded; best blood stallion (30/-), Mr. P. McHugh 1st prize; best draught mare (30/-), Mr. Felix Darragh 1st prize; best blood mare (30/-), Mr. P. McHugh 1st prize; best draught two-year-old stallion (30/-), Mr. Joseph Dunster 1st prize; best two-year-old draught gelding (£1), Mr. John Graham (Avondale) 1st prize; best blood two-year-old colt (20/-), Mr. P. McHugh 1st prize; best blood two-year-old any age (£3), Andrew McGill 1st prize, only one exhibitor; best cow (£3), Evan Evans 1st prize; second best cow (30/-), Evan Evans; best three-year-old heifer (30/-), Joseph Ritchie 1st prize; best fat beast (20/-), Andrew McGill 1st prize; best boar, John Geddes; best sow, John Geddes. The show dinner was a great success, and 40 people were present. Mr. F. R. McCabe occupied the chair, whilst Captain Hart occupied the vice-chair. Donations to the show amounted to £90/16/6, door takings £4/2/4; expenses, prize £63/7/6, other expenses £27/9/7. leaving cash in hand £4/1/9.

The show for 1860 was to be held in Wollongong in January, 1860, and the ploughing match on May 5th, 1860. Prizes for ploughing match: Best executed work, 1st prize £5, second best £3, third best £1. The Society was commanding attention. His Excellency the Governor-General was Patron. President, Mr. C. T. Smith; Vice-President, Mr. Thomas Hale; Alderman Hewlett, Treasurer; James R. Cummins, Secretary; Committee, Councillors Evans, McGill, and Ritchie, and Messrs. Fred. R. Cole, Robert Longmore, Aldermen James Wilshire, J. R. Robson, Lott, Messrs. Evan R. Evans, jun., Thomas Garrett, Richard Dennis, W. D. Wright, Henry Hill Osborne, John Somerville, Robert Wilson, Dr. G. P. Lambert, Messrs. T. A. Reddall, William Kirton, William Osborne, William Spence, Thomas Garrett, M.P., D. W. Irving, A. McKenzie (Ellengown), Andrew Elliott, G. S. Rogers, Andrew Thompson, John Musgrave, James McGill, John Rixon, John Evans, and Michael Devlin. Mr. George Pinchin was appointed collector. With a view of pouring oil on the troubled waters, Mr. Garrett, M.P., hinted that it might be a wise step to hold the next show at Dapto. Mr. C. T. Smith considered it would be useless, as it had been tried and proved a failure. Mr. Robert Haworth considered it would be a wrong move, now that they were established, to go to Dapto. It was then decided to hold the next show in Wollongong on 24th January, 1860, the ploughing match to take place at Dapto. Messrs. Robert Wilson and John Evans, of Shellharbour, were added to the Committee. Messrs. Evan Evans, Joseph Ritchie, and John Rixon were appointed sub-committees to select judges for the forthcoming show.

At the Illawarra A. & H. Society's show, 1860, the judges for horse stock were Messrs. William Keele, Archibald Beatson, and Thomas Wholohan, and gave satisfaction. Both blood and draught horse stock were very superior A chestnut two-year-old blood stallion, bred by Mr. James McGill, got by "Hopping Joe" out of a mare named "Queen," was much admired. Mr. John Smith, of Shoalhaven (formerly of Illawarra) exhibited the well-known race mare "Whynot," a great turf performer. In 1850 she beat Sir Charles in the Maiden Plate. and in the following year, when ridden by Mr. James McGill. she ran neck and neck with "The Plover." Mr. Smith also exhibited the blood stallion Mozart," three years old, in the

aged horse class. His dam was "Whynot." In horned cattle Mr. Andrew McGill exhibited a fine two-year-old bull, equal to anything exhibited in Illawarra, and a remarkably well-bred cow, got by an imported bull out of an imported cow, and was sold to Mr. McGill by Mr. Duncan Beatson, who had purchased her from Mr. Rodd, of Five Dock, Cumberland. Note.—It was said that this cow founded the McGill "Scotch Jock" strain.

The prizes:—Horses: Best draught stallion, Mr. Andrew McGill 1st prize, Mr. Evan Evans 2nd prize; best blood stallion, Mr. Thomas Slavin, 1st prize. Messrs. John Smith, Hugh Gallagher, Jas. H. Evans, John Maxwell, George Osborne also exhibited in this class. Best blood mare, Mr. William Osborne 1st prize. Messrs. John Graham, Jas. H. Swan, and John Smith also exhibited in this class. Best draught two-year-old stallion, Mr. Thomas Coughrane 1st prize. Mr. John Collins exhibited in this class. Best draught two-year-old filly, Mr. Edward Dawes 1st prize. Mr. William James also exhibited. Best blood two-year-old stallion, James McGill 1st prize. Horned cattle: Best bull, any age, Andrew McGill 1st prize, Peter Coleman 2nd prize. Messrs. Jas. H. Swan and William Wilson also exhibited. Best cow, Andrew McGill 1st prize, Mr. Evans Evans 2nd prize. Messrs. Evans exhibited three cows, Samuel Parkes and Joseph Ritchie two cows each. in this class. Best heifer, Mr. Andrew McGill 1st and 2nd prizes. Best fat beast, Mr. Andrew McGill 1st prize, Mr. Samuel Parkes 2nd prize. Mr. Joseph Ritchie also exhibited in this class. Best fat calves, Mr. Samuel Parkes 1st prize. Mr. Parkes had two exhibits, and Mr. John Geddes one exhibit, in this class. Swine: Best boar, Mr. Robert Marshall 1st prize, Mr. W. Brown 2nd prize; best sow, Mr. W. Brown 1st prize, Mr. John Graham 2nd prize. The sum of £71/12/6 was duly paid out in prizes by the Treasurer, and the funds of the Society only amounted to £82/10/3. It will thus be seen that in those times much work was put into these shows of a highly honourable nature.

In 1860 Robert Issel Perrott was President of the Kiama A. and H. Society, and William Irvine, the Secretary. No more impossible men could be selected for those positions. They mixed their own affairs with the business of the Society.

The Berrys, of Coolangatta, confiscated the files of the "Kiama Examiner," the result of a libel action through the proprietors. Messrs. Barr and Pratt. daring to publish a strong address delivered in Wollongong, by Dr. John Dunmore Lang. Dr. George Underwood Alley reported the speech, and Barr and Pratt foolishly published it. Had the speech been delivered in Kiama, they could have done so safely. As it was, every file of the "Examiner" was seized and destroyed, and the printing press carried away.

The loss of the "Kiama Examiner" deprived the Kiama district of its newspaper information to a great extent until the founding of the "Kiama Independent," in 1863.

The pleuro-pneumonia had been introduced into Kiama district by Cook Bros., who had a butchering business in Manning Street, and were leasing Marsden Hill for grazing and slaughtering their beef cattle. It was a serious outbreak, and quite upset the shows.

At a meeting of the Society held on 22nd October, 1860, Mr. C. T. Smith was elected President, Mr. Andrew Elliott, Treasurer, and Mr. John Biggar, Secretary. The following names were added to the previous Committee: Messrs. A. Elliott, R. J. Hales, D. Aitkin, W. F. Lloyd, James Hetherington, Henry J. Marr, Archie Beatson, George Hewlett, and James R. Cummins. Next show to be held on the last Tuesday in January, 1861. Mr. David Williamson Irving suggested to read an essay on "Agriculture" in connection with what was known then as the "O'Connell Classics." A deadlock occurred owing to a technical error in the appointment of the show officials. Eventually there was a committee of management appointed to arrange a general meeting of the members on the 16th September 1861, at which was adopted 14 rules to regulate the Illawarra A. & H. Society. His Excellency the Governor, Patron; President, Mr. Robert Owen; Vice-President, Mr. J. H. Marr; Treasurer, Alexander Elliott; Hon. Secretary, James R. Cummins; Auditors, Messrs. S. D. Lott and D. Aitkin. The prize-list was gone through, and the same prizes were suggested as previous shows, viz.: Best draught stallion, £3; best blood stallion, £3; best bull, any age, £3; best cow, £3; the other prizes being of lesser value, without any addition to the number of classes. Best draught stallion, Thomas Coughrane 1st prize; best blood stallion, Robert Martin 1st prize; best blood mare, Joseph Ritchie 1st prize; best draught two-year-old stallion, W. H. Swan 1st prize; best draught two-year-old filly, Thomas Coughrane 1st prize; best blood two-year-old filly, Thomas Maher 1st prize. Cattle: Best bull, any age,

Andrew McGill 1st prize; best bull, two-years-old, Andrew McGill 1st prize; best cow, Evan Evans 1st prize; best heifer, two-years-old, Andrew McGill 1st prize; best calf, John Geddes 1st prize; best fat beast, Andrew McGill 1st prize. Swine: Best boar, Ben Marshall 1st prize, W. Brown 2nd prize; best sow, John Geddes 1st prize, Ben Marshall 2nd prize.

The entries were as follows:—Thomas Maher, 1 blood mare, 1 blood filly; John Rixon, 1 draught filly, 2-year-old; Bernard McCawley, 1 draught mare; Joseph Ritchie, 1 draught mare, 1 blood mare; John Maxwell, 1 draught mare; Andrew McNeil, 1 bull (aged), 1 2-year-old bull, 3 cows, 1 fat cow, 2 heifers; Evan Evans, 1 2-year-old bull, 1 bull (aged), 1 draught stallion, 2 cows, 1 2-year-old heifer, 1 fat cow; Robert Martin, 1 blood stallion, 1 draught stallion; W. Brown, 1 boar, 1 fat pig, 1 fat calf; W. H. Swan, 1 draught stallion, 2-year-old; Thomas Coughrane, 1 draught stallion, 1 blood stallion; 1 draught mare, 1 draught 2-year-old filly; Ben. Marshall, 1 boar, 1 sow; John Geddes, 1 calf, 1 sow, 1 fat beast; James Hetherington, 1 blood 2-year-old filly.

It will be seen that in aged bulls only one prize was awarded; yet provision was made for a second prize. The same applied in the case of the aged cow class, only one award was made. The judge's remarks were not considered of sufficient merit.

Illawarra A. &. H. Society's Show, 1862. Prize List: Best Draught Stallion, £3; Best Blood Stallion, £3; Best Daught Mare, £1 10s.; Best Blood Mare, £1 10s.; Best Draught 2 years old Stallion, £1 10s.; Best Draught 2 years old Filly, £1; Best Blood Colt, £1; Best Blood Filly, £1; Best Bull, any age, £3; 2nd Best Bull, £1; Best Bull 2 years old, £1 10s.; Best Cow, £3; 2nd Best Cow, £1 10s.; Best Heifer, 2 years old, £1 10s.; 2nd Best Heifer, 2 years old, £1; Best Fat Beast, £1; Best Fat Calf, 10s.; Best Boar. £2; 2nd Best Boar, £1; Best Sow, £2; 2nd Best Sow, £1; Best Fat Pig, £1.

Prizewinners: Best Draught Stallion, Thomas Coughrane; Best Blood Stallion, Robert Martin; Best Blood Mare, Joseph Ritchie; Best Draught 2 years old Stallion, W. H. Swan, Best Draught 2 years old Filly, Thomas Coughrane: Best Blood 2 years old Colt, no exhibit; Best Blood 2 years old Filly, Thomas Maher; Best Bull, any age, Andrew McGill; 2nd Best Bull (no prize); Best Bull 2 years old, Andrew McGill; Best Cow, Evan R. Evans; 2nd Best Cow (no prize); Best Heifer 2 years old, Andrew

McGill; 2nd Best Heifer (no prize); Best Fat Beast, Andrew McGill; Best Calf, John Geddes; Best Boar, Benjamin Marshall; 2nd Best, William Brown; Best Sow, John Geddes; 2nd Best, Benjamin Marshall; Best Fat Pig, William Brown.

Exhibits: Thomas Maher, 1 blood Mare, 1 Blood filly; John Rixon, 1 draught 2 years old filly; Bernard McCauley, 1 draught mare; oJseph Ritchie, 1 draught mare, 1 blood mare; John Maxwell, 1 draught mare; Andrew McGill, 1 fat cow, 2 heifers, 1 aged bull, 1 2 years old bull, 3 cows; Evan R. Evans, 1 draught stallion, 1 aged bull, 1 2 years old bull, 2 cows, 1 2-years-old heifer, 1 fat cow, 1 blood colt, a draught stallion (exhibited by Robert Martin); William Brown, 1 boar, 1 sow, 1 fat pig, 1 fat calf; William H. Swan, 1 draught stallion, 1 2-years-old draught stallion; Thomas Coughrane, 1 draught stallion, 1 blood stallion, 1 draught mare, 1 draught 2-years-old filly; Benjamin Marshall, 1 boar, 1 sow; John Geddes, 1 calf, 1 sow, 1 fat beast; James Hetherington, 1 blood 2 years old filly.

Note.—The Judges were either exacting, or the stock generally were not up to the standard in some instances.

The Shoalhaven Estate A. and H. Society, which was composed only of the tenantry and a few others connected with the estate, was initiated on 1st September, 1863, with Alexander Berry, Esq., Patron; Mr. David Berry, President; Mr. Henry Gordon Morton, Vice-President. Committees of Management (St. Vincent), Messrs. Robert Armstrong, Alexander Aberdeen, William Morrison and James Wallace; (Bolong), Messrs. James McGuire, and Samuel Upton; (Coolangatta), Mr. James Houston; (Broughton Creek), Mr. James Wilson; (Gerringong), Messrs. Henry Lee and James Lang. Mr. James Lang was Treasurer, and Mr. John Bindon Secretary. Eleven rules were adopted, and a long list of subscribers was secured. It would appear, however, that a good many of those who handed in their names to the Committee of Management did not complete their obligations.

List of members: St. Vincent—Alexander Aberdeen, Robert Aberdeen, Robert Armstrong, John James Armstrong, William Bellsham, Hugh Bates, Robert Burrdale, William Connolly, Thomas Condon, John Caffrey, Patrick Caffrey, Alexander Campbell, John Craig, Revd. Father D'Arcy, Charles Caine Dixon, Jeremiah Donohue, Davie Dwyer, Joseph Ephrins, Allen Fleming, Duncan Finlayson, William Gollan (jun), James Gollan, John Gollan, Ronald Gollan, Benjamin Hart, Matthew Hart, Daniel Harris, Isaac Hewitt, John Houston, John Irvine, Geo. Jamieson, Patrick Jullian, John Kennedy, Michael Kennedy, Peter Kelly, Thomas Kelly, Stephen Knapp, Donald Lamond, James Lang, Michael Lenehan, Robert Levlie, Robert Miller, William Cuthbert Morrison, Alexander McIntyre, Alexander McInnes, Lachlan McKinnon, Frank Mordrain, Lachlan McTaggert, Michael Murphy, Christopher Murray, Christopher McLean, Andrew Madden, William Miller, Martin Morrison, Peter McLean, Henry Gordon Morton, Revd. William Mitchell, Andrew Noble, Argus Noble, David O'Keefe, Angus O'Keefe. Cornelius O'Neil, Maurice O'Connor, Edward Pryce, Samuel Potter, Robert Pollock (snr.), Patrick Ryder, John Reid, James Ryan, Arthur Smith, Bernard Shannon, John Shannon, William Truston, Francis Thompson, John Turner, Frederick Walters, James Wallace, David Waddell, John Watts, William Wood, Joseph Williamson, William Anderson Wheatley, Revd. Richard W. Young (Coolangatta), William Berry, David Berry, Cornelius C. Brettell, Geo. Brook, Michael Courtney, Michael, Condon, John Connolly, William Dawes, James Davies, George Davies, Alexander Fraser, William Greenaway, James Houston, William Holden, Smith, Bernard Shannon, John Shannon, Willitt; Bolong—Peter Burke, John Bindon, John Collingwood, Henry Comerford (snr.), Henry Comerford (jnr.).

Pleuro-pneumonia.—A committee was formed in Jamberoo, consisting of Messrs. D. Hartigan, George Wood (jnr.), Alexander Gordon, James English, William Wright, John Cole, Hugh Dudgeon, John Noble, George Tate (jnr.), Joseph Howard, George Watson, Denis McCarthy, John Black, Robert Young, Robert Knight, D. L. Dymock, John Dymock, John Tate (jnr.), Henry Young, William Graham, Walter Curry, Henry Frederick. The objective of this meeting held at Curry's Jamberoo Arms Hotel, 20th July, 1863, was to give a Mr. Hall, who was present, an opportunity of demonstrating that which he claimed, to wit, cure cattle suffering from pleuro-pneumonia, without having to resort to inoculation. Needless to say, he failed to satisfy the committee.

The Shoalhaven Estate A. and H. Society's show, held April 15th, 1864, List of prizes:— Best draught imported stallion, McLean 1st prize; best draught imported mare, Andre De

Mestre, 1st prize; best blood imported stallion, Ette De Mestre, 1st prize; best colonial draught mare, John Elliott, 1st prize; best colonial-bred blood mare—James Thompson, 1st prize; best 2-year-old blood filly, Collingwood, 1st prize; best blood gelding, James McGuire, 1st prize; best Ayrshire bull, Angus McKay, 1st prize; best milch cow, William Gollan, 1st prize; best pair bullocks, — Knapp, 1st prize; best boar, Robert Armstrong, 1st prize; best sow, John Gollan, 1st prize.

The Shoalhaven Estate Ploughing Match, held in the blacksmith's paddock, Numbaa township, 21st June, 1864:—Class 1, horse teams, 1st prize, £5; 2nd prize, £4; 3rd prize, £2. Class 2, bullock teams, 1st prize, £5; 2nd prize, £4; 3rd prize, £2; Class 3, youths, under 18 years of age, bullock teams, 1st prize, £4; 2nd prize, £2; Mr. John Bindon, Secretary.

Kiama A. and H. Society's Ploughing Matches, held in Howard's Flat, Jamberoo, known as the Hermitage Farm. Messrs John O'Meara and Walter Curry had the publican's booth on ground. 1st prize was won by James Black; 2nd prize was won by Thomas Healey; 3rd prize was won by George Tate, jnr. (Mr. George Tate was then a blacksmith in Jamberoo); 4th prize was won by John Murphy. Youths' Match: 1st prize was won by James Bucket; 2nd prize was won by James Healey. A social evening was spent after the matches were over at Walter Curry's Jamberoo Arms Hotel.

First annual meeting of the Shoalhaven Estate was held at the Royal Hotel, Numbaa on 7th September, 1864. Mr. Henry Gordon Morton in the chair, who stated that this society was established on 1st September, 1863. It had 216 members enrolled, 121 had already paid their subscriptions. An exhibition of produce, implements, and live stock was held on 29th day of July, 1864. The following gentlemen gave donations:—Messrs. Andre De Mestre, A. A. Wheatley, of Shoalhaven; Messrs. Henry Whittingham, John Elliott, and George Ballen, of Kiama. The president (Mr. Morton) placed the report before the meeting, which was adopted, on motion by Messrs. William Gollan, jnr., and John Campbell. The balance-sheet showed, by subscriptions, £62; donations and entrance, £7 3s. 6d.; on debit side was printing, stationery, postage, £14 14s. 11d.; individual expenses, £4 18s. 6d.; cash to the society, £5; paid in prizes, £34 14s.; total, £59 18s. 6d.; cash in hand, £9 16s. 1d.; auditors. Messrs. A. A. Wheatley and C. C. Bretell; John Bindon, secretary.

Second annual meeting of the Shoalhaven Estate A. and H. Society, held September 12th, 1865. The following donations were received:—Messrs. Berry Bros., £10; the I.S.N. Co., £5; Messrs. Thomas McCaffery, Hazlett, and Mathews, of Sydney; Messrs. Henry Whittingham, John Farraher, Henry Grey, John Williams, and Robert Miller, of Kiama; Andre De Mestre and John Monaghan, of Shoalhaven gave £1 each. Receipts, £75 14s. 6d. Expenses, £75 12s. 1½d. Balance, 2/4½.

Ploughing matches lapsed owing to the ravages of pleuro-pneumonia among the herds.

The pleuro-pneumonia in the dairy herd was playing havoc with the shows south of Dapto. Then the trouble of getting suitable judges sprung up suddenly. At a show held in an open yard, where the "Kiama Independent" newspaper offices stand to-day, there was a fine display of cattle, in 1864. Mr. Charles McCaffrey, of Jerrara, had some choice cattle bred from the imported stock of Mr. Henry Osborne. They were not valued by the judge. This caused Mr. McCaffrey to remark, "It is plain, judging cattle, like Kissing, goes by favour." There was also much carelessness practised by Secretaries of these shows. The "Kiama Independent," of September the 14th, 1865, put matters honestly before its readers as follows:—"The Agricultural Association which once existed in Kiama, and held several successful shows, exhibitions that were highly creditable to the district, has apparently quite ceased to exist. Even the annual ploughing match, the last surviving portion of the proceedings, which has with something like regularity been held in Jamberoo during late years, was hardly mentioned at the season when it should have taken place last year." No doubt, however, the pleuro-pneumonia was the chiefest cause.

The Shoalhaven Estate Show was held 1st March, 1866. This show was held at Broughton Creek. The horse judges were Messrs. McGill, Waddington, and Thompson.

Best colonial draught entire, William R Hindmarsh, 1st prize; best colonial draught mare, Robert Miller, 1st prize; best colonial draught 2-year-old entire, Francis Grey, 1st prize; best colonial blood mare, John Smith, 1st prize; best colonial blood 2-year-old filly, D. F. McPherson, 1st prize; best colonial blood 2-year-old draught filly, Burradale, 1st prize; best coaching mare (colonial bred), Robert Miller, 1st prize.

ALFRED W. DUNCAN, Berkeley, Unanderra.

PLAYBOY OF BERKELEY.

CHAMPION TEST COW, PRIZE OF BERKELEY.

PRINCESS OF BERKELEY.

BLOSSOM OF BERKELEY.

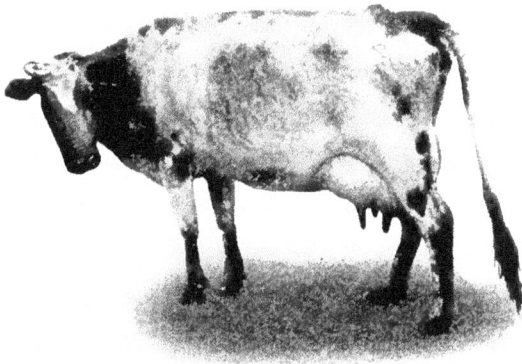

DUCHESS OF BERKELEY.

FUSSIE OF BERKELEY.

Cattle—Judges, Messrs. Henry Grey, Robert Miller, Robert Armstrong, and A. Campbell.

Prior to John Boxell going to Mudgee to buy the Lowe-bred bull, which figured at the Berry and Shoalhaven shows, and sired George Yates' bull Boxer, he had a very excellent herd of dairy cattle of the old Longhorn type. Several of them had white dorsal streaks. They were roan and strawberry cows showing dark hairs throughout their body. From one of those old type cows which displayed the Longhorned Durham character, he bred a red bull that was generally considered the best bull in the Berry district. He then put the Lowe-bred bull into the herd, and gradually lost the old type. Note.—My informant was a neighbour and a personal friend of John Boxell, a man who knew what he was talking about, and a man of much experience in cattle.

Best colonial-bred bull, any age, John Boxell (bred by Lowe, Mudgee), 1st prize; best colonial-bred bull, 2-year-old, Thomas Black, 1st prize; best colonial-bred cow, any age, Robert Tait, 1st prize; best pair of working bullocks, John Grey, 1st prize.

Pigs—Judges, Messrs. Waddington, John Gollan, and Robert Armstrong. Best boar, James Robinson; best sow, William Stewart.

Butter—Mrs. Christie Murray and Miss Stewart won all the prizes.

The Shoalhaven Estate ploughing matches, held on 26th June, 1866.—1st match—Horse teams, 1st prize, £5; 2nd prize, £2 10s.; 3rd prize, £1. 2nd match—Bullock teams, 1st prize, £5; 2nd prize, £2 10s.; 3rd prize, £1. 3rd match —Youths under 18 years, 1st prize, £3; 2nd prize, £1 10s.; 3rd prize, £1.

Ploughing matches at Jamberoo, under the auspices of the Kiama A. and H. Society—John O'Meara 1st prize; Edwin Vidler, jnr., 2nd prize; William Welch, 3rd prize. Youths' Match, under 18 years old, John Collins, jnr., 1st prize; no second prize.

Ploughing match at Whopindilly, Ulladulla, in Mr. Kendall's paddock. Match, bullock teams —1st prize, £5, Thomas Smith; 2nd prize, £3, Stephen Knapp; 3rd prize, £1 10s., Thomas Gover. Judges, Messrs. McLean and Houston.

Mr. John Black, Mayor of Kiama, called a meeting at the Court House, to arrange matters in connection with the Kiama A. and H. Society, for the 20th September, 1866. At this meeting, Mr. John Black (Mayor) took the chair. Mr. John Marks proposed the first resolution: "That in the opinion of this meeting, it is desirable to reorganise the Kiama Agricultural and Horticultural Association." This motion was seconded by Mr. Robert Miller, and carried unanimously. The second resolution was moved by Mr. John Black: "That the following gentlemen form a committee for the purpose of making the necessary arrangements to secure the permanent standing and success, viz., Messrs. John Marks, James Robb, Michael Hindmarsh, James Colley, Robert Miller, jnr., Thomas Chapman, William Moles, John Black, James McGill, David Lindsay Dymock, Samuel Charles, Robert Stobo, George King Waldron, Nicholas Craig, George Adams, William English, George Hindmarsh, James Blow, John McLelland, Henry Fredericks, James Harvison, Samuel Marks, George Gale, Joseph Pike, John Hukins, Walter Curry, John King, Joseph Weston, Stephen Tobin, Henry Lee, George Grey, George Bullen, Thomas McCaffrey, Robert Kendall, William James, Henry Grey, Humphrey Dunster, with power to add to the number." This was seconded by James Harvison, and carried. Mr. Joseph Weston, Hon. Secretary.

Meeting of the Kiama A. and H. Society on 10th October, 1866. Present—Messrs. Robert Miller, jnr., John Black, James Harvison, Nicholas Craig, John Geary, James Spinks, and the Secretary, Mr. Joseph Weston. Mr. John Marks was appointed President, Mr. Robert Miller, Vice-President, Mr. John King, Treasurer, and Messrs. John Black and Joseph Weston. Joint Secretaries. It was decided to hold a show in Kiama, on 27th February, 1867.

The 4th annual meeting of the Shoalhaven Estate A. and H. Society was held on 6th of February, 1867, on the roadside, about two miles south of Gerringong. On the Berry Estate at that time there were 400 tenants. The owners of the estate erected a building for the occasion, 50ft. long and 22ft. wide, of weatherboards and shingle-roof. It was intended for a school. There was also a long row of cattle pens erected. The horse judges were Messrs. Thomas, Thompson, and Sharpe. The prizes were awarded as follows:—

Best blood stallion, £2, George K. Waldron. 1st prize; best draught stallion, £2, Francis Grey, 1st prize; best coaching stallion, £1, John Farraher, 1st prize; best 2-year-old draught colt. £1 10s., George Tate, 1st prize; best blood mare. £1 10s., Joseph York's Nina, 1st prize; best draught mare, £1 10s., D. McLean, 1st prize; best coaching mare, £1 10s., Stephen Tobin, 1st prize; best blood colt, £1, Thomas McIntyre, 1st prize; best blood filly, £1, William Cunningham, 1st prize; best draught colt, £1, Francis McIntyre, 1st prize; best draught filly, £1, William Williams, 1st prize.

Cattle.—Judges, Messrs. Thompson, Grey and Armstrong:—Best bull, any age, £2, George Tate, 1st prize; best bull, any age, £1, Henry Lee, 2nd prize; best cow, £2, Charles Wiley, 1st prize; best cow, £1, Robert Miller, 2nd prize,

In pigs, Messrs. Thomas Black, Thomas McIntyre and William won the prizes.

1866-7.—"After a lapse of a few years," says the "Kiama Independent," "the A. & H. Society show, as recommended by the committee appointed in 1866, was held during February, 1867." This show was a success, and the Show Committee that followed on afterwards aimed at success every year onward. John Black and Joseph Weston were the Joint Secretaries. The show of stock was held in the Market Square, Kiama. The horse judges were Neil Sharpe, Robert Martin, and John Black. The cattle judges were Alexander Gordon, George Hindmarsh, William Brown, Thomas McKenzie, John Thorburn; Dairy and Farm Produce, James Robb, jnr.; Samuel Marks, and Humphrey Dunster.

W. N. Hindmarsh had on exhibition a bull in 2-year-old class. The judges and the public considered he was over the age. Hindmarsh took a declaration that the bull was under 3 years old, and it was accepted by the Committee.

At this show, Henry Fredericks, of Clover Hill, Mount Brandon, had three cows bred by himself in charge of Thomas Alexander. Their respective names were:—"Beauty," color roan; "Stately," colour red; "Nancy," colour red. "Stately" won the 2nd prize. Her hip was out of place, but she possessed a perfect udder. They were of the Henry Osborne strain.

The Committee of the Kiama A. and H. Society for 1868 were:—Messrs. N. Craig, John Geary, William Robb, John Black, Joseph Weston, George Bullen, John Marks (President), Robert Miller (Vice-President). Working Committee—John Marks, John Black, Joseph Weston, N. Craig, George Bullen, William Robb, James Spinks, James Harvison, William English, James Marks, C. D. Young, James Somerville, D. L. Dymock, Samuel Charles, James McGill, Humphrey Dunster, William James, Thomas Black, Robert Miller, Joseph Redford, George Tate; Thomas McCaffrey, Hugh Colley, Edward Parish, George Hindmarsh, John King, George Grey, William Grey, Francis Grey,

James Colley, Dixon King. John King was appointed Treasurer, and John Black and Joseph Weston, Joint Secretaries.

The Committee decided to have but two classes of cattle at the forthcoming show, namely Durhams and Ayrshire. This was the beginning of pure Shorthorn, or, in other words, the beef-shorthorn craze. Arguments were frequent in all public places and at church meetings. It was held by many that as the best dairy cattle in the Illawarra district were a cross between the Durham and Ayrshire, it was plain that the purer these two breeds were kept the better it would be for the dairymen. Henry Fredericks had, at this time, four noted cows named "Nelly Osborne," "Jane Osborne," "Nelly Beatson," and "Jane Beatson," which he could not enter, consequently, he had to either stand out or go into the inner circle, among the pedigreed.

Note.—The writer has not been able to locate the prize-winner at the 1868 Show, held in Market Square, Kiama, for which the following prize list was advertised:—

Horses:—Best draught stallion, £2/2; 2nd best, £1. Best blood stallion, £2/2; 2nd best, £1. Best draught mare, £1/10; 2nd best, £1. Best blood mare, £1/10; 2nd best, £1. Best draught 2-year-old colt, £1/10. Best draught 2-year-old filly, £1. Best blood 2-year-old filly £1.

Cattle.—Best Shorthorn bull, £2/10; 2nd best, £1/10. Best bull 2-year-old, £1. Best Shorthorn cow, £2/10; 2nd best, £1/10. Best Ayrshire bull, £2/10; 2nd best, £1/10. Best Ayrshire bull, 2-year-old, £1. Best Ayrshire cow, £2/10; 2nd best, £1/10. Best Ayrshire heifer, 2-year-old, £1. Best fat beast, £1/10; 2nd best, £1.

For the 1869 Show similar prizes were offered, when T. H. Lee won 1st prize for best Shorthorn bull; and Hugh Colley, of Muskfield, won 1st prize for best Ayrshire bull. Colley's bull was by James Robb's imported Ayrshire bull "The Marquis of Argyle," a very handsome bull, and equally good as a sire. He did much credit to his sire.

Kiama Show, held in Market Square, February 20th, 1869. Over 2000 people present. John Marks, president; James Somerville, secretary. The Kiama Volunteer Fife and Drum Band played lively airs during the day. Stock judges:—James McGill, J. Turkinton, Evan R. Evans, and James Thompson (Burrie). Produce judges:—Gelding, Morton, Morrice, and Allen. The following prizes were awarded:—

Shorthorn cattle:—Best bull, Henry Lee, 1st prize; Thomas Reynolds, 2nd prize. Best bull, 2 years, William Gordon, 1st prize.

Ayrshire cattle:—Best bull, Hugh Colley, 1st prize. Best cow, Evan R. Evans, 1st prize. Best heifer, John Marks, 1st prize.

Milton Show, held Francis McMahon's paddock, March 10th, 1869:—Best bull, Francis McMahon, 1st prize; W. W. Ewin, 2nd prize. Best cow, W. W. Ewin, 1st prize; H. Gumley, 2nd prize. Best 2-year-old heifer, Francis McMahon, 1st prize; Francis McMahon, 2nd prize.

Note.—This was the dawn of a new era—the coming of the beef Shorthorns.

James Spinks exhibited a medium-sized dairy bull, known to his neighbours as the "Clown bull." His dam's name was "The Clown," and was purchased by James Spinks at Robert Johnston's sale, "Fountaindale." She had come down during the years from the Glenlee strain. No better cow could be seen at that time. The Clown bull was a dappled or mottled red and white bull. He was alright in a dairy herd, but nowhere in the show ring of the seventies, among the roans and reds.

Kiama Show Committee for 1870 consisted of John Marks, James Colley, Samuel Charles, Robert Miller, William Moles, John Black, John Colley, Hugh Colley, William Colley, Joseph King, Samuel Marks, George Wood, Junr. (Jamberoo), George Wood (Springhill), Mat. E. Robson, D. L. Dymock, Henry Fredricks, James Spinks, Thomas Fredricks, Nicholas Craig, George Bullen, John Geary, James Somerville, George King Waldron, Joseph Weston, William Budd, James Harvison, Robert Oscar Kendall, John Farraher, William Grey, William English, William Bailey, Senr., William Bailey, Junr., Alexander Emery, Thomas McCaffrey, Thomas Black, James McGuire Smith, George Tate, James Wilson, Junr., James Campbell, Edward Parish, Thomas Blow, Thomas Brown, Hugh Mitchell, Alexander Boyd, Senr., James McGill, William James, Thomas Coughrane, Humphrey Dunster, William Fryer, John Cullen, and Samuel Turner.

At Kiama Show, held on 23rd February, 1870, in Market Square, Kiama, the judges of live stock were:—J. Turkinton, James Monaghan, J. Armstrong, Evan R. Evans, and James Thompson (Burrier).

Best Shorthorn bull, £2/10, Henry Fredricks, 1st prize; £1/10, Mrs. Henry Lee, 2nd prize. Best Shorthorn heifer, £1/10, James Spinks, 1st prize; £1, Thomas Black, 2nd prize. Best bull, 2 years (Shorthorn), £1, M. N. Hindmarsh, 1st prize. Best Shorthorn cow, £2/10, Robert Miller, 1st prize; £1/10, Henry Fredricks, 2nd prize. Best Ayrshire bull, £2/10, Hugh Colley, 1st prize; £1/10, John Honey, 2nd prize. Best Ayrshire bull, 2 years, £1/10, Robert Hindmarsh, 1st prize; £1, John Marks, 2nd prize. Best Ayrshire heifer, 2 years, £1/10, James Robb, 1st prize; £1, Robert Miller, 2nd prize.

Sydney Exhibition stock.—By report dated 8th September, 1870, several prizes were won by Illawarra men; M. E. Robson, 1st prize for cow in milk; E. H. Weston won for best coaching horse; E. H. Weston highly commended for 1-year-old blood horse, "Greyskin"; John Elliott, 1st prize for draught mare.

At Kiama Show held on 15th and 16th February 1871, in Market Square, Kiama:—

Best bull, any age, £3, "Cornet," Robert Hindmarsh, 1st prize; best bull, any age, £2/10, Henry Fredricks, 2nd prize; best bull, any age, age, £1, Richard East, 4th prize; best bull under 2 years old, £2, George Tate, 1st prize; best bull under 2 years old, £1/10, T. and F. Hindmarsh, 2nd prize; best bull, 2 years old, £1, John Russell, 3rd prize; best bull, 2 years old, 10/-, John Russell, 4th prize; best cow, any age, £3, T. and F. Hindmarsh, 1st prize; best cow, any age, £2/10, David Lindsay, 2nd prize; best cow, any age, £1/10, Henry Fredricks, 3rd prize; best cow, any age, £1, David Lindsay, 4th prize; best heifer under 2 years, £2/10, David Lindsay, 1st prize; best heifer under 2 years, £1/10, George Tate, 2nd prize; best heifer under 2 years, £1, George Tate, 3rd prize; best heifer under 2 years, 10/-, T. and F. Hindmarsh, 4th prize; best fat beast, £1/10, William Grey, 1st prize; best fat beast, £1, William Grey, 2nd prize.

Kiama Show, exhibits and prize-winners at Show, 1872. A primitive catalogue.

Judges:—E. De Mestre, William Turkinton, John Badgery, J. Thompson, William Aherne, James Monaghan, W. H. Kerne.

E. H. Weston, blood mare, 2nd prize; E. H. Weston, blood filly, 2 years, 1st prize; M. N. Hindmarsh, draught mare, 2nd prize; William James, crossbred bull, 1st prize; William James, crossbred heifer, 2 years, 1st prize; Robert Miller, crossbred cows, 1st prize; Thomas Coughrane, blood stallion, "Cossack," 2nd prize; Thomas Hindmarsh, Shorthorn bull, aged, 2nd prize; Thomas Hindmarsh, Shorthorn cow, aged, 2nd prize; Thomas Hindmarsh, Shorthorn heifer, 2 years, 1st prize; Thomas Hindmarsh, Shorthorn heifer, 2 years, 2nd prize; Thomas Hindmarsh, crossbred bull, aged; Thomas Hindmarsh, crossbred cow, aged; George Tate, blood colt. "Self Reliance," 1st prize; George Tate, blood filly, "Levena"; George Tate, Shorthorn bull, "Napoleon," 2 years, 1st prize; Robert Hindmarsh, Shorthorn bull, aged, 1st prize; Robert Hindmarsh, crossbred bull, 2 years; John Farraher, blood stallion, "Trump Card," 1st prize; John Farraher, blood mare, 1st prize; John Armstrong, crossbred bull, "Roan," 2nd prize; John Tate, Junr., blood mare, "Village Maid"; Henry Fredricks, crossbred bull; George Tate Hackney, "Darkey"; George Lee, crossbred bull, 2 years, 1st prize; James Fields' crossbred cow, aged, 2nd prize; E. H. Weston, Shorthorn cow, 1st prize; E. H. Weston, Shorthorn bull, 2 years, 2nd prize; John King, Hackney, "Hector"; Thomas Fredricks, crossbred bull; Robert Hindmarsh, Shorthorn heifer, point reserved as to age, 1st prize; Thomas Black, dairy heifer, 1st prize.

Kiama Show exhibits, 1873, and prize-winners:—

Charles Totton, entire colt, 2 years, 1st prize; George Tate, blood colt, sire "Cossack," 2 years, 1st prize; George Tate, Shorthorn bull, 3 years, 2nd prize; George Tate, Shorthorn heifer, 13 months, 1st prize; Robert Miller, cow for dairy purposes; M. N. Hindmarsh, cow for dairy purposes; M. N. Hindmarsh, Hackney, 1st prize; Charles Price, blood filly, 2 years, 1st prize; Thomas Black, Shorthorn heifer, 2 years, 1st prize; John Elliott, blood mare, 1st prize; Fred Hindmarsh, Shorthorn bull, 1 year 1st prize; Fred Hindmarsh, Shorthorn cow, aged, 1st prize; Fred Hindmarsh, Shorthorn heifer, 2 years, 1st prize; Thomas Coughrane, cow, 1st prize; David Lindsay, bull, dairy purposes, 1 year, 2nd prize; Robert Hindmarsh, Shorthorn bull, aged, 1st prize; Robert Hindmarsh, cow for dairy purposes, aged, 2nd prize; Robert Hindmarsh, heifer for dairy purposes, 1 year, 2nd prize; Robert Hindmarsh, blood colt, "Almangor," 1st prize; George Tate, Shorthorn bull, 15 months, 1st prize; Henry Fredricks, bull for dairy purposes, 1 year, 1st prize; Henry Fredricks, heifer for dairy purposes, 2nd prize; Henry Fredricks heifer for dairy purposes 2 years, 1st prize; George Lee, crossbred bull, 1st prize; William James, bull for dairy purposes, aged, 1st prize; William James, heifer for dairy purposes 2 years, 2nd prize; John Farraher, blood stallion,

"Trump Card," 2nd prize; John Farraher, blood mare, 1st prize; George Wood, Jamberoo, blood horse, 1st prize; James Spinks, crossbred bull, 2nd prize; George Wood, Spring Hill, bull for dairy purposes, 2 years, 1st prize Shorthorn; Henry Fredricks, dairy class, heifer, 2 years, 2nd prize; William Gordon, Hackney, "Lennox"; William Gordon, Hackney, "Emu"; E. H. Weston, blood mare, 2nd prize; E. H. Weston, bull for dairy purposes; E. H. Weston, Shorthorn cow, 2nd prize; Peter Quinn, bull, dairy class, 2 years.

Kiama Show exhibits for 1874, and prize-winners:—

Charles Totton, 3-year-old entire, "Britton," sire "Britton's Son"; George Tate, Shorthorn bull, aged, 2nd prize; George Tate, Shorthorn bull, 1 year, sire "Prodigal"; George Tate, dairy bull, 1 year, sire "Napoleon"; George Tate, dairy bull, 1 year, "Napoleon 5th"; George Tate, dairy bull, 1 year, "Conqueror"; George Tate, dairy bull, 1 year, "Napoleon 5th"; George Tate, dairy heifer, 2 years; John Haddon, bull for dairy purposes, aged; William Tate, filly, 2 years, "Bessie Bell"; Joseph Dunster, bull for dairy purposes, 1 year; Joseph Dunster, heifer for dairy purposes, 2 years, 3rd prize; Joseph Dunster, cow for dairy purposes, 1st prize; William James, bull for dairy purposes, 3 years, 2nd prize; W. R. Hindmarsh, Shorthorn cow, 1st prize; W. R. Hindmarsh, Shorthorn bull "Duke of Derrimutt 6th," 2 years, 1st prize; W. R. Hindmarsh, Shorthorn bull, "Duke of Derrimutt 9th," 1 year, 1st prize; Robert Hindmarsh, Shorthorn bull, aged, 1st prize; Robert Hindmarsh, Shorthorn heifer, 1 year, 1st prize; Robert Hindmarsh, dairy cow, aged, 1st prize; Robert Hindmarsh, dairy cow, aged, 2nd prize; John Honey, dairy bull, 2 years, 1st prize; John Johnston, Rose Valley, dairy bull, 1 year, 3rd prize; Mrs. Cole, dairy bull, aged; Fred Hindmarsh, Shorthorn bull, aged, 1st prize; George Wood, Spring Hill, dairy bull, 1st prize; E. H. Weston, Shorthorn heifer, 2 years, 2nd prize; E. R. Evans, bull, aged, dairy purposes; E. R. Evans, cow, aged, dairy purposes; John Russell, heifer, 2 years; David Lindsay, bull for dairy purposes, 1 year, 1st prize; Robert Miller, dairy heifer, 1 year, 2nd prize; James McGill, dairy bull, 2 years; James McGill, dairy heifer, 2 years, 1st prize; Robert Jenkins, Shorthorn heifer, 2 years, 1st prize; John Johnston, Rose Valley, Shorthorn bull, 1 year, 2nd prize; Henry Fredricks, dairy heifer, 1 year, 1st prize; Henry Fredricks, Shorthorn bull, 1 year, 2nd prize.

Neil McGill won 1st prize at Dapto Show in 1874 with a strawberry-roan cow named "Phoebe," sire "Lofty," dam "Old Phoebe." William Moles' bull, the winner of many prizes, was out of "Phoebe." "Old Phoebe" was the choicest of Andrew McGill's cows. For further information about "Old Phoebe" see note below.

Wollongong Show. — At the Wollongong Show held in Market Square in 1860, Andrew McGill exhibited a 2-year-old bull, and a remarkably well-bred cow. She originally belonged to Rodd, of Five Dock, Cumberland, and was said to have been by an imported bull, and out of an imported cow. The cow known in the early seventies as "Old Phoebe" was this Rodd cow.

The Shoalhaven A. and H. Society of the present time was established on 6th March, 1874. James Aldcorn was the first president, and John McArthur was its first secretary. James Monaghan was first treasurer. The formation of the Society was celebrated by a ploughing match on the Terrara Estate, on the 1st July, 1874, and a dinner at night. First-class match.—John Watson, 1st prize; John Monaghan, 2nd prize. Second-class match.— John McAnally, 1st prize; Arthur Smith, 2nd prize. Youths' Match.—John Bates, 1st prize; Alfred Bartlett, 2nd prize. The dinner was held at Isaac's Royal Victoria Hotel. Henry G. Morton presided.

Kiama Show exhibits 1875. Prize winners:— George Tate, blood filly, 2 years, sire "Sir Charles"; George Tate, Shorthorn bull, 1 year, sire "Napoleon"; W. R. Hindmarsh, Shorthorn bull, "6th Duke of Derrimut," aged, 1st prize; W. R. Hindmarsh, Shorthorn bull, sire "6th Duke of Derrimut," 1 year, 1st prize; W. R. Hindmarsh, Shorthorn cow, "Princess," aged; W. R. Hindmarsh, Shorthorn cow, "Kate 2nd"; W. R. Hindmarsh, Shorthorn heifer, "Welcome Brunswick," calved 1/10/1872; W. R. Hindmarsh, Shorthorn heifer, "Queen of Trumps"; James W. Cole, Shorthorn heifer, 1 year, 1st prize; James W. Cole, dairy bull, 1 year, 3rd prize; Thomas Black, dairy cow, 2nd prize; Robert Black, dairy bull, 2 years, 2nd prize; George Wood, Jamberoo, Hackney mare, "Nina"; John Moffitt, Shorthorn bull, 1 year, 3rd prize; William James, dairy bull, aged, 1st prize; M. N. Hindmarsh, Shorthorn heifer, 1 year, 3rd prize; E. H. Weston, Devon bull,

"Victor," aged; Henry Fredricks, Shorthorn heifer, 1 year, 2nd prize; James Spinks, dairy heifer, 1 year, 3rd prize; James Spinks, dairy heifer, 1 year, 2nd prize; John Farraher, blood stallion, "Trump Card"; John Farraher, blood stallion, "Python"; John Farraher, blood mare, "Maid of Erin"; John Farraher, blood colt, "Odd Trick," 2 years; William Bailey, Junr., dairy bull, 3rd prize; Fred Hindmarsh, Shorthorn bull, 2 years, 1st prize; Fred Hindmarsh, Shorthorn cow, aged, 1st prize; Fred Hindmarsh, Shorthorn cow, aged, 2nd prize; Fred Hindmarsh, Shorthorn cow, aged, 3rd prize; D. Robinson, Shorthorn bull, 2 years, 2nd prize; Robert Hindmarsh, dairy cow, aged, 1st prize; Robert Hindmarsh, dairy heifer, 2 years, 3rd prize; Robert Hindmarsh, dairy heifer, 2 years, 2nd prize; Robert Hindmarsh, dairy heifer, 2 years, 1st prize; Robert Hindmarsh, Shorthorn heifer, 2 years, 3rd prize; Robert Hindmarsh, Shorthorn heifer, 2 years, 2nd prize; Robert Hindmarsh, Shorthorn bull, 1 year, 2nd prize; Robert Hindmarsh, Shorthorn bull, 2 years, 2nd prize; John Honey, Shorthorn bull, 2 years, 2nd prize; Duncan McGill, dairy bull, 1 year, 2nd prize; William Johnston, dairy bull, aged 2 years, 1st prize; George Wood, Spring Hill, dairy bull, 2nd prize; George Wood, Spring Hill, dairy bull, 1 year, 1st prize; James Monaghan, blood mare "Hannah'; James Monaghan, blood mare "Kate."

Kiama Show exhibits, 1876. Prize-winners:— John Moffit, Shorthorn bull, 3rd prize; John Kell Tate, blood mare, "Evangeline"; John Kell Tate, blood stallion, "The Barb"; Michael Carberry, dairy bull, 1 year, 3rd prize; Herbert Bartlett, Shorthorn heifer, 1 year, 3rd prize; George Buchanan, dairy cow, aged, 2nd prize; Robert Wilson, dairy bull, aged, 3rd prize; James W. Cole, Shorthorn heifer, 2 years, 2nd prize; James W. Cole, Shorthorn heifer, 2 years, 3rd prize; James W. Cole, Shorthorn heifer, 2 years, 1st prize; James W. Cole, Shorthorn heifer, 2 years, 2nd prize; George Gilbert, Chestnut stallion, "Glencoe," 2nd prize; William James, dairy bull, "Robin Hood," aged, 1st prize; William James, dairy bull, 2 years, 1st prize; Henry Fredricks, dairy cow, aged, 3rd prize; Henry Fredricks, dairy heifer, 2 years, 1st prize; Henry Fredricks, dairy heifer, 1 year, 3rd prize; Henry Fredricks, dairy heifer, 1 year, 2nd prize; Henry Fredricks, dairy heifer, 1 year, 1st prize; Henry Fredricks, dairy bull, 1 year, 2nd prize; M. N. Hindmarsh, Shorthorn bull, 2 years, 1st prize; Robert Miller, dairy cow, aged, 1st prize; Christopher Hetherington, blood mare, 1st prize; John Farraher, blood stallion, "Trump Card," 1st prize; T. J. Roberts, blood stallion, "Terrara," 2nd prize; William Grey, Shorthorn bull, 3rd prize; Duncan McGill, dairy bull, 1 year, 1st prize; W. R. Hindmarsh, Shorthorn bull, "Duke of Derrimut," 1st prize; W. R. Hindmarsh, Shorthorn cow, 3rd prize; W. R. Hindmarsh, Shorthorn cow, 1st prize; W. R. Hindmarsh, Shorthorn heifer, 1 year, 2nd prize; W. R. Hindmarsh, Shorthorn heifer, 1 year, 1st prize; W. R. Hindmarsh, Shorthorn bull, 1 year, 1st prize; W. R. Hindmarsh, Shorthorn bull, 1 year, 2nd prize; Fred Hindmarsh, Shorthorn bull, 2nd prize; Fred Hindmarsh, Shorthorn cow, 2nd prize; Peter Quinn, dairy bull, 2nd prize; Jas. W. Cole, dairy bull, 2 years, 2nd prize.

Referring to the bull "Robin Hood," Mr. D. L. Dymock states:—"In 1876 I was offered 250 guineas for him. Mr. James would not sell—two or three years later he sold his hide for £1." Mr. James when spoken to about "Robin Hood," said:—"It is true, in part. We were offered a big price for the bull, but wanted him for our own use; he died shortly after we went to Alne Bank, Gerringong. It was then discovered that two bulls had previously died from tuberculosis in the stall we had housed "Robin Hood" in. That was about the year 1878."

Illawarra Shorthorns at the opening of the International Exhibition in Sydney in 1876. Class 29, Durhams, aged bulls:—William Warren Jenkins' "Gay Lad," 2nd prize; Henry Hill Osborne's "Alexander," 4th prize. Class 31, Durhams, bulls, 1-year-old. The following animals were exhibited:—William J. Chapman's "Royal Butterfly," (329 N.S.W.H.B.), bred by W. W. Ewin, Ulladulla; W. W. Ewin's "Duke of Brunswick 3rd"; W. W. Ewin's "Duke of Brunswick"; John Moffitt's "Duke," bred by William Rutter Hindmarsh; W. W. Jenkins' "Merry Monarch." In class 31, Richard Lewis Jenkins, M.D., of Nepean Towers, won 1st prize with "Commodore." Class 32, bull. 6 months old and under 1 year, W. W. Ewin's "Duke of Brunswick 5th"; W. W. Ewin's "Duke of Brunswick 4th"; W. R. Hindmarsh's "2nd Duke of Derrimut of N.S.W."; W. R. Hindmarsh's "4th Duke of Derrimut of N.S.W."; W. W. Jenkins' "Eschistina"; W. W. Jenkins' "Alonzo"; William Johnstone's "Duke of Erin." The prizes were won by Robert McDougall's "Count Carisbrook," and

E. B. Woodhouse's "Royal Purple 10th." Class 34, Heifers, 2 years: J. W. and J. T. Cole exhibited "Fairy Queen" and "Spring Blossoms," bred by Henry Fredricks. The prizes were won by R. L. Jenkins' "April Flower," and W. C. Durham's "Village Rose." Class 35, Heifer, 1 year: J. W. and J. T. Cole exhibited "Princess Matilda," bred by Henry Fredricks; Frank A. Thompson "Illawarra Lass"; W. R. Hindmarsh "Duchess of Derrimut." The prizes were won by W. C. Wentworth's "Princess Purple," and Barnes and Smith's "Cherry Ripe." Farmers' class, 35, Cattle not necessarily pure-bred: Bull, 3 years, William Brown's (Dapto) "Grand Turk of Opeke 30th," 1st prize. Class 63, Cow, 3 years, "Cherry Red," bred by Henry Fredricks, 1st prize. The "S.M. Herald," commenting on the cattle at the exhibition, stated: "The splendid show of Durhams and Shorthorns, Mr. W. W. Ewin, of Ulladulla, who showed some good calves; and the Kiama display was also good."

The breeding of beef cattle for exhibition and disposal at the metropolitan shows was very good business for those who could afford the time and money to carry it out. The farmers' classes were a safety valve for those breeders who kept herds of dairy cows to supply milk for the young pedigreed animals. Young bulls and heifers often got the milk of two dairy cows, and there are a number of instances on record where four cows' milk was consumed by a young bull. Those dairy cows of mixed Ayrshire and Devon breeding were served by pedigreed bulls, and the progeny sold to dairymen.

Kiama Show exhibits for 1877:—

Hugh Colley, roan bull, 2 years; George Tate, dairy bull, aged, 2nd prize; George Tate, dairy bull, 1 year, 2nd prize; M. N. Hindmarsh, Shorthorn cow, 3rd prize; M. N. Hindmarsh, dairy cow, 3rd prize; Peter Quinn, dairy bull, aged, 3rd prize; James Johnston, dairy bull, 3 years, no prize; W. R. Hindmarsh, Shorthorn bull, aged, 1st prize; W. R. Hindmarsh, Shorthorn bull, 2 years, 1st prize; W. R. Hindmarsh, Shorthorn bull, 1 year, 1st prize; W. R. Hindmarsh, Shorthorn bull, 1 year, 3rd prize; W. R. Hindmarsh, dairy bull, 1 year, no prize; David Johnston, dairy cow, 3rd prize; Robert Miller, dairy cow, 2nd prize; William James, dairy bull, aged, 1st prize; Michael Carberry, dairy bull, 2 years, 2nd prize; William Grey, dairy bull, 1 year, 2nd prize; Henry Fredricks, dairy bull, aged, no prize; Henry Fredricks, dairy heifer, 2 years, 1st prize; Henry Fredricks, dairy heifer, 1 year, 2nd prize; Henry Fredricks, dairy heifer, 1 year, 1st prize; Henry Fredricks, dairy heifer, 1 year, 2nd prize; Henry Fredricks, dairy heifer, 1 year, 3rd prize; Fred Hindmarsh, Shorthorn bull, aged, 2nd prize; Fred Hindmarsh, Shorthorn cow, aged, 2nd prize; Evan R. Evans, dairy bull, 1 year, 1st prize; Evan R. Evans, dairy bull, aged, no prize; Duncan McGill, dairy bull, 2 years. 1st prize.

Kiama Show exhibits for 1878:—

William James, dairy bull, "Robin Hood," 1st prize; William James, dairy cow, 2nd prize; William James, dairy bull, 1 year, 2nd prize; William James, dairy heifer, 2 years, 1st prize; William James, dairy heifer, 1 year, 2nd prize; George Tate, dairy bull, "Major," 2nd prize; George Tate, dairy bull, "Prodigal," 2 1-3 years, 2nd prize; George Tate, dairy heifer, 2½ years, 3rd prize; Henry Fredricks, 6 dairy heifers, 1st prize and special; No. 10 W. James, h.c.; No. 12, G. Tate, h.c.; John Sproule, dairy bull, 2 years 1st prize; M. N. Hindmarsh Shortberry, dairy bull, 1 year, 3rd prize; Peter Quinn, dairy bull, 3rd prize; John Honey, dairy bull, 2 years, 1st prize; M. N. Hindmarsh, Shorthorn cow, 1st prize; M. N. Hindmarsh, Shorthorn heifer, 2nd prize; M. N. Hindmarsh. dairy cow, 3rd prize; John Nethery, dairy bull, 1 year, 1st prize; Jas. W. Cole, Shorthorn cow, 3rd prize; Jas. W. Cole, dairy heifer, 1 year, 1st prize; Jas. W. Cole, dairy heifer, 1 year, h.c. brand; Henry Fredricks, dairy heifer, 2 years, 2nd prize; Henry Fredricks, dairy heifer. 1 year 3rd prize; W. R. Hindmarsh, Shorthorn bull, 1st prize; W. R. Hindmarsh, Shorthorn cow, 2nd prize; W. R. Hindmarsh, Shorthorn heifer, 1st prize; W. R. Hindmarsh, Shorthorn bull, 1 year, 1st prize; W. R. Hindmarsh, Shorthorn bull, 1 year, 2nd prize; W. R. Hindmarsh, Shorthorn bull, 1 year, 3rd prize; W. R. Hindmarsh, Shorthorn heifer, 1 year, 1st prize; W. R. Hindmarsh, Shorthorn heifer, 1 year, 3rd prize; W. R. Hindmarsh, Shorthorn heifer, 1 year, 2nd prize; W. E. Hindmarsh, dairy cow, 1st prize.

Kiama Show exhibits, 1879:—

M. N. Hindmarsh, Shorthorn heifer, 1 year, 1st prize; Cole Bros., Shorthorn bull, aged, no prize; Cole Bros., Shorthorn cow, aged, no prize; W. R. Hindmarsh, Durham bull, aged, 1st prize; W. R. Hindmarsh, Durham bull, aged, 2nd prize; W. R. Hindmarsh, Durham bull. 2 years, 2nd prize; W. R. Hindmarsh, Durham bull, 2 years, 1st prize; W. R. Hindmarsh, Durham cow, aged, 1st prize; W. R. Hindmarsh, Durham cow, aged, 2nd prize; W. R. Hindmarsh, Durham heifer, 2 years, 1st prize; W. R. Hindmarsh, Durham heifer, 2 years, 2nd prize; W. R. Hindmarsh, Durham heifer, 1 year, 2nd prize; Robert Jenkins, Durham cow, 7 years, no prize.

Kiama Show, 1879. At this show, William R. Hindmarsh won almost all the prizes for Shorthorn cattle, his brother, M. N. Hindmarsh, securing one prize only. This may be said to be the beginning of the end of Shorthorn prizes at the Kiama Shows.

In cattle for dairy purposes:—Best 6 dairy heifers, Henry Fredricks, 1st prize; best 6 dairy heifers, Cole Bros., 2nd prize; best dairy bull, George Tate's "Major," 1st prize; best dairy bull, Peter Quinn's "The Major," 2nd prize; best dairy bull, 2 years old, William James, 1st prize; best dairy bull, 2 years old, William James, 2nd prize; best dairy bull, 2 years old, George Wood (Springhill), 3rd prize; best dairy bull, 1 year old, Henry Fredricks, 1st prize; best dairy bull, 1 year old. W. R. Hindmarsh, 2nd prize; best dairy bull, 1 year old, John Honey, 3rd prize; best dairy cow, Henry Fredricks, 1st prize; best dairy cow, W. R. Hindmarsh, 2nd prize; best dairy cow, Craig and Son, 3rd prize; best dairy heifer, 2 years old, Henry Fredricks, 1st prize; best dairy heifer, 2 years old, Robert Miller, 2nd prize; best dairy heifer, 1 year old, Henry Fredricks, 1st prize; best dairy heifer, 1 year old, Henry Fredricks, 2nd prize.

1879, at the Shoalhaven A. and H. Society's Show on 28th February, 1879:—Best Durham bull, W. R. Hindmarsh, 1st prize; John Green, 2nd prize; best Hereford bull, Ettie De Mestre, 1st prize; J. W. Lee, highly commended; best Devon bull, Ettie De Mestre, 1st prize; best Ayrshire cow, Thomas Connolly, 1st prize; J. Houston, 2nd prize; best dairy bull, George Tate, 1st prize; John Monaghan, 2nd prize; best dairy cow, James Wilson, 1st prize; best dairy heifer, James Monaghan, 1st prize.

The Ulladulla Show, 1879:—Best Shorthorn bull. John Miller, 1st prize; W. J. Chapman, 2nd prize; best Shorthorn cow, W. J. Chapman, 1st prize; David Warden, 2nd prize; Best Shorthorn heifer, 2 years old. Francis McMahon, 1st and 2nd prizes: best Shorthorn heifer. 1 year old, W. H. Wilford, 1st prize; Francis McMahon. 2nd prize; Champion bull, W. J. Chapman;

Champion cow, W. J. Chapman; best dairy bull, Donald Kennedy, 1st prize; John Evans 2nd prize; best dairy bull, 2 years old, Donald Kennedy, 1st prize; best dairy cow, John Miller, 1st prize; John Evans, 2nd prize.

Note.—Donald Kennedy's cattle were Ayrshires. John Evans was a brother of E. R. Evans, of "Penrose," Dapto.

About 1879 a movement was set on foot to do away with prizes for Shorthorn cattle, owing in great measure to several exhibitors, who were poor supporters of the Kiama Shows, from a financial standpoint, winning the giant share of the prize money. In 1881 Robert Miller and Edward Johnston moved to have the Shorthorn classes expunged from the prize list of Kiama Shows. George Somerville and Thomas Fredericks moved an amendment, "That the prizes be continued." William Graham and Edward Johnston wanted to have the cattle divided into two classes. The original motion was lost.

Between 1879 and 1881 a few good Ayrshire bulls found their way into the forefront of the Illawarra Shows. John Lindsay purchased "Earl of Beaconsfield," Henry Hill Osborne purchased "Mokoia," a New Zealand-bred bull; G. K. Waldron was busy introducing J. M. Antill's bull, the champion of champions, "Dunlop." Later other dairymen began to cast round for something better than beef Shorthorns for the dairy, and this caused a return to Devon bulls.

Kiama Show exhibits 1880. Prize-winners: Tate and Coy., Shorthorn cow, "Fairy Queen," 1st prize; Cole Bros., Shorthorn heifer, 1 year, 1st prize.

Kiama Show exhibits for 1881:—

W. R. Hindmarsh, Shorthorn bull, any age, 1st prize; W. R. Hindmarsh, Shorthorn cow, any age, 1st prize; W. R. Hindmarsh, Shorthorn bull, any age, 2nd prize; W. R. Hindmarsh, Shorthorn cow, any age, 2nd prize; W. R. Hindmarsh, Shorthorn bull, 1 year, 1st prize; W. R. Hindmarsh, Shorthorn heifer, 1 year, 2nd prize; M. N. Hindmarsh, Shorthorn heifer, 2 years, 1st prize; M. N. Hindmarsh, Shorthorn heifer, 1 year, 1st prize; Craig and Son, Shorthorn bull, 1 year, 2nd prize.

At Kiama Show, in 1881, J. M. Antill's Ayrshire bull "Dunlop" won chief prize as best Champion bull; 1st as best dairy bull; and the Champion prize as the best bull on the ground. In this latter prize contest he defeated the best bulls of every breed on the ground.

1881. Dr. J. H. Caird's draught stallion "Highlander" and hunting horse "Reuben," buggy horses "Highland Lassie" and "Alma." Denis Kelleher's blood stallion "King of the West," Frank McMahon's hunter "Victor," E. H. Weston's draught stallion "General Clancy," Henry Fredrick's coaching stallion, 2 years, J. G. Lamond's blood stallion "Albury," G. J. Hindmarsh's coaching stallion "Duke of Cleveland," and draught ditto "Young Defiance," M. N. Hindmarsh's blood stallion, aged, Thomas Coughrane's blood stallion, "Sterling," Tate Bros.' hackney "Gay Lad."

Dapto A. and H. Society's Show, 19th January, 1881:—

Horses.—Best draught stallion, E. H. Weston; best blood stallion, Thomas Coughrane; 2nd, best blood stallion, R. T. Jenkins; best draught mare, John Elliott; 2nd, best draught mare, William Kelleher; best blood mare, Cole Bros.; 2nd, best blood mare, Joseph Burgess; best draught 2-year-old stallion, Dr. J. H. Caird; 2nd, best draught 2-year-old stallion, J. F. Griffin; best draught 2-year-old filly, John Elliott; 2nd, best draught 2-year-old filly, E. H. Weston; best blood 2-year-old stallion, James McGill; 2nd, best blood 2-year-old stallion, E. H. Weston; best blood 2-year-old filly. John Shannon; 2nd, best blood 2-year-old filly. A. Staff.

Cattle:—Best bull for dairy purposes, any age, Charles Hore; 2nd, best bull for dairy purposes, any age, James McGill; best bull for dairy purposes, 2-year-old and under 3 years, Cole Bros.; best bull for dairy purposes, 1 year and under 2 years, Cole Bros.; best dairy cow, David Manson; 2nd, best dairy cow, William Piper (Mount Nebo); best heifer, 2 years and under 3 years, David Manson; 2nd, best heifer, 2 years and under 3 years, William Brown; best heifer, 1 year and under 2 years. Cole Bros.

Jerseys or Alderneys:—William Brown and John Lindsay took all the prizes.

Ayrshire cattle:—William Brown, John Lindsay and E. R. Evans took all the prizes.

At a meeting held in Kiama, August 11, 1882, when dealing with section 4, Shorthorns J. T. Cole moved, and Henry Fredricks seconded, "That this section be struck out of the prize list." George Somerville and W. R. Hindmarsh moved an amendment, "That section 4 be retained." After a lengthy debate the amendment was carried.

JOHNSTON BROS., Marksville, Albion Park, Illawarra.

DAIRYMAID'S PRINCE OF MARKSVILLE.

FANNY OF MARKSVILLE.

DAIRY MAID OF MARKSVILLE.

ROSEBUD OF MARKSVILLE.
(No. 1046, I.D.C.H.B.)

FAVOURITE 2nd OF MARKSVILLE.
(No. 1036, I.D.C.H.B.)

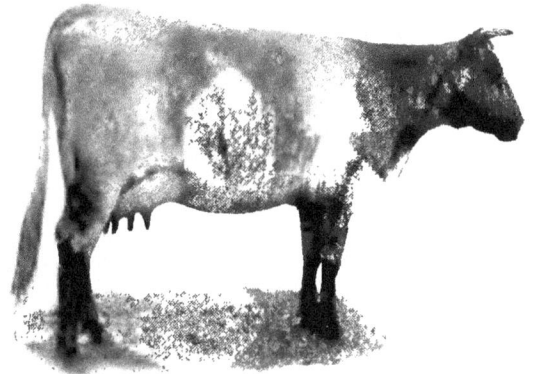

MILKMAID OF MARKSVILLE.

J

At a meeting held 15th June, 1883, section 5, Shorthorns, J. T. Cole moved the omission of this section. This was seconded by Joseph Weston. Dr. John Hay Caird and George Somerville moved to retain section 5. After some discussion the amendment was withdrawn, and the motion carried. No more was heard of the beef Shorthorns at the Kiama Shows. Dairy cattle, or cattle for dairy purposes were in one form or other substituted.

It has been said: "No evil can be removed without opening a door for another evil!" Such was the case in the show business—once pedigreed animals were out of the running all sorts and conditions of false pedigreeing crept in among the lucky prize-winners.

Best dairy bull, Hugh Dudgeon, 1st prize; best dairy bull, J. W. Cole, 2nd prize; best dairy cow, William James, 1st prize; best dairy cow, William Swan, 2nd prize.

THE FOUNDING OF THE BERRY SOCIETY.
(Originally Broughton Creek.)

At a meeting held in the Court-house, Broughton Creek, on 16th October, 1883, there were present James Wilson, Dr. Lewers, J. McKenzie, J. W. Spronle, Jas. Stewart, S. Gall, J. Francis, C. E. Butler, R. E. Walker, A. J. Colley, J. Wiley, J. F. Hooper, and Jas. Boyd. Dr. Lewers moved as follows:—"That this meeting is of opinion that a Horticultural Society should be formed in Broughton Creek to promote the culture of flowers, fruits, and vegetables, and the holding of a periodical show of the same." Jas Stewart seconded, and C. E. Butler supported the motion, which was carried.

Lewis McIntyre was appointed president, Dr. Lewers treasurer, and A. J. Colley secretary. John Grey and John Stewart were appointed vice-presidents. Later on David Berry, Esq., became the patron of the Society. He generously gave the land, and stumped and cleared it free of cost. Then he fenced it, and erected suitable buildings on it. His representative, Alexander Frazer, took an active interest in the affairs of the Society, and anything he (Frazer) suggested to David Berry was quickly carried out. Rules and Regulations were framed, and duly adopted by the Committee, and the Society became a living affair in the midst of a rich pastoral, farming, and horticultural locality.

The Society did not remain as an Horticultural Society for many months. The support given to the movement by the Patron soon stimulated the Committee to spread itself out into sections presided over by willing workers, viz.:—Horses: Bragg, Knox, Frazer, Martin, and Gall. Cattle: John Stewart, H. Graham, R. V. Boyd, John Grey, and Hanlon. Other animals: H. Boyd, T. Burke, Priddle, McIntyre. Farm Produce: Robinson, Graham, English and Knox. Garden Produce: Jas. Stewart, Dr. Lavers, English, Colley and Robinson. Dairy Produce: Grey, Boxell, H. Boyd, Hanlon and Martin. Implements: Gall, Bragg, Frazer, Binks and McIntyre. Manufactures: Lavers, Robinson, Boxell, Jas. Stewart, Grey and John Stewart.

A special prize of £3 was offered by Martin for best Ayrshire bull. Dr. Lavers presented his financial report, and an application was made to Government for a subsidy from the Agricultural Show Fund. It was decided on motion to hold the first show in connection with the Society on 7th and 8th February, 1884. The Patron's new steamer was applied for to lie at Berry wharf all night. A. Campbell, of Shoalhaven Heads, gave £5 as a donation to the show. The Treasurer's report, read at meeting held 15th February, 1884, showed a credit balance of £160. It was announced that in the horse and cattle sections the sum of £60 and £42 was paid in prizes. A conference of the A. and H. Societies in Kiama, 30th May, 1884. First ploughing matches meeting, 14th April, 1884. D. L. Dymock consenting to deliver a lecture before Berry Society, April, 1884.

A Ground Committee, consisting of Bragg, C. Robinson, John Stewart and Alex. Frazer. The question of giving prizes for dairy cattle came before the Committee in 1884, and prizes were set apart for that class of animal in 1885 schedule.

On 10th February, 1884, Mr. William G. Thompson, of Belsley Vale, Dapto, who was at the time President of the Dapto Society, delivered an address on dairy cattle breeding, during which he displayed a strong leaning to the pure Shorthorn. As this address was open to friendly criticism, Mr. John Lindsay, of Kembla Park, said: Mr. James McGill, a good authority, always contended that Mr. Macarthur's dairy herd at Camden was the best dairy herd in N.S. Wales; the Glenlee herd came next in merit, and that both herds were full of Ayrshire blood. Mr. William Cook, of West Dapto, stated that the old type dairy cattle had disappeared from Illawarra twenty years ago. He also favored an infusion of Ayrshire blood. Mr. Evan R.

Evans, of Penrose Villa, disagreed with the President's views, as all the best herds in the colony had Ayrshire blood in them. Both the Glenlee and Camden herds had Ayrshire blood in them, and other noted herds were the same, and he had no doubt but what all our best herds could be traced to an Ayrshire source. The late Mr. Henry Osborne many years ago imported some Durhams, but they appeared to be of a better milking strain than the breed usually is. Durhams are better adapted where feed is plentiful. More than this, he considered them less hardy than other breeds. Mr. George McPhail, West Dapto, spoke in a similar strain, and held that it was beyond doubt that the introduction of Durhams into the district caused 25 per cent. of the present degeneracy in our cattle. Mr. C. J. Cullen briefly supported the President's views. Messrs. David Manson, George Lindsay and John Brown also spoke. The latter advocated an infusion of Devon blood to give constitution. (For full particulars see Illawarra "Mercury" of 12th February, 1884.)

The writer, on November 25th, 1903, wrote Mr. Evan R. Evans, of Dapto, for his views on the origin of his late father's dairy herd. Mr. Evans did not reply but came to Kiama to see me. We had a general chat of a more or less private nature, which need not be published. He (Mr. Evans) had in the meantime written to Mr. John Brown, of Brownville, Dapto, on the subject. The following is a copy of Mr. Brown's reply to Mr. Evans, dated 3rd December, 1903:—"Dear Sir,—In reply to yours of this date, re the early herds of cattle introduced into this district, I beg to state that, as far as I have heard and believe, Dr. Throsby was the first person to bring a mob of cattle into this district, and many others soon followed. The great drought sent them here. I don't know what breed they were, but the cattle of the colony at that time must have been a very mixed breed, brought principally from the Cape of Good Hope. My father brought a good many cattle into the district between 1824 and 1834, and these were mostly small cattle with long thin horns, of different colours, mostly brown, brindle, light roan, and white. There were a few red and white and a few black, and these were about the general run of the cattle that were first brought into Illawarra. Mr. John Wyllie, who obtained a grant of 2000 acres on the north bank of Mullet Creek, which now forms the Canterbury, Newton and Kembla Grange properties, imported two Ayrshire bulls and some cows, and brought them into the dis-

trict, and these, I believe, were the first pure blood or pure breed of cattle that were brought into Illawarra. My father had the greater portion of the Wyllie estate as a cattle run, and his stock were much improved by the cross of the Wyllie Ayrshires. When Mr. Wyllie left the district my father purchased one of the the bulls from him. Mr. Alexander Berry purchased the other bull and the cows, and they went to Coolangatta. In 1843 my father purchased a station and cattle at Kydra, Monaro, and sent the whole of his Illawarra cattle there as improved by the Ayrshire bull. In 1845 Mr. Lomax had some fine red Durham cattle of the milking breed, and a very fine imported roan bull. His herd cows and bulls numbered 60 head. He settled on the Lakelands Estate on Goondarans Creek, where he carried on dairying and cattle breeding. Mr. Lomax must have sold a good many young bulls. My father purchased 10 young bulls and sent them to Monaro. When Mr. Gerard Gerard began dairying he got his cows from Mr. Berry, of Shoalhaven. They were no doubt Ayrshires, and from the original stock imported by Mr. Wyllie. In 1847 my father bought the Glenbog Station, Monaro, with all the cattle. These cattle were most carefully bred from imported stock of the Durham breed, and included a fine imported bull of the same breed. The bull, however, died, and six of the young Lomax bulls were then taken from Kydra to Glenbog. with the result that all, or nearly all, the increases from them were red of a milky quality. About 450 head of these cattle were brought down and sold to the Illawarra farmers in the early fifties. Therefore, Wyllie, Lomax and Brown played a part in founding the Illawarra herds.—Yours, etc., John Brown."

Note.—According to Mr. Evan R. Evans the Lomax red cattle had much Devon blood in them, his late father having used them in his herd.

Meeting held 5th June, 1885. Cow-testing was introduced. The following Herd Book regulations were placed on record:—1st. Parties requiring a test must apply in writing to the Secretary, enclosing fee of 10s for each cow, and a test will be conducted at the owner's residence within 14 days (both inclusive) from receipt of notice to Secretary. 2nd. No cow shall be entitled to a place in the Herd Book which shall not have 66lbs. weight of milk in milkings (consecutive) two mornings and one evening. 3rd. The tester or testers will be supplied with a book. in which shall be entered a full and clear description of every cow that shall have given the standard weight of milk, to include age, name, color, brand and pedigree if possible. The weight of milk for each milking and the total will be entered in duplicate and signed by tester and owner, one of which shall be retained by the Society as a record and the other held by the owner, and each leaf of the testing book shall be stamped with the Society's stamp. 4th. The testing will be conducted during the whole year, with the exception of 14 days prior to each show. 5th. There shall be five prizes given to the five cows yielding the heaviest weight of milk—1st prize £5, 2nd £4, 3rd £3, 4th £2, 5th £1; the owners of prize takers shall exhibit same at annual show on the first day, and the Secretary will notify owners to that effect at least six days prior to show; every cow will be distinguished on the ground by ribbons suitably arranged. 7th. The competition shall be confined to members of the Association, animals to be the property of member entering at least one month previous to show. 8th. Any bull, three of whose progeny are placed on the Herd Book, will be entitled to a place in the Herd Book, also his pedigree (if known), name, age, and other particulars that may be deemed necessary being registered at same time. 9th. Any infringement of any of the above rules will disqualify any beast from obtaining either a prize or a place in the Herd Book.

A. J. COLLEY, Secretary.

LEWIS McINTYRE, President.

1886.—At the Berry Show, 1886, Daniel Boyd won James Martin and Coy.'s gold medal for having won the largest number of prizes at the show.

BROUGHTON CREEK SHOW, 24th FEBRUARY, 1886.

Dairy Cattle.—Judges: Francis McMahon, Donald Kennedy and Henry Fredricks. Best bull—Cole Bros 1st, Charles McCabe 2nd, Robert Hindmarsh 3rd. Bull, 2 years—Daniel Boyd 1st, William Rutledge 2nd and 3rd. Bull, 1 year—Daniel Boyd 1st, James Bros. 2nd. Bull calf—David Thorburn 1st, Daniel Boyd 2nd. Best cow in milk—John Grey 1st, James Bros. 2nd, John Grey 3rd. Best cow (dry)—Daniel Boyd 1st, Daniel Boyd 2nd, William Elliott 3rd, Cole Bros 4th. Heifer, 2 years—John Grey 1st, Daniel Boyd 2nd. Heifer, 1 year—Cole Bros. 1st, Daniel Boyd 2nd. Pen of 4 cows—James Bros. 1st, Cole Bros. 2nd, Daniel Boyd 3rd. Pen of 5 3-year-old heifers—Daniel Boyd 1st, Cole Bros 2nd, James Brown 3rd. Pen of 5 2-year-old heifers—Daniel Boyd 1st, Cole Bros. 2nd, John Boxell 3rd. Pen of 5 1-year-old heifers—John Grey 1st, Patrick Devery 2nd, Daniel Boyd 3rd. Pen of 5 calves (females)—Daniel Boyd 1st, Thomas Gall 2nd, Daniel Boyd 3rd. **Champion cow on ground**—James Bros. (Ayrshire). **Champion bull on ground**—John B. Taylor (Ayrshire).

Pedigree Cattle.—Judges: Evan R. Evans, J. P. Dowling and James Monaghan.

Jerseys—Best bull—John Stewart 1st. Best bull, 2 years old—Thomas H. Lees, 1st. Best bull, 1 year—William James 1st, Albert Taylor 2nd. Best cow—William James 1st, John Stewart 2nd. Best heifer—William James.

Ayrshires—Best imported bull—John B. Taylor. Best colonial bred bull—Robert Graham 1st, George H. Grey 2nd. Best 2-year-old bull—Michael Kenny 1st, Z. Bice 2nd. Best bull, 1 year—Thomas Binks 1st, James Daly 2nd. Best cow—James Bros. 1st, John Grey 2nd. Best 2-year-old heifer—John B. Taylor 1st, John Grey 2nd. Best 1-year-old heifer—Robert Watson 1st, John Grey 2nd.

Devons.—Best Devon cow—Henry Graham 1st and 2nd.

Herefords.—Best bull and cow—David Berry.

Durhams.—Best bull—David Berry. Best cow—Henry Fredricks 1st, James Bros. 2nd. Best heifer, 2 years—George Chapman 1st. Best heifer, 1 year—George Chapman.

Cow giving greatest quantity of milk, three milkings—D. Boyd 1st, H. Fredricks 2nd, James Bros. 3rd. The winning animal gave 91lbs. of milk.

Broughton.—The Society was reorganised in 1888. The name: The Association shall be called the Broughton Creek Agricultural and Horticultural Association. The objects: The objects of the Association shall be the management, encouragement and development of agriculture, horticulture, dairying and other industries, the improvement of live stock, and the introduction into the district of implements and machinery for agriculture, dairying and other purposes. Then followed a series of means and ways by which the above ideals could be effected. In 1888 the new show ground was completed, and a committee, consisting of John Grey, P. H. Morton, Chas. Robinson, John Stewart and Jas. Wilson, was appointed to wait on Mr. Berry's representative, H. G. Morton, regarding the handing over of the ground to the Society. John Boxell, President, 1888. Three days' show in 1889. Ploughing matches same year, 28th June. John Hay became Patron of the Society, November, 1889. John Boxell elected President 1890. Lovegrove Treasurer. Dr. Lewers, Secretary in the absence of A. J. Colley. Mr. Lovegrove pointed out that in 1888 members' subscriptions amounted to £175. The year 1889 reduced the amount to £169. The year 1900 reduced the amount to £148. Donations fell from £94 in 1888 to £50 in 1889, and to £49 in 1890. By way of endowment the Society received in 1888 £103, in 1889 £335, in 1890 £106, whilst the prizes had been steadily on the increase. In horses old Piscator and Lottery had been champions for years. At Kiama five members carried off £120 in prizes, and of these three only contributed 15/6 a year to the funds. Conference of A. and H. Society delegates at Kiama 9th August, 1893. National prizes, four cows in milk, £6 and £4, August, 1892. Special prizes of £7 7s and £3 3s by Mr. Alex. Hay for the five cows (all the bona fide property of the exhibitor) giving the largest yield in one day of milk and butter. Only members of the Berry Agricultural Association residing between the north boundary of the Gerringong municipality and the Shoalhaven River and the Barrengarry Range can compete. Entries to close 31st December, 1895. John Stewart was President. D. Boyd won several awards, Cole Bros., D. Thorburn, John Grey, and James Bros. champion for dairy cow. Henry Graham and David Berry exhibited Devons. Shorthorns were not numerous. H. Fredericks and George Chapman took the honors.

The Berry Champion National Prize of £25 for best five cows tested at exhibition ground in 1896. The product of each cow for one milking to be computed at commercial butter 9d per lb. and skim milk at ½d per gallon.

Breed.	Owner.	Lbs. of Milk.	Butter Fat.	Com. Butter	Skimmed Milk.	Total Value.	Remarks.
						s. d.	
Illawarra.. ..	C. W. Craig	120¼	4.50	6.06	116	5 0¼	1st prize
Half-bred Jersey	D. Hyam & Son	84½	4.30	4.05	80	3 4¼	2nd prize
Illawarra.. ..	Wm. Sharpe	97¾	3.60	3.89	94	3 3½	3rd prize

Prize of £20 for Single Cow—same conditions as before mentioned.

Breed.	Owner.	Lbs. of Milk.	Butter Fat.	Com. Butter.	Skimmed Milk.	Total Value.	Remarks.
						s. d.	
Illawarra.. ..	M. F. Morton	28¾	4.50	1.44	24	1 2	1st prize
¾-bred Jersey ..	C. Waldron	21¼	4.10	.96	17	0 9½	2nd prize
Illawarra.. ..	— Wilson	19¾	3.70	.81	16	0 8	3rd prize
Jersey	C. Price	14½	4.60	.75	10	0 7¼	—
Illawarra.. ..	A. Fraser	21¼	2.60	.60	19	0 6¼	—
Jersey	E. Goody	16¾	3.30	.60	13	0 6	—
Illawarra.. ..	H. Higgins	11½	4.60	.59	7	0 5½	—
Jersey	H. Taylor	11	4.20	.52	7	0 5	—

See page 202—Illustration of C. W. Craig's Five Test Cows

Kangaroo Valley Show, 16th March, 1886. Cattle for dairy purposes.

Ayrshire bull, any age—John Randall 1st prize, Alexander Osborne 2nd prize, James McLelland 3rd prize. Ayrshire bull, 2 years—Michael Kenny 1st prize, George Tate, jun., 2nd prize. Ayrshire bull, 1 year—John Randall 1st prize, Thomas Somerville 2nd prize. Ayrshire cow, any age—John Randall 1st prize, Hugh Hanlon 2nd prize. Ayrshire heifer, 2 years—Thomas Somerville 1st prize, George Tate, jun., 2nd prize. Channel Island bull, any age—Alexander Osborne 1st prize. Channel Island cow, any age—Alexander Osborne, 1st prize, Wesley Vance 2nd prize.

Dairy Division.—Bull, any age—Charles McCabe 1st prize, Henry Timbs 2nd prize. Bull, 2 years—Alexander Morrison 1st prize, James Trimble 2nd prize. Dairy cow, any age—William Black 1st prize, William Kelleher 2nd prize, Charles Graham 3rd prize. Dairy heifer, 2 years—David C. Pryce 1st prize, Tate and Sullivan 2nd prize. Dairy heifer, 1 year—Tate and Sullivan 1st and 2nd prizes. Pen of 5 heifers, 2 years and under 3 years (the property of the owners)—Tate and Sullivan 1st prize, F. Nelson 2nd prize. Pen of 5 heifers, under 2 years (the property of one owner), special prize by Alexander Campbell—F. Nelson 1st prize, Robert Martin 2nd prize. Pen of

4 dairy cows (the property of one owner), special by John Stewart—1st prize. A special by Elliott and Clarke for 4 best dairy cows—George Tate, jun., 1st prize. W. Clarke 2nd prize. A special by John Bailey for best dairy bull—John Randall 1st prize, Alexander Morrison 2nd prize.

MILKING TESTS, 1885-6—F.F. & I. CO.'S PRIZE MILK COW. For Kiama Show, 1886.

Date of Notice.	Date of Test.	Name of Owner	Produce
1885	1885		lbs. oz.
Aug. 1	Aug. 9	Hugh Dudgeon	47.4
Sept. 15	Oct. 6	Henry Fredericks	53
Sept. 22	Oct. 30	Hugh Colley, jun.	51.8
Sept. 29	Oct. 30	Jas. W. Cole	44.8
Oct. 14	Oct. 30	Hugh Colley, jun.	46.12
Nov. 10	Nov. 20	James Bros.	49.8
,,	,,	,, ,,	48.12
Nov. 18	Nov. 24	Henry Spinks	49.4
Dec. 22	Dec. 30	John Lindsay	49.8
,,	,,	,, ,,	46.12
,,	,,	,, ,,	44
1886	1886		
Jan. 1	Jan. 8	John Lindsay	51.8
,,	,,	,, ,,	44.4
,,	,,	,, ,,	44

Mr. Henry Frederick Noble's Prize Heifers, under 3 years.

Date of Notice.	Date of Test.	Owner's Name.	Produce
1885	1885		
Sept.—	Sept 17	Cole Bros.	26.0
,,	,,	,, ,,	35.4
Oct. 1	Oct. 7	Henry Fredericks	31.8
Oct. 22	Oct. 30	James W. Cole	44.8
Nov. 10	Nov. 20	Henry Fredericks	39.8
1886	1886		
Jan. 23	Jan. 30	Hugh Dudgeon	53.0

RESULT OF COMPETITION FOR SPECIAL MILK PRIZES OFFERED BY KIAMA AGRICULTURAL SOCIETY'S SHOW OF 1886.

Henry Frederick's cow	53 lbs. milk in two milkings.
Hugh Dudgeon's cow	53 lbs. ,, ,, ,,
Hugh Colley, junr., cow†	51½lbs. ,, ,, ,,
John Lindsay's cow*	51½lbs. ,, ,, ,,
James Brothers' cow	49½lbs. ,, ,, ,,

†No mention of winner.

* Cow's name, Susan—Jenkins' breed.

COW TESTS OF KIAMA AGRICULTURAL SOCIETY, 1886.

Nos.	Name of Owner.	Color of Cow.	Age.	Milk Test.	Date of Test and Breeding.
1	Jas. W. Cole	—	—	44½ lbs.	——
2	Henry Fredericks	—	—	32½ ,,	——
3	Hugh Colley, junr.	Light roan	—	35 ,,	27th November, 1886.
4	Robert Miller	Light roan	—	36½ ,,	29th October, 1886
5	Thomas Brown	Red	—	38 ,,	25th March, 1887.
6	Hugh Dudgeon	Red	—	35 ,,	——
7	Hugh Dudgeon	Red roan	—	36 ,,	——
8	John Hayter	Dark roan	—	42 ,,	Supposed to be old milking Durham.
9	Hugh Dungeon	Red and white	Under 3 years	37½ ,,	Major strain
10	Hugh Dudgeon	Red and white	,, ,,	37 ,,	Major strain.
11	Jas. W. Cole	—	,, ,,	47 ,,	8th October, 1887.
12	Cole Bros.	—	—	38½ ,,	——
13	Cole Bros.	—	—	—	——
14	C. W. Craig	Red and white	Under 3 years	42 ,,	——
15	C. W. Craig	Roan	,, ,,	41½ ,,	——
16	Stewart Bros.	—	—	46 ,,	30th November, 1887.
17	George Couch	—	—	42½ ,,	30th November, 1887.
18	Daniel Murphy	Red and white	—	48¾ ,,	23rd October, 1889.
19	Edward R. Bigg	—	3 years	35 ,,	Ayrshire.
20	Mrs. Jane Armstrong	Brindle	3 years	46 ,,	29th October, 1890. ¾ Jersey.
21	James Spinks	Red and white	2 years	39½ ,,	5th January, 1892.
22	Spinks Bros.	Red and white	Under 3 years	39¼ ,,	11th June, 1892.
23	John F. Spinks	Dark spotted	Under 2 years	37¾ ,,	Nov., 1892. Bred from Major strain
24	James Bros.	Roan	Under 3 years	43 ,,	10th January, 1893.
25	T. R. M. Moffitt	Red	Under 3 years	37¼ ,,	18th April, 1893.
26	C. W. Craig	Roan	Under 2 years	38¼ ,,	3rd August, 1893. Major strain
27	C. W. Craig	Roan	2 years	35¾ ,,	3rd August, 1893. Major strain.
28	Hugh Dudgeon	Red	Under 3 years	43 ,,	1st Nov., 1893. Major strain.
29	James Bros.	Red with white spot	Under 3 years	43½ ,,	1st June, 1894. Illawarra strain (Prince Charlie).
30	C. W. Craig	Black	Under 3 years	49¾ ,,	29th September, 1894.
31	John T. Young	Red and white	Under 3 years	42½ ,,	——

MILKING COW TESTS IN CONNECTION WITH KIAMA AGRICULTURAL SOCIETY.

Nos.	Name of Owner.	Color of Cow.	Age.	Milk Test	Date of Test.	Pedigree.
1	John Lindsay	Red (Susan) ..	—	51½ lbs.	1st Jan., 1886	District breed
2	John Lindsay	Light roan ..	—	44¼ ,,	9th Jan., 1886	District breed
3	John Lindsay	Dark red ..	—	42 ,,	9th Jan., 1886	District breed
4	Daniel Boyd	Roan	—	58½ ,,	5th May, 1886	
5	Robert Miller	Red	7 years	55 ,,	2nd Oct., 1886	
6	Daniel Boyd	Red	4 years	49 ,,	9th June, 1886	
7	Henry Fredericks ..	Red ..	—	52½ ,,	22nd Oct., 1886	
8	James Sharpe	Roan	—	52¾ ,,	23rd Nov., 1886	
9	James Sharpe	Red and white	—	54¾ ,,	30th Dec., 1886	
10	James W. Cole	Light roan ..	—	59½ ,,	28th Jan., 1887	Durham
11	John Curtis	—	—	62½ ,,	12th Mar., 1887	
12	Daniel Boyd	Roan	5 years	62 ,,	4th May, 1887	
13	Michael O'Gorman ..	Red	—	49 ,,	—	
14	John Lindsay	Red and white	—	59½ ,,	3rd Nov., 1888	¾ Ayrshire
15	John Lindsay	Red and white	—	62½ ,,	14th Nov., 1888	¾ Ayrshire
16	John Lindsay	Red, white face	5 years	68 ,,	12th Dec., 1888	½ Ayrshire
17	Daniel Boyd	Light roan	6 years	69 ,,	29th Jan., 1889	
18	James W. Cole	Light roan ..	6 years	69 ,,	January, 1889	By Commodore
19	James W. Cole	Light spots ..	—	65 ,,	31st May, 1888	
20	J. T. and E. Cole ..	— ..	—	60 ,,	1st Dec., 1887	
21	Roger Murphy	Light roan ..	—	60 ,,	—	
22	Roger Murphy	Spotted ..	—	51¼ ,,	—	
23	W. Sharpe	Roan	7 years	56½ ,,	21st October,	
24	Daniel Boyd	Red and white	7 years	58½ ,,	26th Oct., 1887	
25	Daniel Boyd	Yellow.. ..	6 years	54 ,,	30th Sept., 1887	Sire, Comet
26	John Lindsay	Red and white	—	68 ,,	5th Dec., 1889	
27	John Lindsay	Red and white	6 years	69½ ,,	5th Dec., 1889	
28	James Bros.	Roan	6½ yrs.	60½ ,,	23rd Aug., 1889	
29	James Bros.	Dark roan ..	—	70¼ ,,	23rd Oct., 1889	
30	James W. Cole	Light roan ..	—	77¼ ,,	10th Jan., 1890	Commodore
30½	J. T. Hayter	Red and white	12 years	59¾ ,,	2nd Dec., 1920	Some Antill blood
31	Jas. W. Cole	Light roan ..	—	68 ,,	2nd Jan., 1891	Major strain
32	Jas. W. Cole	Light roan ..	—	57 ,,	24th Jan., 1891	Commodore
33	Hugh Dudgeon	Red	8 years	54½ ,,	24th Jan., 1891	Major strain
34	John Lindsay	Yellow with white back ..	—	70½ ,,	10th June, 1891	Half-bred Ayrshire
35	James Bros.	Red and white	6 years	70¼ ,,	12th Dec., 1891	Major strain
36	Hugh Dudgeon	Light roan ..	5 years	61 ,,	19th Jan., 1892	Major strain
37	James W. Cole	— ..	—	65½ ,,	23rd Jan., 1892	
38	John Lindsay	Red and white	9 years	72½ ,,	26th Nov., 1892	Ayrshire bull, D'ham cow
39	James Bros.	Brown ..	7 years	59½ ,,	10th Jan., 1893	E. R. Williams' breed
40	Hugh Dudgeon	Red	6 years	64½ ,,	17th Jan., 1893	Major strain
41	Hugh Dudgeon	Light roan ..	6 years	60 ,,	17th Jan., 1893	Major strain
42	C. W. Craig	Roan	8 years	68¾ ,,	3rd Aug., 1893	Major strain
43	C. W. Craig	Roan	10 years	53¾ ,,	20th Oct., 1893	Major strain
44	C. W. Craig	Roan	5 years	56¼ ,,	20th Oct., 1893	Major strain
45	Hugh Dudgeon	Spotted ..	10 years	62 ,,	1st Dec., 1893	District breed
46	Hugh Dudgeon	Light roan ..	7 years	62¾ ,,	12th June, 1894	Major strain
47	Hugh Dudgeon	Dark red ..	7 years	56¼ ,,	12th Jan., 1894	Major strain
48	C. W. Craig	Roan	6 years	64 ,,	8th Nov., 1894	Major strain
49	John T. Young	Red and white	aged	64 ,,	22nd Aug., 1895	
50	Hugh Dudgeon	Spotted ..	9 years	65½ ,,	17th Sept., 1895	Major strain
51	Hugh Dudgeon	Red	5 years	63 ,,	26th Oct., 1895.	Major strain

Owner's Name.	Color of Cow.	Age.	Date of Test.	Milk.	Butter.	Pedigree.
				lbs.	lbs. ozs.	
Hugh Dudgeon	Red, white flank	2 years	19th Jan., 1907	34.8	—	Illawarra Durham
Hugh Dudgeon	Red	2 years	16th Oct., 1906	41.8	—	Sire, Gordon Brook bull
Charles Sharpe	Red roan ..	9 years	28th July, 1906	65.8	13 10	Shorthorn
Bailey Bros.	Red and white ..	5 years	21st Nov., 1906	50	—	Illawarra breed
M. J. Hindmarsh ..	Yellow	5 years	7th Dec., 1906	51	—	Grade Guernsey
Thomas James	Light red ..	6 years	21st June, 1905	51	13 9	Jersey-Durham cross
Thomas James	Roan (Rossonus)	11 years	21st June, 1905	43	12 7½	Milking Shorthorn
George Grey	Black and white	4 years	5th Oct., 1905	57	—	Holstein cross
Daniel Murphy	Red	5 years	18th Nov., 1905	53.4	12 4	Milking Shorthorn
W. H. Sharpe	L't roan & white	7 years	23rd Dec., 1905	50.8	12 4	Ayrshire Shorthorn cross

The difficulty of getting hold of reliable pedigrees has been a trouble in Illawarra for years past; to carry cattle pedigrees about in one's head is a gift bestowed on but few. Yet, hundreds profess to know, first hand, everything. Take Edward Gibson's cow, "Handsome." She was calved on Gibson's farm at Figtree, near Wollongong on September 30th, 1884. Colour roan and white. She was then described as being descended from the old Illawarra and the Glenlee cattle, a strain of cattle much admired for the dairy. She won her first prize in class 1 year and under 2 years in 1886; her second 1st prize in class 2 years, and under 3 years in 1887. First prize as a dairy cow at Albion Park in 1888; also 1st prize in dairy cow class at Dapto, same year. She won 1st prize at Wollongong Show in 1889. Her breeding was then given as follows:—"Out of a pure Durham cow, her sire an Ayrshire-Durham, bred by Lindsay Bros." According to Lindsay Bros, the bull in question was "bred by John Lindsay of Kembla Park, Munderra, sire Earl of Beaconsfield, dam an Illawarra cow." Handsome tested gave 50 lbs. of milk per day, averaging 14 lbs. of butter per week.

CATTLE FOR DAIRY PURPOSES.
ILLAWARRA BREED.

Best bull, 3 years and over.—1st prize (£3 or medal), Thomas Love; 2nd prize (£2), Frederick Beggs; 3rd prize (£1 10s.), Robert Jones; 4th prize (£1), John F. Spinks.

Best bull, 2 years and under 3 years.—1st prize (£2), Hugh Thompson; 2nd prize (£1 10s.), John Carberry; 3rd prize (£1), Richard Keevers.

Best bull, 1 and under 2 years.—1st prize (£1 10s.), James Moffitt, jun.; 2nd prize (£1), George Chapman.

Best milking cow.—1st prize (£3 or medal), Thomas Fredericks; 2nd prize (£2), Cole Bros.; 3rd prize (£1 10s.), Craig and Son; 4th prize (£1), Cole Bros.

Best dry cow.—1st prize (£3 or medal), John Curtis; 2nd prize (£2), W. C. Dunster; 3rd prize (£1 10s.), Thomas Love; 4th prize (£1), William Graham.

Best heifer, 2 and under 3 years.—1st prize (£2), Richard Keevers; 2nd prize (£1 10s.), William James; 3rd prize, (£1), Thomas Brown.

Best pen of 4 heifers, under 3 years.—1st prize (£2), J. W. Cole; 2nd prize (£1), Daniel Boyd.

Best pen of 4 dairy cows, any breed.—1st prize (£2 2s.), Cole Bros.; 2nd prize (£1 1s.), J. W. Cole.

Best pen of 4 dairy cows, under 4 years.—1st prize (£2 2s.), Cole Bros.

Best pen of 6 heifers, under 3 years.—1st price (£2 10s.), Daniel Boyd.

Best male animal for dairy purposes, any breed.—1st prize (£5 5s.), Thomas Love's "King Cole,"; 2nd prize (£5 5s.). Craig & Son's "Louie."

Best bull and his progeny (females), 6 in number.—Thomas Brown (sire by "Dunlop").

AYRSHIRE DAIRY CATTLE.

Best Ayrshire bull, 3 years and over.—1st prize (£2 5s.), John B. Taylor; 2nd prize (£1 5s.), Thomas Brown.

Best Ayrshire bull, 1 year and under 2 years.—1st prize (£1 5s.), W. C. Dunster; 2nd prize (£1), James Sharpe.

Best Ayrshire cow, 3 years and over —1st prize (£2 5s.) or medal), Robert Wilson; 2nd prize (£1 5s.), Irvine Martin.

Best Ayrshire heifer, 2 years and under 3 years.—1st prize (£1 15s.), William James; 2nd prize (£1 5s.), Thomas Brown.

Best dairy bull, any age (Special).—1st prize (£4 5s.), John Lindsay; 2nd prize (£1), W. C. Dunster.

In **Jersey** and **Alderney Classes**—Edwin Vidler, Alex. Campbell, William James, William Emery, and Con. Heninger were the principal winners.

The Kiama "Challenge Prize" of 1887 for cows of any of the foregoing breeds and of any age.—1st prize, Cole Bros; 2nd prize, J. W. Cole.

Show Test.—Cow giving largest quantity of milk in 24 hours —1st prize (£10), J. W. Cole's "Violet," 59½ lbs.; 2nd prize (£9 9s.), Daniel Boyd, 58½ lbs.; 3rd prize (£5), Robert Miller, 55 lbs.; 4th prize (£2 2s.), James Sharpe. 54¾ lbs.; 5th prize (£1 1s.), James Sharpe, 52¾ lbs.

Cow giving the largest quantity of butter in test for qualification for Herd-book, during the year 1886.—1st prize (£5 5s.), Spinks Bros., 14¾ lbs.; 2nd prize, (£3 3s.), Cole Bros., 12¾ lbs.; 3rd prize (£2 2s.), Hugh Dudgeon, 12 lbs.; 4th prize (£1 10s.), Hugh Dudgeon, 7½ lbs. *Note.*—This 4th prize cow was "Charmer." She had been milking 9 months, and was at time of test due to calve within two months.

Test for cow, under 3 years old.—1st prize (£2 2s.), Robert Miller, 36½ lbs.; 2nd prize (£1 1s.), Hugh Colley, jun., 35 lbs.

Section I.—Albion Park Show, 1888.

Class 1—James McGill (The Bass), 1st prize; E. H. Weston (Thunderbolt), 2nd prize; George Couch (Emperor), 3rd prize.

Class 2—Henry Allison, John H. Wright, Thomas Charlton, 1st prize; Gabriel Timbs, junr., Charles Weston.

Class 3—Thomas Charlton, George Faulks, Charles Weston, 2nd prize; Charles Weston, 1st prize; Marceau Bros.

Class 4—20 entries—P. Flitcroft, 1st prize; John Saunders, 2nd prize.

Class 5—11 entries—Michael O'Gorman, 1st prize; David Manson, 2nd prize.

Class 6—9 entries—James McGill, 1st prize; P. Flitcroft, 2nd prize.

Class 6a—8 entries—P. Flitcroft, 1st prize.

Class 7—2 entries—Hindmarsh Bros., 1st and 2nd prizes.

Class 8—2 entries—Hindmarsh Bros, 1st prize; Gabriel Timbs, 2nd prize.

Class 9—2 entries—Denis Kelleher, 1st prize.

Class 10—6 entries—Hindmarsh Bros., 1st prize; David Manson, 2nd prize.

Class 11—5 entries—Hindmarsh Bros., 1st prize; Dunster Bros., 2nd prize.

Class 12—2 entries—Hindmarsh Bros., 1st prize; Gabriel Timbs, 2nd prize.

Class 13—2 entries—Marceau Bros., 1st prize; Gabriel Timbs, 2nd prize.

Class 14—4 entries—Hindmarsh Bros., 1st and 2nd prizes.; Cornelius Heinenger, highly commended

Class 15—2 entries—Hindmarsh Bros., 1st prize.

Class 16—6 entries—George Geer, 1st prize. J. Chie, 2nd prize.

Class 17—7 entries—Hindmarsh Bros., 1st prize; James Condon, 2nd prize.

Class 18—3 entries—James Sharpe, 1st prize; J H. Wright, 2nd prize.

Class 19—2 entries—Alexander Fraser, 1st prize.

Class 20—8 entries—John Fraser, 1st prize; Thos. Charlton, 2nd prize.

Section II.

Class 21—14 entries—Thos. Charlton, 1st prize; George Clinch, 2nd prize.

Class 22—17 entries—Charly Weston, 1st prize; John McGlinchy, 2nd prize; — Campbell, highly commended.

Class 23—7 entries—F. Biggs, 1st prize; Charles Barnes, 2nd prize; James Sharpe, 3rd prize.

Class 24—11 entries—Edwin Vidler, junr., 1st prize; Michael Carberry, 2nd prize.

Class 25—12 entries—Dr. Asche, 1st prize; — Booth, 2nd prize; Alex Fraser, 3rd prize.

Class 26—11 entries—Caleb Davies, 1st prize; David Manson, 2nd prize.

Class 27—12 entries—P. Malone, 1st prize; George Geer, 2nd prize.

Class 29—9 entries—Charles Weston, 1st prize; Robert Gordon, 2nd prize.

Class 30—12 entries—C. Braddock, 1st prize; Robt. Osborne, 2nd prize; James Condon, highly commended.

Class 31—12 entries—Robert Jones, 1st prize; Edward Swan, 2nd prize.

Class 32—11 entries—Robert J. Marshall, 1st prize; C Hukins (Dr. Avondale), 2nd prize; A. B. Staff (Duchess) 3rd prize.

Class 33—6 entries—Edward Swan, 1st prize; Michael Carberry, 2nd prize.

Section III.

Class 1—Bulls—Evan R. Evans, 1st prize; F. Biggs, 2nd prize.

Class 2—Duncan McGill, 1st prize; Duncan McGill, 2nd prize.

Class 3—10 entries—W. Mathie, 1st prize; Edward Gibson, 2nd prize.

Class 4—29 entrie—(Cows in Milk) Edward Gibson, 1st prize; John Dudgeon, 2nd prize.

Class 5—21 entries—(Dry Cows) Dunster Bros., 1st prize; John Dudgeon, 2nd prize.

Class 6—28 entries—James Bros., 1st prize; James Bros., 2nd prize; John Brownlee, highly commended.

Class 7—37 entries—J. H. Swan, 1st prize; James Musgrave, 2nd prize; Evan R. Evans, highly commended.

Class 8—14 entries—E. Gibson*, 1st prize; John Dudgeon, 2nd prize.

* Mr. Edward Gibson's Illawarra cow, "Handsome," bred by owner, calved September 30th, 1884; color, roan and white, was described by Mr. Gibson to the Illawarra *Mercury* representatives as having descended from the old Illawarra and Glenlee strains. She won 1st prize at Albion Park Show in 1888 and 1st prize at Dapto Show same year in dairy cow. Mr. Gibson then said:—" She is out of a pure-bred Durham cow by an Ayrshire Durham bull, bred by Lindsay Bros. "Handsome" was a show cow of note in her day, and when officially tested gave 50 lbs. of milk in 24 hours, and 14 lbs. of butter per week. This test was carried out by means of separator and churn, the official system of testing cows at that period. She was full of Devon blood.

Class 9—30 entries—James Musgrave, 1st prize; E. H. Weston, 2nd prize; Dunster Bros., highly commended.

Class 10—20 entries—George Timbs, 1st prize; Michael O'Gorman, 2nd prize.

Class 11—8 entries—Michael O'Gorman (3 cows), 1st prize; John Lindsay (3 cows), 2nd prize.

Class 12—Nil.

Class 13—Con. Heinenger, 1st prize.

Class 14—6 entries—Con. Heinenger, 1st and 2nd prizes.

Class 15—7 entries—Con. Heinenger, 1st and 2nd prizes.

Class 16—5—entries—D. Lindsay, 1st and 2nd prizes.

Class 17—2 entries—D. Lindsay, 1st prize.

Class 18—4 entries—Marceau Bros., 1st prize; Henry Keevers, 2nd prize.

Class 19—6 entries—John Lindsay, 1st prize; George Couch, 2nd prize.

Class 20—6 entries—John Lindsay, 1st prize; Edward Gibson, 2nd prize and highly commended.

Class 21—5 entries—Bulls—Irvine Martin, 1st prize; John Lindsay, 2nd prize.

Class 22—7 entries—Cows—Evan R. Evans, 1st prize; John Lindsay, 2nd prize; Irvine Martin, highly commended.

Class 23—5 entries—John Lindsay, 1st and 2nd prizes.

Class 24—6 entries—John Lindsay, 1st and 2nd prizes.

Class 25—9 entries—Edward Gibson, 1st prize.

Class 26—7 entries—Tests: John Lindsay's cow, 37lbs. 6 ozs., 1st prize; Charles Gower's cow, 28lbs. 2 ozs., 2nd prize; David Manson's cow "Bally," 28lbs of milk, highly commended.

Class 27A—13 entries—John Dudgeon (3 cows milking), 1st prize; Michael O'Gorman (3 cows milking), 2nd prize.

Class 27—13 entries—David Manson (2 cows), 1st prize.

Class 28—3 entries—David Manson exhibited "Gaylad"; no awards.

Class 30—1 entry—David Manson's "Queen." No award.

Class 32—8 entries—J. H. Swan, 1st prize.

Class 33—9 entries—Mick Crowley, 1st prize.

Class 34—5 entries—Mick Crowley, 1st prize; J. Thomas, 2nd prize.

Class 35—10 entries—Evan R. Evans, 1st and 2nd prizes.

Class 36—8 entries—J. Chie, 1st prize; D. Manson, 2nd prize.

Section III.—Cattle for Dairy Purposes.

Class 1—Bull, any age—13 entries—Evan R. Evans, 1st prize; Robert Jones, 2nd prize.

Class 2—Bull, 2 years—4 entries—Edward Gibson, 1st prize; W Mathie, 2nd prize.

Class 3—Bull, 1 year—13 entries—H. Dudgeon, 1st prize; Fred Timbs, 2nd prize.

Class 4—Cow in Milk—13 entries—John Dudgeon, 1st prize; Edward Gibson, 2nd prize; Hugh Dudgeon, highly commended

Class 5—Dry Cow—20 entries—Dunster Bros., 1st prize; Hugh Dudgeon, 2nd prize.

Class 6—Heifer, 2 years—25 entries—William Moles, 1st prize; David Manson, 2nd prize; Edward Gibson, highly commended.

Class 7—Heifer, 1 year—33 entries—Frank Downes, 1st prize; J. Chie, 2nd prize.

Class 8—Bull Calf, 6 months old—8 entries—Charles Barnes, 1st prize; Edward Gibson, 2nd prize.

Class 9—Heifer Calf 6 months old—25 entries—John Dudgeon, 1st prize; Charles Faulks, 2nd prize.

Class 10—4 heifers, 1 and 2 years old—19 entries—James Bros., 1st prize; Edward Gibson, 2nd prize.

Class 11—6 Heifers, 2 years old—5 entries—William Moles, 1st prize; Edward Gibson, 2nd prize.

Class 12—3 Dairy Cows (Special, J. Marks)—10 entries—Edward Gibson, 1st prize; Alex. Fraser, 2nd prize. Michael O'Gorman and John Dudgeon, highly commended.

Class 13—Champion Cow—John Dudgeon, 1st prize; Edward Gibson, 2nd prize. As no tests given, prizes were not awarded.

Class 14—Cow in Milk—5 entries—David Manson, 1st prize; and 2nd prize.

Class 15—Two Heifers, 1 and 2 years old—11 entries—F. Downs, 1st prize; Dunster Bros., 2nd prize.

Class 16—Jerseys and Alderneys: Bull 3 years—3 entries—J. Heinenger, 1st prize; C. Heinenger, 2nd prize.

Class 17—Bull, 2 years—3 entries—C. Heinenger, 1st prize.

Class 18—Best Cow, any age—8 entries—Thomas James, 1st prize; David Lindsay, 2nd prize.

Class 19—Ayrshire Bull, 3 years—James Couch, 1st prize. Edward Gibson, 2nd prize.

HENRY CHITTICK & SONS' STUD, Alne Bank, Gerringong, Illawarra.

PET II OF ALNE BANK.
(No. 409, A.R., I.D.C.H.B.)

BUTTERCUP III OF ALNE BANK.
(No. 218, A.R., I.D.C.H.B.)

FUSSY OF ALNE BANK.

COCKIE OF ALNE BANK.
(No. 96, I.D.C.H.B.)

LINDA 2nd OF ALNE BANK.
(No. 140, A.R., I.D.C.H.B.)

BUTTERCUP II.
(No. 218, A.R., I.D.C.H.B.)

Class 20—Bull, 2 years—1 entry—Irvine Martin, 1st prize.
Class 21—Bull, 1 year—1 entry—Gabriel Timbs, 1st prize.
Class 22—Cow, any age—6 entries—Evan R. Evans, 1st and 2nd prizes.
Class 23—Heifer, 2 years—6 entries—James Bros., 1st prize.
Class 24—5 entries—No awards.
Class 25—Challenge Prize—Evan R. Evans, 1st prize.
Class 26—Bull, under 3 years—Irvine Martin, 1st prize.
Class 31—Shorthorn Bull—4 entries—D. Manson, 1st prize; J. Chic, 2nd prize.
Special—6 Dairy Cows (F.F. & I. Co.)—5 entries—Edward Gibson, 1st prize; Michael O'Gorman 2nd prize.

Kiama Show on 9th and 10th February, 1887, on new show ground, Longbrush Road; 1000 entries. Jas. W. Cole won with Violet, aged 4 years, on 2nd calf. Daniel Boyd was 2nd with a cow of the Scotch Jock strain. Robert Miller was 3rd with a cow by a Cornet bull out of a Major cow. Spinks Bros 4th with a cow bred by Roger Murphy, of Jamberoo, of the Scotch Jock strain. Hugh Dudgeon was commended for a cow by George Tate, sen., of Broughton Village.

Cow giving most milk in 24 hours—1st prize J. W. Cole, 59lb. 8oz.; 2nd prize, Daniel Boyd, 58lb. 12oz.

Cow giving the largest amount of butter per week for Herd Book—Spinks Bros., 1st prize, value £5 5s, 14lb. 10oz.; Cole Bros. 2nd prize, £3 3s, 12lb. 12oz.; Hugh Dudgeon, 3rd prize, £2 2s. 12lb.; Hugh Dudgeon, 4th prize, £1 10s, 7lb. This 4th prize cow was "Charmer," 9 months in milk, 2 months off calving.

1889.—Best bull, J. W. Cole, 1st prize; Spinks Bros., 2nd prize. Bull, 2 years old, Thomas Honey, 1st prize; Robert Jones, 2nd prize; Peter Quinn, 3rd prize. Best cow, J. W. Cole, 1st prize; J. T. Cole, 2nd prize. Best dry cow, J. W. Cole, 1st prize; J. T. Cole, 2nd prize. Best Ayrshire bull, George H. Grey, 1st prize; Robert Wilson, 2nd prize. Alderney or Jersey, best bull, William Emery, 1st prize; Z. Bice. 2nd prize. Best cow, J. Jones, 1st prize; William Emery, 2nd prize.

Kiama A. & H. Society, meeting October, 1889. Report on cow testing by Special Committee. Mr. John James read the following report:—"Your committee, after mature consideration and careful experiment, beg to report that they believe hand separators will give a reliable test in any kind of weather, and recommend, 1st: The adoption of testing by hand separators instead of setting the milk as formerly; 2nd: That two persons be appointed to conduct tests in different localities; one in Jamberoo, and one in Gerringong, it is suggested would be more convenient than the present locality; 3rd: That two days' test be adopted instead of seven days as previously. This is thought may induce more stock owners to compete in entering stock; 4th: That 100 lbs. of milk or 3½ lbs. of butter in two consecutive days be the standard for admission to Herd Book; 5th: That hand-feeding or milk-feeding be not allowed; the feed to be best pasture available, or in times of scarcity, green fodder only; 6th: That the entrance fee be abolished; 7th: The adoption of the Cook System, the person testing to keep a book and enter name, age, colour, brand, breed, feed, state of the weather, and weight of milk and butter, a duplicate leaf to be given the owner of cow tested, both leaves to be signed by person testing and the owner of cow. In the case of a cow passing the standard, the person conducting the test to furnish the secretary with full particulars for entry in Herd Book. Waugh and Josephson, for lending a hand separator, and Frank McCaffrey for conducting the test of a hand separator. H. H. Honey was thanked also. He used one of Martin and Co.'s Alexander machines. "The Australian Ironmonger" was the journal that reported on these tests. G. W. Fuller was then M.P. for the Kiama Electorate, and got £200 for the Kiama Show.

Spring balance for weighing milk in cow tests, January, 1891. B. Lane, 175 lunches at 4/- each, £35.

The point system of judging, adopted July 17th, 1891, and on 28th August, 1891, and £250 was approved of by Minister of Agriculture for district national prizes.

Although the point system of judging was adopted in 1891, the actual arrangement of these points does not appear to have taken effect until after a general conference of the Agricultural Society's delegates who assembled in Kiama, 4/6/'92. It was a representative meeting, as all such things were then and are to this day, and for the matter of that, from the beginning, but nothing seems to have come out of the movement, as the point system is above the mind of the majority of the best. 1890.—Show in Kiama, 16th and 17th January, 1890. Best bull, J. W. Cole, 1st prize; J. T. Cole, 2nd prize. Best bull, 2 years old, Hugh Dudgeon, 1st prize; Thomas Love, 2nd prize. Bull for dairy purposes, any breed and any age, J. W. Cole, 1st and champion. Cow any age and any breed, John Lindsay, 1st prize. Heifer, 2 years old that never had a calf, Craig and Son, 1st prize. Heifer, 2 years old in calf, Michael Murphy, 1st prize; William Sharpe, 2nd prize.

Wollongong Show, 1890 (February.): Dairy cow, Edward Gibson, 1st prize; John Lindsay, 2nd prize. Berry Show, 1890 (12th Feb.): Dairy cow in milk, Daniel Boyd, 1st prize; J. T. Cole, 2nd prize. Champion cow, Daniel Boyd. Heifer, 2 years old, Daniel Boyd, 1st prize and 2nd prize.

1892.—Best bull, John Dudgeon's Reddie, 1st prize. Best bull, 2 years old, E. H. Cole, 1st prize. Best bull, 1 year old, Edward Gibson, 1st prize. Best 4 dairy cows, John Lindsay, 1st prize. Best dairy cow, John Lindsay, 1st prize; Edward Gibson, 2nd prize. Best Ayrshire bull, Irvine Martin, 1st prize; Robert Lindsay, 2nd prize. Best Ayrshire cow, John Lindsay, 1st prize. David Manson, 2nd prize. Alderney or Jersey. Best bull, George Hill, 1st prize; Con. Heninger, 2nd prize. George Hill, of Sydney, was in 1892, interested in the blue metal trade at Bombo, Kiama.

1893.—Kiama Show, January, 1893. Bull, 4 years and over, John Dudgeon's Reddie, 1st prize; Spinks Bros., 2nd prize. Bull, 2 years old, J. W. Cole, 1st prize; Henry Fredericks, 2nd prize. Best cow in milk, John Dudgeon, 1st prize; Hugh Dudgeon, 2nd prize. Champion bull, Spinks Bros. Champion cow, J. T. Cole, 1st prize. Heifer, 2 years old, T. and F. James, 1st prize; James Bros., 2nd prize.

Berry Show, 1893, opened by Lord Jersey. Best dairy bull, John Dudgeon, 1st prize (Reddie); J. W. Cole, 2nd prize. Best cow in milk, John Lindsay, 1st prize, Thomas Somerville, 2nd prize. Bull, 2 years old, Edwin Vidler, 1st prize. Daniel Boyd, 2nd prize. Heifer, 2 years old, R. V. Boyd, 1st prize, John Lindsay, 2nd prize. Champion bull, John Dudgeon. Champion cow, John Lindsay.

Albion Park Show, 1893. Best cow, John Lindsay's (Honeycomb), 1st prize. Best bull, John Dudgeon's (Reddie), 1st prize; Hugh Dudgeon's (Charmer), 2nd prize. Champion cow, John Lindsay's Honeycomb, Hugh Dudgeon, highly commended; heifer, 2 years, T. and F. James, 1st prize; T. James, 2nd prize. Bull, 2 years, Edward Gibson, 1st prize; Michael Boyle, 2nd prize.

Shoalhaven Show, 1893. Best dairy bull, J. W. Cole, 1st prize. Best 2 years old bull, J. W. Cole, 1st prize. Best dry cow, J. W. Cole, 1st prize.

Robertson Show, 1893. Best dairy bull, John Dudgeon's Reddie, 1st prize; J. W. Cole, 2nd prize. Best bull, 2 years John Lindsay, 1st prize, Edwin Vidler, 2nd prize. Champion dairy bull, John Dudgeon's Reddie, J. W. Cole, commended. Best dry cow, J. W. Cole, 1st prize; W. Taylor, 2nd prize.

The Farmers' Slogan

Successful Co-operative Marketing.

A Genuine Co-operative House.

The Berrima District Farm & Dairy Co. Ltd.

401 Sussex Street, Sydney.

For the disposal of all kinds of Farm & Dairy Produce.

Lowest Charges.   Highest Prices,   Cash Bonus.

ARTHUR KNOX, General Manager.

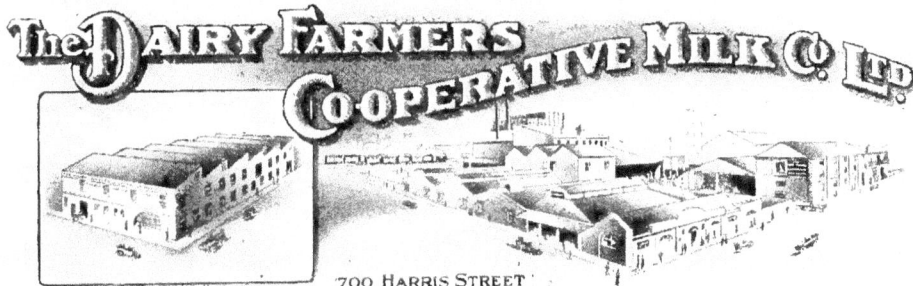

700 HARRIS STREET
ULTIMO
Sydney

Established in 1900   Head Office and City Depot.

Dairy Farmers of Albion Park and Dapto were the Originators of this Company, and afterwards linked up the South Coast from Nowra to Wollongong. The object being to place on the Sydney Market pure fresh Country Milk in unlimited quantities.

Year by Year the business has grown till last Year the output exceeded 5 million gallons.

Depots for receiving, pasteurising and cooling of milk are in operation at **Nowra, Berry, Gerringong, Kiama, Jamberoo, Albion Park, Dapto,** and **Unanderra** on the South Coast, and **Raymond Terrace,** near Newcastle with **Dungog** on the North, while **Moss Vale** is being linked up on the Southern Line.

Milk is conveyed from the Country Depots to the City in large round insulated tanks which prevents high temperatures and insures the freshest and best of milk on arrival

Distributing Depots are established in addition to the **Head Depot** at **North Sydney, Waverley, Balmain, Ashfield, Lindfield** and at **Newcastle** on the North.

The Company is possessed of Freehold Property to the extent of about 1½ acres, in the heart of the City, with ample Railway Siding, and has Buildings, Machinery, Plant, etc, thereon to the value of £150,000.

This is the first and only Co-operative Company of its kind in the Commonwealth.

H. FRYER, General Manager

DAIRY CATTLE BREEDING.

Dairy cattle breeding as a means of living for many people on the land may be considered by the majority of such persons a very simple process indeed. No doubt it is—so long as they as a body do not attempt to soar any higher than the common level. But there are always a few who desire to improve their products by turning their attention to the scientific side of the subject. Such persons very soon find that there are one hundred and one things to be learned that had never entered into their early philosophy. They have learned that in the beginning they knew very little, and that there is an important something they have yet to learn.

There are many keys required to open the door to success in dairy-cattle breeding, simply because there are numerous influences operating on the dairy farm. First we have selection, and after selection comes the judgment of mating and the controlling of inheritance. Environment has its influence, which operates in an even or uneven range, according to other influences. Then we have that mysterious power which operates in animals in various ways, known as the exercise of the functions.

The whole of these difficulties, together with the selection and mating of animals, we have learned from experience that unless a man has loaded dice he cannot always throw a six, and it is useless to use dice for procuring the six if a five is the number required. With the germ-cell it is the same, and much has to be done in this direction by means of mating the parents. Yet we know that there is a ''mean'' within which our operations must be carried on. We very soon learn that poor qualities are apt to crop up where we expect to find good ones. It is the duty of the breeder, then, to reduce the chance of defects by increasing the chances of good qualities; that is to say, loading the dice with special care or due caution.

The laws of inheritance naturally hold the animal kingdom in an orderly, systematic procession. The art of the breeder, therefore, lies in first getting a thorough grasp of his own ambition, so as to reduce his aim to a certain direction. He must then learn the good and bad qualities in his breeding animals and their

powers of transmission. The selection, mating and feeding of dairy cattle is, then, a very simple matter, indeed, on paper; but on the dairy farm it somehow pans out different, and our breeders find that there is always something more to be discovered.

Within the ordinary limits of a family there are certain hereditary peculiarities which constantly reappear, and a certain family likeness unites the members of a family. These physical resemblances are patent, and are looked upon as evidences of the laws of heredity.

The question has often been asked, ''How have breeds been founded?'' And this inquiry has over and over again been answered by asking other questions, namely, ''Why did Charles Colling's 'Hubback' (the grandsire of the bull 'Comet') picked up in a lane; and the 'Godolphin Arabian' (the maternal grandsire of 'Eclipse') purchased from the owner of a water-cart, become the fountain head to which cattle-breeders and horsemen desire to trace the pedigrees of their stock? Why were they selected?'' Just because they possessed, in a marked degree, most of the very best qualities which were desired in a bull and a horse, and because the purchaser believed and acted upon the idea that ''like tends to beget like.''

Right here, then, lies the judgment of the selector. If like tends to beget like in good qualities, why not in the bad? Experience teaches us that with regard to bad or inferior qualities like begets like, and it rolls on with fearful power if the defect be a hereditary one. Here we find the man of an inquiring turn of mind making his way through the crowd. He has selected his bull or an entire, and sets about ascertaining from every reliable resource the family traits of the animal he has selected. Here again the effects of too much inbreeding or too much outbreeding are apt to throw the best judgment out of line, when the progeny comes to be considered later on, and the true worth of the selection laid bare.

With regard to inbreeding—there is always a risk when the males and females from two inbred herds are mated. But when this infusion of two different strains blend, the ill effects of too much inbreeding seem to disappear, and a more vigorous strain is the result. Charles

Darwin saw the effect of mating two inbred animals from different strains and different pastures when he said:—"However little we may be able to discover with regard to the cause, the fact under review shows that the male and female elements must be differentiated to a certain degree in order to unite properly and to give birth to a vigorous progeny. Such differentiation of the sexual elements follow from the parents, and their ancestors having lived during some generations under different conditions of life."

Inbreeding for the Turf was in the past exceedingly simple and may be briefly stated as follows:—1st Inbreeding as the foundation; 2nd outcrossing from inbred blood; and 3rd, returning to same strain after an outcross. By inbreeding, which produced animals successful both at the Turf and the Stud, was meant a re-union, once, twice, or oftener, of strains of same blood, separately as a rule, not more than four steps of generations. This inbreeding was considered to intensify all the prominent characteristics and qualities of the stock, and it was therefore essentially necessary that the blood which is the subject of it should be the best and purest of its kind. Thus it will be seen that great importance was placed on correct pedigreeing early in the history of blood-horse breeding, as it was considered a mistake to adopt inbreeding with animals of impure blood or inferior powers. Take for example:

Sir Hercules, once inbred to the brothers Whalebone and Whisker, at three removes, and twice to their sire, Waxy, is the best and simplest example that could be selected by old-time writers. His sire and dam were second cousins, the grandchildren of own brothers, and his sire before him stood in about the same degree of relationship, being the produce of half-brother and half-sister by Waxy.

Outcrossing which was in the past remarkable for the production of many great racehorses, is the mating of an inbred animal with another of entirely different blood. This may take place from inbred blood on the side of either the sire or dam. Outcrossing has naturally followed continued or close inbreeding, and is therefore an essential part of our breeding theories with all kinds of stock. But it has been found to limit the number of good progeny. Breeders then return to the previously inbred stock, for a good cross can always be introduced, and yet the inbreeding carried on, as may be seen by looking up our blood horses' pedigrees.

It may be desirable to point out that there is an essential difference between cattle and those which apply to the breeding of racehorses. It is not easy to define this difference, it nevertheless exists. With cattle, not only close but continuous mating was originally advocated. Take for our example the long-horned bull Shakespeare, who was produced from only three distinct individuals in four generations, viz:— Westmoreland bull, old Comely (Canley Heifer No. I), and Canley Heifer No. II; and the animals whose names figure in the pedigree, Twopenny (son of West Moreland Bull), and old Comely, Twopenny's own dam, come together once, and Twopenny and the Canley Heifer No. II twice, the grandsire, and the dam of Shakespeare being both by him out of Canley Heifer No.II, and his daughter from his own dam being the dam of Shakespeare's sire; so that the breeding in-and-in, was remarkably close, and remarkably successful in a short space of time.

Now, when inbreeding has been very close or long continued, the cross of unrelated blood seems to be essentially necessary to retain the vigor of the thoroughbred horse and the dairy cow, as they must both be capable of great bodily exertion—one in the direction of high and continuous speed, and the other in long continued milk production. We find examples of the good effects of an outcross, and the returning to close breeding in many of our dairy-herds.

We are never too certain of the breeding ideas of our Illawarra dairymen. They seem to think that this special brand of wisdom should be protected by Patent Rights, yet it is plainly clear that the smartest of them tried to ape the great racehorse breeders from time to time with regard to breeding in-and-in. We know that both Duncan Beaton and Andrew McGill at all risks followed their own respective judgments, so did the elder Evan R. Evans, and purchased or otherwise selected animals from the larger breeders, and carried on breeding and dairying with blood, displaying a variety of colour, but of remarkable even type. Later breeders, for instance William Graham, of Minnamurra and Jamberoo, went in for close inbreeding with the Warrior blood. Warrior, a roan bull, was sired by a big framed bull, bred by his neighbour, Thomas Fredricks. Warrior was a fine type of dairy bull, displaying length and height. He was the sire of that magnificent type of Illawarra Cow "Flower." When Graham Bros. went for an outcross to mate with the much inbred Warriors, they, after much enquiry selected a small sized red bull named Admiral, whose sire was a red bull named Sir Henry, and whose dam was a roan cow bred by Edward Moses. Here we have not only an outcross from a different strain, but an animal whose antecedents were raised under either different climatic conditions or differently arranged soils, as Dairymaid, the dam of Admiral, was bred on the Robertson Tableland, and Sir Henry was bred at Spring-Hill, Wollongong. Dairymaid was bred by Edward Moses, and Sir Henry was bred by Simeon Dudgeon. Both however were breeders of dairy cattle of long standing in the Illawarra district.

"Admiral" was the sire, and "Flower" the dam of "Togo," who in the possession of George Grey of Kiama proved himself to be one of the best sires in Illawarra. Of course there are many very excellent authorities who may disagree with me in this statement. If so, I cannot alter my opinion to please them, as I am working on practical results, and in doing so am quite prepared to allow that two bulls with equal merits will not always produce the same results, and many good bulls have been wasted in the hands of their owners. Harking back to "Togo," and what we are pleased to term the "Togo" influences, when George Grey began dairying he was not blessed with riches—certainly he had knowledge, but his dairy herd although good average dairy cattle, as producers, were a mixed lot with few exceptions. His first lift up was an Illawarra bred bull, bred from stock strictly Illawarra in type and quality, named Ranji. Ranji's G. sire was bred by William Coughrane, senr., of Spring Hill, Wollongong, and his G. dam was bred by the Grahams of Rose Valley, Gerringong—a very choice cow indeed. Ranji certainly moved the herd upwards, yet, we cannot move from the truth, and after a very careful survey of the whole facts of the case, we have to say that "Togo" was one of the most notable bulls ever bred in the Illawarra district.

"Togo's" G.G. dam "Nugget," G. dam "Dairymaid;" and dam "Flower," were of high standard quality. Ranji's G.G. dam, G. dam, and dam were also of a high standard of quality. These six cows possessed good form and contour — hence the high quality of "Togo."

Chance or accidental mating of certain animals have produced excellent results in many instances. When Michael Carberry was living in the vicinity of Kiama, he possessed a very excellent bull; bred by Michael O'Gorman of Albion Park, sired by Volunteer. This bull was on exhibition in Kiama in 1877 and was very much admired. Jerry Daly of Wallaby Hill, Jamberoo had purchased heifers from O'Gorman, and got a bull from Carberry. From one of the O'Gorman cows he raised a young bull by the Carberry bull, which he gave to his neighbour, Mr. Chase, who in turn sold him to Thomas McCarthy, of Druwalla, Jamberoo, who mated him with an excellent cow, purchased from Samuel Risk of Kangaroo Valley. McCarthy sold the old bull to Charley Allen, and in time Stephen Major got possession of the younger bull, and sold him to Jas. W. Cole, who called him "Comet." "Comet" was not a show-bull. It was, however, from that strain of blood that that great show cow "Gold of Coleville" was produced.

Take another example—Edward Smith of Druwalla, Jamberoo, was a dairyman who kept closely to the Henry Fredericks and Dudgeon strains of dairy-cattle. From Edward Smith, C. W. Craig purchased a big lengthy, light roan bull called "Colonel." Smith leased a bull from Hugh Dudgeon by Soger Boy II., and out of "Gazelle." He was known as the Gazelle bull. From the Gazelle, Smith bred John Boyle's "Emperor," from that bull Dixon Cook, on the North Coast, produced some foundation cows.

These and other chance matings not having been carefully recorded at the proper time, decade after decade has left each generation that has followed on since then in a shadowy vale of doubt. The Cattle Associations that are now being perfected will, it is to be hoped, place these chance or accidental matings on record, so that that which was designated "mere chance" may prove the true lines to follow in order to obtain the best possible results.

The influence of the sire on his female progeny, and that of the dam on her male progeny has long since been freely admitted. It is, however, possible to learn too much either way.

There are numerous writers who have expressed their views on the system of selecting dams whilst but few have attempted to define the sires, although the indications of high production in a modified form or degree is to be seen in the sire—Thus a fine bone and deep body is essential in both sexes, together with a thin, flat, broad thigh. The pelvic bones and the prominent spine are necessary in both, as well as a full clear eye. The trouble is that even with these qualities combined in both sire and dam, the offspring may fail to be equal to their parents in general outline and conformity to type and quality from a productive point.

Unfortunately for the investigator or the enquirer after truth our past dairy-cattle records have been loosely kept, and, in some instances purposely faked, then again so few stud animals of either sex have been tested; fewer still have been mated on any seeming scientific basis. This in itself compels most of our writers on stock-breeding to fall back for guidance on the results obtained by the followers of race-horse breeding.

Right here we are at times confronted by a little doubtful pedigreeing. But on the whole we find that certain strains of blood hold good throughout the long list of racing records. It has been stated somewhere that the "Welkin link" in the chain of racing sires may be classed as the weakest link in the chain, and that it proved itself to be the strongest in certain animals.

Be this as it may, we all know that that which is often proved to be weak in theory comes out strongest in practice. This may be explained when we come to consider the many theories that float about among breeders of dairy cattle that pass in a nebulous form over the top-rail of a fence without further notice, no opportunity being available by which these theories could be put into practice. "Procrastination is the thief of time," and one is safe in saying that many brainy men have allowed their opportunities in life to drift away like smoke, to be caught up years later in another form. This may be applied to our racehorse breeders with as much force as to our dairy cattle breeders, and is the cause of many heated discussions with a view to prove whether our horses or cattle are better to-day than those of fifty or sixty years ago, without arriving at the needful result.

During those discussions it was frequently remarked that "most of the breeding went in at the mouth," which was then and is now in part true. But it took modern scientific research to put the whole case before our breeders, and this was not done until serious investigation began to analyse and investigate "Mendelism." Sir Francis Galton was the founder of modern eugenics, adopting a phrase, it is said, from the immortal Shakespeare. He affirmed in effect that every character and every attribute of every living being is the product of "Nature" and "Nurture." By "nature"

he meant all that comes under birth and the pre-natal stage of animal life, heredity, etc., and by "nurture" all that comes under nutrition, care, and training, and ·that both were equally necessary.

An important press writer has stated:—"A point that is sometimes discussed among breeders is whether absolute purity should be maintained in the breeding of stock, even when there are signs of wane of constitutional vigor. This question of the introduction of alien blood is one of the most important with which the expert is called upon to deal. In the improvement of races that sadly need replenishing he is a wise man who uses skilfully the best material at hand. The history of what we now know as pure stock-breeding is redolent of outside crosses, which have been skilfully blended with native blood, and there are very few types which have not borrowed some characteristics from those which nowadays we regard as entirely alien."

The Shorthorn, going back, as it does, over such a long period, has not been free from outside influence, and one can trace in most of the native races a blending of types which has resulted in the making of distinct characteristics. Breeders to-day have reached a higher point than ever Bakewell attained, just as dairymen claim to stand on a higher pedestal than did the dairymen of a previous generation. Yet the principles which Bakewell adopted have been commonly accepted as the best means of attaining the end breeders have in view. These principles, so far as we know, were the concentration of desired characteristics by means of line breeding and breeding in-and-in, which was later on carried too far by many of the shorthorn breeders, namely, Bates and Colling Bros.

Getting down to the theory based on the experiments of the "Abbot Mendel," we are informed by Professor Bateson that "the factors which the individual animal receives from his parents, and no others, are those which he can transmit to his offspring, and if any one factor was received from one parent only, not more than one-half of the offspring on the average will inherit it." This fact has only recently been recognised, even among prominent breeders. It is, therefore, as previously hinted in this article, that breeders have come to see that the dam matters as much as the sire. Hence the importance of breeding from the best.

This is a wholesome reminder to breeders of every class of stock, and may not, perhaps, overturn the old axiom that "the bull is half the herd," but it does emphasise the fact that the best bull that ever lived cannot raise all his produce to his own standard of merit. It is also well to remember that heredity can be expressed in terms of absence and presence alike. Some ingredients possessed by the ancestor are represented and some omitted, and heredity is established by either line of proof. But no case or illustration is established by simple rules.

Here we are confronted with the theory regarding the breeding of that mysterious animal —the general-purpose cow. Hoard's Dairymen of 1-9-16 says:—"One of the peculiarities of the advocates of dual-purpose cattle is that, while they may make a plausible argument and paint an alluring picture of the cow that will please the beef farmer as to form and the dairy farmer as to milk production, yet they always gasp for breath when called upon to submit the proof to critical experience. The dual-purpose delusion was preached for years before the special purpose cow had a single champion in America, yet in all this time the picture of the successful dual-purpose cow has not been visualized on American farms. Her advocates, while gasping for breath, shout 'Bates,' 'England,' 'Across the pond.' After these many years of advocacy of dual-purpose cattle and the trials made in America, they must still rely on Great Britain for proof, if proof it can be called. They cannot point to a single State or community where a successful attempt has been made to realise a dual-purpose ideal." (The same condition of things has prevailed against odds in Australia for upwards of seventy-five years.)

Again Hoard's Dairymen:—"If there is one State that has suffered more than any other from the dual-purpose propaganda that State is Minnesota. Men of strong minds and firm purpose have taught dual-purpose in that State for many years. These men have had the support of still other men who were able to spend large sums of money in trying to prove out the theory. They have sent men up and down the State to argue and convince her people, and how expensive this teaching has been to the farmers of Minnesota and how meagre and unsubstantial have been the results, he who runs may read.

Many communities that owe their prosperity to the special-purpose dairy cow can be found in every State of the Union, and we will be able to say in every county in every State. When will the dual-purpose enthusiasts meet the issue and locate American communities that are prosperous because of dual-purpose cattle? They never have, they do not now, and they never will. It simply can't be done." And so say all of us!

The bull, after all, must be looked at "broadside on"—depth of body, length of the sheath, prominent spine, depth and fineness of flank; above all, look for space between the hook bone and the rib. Without space there the rib cannot grow down and out to give room for the dairy quality that is to be looked for in his female progeny. Beef bulls do not carry this quality, as it tends to increase the offal or waste flesh not desired by the butcher.

The Effect of Feed on a Dairy Cow.

It has been long asserted, and still believed by many dairymen, that a great tendency to feeding is incompatible with a great tendency to milking. While trying to solve this hackneyed assertion, an eminent writer has stated that "the tendency and effect are two very different things," giving as his opinion that the tendency may exist when its effects are wholly or partly destroyed by some counteracting cause, and that if the effects of such counteracting can be removed the other cause may be wholly productive. If it be assumed that a cow, while giving a great quantity of milk, cannot keep herself in good condition, because so great a portion of the food consumed being converted into milk rich in solids the carcase could not be properly supported, it would yet be a rash conclusion to infer from hence that the same animal could not have a great tendency to get fat, and that when dried off cannot keep herself in good condition, and soon produce in corresponding effect, for the effect of the milking tendency having then ceased the other cause, namely, the tendency to fatten, would remain unopposed, provided the same food conditions remained. In theory this may work out nicely, but cattle bred for dairy purposes should not have a great tendency to fatten, as the fat will quickly work itself into the udder, and all the tissues will be affected by it to such an extent that there will be no room left in the udder for the manufacture and storage of any great quantity of milk. It will be carried on to the offspring. And it will soon be observed that the near future generations will be lacking in back udder formation. Some argue from another standpoint, which is very natural, but those who have watched cattle developing must have noticed the good and bad effect that food has on cattle bred for any given purpose.

There is in almost any breed of animals that are raised domestically certain strains of blood which, when closely followed, give that particular strain a title, which we call a family. And it is quite noticeable throughout the history of dairying in Illawarra that the most successful of our breeders to-day can sit down and trace out within a defined circle how they have bred in and out for years without losing sight of the first point of that circle.

Mr. Daniel Boyd, of Broughton Vale, Illawarra, was a dairy farmer whose conservative judgment made his name a name and fame memorable without any desire on his part to be considered notable. The writer visited his farm in 1892, at a time when his herd was considered to be on the wane. He had, however, at that time many very valuable dairy animals —animals that would command attention in any show ring at the present time. They were nearly all blood reds, with the exception of a few spotted red and white and roan cows. The herd might be termed all reds. The type throughout was uniform, but speaking generally they were too high on their legs, caused possibly by too close breeding. He remarked to me that he would have gone outside his own herd for bulls had his neighbours bulls of equal quality to his own. It was plain that he had seen no cattle so pleasing to his eye as his own.

In a conversation with William H. Morrow about the Boyd cattle he said: "I am certain that when the Boyds came to James Robinson's farm at Broughton Vale they brought no roan nor red and white cattle with them. That was in 1871. They had a beautiful red bull and a small herd of female cattle of all ages. A few years afterwards the herd had increased considerably, and there wasn't then three per cent. of broken colored cattle in the whole herd, and as for dairy quality, no better herd could be found in N.S.W. Later on," said Mr. Morrow, "Dan Boyd purchased a few head of cattle, but in quality these animals were very common looking when placed side by side with the reds."

It must be borne in mind that William H. Morrow was a neighbour of the Boyds at Broughton Vale, only a fence between the farms, and that he (Mr. Morrow) is a keen cattle judge, a breeder of high-class dairy cattle, and, above all, a thoroughly reliable authority. He always says what he thinks, and has a happy knack of expressing what he thinks in a clear, concise way, so that there is no possible chance left for misunderstandings.

It would appear that when the British Agricultural Commissioners visited N. S. Wales, some years before Dan Boyd's death, they were taken to see Boyd's dairy herd. They were so pleased with what they saw that they advised Dan Boyd to "continue on the lines he had been following," which may be either termed in-breeding or in-and-in-breeding. Doubtless, Ben Jones and the other British Commissioners were imbued with the spirit of the old time notions, which were then at least a century old, namely, "that races of domestic animals reproduce themselves with great uniformity if inbred, but that the moment one mixed up two different races or breeds, one did something that caused an epidemic of variation," quite forgetting that in practice variations occur so frequently in in-bred races of domestic animals that it is difficult to keep up the standard in many cases without having to resort to continuous culling. Similarity of offspring to their parents may be very marked in dairy cattle, and may extend to all the characters of the race, yet variability appears to be a property peculiar to all animals under domestication. The characters, however, which go to make up a breed or family of dairy cattle are not all of the same kind; some of them are inborn, and will develop under normal conditions of nourishment, naturally others require various kinds of stimuli to produce them. Take as an example the udder of a high-class dairy cow. It may appear to be inborn, and to a certain extent it is so, but it requires great care to keep up to the standard required by our dairymen, and it is done by careful mating and feeding. Consequently we cannot call all its great characters inborn.

"Much obscurity has been due," says Thompson, "to false antithesis between heredity and variation. When we say that 'like begets like,' that offspring tend to resemble their parents and ancestors, we are stating a fact of life. But when we speak of an opposition, such as a tendency to variability which makes offspring different from their parents, we are indulging in verbiage." It has been often demonstrated in dairy cattle breeding that a slight structural peculiarity, such as a nick in both ears at the extreme tips, may persist for several generations. Modifications of bodily structure or habit may also be acquired. They are distinguished from temporary adjustments or accommodations on the one hand and from inborn variations on the other. Change of food and climatic conditions become quickly visible when young heifers are removed from one climate to another, or when food conditions are altered from rich to poor. Nothing more certain than the change in type and of character of cattle.

If an enquirer in search of historical facts, as we understand facts, were to depend on much that has been written about the state of agriculture and stock raising in Great Britain and Ireland one hundred and fifty years ago, his research would not benefit him very much, as the people had not settled upon any fixed ideas about breeding methods, and as a result we find from reports on the animals of the farms that little or no progress was made by way of forming breeding associations on defined lines. In truth, it is doubtful if there existed any defined lines.

It is correct enough to state that one hundred and fifty years ago the pioneers of New South Wales were either unborn or mere school children—many of them unfortunately never saw the inside of a school. Yet it was under such conditions that Captain Phillip founded the first settlement in Australia, on the shores of Port Jackson, A.D. 1788, with a mixed crowd of human beings. He, or the authorities, neglected to send out cattle with the fleet for the development of the settlement, so he called at the Cape of Good Hope and took on board a number of zebu cattle, which were naturally adapted to suit pioneering work.

Later on ships' captains speculated in cattle, horses, sheep, pigs and goats, and many animals were added to the live stock of the settlement in this way. The "zebu" thrived apace, and in the thirties and early forties of last century traces of them were to be found in every settlement in New South Wales.

If we take our lead from the twenties and thirties of last century we will find that mixed types of cattle from every county in Great Britain and Ireland were to be found in the possession of the pioneer settlers. The question then arises—Was that admixture of blood ever eliminated? Neither history nor science could answer in the affirmative, as each animal had necessarily two parents, four grandparents, eight great-grandparents, and sixteen great-great-grandparents, and so on ad infinitum. Breeding influence may control the zebu blood, but, as will be shown elsewhere in this work,

it may be held by careful mating, but always remains as a latent character in the cells.

The actual value that can be placed on arguments relating to dairy cattle breeding must be based on the capacity of the human brain to convey or receive truths. It is very doubtful if one person can convince another of a great and scientific truth by mere words. It is a combination of circumstances which invariably lead men to form an established conviction, which may be claimed to be a relative conception of truth. Our individual experiences are no proof to anybody but ourselves, unless it is persons who have met with similar experiences, and unfortunately such persons are not numerous.

It matters not how sincere an exponent of a new idea in cattle breeding may be, still we have to recognise the fact that no one can be convinced regarding this or that system if they do not earnestly desire to know. The desire to know is the first and most important factor in all questions of research. It is very easy for some men to say "I believe you!" But to know requires an effort, nay, many efforts. Too many trust to past experience, and will not entertain new ideas. They forget that every effort to gain fresh knowledge sensitises the brain, and the moment one's mind is sufficiently sensitised it receives its impression. This rule applies to every line of thought. Some brains are, however, more easily sensitised than others, yet there is a cause for every effect.

In basing my argument on the difficulty of educating people up to any given standard, it is not intended as a slight on their intelligence. This fact is not difficult to explain, when we reflect on those people with only moderate intelligence who have bred many excellent cattle, while others with excellent mentality cannot or have not been able to master the first rudiments of the art. The difference is this: One takes in the whole situation and plods on with the good and the bad combined; the other takes the case bit by bit and rejects it item by item, waiting until a single absolutely conclusive idea turns up, which never does turn up. It is right here that Mendelism can be of great value to breeders of every description of stock, provided that the farms were properly fenced, and that proper pedigrees were then kept of all the breeding animals.

CATTLE SALES.

As all writers are supposed to have an object in view when placing reading matter before their readers, it is but right to state that in this instance a section of this work has been set apart for a review of important auction sales, as being a guide to readers, from which they can draw their own conclusions. Unfortunately auctioneers had to make sales, and in order to do so had often to find buyers and give long terms of credit in many instances—hence animals were often sold and re-sold many times. When a bull got a name, that bull sired in some instances more bulls than the number of cows in his owner's herd!

In 1804 Governor King established his dairy farms—one was situated near Parramatta, and the other at South Creek. His stock brand was K. In the same year Lieutenant Kent left Sydney on a tour of inspection in the Illawarra and Shoalhaven districts. In those days Madagascar cattle were being highly praised owing to their cheapness compared with other breeds. They could then be purchased on the island at £2 per head at six months old, and that Madagascar having a similar soil and climate to New South Wales, they would prosper here. At least this was Lieutenant Brerton's opinion. On 3rd March, 1805, Lieutenant Kent, of H.M.S. Buffalo, is reported to have returned from his tour of the Coast. August 30th, 1807, two cows were shipped from Sydney to Dr. Charles Throsby, at Newcastle. This brings us to the Bligh rebellion, and all the trouble of those who assisted in bringing about his arrest, and subsequent enquiries.

Captain William Cox, Paymaster of the old New South Wales Corps, owned two properties —one at Canterbury, and one at Prospect—together with stock in 1803. Mr. Robert Campbell—"Big Campbell of the Wharf"—sold these farms and a mare and foal, and most of the cattle by auction at Parramatta. The mare and foal brought £380, and the cows averaged £50 each. 1 English bull of the "Hampshire breed," 4 cows, 3 heifers and 1 calf were reserved from sale. These were sold by Mr. Simeon Lord, in 1805.

In the year 1805 Mr. Simeon Lord, Auctioneer, sold out Captain William Cox. The Cox property at that time consisted of fourteen grants of land, comprising in all 775 acres, one Hampshire bull, aged 3 years and 3 months, and 9 bullocks in harness.

Captain William Kent, R.N., suffered severely under the regime of Governor Bligh. He brought from England in H.M.S. Buffalo, 77 head of cattle, 2 horses and 4 mares of the Persian breed. He could lay claim to be one of the earliest importers of merino sheep. Bligh, however, was displeased with him. Kent suffered and died about 1815, when the trustees of his estate sold 60 head of horned cattle (Devon and Alderney crosses) and 300 pure merino sheep.

Cattle sales followed: John Macarthur's cattle, together with a number of fine cows and bulls of the English breed were sold at Parramatta, February 19th, 1809. Dr. Charles Throsby was dead and a practical man was required to take charge of his dairy herd at Parramatta. Captain Antill and Thomas Moore were interested in the sale of the late Andrew Thompson's farm, known as Killarney, on Bardo-Nerung River; Gaudry, of Windsor, was the auctioneer, date of sale, 27th December, 1810. A red cow with hooped horns down to the nose was being advertised for. Thomas Laycock was dead, and his Ayrshire herd was being sold by his executors. The colours of these animals were red and white, flecked. Mr. Bevan, auctioneer, was selling for Mr. Bayley: "Primrose," a full-blooded English cow, 4 years old, with female calf at foot, by Mr. Blaxland's bull, the dam of this cow was imported by Col. Foveaux; "Jenny," a full bred cow, 4 years old, dam "Scott," imported by Captain Scott, in H.M.S. Porpoise, with a female calf at her side of Mr. Blaxland's bull "Raspberry"; a full-blooded cow, 4 years old, dam "Old Daisy," with a female calf at foot by Mr. Blaxland's bull, she had been purchased from Mr. Holt; "Magpie," a granddaughter of the famous "Magpie," by Mr. Connolly's English bull, with a male calf at foot by Mr. Blaxland's bull, "Cherry Longsides"; and a polled cow bred by Mr. Macarthur—a good milker, of great size, and in calf to a thoroughbred bull of Mr. Badgery; 1 2-year-old bull, thoroughbred, from the stock of Captain Kent, a yearling bull out of "Old Daisy," by Mr. Blaxland's bull. Mr. Blaxland's farm was at Prospect, and the date of this sale was 20th December, 1813. Mr. Charles Throsby was agent for Mr. John Jamieson, who had been on a trip to England.

Mr. Bevan was selling on behalf of Captain Richard Brooks, 1400 head of cattle at his Cattle Market, Haymarket, Brickfield Hill, Sydney, 30th March, 1815. In 1815 Captain Kent was dead, and in July of that year, Messrs Oakes and Rouse, auctioneers were selling his stock consisting of 300 sheep and 60 head of pure English bred cattle. Robert Jenkins, auctioneer, selling on 19th January, 1815, a yellow Cape bull, with short horns; also a brindle bull with white breast and back of the buffalo breed. September, 1817, Mr. David Johnston had lost a valuable red and white bull, bred entirely from the stock of Governor William Bligh, the age of the animal being given as 14 months. The first article on cow-testing appears in the Sydney Gazette, June 14th, 1817, by a Mr. Anderson, who suggested that each cow should be tested once a month. At a cattle sale on account of the stock committee of the New South Wales Agricultural Society, one heifer to J. T. Campbell at £25, one heifer to J. T. Campbell at £41, one heifer to J. T. Campbell at £53, one heifer to John Dixon at £36, one heifer to J. T. Campbell at £63, one heifer to John Dixon at £48, one heifer to De Arcy Wentworth at £51, one heifer to Sir John Jamieson at 50 guineas, one bull to Sir John Jamieson at £85, one bull to John Dixon at £107. Date of sale, January, 1825. The ship "Brothers" arrived with cattle for the Australian Agricultural Coy. The ship "Greenock" also arrived with four 4-years-old cows and two 2-years old bulls of the pure Ayrshire breed, also four yearling heifers and two yearling bulls of the pure Ayrshire breed, January, 1824. These Ayrshires were the animals that found a home on John Wyllie's Dunlop Vale Estate, Illawarra, which Mr. John Brown described so often, and whose descendents laid the foundation of Berry's Ayrshire herd at Coolangatta. Importation of brown and brindle cows and bulls, August, 1826, by Mr. De Arcy Wentworth. These were the cattle that Mr. James McGill used to dilate on at the Illawarra A. and H. Society show dinners. Sale of stock per ship "William Shand"—a red Devon, and a piebald Durham to J. T. Campbell, a red Devon to J. T. Campbell, a red Devon to John Dixon, a Devon heifer to J. T. Campbell, a Durham cow to Sir John Jamieson, a Devon bull to John Dixon, date of sale January herd at Parramatta for £1200, consisting of 300 head.

During 1827, 15,000 cows passed from the Hunter River Valley to Liverpool Plains. The Moreton Bay settlement was buying cattle for Queensland. May 1827.—Camden cattle, including Macarthur's, were being offered at from £6 to £12 per head; Illawarra cattle were offered at 4 guineas per head. Surgeon De Arcy Wentworth was dead in 1827, and Mr. Richard Jones bought 1400 head of his Cattle. His Executors offered 1200 heifers in the Estate at £10 per head. Five years' credit was given to bona fide land owners. In 1829 horned cattle in New South Wales dropped to £2 per head. On 1st October, 1829, Mr. Peter Macqueen, of the Segenhoe Estate, Singleton, had for sale at Parramatta eight young Durham bulls. Cattle still continued to drop in value, and during August, 1834, they were selling in the Sydney Markets at from £1 10s. to £5 per head. A serious drought was the cause, yet in Illawarra in 1834 a Gazette report shows that a splendid season prevailed. Cattle were milking well, and the dairies presented a busy appearance—cows giving an abundance of milk. John Terry Hughes bought 50 milking cows from Aspinall and Brown, in Sydney, £10 15s. per head, in 1834; Mr. J. Moore of Baw Baw, Goulburn, selling out 500 dairy cattle of the Durham, Devon and Alderney breed—date of sale, September, 1833. On October 1st, 1833, after the exhibition at Parramatta, two pure Durham bulls for sale. In 1834, John Dixon sold to Alexander Berry 600 head of milk and dairy cows improved from crosses with his Devon stock, 50 red Devon heifers, 20 pure bred Devon bulls. January, 1837, 15 head of high class cows for sale in Sydney, in calf to a bull bred by Mr. Henry Dangar of Neotsfield, Singleton. At Jervis Bay, 250 head of Cattle including 70 dairy cows, bred by William Cox, of Parramatta.

"Sydney Herald" of September, 1831, states: G. T. Palmer offers for sale a considerable quantity of dairy cows, crosses of the best imported Alderney, Lancashire, Suffolk, Devon and Shorthorn herds, during the last 21 years, and may be seen in the Argyle district. Samuel Lyons was selling on same date on behalf of Governor Darling 84 head of milking cows from imported English bred cows and bulls, also 3 Durham bulls.

In September, 1831, 700 head of cattle were to be sold by auction at Shancanmore, the Estate of John Terry Hughes, comprising Ayrshire cows, bulls, heifers and oxen.

About this date the "Sydney Herald" stated that Sir John Sinclair, President of the Agricultural Society of England had said: "The Ayrshire cattle for the dairy is the superior breed—that opinion prevails." The Sydney market was glutted with inferior cattle, 800 head sold in October 1831, at 30/- per head. The ships "Lang" and "Mansfield" arrived in Sydney with valuable live stock for the Imlay Bros., in August, 1832. Cooper and Levy had slaughtered 3,820 head of cattle in Sydney from April to June, 1832.

An important sale of pure Durham bulls in Sydney, bred by Mr. Thomas Potter Macqueen, of Segenhoe, Singleton, on January 15th, 1837: Lot 1, Bravo; Lot 2, Baron; Lot 3, Musleman; Lot 4, Tancard, Lot 5, Mameluke; Lot 6, Meteor; Lot 7, Star; Lot 8, Friar Jack; Lot 9, Ranger; Lot 10, Casper; Lot 11, Rosey Beau; Lot 12, Comet. Comet was represented as the best bull in Australia. his sire cost 1000 guineas in England. At Parramatta, 100 head of dairy cattle, selected from the well-known herd of Mr. George Macleay, the cows were in calf to a Durham bull. Mr. Richard Jones' Cattle at Maitland for sale during May 1837, 550 head of breeding and milking cows and heifers. 12 superior pure bred Durham bulls, including the celebrated imported bull "Roger," a number of cows in calf to Mr. Icely's bull.

Francis O'Brien of Illawarra had for sale a small herd of 30 well-bred dairy cows, by private contract. October, 1837. For sale, October, 1837, 700 head of cattle belonging to the Estate of the late Captain Eber Bunker, at Collingwood. 200 head of Durham milkers in connection with the Toryburn Estate. John Tooth had for sale 674 head of cows, heifers and bulls of the pure Durham breed, also 588 head of cows, heifers, and bulls of the pure Durham and Aryshire breeds mixed, Nov., 1837. Sale of cattle at Ireland's on Parramatta Road, 800 cows and heifers, the majority of which are of the Durham breed. Sale of 11 young Devon bulls at the bazaar, Sydney, Abraham Polack, auctioneer; also on behalf of Mr. T. U. Ryder, 4 pure Durham bulls and 3 heifers. These animals were landed from the ship "Juliet," December, 1837, bearing the highest pedigrees. The bull and one heifer went to Mr. Lawson, for £45, a heifer in calf to Mr. Lawson for £170; heifer to Mr. Lawson, for £125; a cow to Mr. Lawson at £65 Mr. Armstrong, U.S., imported per ship "Achilles," two Durham bulls, one 22 months old and the other 20 months old, both of deep, rich red colour. Mr. Armstrong had a bazaar and a

veterinary hospital in Sydney, and a run for horses and cattle in Illawarra. At Mr. Hart's yards, Sydney, 6 very superior Durham cows, warranted in calf to an imported bull, September, 1839. Mr. J. J. Moore, selling at Baw Baw, Goulburn on 12th September, 1839, 250 cows, 250 heifers, 3 well-bred bulls. They are of the noted Ayrshire, Devon and Durham breeds, very much improved and noted as the most desirable for graziers and breeders of horned cattle.

Sale of dairy cattle at the Segenhoe Estate, Singleton, on January 20th, 1838: 20 cows to James Boman at £21 each; 20 cows to W. McLean at £16 10s. each; 20 cows to A. Fotherinham, £15 10s. each; 20 cows to James Barker, £14 10s. each; 20 cows to A. Fotheringham, £11 each; 20 cows to D. Chambers, £12 each; 20 cows to John Johnston, at £10 10s. each; 20 cows to A. Fotheringham, at £9 10s. each; 20 cows to D. Chambers, £8 10s. each; 20 cows to A. Fotheringham, £8 each; 15 cows to E. Turner, £7 10s. each; 15 cows to E. Turner, £8 each; 15 cows to George Ruat, £7 each, 15 cows to A. Foss, £7 each; 1 cow to George Porter, £15; 15 cows to George Nail, at £6 each; 15 cows to C. Haley, at £6 each; 15 cows to J. Wheeler, £6 each, 15 cows to H. Keek at £5 each; 15 cows to S. A. Bryant, at £4 10s. each; 10 cows to W Shepman, £5 5s. each, 40 cows to James Hale at £4 each; 1 bull calf to John Smith, at £39.

The bull sales at the Segenhoe Estate, Singleton, January 20th, 1838.

The residue of the Segenhoe stock of Durhams improved under the management of Messrs McIntyre and Scomfill, 60 head of delightful milk cows, 130 heifers and 2 bulls. Three head of horned cattle were landed in Sydney in the quarter ending 10th October, 1838, and were valued at £400. Sale of cattle at Underwood's: 1 bull, £67; 1 yearling bull, £21; 1 cow and calf, £67 10s.; 1 Ayrshire cow, £27 10s.; 7 cows, £53 15s.; 11 head of yearlings, £60 10s., sent from Tasmania. Mr. Dawson, of the Reddall Estate, Illawarra, advertised for a cow with blue sides, white belly, back and face. Alexander Berry was the sole executor in the estate of John Dixon, of Dixon's Estate, Nonorrah, and 800 head of Cattle at Camden. Tradition points to Dixon's cattle having been purchased by Alexander Berry, and sent to his Coolangatta Estate, Shoalhaven. This is certain, the type of cattle owned by John Dixon were later plentiful in the Shoalhaven district in after years.

Mr. William Howe, of Glenlee, Campbelltown, purchased at the Segenhoe Estate, near Single-

HENRY SPINKS, Culwalla, Jamberoo, Illawarra.

DAPHNE 2nd OF CULWALLA.
(No. 1726, I.D.C.H.B.)

MABEL OF CULWALLA.

HENRY McGRATH, Greenhills, Nowra, Shoalhaven.

ton, sale on January 20th, 1838, the Shorthorn bull, "Jupiter," for £85. This bull was then 4 years old, and was one of the chief stud bulls owned at the time by Mr. Potter Macqueen. We can note in April, 1841, that Samuel Lyons had for sale in Sydney the celebrated pure Durham bull "Jupiter," bred by Mr. Potter Macqueen, of Segenhoe, Singleton. His sire was "Comet," and his dam was "Durham Nancy." His age was given at 7 years; and if fat would weigh 2000 lbs. Also 4 bulls by Jupiter out of Glenlee cows that have been judiciously crossed by imported bulls for the last twenty years.

A. Polack, at his bazaar, Sydney, January, 1838, 13 Durham and Devon bulls, all pure-bred; also 5 pure Devon bulls and one Durham cow, landed per ship "Spartan." John Tooth, auctioneer, selling 1000 head of cattle at the Cow-pastures, Camden, and 1000 head of cattle on behalf of Mr. Thomas U. Ryder, all Shorthorns, at Belltrees, Hunter River. Abram Polack sold at his yards, Sydney, March 1838: 20 cows to Edward Browne at £320; 20 cows to Edward Brown at £270; 20 cows to Edward Trimnar at £230; 20 cows to G. F. Fenwick, at £210; 20 cows to T. Holmes at £210; 40 cows to T. Holmes at £320; 20 cows to Dr. Thompson at £150; 20 cows to T. Holmes at £150; 25 heifers to George Ruat at £237 10s.; 25 heifers to Edward Brown at £200; 120 heifers to Thomas Holmes at £560. These cattle comprised Mr. Thomas U. Ryder's stud herd. Abram Polack sold at his bazaar, Sydney, 10 very superior bred bulls, including 2 pure Durhams, and 2 pure Devons. At the sale of Sir Richard Bourke's cattle, cows averaged £12 per head, and heifers £8 per head. They were the Rev. Samuel Marsden's breed. Red Polled Norfolks. Mr. Richard Jones had for sale in June, 1829, in the estate of the late Mr. W. E Riley, 20 pure Devon cows, 3 cross-bred bulls, 6 heifers, 6 female calves, 6 male calves, one Indian cow and calf, running at Raby. The imported bulls and heifers per the Ship "Mellish." arrived in Sydney and were on view at Quinn's stables in York Street. They were of the Durham breed, from the stock of one of the finest breeders in England, Mr. Jackson, of Berwick Hall, and were imported by Mr. John Brown, of Pemberton Grange. Mr. Armstrong, V.S., had for sale at his bazaar, Sydney, December, 1829, 5 Durham bulls, 3 Hereford bulls, a pure Ayrshire bull and cow. The Durham bulls were by Mr. George Hobblen's imported bull "Jupiter," purchased at the Segenhoe Estate sale. The Hereford bulls were wrecked in the ship "Dun-

lop," off the Cape of Good Hope. The Duke of Bradford had paid £100 for the service of the sire for one season. The Ayshire bull and cow were imported by Mr. A. Paterson, of Maitland. Sale of cattle belonging to Mr. Thomas Icely and Coy.: 400 dairy cows, in calf and calving, 200 heifers by imported Durham, Devon, and Ayrshire bulls on November 1839. Mr. Icely's stock were famous for the dairy. The Australian Auction Company was formed in December, 1839, and had for sale on behalf of Mr A. B. Spark, 80 cows with calves at foot, 40 2-year-old heifers, 30 heifers 1 year old, 3 very fine bulls. These cattle were in charge of Mr. Thomas Wilson, of Wollongong, Illawarra. Alexander Berry had 1437 head of mixed cattle for sale, of the Durham and Devon breeds, on behalf of the estate of the late John Dixon.

T. W. Smart, auctioneer, had sold the Oldbury herd, 79 cows, 20 heifers, 11 bulls, on 1st October, 1838. The Oldbury Estate was near Sutton Forest, and owned by the late Mr. John Atkinson. Abram Polack sold at his bazaar, Sydney, 25 heifers of the pure Durham and Suffolk breeds, heavy in calf, on October, 1829. Samuel Lyons, auctioneer, selling 500 cows and heifers of the Durham, Devon and Hereford breeds on December, 1839. The Australia Auction Coy. had a capital of £240,000. Shares were £12 each, and the Company was formed by the leading business men and settlers in the Colony. It had for sale, 14th August, 1839, a very superior herd of dairy cows running at Colyer's, Leigh, Bong Bong, comprising 80 cows and 1 superior bull by Dr. Reid's Durham bull, and for sale at the Auction Mart, Sydney, 6 Durham cows, with calves at foot bred by Mr. Macarthur, of Camden, for the dairy. Sale of cattle belonging to the Estate of the late Mr. J. M. Blaxland, September, 1840, consisting of 49 cows and heifers, and 1 imported Durham bull. A Mr Dodds was appointed agent for the Australian Auction Coy. at Maitland.

In September 1840, the Australian Auction Coy. imported, per ship "Mary Ann": "Daisy," a pure-bred Durham cow, calved April, 1835, got by "Scription" out of "Red Daisy"; "Young Albert," her calf, by "Prince Albert," calved 1840; "Mary Ann," a pure-bred Devon cow, with a bull calf at her side, calved August 1840; "Lady Clark," a superior large framed Devon. These cattle were specially selected. A Dodds, agent for the Australian Auction Coy., selling for Mr. Thomas Potter Macqueen, of the Segenhoe Estate, 71 cows of the Durham breed, 60 3-year-old heifers, pure Durhams, 11 2-year-old

Durham bulls, 13 2-year-old heifers, 10 Durham bull calves, 1 bull, 5 years old, 1 bull, 3 years old, 3 1-year-old bulls, 300 very superior cows of the Durham breed in calf to imported Durham bulls and with calves at their side, and 12 superior Durham bulls, in September, 1840. Note—When the compiler of the foregoing notes visited Segenhoe in 1892, there was but little left of the once greatest cattle breeding Estate in New South Wales. If ever the history of Segenhoe is written it will form tragic reading, of which traces could be found then (1892), otherwise the whole settlement wore a neglected appearance. Mr. J. J. Forrester, of Drayton, "St. Patrick's Plains," Singleton, had lost in 1840 from his station, 20 young bulls from 1 to 2 years old of the Devon and Durham breed, missing from 1st January, 1840. The Australian Auction Coy. was selling for Mr. George Macleay of the Cowpastures, 100 dairy cows of an improved breed.

In 1840 John Terry Hughes purchased two pure-bred bulls, 17 and 18 months old respectively, for his estate, Shankamore, near Bringilly, at £420, and in the same year, through the same agency—namely, the Australian Auction Company—Mr. Henry Osborne purchased three very superior bulls, one being described as being by "Knight's old grey bull," one by "Young Favorite," and the third by "Phoenix" (no better blood, it was said, could be found in England) in March, 1840; price paid, £700. Mr. Osborne later on purchased two more bulls—one a roan, the other a red and white, 12 and 15 months old—of the Yorkshire breed. All these animals played an important part among the dairy herds of Illawarra. Some of these animals were probably bred by Hon. Potter Macqueen, Segenhoe, near Singleton, as the Australian Auction Company was his agent. On the other hand, however, it is certain that two Durham cows purchased by Mr. Henry Osborne, of Marshall Mount, Illawarra, were imported direct from England, and sold by Mr. Samuel Lyons from the ship "Earl Grey," and the two Yorkshire bulls mentioned above were landed from the ship "Hope," and also sold by Mr. Samuel Lyons.

The Australian Auction Company had for sale at Maitland, on behalf of Richard Jones, Esq., M.C., 20 young bulls of the Devon and Durham breed, November, 1840. Samuel Lyons had for sale, November, 1840, 500 cows, 270 heifers and 6 bulls. These cattle are of the Ayrshire, Durham, Devon, and Sussex breed, and are remarkable for their dairy quality.

In February, 1840, two pure Durham bulls were landed, per ship "Florentia," from the herd of Mr. Smith, of Primrose Hill, England, and one pure Durham bull, fashionably bred, from the same herd, 21 months old. The A.A. Company, of Port Stephens, sold 26 pure bred Durham cows and six three-quarter Ayrshire-Durham cows, at an average of £40 per head. Note.—It is well to understand that there was a marked distinction between the Australian Auction Company and the A.A. Company; one was merely an agency, the other was pastoral. It was the Australian Auction Company that imported the pure Shorthorn bull (colour white) named "Ella," from Tasmania, for Mr. Alexander Berry, of Coolangatta, in the "Australian Packet." Mr. Thomas Icely had for sale at Stubb auction mart, George-street, Sydney, April, 1840, 50 head of thoroughbred Durham cows, in lots of five each, the whole in calf; two pure-bred Durham bulls, "Comet" and "Christmas." De Loitt & Company had for sale in Sydney, February, 1840, an imported cow of the Durham breed, per ship "Florentia." The Australian Auction Company, in March, 1840, at Maitland, six young Durham bulls and 25 Durham cows in calf to a choice bull, on behalf of Mr. P. P. King, manager of the A.A. Company, Stroud; also 20 good milk cows of the Durham breed, two excellent Durham bulls, and one superior Durham bull bred by Doctor Boman. Samuel Lyons had for sale at his auction mart, Sydney, two thoroughbred Yorkshire-Durham bulls, just landed ex ship "Hope"; one Durham bull calf, and two very superior Durham cows, just arrived per ship "Earl Grey," from England; one very fine English cow, imported per ship "Bengal." The result of this sale was as follows:—One Durham cow to Thomas Walker, £75; one Durham cow, with calf at foot, to Thomas Walker, at £94; two thoroughbred red and white Yorkshire bulls, 17 and 18 months old, to Mr. John Terry Hughes, at £420. Mr. Thomas Walker was a member of the Twofold Bay Company, and Mr. John Terry Hughes owned Albion Park, Illawarra. It was also through the Australian Auction Company that Mr. Henry Osborne, of Marshall Mount, Illawarra, imported his cattle in 1843. The Australian Auction Company had for sale, at mart, Sydney, three very superior Durham bulls—one by Knight's old grey bull, one by "Young Favourite," and one by "Phoenix"—no better blood in England, March, 1840; also, per ship "Competitor," three pure Hereford bulls and four pure Durham bulls. The four pure Durham bulls sold for £600, while two colonial bred bulls sold for £10; two red and white bulls, pure Yorkshire strain, 12 and 15 months old, sold at £210; name of purchaser not given. The Australian Auction Company had for sale, at mart, Sydney, four Durham bulls by imported Durham bulls out of Segenhoe-bred cows, March, 1840. Richard Jones, Esq., M.C., had for sale at his Fleurs Estate, South Creek, a number of superior young bulls of an improved breed for the dairy.

This brings us at once into touch with Mr. David Williamson Irving, of Newton, Illawarra. who was a son-in-law of Mr. William Howe, of Glenlee, who commenced dairying in Illawarra in 1840 with Glenlee bred cattle. The Glenlee cattle had a mixture of the Sussex blood in them. The Sussex is described as being harder to the feel of the hand than the Devon; deeper in colour than even that of the North Devon; they are described as "cherry red," and tip-top milkers. A Gazette notice states: "Mr. Bevin, auctioneer. In the insolvent estate of John Robertson, land and stock at Jerry's Plains; 5 Durham bulls, half-share in a bull, 300 cows; date of sale, 6th May, 1843."

The "Sydney Morning Herald" for 1841 contains such a long list of cattle sales that it is impossible to deal adequately with them in this volume. In passing let us be satisfied with just one, dated 22nd May, 1841: For sale at Oatley's stables (per ship "Mary"), a young bull and heifer of the Shorthorn-Durham breed, pure white in colour, bred by Mr. Henry Barry. The heifer had won the Liverpool (Eng.) Society's medal for 1839. The bull, whose name was "Wellington," sired by "Malibran," calved 27th November, 1839, was descended from the celebrated bull "Comet." "Camelia," the heifer, calved 7th June, 1839. Messrs. Aspinall and Brown were the agents.

Sufficient has been shown in these cattle sale reports taken from the records, and are authentic so far as such records go, that from the earliest times New South Wales received hundreds of valuable animals from the countries of the old world, and that breeders everywhere aimed at breeding cattle to suit their surroundings. They also show us that no one all along those decades from 1800 to 1840 had by any means a monopoly of the wisdom or wealth of cattle. True, some prospered, while others lost. But following on the years, the time was ripe in 1840 for the coming of the emigrant settler, and they came in hundreds, and New South Wales benefited thereby. It was old Illawarra,

however, that led the way from 1840 onward in dairying. It is not by any means an easy task to follow the movement of the early settler and their cattle, as cattle were being constantly sent away in droves to the south as far as the River Murray, and north to the Queensland border. And cattle were returned from those far away places to the western district of New South Wales, where the South Coast settlers had large holdings. The truth is—it is remarkable how we have been able to trace as much of our cattle transactions as we have done. owing to the destruction of the old homesteads, which contained many valuable papers and documents that would have connected the past with the present generation.

Samuel Lyons has for sale, at his bazaar, Sydney, six Durham heifers (sire "Alexander"); one roan bull, whose sire is "Elrington," imported by Mr. Carr in the ship "Alexander" in 1840; a brown filly by Charles Roberts' "Colonel," dam "Medora" by "Whisker," grand-dam by "Model," g.g. dam by "Sheik"; date of sale, 9th May, 1843.

William Boman and William Dawes had a dairy farm for lease, called Bishopgate, opposite Cooper's distillery, in Parramatta-street, Sydney, May, 1843.

Major Wentworth arrived in Sydney from London in the ship "Brackenmoor," May, 1843. He was interested in a consignment of cattle.

On 3rd May, 1843, in the insolvent estate of Mr. John Robertson, land and stock at Jerry's Plains; five Durham bulls and half-share in a bull, 300 head of cows.

On 6th May, Samuel Lyons, selling at his auction mart, Sydney, six Durham heifers, whose sire is "Alexander"; one roan bull, whose sire in "Elrington," imported by Mr. Carr in the ship "Alexander" in 1840.

Note.—On following up the cattle sale advertisements throughout the years it is plain that there were plenty and to spare of speculators who brought out valuable cattle from not only Great Britain and Ireland, but from all the centres of commerce where British ships were trading. A beast purchased in one or other of the markets for, say, £10 could be sold in Sydney, if safely landed, at a profit. It may be termed gambling, but the Stock Exchange is a gamble. Unfortunately we have no authentic records as to who purchased those cattle when sold.

Then cattle came into Illawarra at a time before we had a local press. For example, the Honorable East India Company, in 1850, had an auction mart in Hunter-street, Sydney, under the management of Mr. Thomas E. Jones. Later Mr. Budham Thompson took charge. This company carried out very extensive dealings with shipping men in both horses and cattle in a private way; hence we cannot reach their records during this life.

There were many other such auction companies in Sydney, which enabled wealthy men to get their stock first hand. If the progeny turned out well a pedigree was arranged; otherwise not a word was uttered.

Be all that it may, the auction sales given here are from our newspaper files, and the men who attended many of those sales are still living. What is more, the newspaper files from which they were taken still exist. One notable feature of these auction sales is this. It often happened that those who bought from the original breeders, and then sold the progeny of the purchased, framed most of the pedigrees, in conjunction with the auctioneer.

Many of our stock-breeders when cornered over the pedigree of a bull or a cow, in the crazy days of pure Shorthorns, were ever ready to console an anxious enquirer with these words: "By or out of an A.A. Company's bull or cow," as the case demanded. The writer has had a good deal of experience in working out dairy cattle pedigrees, and always when in doubt—and that frequently happened—asked for the description of the brand used by the A.A. Company, whose headquarters were between three centres of civilisation to-day, namely, Port Stephens, Stroud, and Gloucester, and never once got any really reliable information from anyone. The brand was either AA over CO and CO over AA. The company was established there in 1824. It was through the A.A. Company that John Berry imported the black Argyleshire cattle to Coolangatta. This company had no connection with the Australian Auction Company, of Sydney and Maitland.

1855-6.—Fred. R. Cole, selling for Jas. Armstrong at Keelogues, near Wollongong, a dairy herd (40 cows, 12 heifers, two bulls). He also was selling at Brown's Illawarra hotel yards, Dapto, October 13th, 1855, 40 head of springing heifers, carrying the WC brand, and bred by William Carr at Murramarang. John Collie, selling for Patrick Heffernan, 20 cows and 10 heifers, at Five Island, Oct., 1855. Fred. R. Cole, selling for John Hukins, at Eden Hill, Shellharbour, 20 cows, 3 heifers, 1 bull bred by Captain Addison, November 13th, 1855. John Collie, selling at Barton's hotel yards,

Kiama, November 1st, 1855, 25 springing heifers. John Carruthers, selling at G. Woods' farm, Jamberoo, on November 19th, 1855, 40 dairy cows and 1 bull. Fred. R. Cole, selling at Hyam's late farm at Jamberoo for William Johnston, 30 dairy cows in milk, 10 dairy cows in calf, on 21st December, 1855. Fred. R. Cole, selling at Brown's Illawarra hotel yards, Dapto, on December 13th, 1855, 30 springing heifers, carrying the EE and WC brands, from Murramarang. Cole also announced, on behalf of E. R. Evans, a mob of heifers, bred in New England, and specially selected by Mr. Evans.

1856.—Fred. R. Cole, selling for Henry Osborne, M.C., at Brown's Illawarra hotel yards, on January 7th, 1856, 25 first-class springing cows and heifers, 4 pure-bred bulls, all carrying the HO brand. Fred. R. Cole, selling for William Wilson, at the Macquarie Rivulet, Albion Park, 30 cows, 15 heifers, 2 first-class Shorthorn bulls and 1 Devon bull, equal to imported. Mr. Wilson was a brother-in-law of Mr. William Hawdon, of Kiora, Moruya.

January, 1856.—Fred. R. Cole, selling for Thos. A. Reddall, January 22nd, 1856, 20 head of TXA cows, specially bred by Messrs. Towns and Addison, of Shellharbour. John Collie, selling on Wollongong Showground, 7th February, 1856, 1 very superior bull (4 years old) of the Durham breed, bred by Tritton from the A.A. Company's, of Port Stephens, stock; also 1 red and white bull out of one of the best TXA Durham cows, and by Evan Evans' well-known Durham bull. John Carruthers, selling for William Howard at Jamberoo, 42 cows, 1 superior bull, Feb. 18, 1856. Thos. Rose, selling for Campbell, of Bergalia, 20 cows of the famous Heart brand at Barton's Hotel yards, Kiama, February 13th, 1866. These cows brought £6 per head. Gerard, selling at Higgins' hotel yards, Figtree, near Wollongong, 60 head of springing heifers, bred by Macarthur, of Camden, 13th February, 1856. Gerard, selling for Wyatt and Butler, of Fairy Meadow, same date and place, 15 heifers and 1 Glenlee-bred bull. Fred. R. Cole, selling for Robert Somerville at Dapto on April 3rd, 1856, 29 cows, 5 two-year-old heifers, 1 superior bull got by George Somerville's well-known bull "Major." This bull, "Major," was a white bull, small spots on neck and head, and was given as a present to Mr. George Somerville by Henry Osborne when a calf. Edmond Gerard, selling at Higgins' Mount Kiera hotel yards, near Wollongong, 40 pure Durham cows, bred by James Rodd, of Braidwood.

Several of those who were associated with Henry Osborne's Kangaroo Valley property had the right to rear a few heifers from cows that were allowed for the supply of milk and butter for the family. Among the number were John Tritton and Robert Johnstone. Tritton's brand was JT; Johnstone's brand was RJ. Tritton made the best use of his opportunity, and when he left the Valley to reside on portion of the Avondale Estate, Dapto, he had a fair herd, which he improved, or tried to improve, by buying bulls from the large cattle owners. He became associated in cattle matters with Joseph Dunster; set Dunster up in a butchering business at Shellharbour, and supplied him with cattle. It was from Tritton that Joseph Dunster got his red and white spotted cattle.

In October, 1856, Fred. R. Cole sold, on behalf of David Johnston, of The Meadows, Illawarra, 50 head of pedigreed Durham cattle at Brown's Illawarra hotel yards.

Fred. R. Cole, selling at Brown's Illawarra hotel yards, Dapto, for David Johnston, of The Meadows, 12 superior Durham heifers, on 28th November, 1856.

Fred. R. Cole, selling for Henry Osborne at Brown's Illawarra hotel yards, Dapto, 70 head of fat cattle and springing heifers, 6th January, 1857.

Waldron, selling for Charley Ransome ("Charley the Cobbler") at Stoney Creek, near Jamberoo, 50 head of dairy cows and heifers, May, 1857.

Fred. R. Cole, selling for Evans and Yates, at Brown's Illawarra hotel yards, 60 superior cows and heifers from Murramarang, and 4 superior bulls, Devon and Durham, from 1 year to 2 years old, EE and WC brands.

Fred. R. Cole, selling at Wilson's Store. Macquarie River, Albion Park, on April 8th, 1856, 20 cows, 6 three-year-old heifers, 12 two-year-old heifers, 3 high-bred Durham bulls. Dr. Falder had for sale at his farm, Mount Kiera, near Wollongong, April, 1856, 20 cows and 1 yearling bull that received first prize at the late Illawarra Show. George Somerville. selling at Brown's Illawarra hotel yards. Dapto, 40 cows and heifers and prize bull "Young Major," also 4 young bulls from one to two years old, on April 20th, 1856. Gerard. selling for Wyatt and Baker, a milk walk in Wollongong, 10 cows, and 1 highly-bred two-years-old Ayrshire bull. John Collie, selling at Higgins' Mount Kiera hotel, near Wollongong, 35 springing heifers from the famous herd of James

Throsby, of Bong Bong. T. Rose, selling for John Sharpe, of Bushbank, Kiama, 30 cows and heifers of the noted Gerard Gerard breed. John Collie, selling for Edward Hawdon, of Broulee, at Brown's Illawarra hotel yards, Dapto, 115 cows and heifers, and one bull got by the imported Shorthorn bull "Leslie." Thos. Fowler, selling at Hukins' Four-in-hand Inn, Kiama, on 25th September, 1856, 20 springing heifers of the B and W brand, on behalf of David Berry, of Coolangatta, Shoalhaven. 1858.—John Collie, selling for George Whitton, at Dapto, 40 cows, 33 hand-reared heifers, 2 bulls (one of whom was bred by George Somerville). F. R. Cole, selling for John Graham at Barretts' farm, West Dapto, 36 cows, 10 yearling heifers, 2 choice bulls, 2nd November, 1858. Fred. R. Cole, selling for John Beatson at Macquarie Rivulet stores, 50 choice springing heifers. These heifers had been taken in exchange for goods— the rule of the road in those days. Fred. R. Cole, selling for George Buchanan, at Dapto, 75 head of cows and heifers, 35 young hand-reared heifers, and 4 superior bulls, November, 1858. Mr. Alex. Osborne purchased 100 head of heifers from Messrs. Evans and Ritchie at Murramarang. Fred. R. Cole, selling for David Johnston, of The Meadows, Albion Park, at Brown's Illawarra hotel yards, December 3rd, 1858, 90 head of well-bred heifers, some very forward. 1859.—Irvine and Fowler, selling for Messrs. George and John Noble, at Omego Retreat, Gerringong, on 2nd February, 1859, 20 cows of the HO breed, 7 heifers, and 1 well-bred bull. Fred. R. Cole, selling for David W. Irving, at Newton, Dapto, on 22nd February, 1859, 84 cows and springing heifers, 23 hand-reared heifers, 14 yearling heifers, 2 superior bulls, equal to imported, winners of several prizes. "Sportsman" was a bull of the pure Durham and Devon extraction, was the winner of two first prizes, and was bred by Mr. Evan R. Evans, of Penrose, Dapto. "Glenlee" was bred by Mr. William Howe, of Glenlee, Campbelltown, from a pure Alderney cow. G. K. Waldron, selling for Messrs. W. R. Hindmarch and W. W. Ewing at Alice Bank, Gerringong, March, 1859, 120 cows and heifers. Fred. R. Cole, selling for Messrs. Graham and Armstrong, at Kembla Grange, Dapto, 100 first-class cows, 40 heifers from one to two years old, 10 calves, 2 superior bulls (one by Captain Addison's bull "Dick), and 3 two-year-old bulls. Fred R. Cole, selling for Thomas Clifford, at Mullet Creek, Dapto, 68 first-class cows, 37 two-years-old heifers, 14 one-year-old heifers, 2 four-

K

year-old bulls, 1 two-years-old bull, 3 one-year-old bulls, February, 1859. 1859.—Fred. R. Cole, selling for Captain Hopkins, at West Dapto, and John Weston, West Dapto, known as the Horsley herd, consisting of 40 cows of the Badgery breed. Burt & Co., of Sydney, were selling at their bazaar the prize bull "Louis Napoleon," bred by John Emmerson, of Overdurdale, Darlington, England, calved February 3rd, 1858, colour white, got by Baron Farnly (14,129 C.H.B.), dam Louisa IV. by Red Duke (13,571 C.H.B.), winner of first prizes at Cumberland, Cleveland, and Barnard Castle shows, and h.c. at Yorkshire, March, 1859. Irving and Fowler, selling for John Dean, of Shellharbour, 35 cows, 18 heifers, and 1 bull by Captain Addison's bull "Stewey." F. R. Cole, selling for Duncan Beatson, at Hughes' Station, Albion Park, Macquarie Rivulet, on May 9th, 1859, 80 dairy cows, 20 springing heifers, 30 young heifers, and 6 splendid bulls. Thomas Corser, selling for Patrick Ryan, at Mayfield, Shoalhaven, 20 first-class cows in milk (without calves), 10 choice springers, 50 head of hand-reared cattle from 12 to 18 months old, 1 superior four-years-old Durham bull, and 1 roan Durham bull, two-years-old, May, 1859. G. K. Waldron, selling for William Haslem, at Hukins' Hotel (The Man of Kent), Jamberoo, on 28th January, 1859, 20 heifers and 1 choice bull, 18 months old. Fred. R. Cole, selling for Ephrimus Howe, at Dapto, August, 1859, 40 cows, 8 heifers, and 2 choice bulls. Note.—Mr. Ephriam Howe and David Williamson Irving were brother-in-laws, and they used the same class of cattle and carried on dairying pursuits in Illawarra on, as near as possible, the same lines as that of William Howe, of Glenlee, Campbelltown. Messrs. Collie and Curr, selling at the Mount Kiera hotel yards, near Wollongong, 21 springing heifers, bred by Henry Badgery, of Vine Lodge, Bong Bong. G. K. Waldron, selling for William Brown, at Steam Packet hotel yards, Kiama, on 8th September, 1859, 33 springing heifers, bred in Bong Bong. Fred. R. Cole, selling for James Sleevens, at the Keelogues, near Wollongong, on 29th September, 1859, 50 good cows, 40 head of hand-reared heifers, from 1 to 2½ years old, and 2 high-bred bulls. Messrs. Collie and Curr, selling for James Condon, at Gooseberry Hill, Shellharbour, 73 cows, 15 heifers (two-years-old), 21 yearling heifers, 20 calves, 3 well-bred bulls. G. K. Waldron, selling at Steam Packet hotel yards, Kiama, 31st September, 1859, for David Berry, of Coolangatta, 12 springing heifers.

Messrs. Fuller and Waldron were purchasing weaned calves in Kiama at £1 per head for J. G. and R. Wilson's run at Cambewarra, where grazing could be had for £1 per year. Owing to imported cattle reaching New South Wales, via Victoria, from South Australia, great alarm was felt, as pleuro-pneumonia had broken out in a Mr. Boadle's herd in Victoria, October 6th. 1859. Thos. Fowler, selling Kenneth Finlayson's herd at Bolong, Shoalhaven, 20 cows, 6 springing heifers, and 1 superior bull by Jenkins' imported Durham bull, "Bellins," and out of an imported cow, October, 1859.

Messrs. Collie and Curr, selling at Brown's Illawarra hotel yards, Dapto, October, 1859, 20 springing heifers, on behalf of Martin Larkin, carrying the Messrs. Hassall and Badgery brands. Messrs. Collie and Curr, selling for Mrs. Esther Hughes, of Sydney, at Terry's Meadows, Albion Park, in accordance with the directions in the will of Samuel Terry, 97 cows (milking and springing), and 100 heifers, 6 bulls, on 2nd and 3rd November, 1859. G. K. Waldron, selling for Robert Miller, of Gerringong, at Steam Packet hotel yards, Kiama, on 3rd November, 1859, 4 prime bulls (one being his celebrated Durham-Ayrshire cross bull). The trustees of the late Henry Osborne were selling at the Fermanagh hotel yards, Kiama, on November 10th, 1859, 50 choice springing heifers, described as being of equal quality to those sold by Mr. Osborne the previous year. Christopher Murray, for James Bemill, Gooddog, near Jervis Bay, 5th December, 1859, 1 Durham bull, 3 young bulls, 4 heifers. Fred. R. Cole, selling at Brown's Illawarra hotel yards, Dapto, on account of David Johnston, of The Meadows, Albion Park, 25 choice springing heifers, on December 10th, 1859. Messrs. Collie and Curr, selling for Thomas Farraher, at Stoney Creek, Jamberoo, on 3rd December, 1859, 35 cows, 12 two-years-old springing heifers, 23 yearling heifers, and 1 Devonshire bull —a truly superior animal. For sale at Martyn's bazaar, Pitt-street, Sydney, 14 remarkably fine Durham bulls and 2 very superior cows with calves, said to be the best lot ever imported. Fred. R. Cole, selling for Robert Kerr, at Mount Kembla, 21 choice cows, 8 hand-reared heifers, 2 well-bred bulls. The cows were all carrying the Badgery brand, and were described as very superior. The Cumberland disease had broken out among the dairy cattle in Kiama; East, of East's Prospect farm, had lost four head, John Greenwood five head, Hall of Mount Salem two head, Hindmarsh one beast, Houst, the German, one beast; date January, 1860. This disease had been introduced to Kiama by the Messrs. Cook, butchers, of Kiama, who had a holding at Marsden Hill, Kiama, and had purchased a mob of fat cattle at Wagga Wagga. It spread very quickly, and practically carried off all the animals in the herds mentioned. It may have been pleuro-pneumonia for all anyone knew about cattle diseases then. Pleuro-pneumonia or Cumberland disease (it is difficult to say which). Shortly afterwards, 1862, it ravaged the herds of Andrew McGill and David Johnston at Albion Park; introduced by a man named Stuckey, who was moving a mob of cattle through there to Shellharbour. McGill lost his prize two-years-old bull and several of his show cows, and David Johnston lost over a score of his choicest animals.

Charles Martyn was selling for the executors in the estate of the late **Henry Osborne**, of Marshall Mount, Illawarra, at his bazaar, Pitt-street, Sydney, on 3rd March. 1860, 2 imported Durham cows, 30 superior cows (all from imported stock, pedigrees at sale). A footnote stated: "The late Henry Osborne never spared money in purchasing cattle." On 8th March, 400 cows, 20 bulls, 300 mixed dairy cows, 210 heifers from two to three years old. 400 heifers from 18 months to two years old. These animals were running at Marshall Mount and Kangaroo Valley. 610 head running at Point Station, Jugiong, Murrumbidgee River. The latter lots for absolute sale at Homebush yards, near Sydney. Henry Osborne gathered those cattle and five large holdings in 30 years. The pedigrees of the stud cattle were mislaid, and could not be found, consequently the sale was delayed by the auctioneer until 4th April. 1860. On that date they were sold without reserve, as was the custom when pedigrees were not forthcoming. The two imported cows were "Charlotte" and her dam. "Young Charlotte" was calved on the voyage out in 1856, and at the sale on April 4th, 1860, she was purchased by C. S. Tindall, of Ramornie Station, Clarence River, N.C. She was the dam of "Constance" (see Vol. I. N.S.W. S.H.B., 1872).

Important Sale.

Messrs. Collie and Curr, selling for Daniel Downey, at Eden Hill, Shellharbour, on 14th and 15th February, 1860, 56 cows. 30 heifers from one to three years old, 20 yearling heifers, 4 superior Durham bulls. Eden Hill comprised 840 acres, of which 100 acres was cleared.

William Irvine, selling for S. Mathews. of Shellharbour, on March 21st, 1860, 21 cows. 4 two-year-old heifers, 12 one-year-old heifers, one well bred bull out of McGills' prize cow. Collie and Curr selling for James Kidd at Roden Vale, West Dapto, 40 cows, 32 heifers, one well bred Ayrshire bull, on May 5th, 1860. Collie and Curr selling at Ousley Vale, near Wollongong, for Carnes of Fairy Meadow, on 10th May, 1860; 40 well bred cows, one three-year-old bull by an imported sire. William Irvine selling for W. H. Steadman at Jamberoo on 15th May, 1860, 40 cows, 26 heifers. one shorthorn bull.

Sale at "Retreat," Bringelly.—David Bell, Esq.—300 head of cattle, 10 well-bred bulls, December 1st 1863. John Biggar selling for Robert Miller at Dapto Flour Mills (now Brownsville), 2nd November, 1864; 110 cows, three well bred bulls, cattle purchased from the A.A. Company, Stroud, the Glenlee herd, and the estate of the late Henry Osborne. Miller was leaving for Chatsbury, near Goulburn. D. L. Dymock was selling for A. K. McKay. of Nowra Park, Shoalhaven, 5 bulls, at Steam Packet hotel yards, Kiama, by only imported Ayrshire bull in the Colony; date, 24th November, 1864. G. K. Waldron, selling for John Mitchell, of Mitchell Mount, Kiama, 30 cows and 2 bulls—one by McKay's Ayrshire bull; the other bred by Andrew McGill. 25/11/64.

Note.—When Mr. James Robb's consignment of cattle arrived in New South Wales from Scotland, consisting of one bull (two-years-old) and two cows, they were in due time landed off a steamer at Wollongong (no harbour in Kiama in those days). Mr. Robb sent his son, Hugh, and a servant, George Duffy, to Wollongong to take charge. They did so; but as one of the cows was near calving they journeyed home slowly. Somewhere not far from Albion Park they were joined up by a friend, who persuaded them to leave the cow—in which he evinced great interest—in the paddock until she calved, and stated he would care for her. He did so. But after a few years later Mr. Robb discovered that his would-be friend had a very excellent Ayrshire bull, whilst his bull was a rank duffer. Exchanging calves and foals had become an art in Illawarra long prior to 1860.

G. K. Waldron, selling on behalf of James Robb, of Riversdale, Kiama, at Steam Packet hotel yards, Kiama, on 23rd February, 1865, five Ayrshire bulls by the imported Ayrshire bull "Marquis of Argyle," imported in 1861; pedigree and bills of lading to be seen in Mr.

Waldron's office, Kiama. This was to prove that A. K. McKay's statement about having the only imported bull in the Colony was wrong. Jasper McKay occupied an ancient estate near Jervis Bay, called Cumberton Grange, in 1850. He had a large number of cattle, including a herd of Ayrshires. It was at Cumberton Grange that William W. Wilford gained his colonial experience. He and his brother afterwards carried on dairying at Middle Creek, Kiama, before removing to the Ulladulla district. Jasper McKay was a Magistrate and Crown lands agent. He removed to Nowra Park, and imported several valuable Ayrshires from Scotland. John Biggar, selling for Robert Armstrong, at Avondale, Dapto, adjoining Captain Hopkins' farm, March 29th, 1865, 60 cows, 45 well-bred heifers of various ages, 1 superior-bred strawberry bull. G. K. Waldron, selling for Messrs. W. R. and M. N Hindmarsh, at Alne Bank, Gerringong, 3rd April, 1865, 100 dairy cows, 25 springing heifers, 2 superior-bred bulls. G. K. Waldron, selling for Matthew Feehan, of Braidwood, at Steam Packet hotel yards, Kiama, on 11th May, 1865, 32 springing heifers, carrying the famous BA brand. Charles Wilford, selling at Bramton Grange, Middle Creek, Kiama, 14th June, 1865, 40 cows, 10 heifers, 1 superior bull; Waldron, auctioneer. Bernard Brown was selling for Mrs. De Mestre at Terrara, Shoalhaven, the dairy herd, the dams of which were bred at Glenlee, and their sire was bred by Lee, of Bathurst, by an imported Shorthorn bull. Fred. R. Cole, selling for Archie Graham, at Canterbury, Dapto, on 28th February, 1866, 70 cows, 20 springing heifers from 2 to 2½ years old, 2 superior bulls. G. K. Waldron, selling for Robert Miller, of Gerringong, at Steam Packet hotel yards, Kiama, 3 choice two-year-old bulls (sire bred by Andrew McGill), their dams being McMiller's choicest cows, 8th February, 1866. G. K. Waldron, selling for William Swan, of Gate Farm, Albion Park, on February 20th, 1866, 51 cows, 21 springing heifers, 2 first-class bulls.

On the 26th of June, 1866, Mr. G. M. Pitt, the founder of the firm of auctioneers, Pitt, Son, and Badgery, sold Edward Cox's herd at his saleyards, near Penrith. These cattle were described as being Durhams and Durham and Ayrshire crosses, bred for the dairy, and, according to the late Mr. Evan R. Evans, who purchased three young bulls there, the Durham cross cows in Mr. Cox's herd displayed much dairy quality. From statements made during the year 1880 and later by James McGill and Henry Fredricks, many animals said to have been descended from a bull known as "Major" were actually descended from those Cox-bred bulls.

G. K. Waldron, selling at the Steam Packet hotel yards, Kiama, on 8th March. 1886, 40 heifers, carrying the famous DB brand, bred by David Bell, of Bringelly, Liverpool. G. K. Waldron, selling for William R. Hindmarsh, at Gerringong, on 10th March, 1866, 88 dairy cows. Fred. R. Cole, selling for Joseph Dunster, at Macquarie Rivulet, 11th April, 1866, 50 cows and 2 bulls. G. K. Waldron, selling for Alex. Osborne, at the Albion Park yards, Albion Park, on May 18th, 1866, 30 springing heifers and 4 young bulls, the latter descended from imported stock. G. K. Waldron, selling for Patrick O'Meara, of Middlemount, Jamberoo, 3rd August, 1866, 15 cows, 4 springing heifers, 1 choice bred bull out of John Marks' prize cow "Daisy." G. K. Waldron, selling for the executors of the estate of the late David Johnston, The Meadow, Albion Park, at the Albion Park hotel yards, on 21st September, 1866, 20 head of dairy cows and 20 hand-reared heifers. G. K. Waldron, selling on behalf of the executors of the estate of the late David Johnston, of The Meadows, Albion Park, at the Albion Park hotel yards, on 20th October, 1866, 50 head of well-bred dairy cattle, and 1 well-bred bull. Bernard Brown selling for Ettie De Mestre, at Royal Victoria hotel yards, Terrara, 25 heifers bred by Roberts Bros., of Boro, Argyle, November, 1866. John Biggar, selling for Henry Harris, of "Struggle Farm," West Dapto, 12th December, 1866, 70 cows, 30 heifers, and 2 superior bulls. John Biggar, selling for Duncan Beatson, at Fairy Meadow, near Wollongong, on January 9th, 1867, 40 cows and heifers, 1 choice bull. Bernard Brown, selling for Kenneth Cameron, of Bolong, Shoalhaven, on January 31st, 1867, 10 cows and heifers springing, 5 yearling heifers, 1 Shorthorn bull, 4 years old, by an imported bull, and 1 yearling bull. G. K. Waldron, selling for James Robb, Riverdale, Kiama, at Steampacket hotel yards, Kiama, April, 1867, 17 young Ayrshire heifers and 6 Ayrshire bulls by imported Ayrshire bull "Marquis Argyle." Bernard Brown, selling for Messrs. A. and E. De Mestre at Terrara, Shoalhaven (owing to dissolution of partnership) on 6th, 7th, and 8th April, 1867, 70 well-bred cows, 70 heifers from 1 to 3 years old, 2 bulls 4 years old, 1 bull 2 years old. The report of Messrs.

A. and E. De Mestre's dairy cattle went to show that the original stock were selected from Howe's Glenlee herd, near Campbelltown, and had been bred and preserved by the De Mestre family on the same lines for 20 years. William Howe, of Glenlee, kept Shorthorn, Devon, Ayrshire and Alderney bulls in the herd from time to time, believing as he did in the blending of these breeds on a large scale. Note.—In conversation with Mr. Andre De Mestre at his home, Crookhaven, in the presence of two well-known residents of Shoalhaven, he said: "It was Mr. De Lotte who brought out some of the stud cattle used on the Terrara estate. But," said he, "no animal that was ever on the Terrara estate could equal for dairy quality a cow we used to call 'Waison.' She was a blood-red cow, bred by Waison, of Ulladulla. For years she never left the yard, and her progeny were all good." The Waison red cattle were valued in Ulladulla for many years.

John Biggar, 1867-9, selling for Captain Hopkins, at Benares, West Dapto, 60 prime milkers, 20 heifers from 2 to 3 years old. and 2 well-bred bulls, February, 1867. D. L. Dymock, selling for James Graham, at Waughope, Jamberoo, on 27th May, 1867, 40 cows, 30 heifers, 1 bull bred by Messrs. De Mestre. Terrara, Shoalhaven. D. L. Dymock, selling for James Moffitt, on roadside between Kiama and Jamberoo, 50 choice cows, 18 springing heifers, 15 2-year-old heifers, 10 yearling heifers, 2 well-bred bulls. D. L. Dymock, selling for John Milligan at Gerringong, 60 cows and 1 pure Ayrshire bull. G. K. Waldron, selling for James Robb, of Riversdale, Kiama, at Steampacket hotel yards, Kiama, on 20th August, 1867, 9 splendid Ayrshire bulls by imported Ayrshire bull "Marquis of Argyle." Fred. R. Cole, selling for the executors of the late Andrew Thompson, at Yallah, 120 cows and heifers, 14 calves and 4 bulls, September, 1887. John Biggar, selling for executors of the late Andrew Thompson, at West Horsley, Dapto, 120 cows and heifers, 12 yearling heifers, and 2 bulls, September, 1867. There was evidently two dairy herds in the estate of Andrew Thompson. G. K. Waldron, selling for Duncan Beatson, 30 splendid springing heifers selected from A. Davey's celebrated herd. G. K. Waldron, selling for Andrew McGill, at Meadows, Albion Park, on 25th October, 1867, all his choice herd of dairy cattle, including prize-winning cows and bulls; cows in full milk; 30 heifers. Lease expired. Note.—The McGill herd was not submitted to auction, as the Bartlett family, by

arrangement, purchased the whole of Andrew McGill's stock—a walk-in walk-out sale. They had leased the farm, and purchased everything except the household effects. C. F. Smith, selling for John Evans, at Shellharbour. November 6th, 1867, 10 superior heifers. John Biggar, selling for Frederick Weston, at Duncan Beatson's old farm, Macquarie River, on January 13th, 1869, 15 dairy cows, 5 heifers. John Biggar, selling for Michael Carberry, on 8th March, 1869, 25 cows, 12 heifers from 1 to 2 years old, 6 yearling heifers, one bull bred by Andrew McGill. D. L. Dymock, selling at the Steampacket hotel yards, Kiama, 1 first-class bull, 5 years old, carrying the famous H.O. brand. G. K. Waldron, selling for John Honey, at Saddleback, Kiama, on 14th April, 1869, 50 cows in milk, 15 springing heifers, 35 young heifers, 3 bulls bred by Andrew McGill and McKay, one of the best dairy herds in Illawarra. G. K. Waldron, selling for Alex. Emery at Crawley Forrest, Kiama, on 24th April, 1869, 55 dairy cows, 10 heifers, 2 superior bulls, one an Ayrshire bred by James Robb. the other was bred by John Black. G. K. Waldron, selling for Charles Price, at Woodstock, Jamberoo, on June 4th, 1869, 100 dairy cows, 20 springing heifers, 20 heifer calves, 3 superior bulls. G. K. Waldron, selling at Steampacket hotel yards, Kiama, for Messrs. Williams and Evans, 20 heifers carrying the EE brand, on 27th May, 1869-70. D. L. Dymock, selling for Daniel McIllraith. at Sea View, Kiama, on June 16th, 1869, 80 head of half-bred Ayrshire cows, two Ayrshire bulls. D. L. Dymock, selling for Walter Curry. at James' old farm, Longbrush, Kiama. on June 30th, 1869, 110 cows, 30 heifers in calf, 30 yearling heifers, and three good bulls. D. L. Dymock, selling for John Marks, at Terragong, Jamberoo, on 15th September, 1869, 60 cows in full milk, and two well bred bulls, one was James Robbs' imported Ayrshire bull, Marquis of Argyle. Neil Harper was the purchaser. John Biggar, selling for Evan R. Evans, at Penrose, Dapto, on September 23rd, 1869, 40 cows and heifers. G. K. Waldron, selling for James Stroud, at Tullumbar, Macquarie rivulet, 200 dairy cattle, viz., 90 cows, 30 springing heifers from two to three years old, 23 hand-reared heifers, six bulls Ayrshire, Durham and Herefords. October, 1869. D. L. Dymock, selling for William English, 50 cows, 12 heifers, one bull bred by De Mestre. of Shoalhaven, 8th December, 1869. G. K. Waldron, selling for Stephen Tobin, at Crooked River, Gerringong, on 28th

January, 1870, 21 cows, one good bull and one superior yearling bull. D. L. Dymock, selling for James Colley, at Terragong, Jamberoo, on 31st January, 1870, 31 cows, nine heifers, and one bull, bred by Andrew McGill. G. K. Waldron, selling for Neil Harper at Flat Rock, Jerrara, Kiama, on 25th March, 1870, 30 cows, and one superior bull, James Robb's imported Ayrshire bull Marquis of Argyle. William McIllraith was the purchaser. G. K. Waldron, selling for Joseph Perkins, at Gerringong, on 4th March, 1870, 17 dairy cows and heifers, many of them from imported cows. D. L. Dymock, selling for John McClintock, at Gerringong, on 30th March, 1870, 80 choice cows, 12 heifers in calf, 12 yearling heifers, and two well bred bulls.

G. K. Waldron, selling for John Bartlett at Albion Park (Andrew McGill's old farm), on 23rd April, 1869, 50 cows in milk and 50 heifers (15 springing), 3 well-bred bulls, described as the most valuable dairy herd in Illawarra, including all the noted prize-winning stock of the late Andrew McGill.

In speaking to Mr. John Bartlett about the cattle purchased by his late father from the late Mr. Andrew McGill, re the possibility of pleuro-pneumonia having carried off in 1862 some of the choicest of the late Andrew McGill's prize dairy animals, Mr. Bartlett said:— "Of that I am not in a position to speak. All I know is that my late father bought all the stock, young and old, belonging to Andrew McGill. It was a walk-in walk-out deal. But this I do know, my late father bought far better cattle from Duncan Beatson at that time than he bought from Andrew McGill." This statement has been repeated to the writer several times by Mr. John Bartlett.

G. K. Waldron for the trustee of the estate of the late Ebenezer Russell, 125 picked cows 100 heifers from 1 to 4 yrs. old, 3 splendid Devon bulls. 1 Ayrshire bull, April, 1870. G. K. Waldron, selling for John Evans, of Shellharbour, on 6th May, 1870, 25 cows, 6 springing heifers, and one well bred bull. G. K. Waldron, selling for Thomas Gay, of Fortune Farm, Jerrara, Kiama, 80 cows, 40 heifers, and 2 superior bulls. G. K. Waldron, selling for John Allen, of Albion Park, 25 cows, 11 prime heifers, and 1 Ayrshire bull. G. K. Waldron, selling at Albion Park Hotel yards, Albion Park, September 14th, 1870, 28 springing heifers, district reared. G. K. Waldron, selling for William Alcorn, of Foxground, on 14th October, 1870, 34 cows, 10 forward heifers, 7 yearling heifers, 1 Ayrshire bull, and 1 Durham bull. John

Biggar, selling for Mrs. House, at Johnston's Meadows, Albion Park, on 31st October, 1870, 31 cows, 15 heifers, 2 well bred 2 year old bulls. the progeny of David Johnston's imported stock. C. F. Smith, selling for Robert Jenkins, of Berkeley, on November 14th, 1870, 70 milking cows, 1 bull (a Noble Arthur, bred by Dr. R. L. Jenkins, of Nepean Towers, Campbelltown. John Russell, of Croome, Shellharbour, was the purchaser of the Noble Arthur bull. 5 young Noble Arthur bulls were sold at sale, from Mr. Jenkins' picked cows.

Cattle Purchase. Robert Hindmarsh purchased "Cornet," a blood red bull, for 125 guineas. "Cornet" was bred by William Durham, of Wombo, Singleton, calved 1868, by Sandysyke (imp.) dam Queen of Trumps, by Champion (imp.). Fred Hindmarsh bought Wild Rose, bred by Barnes and Smith, of Dyraaba, Richmond River; calved December, 1868, by Practor (2016), dam Carlisle (15,738), for £57/10/-. George Tate bought Napoleon, bred by Barnes and Smith, for 50 guineas; a dark roan calved October, 1869, by Practor, dam 149, by Prince of Prussia (15,105). William R. Hindmarsh purchased Lady Bird from Barnes and Smith, Dyraaba, Richmond River, for £97/10/-, a roan heifer, calved June, 1869, by Practor (20,516), dam 212, by Prince Imperial (15,193). Alex. Osborne purchased for Barrengarry, Kangaroo Valley, a yearling bull unnamed, and without pedigree.

Metropolitan Show, 1870.

At Metropolitan Show, Sydney, 1871, cattle were said to be of great quality, and the largest display ever seen in Australia. Shorthorns numbered 120 head. Devons were represented by the Tocal Stud, Paterson River; Herefords of poor quality. Alex. Osborne bought two pure Shorthorn heifers, aged 9 and 18 months respectively, for Barrengarry, Kangaroo Valley.

G. K. Waldron, selling for executors in the estate of the late Alderman Robinson, of Broughton Vale, 75 cows in milk, 75 cows and heifers of various ages, 3 superior bulls, on 11th March, 1871. D. L. Dymock, selling for D. L. Waugh, 25 cows and 1 well-bred bull, bred by Henry Frederick. G. K. Waldron, selling for James Robb, sen., at Riversdale, Kiama, on 10th April, 1871; 95 dairy cows, 4 Ayrshire bulls. This was described as the best dairy herd in Illawarra. G. K. Waldron, selling for Wyndham Bartlett, near McGill's, Macquarie River, 80 prime dairy cows, 20 3-year-old heifers, 50 hand-reared heifers, from 1 to 2 years old, 30 calves. Many of these animals are the progeny of Andrew McGill's noted herd.

D. L. Dymock, selling for Jamse Robb, junior, of Clover Hill, near Kiama, at Steampacket Hotel Yards, Kiama, 6 half-bred Ayrshire bulls on 11th March, 1871. G. K. Waldron, selling for Michael Cronan at Macquarie River, Albion Park, 43 dairy cows, 13 heifers, 3 well-bred bulls. The cows were nearly all of the H.O. breed. On 28th March, 1871.—D. L. Dymock, selling for Robert Wilson, adjoining Joseph Dunster's, Shellharbour, 24 cows and 2 bulls of superior quality. April, 1871.—G. K. Waldron, selling for Thomas Cosgrove at Mount Pleasant Farm, Shellharbour, on 26th June, 1871, 100 dairy cows, 50 prime springers, 40 hand-reared calves, 2 bulls, one of whom is well-bred. John Biggar, selling for Evan R. Evans, at the Albion Park Hotel Yards, on 21st July, 1871, 20 choice, well-bred heifers at calving. G. K. Waldron, selling for Alex. Osborne, at Albion Park Hotel Yards, on 4th August 1871, 15 splendid dairy cows, and 15 splendid springing heifers. G. K. Waldron selling for D. Williams at Albion Park Hotel Yards on 16th October, 1871, 20 district-reared heifers. D. L. Dymock, selling for Messrs. John and James Marks at Steampacket Hotel Yards, 2nd November, 1871, 2 superior Shorthorn bulls. giving up raising fat cattle for local markets. John Biggar, selling for Isaac Pearson of Macquarie River. Albion Park, 50 cows, 15 springing heifers, 6 yearling heifers. 3 bulls of superior quality. D. L. Dymock, selling for George Noble, at Omega Retreat, Gerringong, 92 head of dairy cattle and 2 bulls. D. L. Dymock, selling for Messrs. John and William Black, at Jerrara, near Kiama, 50 dairy cows, 20 springing heifers, 2 well-bred bulls, 15 young heifers, March, 1872. G. K. Waldron, selling for Robert Oscar Kendall, at Happy Ville, Kiama. 12th April, 1872, 80 dairy cows, 25 heifers, and 2 capital bulls. D. L. Dymock, selling for James Robb, jun., at Clover Hill, near Kiama, 68 cows. 30 springing heifers, 20 yearling heifers, and 2 well-bred bulls. 8th May, 1872. Bernard Brown, selling for Messrs. D. and A. Hyam, at Nowra Hill. Shoalhaven. 76 choice cows. 85 heifers, 30 hand-reared heifers, 4 well-bred bulls, May, 1872. G. K. Waldron, selling for John Russell, of Croome, Shellharbour, at Steampacket Hotel Yards. Kiama, on 9th May, 1872, 6 young bulls from imported stock—Noble Arthur and Baronet—Shorthorn and Durham. D. L. Dymock, selling for E. H. Weston, of The Meadows, Albion Park, 1 well-bred, roan, Shorthorn bull. Pedigree at sale on 12th December, 1872.

C. T. Smith, selling for Robert Harworth, at Kembla Grange, 100 dairy cows, 50 picked heifers from 1 to 3 years old, and 2 well-bred bulls, December, 1872. John Biggar, selling for Joseph Ritchie at Canterbury, Dapto, 50 cows, 20 2-year-old heifers, 20 yearling heifers, and 3 well-bred bulls, December, 1872. Note: At this sale, Henry Fredricks purchased 10 heifers, and bred from two or three of them. noted bulls. John Biggar, selling for William Gibson, of Charcoal Creek, 85 dairy cows, 25 heifers, 1 superior-bred bull, and 1 extra good, a rich roan, December, 1872. 1873.—John Biggar, selling for William Thompson, of Belsley Vale, Dapto, 70 cows, 32 2-year-old heifers, 16 1-year-old heifers, 1 choice roan bull, 1 yearling bull, a roan. The herd was represented as being of the McGill strain throughout. Thomas McGee, selling for W. R. Hindmarsh, 350 head of dairy cattle—pedigree at sale—cows in calf to his bull Conqueror, now 4 years old. Conqueror cost £150 as a calf, and was sold at sale for £200. Sale held Croobar, Ulladulla.

At the Metropolitan Show in Sydney, 1872. Mr. E. R. Evans, Dapto. Illawarra. bought a pure-bred Durham bull, bred by Messrs. W. and C. Durham, of Singleton, N.S.W., the same people who bred Mr. Robert Hindmarsh's Coronet or Comet. The bull in question was by Balco (imp.). dam California, by Sandysyke. grand-dam California III. (imp.), by Flying Duke, 9.9., dam Careless, by Whittlebury, 9.9.9.. dam California, by Victory, 9.9.9., dam Emily, by Belton, etc. Balco was bred by Edward Rowley, of Liddington House, Gloucester (Eng.), by 4th Duke of Oxford, dam Juliet, by Sol. Sandysyke was bred by Miss Calvert, of Sandysyke, Brampton. Cumberland (Eng.), going back to the English-bred Butterfly. See Coates' S.H.H. Book; and at same sale Mr. Frank A. Thompson purchased a pure-bred Durham heifer. 1873.—John Biggar, selling for Andrew Devlin. Mount Kembla. adjoining Keelogue, 40 cows and 1 prize bull. John Biggar, selling for Mrs. Stroud, at Macquarie Rivulet. 35 cows, 12 heifers, 2 bulls, of good quality. picked by the late James Stroud, February. 1873. G. K. Waldron, selling for John Hamilton at Terry's Meadows, on 17th March, 1873, 50 prime cows. 20 splendid heifers. 1 well-bred bull. The first herd in quality in Illawarra. John Biggar. selling for James Baxter. near Bong Bong road, West Dapto. 30 cows. 30

heifers, 10 poddies, 1 superior bull, 4 years old, bred by Griffiths, of Mittagong. The cows were mostly bred by E. Shipley, carrying the E.S. brand, on 28th March, 1873. John Biggar, selling for John Egan, Sunnyside, near Benares, Dapto, 30 cows, 10 heifers, 1 well-bred bull. Cattle selected from the McGill and Evans' herds, April, 1873. W. R. Hindmarsh, of Ulladulla, bought a Duke of Derrimut bull from Morton, of Victoria, for £700. W. W. Ewin gave £1150 for two heifers, Matilda 10th and Matilda 11th. All three animals were by the Duke of Brunswick. John Biggar, selling for Michael Flanagan, at Woodbrook, American Creek, Dapto, 52 cows, 14 3-year-old heifers, 10 poddies, and 2 bulls, bred by Evan R. Evans. These cattle were carrying the H.H.O. and E.E. brands. John Biggar, selling for E. H. Weston, at Albion Park Hotel Yards, 20 carefully-selected springing heifers, mostly in calf to the Shorthorn bull "Nonsuch," bred by Lee, of Bathurst, and purchased by Mr. Weston at the Sydney Exhibition in 1871. D. L. Dymock, selling for John Seymour, of Shellharbour, 120 prime dairy cows, 50 heifers, 2 bulls, April, 1873. Mr. Seymour was a good judge of cattle, and bred from best bulls.

Cattle sales in connection with the Kiama Show on 4th February, 1875. G. K. Waldron, selling for Frank A. Thompson, of Dapto, Admiral, a light roan bull, 2 years old, sire Prince Royal, dam, Blossom, by Grandmaster, from a pure Lee cow. Young Red Gauntlet, 3 years old, sire Red Gauntlet (imp.), out of a pure A.A. Co.'s cow.

G. K. Waldron, selling on account of William Grey, of Kiama, 2 superior McGill cows, in calf to George Woods' bull Defiance, 1 bull, 1 year old, by a Bartlett bull, and out of a Bartlett cow; 1 bull, 6 months old, by Henry Fredrick's bull out of a superior cow. On behalf of William James, 1 bull, 12 months old, by E. R. Evans' prize bull, and out of a McGill cow; 1 bull, 1 year and 9 months old, by Baronet out of an H.O. cow; 1 bull, 6 months old, by Alexander (imp.), by H. H. Osborne, at great cost, and out of an H.O. cow; on behalf of John Cunningham, 3 splendid cows, the progeny of E.E. cows; two heifers, the progeny of E.E. cows. For Donald Robinson, 1 bull, Prince of Wales, bred by Francis McMahon, of Ulladulla, sire, Frank, dam, a prize cow by Mariner (imp.), Frank, by Frank Gwyne (imp.), dam by Prince of Prussia.

D. L. Dymock, selling for J. W. Cole, 6 young bulls (calves), by the celebrated Major, 1 red

bull, 1 year old, by Royal Butterfly, 1 roan bull (calf), by Baronet. For James Robb, jun., 1 bull, by Cornet. For John Colley, 1 magnificent cow from the celebrated H.O. breed. For Edward Smith, 1 roan bull, bred by Henry Fredricks, 2 roan yearling bulls, bred by Henry Fredricks. For Henry Noble, 1 rich roan bull, by Evans' imported bull, 2 superior cows, choice colours.

G. K. Waldron, selling for W. J. R. Jenkins, 1 bull, Noble Arthur III., sire Noble Arthur (imp.), 1662, C.H.B., dam Princess, by Noble Arthur (imp.), 16,621, C.H.B., grand-dam Cameo (imp.). For Edward Burke, 1 Shorthorn cow, by Evans' bull, out of a first-class cow, 1 handsome cow by James' bull. For E. H. Weston, 6 handsome young bulls, out of Johnston's superior cows, and by the celebrated Shorthorn bulls "Nonsuch" and "Imperial Purple." For William Bailey, 1 rich roan bull, 4 years old, by the celebrated bull "Boxer," bred by John Boxell, dam, a superior H.O. cow. Boxer won six prizes, and was owned by George Tate, sen. (This bull, Boxer, originally called Boxsell, has been referred to by several authorities. Mr. John Tate, of Jamberoo, who milked the Boxer cows on his father's farms, says: "The Boxer cows were bad-tempered, always kicking and dirty." Mr. George Grey, of Greyleigh, Kiama, had a similar experience with cows of the Boxer strains.) Evan R. Evans—4 handsome young bulls, by Balco, sire Balco (imp.), 2 half-bred Devon bulls 15 months old. For Thomas Nelson, 1 superior red bull, (calf) sire bred by Henry Fredericks, dam bred by John Boxsell. For John Seymour, 1 splendid red bull, 6 years old, sire Scotch Jock, and bred by William James, from a first-class cow, 1 red roan bull, 11 months old, out of Princess, a prize taker at the Kiama Show, 1874.

D. L. Dymock, selling for John Honey, red bull, Young Cornet, aged 2 years 4 months, winner of 1st prize, Kiama Show, 1874. For Messrs. D. and N. McGill, the roan-strawberry cow, Phoebe, winner of 1st prize, at Dapto Show, 1874, sire Lofty, dam old Phoebe. 1 roan heifer, 2 years old, by Baronet, a prize taker at Kiama Show, 1874, 1 yearling bull, by Mole's bull. (Mole's bull won many prizes, and sired many winners). For Henry Fredericks, 4 rich roan heifers, by Royal Butterfly, from Major dams 1 year old, 2 roan heifers (calves), by Baronet, dams by Major, purchased by J. W. and J. T. Cole. For Robert Hindmarsh, 6 bulls from 6 to 9 months old, by Cornet, 10 yearling heifers, all reds and roans, by Cornet from EE cows, 3 splendid E.H.W. cows, (these cows were in calf to the 6th Duke of Derrimut), 1 red bull Ruby, sire Cornet, 3 years old H.O. cows, 3 roan bulls, by Sandysyke, 1 heifer in calf to Gipsy Boy (imp). For Edward Johnstone, 1 Durham cow from John Mark's old stock. For M. N. Hindmarsh, 1 heifer 10 months old, by 6th Duke of Derrimut, dam by Evans (imp). (The use made of the H.O. brand in these advertisements since the early sixties is misleading, as after the death of Henry Osborne senr., his sons in Illawarra and Kangaroo Valley used their own brands—Henry's brand was H.H.O.—Alexander's was A.H.O., and Benjamin's B.H.O.)

G. K. Waldron, selling for M. E. Robson, at Rose Valley, Gerringong, 6th March, 1875, 105 cows and spring heifers, 50 heifers from 18 months downwards, 50 calves, by Duke, six months old, by Alexander (imp), 1 bull 6 months old, by Mole's bull, 1 bull six months old, by William James' Scotch Jock.

G. K. Waldron, selling for William Connors at Toolijooa, Gerringong, on 8th February, 1875, 16 dairy cows, 3 heifers 2 years old, 15 first class poddies, 2 well bred bulls.

D. L. Dymock, selling for James Campbell, at Gerringong, on 24th February 1875, 38 cows and 1 bull, by Napoleon.

Thomas Allen, selling for John Allen, at Bloomfield, Ulladulla, on 24th February, 1875, 60 cows, 50 heifers from 12 to 18 months old, 2 superior bulls bred by W. R. Hindmarsh. G. K. Waldron, selling for Thomas McCaffrey, at Jerrara, Kiama, on 17th March, 1875, 26 cows, 19 yearling heifers, 1 first class bull 4 years old, 1 bull 2 years old (Big Ben), bred by Henry Fredericks' sire Royal Butterfly. D. L. Dymock, selling for Cole Bros., at Kiama yards, 6 roan Major bulls 1 year old, 1 roan bull by Baronet, bred by Henry Fredricks, and winner of 1st prize Kiama Show, 1875. D. L. Dymock, selling for Edward K. Tate, of Jamberoo, 56 cows. 23 heifers, 2 well bred bulls, 1 bull, by Napoleon. D. L. Dymock, selling for Messrs. Fredericks and Gordon, at Kiama yards, March, 1875, 30 springing heifers, 7 young bulls by Baronet. 2 young bulls by Royal Butterfly.

John Biggar. selling for Edward Gibson, at Benares, Dapto, on 24th and 25th March, 1875, 140 cows milking and springing, 70 heifers from 1 to 2 years old, 1 bull, Young Shamrock, colour red, calved November, 1872, sire P. H. Osborne's Devon bull Shamrock, dam Cherry, one of the best dairy cows on the Lake Farm. Shamrock was by Red Rover (imp), and bred by Charles Reynolds, of Tocal. Paterson River, N.S.W., 2 2 year old bulls by Evans' imported bull, 1 out of McGill's Queen, and the other bull's dam an excellent McGill cow, 1 bull, 15 months old, by E. H. Weston's Nonsuch, and out of a Weston cow, 1 half bred Devon bull, 15 months old, 4 yearling bulls. Note:—Mr. Gibson having leased Mr. F. A. Thompson's red bull, No. 547, bred by the A.A. Coy. sire, Red Gauntlet (imp.), No 27, 243 C.H.B. out of a pure A.A. Coy's. cow, 100 of the cows and springing heifers are in calf to him. Young Red Gauntlet's stock have sold up to £110, and Young Shamrock is the sire of many of the yearling, and a few of the 2 year old heifers; others are by an Evan Evans bull, whose sire was the bull imported by the late Evan Evans.

Metropolitan Show, Sydney, April, 1875, Class 33, Bulls; 14 exhibits.—R. McDougall's Agemmemon, bred by W. W. Jenkins, Berkeley, Illawarra, sire, Gay Lad, 1st prize. John Honey's Young Cornet, 2 years and 4 mths. old. bred by Robert Hindmarsh, sire Cornet, dam Mealey, bred by Badgery of Sutton Forest, 6th prize. Frederick Hindmarsh's Gipsy Boy (imp) colour roan, aged 2 years and 9 months, bred in Ireland, by R. Challoner, sire Frederick Fitzbooth, dam Daisy Queen, by Knight of Chesnut (26,547 C.H.B.) 7th.

Bull, 6 months and under 9 months, Ben Osborne's Imperial Purple 37th, bred by E. K. Cox, of Penrith, 1st prize. W. W. Ewin's Duke of Derrimut, roan, 10 months and 16 days old, bred by Fred Hindmarsh, sire Duke of Derrimut 6th, dam Vebena, by Young Chancellor (316 N.S.W.), g. dam by Prince Alfred, 5th. W. R. Hindmarsh's Duke of Derrimut 1st of N.S.W., 6th. W. W. Ewin's Field Marshal Booth of N.S.W., colour white, aged 7 months and 10 days, bred by exhibitor, sire Field Marshal Booth, dam Cleopatra, bred by R. McDougall, of Victoria, 7th.

Farmers' prizes.—For farmers holding not less than 100 acres. William James' Robin Hood, red colour, sire by Major (imp.), dam Reddy by Red Rover from an A.A. Company cow, purchased by the late Evan Evans, of Dapto, 1st prize. The "S.M. Herald" remarked that "The three bulls entered were of really excellent quality. Robin Hood looks to have a strong dash of Devon blood in him—a cross that looks in his case to be extremely good." Note.—This is easily explained when we look up the breeding of Red Rover. He was a pure-bred Devon, bred by Frank Reynolds, of Tocal, Paterson River, N.S.W.

Sales of cattle at the Metropolitan Show, 1875:—Henry Badgery, salesman for W. Waddell, to John Miller, of Ulladulla, Tercus No. 312 N.S.W., 23 guineas. For Charles Reynolds to P. H. Osborne, Lord Napier 384 N.S.W., 60 guineas. For R. L. Jenkins to — Wade, Noble Arthur (208 N.S.W.), 27 guineas. Charles Reynolds to Ben Osborne, Brighton (385 N.S.W.), 58 guineas. For J. D. Cox to P. H. Osborne, St. John (321 N.S.W.), 99 guineas. For John Honey, Young Cornet, to — Holt, for 75 guineas. For William Johnstone to — Bercher, Cornet 2nd, for 39 guineas. Note.— The bulls bought by P. H. and Ben Osborne were Devon bulls.

Edward Gibson had a sale at West Dapto on March 24th and 25th, 1875, so it is not clear as to whether he reserved any of his cattle by secret purchase of not. It was certainly a common practice when dairymen were moving from one farm to another to get friends to "buy in," as it was termed, certain favoured animals.

D. L. Dymock, selling for Messrs. Cole at the Kiama yards on 27th April, 1875. 6 young bulls by Major, from choice cows, good colours; for Denis Kelleher, 2 fine bulls, pure red, by Scotch Jock, bred from Dunster's stock.

D. L. Dymock, selling for Evan R. Evans at Kiama yards on 25th May, 1875, 2 bulls, rich roans, one four years, the other five years old, by his well-known imported bull.

D. L. Dymock, selling for Gabriel Timbs at Mount Terry, near Albion Park, on 31st May, 1875, 80 cows, 50 heifers from one to two years old, 1 superior bull (bred by Evan Evans), sire Major (imp.). George Tate, of Broughton village, bought this bull.

D. L. Dymock, selling for Robert Hindmarsh at the Kiama yards, 8th July, 1876, the highly-bred bull Ruby, sire Cornet, aged three years; also Young Ruby, sire Ruby. For William R. Hindmarsh, 1 splendid bull, sire Conqueror, dam a Hereford cow. For Henry Fredricks, 1 splendid bull, by Scotch Jock, out of a McGill cow, and full brother to George Woods' (Springhill) Defiance, and was bred by William James, of Shellharbour; won 1st prize as a yearling at Kiama Show, 1872, beating Robin Hood, and gained 2nd prize 1875.

D. L. Dymock, selling for E. H. Weston, of The Meadows, Albion Park, at the Kiama yards, on 8th July, 1876, 2 Lee bulls.

G. K. Waldron, selling for Alex. Osborne, at Kiama yards on 13th July, 1876, 15 splendid springing heifers and 2 Lee bulls. For William Grey, Mount Salem, 8 prime springing heifers, in calf to a Major bull. D. L. Dymock, selling for William Couch, at Middle Creek, Kiama, 42 cows, 4 heifers, 1 roan bull of the McGill breed, 1 Baronet bull, 1 Dunster bull (both under 12 months old). At Kiama yards, for William R. Hindmarsh, 6 superior heifers, reds and roans, reared from David Warden's noted stock; date of sale, 24th August, 1876.

D. L. Dymock, selling for Thomas Coughrane, at Mount Terry, Albion Park, on 1st September, 1876, 40 choice cows, 10 springing heifers, 30 young heifers, 1 pure bred bull, by W. W. Jenkins' noted bull out of Cox's cow Matilda. D. L. Dymock, selling for James Marks at Culwalla, Jamberoo, 40 superior cows, 1 rich roan bull (bred by Robert Miller) of the McGill breed. At Kiama yards a grand bull, 2 years old, by Major, dam bred by Henry Clarke, of Bergalia. For Henry Fredricks, a rich colored bull by Major, dam a pure bred cow. For Robert Hindmarsh, 5 young bulls, by Cornet out of prime cows; date of sale, 30th November, 1876.

D. L. Dymock, selling for William James at Kiama yards on 29th February, 1876, 30 forward springing heifers, choice colors. For Mr. Thomas Black, at the Longbrush, Kiama, on 8th March, 1876, 40 cows, 10 heifers, 1 Cornet bull, 18 months old. The cows were all by a Cornet bull. For Robert Hindmarsh, at Gerringong, on 20th March, 1876, 44 cows in calf to Major, 1 highly bred bull, 2 thoroughbred cows, 10 heifers by Cornet, and in calf to Major (imp.) 53 soft colored heifers sired by noted bulls, 23 young stock, 1 pure bred bull by Duke of Derrimut, 2 young bulls by Cornet.

D. L. Dymock, selling for George Tate, at Broughton Village, on 27th March, 1876, 70 cows in calf to Major bull, 2 bulls bred by Evan Evans, by Major (imp.). Mr. Dymock has stated, when commenting on the cattle that passed through his hands at auction sales in Illawarra, "I had sold the old Major bull in the Kiama yards for E. R. Evans to Thomas Williams, a few weeks before Gabriel Timbs' sale. At Timbs' sale Robert Hindmarsh ran up Timbs' bull to the last bid, and then he was knocked down to George Tate at £32. The bull was about 4 years old, splendidly developed, and in all respects a Shorthorn of dairy type. In color he was steel or blue roan, with a fringe of brown hair all along his neck and shoulders; hair soft, with a beautiful head;

nice round, short horns, and clear eye; fine forequarters, body good, not so barrel, shaped as Cole's bull Major; not a great size, but well proportioned; in every way a dairy bull."

When selling Tate's herd at Broughton Village, the bull purchased at Timbs' sale was the only aged animal reserved. Tate doubtless had some good cattle in the Kangaroo Valley to mate with him, but he had so many cattle that his herd was a really good one. I do not remember selling the young stock. George Thompson, who had leased the farm, was a heavy buyer at Tate's sale, but it is difficult to say how many of the cows purchased by Thompson were in calf to the Timbs' bull."

G. K. Waldron, selling at Kiama yards on April 6th, 1876, for W. J. R. Jenkins, of Berkeley, 12 handsome JWC (Chisholm-bred cows with calves at foot, by Gay Lad). For James McGill, of Coome, 1 handsome roan bull, 3 years old, by John Lee's celebrated bull Nonsuch out of Lawson's Countess; 1 beautiful red bull, 4 years old, of the genuine old AG (Andrew McGill) breed; 2 handsome, well-bred heifers; 1 very fashionably bred cow, and 3 promising well-bred bulls, 1 year old. For Michael Carberry, 1 beautiful roan bull and 1 heifer, both 1 year old, by George Tate's Major bull—show stock.

D. L. Dymock, selling for William Swan, at Johnstone's Meadows, Albion Park, March 28th, 1876, 51 cows descended from HO stock, 3 well-bred bulls, 30 heifers from 1 to 2 years old, 3 Lee bulls. For William Gordon, of Summer Hill, Kiama, on 3rd April, 1876, 40 cows, 1 roan bull by Major, 1 white bull by Royal Butterfly. For Messrs. Cole, at Kiama yards, on 8th April, 1876, 10 Major bulls from extra good cows. For John Honey, 1 yearling heifer (sire Cornet, dam Butterfly; g. dam by Major, imp.). 1 bull by Young Cornet (dam an EE cow, by Major, imp.—show stock). For Henry Fredricks, 3 yearling bulls by Sir Roger, 2 Major cows. 6 yearling heifers, by Baronet from Major cows. For William Johnstone, of Omega, Gerringong, 1 bull, Duke of Erin, by the 6th Duke of Derrimut, dam by Major (imp.), show stock, in Market Square, Kiama, on 6th April, 1876. G. K. Waldron, for Robert Booth, at Jerrara, Kiama, on 1st May, 1876 120 cows, 20 springing heifers. 60 head young cattle from 1 to 2 years old, 2 highly bred bulls. Messrs. Craig and Son entered into possession of the farm on day of sale, it having been purchased by them from the Messrs. Black and leased to Booth.

Opening of the International Exhibition, Sydney, 1876. The following list of animals from the South Coast was published in the press:—

Class 29, Durham Bulls: W. W. Jenkins' Gay Lad, 2nd place; H. H. Osborne's Alexander, 4th place. Class 31, Durham Bull, 1 year old: W. J. Chapman's Royal Butterfly (329, N.S.W.), W. W. Ewin breeder; W. W. Ewin's 3rd Duke of Brunswick, W. W. Ewin's 1st Duke of Brunswick; John Moffitt's Duke, bred by W. R. Hindmarsh; W. W. Jenkins' Merry Monarch; David Warden's 3rd Duke of Derrimut. In this class R. L. Jenkins, of Nepean Towers, took first place with Commodore; and Robert McDougall, of Victoria, took 2nd place. Class 32, Durham Bull, 6 months and under 12 months: W. W. Ewin's 5th Duke of Brunswick, W. W. Ewin's 4th Duke of Brunswick, W. R. Hindmarsh's 2nd Duke of Derrimut of N.S.W., W. R. Hindmarsh's 4th Duke of Derrimut of N.S.W., W. W. Jenkins' Eschistina, W. W. Jenkins' Alonzo, William Johnstone's Duke of Erin. The prizes were won by Robert McDougall's Count of Carisbrook and E. B. Woodhouse's Royal Purple 10th. Class 34, Durham Heifer, 2 years old: J. and T. Cole exhibited Fairy Queen, Spring Blossom bred by Henry Fredricks. The prizes were won by R. L. Jenkins, of Nepean Towers, with April Flower, and W. C. Durham, of Singleton, with Village Rose. Class 35, Durham Heifer, 1 year; J. T. Cole exhibited Princess Matilda, bred by Henry Fredericks; Frank A. Thompson, Illawarra Lass; W. R. Hindmarsh, Duchess of Derrimut. The prizes were won by Wentworth's Princess Purple and Barnes and Smith's Cherry Ripe.

Farmers' Cattle.—Class 62 (not necessarily pure-bred).—Bull, 3 years: William Brown, of Dapto, Grand Turk of Specke 30th, 1st prize. Class 63, Cow, 3 years: Cherry Red, bred by Henry Fredricks, 1st prize. The "S.M. Herald" commented very favorably on the appearance and quality of Mr. W. W. Ewin's (Ulladulla) Durhams and Shorthorns.

D. L. Dymock, selling at Kiama yards for Cole Bros., 8 pure coloured young bulls by Major. For George Johnstone, 1 red bull by Major, dam bred by Henry Fredericks; date of sale, 20th June. 1876. There were also 2 bulls of the McGill breed advertised for sale, together with a cow belonging to M. N. Hindmarsh—a beautiful roan bred by Henry Clarke, of Bergalia, Moruya. She was the winner of many prizes. and in calf to Major.

G. K. Waldron, selling for John Bartlett, at Kiama yards, on 26th October, 1876, 20 beautiful district reared heifers. principally the progeny of the McGill herd. D. L. Dymock, selling for John Cullen, at Mount Johnstone, Jamberoo, on 10th December, 1876, 45 cows, 40 head of young cattle from 18 months to 2 years old, 1 rich roan bull, by Baronet out of a McGill cow. For Adam Rankin, on Timbs' farm, near Mount Terry, 32 cows, 4 2-years-old heifers, 8 18-months-old heifers, 1 bull highly bred, 1 bull 18 months old, by Red Gauntlet, and 1 18-months-old by Prince William, on November 17th, 1876. For the Misses Wallace, at Woodbrook, Jamberoo, on 20th November, 1876, 32 choice cows, 7 2-years-old heifers, 13 15-months-old heifers, and 2 bulls. The cows were the progeny of the H.O. breed. James Wallace brought cattle with him from Kangaroo Valley, where he had been for a short time managing for the late Henry Osborne.

D. L. Dymock, selling for Frederick Hindmarsh, at Alne Bank, Gerringong, on 13th December, 1876, 72 cows, 11 pure cows and heifers, 14 bulls, pure and half-bred. For John Moffitt, at Toolijooa, on 20th December, 1876, 25 cows, 2 bulls, 1 by Scotch Jack and 1 by Boss.

The Messrs. Anderson Bros. of Bannockburn Station, Inverell, who had been carrying on stud horse and cattle breeding for some years, Bannockburn was 16 miles from the town of Inverell. In 1873 P. W. Anderson, one of the firm, engaged Jonathan Lambert to look after the homestead affairs. In 1878 the brothers decided to establish a small stud of cattle in Illawarra, and a stud of blood horses at Campbelltown. Jonathan Lambert arrived at Dapto, Illawarra, in charge of 16 head of stud Shorthorns, including a pure Shorthorn bull named Viceroy (colour, roan); Phillis, a roan Shorthorn cow; Isabella, a white Shorthorn heifer, and a choice roan cow named Phoebe. There were other animals that came from Victoria in a shipment with stock purchased by W. W. Ewin, of Ulladulla. The farm selected was on the banks of Mullet Creek, which empties into Lake Illawarra. The objective was to breed stud Shorthorn bulls and heifers which were averaging at the high prices in N.S. Wales.

This Illawarra stud was established too late, as stud beef cattle took a fall. The cost of raising fodder had to be contended with. The dairymen with butter at from 7d. to 8d. per lb. had to look for good dairy cows. A few, then as now, were on the lookout for show type animals, but rent-payers had to find dairy cattle. This fact, together with the cost of feeding large framed cattle, created a slump, and

in consequence of the fall of prices Anderson Bros. sold out in October, 1880.

Michael O'Gorman purchased a young roan bull from the Andersons, and called him Clare Boy. This bull, Clare Boy, mated with cows sired by the Gabriel Timbs' bred bull Volunteer, gave O'Gorman many show animals. It is remarkable how many bulls were purchased in this way without a question being asked about the pedigree of either sire or dam. The Anderson Bros. could have supplied pedigree. Buyers used their judgment—with them pedigree did not count.

D. L. Dymock, selling for Henry Fredricks at Fortune Farm, Saddleback, 150 head of cattle, February, 1885. D. L. Dymock, selling for Charles Inskip, at Shellharbour, 40 cows, 7 heifers, 2 bulls bred respectively by William James and Evan R. Evans on February 9th, 1885. D. L. Dymock, selling for Samuel Rink, at Broughton Creek, 100 cows, milking and springing, and 73 3-years-old heifers, 30 yearling heifers, 75 forward heifers, 2 well-bred bulls, on 25th and 26th March, 1886.

D. L. Dymock, selling for John Synott, at Omega, Gerringong, 40 cows and 1 bull, January, 1886. James Beacom had a noted cow and calf at Burrawang, Wingecarribee, in January, 1886, for which he had been offered £50—a very big price in those days. D. L. Dymock, selling for James Swan at Oak Flats, Shellharbor, on January 30th, 1886, 12 young cows and four bulls, Major and other strains of blood. Alex. Campbell, selling at Boyd's Hotel, Cambewarra, 46 heifers bred by Samuel Clarke and E. H. Weston, of Albion Park. D. L. Dymock, selling for Samuel Cooke, at Farraher's farm, Stoney Creek, Jamberoo, on 1st March, 1886, 50 cows, 6 springing heifers and 10 backward heifers. D. L. Dymock, selling for Patrick Raftery, at Tullimbah, Macquarie River, 64 cows, 40 heifers from 1 to 2 years old. These cattle were reported to be of the McGill and Evans strains, 1st March, 1886. D. L. Dymock, selling for Samuel Risk, near Kangaroo Valley, on 25th and 26th March, 1886, 100 cows, 15 prime springers, 75 2-years-old heifers, 3 heifers from 9 months to 1 year old, 2 good bulls. D. L. Dymock, selling for James Bros. at Alne Bank, Gerringong, on 9th and 10th April, 1886, 90 dairy cows, including Alice, the champion cow at Kiama show; Rose, the champion cow at Broughton Creek show; and Duchess, the champion Ayrshire cow of Illawarra; 10 springing heifers and 5 good bulls. This herd was said to be the result of 30 years' breeding. D. L.

Dymock, selling for Matthew Reen, at Avondale, Dapto, on 7th April, 1886, 80 choice cows and 3 bulls. This herd was selected from the herds of Evan R. Evans and Williams, and was mostly of the Major Strain.

It was at Patrick Raftery's and Matthew Reen's sales that William Graham, of Jamberoo, got some of his foundation stock that won prizes for him in after years.

Alex. Campbell, selling for George Tate, jun., Kangaroo Valley, April, 1886, 10 superior springing heifers reared from Major and Dunlop bulls. Mr. Tate had previously purchased a Dunlop Ayrshire bull from Mr. Thomas Brown. D. L. Dymock, selling for John Lindsay, at the Albion Park yards, 13 Ayrshire bulls on 12th April, 1886. D. L. Dymock, selling for Simeon Dudgeon, at Woodbrook, Jamberoo, on 5th May, 1886, 15 choice cows, 25 heifers from 1 to 2 years old, 1 prize bull by Evans (imp.), and from a Major cow (winner of 4 prizes), 3 bulls by Antill's Ayrshire bull, from 1 year to 1½ year old, and 1 yearling heifer out of the test cow. D. L. Dymock, selling for Mrs. Breen, of West Dapto, on 19th May, 1886, 46 cows, 10 forward springers, 8 yearling heifers, the progeny of Major and other noted bulls. Alex Campbell, selling for James McIntyre, at Gerringong, on 20th and 21st May, 1886, 60 cows, 12 forward springers, 50 heifers from 1 to 2 years old, 1 Ayrshire bull, a noted stock-getter.

Dunlop, calved November 1st, 1873. He was bred by D. McLean, of Victoria. Dunlop, in 1874, won 1st prize as a yearling at the National Agricultural Show in Melbourne, 1st prizes in Sydney in 1879, and 1st prize in 1880. At Kiama Show, in 1882, was awarded 1st and Champion bull of all breeds. He won 1st prize in Moss Vale in 1882, at Goulburn in 1882, at Camden in 1882. He took 9 first prizes, and was never beaten in any show ring. He was the property of J. M. Antill, of Jarvisfield, Picton. His sire was Tam-O'Shanter, and his dam was Lady of the Lake, by Donald, g. dam Rose II., by D. McLean's imported bull, g.g. dam Rose, imported by D. McLean.

Dunlop was purchased by James McIntyre, of Crooked River, Gerringong, through G. K. Waldron, auctioneer, in 1883, for £50. From May 23rd, 1878, Waldron was buying Dunlop bulls. Henry Fredricks, of Kiama, bought 3 young bulls; same year Waldron purchased 4 young bulls. In May, 1879, Waldron purchased 4 young bulls—all direct from Mr. J. M. Antill, of Jarvisfield, Picton, for local breeders. Mr.

James McIntyre bred several valuable animals from Dunlop, including Mr. Charley McCabe's bull that won several prizes, and laid the foundation of Mr. Sam Cook's herd on the Richmond River. McCabe called his bull Peter. The Dunlop blood can be traced in with ease through the best herds in Illawarra.

At James McIntyre's sale, Henry Fredericks purchased a very superior blood red cow of the Waison strain. She was in calf to Dunlop. Her calf, a bull, was purchased by Simon Dudgeon, who refused to part with him for years. He was the sire of Sir Henry, who in Denis Kelleher's herd sired Admiral, who in Graham Bros.' herd sired Togo, who in turn made fame for George Grey.

D. L. Dymock, selling for William Graham, on 4th December, 1886, at Tate's Hotel yards, Jamberoo, 23 heifers, 2 years, and 2 2-years-old bulls, of the Commodore breed. W. J. Miller and Coy., selling for Walter Ewin, at Woodstock, Milton, Ulladulla, on 25th and 26th June, 1886, 100 milking and springing cows, 30 empty 2-years-old heifers, and 30 yearlings. Ewin had taken over the Albion Hotel, Nowra. D. L. Dymock, selling for Samuel Cook, at Farraher's Farm, Jamberoo, on 1st March, 1886, 30 choice cows, 10 heifers, 6 springing heifers, Cook going to Richmond River. D. L. Dymock, selling for John Graham, at Kiama Yards, on 2nd February, 1886, 30 grand springers, from Edward Graham's noted stock, all choice colours. D. L. Dymock, selling for James Bros., on 9th and 10th April, 1886, at Alne Bank, Gerringong, 90 cows, milking and springing, including Alice, champion cow at Kiama show; Rose, champion at Broughton Creek Show; Duchess, champion Ayrshire cow of Illawarra, 10 springing heifers, 5 bulls of good kinds. Alexander Campbell, selling at Kangaroo Valley yards, on 15th September, 1886, for George Tate, jun., 10 choice forward springers, reared from Major and Dunlop bulls. D. L. Dymock, selling for William H. Grey, of Saddleback, Kiama, on 2nd April, 1886, 70 superior cows, milking and springing, and two bulls, going to Richmond River. John Stewart, selling for William Grey, April 21st, 1887, at Broughton Creek, 36 grand young cows, milking and springing, 14 yearling heifers, and 1 good young bull. D. L. Dymock, selling for William Fryer, at Mount Terry, 20th March, 1887, 50 cows, milking and springing, 9 heifers, 2 bulls carrying EE brand. John Stewart, selling for Robert McLelland, at Broughton Creek, April 25th, 1887, 40 grand young cows, milking and springing, 12 superior heifers, 1 Ayrshire bull (a prize-winner), and 1 good bull.

D. L. Dymock, selling for J. W. Cole, on 13th July, 1886, at Kiama yards, 12 heifers from prize cows by the prize bull Commodore. D. L. Dymock, selling for Alex. Osborne at Barrengarry, Kangaroo Valley, on 12th November, 1886, 120 milking cows, including Shorthorn, Ayrshire and Jerseys. John Stewart, selling for William Black, at Glen Murray, Kangaroo Valley, on January 14th, 1887, 58 grand cows, some of them prize-winners at the Kangaroo Valley Show, 30 heifers from 9 months to 3 years old, and 3 grand young bulls. Alex. Campbell, selling for Daniel McMillan, at Cabbage-tree Creek, near Nowra, 23 choice cows, 15 choice calves by an Ayrshire bull, and 1 half-bred Ayrshire bull on 28th January, 1887. D. L. Dymock, selling for G. Hempton at Daisy Bank, Dapto, 60 cows, 12 heifers in calf, 10 young heifers, 3 superior bulls. The cows were all of the McGill strain (on 31st January, 1887). D. L. Dymock, selling for Thomas Love at the yards, Kiama, a young bull by King Cole, the champion bull of Illawarra, and out of a test cow. D. L. Dymock, selling for William Buchanan, at Omega, Gerringong, on March 17th, 1887, 100 cows, 6 superior heifers, and 3 bulls. D. L. Dymock, selling for Daniel Boyd, at Kiama yards, 1 roan bull calf, 6 month old, a prize-taker, and out of a prize test cow. John Stewart, selling for R. V. Boyd, 60 heifers from 1 to 2½ years old, and a grand 2-years-old bull bred by J. W. Cole out of a Slasher cow, 5th of April, at Kiama yards. Same day D. L. Dymock was selling, at Kiama yards, for J. W. Cole, 6 young bulls, 8 months old, and 6 young heifers by Slasher. D. L. Dymock, selling for Simeon Dudgeon, at Spring Hill, Wollongong, on 4th May, 1887, 44 cows, 18 heifers and 4 bulls, prize-winners. D. L. Dymock, selling for John Grey, of Broughton Creek, 40 half-bred Ayrshire springers in calf to a pure Ayrshire bull, on 7th June, at Kiama yards. William Osborne and Coy., selling for Henry Giles Irvine at Berkeley on 24th August, 1887, 40 cows, 30 heifers from 1 to 2 years old, 1 bull bred by Edward Gibson. D. L. Dymock, selling for Robert Hindmarsh at Kiama yards on 20th September, 1887, 2 superior bulls bred by James Bros. D. L. Dymock, selling for John Joliffe, of Berkeley, adjoining Couchrane's farm, Unanderra. 60 cows, 70 heifers, from 1 to 2 years old, on 21st October, 1887. Alex. Campbell, selling for Mrs. Elliott, of Broughton Village, November 3rd,

1887, 50 well bred cows, 40 heifers, 1 to 2 years, 2 Ayrshire bulls. These cattle comprised the best dairy strains on the South Coast.

Alexander Campbell, selling for William Thompson, at Forest Lodge, Cambewarra, on 7th February, 1887, 45 first-class cows, 12 springing heifers, 8 yearling heifers, 1 dairy bull, a prize taker. Thompson, going to Bega, D. L. Dymock, selling for George D. Reddall, at Stoney Range, Shellharbor, on 12th January, 1887, 50 cows, milking and springing, 2 springing heifers, and 2 superior bulls. John Stewart, selling for William Black, at Glen Murray, Kangaroo Valley, on January 14th, 1887, 58 grand cows, milking and springing, some of which are prize winners, 30 heifers from 1 to 3 years old, and 3 grand young bulls. Alexander Campbell, selling for Samuel Clarke, jun., of Albion Park, at Kangaroo Valley yards, on January 15th, 1887, 60 beautiful hand-reared heifers from 15 to 18 months old, principally roans and reds, from picked cows—a dealer's collection. D. L. Dymock, selling for Thomas Love, Kiama, on 9th February, 1887, the champion bull King Cole and a young bull by King Cole. D. L. Dymock, selling for Samuel Marks, at Terragong, Jamberoo, on 16th February, 1887, 50 superior cows, 6 springing heifers, 3 bulls. This herd is descended from the McLeay and McGill cattle. Alexander Campbell, selling for Henry Packer, at Barrengarry, Kangaroo Valley, on 28th February, 1887, 80 head of springing and backward heifers, 3 milking cows, and 1 Devon bull. Alexander Campbell, selling for John Wilson at Crooked River, Gerringong, on March 5th, 1888, 60 choice cows, milking and springing, 16 heifers from 18 months to 2 years old, 2 well-bred bulls. Wilson going to Richmond River. D. L. Dymock, selling for George Duffy, of Rosedale, Dapto, on 30th March, 1888, 50 grand milking and springing cows, 45 heifers from 1 to 2 years old. These cattle comprise the oldest and best dairy strains.

D. L. Dymock, selling for John Chie (a son of the sun), at West Dapto, on 22nd and 23rd February, 1889, 85 cows, milking and springing, 15 heifers, 2 prize bulls. D. L. Dymock, selling for William Grey, Kiama, 20 springing heifers, 50 heifers from 18 months to 2 years old, 1 bull of Major breed, on 30th March 1889.

D. L. Dymock, selling for Alexander Osborne at Barrengarry, Kangaroo Valley, on 12th November, 1886, 120 milking and springing cows, including pure bred Ayrshire and Jersey cows, 5 bulls, majority grade cows.

THE ORIGIN OF THE BULL MAJOR.

The Origin of the Bull "Major."—The many doubts that have been expressed about the origin of the bull Major have led to many arguments. It has been so easy to trace cattle importations that few indeed at any period of our history accepted statements right off without proof. If proof were not forthcoming, the old Scotch verdict, "Not proven," would be invariably returned, and the question would then be shelved.

Those of us who doubt much that has been said and written about dairy cattle and dairy cattle breeding cannot in turn expect others to believe us. If then, the writer, who is one of the many unbelieving "Thomases," puts forward a theory regarding the origin of the bull "Major," he is prepared to stand by his theory, as a theory, and will take smilingly all the knocks levelled at him in a true sportive spirit. It is my theory, and the unexpressed theory of older and, therefore, more experienced Illawarramen.

To begin, George Somerville and his family were neighbours of my father and mother, in the County Fermanagh, Ireland. The Somerville family left for Australia in 1838, and settled at Dapto, Illawarra, in 1839, on the opposite side of Mullet Creek to Brownville. My father and mother landed at Marshall Mount, Illawarra, in March, 1841. This will show that several of the old Illawarra men knew exactly the nature and conditions of each other's surroundings, together with the class of stock prevailing at the time.

According to George Somerville Junr., his father in 1849 had a lease of some swampy land near the Lake. A drought was on in the district, and the late Henry Osborne got leave from his father to depasture some of his best imported cattle there. When the drought broke Henry Osborne came to pay for the obligement, and take the cattle back to Marshall Mount. His father refused to take payment from his neighbour, so Henry Osborne forced him to take a white bull calf just dropped out of an imported cow, and by an imported bull. That is positively the origin of at least one bull known in Illawarra as "Major," prior to 1856. From this bull George Somerville bred several young bulls which he disposed of to dairy men, and one for his own use which he called "Young Major." The following is the Messrs. Somerville sale announcements:—Fred. R. Cole selling for Mr. Robert Somerville, at Dapto, on April 3rd, 1856. 29 cows, 5 two year old heifers, one superior bull, got by Mr. George Somerville's well-known bull "Major." Fred. R. Cole selling for Mr. George Somerville Senr., at Brown's Illawarra hotel yards, on April 20th, 1856. 40 cows, 1 heifer, and prize bull "Young Major," 4 bulls from 1 to 2 years old. F. R. Cole was a son of Captain Cole.

According to Mr. George Somerville Junr. Messrs. Evan R. Evans, Thomas Williams, George Whitton, and other residents of Dapto, became the owners of these bulls bred by George Somerville Senr., from the Osborne gift bull. This bull "Major" was evidently the product of imported stock that were highly prized by Henry Osborne. Yet he continued his importations with a view of competing with his neighbours in the local show rings, and seldom parted with his choice animals. In this respect he simply pointed out the cattle he had for sale, placed his price per head on them, and the buyer could either take or leave them. My late father got five heifers from him in 1852, from imported stock, and I have heard of a few similar cases which are scarcely worth recording. William Wilson, a son-in-law of John Hawdon, Moruya, purchased cattle from Mr. Osborne and settled on a farm at Tongarra prior to joining the ministry of the Wesleyan Church. At William Wilson's sale my late father bought a white bull with small blue spots on head and neck, a remarkable fine bull. The Fraser family, of Tongarra, had one of the H.O. white bulls, whose progeny was A.1. Joseph Dunster got his best cattle from old man Fraser. One could easily trace these light roan or white strain of cattle from the herd of Thomas Williams to James Spinks, Kiama Robert Hindmarsh, Gerringong, James Bridges, and York Bros., Gerringong, as they were all generation after generation, invariably white with large scaly markings on the back. They were thin skinned, subject to sun burn, yet pure and simple Illawarra dairy cattle in type and dairy quality. The death of Henry Osborne in the prime of his life was a decided loss to Illawarra.

The sale of cattle in the estate of the late Henry Osborne, of Marshall Mount, Illawarra, was announced in the press as follows:— "Charles Martyn has received instructions from the executors in the estate of the late Mr. Henry Osborne, of Marshall Mount, Illawarra, to sell at his bazaar, Pitt St., Sydney. on 3rd March, 1860, 2 imported Durham cows, 60 superior cows and heifers, 20 bulls, all from imported stock." Note:—"The late Mr. Osborne never spared money in purchasing cattle."

On March 8th, 1860, at Homebush yards, 400 dairy cows, 20 bulls, 300 mixed cows, mostly milkers, 70 bullocks, and 100 steers, running at Marshall Mount and Kangaroo Ground, also 610 head of mixed cattle from Point Station (Jugiong), Murrumbidgee River.

The stock sold on 8th March, 1860, at Homebush yards, were disposed of by Messrs. Richardson and Wrench, of Sydney. The stud cattle were not disposed of by Charles Martyn, until the 4th of April, 1860, when they were sold without reserve, owing to the fact that all pedigrees were lost. Tradition tells us that the two imported cows were Charlotte and her daughter, imported by Mr. Henry Osborne, in 1856. Charlotte's daughter must have been a mere calf when landed in Sydney, in 1856, and strange to say she is the only animal sold in 1860 of which we have a record. She was like her dam, a white cow showing a few roan marks and was calved in 1856, purchased at the sale by Mr. C. G. Tindal, Ramornie, Clarence River. While with Mr. Tindal she produced two heifer calves, "Cowslip," calved June 1st, 1861, and "Constance" calved May 10th, 1862. Both these heifers were like their dam, but not their grand dam in colour, the latter being described by those who often saw her, as being a dark roan of fine proportions. The white colour with the small red markings came from the sire, a characteristic, a certain strain of the H.O. Cattle seems to be one's only proof of the affinity between the Osborne and the old time Evans strain of dairy cattle, yet in the minds of close observers this would carry weight. As to the purchase of the calf at Martyn's bazaar, Sydney, without a pedigree, is also important following as it did so soon after the disposal of the late Henry Osborne's stud herd. The Sydney dairy men were then as now good judges of dairy cattle, and particularly smart dealers.

For many years past the blood of "Major" could scarcely be determined microscopically, yet there is always a few men who are not scientifically well enough informed to let the old legendary stories about that bull remain as mere newspaper copy. Such men delight in dangling such stories in mid-air like Mahomet's Coffin. This "Major" imported talk began in the early eighties when co-operative dairying, and the introduction of new blood among the dairy herds was freely discussed. The value of pure-blooded sires was freely mentioned. And by way of argument two bulls, "Theodore" and "Major" were placed on trial. Following closely these two remarkable bulls by means of comparison a little further, we find that whereas "Major's" pedigree was never published, "Theodore" had an excellent pedigree, his number being (292) in the New South Wales Shorthorn Herd Book, and going straight back to "Bolingbroke" (86). "Major," on the other hand, was reported to have been purchased as a calf at Martyn's Bazaar, Sydney, having been born at sea; and that his dam was imported by Mr. Lee, of Bathurst. The writer went to no end of trouble to ascertain the correctness of that report. but failed to get any information that would show that "Major" had ever been on a ship beyond the one that brought him from Sydney to Wollongong. There are three letters, one each from the brothers Lee— namely, Mr. George Lee. M.L.C., Leeholme. Bathurst. Mr. John Lee. Kelso, Bathurst; and Mr. James Lee. Larras Lake, Molong. which can be examined by anyone desiring to do so. But not content with these letters—having in the meantime discovered that the Messrs. Lee had imported a cow and calf about the period "Major" was brought into Illawarra—another letter was despatched to Mr. James Lee on the subject. The following is a copy of his reply—

"Larras Lake. Molong, March 12th, 1894.

   Mr. Frank MacCaffrey,

   Dear Sir.—I am in receipt of your letter of 9th instant. My father imported the cow you speak of. and she had a calf which was not sold. but brought from Sydney to Bathurst in a crate on a cart, the cow following.—Yours faithfully,

           James Lee."

"Major." however, in the face of the fact that he had no pedigree. was mated with some of the best dairy cows that ever looked through a bail. and the result was that his progeny were second to nothing in the world as milk and butter producers, while "Theodore's" stock, with all their fashionable ancestry, drifted away among the beef Shorthorn breeders and were lost to the dairymen of Illawarra, who might otherwise have turned them to dairy use.

The foregoing was published by me in the "First Century of Dairying" in 1909, pages 172-173, when all the principals were alive. They are all dead now, consequently the old, old story is resurrected, to wit, 1924 A.D.

As no pedigrees were kept, worth the name, as will be seen by running one's eyes over the old Kiama Herd Book records, the subject was not followed seriously. The purpose of keeping pedigree records is not necessarily to give the history of animals. The main purpose is to serve as a guide for the breeder in order to obtain hints in mating; to serve as a means by which performances may be traced in the immediate ancestry of an animal; in all cases to enable a breeder to improve defects. Simple as this system of keeping pedigrees may be to modern breeders, it was not followed in the past by the dairy cattle raisers. Therefore, any endeavour to connect "Theodore" or "Major" with our present-day cattle would be working on the proverbial "A million to one chance" against the effort, mate them as they may.

Licenses granted by the Bench of Magistrates at Kiama, from 1854 to 1884.

Register of Spirit Merchants and Brewers, 1st January, 1854.

Joseph Pike, spirit merchant, stone building, Terralong Street, Kiama; Nathaniel Leathes, spirit merchant, weatherboard house, High Road, Gerringong; Samuel Bonham and George Hunt, Fitzroy Brewery, Collins Street, Kiama; Alexander King, spirit merchant, wooden store, Terralong Street, Kiama; Robert Hall Owen, spirit merchant, wooden house on road side, Jamberoo; Stephen Freeman, spirit merchant, weatherboard house, Manning Street, Kiama; John Allen, spirit merchant, Terralong Street, Kiama; John Goldfinch Brown and Thomas Tempest, spirit merchants, Jamberoo.

Register of Spirit Merchants and Brewers, 1st January, 1855.

Stephen Freeman, spirit merchant, Manning Street, Kiama; Joseph Pike, spirit merchant, Terralong Street, Kiama; Nathaniel Leathes, spirit merchant, Mount Pleasant, Jerringong; John Graham, spirit merchant, Kiama.

John Goldfinch Brown and Thomas Tempest, large wooden store, Jamberoo; John Allen, spirit merchant, Terralong Street, Kiama; William Allen, spirit merchant, at village, Jamberoo; George Hunt, spirit merchant, Shoalhaven Street, Kiama; James G. Wilson and Co., spirit merchants, iron store, Manning Street, Kiama; John and Francis Seager, brewers, Manning Street, Kiama; John Tate, spirit merchant, store, Jamberoo; Charles J. Potts, brewer, Urndcliff, Kiama.

Register of Timber Licenses, 1855.

William Haslim, cedar license, £4; Joseph King, timber license, £2; George Wood, cedar license, £4.

Spirit Merchants and Brewers, Kiama, 1st January, 1856.

John Tate, spirit merchant, weatherboard house, Jamberoo; Thomas Tempest, spirit merchant, weatherboard house, Jamberoo; William Allen, spirit merchant, weatherboard house, Jamberoo; John Allen, spirit merchant, store, Terralong Street, Kiama; Joseph Pike, spirit merchant, store, Terralong Street, Kiama; James W. Wilson and Coy., spirit merchants, iron store, Manning Street, Kiama; Nathaniel Leathes, spirit merchant, High Road, Jerringong, Mount Pleasant; Thomas Fuller, spirit merchant, stone store, Kiama; John and Francis Seager, brewers, Manning Street, Kiama; William Ritchie, spirit merchant, Jerringong.

Brewers and Spirit Merchants for January, 1857.

John Tate, spirit merchant, weatherboard house, Jamberoo Road; Thomas Tempest, spirit merchant, weatherboard house, Jamberoo Road; J. and W. Ritchie, spirit merchants, Jerringong; Nathaniel Leathes, spirit merchant, Mount Pleasant, Gerringong; Joseph Pike, spirit merchant, Terralong Street, Kiama; William Allen, spirit merchant, Jamberoo; John Allen, spirit merchant, Terralong Street, Kiama; J. G. Wilson & Coy., spirit merchants, iron store, Manning Street, Kiama; George Hunt, brewer, Shoalhaven Street, Kiama.

Spirit Merchants and Brewers for 1858.

Joseph Pike, spirit merchant, Terralong Street, Kiama; William Budd, spirit merchant, stone store, Terralong Street, Kiama; J. G. Wilson & Coy., spirit merchants, iron store, Manning Street, Kiama; George Hunt, brewer, Shoalhaven Street, Kiama; John Allen, spirit merchant, Jamberoo; Fuller and Waldron, spirit merchants, Manning Street, Kiama.

Brewers' and Spirit Merchants' Licenses for 1860.

J. W. Smith, spirit merchant, weatherboard house, Manning Street, Kiama; George Hunt, brewer, Shoalhaven Street, Kiama; William Budd, spirit merchant, iron store, Manning Street, Kiama; George L. Fuller, spirit merchant, stone store, Manning Street, Kiama.

Brewers and Spirit Merchants for 1861.

George Hunt, brewer, Shoalhaven Street, Kiama; William Budd, spirit merchant, iron store, Manning Street, Kiama; George L. Fuller, spirit merchant, stone store, Manning Street, Kiama.

Brewers and Spirit Merchants for 1862.

George Hunt, brewer, Shoalhaven Street, Kiama; George L. Fuller, spirit merchant, stone store, Manning Street, Kiama; William Budd, spirit merchant, iron store, Manning Street, Kiama; Joseph King, spirit merchant, central store, Terralong Street, Kiama.

Note same order in 1863. Same in 1864 with the exception of George Hunt, brewer, who had moved to Manning Street. Same order in 1865. Same order 1866. Same order 1867. Same order in 1868. John King took Joseph King's place in 1869, and T. A. Caldwell came into Manning Street, also Alfred Hayden in 1869. In 1870 spirit merchants Alfred Hayden and John King, George Hunt, brewer. In 1871 Gordon, Cunningham and Gordon opened a spirit store in Manning Street. In 1872, Stephen Major joined the ranks, and John King went out, leaving only Alfred Hayden and Stephen Major, spirit merchants, and George Hunt, brewer, in the field. They continued in order from 1872 until 1875. In 1874 Alfred and Ann Hayden were brewers. So was George Hunt in Manning Street. Richard Butter in brick building in Manning Street. In 1877 Samuel Reid opened a spirit store in Terralong Street; Sam Reid and George Hunt only in 1878, 1879, and 1880. In 1881 William Budd and Stephen Major returned as wine and spirit merchants. Budd went out in 1882. Major and Hunt lived on until 1884.

Slaughtering Licenses—Each 2/6.

1854.—George Grey, Jerringong; Samuel Forward, Riversdale; Joseph Hardy, Kiama; Thomas Boxell, Jerringong; John Watson, Kiama; Charles Price, Kiama; Thomas Kendall, Kiama; Michael Hindmarsh, Alne Bank; John Thomas, Shellharbour; William Burless, Gerringong; David L. Waugh, Jamberoo; William Hindmarsh, Alne Bank; James Black, Longbrush; Joseph King, Kiama; Michael Cronan, Terry's River; Alfred Cook, Marsden's Hill; Abraham Kent, Kiama; John Tate, Jamberoo; James Armstrong, Spring Hill; Parnell and Bradney, Woodstock, Jamberoo; John Ledwidge, Jamberoo; Captain Hart, Jamberoo; William White, Riversdale; Thomas S. Kendall, Happy Valley; Joseph Ross, Jamberoo; Laurance O'Toole, Kiama; George Blay, Kiama; Jesse Dodds, Crawley Forest; Thomas Moon, Riversdale; Thomas Wm. Dixon, Jerringong; James Robinson, Jerringong; Alexander Berry, Lee's yard, Jerringong; James Mackay Grey, Omega Retreat. 1856.

HEREDITY.

"**Heredity,**" says Dr. Archibald Reid, "in its chief purpose, and its objects, very clearly, is not as Weismann supposed it to be, viz., to aid production of variations, for variations occur readily in its absence. There are two remaining possibilities. The first is the inheritance of the effects of use and disuse; the second is the actual selection or spontaneous variation that arises at random, though of course not without some cause, and are evenly distributed about a specific mean. It is essential then to understand what characters are transmissible and what are not. Only inborn characters are transmissible."

"The phenomenon of heredity, or the transmission of characters from parents to offspring, is exhibited by all living organisms, both plants and animals. So far as we know living matter, whether it be animal or vegetable, exists in only one form, that is as minute masses of complex jelly like substance known as protoplasms. These minute masses are called cells, and are composed of certain definite parts. Up to a certain stage in the development of an embryo there is no conclusive evidence as to the nature or situation in the cell of hereditary substances representing racial characters."

It has been pointed out by biologists that most mutations with which we are acquainted are due to losses of one, or perhaps even more than one, of the characters of the wild type. De Vries calls these "retrogressive mutations," and they appear to follow the Mendelian law of heredity. It is obvious that a thornless rose would be a different thing from the rose of the hedges, but the difference would be caused by the loss of something—in this case the thorn—and not the addition of any new feature.

But, breeders will say: "Surely new features do appear?" They certainly seem to do so, but according to the authorities on Mendel, they are not really "new qualities" in any proper sense of the word. They are qualities which have all along been there, but have been "inhibited," as it is called, by other qualities, which have prevented them from coming to the front. Hence we sometimes hear heredity described: "That which is in an animal before it is born." Convergence, a term applied to resemblance amongst animals which are not due to direct relationship or genetic affinity; in other words, which are not derived by inheritance from common ancestors, but which result from independent functional adaptation to similar ends. The porcupine and the hedgehog, for example.

Selection.—The theory of natural selection, as propounded by Charles Darwin, which supplies a casual explanation of the processes attending the formation of species in the wider sense; and, therefore, need not be touched upon here. The theory of selection, or Darwinism in the narrower sense is briefly as follows:—A dairy farmer who breeds dairy cattle chooses from the different varieties and definite individuals possessing definite qualities, in order to breed from their intercourse a new type possessing these qualities. There is a similar process in nature, not motived by any purpose. The hypothesis, on which this theory rests, is that the organic species are subject to change. working in various directions in an undefined and unlimited manner. If under certain conditions some varieties are produced, which accommodate themselves better than others to the circumstances of their life, these will triumph in the struggle for existence, and the others will be eliminated. The victors will become more and more prominent by eventually transmitting their qualities to their descendants. But, even in theory this process of development, if unassisted by a higher human intelligence would end in disaster to the dairyman, as the survival of the naturally fittest could not possibly be the most profitable. Hence we have to turn our attention to the great part played by "Nurture," which includes the science of feeding stimuli.

It will thus be seen that "selection" is only one of the principles of the theory of evolution. and, moreover, a subordinate one, which in its very nature bears a negative character, for it only weeds out. The action of natural selection is, however, always essentially negative; it is the survival of the fittest, and the underlying reason for the presence of the fittest must be sought elsewhere, ultimately in the interior laws regulating the evolution of organic life. Yet, the co-operation of the interior and exterior factors is absolutely necessary for any beneficial adaptation. If we do not know, as yet, the interior factors of evolution, it is a defect due to our imperfect scientific knowledge. With scientists the theory of evolution is still in its infancy. Some day Bower's hypothesis of the individuality of the ''Chromosonies'' and their definite modification in the germ cells may yet give the key to open Nature's secrets regarding evolution.

''Heredity,'' according to Herbert Spencer, ''is the capacity of every plant and animal to produce other individuals also of a like kind.'' With regard to dairy cattle characters of the adult are not, however, all of the same kind, some of them are inborn and will develop under normal conditions of nourishment, naturally others require various kinds of stimuli to produce them. We can take a concrete example—the cow's udder. This is produced naturally. But the capacity and the production of a cow's udder can be increased by stimuli, and the characters thus acquired may be termed mutations. Trotting horses have been improved in pace during the last one hundred years. Many may conceive this to be a natural acquirement, whereas it is the result of stimuli. The racehorse Eclipse was the sire of many foals. It has been given to us as a problem in heredity to compare them with him, and to enquire into the vital arrangements. in virtue of which many of them reproduced his remarkable quality of swiftness. He also had a patch on his body, a quite useless spot of colour which reappeared even in the sixth generation of his progeny. One of the most erudite scholars in Europe has said: ''It is a fact that individuals born of the same parents differ to a certain extent, both from their parents and from one another, and it is no less true that the qualities of grand-parents or their collateral relatives latent in the generations past in succession reappear suddenly in the grand-children.''

The minds of scientists are deeply concerned as to the true bearers of hereditary characters. The question is raised: ''Is there a connection, tending to the same aim, between the material bearers of heredity among themselves, and the influence of the outer world, so that the former are modified by the latter and directed into new channels of development.'' As the authority just quoted puts it: ''Such a theory seems to grant that there is a teleological element in the constitution of these material bearers of heredity to which they owe their capacity to responding changes in their constitution, and

adapt themselves to new circumstances by corresponding changes in their constitution, and thereby to effect a regular development of the organic species. This phenomena of heredity is, however, beyond the ken of the average breeder. ''The vital principle that controls what goes on in a diminutive fertilised ovum, is the same time the architect directing the course of the whole resulting process of development, and bringing it to completion by means of the mechanical agencies that are subordinate to him.'' If dairy cattle breeders only knew for certain what material to supply, the art of breeding would be simplified. ''But this little architect is not of himself an intelligent being, he has the power to act in the various cells and in the whole organism, and direct all to their aim, but he does so by virtue of the laws of a higher intelligence superior to our universe, imposed upon living matter when the first organisms came into being. Only an architect of infinite intelligence could possibly construct a machine capable of developing, growing, and propagating itself for millions of years by means of purely mechanical agencies. The reasons for regarding the machine theory as untenable are therefore not theological, but scientific. The fertilised ovum and the organisms proceeding from it have in themselves the vital principles, which uniformly direct the action of the chemico-physical forces of the single atoms towards the higher aim of life. Our praise is due, not to these diminutive unconscious architects, but to the Eternal Creative Spirit that has connected them with matter. It directs the seed of the rose into a rose bush, the hen's egg into a chicken, and the ovum of a cow into a calf. Rose bushes, poultry, and cattle have not always existed. Geology points to the coming into existence of mammals as being in the Cenozoic era, which is the Tertiary age, and that period embraces the pliocene, the miocine, oligocene, and eocine periods.

The first cattle on this earth, so far as we know, were two-horned. How did the polled breeds come into existence? Some day we may get clear insight into these secrets. Mendel considered in the gametes there was either a definite something corresponding to the dominant character, or a definite something corresponding to the recessive character, and that these somethings, whatever they were, could not co-exist in any single gamete. These somethings are usually termed factors. The factor, there, is what corresponds in the gamete in the unit character that appears in some shape or other in the development of the zygote. In the coming into existence, however, of polled cattle (and the same applies to the disappearance of other characteristics), suggests the omission in the gametes of the horn factor, and this at once suggests the idea that the various domestic forms of our cattle have arisen by the omission from time to time of this factor or of that. The puzzling part of this idea, regarding the omission from time to time of the factor which brought about hornless cattle is this: when a polled bull is put with a herd of horned cows the polled character becomes dominant. We must then be prepared to expect that the evolution of domestic varieties of our cattle may come about by a process of addition of factors in some cases, and of substraction in others. But until exhaustive experiments have been carried out scientifically with cattle of various colours, and raised in various forms of domestication, and mated with animals raised in a wild state of Nature to insure purity of blood for crossing purposes we need not look for much beyond an array of scientific contradictions.

As has been stated by Punnett, "The polled character in cattle is dominant to horned, and the occasional appearance of the horned animal is due to the fact (as scientists tell us) that some of the polled herd are heterozygous in this character. When two such individuals are mated, the chances are one in four that the offspring will be horned. Though the heterozygous individuals may be indistinguishable in appearance from the pure dominant, they can be readily separated by the breeding test. For when crossed by the recessive, in this case horned animals, the pure dominant gives only polled beasts, while the heterozygous individual gives equal numbers of polled and horned ones. In this particular instance it would probably be impracticable to test all cows by crossing with a horned bull. For in each case it would be necessary to have several polled calves from each, before they could with reasonable certainty be regarded as pure dominants. But to ensure that no horned calves should come, it is enough to use a bull which is pure for that character. This can easily be tested by crossing him with a dozen or so horned cows. If he gets no horned calves out of these he may be regarded as a pure dominant, and thenceforward put to his own cows, whether horned or polled, with a certainty that all his calves will be polled. Or again, suppose that

a breeder has a chestnut mare and wishes to make certain of a bay foal from her. We know that bay is dominant to chestnut, if a homozygous bay stallion is used with a heterozygous chestnut mare. The roan shorthorn is heterozygous, being a cross between red and white.

"Definite characters for good or ill, whether dominant or recessive, do not disappear in Mendelian inheritance. They persistently reappear in their original purity—permanent progress in cattle breeding is a matter for studying gametes, not of training—as one knowledge of heredity clears away the mists from the hills of doubt, we gradually come to the conclusion that our best animals were not made, but born, like our poets.

"Breeders who have with carefulness evolved a fine herd are often very slow to introduce fresh blood, even when they suspect that they are aproaching the limit of safe inbreeding. But, if Mendelism applies to the organisms bred, then it does not seem as if the introduction of fresh blood need affect the purity of the stock. A cross is effected with a view to secure reinvigoration; the results of the cross may be inbred, and if Mendelism applies, then forms like the original parent will reappear in the next generation, and the forms not wanted can be disposed of.

"No one can, of course, at present say that these simple suggestions will apply where the introduction of fresh blood into a herd of cattle is found to be necessary, but the time has come for trying daring experiments on Mendelian lines or on more approved lines.

All the early beef cattle breeders began with more or less random selections of good specimens of the ordinary stock of their respective localities. A good pedigree was at first simply a pedigree built up of good individual ancestors. The second step was to strengthen the herd by eliminating those animals of poor quality, and to fix excellence by inbreeding and selective breeding. In most cases there seems to have been a critical moment in the history of the herd, when a particularly good sire turned up in each herd. The breeders then used the dominant sire and his male progeny on the different families of cows, composing the herd, until his most excellent blood seemed to permeate the whole. Finally, there seems to have arisen a limit of profitable inbreeding, when new blood had to be introduced. The first bad effects of inbreeding is some loss of size of body, and too much daylight under it. Afterwards comes impaired constitution. If the breeder introduces a strongly inbred sire of a different line, there is a conflict between the two powerful strains, then the type is apt to be destroyed and the progeny sports in all directions.

So long as dogmatic Darwinism held the field with the aid of British and German scientific pressmen, whose chief objective was to prove hypothetically that apes occupied the same place in the universe as proud man, it was futile to speak or write in a style that flattered men of science gifted with the keenest perception, such as Professor St. George Mivart and Sir Oliver Lodge. Those two great scientists set up a reaction only.

During all those years the Abbot Mendel was experimenting quietly with sweet peas. He came across a law in the crossing of species, which has since created widespread discussion, inasmuch as it apparently proves that there is no such thing as spontaneous variation. This discovery struck at the root of the Darwinian theory, as it went to prove that variation in a plant was due to an original form, and that it lay there submissive, until the abeyance of dominant qualities allowed it to come to the fore, whether by accident or design we won't argue.

Professor Bateson says:—"From this experimental proof it is patent that variation consists largely in the packing and re-packing of an original complexity; it is also certain that there is order, be it pre-determined or not, as Mendelism depicts Nature dropping characters and proceeding from complex to less complex forms."

When Bateson first took Darwinism to task seriously he quoted a text of Scripture, viz.:— "All flesh that is not the same flesh, but there is one flesh of men, another flesh of beasts, another of fishes, and another of birds." It may, then, be quite true that man did not descend from an ape. Furthermore, instead of adhering to the fetish that all life started on earth from a single source, it may be safer and saner to say it started from several such sources. This is consistent with the highest ideal of creation.

Sufficient has been stated to show that in breeding farm animals much has to be understood before any real advance in improvements can be made on a large scale, as Mendelism is but the key to unlock hidden secrets that often lie unobserved, yet available and at the command of the searchers who constantly follow the vagaries of cattle breeding. Such men know that a pair of animals when mated with each other for several years seldom give the progeny the same character each mating.

R. C. Punnett states:—"A curious thing in the history of human thought, so far as literature reveals it to us, is the lack of interest shown in one of the most interesting of all human relationships. Few, if any, of the more primitive peoples seem to have attempted to define the part played by either parent in the formation of the offspring, or to have assigned peculiar powers of transmission to them, even in the vaguest way. For ages man must have been more or less consciously improving his domesticated races of animals and plants, yet it is not until the time of Aristotle that we have clear evidence of any hypothesis to account for these phenomena of heredity. The production of offspring by animals was held to be similar to the production of a crop of seed. The seed came from the male, and the female provided the soil. This remained the generally accepted view for many centuries, and it was not until the recognition of the female as more than a passive agent that the physical basis of heredity became established. The recognition was effected by the microscope, for only with its advent was actual observation of the minute sexual cells made possible. After more than a hundred years of conflict, lasting until the end of the 18th century, scientific men settled down to the view that each of the sexes makes a definite material contribution to the offspring produced by their joint efforts. Among animals the female contributes the ovum and the male the spermatozoon."

When complete fusion occurs, the minute embryo of a new animal immediately results. The product of each sex prior to fusion are termed "gametes," or marrying cells, and the individual formed by the fusion or yoking together of two "gametes" is termed a "zygote." The result is a more or less spherical mass of cells adhering to one another, the whole resembling a mulberry. It is termed "morula." the Latin name for mulberry. This solid mass becomes hollow, with cells hanging all round. something like a raspberry with the centre pulled out, and the embryo is now termed a blastula. There are stages in the development from the fertilised ovum, and the stages can be followed until they give rise to the alimentary canal. Yet there is no conclusive evidence as to the nature or situation in the cell of hereditary substances representing racial characters.

It ought to appear patent to a casual observer of nature the variations of form and character, even in the structure of semi-wild animals that are not occasional or minute, but incessant and important, that if there was not some great controlling power ruling these great changes the bovine species would entirely disappear or change before our eyes. To put it plainly, if every organ and function in each concrete specimen that we meet tends to depart from the normal type, how is it that the type remains normal and that these variations persistently arrange themselves about it? The deflections and mutations of a planet prove the existence of the forces which, in spite of them, prescribes a fixed path and position, and unless the minor members of a solar system tended, of their own momentum, to fly off into space, we should not know that there was an overmastering power anchoring them to one centre. If the centrifugal tendency which such variability indicates were all, every varying climate and soil and circumstances on the face of the earth should make its own species, or, rather, there should be no species of ox at all, but a fleeting and evanescent succession of individual forms, like the shape of clouds in a windy sky. It is useless to pretend that the outline which any species constantly exhibits is specially adapted to existing circumstances, for in no two habitats are existing circumstances the same. Plainly, a species is a permanent group of animals framed in all particulars after a single type. We can, therefore, describe the ox species very much as a bull or cow. The ox species, then, is the ultimate mould in which nature cast her first pair—a bull and a cow. And, history tells us that the first animals of the bovine race are the only animals endowed with a pair of horns. The one fact given us is, then, the existence of evidence shows that cattle have possibly been developed from one another. This, so far as it goes, is matter for scientific treatment, and the theory of evolution, within certain limits, has a right to be called a scientific hypothesis. The one element which is claimed to be the mainspring of organic evolution is totally and absolutely wanting in the inorganic, viz.:—the element of strife for "the survival of the fittest."

In Darwin's "Origin of the Species," 6th edition, 1888, vol. ii., p. 305, we find him saying: "There is a grandeur in this view of life,

with its several powers, having been originally breathed by the Creator into a few forms or into one; and that, whilst this planet has gone cycling on according to the fixed law of gravity, from so simple a beginning endless forms, most beautiful and wonderful, have been and are being evolved."

In the words of Professor Huxley: "If the hypothesis of evolution be true, living matter must have arisen from non-living matter; for by the hypothesis the condition of the globe was at one time such that living matter could not have existed upon it, life being entirely incompatible with the gaseous state."

Darwin, Huxley, and Tyndall, together with a host of other scientists, had preconceived notions about spontaneous generation prior to the investigations of the great French savant, M. Pasteur. The modern scientists, with all the most improved appliances at their command, may frame theories, yet there is nothing positive even to them that lies beyond the reach of the instruments at the command of the chemist, the astronomer and the geologist, and the wisest of these say: "We are only on the outer rim of these great wonders of nature." In proof of this Lamark believed in spontaneous generation. Pasteur, it has been shown, pricked that bubble. Again the want of proof of the inheritance of acquired characters is very serious. Theoretically they are transmissible, but in point of fact they are not transmitted. Professor H. F. Osborn says:—"It follows as an unprejudiced conclusion from our present evidence that upon Weismann's principle we can explain inheritance, but not evolution, while with Lamark's principle and Darwin's selection principle we can explain evolution, but not, at present, inheritance. Disprove Lamark's principle and we must assume that there is a third factor in evolution of which we are ignorant."

We can, therefore, pass back to scientists a host of these tangled tales for their further consideration, and while we await their newer views, it would be wise for dairy cattle breeders to put the Abbot Mendel's experiments with peas into operation with their dairy cattle, and test his theory of segregation in common with many of their friends in other parts of the world, secretly and silently, under another name.

THE ILLAWARRA DAIRY CATTLE ASSOCIATION.

The object of this meeting to-day is to form an Illawarra Dairy Cattle Association. And we may at once state that it is no part of this meeting's duty to interfere in any way with any existing dairy cattle associations. Our aim is in one direction, and that direction is, I hope, on parallel lines with all other dairy cattle breeders' associations, to wit, the breeding of the most profitable animal for our district, and experience has taught us that that animal is what is termed a special quality dairy animal. Some men who try to be wiser than us say: "The Illawarra cow is a cross-bred." But on that line of reasoning, the English racehorse was a cross-bred at one period of his history.

To come to our point: We argue that all breeds of dairy cattle must conform to a certain type. Just as all breeds of beef cattle must conform to a type. Take the points of any given breed of dairy cattle, and with the exception of color and the twist of the horn, which are matters of taste in breeding, every good cow, heifer, or bull won't vary much from these points, if the points are adhered to strictly by an intelligent practical judge; and, just as any breed of dairy animal verges too much towards the beef type, so its utility as a dairy animal decreases.

The ideal dairy animal, as represented in most of our best types of Illawarra bred cows and bulls, has beyond doubt a large percentage of Shorthorn and Ayrshire, and, in many instances Devon blood in their veins. Some may have an objection to the Devon. But they must remember that the pale or yellow bred Devon gives exceedingly rich milk, and is equal in many respects to the Guernsey or Jersey for fineness of bone, and the Ayrshire for vitality and constitutional vigor. Unfortunately their milk flow is not great, but their teats are well set and of a rich yellow color. Therefore, no practical man would object to a blend of Devon in a dairy cow, as their color alone is at times recognised as valuable on the best Shorthorn stations in Australia.

Whilst. therefore, we are prepared to accept into our future herd-book cattle of the Ayrshire, Shorthorn, or Shorthorn-Ayrshire crosses, we should not object to a blend of Devon blood in their veins. But we shall with inexorable exactness object to any animal that contains Jersey, Guernsey, Holstein, or any other blood foreign to the three breeds herein specified. The types for bulls and cows we will leave to our executive committee to decide on, and place on paper before finally putting the matter before the members of the Association; the same thing will also apply to the colors to be adopted. The one important matter that must be discussed is that of quality. In all pronounced qualities of a dairy animal there is no one point more important than that of dairy quality. Every practical man aims at the quality of his dairy cattle, and we propose to have a test to cover three periods of a cow's yearly milking, which, of course, will be decided on by the executive committee. Bulls will be admitted also for registration in the herd-book on condition that they are proven to be the sires of good producing cows, and other such conditions as the executive may impose upon them.

We have learned sufficient from past experience that it is not numbers that will make our Association valuable. We must be most exacting in our investigations and ultimately in our tests. The scales and the Babcock Milk-tester will be our practical guide. But as neither is a guide to quality in themselves we have to place ourselves in touch with men who will see that those appliances are properly worked, so as to arrive at accurate results. We want no doubts, no suspicions, nor outside blither; and we want our entries in the herd-book to be what they are represented to be, and neither more or less than they are. As practical, honest men we know what we are doing, and we will do it. We know that our fathers immortalised the name of Illawarra through their dairy herds of cattle, and it is but just and right that we should perpetuate that honored name and hand it down unsullied to posterity

Now, gentlemen, if I am permitted to be somewhat poetic and prophetic, I should and would say in conclusion :—

Our fathers won wealth and fame on every slope, and vale, and plain,
And what our fathers did their sons will do again.

Cattle for dairy purposes, which include bulls, cows and heifers, when placed before us for inspection, with a view of having judgment passed upon them, may be arranged into five divisions as follows:—Head, neck, trunk, fore-limbs, hind limbs. These five divisions are in turn divided into 49 parts. Each of these parts performs important functions, and when any one of these parts is found to be deranged or diseased the animal is more or less said to be unsuited to its purpose. The more vital the part, the more important it is that the animal should be rejected for breeding purposes. This applies, of course, more particularly to those organs which perform the breathing, digestive, and circulating work of the animal, the secretive organ being a combination of the whole.

It does not seem necessary in this connection to give description of all the various parts of our dairy cattle. I am not dealing with the students of any of our Agricultural Colleges, nor their science masters or teachers; I am dealing with practical dairymen, who have met here to-day for a purpose, and that purpose has already been explained.

Although it may be somewhat beyond my scope to attempt to define the points of a dairy cow, heifer, or bull at this early stage of our transactions, a few brief hints may be pardoned.

I should, therefore, as a preliminary to my suggestion on the point system of judging dairy cattle, ask you to imagine a dairy animal of either sex placed in front of you. That animal could be divided, for all practical purposes, into three parts, namely:—Fore-quarter, barrel or middle piece, and hind-quarter. All three are important, and all three should melt or blend together with an ease and grace hardly definable in the character sketch of a beautiful animal. Of these three parts, certainly the more important to a dairyman is the hind-quarter. Then next in importance comes the barrel or middle piece. Then following close up comes the fore-quarter. I should, therefore, arrange a scale of points on those lines as follows:—Hind-quarter 80, barrel or middle piece 60, fore-quarter 40. Total, 180 points.

But it is just possible that we may have to extend these points as follows:—Every cow and bull, having been provided by nature with certain characteristics which have enabled us to distinguish them from other animals, they are at once entitled to, say, 50 per cent. of any scale of points that may be devised for the guidance of the examiners. If, then, the difference in type between a cow and bull or a good dairy cow or bull is put down at 25 per cent. points, we get 75 points as the lowest number of points which will be accepted for entry in the herd-book. The difference again between a good dairy cow or bull and a high-grade show cow or bull will be covered by an additional 25 points.

Note.—This matter was explained at the meeting. Unfortunately examiners did not act up to it. It was, however, the first Cattle Association in Australia to register bulls or the quality of their progeny according to tests.

Illawarra Dairy Cattle Association.
Title.

1. The Association shall be called "The Illawarra Dairy Cattle Association."

Objects.

2. The objects of the Association shall be—
   (a) To maintain the characteristics and improve the Illawarra Breed of Dairy Cattle.
   (b) To collect, verify, and publish information relating to the breed.
   (c) To compile and publish a Herd-Book of the Illawarra Cattle.
   (d) To advocate that prizes be set apart at shows for this breed of cattle, without such necessary distinctions as implied by these words—"grade, miscellaneous, other than pure bred," &c., &c.
   (e) To issue Certificates for such cattle of the breed as shall pass certain standards.
   (f) To promote in any way, not above mentioned, the interests of this breed of dairy cattle.

Council.

3. The affairs of the Association shall be administered by a Council consisting of thirteen members (with power to add to 21), and the President, Secretary and Treasurer.

4. The members of the Council shall be elected annually by members.

5. The Council shall hold its meeting where and when it shall decide.

6. The Council at its first meeting shall form all sub-committees.

7. The next ensuing election shall take place when deemed expedient.

8. At all meetings seven members shall form a quorum.

9. Three days' notice of the meeting shall be sent to every member of the Council, with particulars of business to be transacted thereat.

10. The Council shall have power to make By-laws for the conduct of the Association's affairs.

11. The Council's decision on all matters affecting the Association or its interests shall be final, and the Chairman at any meeting shall have a casting vote in addition to his vote as a member.

Membership.

12. Any dairyman may and shall become a member of the Association upon payment of the sum of 10/6, whereupon he shall be possessed of the rights and privileges of memberhip until the expiry of the then current financial year of the Association, and may join any time during that period by paying full subscription.

13. The subscription shall be due annually in advance, and members whose subscriptions are in arrears shall not be entitled to vote at any meeting.

14. Any member whose conduct in any respect shall be deemed derogatory or prejudicial to the interests of the Association may be expelled by a resolution of the Council to that effect. Twenty-one days' notice of intention to move such a resolution shall be sent to every member of the Council and to the member whose removal is sought, and who shall be entitled to be present at Council's meeting; but if he happen to be a member of the Council he shall not be entitled to vote.

15. The Council may elect as honorary members any person whom they shall consider to have advanced or calculated to advance the objects of the Association.

16. No dairyman can be a member of this Council if he be on the Council of any other Dairy Cattle Association.

Finance.

17. The financial year shall end upon 30th June, 1911.

18. All moneys shall be banked where the Council shall direct.

19. All accounts shall be paid by cheque.

20. All cheques shall be signed by the President, and counter-signed by the Honorary Secretary and Treasurer.

21. All accounts of the Association shall be audited annually by two Auditors appointed by the Council.

22. A balance-sheet showing the position of the Association shall be submitted to the Council at its first meeting after the closing of the financial year, and a copy shall be furnished to every member of the Association.

Honorary Treasurer.

23. This official shall be responsible to the Council for the proper discharge of his duties.

24. He shall be responsible for all moneys received by him on behalf of the Association, and shall forthwith pay such into the Association's Banking Account.

25. He shall have the custody of all property belonging to the Association.

26. He shall be (as also the Secretary) an ex-officio member of the Council, and shall vote at meetings.

27. They shall be elected by the Council and may be removed by the Council.

28. Their term of office shall expire annually after the first Council meeting in July, but they shall be eligible for re-election.

Herd Book.

29. The Association's publications shall be known as the Illawarra Dairy Cattle Herd Book.

30. The Herd Book shall provide for entries of all animals of this breed coming up to the recognised standard.

31. The qualifications for entry in the Herd Book shall be that the name, age color, tests, breeder of each animal, together with the names of the sire, dam, grand-dam, and sire of grand-dam when procurable, be required to be given.

32. The fee payable by members shall be: For bulls 5/-, for cows 2/6.

33. The Council shall have power to amplify or amend the conditions regulating entries for the Herd Book when deemed expedient.

34. All Herd Book entries must be accompanied by a statutory declaration before a Justice of the Peace that the particulars supplied are correct.

Certificates.

35. The Association shall issue a Certificate of "Highly Commended" for such animals as obtain 75 per cent. of points or more on the scale of points authorised by the Council.

36. Examinations for Certificates may be held at any time upon application of owner—by persons approved by the Council as competent judges—provided the animals have previously come up to standard of quality imposed by the Council, which shall be 75 per cent. of points and not less than 12 pounds of butter per week. Conditions: Cows to be milked out in the presence of two officials evening, morning and evening consecutively at equal periods. The whole three milkings to be weighed and samples taken and sent to tester, only the two latter

to be counted for the test, and for every lb. of butter produced per week over and above 12lbs. 5 points are to be added to her scale of points, If in the opinion of the Inspection Committee anything of a suspicious nature in regard to the weights or tests of the three milkings should occur, they are to immediately report same to the Council, who may order another test to be made.

37. The standard for bulls shall be 75 per cent. of points, and that four of his heifers of approved type with not more than 4 permanent teeth shall give not less than 30lbs. milk per day—milk to be up to Government Standard—or 4 cows qualifying for Herd Book.

38. All cattle qualifying for entry in Herd Book shall be branded by the Association's registered brand

39. That a Dairy Register be kept in connection with Dairy Herd Book for cows, to include date of calving, description of calf, sex of calf, whether destroyed or kept, date of service of bull, name of bull, &c., this information to be furnished to the Secretary immediately after each cow calves, and later on when served.

BULLS.

	Points
Head—Showing vigour, elegance of form, male characteristics	20
Forehead—Broad between the eyes, dishing —intelligent	20
Face—In keeping with the forehead—long below the eyes	20
Ears—Of medium size and length, covered with soft hair, yellow inside	10
Eyes—Large, full and bright, but not vicious	20
Horns—Medium size and length, of fine texture, slightly inclined either upward or downward, but going out in line with body	10
Neck—Gracefully joined to head and shoulders, nearly free from dewlap, of good length, strong but not gross, inclined slightly downward	40
Shoulders—Of medium height, free in their action, well rounded, and even on top	30
Chest—Full, free from beef, broad on floor, showing heart and lung room	80
Crops—Full and level with the shoulders, showing a distinctive spine	40
Chine—Straight, broadly developed and open, not inclined to beef	40
Barrel—Well rounded, deep, broad and large underneath	60
Loins & Hips—Full, long, broad and level, hips broad deep and flat	60
Rump—High, long, broad and level, showing prominent pelvic arch	60
Thurl—High and of great width, displaying a roomy pelvis	40
Quarters—Long, straight behind, wide, with full flat sides	60
Flanks—Deep, full, arched and fine, free from fat	20
Legs—Medium length, tapering, bone fine and flat, strong flat arms, broad flat thighs set wide apart, feet medium size, round fine and solid	50
Tail—Reaching to hocks or below, large at setting, tapering finely to a full switch	20
Hair and Handlings—Short, fine, soft, skin mellow and yellow, of moderate thickness	100
Mammary Veins—Long, large, branched, with extensions entering large orifices	100
Rudimentary Teats—Not less than four, brown in color, large and well spread	20
Escutcheon—Large and of fine development according to its kind	30
Scrotum—Of good size, well hung, even size testes	50

MAXIMUM POINTS .. 1000

COWS.

	Points
Head—Showing vigor, elegance of form, and female characteristics	20
Forehead—Broad between the eyes, dishing —intelligent	20
Face—In keeping with the forehead, long below the eyes	20
Ears—Of medium size and length, covered with soft hair, yellow inside	10
Eyes—Large, full and bright, but withal docile	20
Horns—Medium size and length, of fine texture, slightly inclined either upwards or downwards, but going outwards in line with the body	10
Neck—Gracefully joined to head and shoulders, free from dewlap, of good length, strong, flat and fine, clear about the throat and chest	40
Shoulders—Of medium height, free in their action, well rounded and even on top	30
Chest—Full, free from beef, broad on floor, showing heart and lung room	80
Crops—Full and level with the shoulders, showing a distinctive spine	40
Chine—Straight, broadly developed and open, not inclined to beef	40
Barrel—Well developed, deep and broad underneath towards the udder	60
Loin and Hips—Full, long, broad and level, hips broad, deep and flat	60
Rump—High, long, broad and level, showing prominent pelvic arch	50
Thurl—High and of great width, displaying a roomy pelvis	40
Quarters—Long, straight behind, with full flat sides	50
Flanks—Deep, full, arched and fine, free from fat	20
Legs—Medium length, tapering, bone fine and flat, strong flat arm, broad flat thighs, set wide apart, feet medium size, round and solid	60
Tail—Reaching to hocks or below, large at setting, tapering finely to a full switch	20

Hair and Handling—Short, fine, soft, skin mellow and yellow, of moderate thickness   80

Mammary Veins—Long, large, branched, with extensive openings into body   100

Udder—Capacious, flexible, well developed both in front and rear, but not too pendulous, teats well formed, wide apart, of good size   100

Escutcheon—Of good size, of fine quality according to its kind   30

MAXIMUM POINTS .. 1000

BREEDS TO BE RECOGNISED ONLY.

In the blend which compose the Illawarra Breed of Dairy Cattle, whether bulls, cows or heifers, the breeds shall be only Shorthorn, Ayrshire or Devon, but no questions shall be asked as regards the quantity of the blood of either of those breeds in the veins of any animal.

COLORS TO BE RECOGNISED.

The Colors to be recognised only in the Illawarra Breed of Dairy Cattle shall be Red, Red and White Spotted, Light Red, Light Red and White Spotted, Red-roan, Roan, Roan and White, Strawberry Roan, Strawberry Roan and White, White.

A mysterious critic writing to the "Daily Telegraph," dated June 23rd, 1910, stated as follows:—"I notice in your issue of the 16th instant that steps are being taken to preserve the identity, purity, and characteristics of the old Illawarra breed of dairy cattle. This is to be commended, for it is doubtful if better dairy cattle could be found in any part of the world, certainly not in Australia, and this result has been achieved by long and careful breeding and selection for a period extending over 70 years, until the breed has become, as the report justly states 'too good to be merged into others and lost.' But the same report states that Shorthorn, Ayrshire, and Devon bulls may be used and no questions shall be asked as to quantity of blood of any of these breeds to be found in the veins of any animal. This is much to be regretted, if the purity of the breed is to be maintained," &c.

This brought forth the rejoinder from the Hon. Sec. (dated 25th June, 1910) of the I.D.C. Association:—"Your correspondent writes as if he was fearful lest the Council of the Illawarra Dairy Cattle Association are going to tumble into pitfalls of their own construction with regard to the future of the Illawarra breed of cattle. He may, however, set his mind at rest on that score, as we are going to do the right thing, namely, stand by and sustain the reputation of our dairy cattle in future. To begin, we do not recognise the bull called 'Major' as the origin of the Illawarra breed of dairy cattle. The bull was one animal, and one only, among hundreds of bulls that have been used for breeding purposes in the Illawarra district. Neither do we advocate the use of Shorthorn, Ayrshire, or Devon bulls. But we are honest enough to admit that 65 to 70 years ago, and later, the blend of blood that was prominent in Andrew McGill's herd—those deep red cattle with a white blaze on the flank or side—was worked in from three strains, &c. . . . Type and quality are our chief objects, and we are, therefore, going to attain and maintain the end we have in view."

In this matter, "We ask no question." Critics from within and without the ranks of the I.D.C.A. were sorely perplexed. The fact that the examiners had to exercise caution in passing animals into the herd-book did not seem to appeal to them, and the fun of the thing was that the critics did not see the joke. Take one of scores of our Illawarras and see if an anatomist could calculate the amount of those three breeds circulating through its veins.